The Food Lover's Guide to France

PATRICIA WELLS

Assisted by JANE SIGAL
and SUSAN HERRMANN LOOMIS
Photographs by JOSEPH KUGIELSKY
Maps by EMILY WEINER

Workman Publishing, New York

*Once again
for Walter,
for all the same reasons*

Library of Congress Cataloging-in-Publication Data
Wells, Patricia.   The food lover's guide to France.
Includes index.   1. Restaurants, lunch rooms, etc.—France—Guide-books.
2. Grocery trade—France—Guide-books.
3. Cookery, French. 4. Hotels, taverns, etc.—France—Guide-books.
5. France—Description and travel—1975—Guide-books. I. Title
TX910.F8W382 1987   647'.9544   86-40547   ISBN 0-89480-306-9 (pbk.)

Book design: Susan Aronson Stirling
Front Cover and book photographs: Joseph Kugielsky
Maps: Emily Weiner

Workman Publishing Company, Inc.
1 West 39th Street
New York, NY 10018

Manufactured in the United States of America
First printing April 1987
10   9   8   7   6   5   4   3   2   1

The recipe for "Le Succès de Bernachon" originally appeared in *La Passion du
Chocolat* (Flammarion, Paris, 1985); the "Salade de Lapereau à l'Auberge de l'Ill"
originally appeared in *Les Recettes de l'Auberge de l'Ill* (Flammarion, Paris,
1982). Both are reprinted with permission of the publisher. A
version of "Berawecka" originally appeared in Elizabeth Schneider Colchie's
Ready When You Are (Crown, New York, 1982)
and is reprinted with permission of the author.

Portions of this book have appeared in some form in *The New York Times*, the *International
Herald Tribune*, and *Travel & Leisure* magazine.

Front cover photographs: *Top left*, Maurice Bernachon, of Bernachon chocolate in
Lyons. *Top right*, At the Durand farm in Camembert. *Bottom left*, The Georges Blanc
meringue dessert. Back cover photographs: *Top left*, At the night market in Bayonne.
Bottom left, The Grand Café des Négociants in Lyons. *Bottom right*, At Gérard Boyer's in Reims.

Acknowledgments

Even before the companion to this book—*The Food Lover's Guide to Paris*—rolled off the presses, my file cabinets were bulging with the clips and notes, menus and wine lists I had begun to collect from my journeys throughout France. This book was begging to be written. But it could not have been conceived, researched, or completed without the generous and enthusiastic support of so many fine people.

Most of all, I want to thank the hundreds of French men and women—the bakers and cheesemakers, chefs and farmers—who so eagerly gave up their time to help me document their lives, and thus the gastronomy of contemporary France. My life has been immeasurably enriched by them, and I want to give special thanks to Pierre, Jany, and Arlette Gleize of restaurant La Bonne Etape in Château-Arnoux; Jules Roux-Daigue, the Beaufort cheesemaker from Bellecombe-Tarentaise; Maurice and Jean-Jacques Bernachon, chocolate makers in Lyon; Maurice and Paule Bal, retired farmers in Flaxieu; Marie-Claude Gracia, chef at La Belle Gasconne in Poudenas; Jean-Marc Fognini of the tourist office in Bourg-en-Bresse; Adrien Sordello of restaurant Bacon in Cap d'Antibes; Philippe Garrigue of the tourist office in Salers; and to Paul Bocuse, who in his own unique way has encouraged all of us who love France and French food to know it just a little bit better.

There is no job description to cover the various tasks Jane Sigal performed during the creation of this book. On the road, she did her best to navigate us over mountain roads, down country paths, and up to the right farmhouse or country *auberge*. She helped me rock rental cars out of ditches in Normandy, scrape ice off the windshield in the Jura, and sang with me to stay alert in the middle of the night as we drove down dark and rainy roads in the Loire. Back in Paris, she played detective, persistently tracking down the craftsmen and the artisans we knew had to be out there, spending endless hours on the telephone, checking and rechecking addresses, hours, spellings, and accents, all the while keeping the mountains of clips and files in order.

In Seattle, Susan Herrmann Loomis remained a cheery, enthusiastic colleague, reworking the recipes I tested in France, then testing and retesting, searching for proper substitutes in the American marketplace.

There were others who assisted at various steps along the way, and I would like to thank Colette Seiler, Dewey Markham, Jr., and Kevin Ryan for agreeing to become part of this project.

My good friend the wine merchant Kermit Lynch has been an invaluable resource, and I will always be grateful for the role he has played in my wine education, not to mention wine enjoyment.

But all these words would never have seen the light of day were it not for the trust of my publisher, Peter Workman, or the careful attention of my editor, Suzanne Rafer. Thanks also to Paul Hanson, Susan Aronson Stirling, and Barbara Scott-Goodman for the lovely design of the book, and to Kathie Ness for her cheerful telephone voice and her attentive editing.

Many people were kind enough to share special addresses with me, and I want to particularly thank Ghislaine Bavoillot of Flammarion in Paris and Carole Bannett of the Lee Bailey department at Saks Fifth Avenue in New York. Also thanks to Henry Voy of La Ferme Saint-Hubert in Paris for supplying many of the French cheeses pictured in this book, and to Steven Spurrier of Caves de la Madeleine in Paris for supplying many of the wines.

Over the years, many people have knowingly and unknowingly assisted me in my work, and I want to thank them here. Special thanks to Arthur Gelb, Mike Leahy, and Nora Kerr at *The New York Times,* and to Lee Huebner at the *International Herald Tribune.* I owe a special debt of both personal and professional gratitude to Julia Child and Craig Claiborne, who, by paving the way, made it possible for me to develop the career that I have today. I am grateful, as well, to my literary agents, Susan and Robert Lescher, for their continued encouragement and support.

Many friends played a major role, serving as fellow travelers and eager dinner companions, offering constant moral support over the years. I want to particularly thank Susy Davidson, Rita Kramer and Dr. Yale Kramer, and Catherine O'Neill and Richard Reeves for their very special and meaningful friendships. Most of all, I am grateful to my husband, Walter, whose endless patience, support, and love have carried me through the longest of days.

Contents

Recipe Contents

A Taste for France

Over the past two years, I have journeyed 50,000 kilometers throughout France, some 30,000 miles on high-speed trains and slow mountainous roads, interviewing hundreds of men and women, discussing the elements that are basic to France's tradition of gastronomy. I have talked with Loire Valley goat farmers and Roquefort cheesemakers, Breton crêpe makers and France's best chefs, scallop and lobster fishermen, certifiably insane bakers, *escargot* processors, sea salt rakers, walnut oil pressers, winemakers, cheese agers, pig wholesalers, and two brothers who make a living growing zucchini blossoms. Along the way I've worked beside many of them—curing a 300-pound pig, conserving *foie gras,* digging in icy soil to unearth black truffles, learning to distinguish edible wild mushrooms from the deadly ones. And in towns all along France's two coasts, I have gotten up in the middle of the night to greet fishermen as the sun came up, arriving with their catch of anchovies, sardines, or fresh white tuna.

Wherever I went, I searched out the most authentic and the best, and this invariably brought me to the "little guys," the artisans, farmers, and producers who work independently. As a consequence, I spent a lot of time in villages too small to rate their own postal code and talked with Frenchmen far removed from the excitement of Paris and the glamour of the country's famous kitchens.

Throughout my journeys, I searched for answers to two basic questions.

The first was how, in this homogenized world, has France managed to retain its undisputed role as the maker, the shaper, the ruler of Western cuisine? Others challenge it—Italy notably has a joyous gastronomic tradition and there are remarkable tables in that sensuous country. And elements of American cooking are emerging in many noteworthy ways. But France's cuisine remains the standard by which all others are measured, to which all others are compared.

The second question is, can all this continue? Already, in the decade or so I have been traveling and living in France, I have seen anonymous chain supermarkets squeeze out small vendors whose produce was fresher and far more attractive. I have watched the trend develop for cheeses whose taste has nothing over Velveeta, and I have mourned as neighborhood *traiteurs* and *charcuteries* disappeared in favor of trendy fast-food eateries.

As I carefully researched, then documented, the gastronomy of contemporary France, I asked dozens of specific questions whose answers would reflect on those two primary ones. All the while, I focused on the present rather than the past, on reality rather than the myths that have outlived the past.

In many ways, I began this project because, as a journalist trained to seek out the facts, I found myself constantly frustrated by the fact that so much of the "common knowledge" about French gastronomy was sheer invention. I discovered that the "primary source" for some of the authors I had respected turned out to be the Michelin Green Guides, and that their descriptions of methods and practices were poetry or fantasy—or just plain misinformation. I was determined to avoid the appeal of mythmaking and to try to inform readers about how things are today rather than romanticizing the past.

Along with concentrating on the present, I operated on the premise that any cuisine has its source in the tastes and traditions of a nation, not simply in the kitchens of its elegant restaurants, and that its fields and vineyards are more important to preserving those tastes and traditions than its grandest chef. I don't know that I have arrived at final answers to my questions, but I do have clues and leads, vivid impressions and, of course, opinions.

I quickly came to the realization that no matter how exhausted I was from getting up early to greet a fisherman with his catch, or to interview a baker as his first batch of bread went into the oven, the person I was interviewing probably worked much longer hours and much harder, physically, than I ever could. Moreover, the next day, the day after that, and the next year and the next decade, he would go back to that job with thoroughly unrestrained dedication.

And if there is one theme I heard time and again, it was the three simple phrases I heard repeated from Alsace to Brittany, from Gascony to the Alps of Provence: "We do not count our hours. We love our work. We think that it has value." In part, that was because

I was talking to the little guys—the men and women who them-selves raise the *mesclum,* pick the grapes, cure the olives, dry the plums, knead the bread, smoke the sausages, or age the cheeses that have come to mean, in our gastronomic minds, France.

For most of the people I talked with, their involvement with food is not a job. It is a passion, an emotion and an involvement that lie somewhere between deep love and religious zeal. There is the fish chef who told me he dreamed about fish every night, and who spends five hours each day in the market in Cannes, selecting each fish he serves in his restaurant. There's the Beaufort cheese-maker who rejects artificial insemination of his cows because, he insists, only contented cows give great milk. (Besides, he was so proud of his bull.)

These people aren't doing it for money, because they really don't earn a great deal, or for prestige, because farm work is short on that. They are motivated by unlimited zeal for what they do and by centuries of tradition.

I don't know that this sort of fascination, respect, and knowl-edge will last forever—industrialized food continues to make inroads in France, working to confuse the palate or even destroy it. And the market for processed quick-and-ready food expands as—I regret to say it—French society becomes more Americanized.

There were times, of course, when searching out the little guys was not enough. Good intentions, hard work, and low-grade flour will still make bad bread. Cheese made from milk that's been pumped, chilled, churned, and reheated just won't turn out as well as cheese made from milk still warm from the cow. And even the cheese that is made with this wonderfully fresh milk won't taste wonderful unless it's been given time to age.

Despite such negative factors, regional cuisine is alive and well and even enjoying a resurgence. Throughout the country, authentic regional restaurants are thriving while their flashier homogenized competitors struggle for a clientele. In the Savoie you can still find restaurants serving an honest *friture* of tiny fish fresh from the alpine lakes. Along the French-Spanish border, near the village of Céret, there's a restaurant that still serves a traditional *cargolade,* a wonderfully hearty assortment of snails, pork sausages, lamb, and blood sausage, all grilled over an open fire fed with vine cuttings. In Normandy's markets, that day's catch of shrimp still squiggles in the fishmonger's bins, and great brasseries nearby still prepare them *à la minute.* You can still get daubed-out in Provence, lobstered-out in Brittany, eat your fill of goose hearts in Gascony. There's no paucity of great regional fare—just of the time and the temperament to seek these places out.

Another encouraging aspect is that gastronomic history is not being forgotten. The *tarte Tatin* at the Hôtel Tatin in Lamotte-Beuvron may not merit a special trip, but it really is pretty good. And if you do go there to dine, you can see the stove where those sisters supposedly invented that wonderful upside-down apple tart. I certainly wouldn't be ashamed to serve the omelet I sampled at La Mère Poulard in Le Mont-Saint-Michel, where ladies in long dresses still prepare those time- and tourist-honored dishes in long-handled pans over an oak-wood fire. Quality is a tradition in French cuisine, and the French respect for both quality and tradition will help protect the nation's gastronomy for a long time.

Which is not to say it will be preserved intact. In my travels I have encountered a variety of deceptions, situations that are not quite what they seem. It may be something as small as the fact that the majority of the truffles preserved in the Périgord actually come from the other side of France, in northern Provence. These "cans of worms"—the label on the file I put them into as I worked on sorting them out—add up to a basic, disappointing discovery: Many of the products that have made French cuisine famous no longer come from France. That *foie gras* you rave about in Michelin-starred restaurants? There's a 75 percent chance it came from Hungary, or Poland, or Israel. Those luscious *escargots?* Probably from Hungary. The frog's legs? From Yugoslavia. The *brochet* in your *quenelles?* Canada. The mustard grain in your Dijon mustard? From Kansas.

Authenticity of origin is a hard question to deal with. Were the products better when they were French? No doubt they were. Food is invariably better the closer it's prepared to its source. But how much better? My decade here isn't enough for me to answer that. Besides, there are other complications. I showed rather serious disappointment when a restaurateur in Brittany told me that most of her scallops come from Irish waters and that her lobsters did not carry a French passport. Her only response was, "Let's not push the matter. After all, people have to have their dreams."

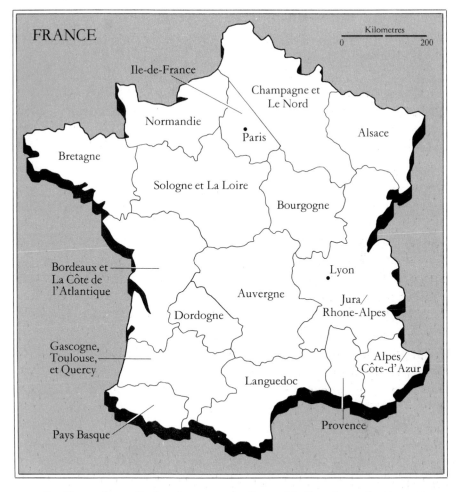

FRANCE

Kilometres
0   200

Ile-de-France

Champagne et
Le Nord

Normandie

Paris

Alsace

Bretagne

Sologne et La Loire

Bourgogne

Bordeaux et
La Côte de
l'Atlantique

Lyon

Auvergne

Jura/
Rhone-Alpes

Dordogne

Gascogne,
Toulouse,
et Quercy

Alpes/
Côte-d'Azur

Languedoc

Provence

Pays Basque

Scallops from Ireland, mussels from Holland, and olives from
Spain may not destroy French cuisine or end its traditions. But the
effects of the contemporary economic order are shattering some
aspects of regional gastronomy. Sheep farmers in the Pyrénées can't
compete with British lamb and are abandoning the land. Olive
growers in the Drôme can't survive both the hard freezes that end
production for years and less expensive imports from Spain. The
economic cooperation brought about through the Common Market
has indisputably raised living standards throughout Western Europe. But the EC's agricultural policy is leading to a steady,
irreversible industrialization of farm practices. Inevitably this will
mean that the price difference between a farm-raised chicken from
Bresse and a factory-produced one will drive all but the most

committed Bresse poultry farmers out of business. That a *poulet de Bresse* will become as rare as caviar and just as unaffordable is truly lamentable.

Yet basically I came away from my research with my optimism intact. In another generation, I doubt there will still be farmers in the mountains of Cantal, milking their cows by hand, living in stone shacks that lack electricity and running water. Old Tante Paulette and Tante Yvonne won't be feeding us their *poulet au vinaigre* or *daube provençale,* but someone will come along to fill their shoes.

Certainly frozen-food sections will grow in supermarkets, that drive-in *baguette* shop I saw in Avignon will no doubt breed offspring, and there's no question that McDonald's and Love Burger are here to stay.

But a good percentage of the authentic, dedicated food people I've met over the past two years will be around to see the new century in, and I'm convinced that the passions of men like Paris bread baker Lionel Poilane and Lyon chocolate maker Maurice Bernachon will not only get us through just a little bit longer, but will inspire successors who are determined not to let their teachers down.

Paris, France
February 1987

Dining Out in France

This is a personal guide, and whenever I had to decide whether or not to include an establishment I asked myself one question: Would I want to go back there again? If the answer was no, the listing was discarded.

Thus every listing has been personally selected and visited by me, and each one can be considered a recommendation. Many well-known restaurants are not included here, and in most cases, that absence is intentional.

In the selection of places to dine in each region, I have worked to create a balanced list of restaurants that represent a variety of dining styles, of prices, and of atmospheres, ranging from small snack spots to the grand special-occasion restaurant. My hope is that if you travel with this book for several days to a week in a particular region, when you leave you will have sampled a representative range of what that area has to offer.

The variety of restaurants listed in this book are not easy to categorize. While restaurants in Paris can quite clearly be classified as cafés, bistros, brasseries, and restaurants, I have found that each region of France tends to impose its own personality and customs on restaurant styles. Additionally, since almost all establishments listed here tend to be family run, they take on the personality of the chef and his or her family. Thus we have fish shacks in the Pays Basque, country cafés in Normandy, and in Alsace, an Adidas employee dining room that opens to the public after the staff has eaten.

Restaurants

Basically, this book contains five types of restaurants:

Ferme-Auberge: Meals taken in the family's home, where rooms are also generally available. Expect to pay about 100 francs per person.

Quick regional fare: This includes street food (such as *socca* in Nice and snacks from pizza trucks at the markets throughout Provence) as well as such casual restaurants as *crêperies* in Brittany and *flamme-kueche* restaurants in Alsace. Expect to pay about 50 francs per person.

Small family restaurant: The country equivalent of a big-city bistro, this is usually an informal restaurant serving varied regional fare. Restaurants in this category range from extremely casual affairs with bare wooden tables and paper tablecloths (the sort of place where you would feel comfortable in blue jeans) to those with linens and fresh flowers. Like the big-city bistro, meals at small family restaurants tend to be relatively inexpensive, and there is usually a range of fixed-price menus. Wines in all of these tend to be regional and are generally reasonably priced. Expect to pay anywhere from 75 to 200 francs per person.

Brasseries: Brasseries tend to be big-city establishments, and one finds few outside of Paris. Those that do exist generally follow the custom of offering beer on tap, usually serve raw fish and shellfish, and keep rather flexible, and late, hours. Brasserie fare is also inexpensive. Expect to pay about 200 francs per person.

Restaurants: Here the range of prices and styles is broad, and country restaurants vary from attractive homey cottages to grand and elegant *châteaux.* Food may vary from earthy regional fare to a very refined cuisine. And, depending upon the price range, they may vary from everyday restaurants to those to reserve for very special occasions. Prices can range from 200 to 600 francs per person.

Reservations

I follow two strict rules of etiquette regarding reservations: I always make a reservation, and if I cannot honor the reservation, I call to cancel. Many diners—Americans in particular—have the habit of reserving at several restaurants for a given meal so they can decide at the last minute where they would prefer to go. This works for large, busy establishments with a high turnover. But most restaurants in France are small family affairs, and generally there is not more than one seating for a given meal. This means that if you have reserved a table and do not show up, that table will most likely go empty for the evening. French restaurateurs report that this is an ever-increasing problem, with Americans making up the bulk of the "no-shows."

When traveling, it is not always possible to arrive at the appointed hour. If you will be late, etiquette suggests that you call to announce your delay.

Dining hours

Set aside plenty of time for dining in France. Although times have changed some—more and more restaurants offer a *menu rapide,* usually a single main course—expect to spend anywhere from one to three hours at table for a substantial lunch or dinner. If you have a tight schedule and want to be in and out within thirty minutes to an hour, then visit a café, tea salon, wine bar, or brasserie—but don't attempt to rush through a meal at a serious restaurant.

Dining hours for restaurants outside of Paris are generally earlier than Parisian dining hours. You can expect to begin lunch around noon or 12:30 P.M., and the dinner hour often begins as early as 7 P.M. Each restaurant listing in this guide notes the time at which the last order is taken at lunch and dinner. If you intend to arrive earlier or later than conventional dining hours, it is always advisable to call to announce your intentions.

Paying the bill and tipping

When it comes to paying restaurant bills in France, you need to remember only one fact: You are never required to pay more than the final total on the bill. *Service* is roughly the equivalent of a tip. But while a tip is optional, *service* is not. *Service* ranges from 12 to 15 percent, depending upon the class of the restaurant, and it may or may not be included in the price of individual dishes as listed on the menu; but it will always be added to the final bill before it is presented. When the menu says *service compris* (service included, often listed as *s.c.* in the fine print at the bottom of a menu), that means the 12 to 15 percent service charge has been built into the price of each dish. When the menu says *service non compris* (service not included) or *service en sus* (service in addition), the *service* will be added to the total after the food and wine have been added up. Either way, the bottom line is what you pay. Etiquette does not require you to pay more. However, if you have particularly enjoyed the meal, if you feel that the maître d'hôtel or *sommelier* has offered exceptional service, and if you are in a particularly generous mood, then you might leave an additional tip of up to 5 percent of the total. Tipping in cafés, tea salons, and bars is similar: *Service* is included but you may wish to leave a few extra francs.

Credit cards

Throughout France, an increasing number of establishments accept credit cards. But if you are totally dependent upon credit cards as a means of payment, it is a good idea to confirm credit card information when reserving. If you are sharing a bill with another person or couple and you both wish to pay by credit card, most restaurants will agree to divide the bill between two cards. Out of kindness to the waiters and the *sommelier,* any tips (beyond the obligatory 12 to 15 percent for *service*) should be left in cash. I have found that increasingly, as foreign exchange rates fluctuate, many establishments do not accept traveler's checks.

A private room

Many restaurants offer private rooms, large and small, for anywhere from eight to several hundred people. In some restaurants the rooms are particularly elegant and well appointed. Others may be drab, uncomfortable, and less appealing than the restaurant's main dining room, so it is a good idea to see the room before making plans.

There are advantages and disadvantages to reserving a private room. One advantage, of course, is privacy, and it makes it easier to organize a special feast, discussing and preparing beforehand the complete menu, including the wines. The main disadvantage is that you must plan several weeks ahead and in most cases will need a French-speaking person to make the arrangements. Also keep in mind that since your group will be set apart from the main dining room, you will miss much of the "theater" and ambience that goes with the dining experience. There is no extra charge for private rooms, and in many cases the total bill will be less than if the group chose from the regular menu. Where private rooms are available, such facilities are noted with the restaurant description.

Ordering

There are many things to consider when one sits down at a table to order. The first questions I ask myself are "What's likely to be fresh? What is in season? What dishes are typical of the region?" I wouldn't think of ordering *choucroute* in Lyon, *bouillabaisse* in Normandy, or *cassoulet* in Provence. When visiting an area, it always helps to visit local markets to see for yourself. Then you can anticipate the farm-fresh asparagus, first-of-season strawberries, or fresh Saint-Pierre.

In my restaurant descriptions, and through the list of each establishment's specialties, I have tried to help the reader understand what dishes the restaurant is most proud of, and which ones I have most enjoyed.

In considering freshness, note that when there is a *plat du jour*, or daily special, this is almost always the best bet, assuming that it is a dish to your liking.

Butter

Most restaurants offer butter at the table, but few small establishments do. If you don't see butter, simply ask for it. Only at the smallest cafés will there be an extra charge. Since the French do not ordinarily butter their bread, restaurants do not systematically offer it—unless you order a dish that generally calls for buttered bread, such as *charcuterie* or the cheese course. Almost all French butter is sweet butter except in Brittany, where the butter is generally salted.

Coffees, teas and artificial sweeteners

The French have very specific coffee drinking habits. Many Frenchmen begin their day with a *café au lait*—usually lots of hot milk with a little bit of coffee. During the rest of the day they drink either black coffee (usually sweetened), or *café crème* (coffee with steamed milk). But in restaurants, the coffee taken after meals is always black coffee, never coffee with added milk. Most restaurants will provide cream or milk if requested for tea or coffee, but some will not. In France, coffee is always taken at the very end of the meal (not with dessert), served almost as a course of its own. In finer restaurants, chocolates and/or *petits fours* might also be served. Brewed decaffeinated coffee (not freeze-dried) is almost always available at restaurants (though not at all village cafés). Simply ask for a *déca*, a *décaféiné*, or a *faux café*. Tea and herb teas (known as *infusions*) are most often of the tea bag variety. However, at finer restaurants one can find excellent freshly brewed herb teas, often of herbs picked right from the garden. Most restaurants do not offer artificial sweeteners, but small tablets of artificial sweetener can be purchased at almost any pharmacy. The major brands are Canderel, Aspartam, Pouss'Suc.

Fish, meat and poultry

Almost all fish, meat, and poultry tastes better when cooked on the bone. If you have problems with boning fish, ask if the fish dish you are ordering is boned *(sans arêtes)*, and if not, ask the waiter to debone it before serving *(enlevez les arêtes)*. The French prefer their meat and some poultry (particularly duck) cooked quite rare. But if rare meat or poultry bothers you, ask for it *bien cuit* (well done). Be prepared for the waiter to wince. (For rare meat, order it *saignant;* for medium, *à point*.)

Salt and pepper

Some chefs are insulted if diners alter their creations with additional seasonings, and so do not offer salt and pepper at the table. If you don't see salt or pepper, just ask for it. But do be sure to taste the food before reaching for the mill or shaker.

Water

Because the French consume so much bottled water, people still wonder whether it is safe to drink the tap water. Of course it is. The French simply sometimes prefer the taste, effervescence, and/or healthful qualities of mineral and spring waters. All restaurants will serve tap water *(une carafe d'eau)* free of charge. Mineral water, which you will pay for, comes either still *(plate)*, or with bubbles *(gazeuse)*. If you order Perrier brand mineral water, don't be surprised if only small bottles are available. The French consider Perrier too gaseous to drink with meals, so most restaurants stock only small bottles for drinking as an *apéritif* or with mixed drinks.

Wine and liquor

This is one area where I firmly advise you to follow the rule "When in France, do as the French do." Most Frenchmen do not drink hard liquor before meals, and few restaurants are equipped with a full bar. If you are accustomed to having a cocktail before meals, try to change your habits during your visit to France. The liquor will numb your palate for the pleasures to follow, and requests for a martini or whiskey before a meal will not put you in good stead with the waiter or with management. Almost all restaurants offer a less-alcoholic house cocktail—most often a Kir, a blend of white wine or Champagne and *crème de cassis*. I personally dislike most of these concoctions (which can be expensive and run up the bill) and always ask for the wine list when requesting the menu. Then I usually order as an aperitif a white wine that will be drunk with the meal, or at least with the first course.

Selecting wines

Most of what I know about wines I've learned from tasting, tasting, tasting in restaurants. I study wine lists, keep track of prices and favorite food and wine combinations, and am always eager to sample a wine that is new or unfamiliar to me. The joy of traveling in various regions is that even the most modest restaurants will offer a selection of the regional wines. And though prices may not always be lower than elsewhere in France, there is usually something new to discover.

Although I have found some *sommeliers*, or wine stewards, to be outrageously sexist, generally I haven't found them to be unfair or unwilling to help when I sought information or assistance. If you don't know a lot about wine, ask the *sommelier*'s advice. Give him a rough idea of your taste and the price you would like to pay. This assumes, of course, that you share a common language. If you do not, simply ask whether there is a *vin de la maison* (house wine).

If you are knowledgeable about wine, you will want to study the wine list. Don't allow yourself to be pressured or bullied into making a quick decision (this isn't always easy). Often I narrow my choice down to two or three equally priced wines, then ask the *sommelier* to make the final selection.

Prices for wines vary drastically from restaurant to restaurant: Some have large long-standing wine cellars, others are just getting started. I love wine and consider it an essential part of any meal.

When dining in a bistro or brasserie, I often order the house wine, by either the carafe or the bottle, and of course always concentrate on the wines of the region. Although it is sometimes difficult, I generally try not to pay more than 200 to 250 francs a bottle for wine. In France, the general rule of thumb is that one third of the final bill should be for wine. That is, if you are paying 400 francs for a meal for two, about 135 francs of that will be spent on wine.

Comments

I welcome all reader comments and suggestions, and whenever possible will respond with a personal note. All remarks should be sent to: Patricia Wells, c/o Workman Publishing, 1 West 39 Street, New York, NY 10018.

How to Use This Book

The following diagram offers detailed instructions on how to read a town listing and an establishment listing.

BEUVRON-EN-AUGE *(Calvados)*

Caen 31 k, Paris 224 k, Pont-l'Evêque 32 k.

(City, town, or village) *(Département)*

(Distance in kilometers to nearby towns and to Paris)

RESTAURANT — (Type of establishment)

LE PAVE D'AUGE — (Name of establishment)
Beuvron-en-Auge, 14430
    Dozulé. — (Street address, or in this case, name of town, postal
(31.79.26.71). code, and name of town where mail is distributed)
Last orders taken at 1:45 P.M.
    and 9 P.M. (Telephone number)
Closed for dinner Monday
    and Tuesday, and
    mid-January through (Latest times that you may order at lunch and
    February. dinner)
Credit cards: AE, V.
Some English spoken. (Weekly closing days and vacation periods)
125- and 220-franc menus.
    A la carte, about 250
    francs. (Credit cards accepted; see list of abbreviations)

SPECIALTIES:
Fish and *poulet Vallée d'Auge* (Someone on the premises speaks some English)
(chicken with cream and
cider). (Prices of set menus, which do not always include
wine and service. Average price of a meal à la carte,
wine and service included)

(Specialties recommended by the restaurant)

Alphabetizing

Within each chapter, entries are listed alphabetically by town. Within towns, entries are grouped within their type of establishment *(restaurant, fromagerie, boulangerie)*.

Markets

Since I feel that a visit to an open-air fruit and vegetable market is essential to the understanding of any area, I have attempted to list all the important markets within each region. So the reader may easily find these markets while traveling, they are listed in two places. The "When You Go" box in each chapter offers a general Monday through Sunday listing, noting markets for all the towns a traveler might be likely to visit in the region. The liveliest markets are marked with an asterisk. Second, when the town is mentioned for another reason (a restaurant, a cheese shop), the market day, hours, and location are noted under the town listing.

Fairs and Festivals

The list of fairs and festivals is selective. I have tried to limit it to those that are directly food-related, or to those at which special regional fare is likely to be served. In many cases the dates change from year to year, so I have not listed exact dates for each fair and festival. When you are in the region, contact either the local *office de tourisme* (tourist office), the *syndicat d'initiative* (the equivalent of the chamber of commerce), or the *mairie* (city hall) for detailed information.

What Is a Département?

France is divided into ninety-five *départements,* areas roughly equivalent to a state in the United States. Each *département* has a name, and is numbered in a rather rough alphabetical order, beginning with the Ain (01) and ending with the Val-d'Oise (95). The first two digits of all postal codes and the final two digits on automobile license plates match the *département* numbers. For example, the postal code for Bourg-en-Bresse, the capital of the Ain *département,* is 01000. the last two digits of a license plate from the Ain will be 01.

    Départements are then put together to make administrative regions. For example, the region of Brittany *(Bretagne)* includes four *départements:* Finistère (29), Côtes-du-Nord (22), Morbihan (56), and

Ille-et-Vilaine (35). In this book, I have roughly followed the administrative boundaries for regions. But since this is not a book about government, but about gastronomy and travel, the boundaries are rather more loosely defined.

MICHELIN ALERT

Michelin's Green Guides are currently being updated, with some changes in titles and boundaries of the areas covered. In each chapter, under "When You Go," we have listed the new title. However, your bookstore might still have the old edition in stock. Check the map on the back of the Green Guide against the *Food Lover's Guide* map for that region, to be sure that the geography coincides.

ESTABLISHMENT GLOSSARY

Affineur: cheese ager

Bistro à Vin: wine bar

Boulangerie: bakery

Charcuterie: prepared foods to go

Chocolaterie: chocolate shop

Confiserie: candy shop

Eaux-de-Vie: fruit brandies

Ecole de Cuisine: cooking school

Ecole de Vin: wine school

Ferme-Auberge: farmhouse dining

Folklorique: regional folklore

Fromager: cheesemaker

Fromager-Affineur: cheesemaker-ager

Fromagerie: cheese shop

Librairie: book shop

Marché: market

Musée: museum

Pâtisserie: pastry shop

Potager: kitchen garden

Pour la Maison: housewares

Salon de Thé: tea salon

Spécialités Régionales: regional specialties

Stand de Pâtisserie: pastry stand

Vigneron: vintner

Vin, Bière, Alcool: wine, beer, and liquor shop

Winstub: wine bar (in Alsace)

When Should I Travel?

The French all continue to take their vacations at the same time, which means that during Easter and the months of July and August, roadways, hotels, and restaurants are likely to be crowded. Although it is always advisable to reserve ahead, it is essential during these periods. The "When You Go" box suggests the best time to visit each region.

A Word on French Holidays

Holidays are sacred to the French, and they seem to have an awful lot of them. When traveling during holiday periods, be certain to reserve well in advance, for that's when the French like to travel too. Be forewarned that both trains and highways tend to be crowded on the weekends preceding and following most holidays. The official French holidays include January 1; *Pâques* (Easter Sunday); *Ascension* (Holy Thursday, the fortieth day after Easter), *Pentecôte* (Pentecost, the seventh Sunday after Easter), May 1, July 14, August 15, November 1, November 11, and December 25. Note that there are also two weeks of school holiday in February, when many establishments close for vacation.

Abbreviations

The following abbreviations are used for credit cards in the listings:

AE: American Express
DC: Diners Club
EC: Eurocard or MasterCard
V: Visa or Carte Bleue

The following abbreviations are used in the recipes to indicate weights and measures:

cm: centimeter
mm: millimeter
g: gram
kg: kilogram
ml: milliliter

A Word on the Recipes

Like the selection of establishments in this book, the choice of recipes is highly personal. I looked for recipes that typified each region and establishment, keeping in mind cost, time, and availability of ingredients. Note that all recipes were first tested by me, in France and with French ingredients, then by Susan Herrmann Loomis in the United States, with American ingredients.

Bretagne
BRITTANY

A grilled lobster feast in Cléden-Cap-Sizun.

Sporting magestic clouds, dramatic double rainbows, and sunsets bold enough to warm the coldest of hearts, Brittany is a land that's appealingly exotic, fittingly ceremonial, and forthrightly a country of its own. Brittany is where you travel when there arises that irresistible urge to go to the sea, and where you go to get to the heart of the matter.

In a day when much of what we eat is pitifully anonymous—we so seldom really know very much about the true origin or freshness of most of our food—it's a rare pleasure to walk out to fishing ports like Guilvinec and greet the colorfully painted boats as they float into view, then watch fishermen unload wicker baskets full of shiny sardines, squiggling pink langoustines, shimmering skate, sweet meaty crabs just seconds from the sea; to see buckwheat *galettes* turn from batter to aromatic, tangy snacks right before your eyes; to pass man-made mountains of glistening crystals of ivory sea salt along the Guérande peninsula and finally make the mental connection between the sea and that everyday seasoning; to down platters full of tiny Belon oysters at water's edge, overlooking the very beds in which they were lovingly plumped; and after all this to say to yourself, this is as fresh as it's ever going to be.

So now I cannot look at a lobster without thinking of the

lobster fisherman I met at the port of Erquy and wonder, was there a violent storm today, or did he venture into the waters, and if so, as he made the rounds checking his lobster traps, did his eyes glow with pleasure or disappointment?

As I cook, tossing grains of salt into pots of boiling water, I think of Jérome, the *paludier,* or salt marsh worker, I met on Brittany's southern coast and marvel that in this day and age, people can still make a living gathering salt from the sea—and frankly, I'm grateful that they do.

I don't hold with those who wrinkle their nose in disdain at Breton cuisine. Is there no merit, no talent, in the process of gathering, selecting, presenting, this remarkable bounty of fish and shellfish, whether it be cooked or raw?

The summer was just ending when I first began my acquaintance with this jagged chunk of land that juts out into the water, with the English Channel to the north, the Bay of Biscay to the south, the vast expanse of the Atlantic Ocean to the west.

On that first visit, my husband and I and our friends shared a weeklong serendipitous adventure, filled with walks along sandy beaches, jogs along lighthouse roads, and days spent stalking pastry shops and markets, evenings feasting at table.

Soon we found that Brittany offered just about everything we were looking for: There would be time for grilled lobster and sea-fresh oysters, and moments for antique-shopping on the picturesque Rue Kéréon in Quimper. We could play at tourist when we wanted to, wandering through museums, and we could while away time at cafés when our spirits needed space and calm.

We met the first Saturday of September in the lively walled town of Saint-Malo, where the beaches and twelfth-century ramparts were still crawling with tourists, eager for one last dose of leisure and sunshine before summer faded into fall. My husband and I drove out from our home in Paris and snacked on buckwheat *galettes* and bubbling cider at a *crêperie* overlooking the Emerald Coast as we waited for our friends to arrive on one of the huge ferries that shuttle travelers back and forth from England.

And for the next seven memorable, sun-filled days—in our minds, the time seemed more like one marvelous month—we played. We intentionally left the itinerary flexible, mapping out a list of restaurants, one for each evening, and agreed that lunch would be constructed informally from markets we found on our journeys.

Brittany is a newcomer, so to speak, that wasn't annexed to France until 1532, later than many other provinces. Even today its people remain Breton first, French second, guarding jealously their own language, customs, and culture. (Recently I received a brochure for a Christmas card with a greeting that could be printed in five languages: English, French, Spanish, Italian, and Breton!)

As we toured, we fell in love with Belle-Ile-en-Mer, where we jogged for miles along flat roads at dusk, the beams from nearby lighthouses swirling in the sky. As we cooled down after the run, we found hedges of wild blackberries hugging the roadside, there for the picking for our pre-dinner snack.

As it turned out, Belle-Ile looks a lot the way I imagined all of Brittany to be: quaint, flat, slightly wild and dramatic, but welcoming as well. No highways, maybe a supermarket, just a handful of restaurants and shops. A place to be by yourself, study nature, wander, get involved in the mysteries of this still mysterious land.

On that first trip, we donned our tourist caps as we wandered with throngs through picture-postcard towns like Pont-Aven, with its squat gray stone cottages ribboned with poppies (where we staged our own *dégustation* of crisp, flaky, buttery *kouign-amann* from among the village pastry shops), and Quimper (where we resisted, but barely, the charming local pottery), taking in, as my friend likes to say, *un peu de shopping, un peu d'histoire.*

We drove out to the western tip of Brittany for a windy, mystical walk to the stormy Pointe du Raz (Michelin justifiably rates this a three-star site) and posed for pictures in front of the statue of Our Lady of the Shipwrecked *(Notre-Dame-des-Naufragés).*

We were struck by the visible influence and importance of the Catholic church: It seemed that every weekend a different village would be hosting a *pardon,* the annual festival held for the patron saint of a church, and everywhere roadside shrines and larger-than-life-size crucifixes caught our eyes.

Brittany lured us back again, and on later visits the reality of modern life hit us hard as we arose before sunrise to greet the huge industrial fishing boats that chugged into the port of Douarnenez, where equally sleepy-eyed merchants—the wholesalers, or

middlemen—bid for entire lots of glistening fish piled helter-skelter into huge gray plastic basins. Much of the fish appeared to us as sad and battered, and we wondered what it might look like the next day, and the day after, as merchants hawked it along the market streets of Paris. We swallowed hard, accepting the fact that our small-fry independent fishermen were indeed a minority here.

No matter where we went in Brittany, it seemed we were forever plotting toward the day we'd next return, to help trawl for the prized *coquille Saint-Jacques* in the scallop-rich Saint-Brieuc bay, run again along the lighthouse roads of Belle-Ile, and, for one more time in our lives, tie those big white bibs around our necks and regale ourselves with a surfeit of fresh, rich, meaty Breton lobster.

WHEN YOU GO

Michelin Green Guide: *Brittany* (available in English).

Getting there: Air Inter offers three daily 1-hour flights to Lorient, leaving from either Paris's Orly Ouest airport or from the Roissy (Charles-de-Gaulle) airport. About a dozen trains a day make the 4-hour trip from the Gare Montparnasse to the city of Rennes; then many continue on to Saint-Brieuc, Brest, Lorient, and Nantes. Cars can be rented at the airport and train stations. From Paris by car, Brittany is about a 6-hour drive.

Getting around: Michelin map 230 (Bretagne/Brittany).

Best time to visit: Brittany is best visited from late spring to early fall. If traveling in July and August—when all of France seems to be on vacation and as close to the ocean as possible—be sure to reserve well in advance. Sun lovers will be happy to know that during the long days of summer, sunset is deferred until almost 11 P.M. Note that a number of establishments close off-season, mid-October to mid-March.

Required reading: There are two marvelous books in English on Brittany: Eleanor Clark's *Oysters of Locmariaquer* is a loving account of summers spent there with her husband, Robert Penn Warren, and their children. The excellent *Horse of Pride: Life in a Breton Village* by Pierre-Jakez Hélias is essential reading for anyone interested in the everyday culture of France in general, Brittany in particular. The book, known as *Le Cheval d'Orgueil* in French, follows the dramatic changes that have taken place in French society since the turn of the century.

MARKETS
(Liveliest markets are marked with an asterisk.)

Monday: Auray, Brest, Combourg, Concarneau, Douarnenez, Ploërmel, Pontivy, Questembert, Redon, Saint-Malo, Saint-Quay-Portrieux, Vitré (except holidays).

Tuesday: Belle-Ile-en-Mer, *Brest, Dinard, Guilvinec, Guingamp, Hédé, Landerneau, *Locmariaquer, Loctudy, Paimpol, Pont-Aven, Pont l'Abbé, Quintin, Saint-Malo, Saint-Pol-de-Léon, Trinité-sur-Mer, Le-Val-André.

Wednesday: Brest, Carnac, Landivisiau, Lorient, Montauban, Pont l'Abbé, Quimper, Riec-sur-Belon, Saint-Brieuc, *Saint-Malo, Tréguier, Vannes.

Thursday: *Brest, Châteaugiron, Dinan, Dinard, Hennebont, Lamballe, Lannion, Locminé, Malestroit, Névez, *Pont-l'Abbé, La Roche-Bernard, Rosporden, Saint-Aubin-du-Cormier, Saint-Malo, Sarzeau.

Friday: Belle-Ile-en-Mer, *Brest, Bruz, *Concarneau, Douarnenez, Fouesnant,*Guingamp, Landerneau, Perros-Guirec, *Ploërmel, Pont l'Abbé, Quimperlé, *Saint-Malo, Saint-Quay-Portrieux, *Trinité-sur-Mer.

Saturday: Brest, *Dinard, Dol-de-Bretagne, Erquy, Fougères, Guingamp, *Landerneau, Locmariaquer, *Lorient, Morlaix, *Névez, Plouescat, Pont l'Abbé, Port-

Louis, Quiberon, *Quimper, *Rennes, *Saint-Brieuc, *Saint-Malo, Saint-Méen-le-Grand, *Vannes.

Sunday: Cancale, *Carnac.

FAIRS AND FESTIVALS

Third Sunday in July: *Fête des Pommiers* (apple tree festival), Fouesnant.

August 15: *Fête de la Mer* (sea festival), Le Croisic.

Third Sunday in August: *Fête des Filets Bleus* (festival of the blue fishing nets), Concarneau.

Beginning of October: *Fête des Boudins* (sausage festival), Nozay.

Mid-October: *Fête des Châtaignes et du Vin Nouveau* (chestnut and wine festival), Nantes.

Patrick Moncey at the Créperie des Artisans, Dinan.

BATZ-SUR-MER *(Loire-Atlantique)*

La Baule 7 k, Nantes 87 k, Paris 452 k, Saint-Nazaire 30 k.

SPECIALITES REGIONALES

LA SALORGE DE GUERANDE
Rue des Marais-Kervalet,
44740 Batz-sur-Mer.
(40.23.92.99).
Open 8 A.M. to noon and 1:30 to 5:30 P.M. Closed Saturday, Sunday, and the last week of December.

A harbor scene along the Brittany coast.

When visiting the region, do take time to drive along the strange and impressive rectangular basins of the Guérande peninsula, including the villages of Batz-sur-Mer, Kervalet, Saillé, and Guérande. Here, from June through mid-September, the local *paludiers* trap the seawater in shallow beds, allow it to evaporate, then rake, and stock in gigantic mounds, the natural gray *sel de mer,* or crystallized sea salt. Even rarer is the more refined, delicate *fleur de sel,* the grayish white salt collected from the top surface of the evaporating beds. With the faint perfume of violets, this is the salt favored by France's best bakers and chefs. Throughout the area, you'll find roadside stands offering salt as well as the region's famed onions and potatoes. Breton sea salt can be purchased here. Note that it can also be found in most health food stores and many specialty shops throughout France.

BELLE-ILE-EN-MER *(Morbihan)*

Quiberon 18 k (half-hour boat ride).

Market: Tuesday and Friday, 8 A.M. to noon,
Place de la République, Le Palais.

RESTAURANT

CASTEL-CLARA
Goulphar, Bangor, 56360 Le
   Palais, Belle-Ile-en-Mer.
(97.31.84.21).
Last orders taken at 1:30 P.M.
   and 9:30 P.M.
Closed mid-October
   through mid-March.
Credit cards: AE, V.
Terrace dining.
Private dining room for 20.
English spoken.
175-, 195-, and 230-franc
   menus. A la carte, 260
   francs.

SPECIALTIES:
*Soupe de palourdes à la fleur de
thym* (clam soup flavored with
thyme), *homard grillé* (grilled
lobster), *langouste grillée*
(grilled spiny lobster),
mille-feuille tiède (warm layered
puff pastry).

Here, overlooking one of Brittany's most breath-taking sea views, you'll feast on some of the best of the region's fare, selected and prepared by the young and ambitious chef, Yves Pérou. His tender lamb is raised right on the island, most of the vegetables come from the garden he and wife tend, and the remarkable *coquilles Saint-Jacques,* lobster, and oysters are purchased directly from the thirty or forty fishermen who still inhabit Belle-Ile.

The food here is simple, at times sublime: perfectly grilled lobster; a light and creamy clam soup infused with thyme; and delicious roast lamb. For dessert, sample his warm layered puff pastry filled with plump fresh raspberries.

GIVE US THIS DAY OUR DAILY BREAD

"Those who made their own bread were well aware of the price involved. Sweat and anxiety. And a kind of religion as well. They would always make the sign of the cross on the bottom of each round loaf. Some of the old people would still cross themselves before cutting into it. And you'd have had to watch them eat it to realize that they were observing a rite. They would sniff it, chew it slowly, then savor it, deep in thought. The crumbs that fell on the table were carefully gathered up into their palms, and every last one of them was gobbled up. To them bread was their body. Otherwise, they weren't hard to please."

The Horse of Pride: Life in a Breton Village,
Pierre-Jakez Hélias

Oysters

The French have a saying, "You can't love oysters without loving Brittany," and I'd say that the reverse must also be true: I can't imagine going to Brittany and not enjoying my fill of sea-fresh oysters.

The "R" months: Contrary to what most people believe, there is nothing unhealthy about eating oysters during the months without an "R," that is, from May through August. But there is still good reason to confine one's oyster consumption to the months from September through April: During the warm summer months when oysters spawn, they lose much of their flavor and texture, as their meat becomes very soft and milky.

Bigger is not better: Size has nothing to do with the gustatory quality of an oyster. Just as the soil in which grapes are grown affects the ultimate character of a wine, the determining factors in the final taste qualities of an oyster are the salinity, makeup, and temperature of the water in which it is raised, as well as of the salt ponds or rivers in which it is aged. Since oysters are usually priced according to size—the largest are always the most expensive—it pays to fall in love with the little guys. In France the *papillon,* or "butterfly" oyster, is increasingly in vogue. These small, plump, crinkle-shelled *creuse* oysters are fattened in the *claires* (oyster beds) of Marennes, down the coast toward Bordeaux. Smaller and less expensive than most *creuses,* the *papillon* nonetheless offers the distinctive creamy sweetness of its pedigree.

Plates or *creuses?* While the flat, or *plates,* oysters—of which the Breton Belon is the best known—remain the most prized and the most expensive French oyster, they are becoming increasingly rare because of a mysterious parasite that first appeared off the coast of Quiberon in 1978. Due to disease and disaster, annual production has declined from 21,000 tons in 1960 to the current 1,500 tons. All this means it's time to discover the abundant and less expensive crinkle-shelled *creuse* oyster, of which France produces about 100,000 tons each year. Among the best *creuses* are the *spéciales* from the aging beds near La Rochelle and Marennes-Oléron (slightly south of Brittany), where they feast on microscopic blue algae for several months, becoming richer, greener, and more flavorful.

Cooking with oysters: When cooking with oysters, the best are medium- to large-size *creuses.* Small oysters are easy to overcook, and are more likely to fall apart when heated.

White wine or red? The white Gros-Plat and Muscadet are the traditional oyster wines, because their flintiness and acidity marry well with the iodine-rich shellfish. But why not experiement with other whites, such as a rich Cassis, or with reds, such as Saumur-Champigny or Bandol?

Dead or alive? To verify that it is just-out-of-the-water fresh, gently touch the edge of the oyster with the tines of your fork. If the oyster contracts perceptibly, it is lively and at its peak. If you're opening the oysters yourself, you'll find the fresher the oyster, the harder it is to open, for the lively muscles contract.

CANCALE *(Ille-et-Vilaine)*

Avranches 59 k, Le Dinan 34 k, Le Mont-Saint-Michel 46 k, Paris 396 k.

Market: Sunday, 8 A.M. to 1 P.M., Rue de la Marine, behind the church.

RESTAURANT

**RESTAURANT DE
BRICOURT**
1 Rue Duguesclin, 35260
Cancale.
(99.89.64.76).
Last orders taken at 1:30 P.M.
and 9:30 P.M.
Closed Tuesday, Wednesday,
and December through
February.
Credit cards: V.
Terrace dining.
English spoken.
84-franc menu Monday
through Friday. A la
carte, 250 francs.
Reservations essential.

SPECIALTIES:
Huîtres plates tièdes (warmed
flat oysters), *homard rôti* (roast
lobster).

My heart warms when I think of a spectacular lunch here, one rainy day in August. My palate was reeling from the marvelous flavors, aromas, and combinations set before me by chef Olivier Roellinger, who has turned his boyhood home into a charming, elegant restaurant with just ten tables and a garden out back. The decor—very pink, with lovely tiled fireplaces and Fragonard-like wall murals—is plush in a homey sort of way and warmly envelops you in comfort and security. The chef's passion for food is evident with every bite. A salad of smoked salmon and the freshest tiny bay scallops; little balls of crabmeat wrapped in cabbage leaves and topped with a sauce of fresh coriander; a spectacular marriage of clams, first-of-season *cèpes,* and thinly sliced potatoes bathed in a fine shallot-rich sauce, all convinced me that this man has a rare talent indeed. His desserts are equally inventive and appealing. I'll not soon forget his *gratin d'abricots*, a warm blend of fresh green plums, yellow plums, and apricots, covered with a gratin of almond cream and served with a scoop of strong buckwheat honey ice cream—a spectacular contrast of hot and cold, sweet and tangy. Note that space is limited and reservations are essential.

*Marketing along the streets of old
Dinan.*

CLEDEN-CAP-SIZUN *(Finistère)*

Audierne 10 k, Douarnenez 32 k, Paris 601 k, Quimper 45 k.

RESTAURANT

L'ETRAVE
Place de l'Eglise,
  Cléden-Cap-Sizun, 29113
  Audierne.
(98.70.66.87).
Last orders taken at 1:30 P.M.
  and 8:30 P.M.
Closed Wednesday, and
  October until Easter.
No credit cards.
50–, 108–, and 150– franc
  menus. A la carte, 200
  francs.

SPECIALTIES:
Araignée farcie (stuffed spider
crab), *homard grillé à la crème*
(grilled lobster with cream),
langoustines grillées (grilled
langoustines).

Good times at L'Etrave.

O ne of my favorite finds in the region is this little village restaurant not too far from the stormy Pointe du Raz and the port of Audierne.

Even after years of living in France, I remained partial to Maine lobster, finding the French variety either too stringy and tough, too dry, or too delicate to send up raves that equal the *homard*'s generally high price. All that changed some years ago, after sampling L'Etrave's incredible grilled lobster. Here the *homard à la crème* is served up on giant platters, still bubbling as it enters the dining room. (The chef cuts the lobster in two, douses it with cream, and grills it for just five or six minutes under a sizzling fire.)

Skip the rest of the offerings (forgettable stuffed crab, ordinary lamb, dreadful bread), but order up a bottle of chilled Muscadet, and enjoy!

DINAN *(Côtes-du-Nord)*

Avranches 67 k, Lorient 151 k, Paris 393 k, Rennes 51 k, Saint-Brieuc 58 k, Saint-Malo 29 k.

Market: Thursday, 9 A.M. to noon (3 P.M. in July and August), Place Duguesclin and Place du Champ.

RESTAURANT

CREPERIE DES ARTISANS
6 Rue Petit-Fort, 22100
    Dinan.
(96.39.44.10).
Last orders taken at 2:30 P.M.
    and 10:30 P.M.
Closed Monday (except
    during July and August),
    and October until Easter.
Credit card: V.
Terrace dining.
A la carte, about 50 francs.

SPECIALTIES:
Breton crêpes (here, thin
wheat pancakes) and *galettes*
(here, thin buckwheat
pancakes).

In the old section of Dinan, not far from the walled city of Saint-Malo, Patrick Moncey serves some of the region's best-tasting crêpes and *galettes*, thin, lacy pancakes best enjoyed plain or with a touch of butter. This folkloric half-timbered house, decorated with bright blue shutters and set on a steep cobblestone street lined with craft shops, is a fine place to come for a snack, sharing the long wooden tables with friends as well as strangers. This is the place to sample the local *lait ribot*, a sort of Breton buttermilk, into which you dip a bite of crêpe or *galette*. A single criticism: The kitchen sanitation here is not of the highest order.

DINARD *(Ille-et-Vilaine)*

Dinan 22 k, Lamballe 47 k, Paris 413 k, Rennes 72 k.

Market: Tuesday, Thursday, and Saturday, 8:30 A.M. to 1 P.M. (3:30 P.M. in July and August), Place Paul-Crolard.

SPECIALITES REGIONALES

GERARD PERRIER
Résidence les Pins, 35800
    Dinard.
(99.46.13.99).

SPECIALTY:
Pêche (fishing).

Chatty, outgoing Gérard Perrier loves boats, fishing, and people, so he combines all his passions by organizing fishing expeditions for those who want to fish, or just watch. Guests are invited to go out with this blond Breton fisherman/hotel owner, who says he was "born with a fishing pole in his hand," to fish—depending upon the season—for lobster, crab, mackerel, and *bar à la ligne* (sea bass caught with a fishing line, not a net). As with everything in Brittany, hours depend upon the tide, but he usually likes to leave around 8 in the morning. His boat is out from March to November, although the best months are June to November. The charge is 500 francs for a half-day (4 hours) or 800 francs for a full day (8 hours), and includes the price of gear, clothing, and lunch. He takes a maximum of six, but if everyone wants to fish, he prefers to limit the number to three.

DOUARNENEZ *(Finistère)*

Brest 75 k, Châteaulin 26 k, Paris 575 k, Quimper 22 k.

Market: Monday and Friday, 9 A.M. to 4 P.M., Place de la Résistance.

PATISSERIE

LE MOIGNE
86 Avenue de la Gare, 29100
  Douarnenez.
(98.74.01.07).
Open 11:30 A.M. (9:30 A.M.
  in July and August) to
  7:30 P.M. Off-season
  closed Sunday through
  Thursday.

A hike up the hilly streets of picturesque Dinan.

Throughout Brittany, pastry shop windows are filled with that relentlessly rich and buttery yeast cake known as *kouign-amann* as well as the popular *far breton* (see recipe, page 50), a homey flan rich with eggs and marinated prunes. But the offerings at Le Moigne are the best and freshest I know in the region, and well worth a detour. (*Note:* Their products can also be found on Thursdays at the Place Gambetta market in Pont-l'Abbé.)

ERQUY *(Côtes-du-Nord)*

Lamballe 23 k, Plancoët 30 k.

Market: Saturday, 8 A.M. to noon, Place de l'Eglise.
Fish market: Daily, according to the tide, Port d'Erquy.

An authentic, lively fishing port on the Baie de Saint-Brieuc, Erquy's waters offer some of France's finest scallops, sea urchins, *praires* (tiny clams), the tiny bay scallops they call *olivettes,* as well as periwinkles, mussels, tiny *amandes* clams, lobster, turbot, sole, codfish, and sea bass. It's fun to just hang around the port in season, stopping at the local cafés for platters of oysters, watching the fishing boats putter in and out.

GATEAU BRETON
BRITTANY BUTTER CAKE

The rich and lightly salted butter of Brittany and fat, fresh farm eggs help make this one of France's most popular desserts. The gâteau breton is a cinch to make, and, though it's insufferably rich, it's the sort of sweet to save for a rare and special treat.

6 large egg yolks, lightly beaten

2 cups (280 g) all-purpose flour (do not use unbleached)

1 cup (1 pound; 240 g) lightly salted butter, cubed, at room temperature

1 ¼ cups (250 g) sugar

1. Preheat the oven to 375°F (190°C). Butter a round 9-inch (23 cm) cake pan.

2. Reserve 1 teaspoon of the egg yolk to use for a glaze.

3. Place the flour in a large, shallow bowl and make a well in the center. Add the butter, sugar, and remaining egg yolks to the well and mix them until smooth with your fingertips. Gradually work in the flour, using your fingers. Knead rapidly and thoroughly until the mixture is smooth and resembles a soft cookie dough.

4. Flour your hands and gently press the dough into the buttered pan. Brush the cake with the reserved egg yolk and use a fork to make a lattice design on the top.

5. Bake 20 minutes. Reduce the oven to 350°F (175°C) and bake until the cake is golden brown, about 30 minutes longer.

6. Remove the cake from the oven and let it cool to room temperature before unmolding. *Gâteau breton* is best eaten the day it is baked, but it may be stored for several days in an airtight container.

Yield: One 9-inch (23 cm) cake.

GUILVINEC *(Finistère)*

Pont-l'Abbé 11 k, Quimper 30 k.

Market: Tuesday, 9 A.M. to noon, Place de l'Eglise.
Fish market: Daily, according to the tide, Port du Guilvinec.

This is the place to go see Brittany with the locals, to don yellow slickers and blue rubber boots and trek on out to the southwestern end of the peninsula to this lively fishing port, where each afternoon just minutes past 5, a score of brightly painted wooden boats slip into the port, cradling, among other fish and crustaceans, wicker baskets filled to the brim with pale pink, squiggling live langoustines. It's a festive moment as the fishermen quickly unload their catch, while dozens of onlookers crowd about to take pictures, touch a live *langoustine,* or simply to greet these men of the sea as they return from another day's work. Visitors can stay to watch the wholesale fish auction, or *criée,* which begins even as the fishermen are still unloading.

SPECIALITES REGIONALES

COOPERATIVE DES MARINS
At the port, next to the *criée,* 29115 Guilvinec.
(98.58.10.31).
Open 8 A.M. to noon and 2 to 6 P.M. Closed Saturday afternoon and Sunday.
Credit card: V.
International mail orders accepted.

SPECIALTY:
Folklorique (regional folklore).

A great shop for all sorts of fishermen's gear and clothing, including marvelous sturdy wire and wicker baskets, thick wool Breton sweaters, colorful boots and slickers.

AN OVERDOSE OF SALMON

"Because of the peasants' decided preference for meat, they usually scowled at the idea of fish, which they were doomed to eat every Friday, the day of abstinence. It was thus 'Lenten and penitential' fare. But also, it didn't retain the body's heat, as would a slice of salt pork. Food for the poor and the miserly. Not so very long ago, the farmhands along the banks of the Aulne stipulated in their contracts that their employers would not make them eat salmon more than twice or three times a week. There was good reason to swallow it down once, to do penance for one's sins, and a second time to show one's good will; but even three times was a bit much."

The Horse of Pride: Life in a Breton Village,
Pierre-Jakez Hélias

HENNEBONT *(Morbihan)*

Concarneau 59 k, Lorient 10 k, Paris 487 k; Quiberon 42 k, Quimperlé 26 k.

Market: Thursday (Wednesday when a holiday falls on Thursday), 8:30 A.M. to 12:30 P.M., Place du Général-de-Gaulle, Place du Maréchal, Rue Trottier.

RESTAURANT

**CHATEAU DE
LOCGUENOLE**
56700 Hennebont.
(97.76.29.04).
Last orders taken at 1:30 P.M.
and 9:30 P.M.
Closed mid-November
through February.
Credit cards: AE, DC, V.
Private dining room for 5 to
20.
English spoken.
185–, 260–, and 340–franc
menus. A la carte, 400
francs.
SPECIALTIES:
Change with the seasons.

In a proud but somewhat tattered *château* situated at the edge of the Blavet river, a very creative chef makes good use of the local Breton products. We sampled delicious bite-size buckwheat crêpes *(petites galettes de sarrasin)* filled with fresh crabmeat and served in light curried butter sauce; turbot sautéed with chunks of artichokes; and whole roast *lotte,* or monkfish, infused with bacon and cream and served with sautéed tiny local potatoes. (Directions: 4 kilometers south of Hennebont on the D781.)

KERASCOET *(Finistère)*

Concarneau 17 k, Paris 536 k, Pont-Aven 12 k, Quimper 39 k.

RESTAURANT

**CREPERIE DES
CHAUMIERES**
Hameau de Kerascoët,
29139 Névez.
No telephone.
Last orders taken at 10:30
P.M.
Open daily July through
August; closed the rest of
the year.
No credit cards.
50 francs.

SPECIALTIES:
Crêpes farcies (stuffed crêpes),
soupe de poisson (fish soup).

Wend your way to this fairytale village filled with impeccably restored *chaumières,* or thatched-roof cottages, and you won't be disappointed. Then sample the thin, delicious crêpes—try one with butter, or for heartier appetites a *complète* (one filled with ham, cheese, and egg)—and sip a bit of cider. Across the street from the *crêperie,* note the beautiful restored community bread oven.

PAIMPOL *(Côtes-du-Nord)*

Guingamp 28 k, Lannion 33 k, Paris 496 k, Saint-Brieuc 45 k.

Market: Tuesday, 5 A.M. to 12:30 P.M.,
Place du Martay, Place Gambetta, Place du Verdun.

RESTAURANT

CHATEAU DE
    COATGUELEN
Pléhédel, 22290 Lanvollon
(96.22.31.24).
Last orders taken at 1:30 P.M.
    and 9 P.M. (9:30 P.M. in
    July and August).
Closed Tuesday and
    Wednesday lunch, and
    the second week in
    January through March.
Credit cards: AE, DC, V.
Private dining room for 45.
English spoken.
130–, 180–, and 280–franc
    menus. A la carte, about
    320 francs.

SPECIALTIES:
Huîtres chaudes au cidre et aux
poireaux (warm oysters with
cider and leeks), *feuilleté de*
langoustines à la citronelle
(langoustines in puff pastry
with lemon grass), *papillote de*
homard aux algues (lobster and
seaweed cooked in parchment
paper), *petit canard rôti au miel*
et au vinaigre (roast duck with
honey and vinegar), *tarte glacée*
à la menthe (frozen mint pie),
soufflé glacé au Grand Marnier
(frozen Grand Marnier
soufflé).

A moment of calm along the Brittany coast.

A great find along Brittany's northern coast, the Château de Coatguelen is a rustic, pleasantly appointed *château* about 10 kilometers (6 miles) from the coastal village of Paimpol. The chef, Louis Le Roy, and his staff deserve a huge bravo for freshness and attention to detail. He bakes his own deliciously wheaty rolls (served with irresistible salted Breton butter), offers tiny, delicate *creuses du Trieux* oysters, and serves such simple dishes as grilled *rouget* (miniature red mullet) accompanied by deep-fried zucchini blossoms. The spotless blue and white dining room offers views of the *château's* swimming pool and nine-hole golf course, and the service by the young fresh-faced Breton women could not be more attentive. If it's on the menu, try the wholesome *mousse de dorade,* a lively, dense, and full-flavored fish mousse, or the *huîtres chaudes au cidre et aux poireaux,* a blend of briny oysters, leeks, and tangy cider. Portions are generous.

PONT-AVEN *(Finistère)*

Concarneau 15 k, Paris 527 k, Quimper 32 k, Quimperlé 17 k.

Market: Tuesday, 8:30 A.M. to 1:30 P.M., Quai Théodore-Botrel (July and August), Place de l'Hôtel-de-Ville (off-season).

RESTAURANTS

RESTAURANT MOULIN DE ROSMADEC
29123 Pont-Aven.
(98.06.00.22).
Last orders taken at 2 P.M. and 9 P.M.
Closed Wednesday, Sunday dinner off-season, the last two weeks in October, and February.
No credit cards.
Terrace dining.
Air-conditioned.
Private dining rooms for 15 and 35.
88- and 200-franc menus. A la carte, 350 francs.

SPECIALTIES:
Homard grillé (grilled lobster), *suprême de sole Champagne* (sole with Champagne sauce), *crêpes flambées* (flamed dessert crêpes).

If there's one reason to spend a few days in Brittany, that reason is lobster. It's not a food most of us can afford to crave with any regularity, but everyone, once in his life, should be allowed to have his fill. At this charming, old-fashioned mill right in the center of Pont-Aven (the decor and ambience remind me of a cozy New England lodge), I was lucky enough to sample a superb female lobster bursting with an honest surfeit of rich, caviar-like roe, offering a contrast in intensity, flavor, and texture to the sweet and firm white lobster meat. At the same meal I also sampled the freshest, most flavorful artichoke one might imagine. The shower of fresh morel mushrooms that topped this giant artichoke bottom was almost superfluous, for one could not stop concentrating on the brilliant, intense artichoke flavor. For dessert, sample the sublime warm apple tart.

LA TAUPINIERE
29123 Pont-Aven.
(98.06.03.12).
Last orders taken at 1:30 P.M. and 9:30 P.M.
Closed Monday dinner except July and August, second week in March, and Tuesday from mid-September through mid-October.
Credit cards: AE, DC, EC, V.
Air-conditioned.
About 300 francs.

SPECIALTIES:
Langoustines grillées au feu de bois (langoustines grilled on a wood fire), *jambon frais grillé* (grilled fresh ham).

La Taupinière, on the road to Concarneau just west of Pont-Aven, is one of my favorite Breton restaurants. It's at the same time large and cozy, welcoming and unimposing. With its chic clientele and self-conscious decor, it reminds me very much of a California-style restaurant. Yet it is Breton to the core. Here giant langoustines are grilled over an open wood fire, ready for diners donned in elegantly embroidered cotton bibs to attack the spiny pincers, to fold back the armoured tail to reveal the sweet, delicate, cloud-like meat that is best enjoyed all on its own, with perhaps a chilled glass of Riesling (the Zind-Humbrecht, Côte-de-Brand, is a remarkable match). I love, as well, their carpaccio of tuna *(thon frais mariné au citron vert)*—a lively first course of fresh tuna "cooked" in lime juice and sprinkled with fresh leaf coriander (see recipe below). Don't neglect the traditional combination of ham (here it's grilled over the wood fire) and white beans. If ever there was a time when the quality of the ingredients made a dish, this is it!

THON FRAIS MARINE AU CITRON VERT LA TAUPINIERE
LA TAUPINIERE'S TUNA MARINATED WITH LIME JUICE

This dish is from one of my favorite Breton restaurants, the beautiful, cottage-like La Taupinière, just outside the village of Pont-Aven. The chef there serves a lively, full-flavored carpaccio of tuna, which is "cooked" in fresh lime juice. The addition of fresh coriander leaves is a touch of genius. Be sure to have some good fresh bread on hand for toasting.

1 pound (500 g) center-cut tuna fillet, dark meat and connective tissue trimmed away
Handful of fresh coriander leaves
¼ cup (60 ml) freshly squeezed lime juice
½ cup (125 ml) extra-virgin olive oil
Salt and freshly ground black pepper to taste
Lime wedges for garnish

1. Wrap the tuna in plastic wrap and freeze for 10 minutes. Rinse and thoroughly dry the coriander leaves. Coarsely chop half of the leaves. Set aside the remainder for a garnish.

2. Prepare the marinade: Whisk the lime juice, oil, salt, pepper, and chopped coriander leaves together.

3. Using a pastry brush, paint 6 dinner plates with the marinade. Sprinkle the plates with salt and pepper, then refrigerate for about 15 minutes.

4. Remove the tuna from the freezer and slice as thinly as possible, about ⅛-inch (3 mm) thick. Arrange the tuna slices, without overlapping, on the chilled plates. Season the tuna generously with salt and pepper, then brush again with the marinade. Refrigerate for 30 minutes before serving.

5. Serve the tuna slightly chilled, garnished with lime wedges, whole coriander leaves, and warm toasted bread.

Yield: 6 servings.

Kouign-amann from Pâtisserie Kersale.

PATISSERIE

PATISSERIE KERSALE
Place de l'Hôtel-de-Ville,
   29123 Pont-Aven.
(98.06.00.61).
Open 7 A.M. to noon and
   2:30 to 7 P.M. Closed
   three weeks in February
   and two weeks in
   September.

A busy little pastry shop with some truly deli-cious, fresh buttery yeast cakes known as *kouign-amann.*

SPECIALITES REGIONALES

LES SOURCES DE L'AVEN
9 Place de l'Hôtel-de-Ville,
   29123 Pont-Aven.
(98.06.07.65).
Open 9 A.M. to noon and 2
   to 7 P.M. Closed
   Wednesday from
   September through June.
No credit cards.

A pleasant—if touristy—specialty shop offering a good selection of regional products, includ-ing homemade butter cookies and *kouign-amann* (a sugary, buttery folded yeast cake).

PONT-L'ABBE *(Finistère)*

Douarnenez 33 k, Paris 568 k, Quimper 20 k.

Markets: Tuesday through Saturday, 9 A.M. to noon, covered market, Place de la République; Thursday, 9 A.M. to noon, open-air market, Place de la République and truck farmers' market, Place Gambetta.

Between bites, make time for a Thursday visit to the truck farmers' market in Pont-l'Abbé's Place Gambetta, where diminutive gray-haired ladies still hobble along village streets wearing traditional crocheted shawls, black and white polka-dot skirts, and the lacy white ceremonial headdresses known as *coiffes*. Here chatty *maraîchers* sell fresh-picked artichokes from the back of their trucks for 1 franc each and local housewives offer baskets full of fresh and nutty buckwheat crêpes, while others sell homemade blackberry jam.

STAND DE PATISSERIE

LE MOIGNE
At the Place Gambetta market from Easter to All Souls' Day.

An ice-cream break in Pont-Aven.

If you're in the mood for a mid-morning snack, you can buy a buttery and still-steaming *kouign-amann* "imported" from the Le Moigne shop in Douarnenez and take it to the local café for pairing with a bracing espresso.

FAR BRETON AUX PRUNEAUX DE PONT-L'ABBE
BRITTANY PRUNE FLAN FROM PONT-L'ABBE

One rainy Thursday in August, while wandering about the charming Pont-l'Abbé market, I passed a pastry stand as a trio of saleswomen busily unpacked a small truck full of warm, still-steaming far breton. *I bought a slice, headed straight for the nearest café, and enjoyed one of the more memorable breakfasts of my journey through France. On returning home, I tested and tested and tested until I got this homey French dessert to taste just the way I remembered. Since the recipe calls for vanilla-flavored sugar, you'll need to prepare some several weeks in advance of making this flan for the first time. Make plenty—using one emptied pod for each cup of sugar. Once you do, a* far breton *is a quick, pleasing dessert that can be tossed together in minutes.*

1⅓ cups (200 g) dried prunes, pitted
2 tablespoons rum
Seeds from 1 vanilla bean
½ cup (70 g) unbleached all-purpose flour
½ cup (100 g) vanilla-flavored sugar (see Note)
5 large eggs
2 cups (500 ml) warm milk
1 tablespoon butter for the baking pan

1. Preheat the oven to 450°F (230°C).

2. Add the prunes and rum to the seeds from 1 vanilla bean and let sit for at least 15 minutes to allow the prunes to absorb the liquor. (If time permits, the prunes may marinate for several hours.)

3. Place the flour, sugar, and eggs in a large mixing bowl and beat with a wire whisk until blended. While still beating, slowly add the warm milk, then stir in the prunes with rum.

4. Butter a 10½-inch (27 cm) straight-sided ceramic baking dish. Carefully pour the batter into the pan. Bake for 10 minutes, then reduce the heat to 350°F (180°C) and bake 25 minutes longer. Serve the flan warm or at room temperature from the baking dish, cutting it into wedges.

Yield: One 10½-inch (27 cm) flan.

Note: To prepare vanilla sugar, place a vanilla bean in the sugar canister, figuring 1 bean for each cup of sugar. The vanilla sugar may be kept indefinitely, adding additional "used" beans to flavor the sugar.

POUR LA MAISON

BOUTIQUE LE MINOR
3 Quai Saint-Laurent, 29120
  Pont-l'Abbé.
(98.87.07.22).
Open 9 A.M. to noon (12:30
  P.M. in July and August)
  and 2 to 7 P.M. Closed
  Monday off-season.

An exceptional shop offering regional hand- and machine-embroidered linens, including very elegant lobster bibs that would be perfect gifts.

Vacation-time strolls along the port.

MUSEE

MUSEE BIGOUDEN
Château de Pont-l'Abbé,
  29120 Pont-l'Abbé.
(98.87.24.44).
Open 9 A.M. to noon and
  2 to 6:30 P.M. Closed
  October through May,
  Sunday, and holidays.
Admission: About 4 francs
  for adults; about 1 franc
  for children under 16,
  students, and groups.

Pont-l'Abbé is the capital of the Bigouden district of Brittany, with some of the most original and attractive costumes in the region. The museum offers collections of local costumes and models of Breton boats.

QUIMPER *(Finistère)*

Brest 72 k, Lorient 66 k, Paris 553 k, Rennes 204 k, Saint-Brieuc 130 k.

Markets: Wednesday and Saturday, 8:30 A.M. to 6 P.M., covered market, Place Laennec; 9 A.M. to 6 P.M., open-air market, Quai Steir.

PATISSERIE

ANDRE ROLLAND
13 Rue Kéréon, 29000
  Quimper.
(98.95.21.40).
Open 8:15 A.M. to 7:15 P.M.
  Closed Sunday, Monday,
  and the last week in June
  through mid-July.
Credit card: V.

Don't leave Quimper without a coffee and *kouign-amann* break at this spotless pastry shop/tea salon. Note the lovely old wooden shop sign and sculptures just above the door.

POUR LA MAISON

JACQUES BIOLAY
8 Rue Elie-Fréron, 29000
    Quimper.
(98.95.33.84).
Open 9 A.M. to noon and 2
    to 7 P.M. Closed Sunday
    and Monday.

Atraditional hardware store where you can find locally ground buckwheat flour (in July and August only) and equipment for making those authentic buckwheat crêpes.

FAIENCERIE KERALUC
14 Rue de Troménie, 29000
    Quimper.
(98.90.25.29).
Open 9 A.M. to noon and 2
    to 6 P.M. Closed Saturday
    and Sunday.
Credit card: V.
International mail orders
    accepted.

Paris Connection:
    QUIMPER FAIENCE
84 Rue Saint-Martin, 75004
    Paris.
(42.71.93.03).

Since 1690, Quimper has been known for its decorative folkloric pottery, which can now be found on just about every street corner in town. This is perhaps the best-known shop for browsing and buying.

Summer snacks at the Crêperie des Artisans.

MUSEES

FAIENCERIES QUIMPER
Rue Haute, 29000 Quimper.
(98.90.09.36).
Open 9:30 to 11 A.M. and
    1:30 to 4 P.M. The last
    visit is at 3 P.M. Closed
    Saturday, Sunday, and
    December 24 after 11
    A.M. through the first
    week in January.
Admission: 12 francs for
    adults, 6 francs for
    children.

Aworkshop and museum devoted to the popular, colorful, folkloric pottery of the region, where old and new pottery can be viewed side by side. (Directions: In the Loc Maria neighborhood of Quimper; in the direction of Bénodet as you leave the center of town.)

MUSEE BRETON
1 Rue Roi-Gradlon, 29000
　Quimper.
(98.95.21.60).
Open 9 A.M. to noon and 2
　to 5 P.M. Closed Monday,
　Tuesday, and holidays.
Admission: 10 francs for
　adults, 5 francs for over
　60 and under 18, under
　11 free.

This museum is worth visiting simply for its architectural merit. The former bishop's palace has been beautifully restored to show to best advantage the stunning collection of Breton furniture and artifacts, Quimper pottery, and local costumes.

RIEC-SUR-BELON *(Finistère)*

Concarneau 19 k, Paris 523 k, Quimper 38 k, Quimperlé 13 k.

Market: Wednesday, 8:30 A.M. to 1 P.M., Place du Docteur-Yves-Loudoux.

RESTAURANTS

CHEZ JACKY
29124 Riec-sur-Belon.
(98.06.90.32).
Last orders taken at 3 P.M.
　and 9:30 P.M. (10 P.M. in
　July and August).
Closed Monday, and
　October through March.
No credit cards.
Private dining room for 50.
English spoken.
About 175 francs.

S P E C I A L T I E S :
Plateau de fruits de mer (raw
and cooked shellfish platter).

This is a roll-up-your-sleeves, let-down-your-hair kind of place. Something happens to people when they're in a roomful of happy, hearty eaters all picking up their food with their hands: They concentrate so, there's hardly time for chatter. Jazz music plays quietly in the background while diners busy themselves extracting delicate meats from multicolored shells. From time to time the sun glares in, a bright blue or yellow boat rolls into the cove, and dozens of faces glow with contentment.

An internationally loved landmark, Chez Jacky is a quintessential waterside fish restaurant nestled in a cove along the Belon river. You're unlikely to find Belon oysters much fresher than this: After the rare flat bivalves have spent eight to ten months growing up in the sea, they come home to live out their lives in the Belon river, where the shallow, warmish blend of salt water and fresh water helps them develop their distinctly sweet, creamy flavor. They might spend up to three years aging in oyster beds adjacent to the restaurant, growing bigger and fatter, until they're ready to be harvested and brought to table at Chez Jacky.

Do go for the *plateau de fruits de mer,* laden with langoustines and bite-size *crevettes,* clams *(palourdes, amandes, vernis),* mussels, perwinkles, Belon oysters, crinkle-edge *creuses* oysters, and the spider crab known as *araignée de mer.* (Directions: on the right bank—*rive droite*—of the Belon port.)

CHEZ MELANIE
Place de l'Eglise, 29124
  Riec-sur-Belon.
(98.06.91.05).
Last orders taken at 1:30 P.M.
  and 9:30 P.M.
Closed Tuesday, and
  November and
  December.
Credit cards: AE, DC.
Private dining room for 10.
90–, 180–, and 300–franc
  menus. A la carte, 275
  francs.

SPECIALTIES:
Huîtres de Belon (Belon
oysters), *palourdes farcies*
(stuffed clams), *homard flambé
à l'Armagnac* (lobster flamed
with Armagnac).

Historically, one of Brittany's favorite lobster eateries is the quaint old-time Chez Mélanie right on the church square in Riec-sur-Belon. It was with Mélanie that Curnonsky, the famed French gastronome, spent a good deal of time during the 1940s, often consuming here his single daily meal, which at times must have consisted of Belon oysters and grilled lobster. Both the decor and the style of cuisine at Mélanie's remain pure 1930s, and like La Mère Poulard in Le Mont-Saint-Michel and the Hôtel Tatin in Lamotte-Beuvron, it stands as a landmark to French gastronomy, truly a restaurant out of another era. Today the food may lack the spark and glistening freshness of other Breton restaurants, but the dining room (filled with some exceptional artwork exchanged, over the years, for room and board) serves as a rare living museum to old-time gastronomy.

SAILLE *(Loire-Atlantique)*

La Baule 3 k, Guérande 4 k, Nantes 71.5 k, Rennes 134 k,
Saint-Nazaire 16 k.

MUSEE

MAISON DES PALUDIERS
Rue du Ber, Saillé, 44350
  Guérande.
(40.42.22.28).
Open 10 A.M. to noon and 2
  to 7 P.M. July and August;
  2 to 6 P.M. mid-May
  through June. Closed
  September through
  mid-May.
Admission: About 7 francs
  for adults, 3 francs for
  children.

A tiny museum filled with tools, engravings, furnishings, and costumes that help explain the daily life of the local *paludiers,* or salt marsh workers. There is also a slide show to demonstrate contemporary methods of salt collection.

SAINTE-ANNE-LA-PALUD *(Finistère)*

Brest 66 k, Châteaulin 19 k, Douarnenez 16 k, Paris 570 k, Quimper 25 k.

RESTAURANT

HOTEL DE LA PLAGE
Sainte-Anne-la-Palud,
   29127 Plonévez-Porzay.
   (98.92.50.12).
Last orders taken at 1:30 P.M.
   and 9 P.M.
Closed mid-October
   through the first week in
   April.
Credit card: V.
Terrace dining.
Private dining room for 40.
English spoken.
160-franc menu Monday
   through Saturday; 190-
   and 280-franc menus
   Sunday and holidays. A
   la carte, about 275
   francs.

SPECIALTIES:
All fish, lobster, and spiny
lobster.

Geranium-filled window boxes and sturdy Breton structures.

The compact beach of Sainte-Anne-la-Palud is one of those hauntingly lonesome yet thoroughly romantic spots that seem to shout out "You have now reached the end of the earth: Sit up and take notice!" One evening we sat in the dining room of the Hôtel de la Plage, which hugs the sandy beach, and sipped Champagne as a dramatic sun blazed its final blood-orange rays of light. You wouldn't have to twist my arm to get me back there again! That evening we sampled remarkably meaty and sweet local crab, mountains of langoustines (both served as part of the *plateau de fruits de mer*), and beautifully grilled *langouste,* allowing one to compare the delicate meat of the langoustine with the denser, more chewy meat of the clawless spiny lobster.

Those in France who are fickle are said to have *"un coeur d'artichaut,"* and perhaps the artichoke itself is fickle, for it is said to have been a beautiful girl whom a jealous god transformed into the sturdy weed.

Artichokes, particularly their hearts, are popular in France and are most often steamed or blanched and used as a small, deliciously nutty cup to hold salads or creamy sauces. French farmers in the westerly tip of Brittany supply about 8 percent of the 750,000 tons of artichokes consumed each year; the rest are imported from Italy and Greece.

Normandie
NORMANDY

At the Durands': farm-fresh Camembert, from Camembert.

Normandy, the land of Calvados, Camembert, and cider, just can't help looking as though it's posing for a picture postcard. Rolling hills so green they make your eyes hurt. The proverbial lazy cow—black and white, brown and white, sometimes just brown—immobilized beneath an apple tree just about to burst into flower. Classic metal milk cans standing elbow-to-elbow at the edge of the driveway. The rural mailman pedaling about on a tattered bicycle, delivering bad news, good news, and bills to half-timbered houses, where he'll stop for a sip of Calvados and to chat about the price of milk, the winter's frost damage, this year's apple crop.

Visually, Normandy won't let you down. When you go, bring with you those wonderfully romantic images and as you drive down the two-lane country roads (look for the ones whose numbers are preceded by a D, then take those outlined in green, meaning it's a scenic drive), you'll see, it's all laid out for you. Nothing's made up. It's real, it's rural, it's earthy. And just a gentle ninety-minute drive from Paris.

It looks so good it could make one forget that much of the Calvados produced today is little more than bland-tasting firewater. The Camembert, sprayed with penicillium to make it age faster, is sold so young, so white, that much of it has little character. And who likes to think of all that rich, golden milk being transformed into a cooked-out, ultra-pasteurized liquid? As for Normandy restaurants, well, the reputation's never been very strong.

Gastronomically speaking, you will have to swallow a bit of reality, but be patient, shift focus a bit, and all will go well. A lot has changed here during the past century. There's barely a *boulanger* who still bakes the regional *pain brié,* the dense, solid white loaf that, until World World I, was about the only bread found in the region. There are only two or three farmers left making old-fashioned farmhouse Camembert. Local farmers found it too difficult to make a totally consistent product, one that could compete with the standardized, and more reliable, Camembert made in large industrial cooperatives. People in the Pays d'Auge area around Deauville talk about the one farmer who still makes his own spicy elastic Livarot, but no one admits to knowing his name or exact whereabouts. Until World War II, all Pont-l'Evêque was farmhouse Pont-l'Evêque, whereas today only a few farmers turn the freshest cow's milk available into solid, fragrant, supple orange squares. The rest is made industrially.

When you know this, it comes as no surprise to find that the regional cuisine has fallen on hard times. Think traditional Normandy food and you think butter, cream, duck, and organ meats like tripe and the tripe sausage known as *andouillette.* Not exactly the way we want to eat very often nowadays.

But the contemporary picture is not nearly as dim as it might seem. Travelers who want to touch base with the solid, square-jawed, outgoing Norman farmers have plenty of opportunities. The quantity may have declined, but quality can still be found in tiny farmhouses selling cider and fiery Calvados, in cheese and bread shops in towns like Honfleur and Deauville, off narrow, solitary roads where farmers group together in converted barns to sell their butter and cream, cider vinegar and honey, cheese, chickens, and *confiture.* Every now and then you'll run into a string of goats, historical strangers in a region where the cow has long been king. You'll known that fresh, delicate goat cheese can't be far behind.

Fortunately, many of the authentic traditional foods—the cool, crisp pear or apple cider, the fiery apple brandy, the renowned sweet butter of Isigny, the pale golden *crème fraîche,* the buckwheat or *sarrasin galettes,* the hot apple tarts—are easily found at the local cafés and restaurants. Stop at any of the port towns from Cherbourg to Honfleur for a feast of *fruits de mer*—a giant platter that might include fresh briny oysters from Saint-Vaast, tiny shrimp from Deauville and Trouville, and bright vermillion mussels from Villerville. Wherever you go, save room for the cheese course (or make a meal of cheese, cider, and slices of rye bread), sampling the soft and creamy Pont-l'Evêque, the pungent rounds of Livarot, and of course, the world-famous Camembert.

In villages like Beuvron-en-Auge and in towns like Rouen, one now finds young chefs who are wide awake and ready to deliver the fresh, healthy food we search out today, while open-air markets still excite us with variety and regional authenticity.

Perhaps my favorite market in all of Normandy can be found on Wednesdays and Sundays in the charming village of Trouville-sur-Mer. The market's a wonderfully lively affair, set up along the Touques river, where fishermen come right up to the docks to unload their fish. You'll find the freshest of sole, lemon sole, and the flat fish called plaice, as well as local mussels, oysters, crabs, and fingernail-size, live, squiggling shrimp. Elsewhere along the long, narrow, outdoor market, you may find rare white strawberries, wicker baskets full of fresh fruit (one day in July, we spotted red currants, cherries, raspberries, black currants, strawberries, and Chinese gooseberries), not to mention homemade *boudin* (blood sausage), fresh farm eggs, and enough farm-made Normandy cheeses to renew one's hope that the region's food traditions have not all been taken over by industrialization.

A single word on timing: The region is jokingly called Paris's 21st *arrondissement.* From Friday through Sunday from early spring to late fall, thousands upon thousands of Parisians desert the capital and descend upon Normandy. On weekends restaurants and hotels fill up early, but in midweek you'll often have it all to yourself.

WHEN YOU GO

Michelin Green Guide: *Normandy* (available in English).

Getting there: Most spots in Normandy are just a few hours' drive from Paris. There are also ten trains daily from the capital to Dieppe, half a dozen to Deauville, and at least seventeen to Rouen; the journey to all three destinations is about 2 hours. Approximately six trains daily make the 4- or 5-hour journey to Le Mont-Saint-Michel. All trains leave from Paris's Gare Saint-Lazare. Cars can be rented at the train stations.

Getting around: Michelin map 231 (Normandie/Normandy).

Best time to visit: Because of its proximity to Paris, Normandy is active year-round. Apple-blossom time in May is spectacular, and the beaches of Deauville are particularly attractive, as well as crowded, during the summer months.

MARKETS
(Liveliest markets are marked with an asterisk.)

Monday: Deauville (July to mid-September), Gisors, Pont-Audemer, Pont-l'Evêque, Saint-Pierre-sur-Dives, *Vimoutiers.

Tuesday: L'Aigle, Bagnoles-de-l'Orne, Balleroy, Beuzeville, Caen, Deauville, Dieppe, Lessay, Rouen, Le Tréport, Villedieu-les-Poêles.

Wednesday: Cabourg, Caen, Deauville (July to mid-September), Dieppe, Eu, Granville, Orbec, Rouen, Saint-Hilaire-du-Harcouët, *Trouville-sur-Mer, Vernon, *Yvetot.

Thursday: Alençon, Bellême, Caen, Conches-en-Ouche, Coutances, Deauville (July to mid-September), Dieppe, Etretat, La Ferté-Macé, Forges-les-Eaux, Houlgate, Livarot, Lyons-la-Forêt, Rouen.

Friday: *Caen, Deauville, *Eu, Gisors, Pont-Audemer, *Rouen, Valognes, Vimoutiers.

Saturday: *Alençon, Les Andelys, Avranches, *Bagnoles-de-l'Orne, Bayeux, Caen, Caudebec-en-Caux, Deauville (July to mid-September), *Dieppe, *Dives-sur-Mer, Domfront, Falaise, Fécamp, *Granville, Honfleur, Louviers, Mortagne-au-Perche, Mortain, Neufchâtel-en-Bray, *Orbec, *Rouen, Saint-Lô, Saint-Sever, *Le Tréport, Yvetot.

Sunday: *Caen, Deauville (July to mid-September), Pont-d'Ouilly, *Rouen, *Trouville-sur-Mer.

First Sunday of the month from October or November through April: *Marché aux Pommes* (apple market), Sainte-Opportune-la-Mare.

FAIRS AND FESTIVALS

Last weekend in March: *Foire au Boudin* (sausage fair), Mortagne-au-Perche.

May 1: *Concours National des Meilleures Tripes* (national tripe contest), Longny-au-Perche.

One day in May: *Foire aux Moules* (mussel fair), Le Tréport.

Ascension weekend: *Grande Fête Normande* (festival of Normandy), Etretat.

Sunday nearest May 30: *Fête de Jeanne d'Arc* (Joan of Arc festival), Rouen.

Last weekend in May: *Foire aux Cerises* (cherry fair), Vernon.

One day in June: *Fête du Cidre* (cider festival), Auffay.

Second weekend in July: *Fête du Poiré* (sparkling pear wine festival), Mantilly.

Last Sunday in July: *Fête du Camembert* (Camembert festival), Camembert.

Last Sunday in August: *Fête de la Moisson* (harvest festival), Illeville-sur-Montfort.

Second weekend in September: *Foire Saint-Croix* (traditional local fair), Lessay.

Mid-September: *Foire de l'Agriculture Normandie-Maine* (Normandy-Maine agricultural fair), Alençon.

Last weekend in September of even years: *Fête du Cidre* (cider festival), Caudebec-en-Caux.

Mid-October: *Journées Mycologiques* (mushroom-hunting days), La Ferté-Macé; *Exposition Mycologique* (wild mushroom exhibit), Brionne.

First weekend in November: *Foire aux Harengs* (herring fair), Dieppe.

December 6: *Foire Saint-Nicholas* (Saint Nicholas Day fair), Evreux.

The Auberge les Deux Tonneaux, Pierrefitte-en-Auge.

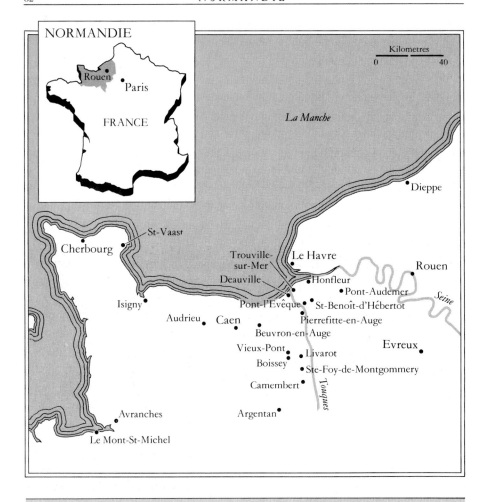

AUDRIEU *(Calvados)*

Caen 15 k, Paris 240 k.

RESTAURANT

CHATEAU D'AUDRIEU
Audrieu, 14250
  Tilly-sur-Seulles.
(31.80.21.52).
Last orders taken at 1:30 P.M.
  and 9:30 P.M.
Closed Wednesday,
  Thursday lunch, and
  early January through
  mid-March.

In the calm and tranquil countryside of Audrieu, halfway between Caen and Bayeux, an excellent choice for a place to dine is the Château d'Audrieu. The eighteenth-century family *château* was transformed into a luxurious but unpretentious hotel and restaurant in 1976, and soon became part of the Relais et Châteaux group. The neatly ordered garden provides the artichokes and purple-topped chives, raspberries and strawberries, regal calla

Credit card: V.
Private dining room for 50.
English spoken.
130- (weekday lunches
  only), 250-, and
  315-franc menus. A la
  carte, 350 francs.

lilies and fiery orange poppies that find their way
into the kitchen and dining room. Specialties include *boudin blanc de pied de veau* (calf's-foot sausage), *chaud-froid d'huîtres à la julienne de betteraves*
(cold cooked oysters with beets), and *salmis de
pigeonneau au jus de mûre* (pigeon stew with blackberry sauce).

BEUVRON-EN-AUGE *(Calvados)*

Caen 31 k, Paris 224 k, Pont-l'Evêque 32 k.

RESTAURANT

LE PAVE D'AUGE
Beuvron-en-Auge,
  14430 Dozulé.
(31.79.26.71).
Last orders taken at 1:45 P.M.
  and 9 P.M.
Closed for dinner Monday
  and Tuesday, and
  mid-January through
  February.
Credit cards: AE, V.
Some English spoken.
125- and 220-franc menus.
  A la carte, about 250
  francs.

SPECIALTIES:
Fish and *poulet Vallée d'Auge*
(chicken with cream and
cider).

Le Pavé d'Auge chef, Odile Engel.

Odile Engel, chef at Le Pavé d'Auge, is one of a
small group of young, dedicated, and ambitious chefs working in Normandy today. Here in a
charming restored village of 276 inhabitants, in an
appealing restaurant created in a rebuilt covered
market, she offers a style of cooking that's at once
personal, creative, regional, and inviting.

Each morning, she's up at dawn to visit the
criée, or fresh fish auction, in nearby Caen. If, as is
often the case, the fishermen are land-bound because of bad weather at sea, it sends Madame Engel
into a tizzy.

"I couldn't remember the name of the chef
who committed suicide because the fish didn't
come, but I called one of my fish suppliers and told
him if he didn't get me some fish quick, he'd have
one dead client," she once told me, referring to the
tale of Vatel, the legendary seventeenth-century
maître d'hôtel who committed suicide when the

fish failed to arrive for a banquet.

Fortunately Madame Engel's wholesaler responded; to fend off disaster he drove to Brittany, where the fish was in plentiful supply. Thanks to the chef's tantrum, diners were able to feast on turbot in a just-right cider vinegar sauce, meaty mussels in a delicate cider and cream sauce, thick filets of Saint-Pierre bathed in a light blend of tomato *coulis* and butter. Don't come here expecting classic, stratified, complicated sauces, photogenic pastries, or hand-carved baby vegetables. As the chef explains, she likes to think of her food as home cooking, and though it's nothing like what most of us cook day in and day out, it has an unedited, homespun quality. The menu is strong on fish, but there's also a fine assortment of meat and poultry dishes, a daily pastry or two (the fresh-from-the-oven lemon tart was exquisite), and a good regional cheese platter (try the mature Pavé d'Auge). There's also a marvelous selection of authentic farm Calvados. Sample either the fine David or the Dupont label. To visit Calvados distilleries in the region, ask Monsieur Engel for a *"Route du Cidre"* map noting addresses of the best local farm cider and Calvados.

VIN ET ALCOOL

MARCEL-JEAN DAVID
Beuvron-en-Auge, 14430
  Dozulé.
(31.79.23.05).
Open daily 9 A.M. to 7 P.M.
  Easter through
  September. Off-season
  call first to ensure
  someone will be there to
  greet you.
Will ship internationally.

One of the best addresses I know for the powerful, pungent local apple brandy, or Calvados, distilled the old-fashioned way, over a slow-burning wood fire. (Directions: just northeast of Beuvron-en-Auge on the D146.)

A Norman farm, in the land of Camembert.

BOISSEY *(Calvados)*

Caen 40 k, Paris 200 k, Rouen 150 k.

FROMAGER-AFFINEUR

DENIS THEBAULT
Boissey, 14170
  Saint-Pierre-sur-Dives.
(31.20.64.00).
Open 8:30 A.M. to 4:30 P.M.
  Closed Saturday and
  Sunday.
Will ship in France.

Normandy: a coastal view.

In 1982 the young Denis Thébault restored a cheesemaking dairy that had been closed for more than twenty-five years, and began gathering cow's milk from about a dozen local farmers to transform into Livarot and Pont-l'Evêque. The flat discs of Livarot are made each morning, combining that morning's milk and the milk from the night before. The Livarot is aged on damp planks of fir, washed with salted water and left at least two months in his cold, humid aging cellars. From the same fresh morning milk, Monsieur Thébault prepares his Pont-l'Evêque, which is formed into squares, brushed regularly, and aged for a month. (Directions: just south of Boissey on the D154.)

CAMEMBERT *(Calvados)*

Argentan 20 k, Livarot 14 k,
Fête du Camembert (Camembert festival): last Sunday in July.

FROMAGERS

DURAND–LA
  HERONNIERE
Camembert 61120
  Vimoutiers.
(33.39.08.08).
Open daily 10 A.M. to noon
  and 2 to 6 P.M.

The Robert Durands are one of the last families to make farm Camembert, and even if their cheese doesn't taste like other Camemberts (the version I sampled was very clean, slightly salty, mildly aromatic), their farm is worth a detour.

MICHEL DELORME
Camembert 61120
  Vimoutiers.
(33.39.12.56).
Open 2 to 6 P.M. Closed
  Saturday and Sunday.
Visits to see the
  Camembert-making
  process can be made by
  appointment.

Until 1981 Andrée and Michel Delorme sold all their milk to the local cooperative, but then they decided they could earn a better living making farm Camembert. Now they transform their milk into 120 to 150 little wheels each day, working out of a small two-room building behind their house. I liked their Camembert—it's a "fat" cheese, spilling out of its wooden box, with a homemade sort of look. The Delorme cheese isn't a classic Camembert—it lacks the smooth elegance of the modern-day version—but it has a clean, lactic aroma and a good hearty flavor.

DEAUVILLE *(Calvados)*

Caen 47 k, Le Havre 75 k, Paris 207 k, Rouen 91 k.

Market: Daily July through mid-September, 8 A.M. to 1 P.M., Place Morny; Tuesday and Friday mid-September through June, 8 A.M. to 1 P.M., Place Morny.

The Wednesday market in Trouville-sur-Mer, right across the bridge from Deauville.

SPECIALITES REGIONALES

LA FERME NORMANDE
Place du Marché, 14800
  Deauville.
(31.88.17.86).
Open daily 9 A.M. to 1 P.M.
  and 3 to 8 P.M. mid-June
  through mid-September;
  10 A.M. to 2 P.M. and 5 to
  8 P.M. off-season. Closed
  Sunday afternoon and
  Monday off-season, and
  early January through
  mid-February.
Will ship in France.

Look for this shop, just across the street from Deauville's charming market. It's the spot to find a fine assortment of Normandy's best cheeses, as well as good cider vinegar and a selection of apple brandy, or Calvados.

HONFLEUR *(Calvados)*

Caen 63 k, Le Havre 57 k, Paris 192 k, Rouen 76 k.

Market: Saturday, 8 A.M. to noon, Place Sainte-Catherine.

RESTAURANT

LA FERME SAINT-SIMEON
14600 Honfleur.
(31.89.23.61).
Last orders taken at 2 P.M. and 9:30 P.M.
Closed Wednesday lunch from mid-November through mid-March, except holidays.
Credit card: V
Terrace dining.
Private dining room for 60.
English spoken.
200-franc menu (lunch only except Sunday and holidays). A la carte, 400 francs.

SPECIALTIES:
Fish: *chausson de homard Prieur* (lobster in puff pastry), *sole normande* (sole with mussels, mushrooms, and shrimp).

This solid, old-fashioned Norman hotel-restaurant has had its ups and downs, but I love nothing better than spending a warm spring or early summer afternoon lunching here on the terrace, enjoying light food, simply prepared, featuring the area's best fish and shellfish, poultry, fruits, and cheese. Recommended are the first course of marinated salmon trout and *bar,* the main course of grilled turbot, and a very moist and delicate saddle of rabbit with a *confit* of shallots. Save room for the cheese course—limited to the finest local varieties—as well as the warm and flaky apple tart, accompanied by an entire pot of thick, golden *crème fraîche.* (Directions: just outside Honfleur on the D513.)

BOULANGERIE

LA PANETERIE
22 Rue de la République, 14600 Honfleur.
(31.89.18.70).
Open 6:30 A.M. to 1 P.M. and 2 to 8 P.M. Closed Monday.

Baker Louis David reigns as the best-known *boulanger* in Honfleur, perhaps in all of Normandy. (In a local restaurant, I once asked a young waiter if I was eating Monsieur David's bread and he laughed. "It's about the only bread you're likely to find in Honfleur" was his reply.) La Paneterie, along the village's main street, is a real show-stopper. Monsieur David offers eighteen kinds of bread, including a coarse and rustic seven-grain loaf perfect for eating with cheese and cold cuts, and a slightly sweet dark rye for pairing with local oysters. There's also the regional *pain brié,* a rectangular loaf that's made without salt and kneaded extensively, producing a very white, dense bread made to eat with tiny shrimp and plenty of salted butter.

LIVAROT *(Calvados)*

Caen 47 k, Paris 192 k.

Market: Thursday, 9 A.M. to noon, Place Xavier de Maistre.

FROMAGER–AFFINEUR

BERNARD GRAINDORGE
42 Rue du Général-Leclerc,
    14140 Livarot.
(31.63.50.02).
Open 8:30 A.M. to noon and
    1:30 to 5:30 P.M. Closed
    Saturday and Sunday.

Graindorge, a major cheesemaker and ager in the region, is *the* name in Livarot and Pont-l'Evêque. Those interested in the cheese-aging process may visit the cheese-aging cellar by appointment.

SPECIALITES REGIONALES

FERME DU HERICOURT
3 Rue Marcel-Gambier,
    14140 Livarot.
(31.32.00.40).
Open 8 A.M. to 7 P.M. Closed
    Sunday afternoon and
    Monday.
Will ship in France.

One of the best addresses in the region for finding the finest dairy products, including Michel Touzé's Pavé d'Auge and Pont-l'Evêque, Camembert from the Isigny cooperative, Graindorge Livarot, as well as local honey and cider.

LE MONT-SAINT-MICHEL *(Manche)*

Avranches 22 k, Dinan 54 k, Paris 326 k.

RESTAURANT

LA MERE POULARD
50116 Le Mont-Saint-
Michel.
(33.60.14.01).
Last orders taken at 3 P.M.
and 9:30 P.M.
Open daily.
Credit cards: AE, DC, V.
English spoken.
130- and 260-franc menus.
A la carte, 300 francs.

SPECIALTIES:
Langouste rose grillée (grilled
spiny lobster), *carré d'agneau*
(rack of lamb), *omelette "mère
poulard"* (puffy omelet cooked
in a long-handled pan over a
wood fire).

Le Mont-Saint-Michel.

For years I put off visiting this famous landmark,
a monument to French culinary tradition, assuming that it would be one of those tourist traps
filled with busloads of indifferent diners. How
wrong I was! I must admit a weakness for anything
cooked over an open fire, and the idea of young,
prettily dressed women cooking omelets in long-
handled pans over a real wood fire is one I couldn't
reject out of hand. Well, I fell in love with this large,
spotless country restaurant right at the foot of Le
Mont-Saint-Michel. I visited one evening in late
August, and the dining room was filled with well-
dressed couples here for the same reason I was, to
take part in the Mère Poulard history, to live a little
bit in the past. The reputation of La Mère
Poulard—who died in 1931 at the age of eighty—
was built around a single menu, one that always
included an omelet, ham, fried sole, lamb and
potatoes, roast chicken and salad, and dessert. But
it's the omelet—creamy, golden, and puffy, almost
like a soufflé—that keeps us all coming back. At
mealtime, even from the street, you can watch the
omelet makers at work and listen to the rhythmic
beating of eggs in shiny copper bowls, and see that
there's no mystery in the dish. We also enjoyed the
tender local lamb, served with the flavorful dried
green beans (see recipe, following page).

GIGOT AUX CHEVRIERS LE MONT-SAINT-MICHEL
LEG OF LAMB WITH WHITE BEANS FROM
LE MONT-SAINT-MICHEL

Gigot, *or leg of lamb, is unquestionably one of France's finest cuts of meat. Whether it's better paired with a crusty potato gratin or served with a sturdy helping of full-flavored beans is really a question of taste. This version, prepared after a memorable dinner at the famous La Mère Poulard in Le Mont-Saint-Michel, is one of my favorite wintertime dishes. Traditionally,* gigot aux chevriers *is made with the small dried green beans known as* chevriers *or* flageolets, *but small white pea beans or Great Northern beans may be substituted.*

Beans:
1 pound (500 g) dried
  flageolets or other
  white dried beans
2 bay leaves
1 medium onion,
  peeled but left whole
1 teaspoon fresh thyme
  leaves
1 tablespoon salt

**Tomato and onion
sauce:**
3 tablespoons (1 ½
  ounces; 45 g)
  unsalted butter
2 medium onions
  (about 8 ounces;
  250 g), coarsely
  chopped

1. Prepare the beans: Rinse the beans carefully, picking them over to remove any pebbles. Place the beans in a large heavy saucepan, cover with boiling water, and let sit for 1 hour. Drain the beans and add fresh water to cover. Heat the beans to a slow boil over medium heat, skimming off any foam that rises to the top. Add more water if necessary. When all the foam has been skimmed off, add the bay leaves, onion, and thyme and cook for about 30 minutes. Stir in the salt, then continue cooking until the beans are tender. The cooking time will vary depending upon the freshness of the beans; fresher beans cook more quickly than older ones. They usually take about 1 ½ hours of total cooking time. Drain, cover, and set aside.

2. Meanwhile, prepare the tomato and onion sauce: Melt 2 tablespoons of the butter in a large deep skillet over low heat. Add the onions and garlic and stir until the onions are thoroughly coated with butter. Cover and cook slowly for 30 minutes, shaking the pan frequently. When cooked, the onions should be soft, tender, and pale golden.

PIERREFITTE-EN-AUGE *(Calvados)*

Caen 45 k, Deauville 14 k, Paris 175 k, Pont-l'Evêque 5 k.

CAFE

**AUBERGE LES DEUX
  TONNEAUX**
Pierrefitte-en-Auge, 14130
  Pont-l'Evêque.
(31.64.09.31).
Meals and snacks served
  from 12:30 P.M. to 7:30
  P.M. (8 P.M. May through
  August).

I love visiting Normandy in the late spring, when the pear and apple blossoms are at their peak. Then there's always time for a bucolic drive and a snack at this honest-to-goodness country *café-tabac,* a side-of-the-road thatched-roof cottage known as Les Deux Tonneaux. The village of Pierrefitte-en-Auge, just outside the brand-name town of Pont-

8 cloves garlic, cut crosswise into thin slices

10 medium tomatoes (about 2 pounds; 1 kg), peeled, cored, seeded, and coarsely chopped

1 teaspoon fresh thyme leaves

Salt and freshly ground black pepper to taste

Lamb:

1 leg of lamb, bone in, 6 to 7 pounds (3 to 3.5 kg)

Salt and freshly ground black pepper to taste

6 cloves garlic

Small handful fresh thyme leaves

3. Stir in the tomatoes and thyme. Increase the heat to medium and cook uncovered until the tomatoes are softened but still in whole pieces and the ingredients are thoroughly combined, about 10 minutes. Season to taste and set aside.

4. As the beans and sauce are cooking, prepare the lamb. (The beans can be prepared several hours ahead of time and reheated at serving time.)

5. Preheat the oven to 400°F (205°C).

6. Trim the thicker portions of fat from the leg of lamb. Season with salt and pepper and place in a large roasting pan. Roast uncovered for 1 hour or until it measures 112°F (45°C) on a meat thermometer inserted in its thickest part. (For well-done lamb, cook an additional 30 to 40 minutes.) While the lamb is cooking, finely chop the garlic and thyme and mix them together. Ten minutes before the lamb is to be removed from the oven, sprinkle the garlic mixture evenly over the lamb. Remove the lamb from the oven and let sit 20 minutes before carving. Degrease the pan juices.

7. Combine the beans and the tomato and onion sauce. Taste and adjust seasoning and cook 10 minutes longer to allow the flavors to blend. Just before serving, stir in the degreased pan juices from the lamb and the remaining 1 tablespoon butter. Slice the lamb and serve with the beans.

Yield: 8 to 10 servings.

Closed Monday and September.
Credit card: V.
Garden dining.
Private dining room for 45.
35 francs for a snack; 100 francs for a meal.

SPECIALTIES:
Ham, *rillettes*, omelets, cheese, cider, *poulet de ferme rôti* (roast farm chicken for three, to order a day ahead), *tripes à la mode de Caen* (beef tripe, carrots, onions, leeks, and spices cooked in water, cider, and Calvados).

l'Evêque, has everything the traveler might want this time of year: a smashing view, cows, fruit trees, a church and tiny cemetery, and a rooster that doesn't seem to be able to tell day from night, he just keeps on crowing. Les Deux Tonneaux is all done up in red-and-white-checked curtains and oilcloth, and the home cider comes right from a giant keg in the wall behind the bar. The paper-thin crêpes are good, especially if you love them soaked in Calvados. (Directions: From Pont-l'Evêque take the D48 toward Lisieux about 3 kilometers to a small lake. One kilometer past the lake, take the road on the right to Les Deux Tonneaux.)

Criteria for a Perfect Camembert

"*G*astronomically, there is no comparison between cheese made from raw milk and that made from pasteurized milk. For it is the bacteria in the milk—the same bacteria that are destroyed in the heat of pasteurization—that help give cheese much of its distinctive flavor and allow the cheese to develop, to grow, to ripen as it ages."

CAMEMBERT, APRIL 24—Until the 1950s, virtually all French cheese was made with raw milk. Today about 95 percent of the nation's 200-odd varieties of cheese are prepared with longer-keeping, but less flavorful, pasteurized milk.

Of the 160,000 tons of Camembert produced in France each year, less than 5 percent is prepared with fresh raw milk, and almost all of that is made by hand in small *laiteries,* or dairies. An insignificant amount is made on two or three farms here in Camembert, the village that gave its name to France's most popular cheese. The remaining 95 percent, all produced industrially, is quite literally manufactured by machine, with pasteurized milk.

But does it really matter what kind of milk is used? Unquestionably.

Gastronomically, there is no comparison between cheese made from raw milk and that made from pasteurized milk. For it is the bacteria in the milk—the same bacteria that are destroyed in the heat of pasteurization—that help give cheese much of its distinctive flavor and allow the cheese to develop, to grow, to ripen as it ages. Any pasteurized-milk cheese, including Camembert, is doomed from the beginning. No matter how it is treated—with care or with abandon—the end result will be a cheese that is nondescript, inoffensively bland, and absolutely consistent, with a texture that is about as appealing as partly dried plaster. French food writers even talk of cheese with an "industrial flavor," that is, no flavor at all.

So why would anyone bother with cheese from pasteurized milk? The reasons are both practical and economic. From the consumer's point of view, pasteurized-milk cheese is less expensive, more widely available, and longer lasting. In some countries, such as the United States, it may be all that is available: U.S. law prohibits the sale of cheese made with raw milk unless it has been aged at least sixty days. Camembert is not.

Oddly enough, today even the lack of flavor has appeal. During recent years the French have begun to display a distinct preference for blander cheese. One wonders which came first, the onslaught of pasteurized-milk cheese or the consumer's drift toward blandness.

One young cheesemaker recently told me: "Over the past five years, I've seen the Parisian taste for cheese change drastically. Parisians want cheese that contains less fat, that is briefly aged and mildly flavored. If I tried to ship to Paris the same kind of cheese I sold here five years ago, no one would buy it."

From the producer's point of view, cheesemaking is simplified—and far less risky—with pasteurized milk. Pasteurized milk keeps longer, is available year-round, and lends itself to industrial production and a five-day week. Moreover, once the cheese is produced, it requires much less care, almost no day-to-day attention, and offers the consumer a thoroughly consistent product.

In contrast, small farms producing cheese with raw milk must take into consideration the natural seasonal variation in milk quantity, quality, and fat content, which results in a variable product that is not 100 percent consistent in appearance, texture, or flavor. Also, raw-milk cheese requires constant, daily care, not just five but seven days a week.

As cheese makes its way from dairy to supermarket or *fromagerie,* the distinctions between the raw-milk and pasteurized cheese become even more pronounced. Once the delicate and fragile raw-milk Camembert reaches the market, it has only eight or nine days of life left. If it sits around too long, it dries up, turns a dull, rusty brown, sags in the center, and takes on a striking, pungent scent of ammonia.

It takes a strong will and lots of inattention to kill a pasteurized-milk cheese. That pasteurized-milk Camembert can sit around for five or six weeks relatively unchanged, with virtually no attention save refrigeration.

Assuming that one sets out in search of a fine raw-milk Camembert, where does one begin?

In most cases, the cheese merchant will not allow you to touch, to smell, to actually look at the unwrapped, naked disc of Camembert. You pretty much have to trust the merchant or the *affineur,* who takes care of aging the cheese once it has left the farm. A properly made ripe Camembert should fill its box roundly and plumply. It should have a fresh, fragrant aroma and should not smell of ammonia. Its rind should be slightly bumpy, mostly white with reddish-rust crinkles. The taste should be straightforward, fresh, uncomplicated, and mild—but never bland. When you cut into a ripe Camembert, it should not run all over the place; rather, it should exude a rather slow, visible sigh. Runny, or *coulant,* Camembert suggests the cheese was not properly dried as it aged; the cheese retained too much water and excessive lactic fermentation has taken place.

What, exactly, is the merchant looking for when he rummages around his larder, pushing and pressing until he finds a Camembert that is *fait à coeur?* Camembert ripens from the outside in. The cheese is fully cured and ready to eat when the center is just as soft as the rest of the cheese. If the exterior looks fine but the surface is very uneven, the cheese has ripened unevenly and probably will never reach the point of perfection.

Most Camembert is sold a bit young and needs a few days of aging at home. To do this, leave the cheese in its container, wrap it in a damp cloth, and leave it in a cool place (but not the refrigerator) for up to three days. The cheese should be checked each day and should be consumed as soon as it is fully cured, preferably with a crisp *baguette* and a glass of young red Côtes-du-Rhône. Once a Camembert has been cut, it will not continue to age, but it can be kept for up to a day and a half, well wrapped and refrigerated. Some raw-milk Camembert labels to look for include Moulin de Carel, Lanquetot, and Camembert Normand from the Cooperative d'Isigny.

PONT-AUDEMER *(Calvados)*

Caen 74 k, Le Havre 48 k, Paris 168 k, Rouen 52 k.

Market: Monday and Friday, 8:30 A.M. to 5 P.M., Rue de la République.

FROMAGERIE

JOLLIT
7 Rue Gambetta, 27500
Pont-Audemer.
(32.41.04.98).
Open 8:45 A.M. to 12:30 P.M.
and 2:15 to 7:30 P.M.
Closed Sunday afternoon
and Tuesday.

One of the most-respected cheese shops in Normandy, offering local cow's- and goat's-milk cheeses, including Pont-l'Evêque, Livarot, Camembert, and Neufchâtel.

PONT-L'EVEQUE *(Calvados)*

Caen 48 k, Deauville 11 k.

Market: Monday, 10 A.M. to 12:30 P.M., Place Foch.

BOULANGERIE/ PATISSERIE

MICHEL THOMAS
61 Rue Saint-Michel, 14130
Pont-l'Evêque.
(31.64.04.08).
Open 8 A.M. to 8 P.M. Closed
Tuesday and one month
during the year.

If you happen by Pont-l'Evêque on market day, stop in for one of Michel Thomas's delicious, prize-winning brioches.

Trouville-sur-Mer: Brasserie Les Vapeurs.

ROUEN *(Seine-Maritime)*

Caen 124 k, Le Havre 88 k, Paris 139 k.

Markets: Tuesday through Sunday, 7 A.M. to 1 P.M., Place du Vieux-Marché;
Friday, 8 A.M. to noon, Place Saint-Marc; Saturday, 8 A.M. to 5 P.M., Place
Saint-Marc; Sunday, 8 A.M. to 1 P.M., Place Saint-Marc.
Fête de Jeanne d'Arc (Joan of Arc Festival): Sunday nearest May 30.

RESTAURANTS

RESTAURANT GILL
60 Rue Saint-Nicolas, 76000
Rouen.
(35.71.16.14).
Last orders taken at 1:45 P.M.
and 9:45 P.M.
Closed Sunday, Monday
lunch, two weeks in
winter, and late August
through mid-September.
Credit cards: AE, DC, V.
English spoken.
260-franc menus. A la carte,
350 francs.

SPECIALTIES:
Ravioles de langoustines
(langoustine raviolis), *nage de
rougets aux asperges et aux huîtres*
(red mullet with asparagus
and oysters), *pied de porc aux
lentilles* (pig's foot with lentils),
pigeon à la rouennaise (pigeon
stuffed with its own liver and
served with a blood-thickened
sauce).

One of a handful of young French chefs to watch today is Gilles Tournadre, a bright, conscientious man who began to develop a following in the early 1980s when he was chef at the lovely Château d'Audrieu, not far from Caen. In 1985 chef Tournadre moved off on his own, establishing Restaurant Gill right in the center of the city's charming maze of pedestrian streets. His small, ultra-contemporary dining room, decorated in shades of pale pink, blue, and brown, has a smart and serious look, and service is cheery and professional.

Even long after a visit, I can still see and taste every dish I've sampled at Gill. When was the last time you tasted sole that actually had some character? Do you remember the last restaurant meal, or any meal for that matter, where every bite from start to finish actually made you sit up and take notice?

Tournadre has a special sort of gift, a gift not only for making you aware of that sculpted leaf of mint resting atop the strawberry-filled puff pastry, but for making sure the herb is so fresh, your palate cannot fail to register the flavor. He can take the most mundane of dishes—a *panaché de poissons* or a simple *blanc-manger*—and transform it into a gustatory symphony.

What's best is that he does all this not with a larder of spices, not with a bombardment of sauces, but, quite simply, with freshness. His *panaché de poissons* has an almost breathless visual beauty, a play of vibrant orange salmon, oyster-white *lotte,* alabaster sole and *barbue,* and glistening red *rouget.* The fish is so fresh, and treated with such respect, that each bite makes your palate tingle.

Even his platter of *ravioles de langoustines*—a

dish made famous several years ago by Joël Robu-chon of Paris's Jamin—was exceptional. The giant ravioli are made of perfect pasta dough, filled with moist, cloud-like mouthfuls of langoustines.

I ordered the *blanc-manger* almost as a challenge. If that classic children's dessert could excite the palate, this chef would gain a convert. He did. Instead of a bland, faintly almond dessert with that unmistakable gelatin wobble, Tournadre offered one that captured the pure essence of almonds, marked with cream, dotted with strawberries, raspberries, and red currants, and surrounded by a bright-flavored strawberry *coulis.*

BERTRAND WARIN
7–9 Rue de la Pie, 76000
   Rouen.
(35.89.26.69).
Last orders taken at 2 P.M.
   and 10 P.M.
Closed Sunday dinner,
   Monday, two weeks at
   Christmas and New
   Year's, and August.
Credit cards: AE, DC, V.
English spoken.
105– and 260–franc menus.
   A la carte, 350 francs.

SPECIALTIES:
Change with the seasons.

Fresh mussels from the Normandy coast.

Hidden in one of the streets that fan out from the Place du Vieux-Marché is Bertrand Warin, a tiny, elegant restaurant that's perfect for an extended Sunday lunch on your way back from a weekend in the country.

Go with a lot of time on your hands, for although service is friendly and accommodating, it is extremely slow. Of the more than a dozen dishes sampled here, almost all were memorable, noticeable for their imagination and careful execution. Only oversalting sadly marred a few.

Dishes that stand out most include the *rougets en habit vert* (a first-course salad of tiny whole *rougets* wrapped in strips of leek and set on a bed of dressed greens); the *salade de langoustines et de mangue* (a copious langoustine and mango salad served with a healthy dose of greens); and the *enveloppe de saumon aux huîtres* (a lively marriage, consisting of warm oysters sandwiched between thick slices of fresh salmon). Both the *courgettes en fleurs aux girolles* (stuffed squash blossoms showered with fresh wild mushrooms) and the *noisettes d'agneau à l'estragon* (lamb nuggets with tarragon sauce) were well executed, but salt, regrettably, dominated.

Desserts here are imaginative and above average. The unusual *beignets de melon,* chunks of fresh melon dipped in batter and quickly fried, were remarkably light and not the least bit greasy, and the *trois tartelettes* offer a nice change from the classic fruit tart—Chef Warin presents a trio of delicate raspberry, lemon, and kiwi tarts, with a good *pâte sablée* base. I'm not sure what he did with the kiwi, but it's the first time that the normally bland fruit didn't make me say "So what?"

The setting here is gracious and harmonious, and there's no question that you're in Normandy. The carefully restored cottage-like restaurant is reached through a courtyard, and the small dining room is attractively and simply adorned with wooden beams, mirrors, and pleasant oil paintings, with the tables looking onto a welcoming garden.

SAINT-BENOIT-D'HEBERTOT *(Calvados)*

Honfleur 16 k, Pont-l'Evêque 9 k.

SPECIALITES REGIONALES

PIERRE LECESNE
Saint-Benoît-d'Hébertot,
14130 Pont-l'Evêque.
(31.64.03.47).
Open daily 8 A.M. to noon
and 2 to 6 P.M.
Will ship internationally.

S P E C I A L T Y:
Calvados (apple brandy).

Normandy markets, the scent of summer melons.

This is just one of many farms you'll find selling products from roadside stands or barns. Pierre Lecesne and his wife, Christiane, still make their own cider and Calvados, selling all they can produce direct from their farm. On their flat and gently rolling seventy-acre farm planted with apple trees that are thirty or forty years old, they produce a variety of ciders—ranging from *doux* (about 2 percent alcohol), to *brut* (about 4 percent alcohol), to the more powerful *cidre bouché,* a cool and bubbly 6-percent-alcohol drink that's more powerful than beer but less alcoholic than wine, and goes down so well on a warm day. "We used to have a dairy farm," Madame Lecesne explained one day as she glued labels to newly filled bottles of cider. "But you know, this is wonderful. We have more daily contact with other people, and besides, picking apples is a lot more fun than milking cows!"

GIGOT D'AGNEAU A LA BOULANGERE
BAKER'S WIFE'S LEG OF LAMB

This is a simple, satisfying dish to make, and one I serve often in the fall and winter months, since it rarely appears on restaurant menus. It's the sort of one-dish meal that French village women used to bring to the local baker for cooking in the community's bread oven, thus the name. As the lamb cooks, its wonderful juices drip into the potato gratin. Just be certain that you use a gratin dish that will easily hold this quantity of potatoes, as well as the lamb. Serve with a solid red wine, such as a Côtes-du-Rhône-Villages or Châteauneuf-du-Pape.

4 pounds (about 8
   medium; 2 kg)
   potatoes, peeled and
   very thinly sliced
2 teaspoons salt, plus
   additional to taste
1 quart (1 liter) milk
Freshly ground black
   pepper to taste
Handful fresh parsley
6 large cloves garlic
1 leg of lamb, bone in,
   6 to 7 pounds (3 to
   3.5 kg)

1. Preheat the oven to 400°F (205°C).

2. Place the potatoes, 2 teaspoons salt, and the milk in a large saucepan. Heat to a boil over medium-high heat, stirring occasionally so the potatoes do not stick to the bottom of the pan. Reduce the heat to medium and cook, stirring from time to time, until the potatoes are tender, about 15 minutes. Season with pepper. Remove from the heat and set aside.

3. Meanwhile, prepare a *persillade* by finely chopping the parsley and garlic and mixing them together.

4. Sprinkle half the *persillade* in the bottom of a large oval gratin dish, about 16 x 10 x 2 inches (40.5 x 25.5 x 5 cm). Spoon the potato mixture into the pan and sprinkle with the remaining *persillade*.

5. Trim the thicker portions of fat from the leg of lamb. Season with salt and pepper and place the lamb on top of the potatoes.

6. Roast uncovered for 1 hour or until it measures 112°F (45°C) on a meat thermometer inserted in its thickest part. (For well-done lamb, cook an additional 30 to 40 minutes. Be sure to remove the potatoes so they do not overcook. Keep them warm while waiting for the lamb.) Do not turn the lamb.

7. Remove the dish from the oven and let sit 20 minutes before serving.

8. Carve the lamb into thin slices and arrange on warmed dinner plates or on a serving platter with the potatoes alongside.

Yield: 8 to 10 servings.

SAINTE-FOY-DE-MONTGOMMERY *(Calvados)*

Caen 50 k, Deauville 50 k, Livarot 4 k, Paris 185 k.

SPECIALITES REGIONALES

MARC DE LESDAIN
Sainte-Foy-de-Montgommery,
  14140 Livarot.
(31.63.53.07).
Open daily 9 A.M. to 7 P.M.
Will ship in France.

SPECIALTY:
Calvados (apple brandy) and
cider.

A good address to know for farm cider as well as excellent homemade Calvados.

TROUVILLE-SUR-MER *(Calvados)*

Caen 43 k, Le Havre 74 k, Paris 206 k, Pont-l'Evêque 11 k.

Market: Wednesday and Sunday, 9 A.M. to 1 P.M., Boulevard Fernand-Moureaux.

BRASSERIE

BRASSERIE LES VAPEURS
160 Boulevard
  Fernand-Moureaux,
  14360 Trouville-sur-Mer.
(31.88.15.24).
Continuous service, noon to
  midnight.
Closed January, and Tuesday
  dinner and Wednesday
  from mid-November
  through early December.
Credit card: V.
Sidewalk dining.
English spoken.
150 francs.

SPECIALTIES:
Moules (mussels), *crevettes grises*
(tiny shrimp), sole, *raie*
(skate).

Just across from the fish market at the port of Trouville there's a marvelous Art Deco brasserie that's been billed as the Brasserie Lipp of Normandy. If I were Gérard Bazire, the owner of Les

Vapeurs, I'd take the comparison as an insult. The food at Les Vapeurs is infinitely better.

Spots like this are rare. Les Vapeurs is just a simple brasserie, but the owner cares about everything, from the flowers to the fresh and flavorful *baguettes,* from the wine list to the humorous, colorful menu. Even the coffee gets special attention.

This is one of the few places I know where you can get truly fresh shrimp—you'll see them live at the market across the street. At Les Vapeurs they cook the tiny *crevettes grises* quickly, sprinkling them with sea salt and lots of coarse black pepper. The shrimp are served piping hot, ready to be eaten with superb local butter, those tasty *baguettes,* and a few sips of chilled Muscadet-sur-Lie. The offerings of fish and shellfish change according to the season and the catch of the day, but their grilled sole is so fresh and full-flavored you'll think they've discovered a new species, and even the rather maligned *carrelet,* or European flounder, reaches new heights.

There's an excellent local cheese selection, including a fine Lanquetot brand Camembert and Lepeudrie Pont-l'Evêque from nearby Tourgeville.

The stern-faced waitresses may give you a hard time, but the bark is worse than the bite, and besides, this is such a great spot for people-watching, they could almost get away with charging admission. Les Vapeurs is the kind of place one could imagine going back to time and time again, to try all those good-looking dishes—the platters of oysters, the golden *frites* and steaks grilled over a wood fire, even the simple omelets—that neighboring diners are consuming with relish.

A fisherman prepares his nets, along the port of Trouville-sur-Mer.

Selling shellfish, fresh from the sea.

VIEUX-PONT *(Calvados)*

Caen 40 k, Deauville 60 k, Livarot 11 k.

FROMAGER

MICHEL TOUZE
Vieux-Pont, 14140 Livarot.
(31.20.78.67).
Open 8 A.M. to noon. Closed
   Sunday.
Will ship in France.

If time and energy permit, take a winding D-road drive to the sleepy crossroads of Vieux-Pont, where you'll find Michel and Thérèse Touzé at work each morning milking some eighty multicolored Norman cows, turning liter after liter of milk into farmhouse Pont-l'Evêque. "It's really just a tiny enterprise, not much to see," Michel Touzé warned when we telephoned for an appointment. That's just what we were after. In a spotless whitewashed barn, Monsieur Touzé and his young assistant, cheesemaker Patrick Bove, transform their milk into the soft, squarish Pont-l'Evêque as well as the lesser-known Pavé d'Auge. Monsieur Touzé explains that it takes three liters of milk to turn out a single Pont-l'Evêque, six liters for a large Pavé d'Auge. "We sell almost all of our cheese locally," the cheesemaker explained proudly. "People drive up with a picnic cooler and buy enough for their family and all their neighbors. There's enough demand, and what's more, it costs me a fortune to transport the cheese to Paris."

CHEESES OF NORMANDY

1. LIVAROT: Elastic, pungent, and rather spicy thick discs of cow's-milk cheese, traditionally wrapped in military-like stripes of willow (now generally paper), giving Livarot the name "little colonel." This washed-rind cheese is generally of raw milk. The best is aged in very damp, cool cellars for at least one month, giving the cheese a very shiny and reddish golden crust.

2. BRILLAT-SAVARIN: A "new" cheese by French standards, this high-fat (75 percent), supple cow's-milk cheese was invented during the 1930s by cheese merchant Henri Androuët. The fat disc sports a white rind and offers a smooth, very buttery flavor.

3. PAVE D'AUGE: A thick, ochre-colored square of rich cow's-milk cheese, aged in humid cellars where it is regularly washed with salted water, making for a very moist, soft cheese. The best Pavé d'Auge has a spicy, tangy flavor.

4. CAMEMBERT DE NORMANDIE: Supple, fragrant, and fruity discs of cow's-milk cheese, the best of which is made of raw milk in small dairies and aged for at least three weeks. Look for cheese with a brightly pigmented, rust-tinged rind. Camembert is sold in a distinguishing wooden box, a marketing idea created in 1880 so that travelers, as well as French soldiers, could carry Camembert with them on journeys. Beware of lily-white versions known simply as Camembert, not Camembert de Normandie.

5. PONT-L'EVEQUE: Very tender, fragrant squares of cow's-milk cheese, the best of which is made from the freshest cow's milk from the rich pastureland along Normandy's Touques river. The cheese has a pungent, earthy aroma, and is aged for a minimum of two weeks.

Champagne et Le Nord
CHAMPAGNE
AND THE NORTH

A touch of the North, crisp greens and carrots.

When I think of the Champagne region I think of gently rolling fields of golden wheat, of unhurried weekends in the country with plenty of time for mushroom hunting in the dampened woods, for tiptoeing about awesome stone cathedrals, for leisurely dining with family and friends.

The North—a flat, compact, rural area dotted with low, square, red brick farmhouses—reminds me, not surprisingly, of Belgium, and calls to mind steaming mounds of mussels and frothy mugs of beer.

Both areas are a gold mine for cheese: From the North come all those earthy, pungent, brightly colored cow's-milk cheeses that make you want to curl up by the fire on a gray winter's day, snacking on country bread and a pungent Maroilles, sipping beer or maybe even the traditional gin. The delicate selections from Champagne, on the other hand, seem to fit the area's gentle, rather elegant image, with its soft, mellow Brie and bloomy Chaource.

No matter where one goes in either Champagne or the North, no location is more than a few hours' drive from Paris, making for compact day trips.

One Sunday in September we boarded the train to Lille, to see the city and wander about the old town during the annual *Grande Braderie,* a sort of do-as-you-wish day when people clean out their attics and set up makeshift stands on the streets. We bought colorful hand-knit children's sweaters for a pittance, hovered over the antique book stalls in the center of town, and then feasted on the daily special, mussels and fries—about the only food you'll find in Lille on the first Sunday in September! By twilight the streets were filled with mountains of mussel shells, and the flea market went on through the night.

The North, of course, includes the coastal towns of Boulogne-sur-Mer, Le Touquet-Paris-Plaza, and Calais, which have become, due to their proximity to the British shores, more like England than parts of England. English is spoken everywhere, and in restaurants and markets it seems that the British day-trippers easily outnumber the French.

My favorite northern town of all is Amiens, famed for its stunning Gothic cathedral and the *hortillonnages,* a vast series of fruit and vegetable plots cultivated amidst a maze of canals at the northeastern edge of town. One afternoon we wandered through this old town, around the cathedral, where they were restoring the marketplace along the Somme river. Chickens wandered through the alleyways as craftsmen worked slowly to restore the small, modest brick homes that appeared to be no more than one room wide and two tiny rooms deep.

We toured the *hortillonnages*—via Rue de Verdun by car, the Chemin de Halage by foot—and watched the gardeners peacefully preparing their plots for the winter.

Anyone who appreciates gardening will love the *hortillonnages,* one of the most spectacular and soothing "microclimates" I know, a stretch of land that attracts migratory birds—including robins and sparrows, herons and wild mallards—with canals full of eel and pike, aquatic plants like water lilies and iris, and, of course, those flat, verdant plots of cauliflower and leeks, spring peas and sorrel. What a pleasing rural touch a few steps from central Amiens, a city of some 130,000 inhabitants.

Until the birth of the railroad—when produce from the south of France began to compete with the locally grown fruits and vegetables—these romantic "floating gardens" supplied all of

Amiens with the freshest of radishes, carrots, apples, and pears, all delivered by boat to the *marché d'eau* (water market) at Place Parmentier near the cathedral.

Today, sadly, the *hortillonnage* culture is dying out: Less than sixteen full-scale gardens remain. It is, one must agree, a rather impractical way to make a living. Many plots have been bought up by nurserymen, who raise fruit trees and flowers for the wholesale market.

The land on which the Amiens cathedral was built was donated by a farmer who gave up his artichoke fields for the church. Perhaps that gargoyle projecting from the gutter of Notre-Dame is that farmer, a primitive carved figure stooping under the weight of his hefty wicker baskets bursting with an assortment of fresh produce, ready for the market.

WHEN YOU GO

Michelin Green Guides: *Champagne/Ardennes, Flandre/Artois/Picardie,* and *Environs de Paris.*

Getting there: Most cities in Champagne and the North are an easy drive from Paris.

Getting around: Michelin maps 241 (Champagne/Ardennes), 236 (Nord/Flandre-Artois-Picardie), and 237 (Ile-de-France/Paris Region).

Best time to visit: The region is at its prettiest, and most active, from Easter through October, though main cities such as Reims and Lille are worth visiting year round.

MARKETS

(Liveliest markets are marked with an asterisk.)

Monday: Chaource, Monthermé, Montmirail, Verzenay.

Tuesday: Chaource, Charleville-Mézières, La Ferté-sous-Jouarre, Lille, Montmirail, Rocroi (except the first Tuesday following the first Monday of the month), Vertus.

Wednesday: Arras, Boulogne-sur-Mer, Calais, Châlons-sur-Marne, Chaource, *Coulommiers, Fère-en-Tardenois, Fumay, Lille, Montmirail, Reims, Sedan, Soissons.

Thursday: *Abbeville, Amiens, Avize, Calais, Chaource, *Charleville-Mézières, Laon, Lille, Montmirail, Rethel, Saint-Dizier, Le Touquet-Paris-Plage, Vitry-le-François.

Friday: Avesnes-sur-Helpe, Ay, Chaource, La Ferté-sous-Jouarre, Langres, Lille, Montmirail, Le Quesnoy, Reims.

Saturday: Abbeville, *Amiens, *Arras, *Boulogne-sur-Mer, *Calais, *Châlons-sur-Marne, Chaource, *Charleville-Mézières, Coulommiers, Epernay, Laon, *Meaux, Montmirail, Reims, *Saint-Dizier, *Sedan, Sézanne, *Soissons, *Le Touquet-Paris-Plage, *Troyes.

Sunday: Calais, Chaource, Coulommiers, *Lille, Montmiral, *Reims, Troyes.

FAIRS AND FESTIVALS

Sunday before Easter: *Foire Internationale aux Vins et aux Fromages* (international wine and cheese fair), Coulommiers.

Second Sunday in April: *Foire du Printemps* (traditional local fair), Bapaume.

Last Sunday in April: *Foire au Cresson* (watercress fair), Lécluse.

One day in May: *Fête des Crustacés* (shellfish festival), Wimereux.

Pentecost: *Foire à la Sardine* (sardine fair), Prez-sous-Lafauche.

Third Sunday in June: *Fête des Fraises* (strawberry festival), Verlinghem.

Last Sunday in June through the following Friday: *Fête des Fraises* (strawberry festival), Samer.

First Sunday in July: *Fête des Myrtilles* (blueberry festival), Les Mazures.

First Sunday after July 5: *Fête de Gayant* (festival of giants), Douai.

Last two weeks in July: *Fête du Poisson* (fish festival), Boulogne-sur-Mer.

One day in August: *Fête de la Moule* (mussel festival), Wimereux.

Sunday before August 15: *Fête de la Flamiche* (cheese tart festival), Maroilles.

Last Sunday in August: *Foire à l'Ail* (garlic fair), Locon.

First Sunday in September: *Foire à l'Ail* (garlic fair), Arleux; *Fête de l'Andouille* (chitterling sausage festival), Aire-sur-la-Lys; *Foire aux Fromages* (cheese fair), La Capelle; *Foire à la Mirabelle* (plum festival), Prez-sous-Lafauche.

First Sunday and Monday in September: *La Grande Braderie* (a citywide flea market and mussel and French-fry festival), Lille.

Early September: *Kermesse de la Bêtise* (traditional local fair), Cambrai.

Second Sunday in September: *Foire aux Aulx* (garlic fair), Bapaume; *Foire aux Oignons* (onion fair), Nouvion-le-Comte.

Last weekend in September: *Salon du Champignon* (mushroom conference), Sainte-Menehould.

Last Sunday in September: *Foire Saint-Michel* (sausage fair), Fumay.

First Sunday in October: *Foire aux Pommes* (apple fair), Neuilly-Saint-Front.

Early October: *Fête du Houblon* (hops festival), Steenvoorde.

Mid-October: *Fête de la Pomme et du Cidre* (apple and cider festival), Saint-Augustin.

Third Sunday in October of even years: *Foire aux Fromages* (cheese fair), Chaource.

Last Sunday in November: *Fête des Oignons* (onion festival), Nogent-l'Artaud.

Weekend before Christmas: *Fête de la Dinde* (turkey festival), Licques.

AMIENS *(Somme)*

Lille 115 k, Paris 148 k, Reims 156 k.

Markets: Thursday and Saturday, 7 A.M. to sunset, Place du Marché; Saturday,
7 A.M. to noon, Place Parmentier.
Hortillonnages tour: For an hour-long guided boat tour of the *hortillonnages,*
contact *"Embarcadère le Week-end,"* 54 Boulevard Beauvillé (22.92.12.18),
80000 Amiens. Tours are held from April through mid-September.

RESTAURANT

**RESTAURANT DU PRE
PORUS**
95 Rue Voyelle, 80000
Amiens.
(22.46.25.03).
Last orders taken at 2 P.M.
and 10 P.M.
Closed Monday dinner,
Tuesday, and February.
Credit cards: AE, V.
Terrace dining.
Private dining room for 15
to 200.
75-, 95-, and 140-franc
menus. A la carte, 130
francs.

After visiting the cathedral in Amiens and touring the *hortillonnages*—the market gardens set along the canals—stop for lunch at this large, casual, old-fashioned waterside restaurant known as a *guinguette.* The food here is simple and authentically regional, service is friendly, and if the weather's fine you can dine on the terrace. Try the local *flamiche aux poireaux,* a vegetable tart filled with leeks, cream, and cheese, or the *ficelle picarde,* a thin crêpe wrapped around a slice of ham and topped with a cheesy cream sauce. The *coq à la bière* was delicious, with a most pleasant beery taste. (Directions: just east of Amiens, left off the Rue de Verdun.)

BOULOGNE-SUR-MER *(Pas-de-Calais)*

Amiens 123 k, Calais 34 k, Lille 115 k, Paris 243 k.

Market: Wednesday and Saturday, 7 A.M. to 12:30 P.M., Place Dalton.
Fête du Poisson (fish festival): last two weeks in July.

FROMAGERIE

PHILIPPE OLIVIER
43-45 Rue Thiers, 62200
Boulogne-sur-Mer.
(21.31.94.74).
Open 8:30 A.M. to 12:30 P.M.
and 2:30 to 7:30 P.M.
Closed Monday.
Will ship in Europe.

Philippe Olivier, an *artisan-affineur,* or craftsman and cheese ager, is intensely passionate about his work and operates one of the most spectacular cheese shops in all of France. I wish more cheese merchants were like Monsieur Olivier: He works hard to educate his customers, offering a regular newsletter and filling his shop with signs and notes concerning each of his more than 200 different varieties of cheese. I also love the fact that he offers his cheese at various stages of aging, always encouraging clients to go for the well-aged versions, which usually have more character and depth. His long, narrow shop has a festive, enticing air and you'll want to buy "one of each." I'm not, however, fond of all of his "doctored" cheeses, such as Camembert with Calvados, or Brie layered with blue cheese.

FERE-EN-TARDENOIS *(Aisne)*

Paris 110 k, Reims 45 k.

Market: Wednesday, 8 A.M. to noon, Place Aristide-Briand.

RESTAURANT

**HOSTELLERIE DU
CHATEAU**
02130 Fère-en-Tardenois.
(23.82.21.13).
Last orders taken at 2 P.M.
and 9 P.M.
Closed after lunch January 1
through February.
Credit cards: AE, DC, V.
Private dining room for 20.
English spoken.
250– (weekdays) and
380–franc menus. A la
carte, 300 francs.

SPECIALTIES:
Change with the seasons.

Marketing in château-*style splendor.*

Much of the joy of travel in France revolves around the idea of romantic weekend lunches in the country, and one of my favorite excursions is the short trip to this baronial nineteenth-century *château,* where you can't help but feel a bit special. Take a window seat in the richly paneled dining room: On one side you'll have a view of newly plowed hills, on the other a view of the formal gardens. Pink damask tablecloths and a single pink rose floating in a crystal bowl add a romantic, elegant touch. Service here is properly attentive, but if you want to be left alone with the view and your companions, no one here will press you. The menu changes regularly, but the foods I've loved best include the *foie de canard chaud à la croque au sel* (sautéed duck liver enveloped in wilted spinach leaves, served with little mounds of coarse salt, coarsely ground black pepper, and finely minced herbs, for dipping) and the *tartare de loup et saumon* (thin slices of bass interlaced with salmon).

SOUPE DES HORTILLONS
GARDEN VEGETABLE SOUP

One of the most breathtaking tours in all of France is the walk along the hortillonnages, *the picturesque market garden plots built between a series of crisscrossing canals on the outskirts of the city of Amiens. Here the local farmers, or* hortillons, *grow all sorts of fresh vegetables, perfect for turning into a fresh, warming soup. This is a time-consuming dish, for all the fine chopping takes some patience. As ever, success depends upon the freshness of ingredients, freshly grated top-quality cheese, and plenty of fresh herbs. Be certain to serve the soup piping hot in warmed bowls. Do not be tempted to cook the beans and peas with the soup. Because they are cooked separately and refreshed, they remain beautifully green and fresh tasting and offer a nice contrast in color, texture, and flavor to the rest of the vegetables.*

3 leeks, white and light green parts, well rinsed and dried

3 ribs celery

3 medium carrots, peeled

3 medium turnips, peeled

8 medium potatoes, peeled

3 tablespoons (1½ ounces; 45 g) unsalted butter

2½ quarts (2.5 liters) water

Salt to taste

Freshly ground black pepper to taste

8 ounces (250 g) fresh green beans, trimmed and cut into ¾-inch (2 cm) pieces

2 cups (500 ml) fresh or frozen sweet peas

Large handful mixed fresh herbs, preferably chervil, tarragon, parsley, and basil, finely chopped just before serving

1 cup (250 ml) freshly grated Parmesan

8 slices country-style bread, toasted

1. Cut the leeks, celery, carrots, turnips, and potatoes into ¾-inch (2 cm) cubes.

2. Melt the butter in a large, heavy-bottomed stockpot, over low heat. Add the leeks, celery, carrots, and turnips; cover and cook gently until very soft, about 20 minutes. Stir from time to time to make sure that nothing sticks or colors. Add the water and salt and heat to a boil. Reduce the heat and simmer covered for 10 minutes. Add the potatoes and simmer until the potatoes are tender but still intact; about 10 minutes longer. Taste for seasoning and salt and pepper to taste.

3. Meanwhile, cook the green beans and peas in separate pans of boiling salted water just until tender, about 2 to 3 minutes each. Drain and refresh with cold running water.

4. To serve, ladle the soup, then the peas and beans into warmed soup bowls. Sprinkle with the fresh herbs and freshly grated cheese. Pass the bread separately.

Yield: 8 servings.

FONTENELLE *(Aisne)*

Cambrai 58 k, Maroilles 16 k.

AFFINEUR

ETABLISSEMENTS
 DUCORNET
Fontenelle, 02170 Le
 Nouvion-en-Thiérache.
 (23.97.05.01).
Open 8 A.M. to noon and
 1:30 to 5:30 P.M. Closed
 Saturday, the last week in
 December, a week at
 Easter, the week of July
 14, and the week of
 August 15.

Market day in the Champagne region.

Since 1830 the Ducornet family has tended to the aging of the local golden-orange Maroilles, made on the farms scattered about this flat and picturesque land. The farmers bring in their fresh white cow's-milk cheeses at about one week of age, then Roland Ducornet—a dedicated professional—takes care to wash them, turn them, brush them with salt, bringing them to life in his ancient vaulted brick-and-stone cellars kept humid with water tapped from a natural spring. He also ages Dauphin, the cheese that's shaped like a dolphin; the pepper-and-tarragon-flavored Boulette d'Avesnes, made with the leftover "seconds" of Maroilles and formed into a cone; and Vieux Lille, cheese made in the same manner as Maroilles, only it is salted more, then aged on wooden shelves in very cold and damp cellars (the cheese is brushed with a salt solution every two weeks and left to age for a full six months until it is stinking ripe—a strong, rugged cheese that literally attacks the palate). Note that this is not a cheese shop, but rather a cheese-aging farm, though cheese can be purchased directly from Monsieur Ducornet.

LILLE *(Nord)*

Amiens 115 k, Arras 52 k, Boulogne-sur-Mer 115 k, Paris 219 k.

Selected markets: Wednesday, Friday, and Sunday, 8 A.M. to 2 P.M., Marché Wazemmes, Place du Concert; Tuesday, Thursday, and Sunday, 8 A.M. to 2 P.M., Place de la Nouvelle-Aventure.
La Grande Braderie (a citywide flea market and mussel and french-fry festival): First Sunday and Monday in September.

RESTAURANT

A L'HUITRIERE
3 Rue des Chats-Bossus,
   59000 Lille.
(20.55.43.41).
Last orders taken at 2:30 P.M.
   and 9:30 P.M.
Closed Sunday dinner and
   the last week in July
   through August.
Credit cards: AE, DC, V.
Air-conditioned.
Private dining room for 10
   to 40.
English spoken.
400 francs.

SPECIALTIES:
Seafood; *agneau de Paulliac*
(southwestern lamb).

The lively old town of Lille sports numerous old-fashioned storefronts, and this combination fish shop and restaurant on "the str?et of the hunchbacked cats" provides one of the best dining experiences in the city. You enter a stunning Art Deco blue and gold mosaic-tiled fish shop, then move into a warm, bourgeois dining room filled with smartly dressed customers enjoying platters of Colchester oysters, the most delicate of fresh braised sardines (you'll never be able to face the canned version again!), mountains of meaty steamed mussels, the freshest Saint-Pierre, or John Dory, and in the fall and winter months, tender roast wild duck.

MAROILLES *(Nord)*

Amiens 80 k, Lille 100 k.
Market: Tuesday, 9 A.M. to 1 P.M., Place de l'Eglise.
Fête de la Flamiche (cheese tart festival): Sunday before August 15.

FROMAGER

FERME DU VERGER
   PILOTE
59550 Maroilles.
(27.84.71.10).
Open 9 A.M. to 8 P.M. Closed
   Christmas Day only.
Credit card: V.

The Verger Pilote farm is one of the strangest combinations I know, sort of one-stop shopping for the Maroilles cheese lover. This is an honest working farm, where they make a very pleasant Maroilles and offer tours of the cheese-making facilities and the stone aging cellars. (Directions: just west of Maroilles on the D959.)

TARTE AU MAROILLES
MAROILLES CHEESE TART

One sunny Indian summer afternoon, while driving through the village of Maroilles, I was lured by the café signs advertising Tarte au Maroilles. *Moments later, I regretted my impulsiveness, as the café owner retrieved a sad-looking tart from her microwave oven. Warmed cardboard must certainly taste better. Later that day a Maroilles cheesemaker offered me a recipe for the real thing. From the list of ingredients, the tart looks awfully rich, but, in the end, it's a very delicate, elegant little tart. I love the way the brioche-like dough puffs up, forming a nice pillow for the golden brown, fragrant topping. It makes a nice lunch or brunch dish, served with a watercress salad alongside. If you cannot find Maroilles cheese, substitute an equal amount of either ripe Véritable Chaumes or extra-sharp Cheddar cheese.*

Dough:
½ cup (125 ml) lukewarm milk
2 ½ teaspoons or 1 package active dry yeast
2 to 2 ¼ cups (280 to 315 g) unbleached all-purpose flour
½ teaspoon salt
2 large eggs
6 tablespoons (3 ounces; 90 g) unsalted butter, at room temperature

Topping:
1 small ripe Maroilles cheese, (about 8 ounces; 250 g) or 8 ounces (250 g) ripe Véritable Chaumes or extra-sharp Cheddar cheese
1 large egg
1 large egg yolk
½ cup (125 ml) *crème fraîche* (see Recipe Index) or sour cream
2 tablespoons (1 ounce; 30 g) unsalted butter
Salt and freshly ground black pepper to taste
Freshly grated nutmeg to taste

1. Prepare the dough: Place the milk, yeast, and ¼ cup (60 g) of the flour in a large mixing bowl. Stir until thoroughly blended and let sit to proof the yeast, about 5 minutes.

2. Stir in the remaining flour, the salt, and eggs and mix thoroughly. Gradually work in the butter, then turn the dough onto a floured surface. Knead until smooth, about 5 minutes, adding additional flour as needed. The dough should be soft and slightly sticky.

3. Place the dough in a large bowl, cover, and let rise at room temperature until doubled in bulk, about 1 ½ hours.

4. Preheat the oven to 375°F (190°C). Generously butter a 10 ½-inch (27 cm) round ceramic baking dish.

5. Punch the dough down and spread the dough over the bottom of the baking dish. Do not build up the sides as you would for a normal tart.

6. Prepare the topping: If the Maroilles rind is particularly hard, remove it. Otherwise cut the cheese into thin slices and arrange them evenly on top of the dough. (If using Véritable Chaumes, remove the rind.)

7. Whisk the egg, egg yolk, and *crème fraîche* in a small mixing bowl until well blended. Pour this mixture over the cheese and spread it to the edge of the dough.

8. Dot the top with the butter and sprinkle generously with salt, pepper, and nutmeg.

9. Bake until the top is brown and bubbly, about 35 minutes. Cut the tart into wedges and serve.

Yield: One 10 ½-inch (27 cm) tart.

Visiting the Great Champagne Houses

Beneath the cities of Reims, Ay, and Epernay lie the ancient, vast Champagne aging cellars, where hundreds of thousands of bottles of white wine are tilted and turned for months, then left on their sides, undisturbed for years, before surfacing as the world's most famous sparkling wine.

Veuve Clicquot, Taittinger, Moët et Chandon, and several others of France's grand Champagne houses offer guided tours of their cellars. Note that it's chilly underground, and the tours usually involve a fair amount of walking and climbing (except at Mercier and Piper-Heidsieck, where a small train takes visitors around!), so bring a sweater and comfortable shoes. Admission is free and English is generally spoken at these establishments:

Bollinger, 4 Boulevard Maréchal-de-Lattre, 51160 Ay. (26.55.21.31). Open Monday through Friday by appointment.

De Castellane, 57 Rue de Verdun, 51200 Epernay. (26.50.12.34). Open Monday through Friday by appointment. Closed August.

Charles Heidsieck Henriot, 3 Place des Droits-de-l'Homme, 51100 Reims. (26.85.03.27). Open by appointment. Closed August.

Heidsieck Monopole, 83 Rue Coquebert, 51100 Reims. (26.07.39.34). Open by appointment. Closed August.

Lanson, 12 Boulevard Lundy, 51100 Reims. (26.40.36.26). Open Monday through Friday by appointment.

Laurent-Perrier, 8 Avenue de Champagne, 51150 Tours-sur-Marne. (26.58.91.22). Open Monday through Friday by appointment. Closed August.

Mercier, 75 Avenue de Champagne, 51200 Epernay. (26.54.71.11). Open 10 A.M. to 12:30 P.M. and 2 to 5:30 P.M. Monday through Friday; 9:30 A.M. to noon and 2 to 6 P.M. Saturday; 9:30 A.M. to 12:30 P.M. and 2:30 to 5:30 P.M. Sunday and holidays. Closed November through the Sunday preceding Easter. Mercier offers a visit by train through their extensive cellar.

Moët et Chandon, 20 Avenue de Champagne, 51200 Epernay. (26.54.71.11). Open 10 A.M. to 12:30 P.M. and 2 to 5:30 P.M. Monday through Friday; 9:30 A.M. to noon and 2 to 6 P.M. Saturday; 9:30 A.M. to 12:30 P.M. and 2:30 to 5:30 P.M. Sunday and holidays. Closed November through the Sunday preceding Easter.

Mumm, 29 Rue du Champ-de-Mars, 51100 Reims. (26.40.22.73). Open 9 to 11 A.M. and 2 to 5 P.M. Monday through Friday.

Perrier-Jouët, 28 Avenue de Champagne, 51200 Epernay. (26.55.20.53). Open Monday through Friday by appointment.

Piper-Heidsieck, 51 Boulevard Henri-Vanier, 51100 Reims. (26.85.01.94). Open daily 9:30 to 11:30 A.M. and 2 to 5:30 P.M. April 11 through November 11. Closed Saturday and Sunday November 12 through April 10. Piper-Heidsieck offers a visit by train through their extensive cellar. Reservations required.

Pol Roger, 1 Rue Henri-Lelarge, 51200 Epernay. (26.55.41.95). Open Monday through Friday by appointment.

Pommery, 5 Place Général-Gourard, 51100 Reims. (26.05.05.01). Open 9 to 11 A.M. and 2 to 5 P.M. Monday through Friday; 10 to 11 A.M. and 2 to 5 P.M. Saturday and Sunday.

Louis Roederer, 21 Boulevard Lundy, 51100 Reims. (26.40.42.11). Open Monday through Friday by appointment.

Taittinger, 9 Place Saint-Nicaise, 51100 Reims. (26.85.45.35). Open daily 9 to 11 A.M. and 2 to 5 P.M. March through November. Closed Saturday December through February.

Veuve Clicquot, 1 Place des Droits-de-l'Homme, 51100 Reims. (26.85.24.08). Open 9 to 11 A.M. and 2 to 5 P.M. Open by appointment in August. Closed November until Easter.

Grace and grandeur at Gérard Boyer's.

MONTREUIL-SUR-MER *(Pas-de-Calais)*

Boulogne-sur-Mer 38 k, Lille 112 k, Paris 206 k.
Market: Saturday, 9 A.M. to 12:30 P.M., Grand Place.

Authentic raw-milk Brie.

RESTAURANT

CHATEAU DE
  MONTREUIL
4 Chaussée Capucins, 62170
  Montreuil-sur-Mer.
(21.81.53.04).
Last orders taken at 2 P.M.
  and 9:30 P.M. (10:30 P.M.
  on Saturday).
Closed Thursday lunch
  (except July and August),
  and mid-December
  through January.
Credit cards: AE, DC, EC, V.
Terrace dining.
Private dining rooms for 16
  and 22.
English spoken.
220–franc menu at lunch
  only. A la carte, about
  300 francs.

SPECIALTIES:
*Mousseline d'huîtres à la
ciboulette* (oyster mousseline
with chives), *pavé de saumon à
l'huile d'olive vierge* (salmon
cooked in virgin olive oil),
canette de Barbarie aux épices
(duck with spices).

This large, appealing manor house offers some of the best food in the North. Chef Christian Germain and his English wife, Lindsay, have succeeded in combining Relais et Châteaux elegance with a personalized hominess. One warm evening in early fall, I sat in this cozy dining room and enjoyed one of the more truly satisfying meals of my life: the simplest roast local chicken served with a healthy dose of sautéed wild mushrooms and a few glasses of hearty red Bandol. There's also a fine assortment of cheese from cheese ager Philippe Olivier.

REIMS *(Marne)*

Château-Thierry 58 k, Epernay 27 k, Lille 208 k, Paris 142 k.

Markets: Sunday, 8 A.M. to 12:30 P.M., Avenue Jean-Jaurès; Wednesday, Friday, and Saturday, 6 A.M. to 1 P.M., covered market, 50 Rue de Mars. Flea market: First Sunday of each month (except August), 8 A.M. to 5 P.M., Place du Boulingrin.

RESTAURANT

GERARD BOYER
(Les Crayères) 64 Boulevard
  Vasnier, 51100
  Henri-Reims.
(26.82.80.80).
Last orders taken at 2 P.M.
  and 9 P.M.
Closed Monday, Tuesday
  lunch, and the last week
  in December through
  mid-January.
Credit cards: AE, V.
Terrace dining.
Air-conditioned.
Private dining room for 25.
English spoken.
About 550 francs.

SPECIALTIES:
Change with the seasons; *petit chou farci aux langoustines* (cabbage leaf stuffed with langoustines), *suprême de canard rouennais aux poires et au gingembre* (duck breast with pears and ginger).

Chef Gérard Boyer.

Understated, discreet, and refined are the words to describe Gérard and Elyane Boyer's restored eighteenth-century-style *château* in the heart of Champagne country. Just at the edge of Reims, the Boyer *château* is a 90-minute drive from Paris, fine for a day's jaunt or for stretching into a relaxing overnight journey. The *château,* actually built in 1900 by the Pommery family of Champagne fame, has been restored and redecorated in exquisite taste, allowing guests all the comforts of the twentieth century while retaining the charm and elegance of a France of days past. Guests are free to roam about the bright and airy *château,* situated in the center of a huge park enveloped in greenery, with trees imported from all over the globe. Look carefully at the exterior and you'll find stone carvings of cheery cherubs, roses, and of course the clumps of Pinot Noir and Pinot Chardonnay grapes that go into making the Champagne that has long cast a spell on the world. The restaurant's wine list includes some 122 Champagnes, varying in size, age, and price. The food—elegant without being precious, simple without being simplistic, light without sacrificing flavor and character—is in keeping with the style of the *château*. The dining room is actually a series of three rooms decorated in muted shades of cream and terra-cotta, the most exquisite of which is paneled in wood and looks out over a rotunda-like winter garden that faces the neatly ordered park and terrace. Everywhere there are fresh flowers, silver candelabra, Chinese ginger jars, marble mantels, and mirrors. Over the years, the dishes I've most enjoyed here include Boyer's *fricassée de champignons sauvages* (a simple but exquisite blend of varied wild mushrooms, delicately sautéed and sauced with a touch of cream); his light and flavorful grilled Saint-Pierre (fresh, flaky, and perfectly grilled John Dory, set on a bed of red onion *confit*—see recipe, facing page); and the very elegant and soothing mussel soup touched with cream and saffron (see recipe, page 102). Of course each meal includes a stunning cheese course, made up of the area's most famous selections, all prepared with raw cow's milk. You'll find the creamy, almost fruity Chaource, with its snowy, dimpled white rind; the spicy Langres, shaped like a sunken crater, with a yellow-orange rind; Maroilles, with its tangy, subtle nuttiness; and of course Brie, of reddish brown complexion with a bright, fruity flavor. Throughout the meal, chef Boyer offers a superb country sourdough bread, made to his specifications by a local baker.

Château *élégance*, chez *Boyer.*

FILET DE SAINT-PIERRE AUX OIGNONS CONFITS ET AU BEURRE DE TOMATES GERARD BOYER
GERARD BOYER'S JOHN DORY WITH ONION CONFIT AND TOMATO BUTTER

This is a light, flavorful fish preparation that could be made with any fish fillets. While chef Gérard Boyer in Reims prepares it with the delicious white Saint-Pierre, or John Dory, Alaska snapper and red snapper make excellent substitutes. Much of the work can be done in advance and the dish completed as the fish broils.

Onion *confit*:
4 medium red onions, minced
1 ¼ cups (310 ml) dry red wine, preferably Côtes-du-Rhône
¼ cup (60 ml) best-quality sherry wine vinegar
¾ cup (185 ml) water
Salt and freshly ground black pepper to taste
1 teaspoon mild honey
1 teaspoon unsalted butter

Tomato butter:
10 medium tomatoes, cored and quartered
1 tablespoon (½ ounce; 15 g) unsalted butter

2 pounds (1 kg) John Dory, Alaska snapper, or red snapper fillets, skinned
1 teaspoon virgin olive oil

1. Prepare the onion *confit:* Combine the onions, wine, vinegar, water, salt, and pepper in a large saucepan. Cook uncovered over low heat, stirring occasionally, until all the liquid is absorbed and the onions are very soft and sweet, about 45 minutes. Stir in the honey and butter and check seasoning. (This can be done up to one day in advance. Refrigerate and reheat just before serving.)

2. Prepare the tomato butter: Purée the tomatoes in a food processor. Press the purée through a fine-mesh sieve, reserving only the juice and strained pulp. Pour into a small saucepan and reduce by two thirds over medium heat. Whisk in the butter until completely blended. Season to taste with salt and pepper. Keep warm.

3. Preheat the broiler.

4. Season the fish with salt and pepper and sprinkle with the oil. Broil until the fish is opaque and still resilient, not soft or overly tough, about 4 minutes on each side.

5. Heat the onion *confit* and spoon onto 4 warmed dinner plates. Pour the warm tomato butter around the onion *confit* and top with the broiled fish. Serve immediately.

Yield: 4 servings.

CHAMPAGNES OF CHAMPAGNE

1. MOET ET CHANDON: The largest, and still one of the most prestigious, Champagne houses. Their best-known Champagne is the vintage Dom Perignon.

2. KRUG GRANDE CUVEE: One of the smallest Champagne houses, producing a luxurious, opulent Champagne that's generally light, elegant, with a very faint aroma of vanilla. Krug's Champagnes are aged longer than most, giving them a very refined, artful quality.

3. ROEDERER CRISTAL 1981: For big, creamy, classic Champagne, try the prestigious Cristal or the pale Cristal Rosé.

4. BILLECART SALMON BRUT ROSE: I guess it's just a coincidence that this elegant, perfumed *rosé* is a pale salmon color. One of the more delicate and fruity Champagnes I know, full of tiny bubbles, with an aftertone of raspberries and strawberries.

5. LAURENT PERRIER: A large, well-known house producing quantities of well-made Champagnes. Their non-vintage Champagne is generally one of the best buys in Champagne. But if money is no object, celebrate with the elegant, refined *cuvée* Grande Siècle.

6. BOLLINGER: The Bollinger name is synonymous with prestige, class, and authority. Try especially the luxury *cuvée* Tradition, a classic, complex, robust Champagne designed to help memorable events live on, long after you've taken your last sip.

7. J. LASSALLE: Jules Lassalle is a personal favorite, one of the rare Champagnes made by a single individual (he transforms his grapes into Champagne in the cellar under his house). This small independent firm offers a variety of very graceful, classic Champagnes, ranging from a mature Cuvée Angeline to a very aromatic *brut rosé*.

CHEESES OF CHAMPAGNE AND THE NORTH

1. MAROILLES: Thick, soft squares of moist cow's-milk cheese, with a very vigorous tangy flavor and strong bouquet. As Maroilles is aged in very humid cellars for two months, the rind turns a shiny, pale brick red. Historically made of raw milk on small farms, then brought to centrally located aging cellars, where professional *affineurs* handled the aging and marketing.

2. CHAOURCE: Known since the fourteenth century, this soft and fruity cylindrical cow's-milk cheese brings with it a faint scent of mushrooms and cream. A buttery, rich cheese with a 50 percent fat content.

3. BOULETTE D'AVESNES: A bright conical cheese made from visually defective pieces of Maroilles: Cheese agers select young Maroilles that may have a few bumps or knicks, then knead the Maroilles "dough" with tarragon and pepper and shape it into a cone. The cheese, traditionally colored red with paprika, is then wrapped in foil and cured for two months. A cheese that demands a strong accompanying beverage, such as beer or the traditional gin.

4. ROLLOT: An aromatic, spicy cow's-milk cheese, similar to Maroilles, with a smooth, glossy ochre-yellow rind. This soft washed cheese is shaped into small cylinders, or more commonly, in the folkloric form of a heart.

5. BRIE DE MELUN: Similar to, but smaller than, Brie de Meaux, any cheese called Brie de Melun must be made of raw cow's milk and aged at least one month on straw mats. The best has a persistent earthy aroma, a very fruity bouquet, and a crackly, rust-colored rind.

6. BRIE DE MEAUX: The flat cow's-milk cheese that, at its best, tastes faintly of hazelnuts has long been considered the "king of cheese." Brie appears around the world, in many shapes and forms, but only Brie made with raw cow's milk in the region of Meaux has the right to the appellation Brie de Meaux.

SOUPE DE MOULES AU SAFRAN GERARD BOYER
GERARD BOYER'S MUSSEL SOUP WITH SAFFRON

This creation of chef Gérard Boyer of Reims is one of those wonderfully surprising recipes that sound rather ordinary but taste so special. For those who love to begin with an elegant soup, it's an especially fine opener.

Garnish:

1 orange

2 leeks, white part only, cut into fine julienne strips

2 carrots, peeled and cut into fine julienne strips

1 rib celery, cut into fine julienne strips

Soup:

4 pounds (2 kg) mussels

2 shallots, minced

1 leek, white part only, well rinsed, dried, and minced

⅔ cup (165 ml) dry white wine

½ cup (125 ml) *crème fraîche* (see Recipe Index) or heavy cream, preferably not ultra-pasteurized

6 tablespoons (3 ounces; 90 g) unsalted butter

Large pinch saffron threads

Salt and freshly ground black pepper to taste

1. Prepare the garnish: Carefully cut the zest (colored part of the peel) from the orange, being sure not to get any of the white pith. Cut the zest into fine julienne strips.

2. Drop the zest into a small saucepan of boiling water. As soon as the water boils again, remove the zest. Repeat this one more time with a fresh pan of water. Refresh the zest under cold running water, drain on paper towels, and set aside.

3. Drop the julienned vegetables into a large pan of boiling water, return to a boil, and drain at once. Rinse with cold running water and drain well. Set aside. (The orange peel and the vegetables could be prepared several hours in advance. Keep them covered so they remain moist.)

4. Prepare the soup: Thoroughly scrub the mussels and rinse with several changes of water. Beard the mussels. (Do not beard the mussels in advance, or they will die and spoil.)

5. Heat the shallots, leeks, and wine in a 6-quart (6-liter) Dutch oven over high heat to a boil. Add the mussels and cook covered just until they open, about 5 minutes. Remove from the heat and strain, reserving the liquid. Let the mussels cool.

6. When the mussels are cool enough to handle, remove them from their shells and set aside. Discard any mussels that have not opened.

7. Pour the mussel cooking liquid into a medium saucepan and reduce by half over medium heat. Add the *crème fraîche* and reduce slightly. Whisk in the butter, tablespoon by tablespoon, until it is completely incorporated. Add the orange zest, julienned vegetables, and mussels. Season with the saffron, salt, and pepper. Serve immediately in warmed shallow soup bowls.

Yield: 8 servings.

Alsace
ALSACE

S'Bretschtelle Eck, where some say pretzels, *some say* bretzels.

Alsace, that narrow, vineyard-rich plain defined by the Rhine river on the east, the Vosges mountains on the west, is one of France's most fun-loving regions, the home of pretzels and sauerkraut, white wine and food fairs, a place where everyone, it seems, knows how to have a good time.

Despite this frontier's rather complicated history—throughout much of its existence, invasion and occupation have been the rule, not the exception—there is nothing terribly complicated about Alsatian cooking. It's a cuisine that combines the robust earthiness of German fare with the subtleties of French cooking. Translated here, it is basic peasant fare, a cold-weather, soul-satisfying cuisine based on potatoes, fresh and cured pork, rye breads with cumin, cabbages, wild mountain berries, and pale golden wines. But don't take this to mean that the food lacks flair, sophistication, or subtlety. Few wines in the world can match Gewürztraminer for finesse and breeding; the region's clear fruit brandies, or *eaux-de-vie*, clearly have no equal; and I know of few regional desserts as elegant as a great Alsatian cheesecake, known as the *tarte au fromage blanc*.

Over the years I've returned to Alsace time and again, most often with food, wine, and folklore in mind. There have been autumn journeys through the famous wine villages, those storybook

towns like Eguisheim, Riquewihr, and Ribeauvillé, with their steep-roofed houses sporting window boxes filled with geraniums.

There's a very welcoming, roll-up-your-sleeves quality about most spots in Alsace, where wine bars become *winstubs,* cafés and bars turn into *tavernes,* and at many restaurants you're likely to be seated on benches, sharing long wooden tables with fellow revelers.

I'm also fond of Alsace because it's a bread lover's land. Here breads and pastries are proudly homemade, not "store-bought" as in much of the rest of France. The home bread oven, a dying tradition in much of France, still reigns—though instead of the huge stone structures found elsewhere in the country, the Alsatian ovens are long, narrow metal affairs, used mainly to bake the thin-crusted cream, bacon, and onion tart known variously as *flamme-kueche* and *tarte flambée*.

The very best season to visit Alsace is fall harvest time, when Sunday after Sunday, villages like Krautergersheim and Munster, Plobsheim and Mutzig, bathed in blue skies and autumn glory, celebrate the season's bounty, toasting to new wines and fresh sauerkraut, red currants and blood sausage. In Alsace, even turnips have their day.

WHEN YOU GO

Michelin Green Guide: *Alsace et Lorraine/Vosges.*

Getting there: Air Inter offers about six daily hour-long flights to Strasbourg, leaving from Paris's Orly Ouest airport. The same journey by train, leaving from the Gare de l'Est, takes 4½ hours; there are at least ten trains daily. Trains also leave from Paris's Gare de l'Est for Colmar at least fourteen times daily; the journey varies from 4½ to 6 hours, depending on the train. There are no flights to Colmar. Cars can be rented at the airport and train stations.

Getting around: Michelin map 242 (Alsace et Lorraine).

Best time to visit: From late spring to late fall, Alsace is at its flowery, and festive, best.

MARKETS

(Liveliest markets are marked with an asterisk.)

Monday: Benfeld, Commercy, Kaysersberg, Molsheim.

Tuesday: *Bar-le-Duc, Guebwiller, Haguenau, Lunéville, Metz, Mulhouse, Munster, Nancy, Ribeauvillé, Sélestat, Strasbourg.

Wednesday: Brumath, Duttlenheim, Epinal, Metz, Nancy, Soufflenheim, Strasbourg, Vittel.

Thursday: Altkirch, Bar-le-Duc, Colmar, Erstein, *Gérardmer, Lunéville, Metz, Mulhouse, Nancy, Obernai, Saverne, Schiltigheim, Wissembourg.

Friday: Baccarat, Commercy, Guebwiller, *Haguenau, Lapoutroie, Metz, Mutzig, Nancy, Niederbronn-les-Bains, Plobsheim, Riquewihr, Rosheim, *Strasbourg, Turckheim, Verdun.

Saturday: Bar-le-Duc, Barr, *Colmar, *Epinal, Gérardmer, *Lunéville, *Metz, *Mulhouse, *Munster, *Nancy, Pfaffenhoffen, Ribeauvillé, Rouffach, *Strasbourg, Thann, *Vittel, *Wissembourg.

FAIRS AND FESTIVALS

Third Monday in February: *Foire aux Andouilles* (chitterling sausage fair), Le Val-d'Ajol.

Third Saturday in March: *Foire aux Harengs* (herring fair), Rupt-sur-Moselle.

Easter Sunday and Monday: *Foire Annuelle du Pâté Lorrain* (annual pâté fair), Châtenois.

Sunday closest to April 20: *Fête des Jonquilles* (daffodil festival), Gérardmer.

Last weekend in April: *Foire aux Grenouilles* (frog fair), Vittel.

Late April or early May: *Fête de l'Escargot* (snail festival), Osenbach.

Last weekend in April and early May: *Foire de Printemps* (spring fair), Strasbourg.

Month of May: *Fête de la Quiche* (quiche festival), Mirecourt.

May 1: *Fête du Printemps et Foire Régionale aux Vins* (spring festival and regional wine fair), Molsheim.

Second weekend in May: *Foire aux Escargots* (snail fair), Martigny-les-Bains.

Monday of Pentecost: *Foire* (international folklore festival), Wissembourg.

Third Sunday in May: *Foire Gastronomique* (gastronomic fair), Bulgnéville.

Second Sunday in June: *Foire à la Chipolata* (sausage fair), Lamarche; *Fête du Kugelhopf* (*kugelhopf* festival), Ribeauvillé.

Mid-June: *Fête de la Cerise* (cherry festival), Westhoffen; *Fête de la Truite et de la Glace Plombières* (trout and ice cream festival), Plombières-les-Bains.

June 21: *Marché au Pain d'Epices* (spice bread market), Gertwiller; *Procession de la Fête-Dieu* (parade in Alsatian costume), Geispolsheim.

Third weekend in June in even years: *Foire à la Quiche Lorraine* (quiche lorraine fair), Dombasle-sur-Meurthe.

Third or fourth Sunday in June: *Festival de la Rose* (rose festival), Saverne.

Last weekend in June: *Foire à la Frite* (French-fry fair), Girancourt.

Last weekend in June and first weekend in July: *Fête de la Tarte au Fromage* (cheesecake festival), Orbey.

Early July: *Fête de la Griotte* (cherry festival), Uffholtz.

First Sunday in July: *Fête du Fromage Blanc et des Traditions Rurales* (cheese and folklore festival), Sarrebourg.

Next to last weekend in July: *Foire aux Vins et Fête Folklorique* (wine fair and folklore festival), Ribeauvillé.

Last Saturday in July: *Fête de la Poitrine Farcie* (stuffed veal breast festival), Thann.

Month of August: *Fête de la Truite* (trout festival), Andlau.

First Sunday in August: *Fête de la Myrtille* (blueberry festival), Dabo.

August 5: *Foire aux Vins et Représentations Folkloriques* (wine fair and folklore festival), Colmar.

Second Sunday in August: *Corso Fleuri et Foire aux Vins* (parade and wine fair), Sélestat.

Mid-August: *Messti* (local festival and wine fair), Gertwiller.

Next to last weekend in August: *Kilbes* (wine fair), Gueberschwihr.

Around August 25: *Fête de la Mirabelle* (plum festival), Darney.

Last week in August: *Fête du Houblon et Semaine Gastronomique* (hops festival and food week), Haguenau.

Last Sunday in August: *Fête du Sucre* (sugar festival), Erstein; *Fête du Maïs* (corn festival), Bossendorf.

Late August or early September: *Fête de la Mirabelle* (plum festival), Metz.

First three days in September: *Journées de la Choucroute* (sauerkraut days), Colmar.

First Sunday in September: *Fête des Ménétriers* (fiddlers' festival), Ribeauvillé; *Fontaine de la Bière* (beer fountain), Mutzig.

First three Saturdays in September: *Fête de la Choucroute* (sauerkraut festival), Geispolsheim.

Mid-September: *Fête de la Groseille* (red currant festival), Bar-le-Duc.

Last Sunday in September: *Foire aux Oignons* (onion market), Brumath.

Last weekend in September and first Saturday in October: *Fête à la Choucroute* (sauerkraut festival), Krautergersheim.

Last weekend in September and first weekend in October, or first two weekends in October: *Journées d'Octobre* (October days), Mulhouse.

First Sunday in October: *Fête de la Planchette Paysanne* (food festival), Plobsheim; *Fête des Vendanges* (grape harvest festival), Barr.

Second Sunday in October: *Grande Fête du Raisin* (grape festival), Molsheim; *Foire au Boudin* (blood sausage fair), Monthureux.

Third Sunday in October: *Fête des Vendanges* (grape harvest festival), Obernai and Marlenheim; *Messti* (local festival), Merkwiller.

Early October: *Fête de la Tourte* (pie festival), Munster.

First and second Saturday nights in November: *Fête du Navet* (salt turnip festival), Lipsheim.

Around December 14: *Fête de la Sainte-Odile* (Saint Odile's Day festival), Obernai.

BASSEMBERG *(Bas-Rhin)*

Sainte-Marie-aux-Mines 32 k, Sélestat 17 k.

EAUX-DE-VIE

DISTILLERIE MASSENEZ
067 Dieffenbach Val,
   Bassemberg, 67220 Villé.
(88.85.62.86).
Open 8 A.M. to noon and 2
   to 5:30 P.M. Closed
   Saturday afternoon and
   Sunday.

Massenez is one of the most respected names in clear fruit brandies, or *eaux-de-vie*. Try especially their *framboise* (raspberry), *poire* (pear), *kirsch* (cherry), and *mirabelle* (plum).

COMMERCY *(Meuse)*

Metz 71 k, Paris 259 k, Toul 32 k.

Market: Monday, 9 A.M. to 12:30 P.M., Place Charles-de-Gaulle.

PATISSERIE

MAISON GROJEAN
8 Place Charles-de-Gaulle,
   55200 Commercy.
(29.91.25.16).
Open 8:45 A.M. to noon and
   2 to 7 P.M. Tuesday
   through Saturday; 9:30
   A.M. to noon and 2 to
   6 P.M. Sunday. Closed
   Monday.

This is perhaps France's major baker of *madeleines,* those oval, shell-shaped lemon tea cakes made famous by Marcel Proust (see page 127).

Along the river l'Ill.

EGUISHEIM *(Haut-Rhin)*

Belfort 71 k, Colmar 7 k, Mulhouse 39 k, Paris 448 k.

RESTAURANT

CAVEAU D'EGUISHEIM
3 Place du Château-
   Saint-Léon, 68420
   Eguisheim.
(89.41.08.89).
Last orders taken at 2 P.M.
   and 9 P.M., but *foie gras,*
   ham, and onion tarts are
   served all afternoon.
Closed Wednesday dinner,
   Thursday, the first ten
   days in July, and
   mid-January through
   February.
Credit cards: AE, DC, V.
Private dining room for 8.
Some English spoken.
105- and 160-franc menus.
   A la carte, 200 francs.

SPECIALTIES:
Choucroute (sauerkraut, various
sausages, bacon, pork, and
potatoes), *tarte à l'oignon*
(onion tart), *baeckeoffe*
(Alsatian stew of wine, beef,
lamb, pork, potatoes, and
onions), game in season.

The Caveau is a folksy, friendly sort of spot, with bare wood floors and tavern-style chairs, and on Sunday, tables are filled with local families out for a good feast. It's one of my favorite spots for a wintry Alsatian Sunday lunch. Reserve a table overlooking the charming village church and the window boxes filled with geraniums, and order their heaping platter of *choucroute,* a classically good version that includes ham hocks, plain Strasbourg sausage and smoked Colmar sausage, mildly smoked bacon, and a good slab of pork. The meats are arranged "pyramid-style" on top of the sauerkraut, a signal that this is an all-you-can-eat affair. If sauerkraut is not to your liking, try their hearty *baeckeoffe,* here made with delicious local potatoes and hearty portions of beef and pork, all baked in and served from a colorful traditional Alsatian earthenware terrine. With the meal, sample Léon Beyer's Riesling, a wine with a good deal of depth and charm. Dessert offerings include a rather gummy and unpleasant blueberry tart *(tarte aux myrtilles),* and a very sweet Alsatian yeast cake, or *kugelhopf,* soaked in rum and served with a healthy topping of whipped cream.

HINSINGEN *(Bas-Rhin)*

Paris 406 k, Sarreguemines 22 k, Strasbourg 90 k.

RESTAURANT

LA GRANGE DU PAYSAN
8 Rue Principale, 67260
   Hinsingen.
(88.00.91.83).
Last orders taken at 2 P.M.
   and 10 P.M., but the wine
   bar is open all day for
   snacks, wine, and beer.

About an hour's drive northwest of Strasbourg, in the middle of Alsatian farm country, there is a marvelously homey and unusual restaurant, where just about everything served—from the sparkling fresh cream in the *flammekueche* to the wheat used to make the dough—comes from this modest model farm. The large cabin-style dining room is full of

Closed Monday.
Credit card: V.
Enclosed terrace dining.
Private dining rooms for 15, 20, and 45.
English spoken.
60- and 178-franc menus. A la carte, 100 francs.

SPECIALTIES:
Alsatian and farm produce. *Flammekueche,* the Alsatian cheese and onion tart, is served Wednesday, Friday, and Saturday nights and all day Sunday. *Porcelet dans le four,* or oven-roasted farm piglet, is served for Saturday dinner and Sunday lunch.

wood and beams and decorated with antique farm implements, wagon wheels, and a giant stone fireplace. For the warmer months there's a bright, flower-filled veranda that overlooks neighboring farms and the village church. As far as the food is concerned, you're not likely to find more authentic Alsatian fare. If you're looking for a delicious *flammekueche,* you need search no farther: paper-thin crust, the freshest *fromage blanc,* thin slices of bacon (neither too salty nor too fatty), and a delicate dose of onions. At La Grange du Paysan the tart is served on heated platters, so the *flammekueche* stays warm as you eat it. As a main course, try the fine *poularde au riesling,* a farm-raised hen cooked in a delicious Riesling wine sauce. Even though the Rieger family cures its own ham, I found that the specialty of ham and wild morel mushrooms tasted bland and commercial. The bread is homemade, the house Riesling is remarkable, and on weekends you can sample a whole roast piglet, cooked in the Alsatian wood-fired bread oven out back. Note that sausages, ham, and cheese can all be purchased to take home.

ILLHAEUSERN *(Haut-Rhin)*

Colmar 17 k, Paris 442 k, Sélestat 13 k, Strasbourg 60 k.

RESTAURANT

AUBERGE DE L'ILL
Rue de Collonges, Illhaeusern, 68150 Ribeauvillé.
(89.71.83.23).
Last orders taken at 2 P.M. and 9 P.M.
Closed Monday and Tuesday November through March; Monday night and Tuesday April through October; February; and the first week in July.

Willows and the river, the Auberge de l'Ill.

Credit cards: AE, DC.
Air-conditioned.
Private dining room for 10.
English spoken.
270- (at lunch on weekdays),
   300-, 370-, and 410- franc
   menus. A la carte, 450
   francs.

SPECIALTIES:
Saumon soufflé (salmon *filet*
filled with a soufflé of pike),
*noisette de chevreuil mousseline de
grenouilles* (sliced venison with
frogs' legs mousseline), *feuilleté
pigeonneaux aux choux et aux
truffes* (pigeon, cabbage, and
truffles in puff pastry).

Of all the grand restaurants in France, one of the most international, and perhaps the most understated, is the idyllic Auberge de l'Ill, less than an hour's journey from Strasbourg.

The Auberge de l'Ill is also one of France's more consistent restaurants, a consistency that is backed by hard work, character, a sense of purpose, a solid family netting. Father and son, Paul and Marc Haeberlin, work quietly in tandem in the kitchen while Jean-Pierre—the brother, the uncle—plays supporting role of perfect host.

Here, seated near the window overlooking the weeping willows and the narrow Ill river, one should be prepared for a few hours of pampering.

Anyone searching for clues as to what makes a restaurant great should begin by examining the Haeberlin menu. If offers a finely tuned selection of classical and regional fare, food designed to please almost any palate. There's a creative use of locally popular ingredients: Chunks of salty smoked *lardons,* or bacon, hearty green lentils, puckery red rhubarb, all appear in proper proportions.

Some of the finest dishes sampled on the last visit included a cream of asparagus soup adorned with bite-size *profiteroles,* or cream puffs, and a sprinkling of Iranian caviar; a warm salad of delicate *merlan,* or whiting, served with a frivolous *friture* (something akin to tempura) of vegetables, and mixed with a stunning coriander-flavored vinaigrette; and top-quality lamb cooked in a wrapping of strudel dough.

And should the *salade de lapereau* (rabbit salad) appear on the menu, do try it, with one of the Haeberlins' vast assortment of local white Rieslings (see recipe, following page).

Desserts nicely complement the rest of the meal. The classic *profiteroles* were as good as that satisfying dish can ever be, and I doubt that many pastry chefs will want to compete with the Haeberlin rendition of rhubarb tart—warm layered puff pastry with bright-flavored rhubarb oozing over the edges and flowing into a pool of Sauternes-infused sauce. The wine list is worth the detour and the normal six-week wait for a table.

SALADE DE LAPEREAU L'AUBERGE DE L'ILL
AUBERGE DE L'ILL'S RABBIT SALAD

This elegant salad has become a classic at the breathtaking Alsatian restaurant Auberge de l'Ill. I first sampled it years ago on my very first visit to this romantic spot along the Ill river. It may well have been the first time I sampled rabbit, but certainly not the last. Serve this dish with a chilled crisp Riesling and perhaps some grilled homemade bread.

1 fresh rabbit (2½ to 3 pounds; 1 kg 125 g to 1 kg 350 g), cut into serving pieces, liver and kidneys reserved

Salt and freshly ground black pepper to taste

5 tablespoons (2½ ounces; 80 g) unsalted butter

2 medium onions, thinly sliced

2 carrots, thinly sliced

2 cups (500 ml) dry white wine, such as Riesling

3 medium tomatoes, quartered

2 bay leaves, crushed

1 sprig fresh thyme

1 sprig fresh rosemary

1 sprig fresh parsley

1 clove garlic, lightly crushed

3 tablespoons best-quality sherry wine vinegar

1½ tablespoons imported Dijon mustard

¼ cup (60 ml) extra-virgin olive oil

1 whole truffle (optional)

2 quarts (2 liters) mixed salad greens, preferably lamb's lettuce, young curly endive, and oak-leaf lettuce

1. Season the rabbit pieces liberally with salt and pepper. Melt 4 tablespoons butter in a large deep skillet over medium-high heat until it is hot but not smoking. Add the rabbit without crowding the pan and thoroughly brown on all sides. Add the onions and carrots and brown them lightly. Very slowly pour in the wine, then add the tomatoes, bay leaves, fresh herbs, and garlic. Cover the skillet, reduce the heat to medium, and cook until the rabbit is cooked through, about 20 minutes.

2. Remove the rabbit pieces and let them cool. Then carefully tear the meat from the bones with your fingers. Cut the meat into bite-size morsels. Discard any tough or gristly meat.

3. Strain the cooking liquid, discarding the herbs and vegetables. Pour the liquid (you should have about 2 cups; 500 ml) into a large, heavy-bottomed saucepan and reduce over high heat to about ½ cup (125 ml).

4. While the liquid is reducing, blend the vinegar, mustard, and oil. While the reduced liquid is still warm, whisk in the vinegar mixture and season to taste with salt and pepper. (The dish can be prepared ahead of time up to this point. If the sauce is prepared ahead, reheat over low heat just until warm.) Just before serving the salad, chop the truffle finely, add it and any truffle liquid to the warm sauce, and mix well.

5. Melt the remaining 1 tablespoon butter in a small skillet over medium-high heat. Add the liver and kidneys and sear quickly. They should still remain rosy inside. This will take just about 1 minute. Transfer to a cutting board and slice.

6. To serve, toss the rabbit pieces with several tablespoons of the sauce to moisten the meat. Season to taste. Toss the greens with the remaining sauce and divide the dressed salad among 6 large dinner plates. Arrange the rabbit pieces on top of the greens, then add slices of liver and kidney. Serve immediately.

Yield: 6 servings.

ITTENHEIM *(Bas-Rhin)*

Strasbourg 13 k.

RESTAURANT

HOTEL AU BOEUF
Ittenheim, 67370
   Truchtersheim.
(88.69.01.42).
Last orders taken at 1:45 P.M.
   and 9:15 P.M.
Closed Monday, mid-June
   through mid-July, and
   the last ten days in
   December through the
   first three weeks in
   January.
Credit card: EC.
Private dining room for 80.
Some English spoken.
50-, 75-, 80-, and 120-franc
   menus. A la carte, 150
   francs.

SPECIALTIES:
Choucroute garnie (sauerkraut,
various sausages, bacon, pork,
and potatoes), *coq au pinot noir*
(chicken in wine sauce), *tarte
flambée* (thin tart with cream,
bacon, and onions, served at
dinner only), *foie gras d'oie*
(fattened goose liver), *potée
alsacienne* (hearty soup of pork
and vegetables, special order
only), fish and game in season.

During my last visit to Alsace, I spent days searching out the best *tarte flambée,* the Alsatian cream, onion, and bacon tart also known as *flammekueche* (see recipe, page 123). The Hôtel au Boeuf version, with paper-thin dough topped with lots of *fromage blanc,* received very high marks, as did their presentation: Guests are invited to wander over to the open kitchen, to watch as the young chefs shuffle the huge bubbly tarts in and out of the wood-fired oven. The tarts are turned out onto large wooden boards, then brought to the table, to be sampled while they're hot. This is a wonderfully casual spot, where crowds of young people come to make a meal out of *tarte flambée,* ordering one tart after another along with carafes of local white wine. Those with more hearty appetites will welcome their superb platters of *choucroute*—you can choose the six-meat or the nine-meat version—as well as a warming *pot-au-feu* served in a procession of courses: At your elbow the waitress sets a traditional Alsatian earthenware terrine, steaming with a meaty bouillon laced with beef, carrots, tasty liver dumplings, and turnips. Next there's a platter of raw vegetables and a fine *céleri remoulade,* grated celeriac in a tangy mayonnaise. Just dig in and enjoy.

*Sweet temptations from
Strasbourg's Christian.*

BERAWECKA
ALSATIAN PEAR BREAD

Laden with luscious dried pears, berawecka (also called bierwecke) is a specialty of the village of Kaysersberg, where it is made during the winter holidays and served at home with a glass of cherry brandy, or kirsch. When making this bread, don't be alarmed at the quantity of fruits and nuts. As you begin kneading them into the dough, you'll say "No way is all this going to fit into this dough." But, voilà, it does.

1 ½ cups (190 g) dried
    pears, cut into pea-
    size pieces
1 cup (130 g) small
    dark currants
½ cup (90 g) dried
    figs, cut into pea-size
    pieces
½ cup (80 g) pitted
    prunes, cut into pea-
    size pieces
⅔ cup (165 ml) hot tap
    water
⅓ cup (80 ml) kirsch,
    pear eau-de-vie, or
    brandy
¼ cup (60 ml) honey
Grated zest (peel) of 1
    lemon

1. The day before making the bread, combine the pears, currants, figs, and prunes in a medium bowl. Place the hot water, kirsch, honey, and lemon zest in a small bowl and stir until well blended. Pour the liquid into the dried fruit mixture and toss to coat thoroughly. Cover with plastic wrap and let sit for about 12 hours, stirring occasionally. The fruits should absorb most of the liquid.

2. The next day, place the yeast, water, and 1 cup (140 g) of the flour in a large mixing bowl or the bowl of a heavy-duty mixer. Stir until thoroughly blended, then set aside to proof the yeast, about 5 minutes.

3. Add the egg, cinnamon, fennel, and salt to the yeast mixture and blend thoroughly. Gradually stir in enough of the remaining flour to make a soft dough. Knead the dough on a well-floured surface, adding as much of the remaining flour as needed to prevent sticking, until the dough is elastic. Place the dough in a bowl, cover, and let rise until doubled in bulk, about 1 hour.

KAYSERSBERG *(Haut-Rhin)*

Colmar 11 k, Munster 26 k, Paris 433 k.

Market: Monday, 8 A.M. to noon, Place Gouraud.

BOULANGERIE/
PATISSERIE

AU PECHE MIGNON
67 Rue du Général-
    de-Gaulle, 68240
    Kaysersberg.
(89.47.30.40).
Open 8 A.M. to 6:30 P.M.
    Closed Monday and the
    last week in January.

Years ago, Elizabeth Schneider, an American colleague, wrote so enthusiastically of an Alsatian Christmas fruit bread that I couldn't wait to try it myself. The bread, known as *berawecka,* is a specialty found in the village of Kaysersberg only at holiday time. I'm totally in love with the version from Au Péché Mignon (see recipe above).

2 ½ teaspoons or 1 package active dry yeast
1 cup (250 ml) warm water
3 to 3 ½ cups (420 to 490 g) unbleached all-purpose flour
1 large egg
2 teaspoons ground cinnamon
1 teaspoon freshly ground fennel seeds
1 teaspoon salt
½ cup (70 g) unblanched almonds, coarsely chopped
½ cup (60 g) hazelnuts, coarsely chopped
½ cup (50 g) walnuts, coarsely chopped

Glaze:
1 large egg yolk
1 teaspoon water

2 tablespoons butter, for buttering baking sheet

4. Meanwhile, drain the fruit in a sieve set over a bowl; reserve the syrup.

5. Punch the dough down. Gradually knead the fruits and nuts into the dough, using additional flour as needed to prevent the dough from sticking. The dough will be very moist, and the fruit and nuts will break holes in the dough, but keep kneading until the dough is workable.

6. Divide the dough in half and shape each half into a narrow loaf about 12 inches (30 cm) long. Cover and let rise until doubled in bulk, about 1 hour.

7. Preheat the oven to 375°F (190°C).

8. Prepare the glaze: Whisk the egg yolk, water, and reserved fruit syrup together and brush this glaze thoroughly over the tops and sides of the loaves. Place the loaves on a buttered baking sheet.

9. Bake until well browned, about 45 minutes. Transfer the bread to a wire rack to cool completely. Serve toasted, with butter and honey.

Yield: 2 loaves.

LANDERSHEIM *(Bas-Rhin)*

Molsheim 22 k, Paris 462 k, Strasbourg 25 k.

RESTAURANT

AUBERGE DU KOCHERSBERG
Landersheim, 67700 Saverne.
(88.69.91.58).
Last orders taken at 1:45 P.M. and 9:30 P.M. (At lunchtime the dining room does not open until 1 P.M., but guests are invited to have a drink in

Leave it to the French to create a classy looking restaurant in a former hunting lodge that also doubles as an employees' canteen! Here we are at the Adidas—of sporting gear fame—dining room, a ballroom-size Wagnerian affair with wooden ceilings and walls and a fabulous bar with a stunning blue and white ceramic beer tap. Before noon, the company's 450 employees lunch on simple fare at bare wooden tables and with stainless-steel utensils.

the bar beginning at 12:30 P.M.)

Closed Sunday dinner, Tuesday, Wednesday, mid-February to mid-March, and late July to mid-August.

Credit cards: AE, V.

Air-conditioned.

English spoken.

180-, 250-, and 310-franc menus. A la carte, 350 francs.

SPECIALTIES:

Terrine de foie gras, noisettes de chevreuil aux baies sauvages (sliced venison with wild berries, during hunting season), *assiette de poissons grillés façon Armand Roth* (platter of grilled fish).

At 12:30 sharp, the tables are covered with lace napery, the silver's laid out, and a new staff of cooks and waiters takes over. The food is far from spectacular (the nicest dish we sampled was a platter of marinated salmon and smoked haddock, served with a stunning horseradish sauce), but there are some thoughtful touches. Ask for tea and the waiter arrives with an entire cart, offering a selection of freshly brewed Indian and Chinese teas and four herb teas. Obviously many dine here just to have a go at the spectacular wine list. The *cave* is stocked with some 80,000 bottles, including 38 different Rieslings, and the four-tiered *eaux-de-vie* cart features some 50 kinds of local fruit brandy, including the popular Massenez brand.

LAPOUTROIE *(Haut-Rhin)*

Colmar 19 k, Munster 29 k, Paris 225 k, Ribeauvillé 21 k.

Market: Friday, 8 A.M. to noon, Place de la Mairie.

RESTAURANT

LES ALISIERS
5 Le Faudé, 68650 Lapoutroie.
(89.47.52.82).

Last orders taken at 2 P.M. and 9 P.M.

Closed Monday dinner, Tuesday, and mid-November through Christmas.

Credit card: V.

Terrace dining.

English spoken.

100 francs.

SPECIALTIES:

Choucroute (sauerkraut, various sausages, bacon, pork, and potatoes), *quenelles de foie* (liver dumplings), *jarret de porc braisé* (braised pork knuckle).

Les Alisiers is a rustic *auberge* high in the Vosges mountains, reached via narrow, winding roads where you'll pass trout fishermen, groups of hikers, and bright meadows full of healthy-looking Holsteins. Come for the clean mountain air and honest home cooking, and you won't be disappointed. This converted farmhouse offers a welcoming wood-beamed dining room and a warming fire, the perfect place to be when you're sampling Ella Degouy's excellent regional cooking. Try the *pommes de terre coiffées au munster fondu,* little potatoes topped with thin shavings of local Munster cheese and a sprinkling of onions. One serving is enough for two, and can be ordered as a first course or a filling side dish. Equally fresh and hearty is the *jarret de porc,* a meaty pork knuckle that's been slowly simmered, then gently browned, so it's properly crisp and crackling.

AFFINEUR

JACQUES HAXAIRE
18 Rue du Général-Dufieux,
   68650 Lapoutroie.
(89.47.50.76).
Open 8 A.M. to noon and 1
   to 6 P.M.

Unquestionably the place to find the finest Munster I know. On one Sunday in autumn, we made the long drive back from Alsace to Paris, arriving home late and famished. Luckily we had the means to soothe the pain: We devoured one of Haxaire's beautifully aged Munsters, sipped chilled Gewürztraminer, and snacked on crusty rye bread. Such a feast there's never been. And I can't imagine a better way to extend happy travel memories.

EAUX-DE-VIE

**GILBERT MICLO
DISTILLERIE**
68650 Lapoutroie.
(89.47.50.16).
Open 8 A.M. to noon and 2
   to 6 P.M. Closed Saturday
   and Sunday.
Will ship in France.

SPECIALTY:
Eaux-de-vie (fruit brandies).

A good address to know for top-quality fruit brandies, or *eaux-de-vie*. Among Miclo's specialties are *framboise* (raspberry), *houx* (holly), *mirabelle* (plum), *kirsch* (cherry), *myrtille* (blueberry), *alisier* (a local wild berry with the taste of bitter almonds), and *poire Williams* (pear). (Directions: on the N415 at the eastern exit for Lapoutroie.)

MARLENHEIM *(Bas-Rhin)*

Haguenau 35 k, Molsheim 12 k, Paris 466 k, Strasbourg 20 k.

Fête des Vendanges (grape harvest festival): third Sunday in October.

RESTAURANT

HOSTELLERIE DU CERF
30 Rue du Général-de-
   Gaulle, 67520
   Marlenheim.
(88.87.73.73).
Last orders taken at 2 P.M.
   and 9:30 P.M.
Closed Monday, Tuesday,
   and January.
Credit cards: AE, DC, V.
Terrace dining.
Private dining rooms for 15
   and 25.

Hostellerie du Cerf, an easy fifteen-minute drive from the center of Strasbourg, is one of those rare, satisfying family places, where everyone seems to be looking after your best interests and the food has an authentic regional flair.

Summer and early fall is the best time to visit, for then the geraniums and umbrella-topped tables decorate the stone courtyard of this old half-timbered farmhouse. At the same time, Robert Husser's garden will be sprouting with fresh greens, herbs, tender vegetables, and even walnuts to em-

English spoken.
160- (at lunch on weekdays),
220-, and 310-franc
menus. A la carte, 300
francs.

SPECIALTIES:
Poisson du marché (here, fresh
fish from Brittany), *noisettes de
chevreuil et faisan* (sliced
venison and pheasant, during
hunting season).

bellish the daily menus.

It's hard to know who is more fortunate in the family, father Robert or son Michel. Robert is lucky enough to have the time to putter around in his garden, casually greet guests, and take care of the hotel and restaurant accounting while son Michel is free to create to his heart's content.

The pleasing menu carefully blends the local specialties—everything from the omnipresent Alsatian headcheese known as *presskoph* to veal kidneys and *spaetzles,* or dumpling-like Alsatian noodles— with an appealing assortment of superbly fresh fish and shellfish, much of it coming from Guilvinec on the coast of Brittany. This means diners can have it both ways: Indulge a bit in the hearty fare of Alsace, moderate a bit with delicate *rouget,* sole, vibrant salmon, or cloud-like langoustines. This is, after all, what *nouvelle cuisine* was really meant to be.

A typical meal might begin with a superb pair of regionally inspired appetizers: bite-size *flamme-kueche* (cream and onion tart, here prepared with elegant puff pastry), and apples and *boudin noir* (blood sausage) tucked into a whisper of brioche.

If it's on the menu, do order the *salade de presskoph grand-père Wagner,* a traditional dish named after Robert Husser's grandfather, the founder of Hostellerie du Cerf. It's hard to imagine a finer marriage of regional and *nouvelle* cuisine. The fresh, delicious headcheese is cut into little rectangles, arranged like a still life on a bed of pungent dandelion greens, and garnished with crispy bacon squares, cherry tomatoes, a perfectly poached egg, and a serious vinaigrette (see recipe, facing page).

For a main course, I can't recommend too strongly the *darnes de saumon aux lentilles et lardons à la crème de raifort.* Satisfying fare it is: fresh salmon larded with bacon, set on a bed of creamy lentils, awash in a pungent sauce enriched with fresh horseradish (see recipe, page 120).

Dessert offerings are equally impressive, with a fine *tarte aux pommes* (thin but flavorful, enriched by a dollop of freshly whipped cream) and their house specialty, thin crêpes wrapped around pungent but pleasing alcohol-infused cherries, served with *fromage blanc* ice cream and a fresh raspberry *coulis.*

SALADE DE PRESSKOPH HOSTELLERIE DU CERF
HOSTELLERIE DU CERF'S SALAD OF DANDELION GREENS, HEADCHEESE, ONIONS, AND BACON

This is one of those lovely nouvelle *cuisine–inspired interpretations of a classical Alsatian first course, a creation of chef Robert Husser of the charming Hostellerie du Cerf in Marlenheim.* Presskoph *is Alsatian pork headcheese, traditionally prepared just before Christmas when the pig was slaughtered. It is normally sliced from a loaf and eaten as a first course with a vinaigrette. This is chef Robert Husser's lightened interpretation, which is more greens and vegetables than headcheese. I love the play of colors, textures, and flavors here and the way the poached egg is absorbed into the vegetables. The creamy vinaigrette has just the right piquancy and stands up well to the headcheese and bacon.*

Salad:
4 handfuls (200 g) dandelion greens, or mixed greens
4 large scallions
1 slice (3 ounces; 100 g) headcheese
Handful mixed fresh herbs, preferably chervil, tarragon, and chives, snipped
24 cherry tomatoes
4 ounces (125 g) slab bacon or side pork, rind removed

Creamy vinaigrette:
2 teaspoons imported Dijon mustard
2 teaspoons freshly squeezed lemon juice
1 tablespoon best-quality red wine vinegar
2 tablespoons *crème fraîche* (see Recipe Index) or sour cream
3 tablespoons virgin olive oil
Salt and freshly ground black pepper to taste

4 large eggs, at room temperature
½ teaspoon vinegar
3 tablespoons snipped fresh chervil

1. Prepare the salad: Stem, rinse, and dry the greens. Slice the scallions into rings, and cut the headcheese into bite-size cubes. Layer the greens, scallions, headcheese, herbs, and tomatoes in a large, shallow salad bowl.

2. Cut the bacon into bite-size cubes and place in a large skillet. Adding no additional fat, cook, stirring frequently, over medium-high heat until crisp. Drain the bacon on paper towels and add to the salad. Discard the fat.

3. Prepare the vinaigrette: Whisk the mustard, lemon juice, and vinegar together in a small bowl. Add the *crème fraîche* and oil and whisk until emulsified. Season with salt and pepper.

4. Poach the eggs: Heat 3 inches (8 cm) water and the vinegar to a boil in a large shallow sauté pan. Turn off the heat and immediately crack one egg directly above the water. Carefully open the shell close to the water's surface, so the egg slips into the water in one piece. Repeat with the remaining eggs. Immediately cover the pan with a tight-fitting lid to retain the heat. Allow the eggs to cook for 3 minutes before lifting the lid. The eggs are ready when the whites are opaque and the yolks are covered with a thin, translucent layer of white. Using a flat perforated spatula, carefully transfer the eggs to a shallow bowl of cold water to stop the cooking.

5. Dress the salad, tossing thoroughly. Divide it among 4 large dinner plates and spread out the ingredients so that they form a rather flat, even bed on which to place the poached egg. Using a spatula, carefully place each egg in the center of one salad. Sprinkle with chervil and freshly ground pepper and serve.

Yield: 4 servings.

DARNES DE SAUMON AUX LENTILLES ET LARDONS A LA CREME DE RAIFORT HOSTELLERIE DU CERF
HOSTELLERIE DU CERF'S SALMON WITH LENTILS, BACON, AND HORSERADISH CREAM

As I research a trip, I generally gather as many menus as I can from the region, so I have a pretty good idea of what's in store. I clearly remember how the title of this dish jumped out at me when I opened the menu for the Hostellerie du Cerf in Marlenheim. Anyone who thought to combine salmon, lentils, and fiery horseradish—three of my favorite foods—would be certain to get high marks. Of course, it was the first dish I ordered once I got to the Husser family's warming restaurant. I wasn't the least bit disappointed.

Lentils:
1 cup (175 g) lentils
2 tablespoons (1 ounce; 30 g) unsalted butter
1 carrot, peeled
1 onion
1 rib celery
1 leek, well rinsed
3 cups (750 ml) chicken stock, or water
1 cup (250 ml) dry white wine, such as Riesling
Salt and freshly ground black pepper to taste

Horseradish cream:
¾ cup (185 ml) *crème fraîche* (see Recipe Index) or heavy cream, preferably not ultra-pasteurized
3 tablespoons prepared horseradish

Salmon:
2 teaspoons olive oil
6 ounces (180 g) slab bacon or side pork, rind removed
1 pound (500 g) salmon fillets, cut into 4 rectangular portions
Minced fresh herbs for garnish, preferably chervil and flat parsley

1. Finely mince the carrot, onion, celery, and leek.

2. Prepare the lentils: Rinse the lentils and pick over carefully, discarding any pebbles you may find. Melt the butter in a medium saucepan over medium-low heat. Add the minced vegetables and cook covered, stirring occasionally, until soft, 3 to 4 minutes. Add the lentils, chicken stock, and wine. Heat to a boil, reduce the heat, and simmer uncovered until the lentils are tender, about 40 minutes. Season with salt and pepper, and keep the lentils warm.

3. Prepare the horseradish cream: Combine the *crème fraîche* and the horseradish in a small saucepan and simmer gently until well blended. Keep warm.

4. Cut the bacon into bite-size cubes and place in a large skillet. Using no additional fat, cook, stirring frequently, over medium-high heat until crisp. Drain the bacon on paper towels and set aside. Discard the fat.

5. Brush a ribbed cast-iron griddle with oil. Heat over medium-high heat. Season the salmon on both sides with salt and pepper. Grill the fish just until the flesh is opaque and still resilient, not soft or overly tough, about 4 minutes each side, depending upon the thickness of the fish. (The fish may also be grilled under a broiler or on an outdoor grill.)

6. To serve, using a slotted spoon, divide the lentils among 4 warmed dinner plates. Place the salmon on top and spoon the sauce all around the lentils. Sprinkle the salmon with the bacon and shower each plate with a sprinkling of herbs. Serve immediately.

Yield: 4 servings.

OBERNAI *(Bas-Rhin)*

Colmar 45 k, Molsheim 10 k, Paris 486 k, Sélestat 23 k, Strasbourg 30 k.

Market: Thursday, 8 A.M. to noon, Grande Place.
Flea market: Ascension weekend and the weekend of Novermber 1, Salle de Fêtes d'Obernai. *Fête des Vendanges* (grape harvest festival): third Sunday in October. *Fête de la Sainte-Odile* (Saint Odile's Day festival): around December 14.

RESTAURANT

LA HALLE AUX BLES
Place du Marché, 67210 Obernai.
(88.95.56.09).
Last orders taken at 2:30 P.M. and 10 P.M. (11 P.M. in summer).
Open daily.
Credit cards: AE, V.
Terrace dining.
English spoken.
150 francs.

A big fun-filled barn of a place—actually a restored ancient grain market—a bit on the touristy side, but then, sometimes travelers can play tourist as well. A good place to go with a group to down *choucroute,* carafes of smooth local Sylvaner, and the good local headcheese known as *presskoph.* In the evenings they serve the Alsatian cream and onion *tarte flambée.*

POUR LA MAISON

DIETRICH
Place du Marché, 67210 Obernai.
(88.95.57.58).
Open 8 A.M. to noon and 2 to 6 P.M. Closed Sunday.
Credit Card: V.

A great old-fashioned hardware store, filled to the brim with folkloric Alsatian pottery, wooden tools, and charming wooden carts for hauling wood—or kids.

The streets of old Strasbourg.

STRASBOURG *(Bas-Rhin)*

Colmar 69 k, Mulhouse 113 k, Obernai 30 k, Paris 488 k, Sélestat 47 k.

Markets: Tuesday and Saturday, 8 A.M. to 1 P.M., Boulevard de la Marne;
Wednesday and Friday, 8 A.M. to 1 P.M., Marché Sainte-Marguerite,
Rue de Molsheim.
Flea market: Wednesday and Saturday, 8 A.M. to 6 P.M., Rue du Vieil-Hôpital.
Foire de Printemps (spring fair): last weekend in April and early May.

RESTAURANTS

L'AMI SCHUTZ
1 Ponts-Couverts, 67000
   Strasbourg.
(88.32.76.98).
Last orders taken at 2:30 P.M.
   and 10:30 P.M.
Closed Sunday dinner and
   Monday.
Credit card: V.
Terrace dining.
English spoken.
115-franc menu. A la carte,
   150 francs.

SPECIALTIES:
Alsatian.

Cheery times at L'Ami Schutz.

A rustic, unpretentious regional restaurant serving a wholesome, hearty *choucroute,* a dish that here includes smoked pork chops and slab bacon, as well as the knockwurst-like *saucisse de Strasbourg.* You'll find yourself seated at long communal tables, making for casual dining.

L'ARSENAL
11 Rue de l'Abreuvoir,
   67000 Strasbourg.
(88.35.03.69).
Last orders taken at 2:30 P.M.
   and midnight.
Closed Saturday, Sunday, and
   mid-July through
   mid-August.
Credit cards: AE, EC, V.
Private dining room for 12
   to 18.
English spoken.
135-franc menu. A la carte,
   175 francs.

A busy, bustling, classy sort of bistro filled with well-fed businessmen, the sort who always know how to search out the real thing. So when you've tired of the *choucroute* circuit, reserve a table here to sample an amazing variety of historically inspired Alsatian cuisine. The menu is brief, and it changes from day to day, but you'll find everything here, including superb ham in sweet and sour sauce, roast wild boar, *soupe aux cochonailles* (a great broth filled with bits of bacon and cubes of blood sausage), and a salad of herring and lentils.

FLAMMEKUECHE
THIN-CRUSTED CREAM, ONION, AND BACON TART

Flammekueche *is one of Alsace's most fabulous regional dishes. Also known as* tarte flam-bée, *this is much like an Alsatian pizza, only instead of tomatoes and sausages, you spread thin, thin dough with* fromage blanc *and* crème fraîche, *nuggets of bacon, and thin rounds of onion. In the area around Strasbourg, people go out for* flammekueche *the way the rest of the world goes out for pizza. It's eaten as a first course or as a filling snack, always washed down with plenty of local white wine. Ideally the dough should be so thin you can curl up the slice and eat it like a crêpe, out of hand. The best tarts are baked in huge wood-fired ovens, but I've not found anyone who rejected the version baked at home in a gas or electric oven!*

1 medium onion, sliced into thin rounds
½ cup (125 ml) cottage cheese or ricotta, whipped in blender
½ cup (125 ml) *crème fraîche* (see Recipe Index) or sour cream
Salt and freshly ground black pepper to taste
8 ounces (250 g) Basic Bread Dough (see Recipe Index)
6 ounces (180 g) slab bacon or side pork, rind removed, cut into matchstick-size pieces

1. Preheat the oven to 450°F (230°C).

2. Combine the onions, cheese, *crème fraîche,* salt, and pepper and let sit for about 15 minutes to soften the onions.

3. Roll the dough on a lightly floured surface into a 10½-inch (27 cm) circle and place it on a round baking sheet.

4. Spread the onion mixture over the dough right to the edge. Sprinkle the bacon evenly over the top, then sprinkle generously with pepper.

5. Bake just until the dough is crisp, 15 to 20 minutes. Serve immediately.

Yield: One 10½-inch (27 cm) tart.

WINSTUB

TIRE-BOUCHON
5 Rue des Tailleurs-de-Pierres, 67000 Strasbourg.
(88.32.47.86).
Last orders taken at 2 P.M. and 11 P.M..
Closed Sunday, Monday lunch, three weeks in June, and one week in late December.
Credit card: V.
Air-conditioned.
English spoken.
80 francs.

A wonderfully authentic Alsatian wine bar, just steps from the famous cathedral. Stop in for Saturday lunch after touring the flea market just a few steps away. Sip the everyday local white, Edelzwicker, as you feast on bacon omelets *(omelettes au lard); salade de gruyère* (cheese and shallots in a mustardy vinaigrette—see recipe, page 130); and a fabulous *tarte au fromage,* a cheesecake that's light, but far from lightweight.

*Strasbourg's Notre-Dame
cathedral.*

SALON DE THE

CHRISTIAN
10 Rue Mercière, 67000
   Strasbourg.
(88.22.12.70).
Open 7:30 A.M. to 6:30 P.M.
   Monday through Friday;
   7 A.M. to 5 P.M. Saturday.
   Closed Sunday.

How's this for temptation? In order to reach Christian's classy second-floor tea salon, you must pass through their impeccable pastry shop, where the aroma of rich bitter chocolate wafts through the air. You cross a flagstone courtyard, climb a winding staircase, and are greeted by soft classical music, cheery waitresses dressed neatly in black and white, oil portraits on the walls. Take a table by the window, with a fine view of the Notre-Dame cathedral, and admire the tidiest of cakes and tarts, arranged like jewels in the glass case that rests, like a throne, in the center of the room. Try especially the rich, soothing *tarte aux pommes amandes,* filled with apples, white raisins, cinnamon, and slivered almonds.

Alsatian Winter's Meal

"Although choucroute *can properly be served year round, and is, there's something about the crispness and heartiness of the dish that calls for falling leaves and roaring fires."*

STRASBOURG, SEPTEMBER 25—An early sign of fall in the Alsatian wine villages that spread out from the Rhine river to the crest of the Vosges mountains is a prominent market sign announcing *"Nouvelle Choucroute."* This means the season's first batch of sauerkraut, still a bit crunchy and with just a hint of acidity, is in the market, ready to be garnished, then roasted, with an array of salted and smoked pork, lean bacon, and perhaps half a dozen different sausages, all to be washed down with plenty of crisp and chilled local white Riesling.

The dish itself is properly known as *choucroute garnie à l'alsacienne,* but all over the world people simply call it *choucroute.* Because it's an earthy, peasant-style dish, there's no single authentic recipe or preparation. On one point most cooks agree: A proper *choucroute* must contain lean slab bacon, preferably smoked, pork loin or shoulder, smoked or not, and an assortment of fresh and smoked sausages, preferably three different varieties. And, of course, sauerkraut.

The origins of *choucroute* are perfectly logical. The ingredients are all native to Alsace, and the cabbage, pork, and potatoes—all hearty foods that can be easily stored or preserved to offer nourishment throughout the long winter—are essential to the Alsatian larder. Since the Middle Ages, Alsatians have been known for their pork products—ham, lean bacon, pork shoulder and knuckles—often salted, then lightly, delicately smoked, and often combined in a single dish. On the slopes of the Vosges, farmers used *sapin,* or fir, to impart the rich smoky flavor; in the flat plains along the Rhine, they chose *bois de cerisier,* or cherry wood. Today in *charcuteries* in and around the Alsatian wine villages, one can still find fir-smoked ham with a rich home-smoked flavor all its own.

The best *choucroute* begins with the best sauerkraut: fresh fall cabbage that's been finely shredded, covered with a mild salt brine, and then left to ripen for several weeks in a cool cellar. The choice of meats is limited only by imagination and availability. Today one finds *choucroute* that includes ham hocks and blood sausage; pig's ears, brains, and tail; liver dumplings; and caraway-flavored pork. And although *choucroute* can properly be served year round, and is, there's something about the crispness and heartiness of the dish that calls for falling leaves and roaring fires.

How does one tell the good *choucroute* from the bad? A proper *choucroute* is remarkably digestible, not too bland, not too acidic, neither fatty nor greasy. When properly prepared, it's neither dried out from overcooking nor swimming in acidic or watery juices. The meats and sausages should be gently smoked but not so much that they overwhelm the dish, and there should be enough variety in the meat to prevent boredom. White potatoes should be boiled or steamed, and not cooked to a bland mush. The biggest problem in most versions is acidity: Either the sauerkraut is so acidic that it brings on instant indigestion or so bland that it might as well be shredded paper. You know the sauerkraut is at its best when it complements, as well as compliments, a glass of chilled Alsatian Riesling.

BOULANGERIES

S'BRETSCHTELLE ECK
3 Rue de Haguenau, 67300
   Schiltigheim.
(88.83.46.06).
Open 6:30 A.M. to noon.
   Closed Sunday.

We strolled into this little pretzel bakery one cold, dark morning in March, arriving around 6:45 to the sound of huge yeasty pretzels crackling and popping, fresh from the oven. Here in a suburb of Strasbourg, thirty-one-year-old Dominique Pronner and his partners are among the last of the Alsatian bakers to fashion pretzels the old way, forming the stiff dough into bands, shaping the bands into traditional crossed-arm shapes, dipping the unbaked pretzels into salt water so they'll come puffy and shiny from the steaming-hot ovens. Each day (except Sunday), from 1 in the morning until around 9, they roll, shape, and bake some 4,000 pretzels. (For directions, call the *boulangerie*.)

**BOULANGERIE CHARLES
   WOERLE**
10 Rue de la Division-
   Leclerc, 67000
   Strasbourg.
(88.32.00.88).
Open 6 A.M. to 7 P.M. Closed
   Sunday.

This shop is a real show-stopper, with beautiful, museum-like display windows honoring the myriad of sizes and shapes of Alsatian breads and pastries. They're most proud of their yeasty *kugelhopf*, studded with almonds and raisins and laced with just a touch of local fruit brandy.

MUSEE

MUSEE ALSACIEN
23 Quai Saint-Nicolas,
   67000 Strasbourg.
(88.35.55.36).
Open 10 A.M. to noon and 2
   to 6 P.M. April through
   October; 2 to 6 P.M.
   November through
   March. Closed Tuesday.
Admission: 6 francs for
   adults, 3 francs for
   children under age 16
   and per person for
   groups of over 25.

Even if you've only a passing interest in Alsace, set aside an afternoon to wander through this exceptionally charming, well-ordered folk museum, right next to the river Ill. This restored eighteenth-century half-timbered house features a series of maze-like rooms, from kitchen to wine *cave*, bedroom to cheese-aging cellar. The museum truly helps you get a sense of the culture as you view all those decorative as well as practical objects in the context of their everyday use. Note especially the arrangement of colorful regional pottery and the marvelous collection of *poêles*, giant cast-iron stoves, still found in use throughout the region.

Of Memories and Madeleines

"*One could almost call the* madeleine *France's national cookie, it has taken such an honored place in custom and history.*"

COMMERCY, APRIL 15—Someone once described it as the cookie with the greatest literary clout. Indeed, one wonders where the moist and golden little tea cake called the *madeleine* would be without Marcel Proust.

How could such a simple blend of sugar, butter, eggs, flour, and a touch of lemon unleash the flood of memories that filled those volumes of prose we know as *Remembrance of Things Past?* For Proust, the memories began one wintry day when his mother sent out for "one of those squat, plump little cakes called *petites madeleines* which look as though they had been moulded in the fluted valve of a scallop shell." With his *madeleines* Proust drank an infusion of *tilleul,* a tea prepared from the dried blossoms of the linden tree.

Proust continued: "I raised to my lips a spoonful of the tea in which I had soaked a morsel of the cake. No sooner had the warm liquid mixed with the crumbs touched my palate than a shudder ran through me and I stopped, intent upon the extraordinary thing that had happened to me. An exquisite pleasure had invaded my senses."

One could almost call the *madeleine* France's national cookie, it has taken such an honored place in custom and history. Today, as in Proust's time at the turn of the century, the golden cakes are found next to the cash register of pastry shops all over the country.

It's hard to know how much Proust influenced or was influenced by custom. Like almost everything in France, there is an etiquette, a ritual, to eating *madeleines.* Even the best, freshest *madeleine* has a dry, almost dusty aftertaste when eaten by itself. To be truly appreciated—to invade the senses with an exquisite pleasure—*madeleines* must be dipped in tea, ideally the fresh and slightly lime-flavored *tilleul,* which releases the fragrant, flavorful essence of the little cake. Coffee just isn't the same.

Unlike Proust's vivid memories, the history of the *madeleine* is slightly clouded. The story promoted by commercial *madeleine* makers in the town of Commercy goes like this: In 1756 King Stanislas of Lorraine was hosting a luncheon. His chef stormed out of the kitchen near the end of the meal, without having prepared dessert. A young assistant saved the day by preparing a little cake her grandmother made at home in Commercy. The king and his guests were so delighted that they named the cake after the girl, Madeleine.

Another version suggests that the little cakes were invented by Avica, Talleyrand's famous pastry cook, and still another insists that Marie Leczynska, the wife of Louis XV, perfected them with the advice of her cook, Madeleine.

The cake is still linked to the town of Commercy, where a large number of commercial *madeleines* are produced. The most famous brand, A La Cloche Lorraine, produced by Maison Grojean, is packaged in handsome oval wooden boxes and sold in specialty shops all over France. The company, which began in 1928 with a single worker, now has 120 employees who produce some 120 million *madeleines* each year.

WEITERSWILLER *(Bas-Rhin)*

Haguenau 32 k, La Petite-Pierre 8 k, Strasbourg 51 k.

FERME-AUBERGE

ZUEM DORFWAPPE
3 Rue Principale, 67340
   Weiterswiller.
(88.89.48.19).
By reservation only, three
   days in advance for
   groups of 5 or more.
Closed January.
Private dining room for 30
   to 50.
English spoken.
60-franc menu only.

S P E C I A L T I E S :
Baeckeoffe (stew of wine, beef,
lamb, pork, potatoes, and
onions), *jambon au riesling*
(ham with Riesling), *tarte
flambée* (cream, onion, and
bacon tart, served Saturday
and Sunday nights only).

Farm-fresh tarte flambée, *from
Fernand and Simone Bloch.*

Can there be a better place to sample authentic
regional cooking than on a working farm where
they raise their own chickens, cows, pigs, and
sheep, make farm cheese, and bake breads and tarts
in an Alsatian bread oven? Since 1980 the outgoing
Fernand and Simone Bloch have invited guests into
their farmhouse to share their table, offering hearty
portions of *baeckeoffe;* delicate *fernkase,* a young
cheese shaped like a flying saucer and sprinkled
with coarsely ground pepper; and exceptional
cheesecake, prepared with homemade *fromage blanc*
and the freshest farm eggs.

WINES OF ALSACE

1. MUSCAT (ROLLY-GASS-MANN): I first discovered this lovely aperitif while dining one cold winter's night at the Auberge de l'Ill in Illhaeusern. The Muscat is a clean, fresh, aromatic wine that offers a nice change and a good regional touch.

2. RIESLING (TRIMBACH): I love Riesling, Riesling, and more Riesling: It's wonderful as an aperitif, great with a variety of foods, and I don't know of a more reliable and flavorful wine for cooking. The Trimbach Riesling, particularly the special *cuvées,* are spicy, rich, and concentrated. Other Riesling names to look for include Léon Beyer, Faller–Domaine Weinbach, Hugel, and Zind-Humbrecht.

3. GEWURZTRAMINER (HU-GEL): This spicy, exotic, zingy wine is one I wish more people would learn to love, for a good Gewürztraminer offers true pleasure, with its bouquet of almonds. It's an opulent wine that retains a rustic character. Sample it with a well-aged Munster or warm *foie gras,* and be prepared to die and go to heaven. Other names to look for include Zind-Humbrecht, Trimbach, and Faller–Domaine Weinbach.

CHEESE OF ALSACE

MUNSTER: Golden, moist, flat discs of cow's-milk cheese, the best of which is *fermier,* or farm cheese, made in the Vosges mountains during the summer and early fall. With its brick-red rind and strong, penetrating aroma, Munster is a perfect accompaniment to the spicy white Alsatian Gewürztraminer wine.

SALADE DE GRUYERE
CHEESE AND SHALLOTS IN VINAIGRETTE

Nearly every wine bar and brasserie in Alsace serves this typically regional salad. Depending upon the quality of ingredients used, the salad may vary from banal to delicious. Be certain to find the best-quality French or Swiss Gruyère available.

Vinaigrette:
3 tablespoons best-quality red wine vinegar
1 tablespoon imported Dijon mustard
Salt and freshly ground black pepper to taste
5 tablespoons extra-virgin olive oil

Salad:
14 ounces (400 g) Gruyère cheese
4 shallots, sliced into very thin rounds
Finely minced fresh parsley, for garnish

1. Prepare the vinaigrette: Whisk the vinegar, mustard, salt, and pepper together in a small bowl. Add the oil and whisk until emulsified.

2. Coarsely grate the cheese. Toss the cheese and shallots together in a medium bowl, then add the vinaigrette and toss until the ingredients are thoroughly coated. Let sit covered at room temperature at least 30 minutes to allow the flavors to blend.

3. To serve, sprinkle generously with parsley, toss, and divide among 4 individual salad plates.

Yield: 4 servings.

Sologne et La Loire
SOLOGNE AND THE LOIRE

Almond-rich pithiviers *from—where else—Pithiviers.*

I can't help but think of the Loire as France's "well-bred" region. Everything here—the architecture, the food, the scenery, even the character of the people—has a gentle, well-mannered, self-assured quality. It's the kind of place that makes you feel secure, and maybe even just a bit pampered. *Châteaux* abound for visiting, for wandering, for spending the night. Lazy rivers and narrow one-way bridges add a pleasant aura of romance.

Even the food here has a soft, rounded quality, foods that make me think of the daffodil days of spring and blue skies of summer. There are delicate mushrooms cultivated in mammoth caves near the town of Saumur. Rosy-fleshed salmon plucked from the roving Loire river. Pure, pure white asparagus that grow swaddled in darkness in fine, sandy soil, pushing through the earth as the world is just beginning to awaken. The land that isn't good for grapes is turned over to goats, so we find an abundance of fresh goat cheese with its fleeting, elusive character. If feathers had flavor, they would taste like young *chèvre*. Even the wines, like Vouvray, Savennières, Sancerre, blend naturally into the landscape of the meal.

From spring until fall, when the Loire is abundant with fish, local cafés post signs announcing *"La Friture est Arrivée,"* meaning that someone has caught the various smelt-like fish—tiny *éperlans, goujons,* and *gardons*—that are dipped in milk and seasoned flour, fried, and mounded on large heated platters.

If spring and summer are for touring the vast stretch of land along the Loire river, then autumn is the shining season for another region—the game- and mushroom-rich Sologne, an ancient province that begins just south of Orléans.

During the first nine months of the year, nature and man seem to collaborate, nurturing the dense forest of oak, birch, and chestnut, the flat fields of wheat and millet, even the wild blackberries, to ensure the survival of the plenitude of game that roams this solitary land.

In October, the misty, mysterious Sologne comes alive with the sights and sounds of the green-collared mallard duck known as *col vert,* the hare that runs faster than the proverbial fox, the boar, pheasant, partridge, deer, and miniature quail. Veritable hedges of wild mushrooms—miniature *mousserons,* hefty *cèpes,* cylindrical white *coprins chevelus*—appear to pop up overnight by the roadside, while purplish pink heather grows without restraint, adding delicacy to a land that was once untamed.

The hunting season begins October 1, and lasts well into February. Visitors to the region will find the abundance of game and mushrooms reflected on restaurant menus, and between meals will want to visit the wild game park of Chambord and the *châteaux* of Chambord and Cheverny. There is a major food festival as well, during the final week of October, when Sologne's capital of Romorantin comes alive with marching bands and costumed dancers for the *Journées Gastronomiques,* when both professional and amateur cooks show off everything from a smoked haunch of wild boar to the French equivalent of pumpkin pie, *tarte à la citrouille.*

Throughout the season, pastry shops and *charcuterie* windows display open-faced pumpkin pies and double-crusted savory pumpkin tarts, terrines of pheasant and wild hare, and imaginative sausages that blend game with mushrooms.

On a recent journey into the Loire, I drove out to the hamlet of Epiré, where one of the region's more charming wine cellars is hidden in the cool basement of the former village church. Here the

white Savennières wine called Château Epiré, made uniquely from the *chenin blanc* grape, is aged in old oak barrels; each tiny plot of the vineyard gets its own cask. When customers come in to buy the wine, cheery cellarmaster Robert Daguen—who has overseen the *château*'s winemaking since the 1940s—will urge them to sip samples from half a dozen different casks, allowing clients to select the one that catches their fancy. In the end, I, like so many others, drove off with more cases than I'd intended to buy. Months later, as I sipped this handsome, handmade wine, I'd be able to think back to the couple picnicking under the shade tree near the little church, remember the enchanting sound of the cuckoo that sang as the cellarmaster filled my glass, and could rest assured that a tiny corner of gentle old France would be waiting for me the next time I headed back to the Loire.

WHEN YOU GO

Michelin Green Guide: *Châteaux of the Loire* (available in English).

Getting there: Most spots in the Loire valley are an easy 2- to 3-hour drive from Paris. All trains to the region leave from Paris's Gare Austerlitz: Orléans is about an hour away, with some twenty-four trains leaving daily; Tours is about 2 hours away, also with some twenty-four trains leaving daily; the trip to Bourges takes about 2½ hours, with about eight trains daily. Cars can be rented at the train stations.

Getting around: Michelin maps 232 (Pays de Loire), 238 (Centre/Berry-Nivernais), and 237 (Ile-de-France).

Best time to visit: Generally, May to October is the prettiest and liveliest time to visit the Loire, though a late fall or winter visit to the Sologne is highly recommended, to sample that region's abundance of game and wild mushrooms.

MARKETS
(Liveliest markets are marked with an asterisk.)

Monday: Bellegarde, Bonneval, Bourges, Montrichard, Richelieu, Les Rosiers, Sully-sur-Loire, Tours.

Tuesday: Angers, Blois, Bourges, Bourgueil, Loué, Le Mans, *Montbazon, Montreuil-Bellay, Orléans, Sancerre, Thouars, Tours, Valençay.

Wednesday: *Angers, Azay-le-Rideau, *Blois, *Bourges, Fay-aux-Loges, *La Flèche, Fontevraud-l'Abbaye, *Gien, *Joué-lès-Tours, *Loches, Le Mans, *Montargis, *Montoire-sur-le-Loir, *Rochefort-sur-Loire, *Romorantin, Saumur, Tours.

Thursday: Angers, Blois, *Bourges, Bracieux, La Chartre-sur-le-Loir, Château-dun, Châtillon-sur-Indre, Chinon, La Ferté-Saint-Aubin, Le Grand-Pressigny, Joué-lès-Tours, Lorris, Le Lude, Le Mans, Meung-sur-Loire, Nogent-sur-Vernisson, Orléans, Saumur, Selles-sur-Cher, Tours.

Friday: Angers, Bourges, Châteauneuf-sur-Loire, Lamotte-Beuvron, *Le Mans, Montbazon, *Montrichard, *Richelieu, Romorantin, Sainte-Maure-de-Touraine, Saumur, *Thouars, Tours, *Vendôme.

Saturday: *Angers, Aubigny-sur-Nère, Beaugency, *Blois, *Bourges, *Gien, *Joué-lès-Tours, Loches, Le Mans, *Montargis, *Orléans, Pithiviers, Romorantin, Saint-Aignan, Sancerre, Saumur, *Tours.

Sunday: *Angers, Blois, *Bourges, La Flèche, Joué-lès-Tours, Langeais, Menetou-Salon, *Meung-sur-Loire, *Tours.

FAIRS AND FESTIVALS

First weekend in April: *Le Pot Bouilli* (*pot-au-feu* festival), Savigné-l'Evêque.

May 1 or following weekend: *Foire aux Fromages* (cheese fair), Sancerre.

One week in early May: *Journées Gastronomiques* (food fair), Châteauroux.

First week in May: *Fête de Jeanne d'Arc* (festival of Joan of Arc), Orléans.

First weekend in May: *Foire aux Andouillettes* (chitterling sausage fair), Mennetou-sur-Cher.

Saturday, Sunday, and Monday of Pentecost: *Foire au Vin* (wine fair), Sancerre.

June: *Fête à la Friture* (deep-fried-fish festival), Souzay-Champigny.

Second Sunday in June: *Foire aux Andouilles* (chitterling sausage fair), Jargeau.

Third weekend in June: *Fête à la Tomate* (tomato festival), Sainte-Gemmes-sur-Loire.

Around July 20: *Fête des Moissons* (harvest festival), Saint-Denis-d'Orques.

July 26 (Saint Anne's Day): *Foire à l'Ail et au Basilic* (garlic and basil fair), Tours.

Third Sunday in July: *Foire à l'Ail* (garlic fair), Bourgueil.

Last weekend in July: *Fête de la Grenouille* (frog festival), Vendoeuvres.

Last Sunday in July: *Fête des Grappes Nouvelles* (grape festival), Verdigny.

August: *Marché Médiéval* (medieval market), Chinon.

Second Sunday in August: *Fête des Moissons* (harvest festival), Angrie.

August 21 and 22: *Caves Ouvertes* (open-cellar days), Menetou-Salon.

Last weekend in August: *Fête de l'Ecrevisse* (crayfish festival), Aigurande.

Last Sunday in August: *Journée des Vins de France* (wine fair), Sancerre.

First Wednesday in September: *Foire aux Melons* (melon fair), Amboise.

First Friday in September: *Foire aux Oignons* (onion fair), Le Mans.

First weekend and following Monday in September: *Fête du Chausson aux Pommes* (apple turnover festival), Saint-Calais.

September 25, 26, 27: *Foire aux Fromages* (cheese fair), Bruère-Allichamps.

Last weekend in September: *Fête à la Citrouille* (pumpkin festival), Millançay.

October 10: *Exposition de Champignons Sauvages* (wild mushroom exhibit), Menetou-Salon.

Last weekend in October: *Journées Gastronomiques,* Romorantin.

Last Sunday in October: *Foire aux Huîtres* (oyster fair), Sancerre.

Late October: *Foire aux Pommes* (apple fair), Azay-le-Rideau.

AZAY-LE-RIDEAU *(Indre-et-Loire)*

Chinon 21 k, Paris 258 k, Saumur 46 k, Tours 28 k.

Market: Wednesday, 8:30 A.M. to 12:30 P.M., Place des Halles.
Foire aux Pommes (apple fair): late October.

RESTAURANT

GRAND MONARQUE
Place de la République,
    37190 Azay-le-Rideau.
(47.45.40.08).
Last orders taken at 2 P.M.
    and 9 P.M.
Closed mid-November
    through February.
Credit cards: AE, V.
Terrace dining.
Private dining rooms for 25
    and 60.
English spoken.
82- to 190-franc menus. A la
    carte, 200 francs.

After a wander through the hilly streets of Azay-le-Rideau, stop for lunch or dinner at this cozy hotel-restaurant that's been in the same family since 1900. Here you'll find small-town French hospitality and an outgoing maître-d'hôtel who will compliment you on your French and suggest that you discover their worthwhile local white wine, Azay-le-Rideau. If the weather is good, pick a table on the shaded terrace, enjoying blue skies, blue linens, and refreshing though undramatic local fare: a fresh green salad dressed in a walnut oil vinaigrette, Loire river salmon topped with a delicate soufflé, a platter of goat cheese, and outstanding *baguettes*.

BRACIEUX *(Loir-et-Cher)*

Blois 18 k, Orléans 53 k, Paris 183 k, Romorantin 32 k.

Market: Thursday, 8 A.M. to 1 P.M., La Vieille Halle.

RESTAURANT

LE RELAIS
1 Avenue de Chambord,
    41250 Bracieux.
(54.46.41.22).
Last orders taken at 1:30 P.M.
    and 9 P.M.
Closed Tuesday dinner,
    Wednesday, and the third
    week in December
    through the first week in
    February.
Credit card: V.
Terrace dining.
180- to 300-franc menus. A
    la carte, 300 francs.

Le Relais is a magnificent old coaching inn where guests once stopped to stretch their legs while changing horses. Today Bernard and Christine Robin are working to make this an impeccable and modern restaurant. It is flanked by the wooded wild game preserve of Chambord on one side and their own carefully tended garden of herbs and greens on the other. The cooking here focuses on some of the Sologne's best regional culinary attractions. During the last visit, we sampled a delicate terrine of carp, wild duck with a sweet and sour sauce laced with cherries, and an abundant assortment of cheeses, including no fewer than ten perfectly aged local goat cheeses, ranging from a delicate young farm *chèvre* to the firm and distinctive Selles-sur-Cher, made just a few kilometers away. Until just a few years ago, most grapes grown in the immediate vicinity were vinified for home consumption, but now one can sample, at restaurants such as Le Relais, the fruity and acidic young white Cheverny, made from the *Romorantin* grape first grown during the sixteenth century. End the meal with the homey and delicious multilayered *gâteau opéra,* a layered chocolate and coffee confection that's certain to ensure sweet dreams and fond memories.

GIEN *(Loiret)*

Auxerre 87 k, Bourges, 76 k, Orléans 64 k, Paris 152 k, Vierzon 73 k.

Markets: Wednesday, 8 A.M. to 12:30 P.M., behind the PTT (post office); Saturday, 8 A.M. to 12:30 P.M., Place de la Victoire.

RESTAURANT

HÔTEL DU RIVAGE
1 Quai de Nice, 45500 Gien.
(38.67.20.53).
Last orders taken at 2 P.M. and 9:15 P.M.
Closed the last three weeks in February through the first few days of March.
Credit cards: AE, DC, V.
Private dining room for 45.
English spoken.
75- (weekdays only), 125-, 145-, and 235-franc menus. A la carte, 250 francs.

S P E C I A L T I E S :
Feuilleté d'escargots au Sancerre (snails in puff pastry with Sancerre), *sandre de Loire aux pointes d'asperges* (perch-like fish from the Loire with asparagus tips), *ris d'agneau au vinaigre de cidre et miel* (lamb sweetbreads with cider vinegar and honey).

While wandering about the *château* country, the clean and manageable town of Gien is definitely worth a stop for lunch or dinner. The *quais* along the wide stretch of the Loire are perfect for a long and tranquil stroll, and the restaurant of the Hôtel du Rivage offers a good view of the river. It's a cheerful, sparkling spot decorated in shades of blue and mauve, a pleasant and inexpensive restaurant filled with a faithful clientele. The young waitresses are outgoing and attentive, and you'll find honest local fare, such as snails cooked in the region's Sancerre wine and *coq au vin* prepared with the fruity red Chinon. Fish and shellfish offerings include a chilled mussel soup flavored with basil, sea trout with sorrel sauce, fresh salmon with wild morel mushrooms, and a simple grilled sole. There is also a stunningly fresh and well-chosen selection of regional cheese, and good local wines that don't often appear on wine lists outside the area. Here you can sample as an aperitif the finest sweet wine of the Anjou, Bonnezeaux. Chilled, it reminds me of taffy apples, or better yet, a Granny Smith apple that's been injected with honey—sweet and tart at the same time.

POUR LA MAISON

FAIENCERIE DE GIEN
78 Place de la Victoire,
    45500 Gien.
(38.67.00.05).
Open 9:30 to 11:30 A.M. and
    2 to 5:30 P.M. Closed
    Sunday.
Credit card: V.

The only problem at this warehouse-style pottery factory, which offers seconds of the famous *faïence de Gien,* is trying to limit the number of items you'd like to take home with you. Shoppers can take a supermarket cart and ramble at will, selecting from among dozens of bright, contemporary dinnerware patterns, a variety of tiles, and an assortment of tableware. Prices here are not substantially lower than in the shops in town, but there's a much wider selection.

IF YOU CAN'T BEET IT, COOK IT

I had spent a lot of time in France before realizing that I rarely saw raw beets in the market. More often than not, red beets are sold already cooked right from the market stall, sometimes even steaming, sometimes vacuum-packed in thick plastic for longer storage.

I have found mention of this curious custom as far back as the 1830s, when the beetroot of Provence was sold precooked, for salads. According to produce farmers who grow red garden beets—the majority of whom can be found in the Loire valley —the custom was revived after World War II as a means of conserving domestic fuel. Since beets take a long time to cook, it was more efficient for market garden farmers, or *maraîchers,* to cook the beets in huge vats, right from the field, and sell them ready to eat. It was also, of course, a good sales technique, for cooked beets require practically no preparation. Today raw beets are primarily found in health food stores.

Cooked or raw, France enjoys its beets— almost always cut into matchsticks and tossed with salt and vinegar—and produces about 78,000 tons each year. A French housewife's tip: To keep cooked beets fresh for salads, sprinkle them with a bit of red wine vinegar, and refrigerate. If you do find yourself cooking beets, they will peel more easily if you plunge them into cold water as soon as you take them off the stove.

LAMOTTE-BEUVRON *(Loir-et-Cher)*

Blois 59 k, Gien 57 k, Orléans 36 k, Paris 167 k, Romorantin 40 k.

Market: Friday, 9 A.M. to 12:30 P.M., Place de l'Eglise.

RESTAURANT

HOTEL TATIN
5 Avenue de Vierzon, 41600
   Lamotte-Beuvron.
(54.88.00.03).
Last orders taken at 2 P.M.
   and 9 P.M.
Closed Sunday dinner,
   Monday, and the last
   three weeks in January
   through the third week
   in February.
Credit card: V.
Terrace dining.
Private dining room for 25
   to 30.
English spoken.
65-, 95-, and 125-franc
   menus. A la carte, 150
   francs.

SPECIALTIES:
Regional: game, Loire fish,
tarte Tatin (upside-down apple
pie).

The Hôtel Tatin: of happy moments, of tarte Tatin.

The Hôtel Tatin is a modest spot where residents fill a bright dining room decorated with a tattered tapestry, deer heads, and fresh gladiolas. The menu is typical of the plain and homey restaurants in the region. Order with care, and you should not go away disappointed. Among the choices are simple green salad, a decent trout sprinkled with almonds, a tray filled with some good regional goat cheese, and a fruity local red wine, Saumur-Champigny from the Château de Chaintres.

How does the *tarte Tatin* rate? It's authentic, all right. Warm, golden, nicely caramelized, with the apples cut into big chunks. The thin pastry lacks flavor, but that shouldn't stop one from making the pilgrimage. (See The Tart That Became a Legend, page 147, and recipe, following page.)

TARTE DES DEMOISELLES TATIN
TART TATIN

This is the simplest, most foolproof tarte Tatin recipe I know. A perfect tarte Tatin should be nothing but well-caramelized apples and a layer of thin pastry. Use the best baking apples available. Short of that, use Golden Delicious apples, which are quite flavorless but nonetheless produce a delicious tart when they are properly caramelized. The apples remain in huge chunks, making for an honest, rustic tart. The clear glass baking dish allows you to see if any apples are sticking as you turn out the tart. This may seem like a lot of apples for a single tart, but they cook down quickly.

8 tablespoons (4 ounces; 120 g) unsalted butter
7 to 8 cooking apples (about 2¾ pounds; 1.25 kg), preferably Jonathan or Granny Smith, peeled, quartered, and cored
1 cup (200 g) sugar
Basic Short-Crust Pastry (see Recipe Index)

1. Preheat the oven to 425°F (220°C).

2. Melt the butter in a deep 12-inch (30 cm) skillet over medium-high heat. Add the apples and sugar and stir to combine. Cook for 20 minutes, stirring carefully from time to time so the apples and sugar do not stick. Increase the heat to high and cook until the apples and sugar are a deep golden brown, about 10 minutes longer. Watch carefully to be sure that the apples and sugar do not burn. (If you do not have a pan large enough to cook all of the apples, cook them in 2 smaller skillets, dividing the apples, butter, and sugar evenly.)

3. Literally pile the apples into an unbuttered round 10½-inch (27 cm) glass baking dish.

4. Roll out the dough slightly larger than the dish and place it on top of the apples, tucking a bit of the dough around the edge into the dish.

5. Bake until the apples bubble and the pastry is golden brown, about 20 minutes.

6. Remove the tart from the oven and immediately invert it onto a large heatproof serving platter. Serve warm or at room temperature.

Yield: One 10½-inch (27 cm) tart.

MONTARGIS *(Loiret)*

Auxerre 79 k, Chartres 118 k, Fontainebleau 51 k, Orléans 71 k, Paris 113 k.

Markets: Wednesday, 8 A.M. to noon, Place Girodet; Saturday, 8 A.M. to 6 P.M., Place de la République.

CONFISERIE

MAISON DE LA PRASLINE
45 Place Mirabeau, 45200
  Montargis.
(38.98.63.55).
Open 8:30 A.M. to 12:30 P.M.
  and 2 to 7:30 P.M.
  Tuesday through
  Saturday; 9:30 A.M. to
  12:30 P.M. and 2:30 to
  7:30 P.M. Sunday and
  Monday.
Credit cards: AE, V.
Will ship in France.

Montargis is famous for its irresistible grilled and sugar-coated almonds. The celebrated *praslines de Montargis* are sold throughout France in pastry and candy shops, but it is here, at the historic Maison de la Prasline, across the street from the eighteenth-century Church of the Madeleine, that the candies were first made centuries ago. The *prasline*—also called praline—was named for a certain Duc de Plessis-Praslin, a seventeenth-century ladies' man who divided his time between boudoirs and battlefields, and sweetened his relationships by handing out sugar-coated almonds. The ladies apparently loved them so, they named the sweets after the duke, whose cook settled in Montargis in 1630. The elegant boutique that exists today is a reconstructed version of the original candy shop, with its fleur-de-lis tiled floors and decorative interior created by the famed French architect Viollet-le-Duc.

Leeks, or *poireaux,* seduce the palate with their sweet flavor that blends onion and garlic. The sleek green and white vegetable appears in French markets year-round but is especially appreciated from October to April, when most of the 230,000 tons of leeks grown annually—largely in the Loire and the North—are consumed in everything from soups to tarts. Because the inexpensive root vegetable resembles, at least in form, the costly asparagus, the leek is known in France as *"l'asperge du pauvre"*—the poor man's asparagus—and they have a power that goes beyond cuisine: If someone stands you up, you *"faits le poireaux."* If you're late for a rendez-vous, you're likely to be accused of making someone *"poireauter,"* or wait standing like a leek.

MONTBAZON *(Indre-et-Loire)*

Chinon 41 k, Paris 247 k, Saumur 67 k, Tours 13 k.

Markets: Tuesday, 8 A.M. to noon, Place de la Mairie; Friday, 3 to 8 P.M., Place des Anciens-Combattants.

RESTAURANT

CHATEAU D'ARTIGNY
37250 Montbazon.
(47.26.24.24).
Last orders taken at 2:15 P.M. and 9:15 P.M.
Closed December through the first week in January.
Credit card: V.
Private dining room for 8 to 30.
English spoken.
210- and 255-franc menus.
A la carte, 350 francs.

SPECIALTIES:
Soupe de queues de boeuf aux légumes du pot (oxtail soup with vegetables), *noix de Saint-Jacques au citron vert* (scallops with lime), *brouet de poissons de rivière au Vouvray* (river fish with Vouvray), *aile de raie aux coquillages* (skate with shellfish), *filet de boeuf au vin de Chinon* (beef filet with Chinon).

The romantic elegance of Château d'Artigny.

One spot that brings together all the finest qualities of the gentle Loire is the proud and elegant Château d'Artigny. As you take the long, shaded drive up to the *château,* arriving just as the sun begins to set, you realize that if places like this did not exist in reality, they would exist in the mind of each romantic soul who has ever toured the *châteaux* of the Loire. Even if you don't spend the night, reserve a table in the grand central rotunda dining room and hope that the skies will be clear and sparkling. I'd love to know how many marriages have been proposed at these tables, how many events have been celebrated. One evening I sat and watched a handsome middle-aged French couple at table. They were both dressed in pink—she in a simple bright-rose sheath, he in a pale pink shirt. By chance I glanced over just as they clinked glasses holding raspberry-colored cocktails. At that very moment, the sunset burst through the arched windows of the dining room, spreading a stunning haze of orange and rose. There was no need to listen in on the conversation—their joy and air of celebration radiated from the table.

The Château d'Artigny experience is a very special one: the setting, the service, and the accommodations could scarcely be improved, and the food is, as the French say, *correct*. Nothing to write home about, but not a cuisine that's likely to leave you disappointed. Dishes I've enjoyed here include the ravioli of caviar, a single caviar-filled ravioli swimming in a delicate sauce, surrounded by chunks of langoustine and sole; and the old-fashioned *épigramme d'agneau,* nuggets of lamb and two tiny lamb chops, breaded and fried, paired with lamb sweetbreads and tongue. It's a complex dish that seems right in these surroundings, the proper food to enjoy in a grand *château* set in the midst of an immense park. The wine list is an impressive tome that includes not only a wide range of Bordeaux spanning the past several decades, but just about every wine you're likely to encounter in the Loire. A lovely white to sample is Gaston Huet's Vouvray, a wine with plenty of finesse which goes well as an aperitif as well as with a meal. (Directions: From Montbazon take the D17 2 kilometers in the direction of Azay-le-Rideau. There is a sign to the *château*.)

POIRES MARINEES AU CITRON
LEMON-MARINATED PEARS

There are few dishes as simple and delicate as this blend of ripe, ripe pears marinated in lemon or lime juice with just a touch of sugar. It's always a great hit and one sweet I like to have on hand for unexpected guests. I first sampled the dessert while a guest in a private home near Valençay, the town that's home to the chalky goat cheese of the same name, that is shaped like a truncated pyramid. This, of course, would be delicious served with a dollop of fresh, delicate goat cheese, but a touch of whipped cream would be a worthy substitute.

6 firm ripe pears, peeled, cut into eighths, and cored
1 cup (250 ml) freshly squeezed lemon or lime juice, or enough to cover the pears
2 tablespoons sugar or to taste

Combine the pears with the lemon or lime juice and sugar to taste in a shallow 6-cup (1.5 liter) bowl. Refrigerate covered 24 hours. Remove from the refrigerator just before serving.

Yield: 4 to 6 servings.

PITHIVIERS *(Loiret)*

Chartres 73 k, Fontainebleau 45 k, Montargis 45 k, Orléans 43 k, Paris 82 k.

Market: Saturday, 9 A.M. to 6 P.M., Place des Halles.

PATISSERIE

A LA RENOMMEE
5 Mail Ouest, 45300
  Pithiviers.
(38.30.00.24).
Open 6:30 A.M. to 8 P.M.
  Closed Wednesday, two
  weeks in February, and
  three weeks in
  September.

Pithiviers, *fresh from the oven.*

Travelers driving from Paris to the Loire valley might well want to make a brief gastronomic detour to the historic town of Pithiviers, where one finds the famous almond-paste-filled puff pastry tarts that take their name from the town. But there's another even rarer local pastry: *pâté d'alouette,* or lark pâté, a rather earthy but delicious preparation that may not be to everyone's taste. This is the land of the lark, and for as long as anyone can remember, local bakers have prepared them in pâtés. A whole unboned lark, head and all, is stuffed with forcemeat, sometimes even *foie gras* or truffles, then wrapped in pastry and baked. The result is a rich, gamey, rare treat. But since lark hunting has been outlawed since 1982 (the birds were traditionally caught with huge nets in open fields), the supply is exceptionally limited. The chef at the A la Renommée pastry shop won't say exactly how they get their larks, but he indicates that their stock is dwindling. If they're out of larks that day, settle for the sweet *pithiviers,* which they cut into thick slices from a single oversized tart on the counter. They slice it while it's still warm, and it oozes with thick, rich, pure almond paste, not the almond-extract-flavored imposter found elsewhere.

ROMORANTIN *(Loir-et-Cher)*

Blois 41 k, Châteauroux 67 k, Orléans 68 k, Paris 199 k, Tours 90 k,
Vierzon 33 k.

Markets: Wednesday, 8 A.M. to 6 P.M., Place de la Paix, Place du
Général-de-Gaulle, Rue de l'Ecu; Friday, 8 A.M. to 1 P.M., Cité des Favignolles;
Saturday, 8 A.M. to 1 P.M., Place du Général-de-Gaulle.
Journées Gastronomiques (food festival): last weekend in October.

RESTAURANT

**GRAND HOTEL DU LION
D'OR**
69 Rue Georges-
Clemenceau, 41200
Romorantin.
(54.76.00.28).
Last orders taken at 2 P.M.
and 9 P.M.
Closed January through
mid-February.
Credit cards: AE, V.
Private dining room for 30.
English spoken.
87- (weekdays only), 140-,
and 380-franc menus. A
la carte, 450 francs.

S P E C I A L T I E S :
Change with the seasons.

Chef Didier Clément, back from the market.

The romance of the Loire seems to have touched
the Grand Hôtel du Lion d'Or. Several years
ago chef Didier Clément came to take charge of the
kitchen, and love blossomed between him and the
owners' daughter, Marie-Christine. They married,
securing for themselves, and for diners, a certain
assurance that all will continue smoothly here for a
good long while. In the spring, chef Clément offers

some of the region's finest fat white asparagus, while in autumn and winter the menu is a veritable festival of hearty wild game and delicate wild mushrooms. From the second you set foot inside this charming former coaching inn, you feel taken care of, attended to. Marie-Christine's mother, Madame Barrat, is as stern as she is soft-hearted, often suggesting, sometimes almost demanding, that you try a certain dish, a particular wine. She is not likely to steer you in the wrong direction, so when she recommends her son-in-law's first-course salad of spinach, wild *girolles* mushrooms, and tiny *rougets,* or red mullet, the *crépinette* of pigeon in cider vinegar, or a finely aged Vouvray, follow her advice, and you're certain to leave the Lion d'Or with a smile on your face.

Sweet and glistening, tarte Tatin.

PATISSERIE

RAYMOND CARRE
38 Rue Georges-
   Clemenceau, 41200
   Romorantin.
(54.76.12.37).
Open 8 A.M. to 12:45 P.M.
   and 2:30 to 7:15 P.M.
   Closed Monday, two
   weeks in February, and
   three weeks in July.

This is *tarte Tatin* country, and one of the finest upside-down apple tarts of my memory came from this little shop in the charming town of Romorantin.

The Tart That Became a Legend

"*T*he celebrated French gastronome Curnonsky even rode the train from Paris to Lamotte-Beuvron to taste for himself the famous *tarte* Tatin. We do not know whether he was pleased."

LAMOTTE-BEUVRON, MAY 22—How does a dish become legend? In the case of the French apple pie known around the world as *la tarte des Demoiselles Tatin,* the trail begins in this insignificant agricultural village, a quiet town of 4,400 inhabitants in the forested hunting region of the Sologne.

Here, across from the train station, stands a sturdy stucco building called Hôtel Tatin, the spot where Stephanie and Caroline Tatin reportedly invented the caramelized upside-down apple pie that bears their family name.

This much is fact: Sometime during the 1850s the sisters left a nearby village for Lamotte-Beuvron and built the Hôtel-Terminus Tatin, which soon became a wayside stop for hunters and others traveling from Orléans to Vierzon. The sisters remained there until 1907, when they sold the hotel, leaving behind the fame of their rustic apple tart.

The rest of the legend is unverifiable, but amusing. One day Caroline, the cook and the younger of the sisters, was preparing an apple tart. She had cooked the apples in butter and sugar and, in haste, turned the mixture into a pastryless pie tin. Choosing not to retrace her steps, she improvised by placing the dough on top of the cooked apples. She baked the pie, removed it from the oven, and turned the tart over, creating, *voilà, tarte renversée.*

Now many a culinary historian will tell you that she never invented anything at all, that throughout France housewives had been making *tarte renversée* for years, but it was not until the Tatin sisters' apple pie became famous that it was given a proper name. The celebrated French gastronome Curnonsky even rode the train from Paris to Lamotte-Beuvron to taste the famous *tarte Tatin.* We do not know whether he was pleased.

At any rate, the Hôtel Tatin is alive and well today, complete with the same coal- and wood-burning blue-tiled stove in which the sisters baked their pies. Today the chef, Gilles Caillé, who bought the hotel in 1968, bakes about ten tarts each day in a conventional gas oven.

As a member of the local gastronomic society—*La Confrérie des Lichonneaux de Tarte Tatin*—which upholds the reputation of the village's pie, Monsieur Caillé prepares his dessert according to the club's stipulations. "A *tarte Tatin* is butter, sugar, apples, pastry, and lots of know-how," he says, adding that ideally the tart should be made with France's best cooking apple, the *reine des reinettes,* but when they're not available, as in the summer, he opts for the more banal Golden Delicious. Contrary to the customary recipe, in which the apples are first cooked in sugar and butter atop the stove, Monsieur Caillé combines raw apples, butter, and sugar in a tin-lined copper mold. He covers the mixture with a fine layer of *pâte sucrée,* or sweetened short crust, and bakes it until all is brown, bubbly, and caramelized.

LES ROSIERS *(Maine-et-Loire)*

Angers 30 k, Cholet 62 k, La Flèche 44 k, Paris 288 k, Saumur 15 k.

Market: Monday, 8 A.M. to noon, Place du Mail.

RESTAURANT

JEANNE DE LAVAL
54 Rue Nationale, Les
    Rosiers, 49350 Gennes.
(41.51.80.17).
Last orders taken at 2 P.M.
    and 9:30 P.M.
Closed Monday (except
    holidays) and January
    through mid-February.
Credit cards: AE, DC, V.
Terrace dining.
Private dining room for 15
    to 20.
English spoken.
150- and 300-franc menus.
    A la carte, 350 to 400
    francs.

SPECIALTIES:
Poissons de la Loire au beurre
blanc (Loire river fish with
sauce of white wine, shallots,
and butter), *poulàrde de Loué à*
l'estragon (chicken with
tarragon), *foie gras de canard*
(fattened duck liver).

Today Loire river salmon is one of France's greatest delicacies. It is hard to imagine that there was a time when the salmon was so plentiful that workers in the region were protected from being served the rich, fatty, flavorful fish at each and every meal! If you are fortunate, they will be serving it the day you arrive at the old-fashioned *auberge* Jeanne de Laval. Installed on their brightly flowered terrace after passing through the well-worn, but far from shabby, dining room, you'll swear that time had stopped somewhere in the 1950s. Here you could easily believe that *nouvelle cuisine* had never been invented. As eager, bright-faced waitresses scurry about, the voice of the chef, Michel Augereau, booms from the adjacent kitchen. The offerings could not be more traditional. The autumn and winter months bring roast pheasant and wild hare stews; Loire salmon is generally available from mid-February until the end of June; through the spring there is white asparagus with hollandaise and the perch-like Loire river *sandre,* served with an exceptional *beurre blanc.*

SAINT-THIBAULT *(Cher)*

Bourges 41 k, Pouilly-sur-Loire 13 k, Sancerre 5 k.

RESTAURANT

L'ETOILE
2 Quai de la Loire,
    Saint-Thibault, 18300
    Sancerre. (48.54.12.15).
Last orders taken at 2 P.M.
    and 9 P.M.
Closed Wednesday and
    mid-November through
    February.

L'Etoile, an overgrown porch of a restaurant along the Loire, typifies the unself-consciousness of this refreshing little area around the village of Sancerre, home of the dry, flinty, and ever-popular Loire valley white wine. The restaurant offers a variety of fish and meat dishes cooked over a charcoal fire in the main dining room, and

No credit cards.
Terrace dining.
Private dining room for 25 to 30.
A little English spoken.
75-, 195-, and 150-franc (Sunday only) menus. A la carte, 220 francs.

SPECIALITIES:
Matelote d'anguilles (eel stew), *andouillette grillée au Sancerre* (chitterling sausage grilled with Sancerre).

there's a little terrace for summer or fall dining. The house Sancerre is crisp and *correct,* and one could do worse than spend an extended afternoon sipping wine and lingering over a lunch of simple grilled sole (albeit from the sea) and freshly cooked French fries. L'Etoile's cheese tray includes an assortment of local goat cheeses, some fresh and mild, some *demi-sec* and only slightly pungent, still others brittle, strong, and hard enough to crack a tooth. The Sancerre and the local goat cheese have the same effect on the palate: They are dry, force a bit of a pucker, and leave a surprisingly pleasant though distinct aftertaste—of straw!

SANCERRE *(Cher)*

Bourges 46 k, La Charité-sur-Loire 26 k, Paris 199 k, Salbris 75 k, Vierzon 71 k.

Market: Tuesday and Saturday, 8:30 A.M. to noon, Place de la Mairie. *Foire aux Fromages* (cheese fair): May 1 or following weekend. *Foire aux Vin* (wine fair): Saturday, Sunday, and Monday of Pentecost. *Journées des Vins de France* (wine fair): last Sunday in August. *Foire aux Huîtres* (oyster festival): last Sunday in October.

RESTAURANT

AUBERGE ALPHONSE MELLOT
16 Nouvelle Place, 18300 Sancerre.
(48.54.20.53).
Last orders: continuous service from noon to 7:30 P.M.
Closed Wednesday and mid-December through mid-January.
Credit cards: EC, V.
Covered terrace dining.
English spoken.
65-franc menu. A la carte, 90 francs.

A simple place in the center of this famous wine village, where you can sample Alphonse Mellot's excellent Sancerre with the local Crottin de Chavignol goat cheese and a tasty ham omelet.

Basketry, a Loire Valley specialty.

SAUMUR *(Maine-et-Loire)*

Angers 45 k, Cholet 66 k, La Flèche 31 k, Le Mans 94 k,
Paris 293 k, Tours 66 k.

Markets: Wednesday, 8 A.M. to 1 P.M., Place du Clos-Grolleau; Thursday, 8 A.M.
to 1 P.M., Avenue du Général-de-Gaulle; Friday, 8 A.M. to 1 P.M., Quartier du
Chemin-Vert; Saturday, 7 A.M. to 1:30 P.M., Place Saint-Pierre.

MUSEE

**MUSEE DU
  CHAMPIGNON**
Saint-Hilaire-Saint-Florent,
  49400 Saumur.
(41.50.31.55).
Open daily 10 A.M. to noon
  and 2 to 6 P.M. March to
  mid-November.
Admission: 13 francs; about
  9 francs for children
  under age 14, and 10
  francs for groups of more
  than 25.

Louis Bouchard in his damp mushroom caves.

Between meals and visits to Loire valley *châteaux* and vineyards, a tour of the region's fascinating mushroom-growing caves is in order. As you drive along the banks of the Loire, you'll be amazed at the number of troglodyte dwellings built into the porous volcanic rock of the region. The caves were originally created when mammoth stones were cut out of the rock mountains to build the great cathedrals and *châteaux* of the Loire. The quarrying created an ideal damp and cool space to serve as a wine cellar and, later, for growing mushrooms. You can easily spend an hour at Louis Bouchard's mushroom-growing museum, where you can wander at will through the expansive underground caves, passing beds of the famous *champignons de Paris* at various stages of development. Currently they are also experimenting with cultivating *pleurotes,* the very delicate, soft, feathery-edged mushrooms. At the end of the tour, visitors can purchase fresh, dried, and preserved mushrooms, as well as local wines. (Directions: located on the left bank of the Loire, on the D751, about 5 kilometers west of Saumur.)

TOURS *(Indre-et-Loire)*

Angers 106 k, Chartres 140 k, Le Mans 82 k, Orléans 112 k, Paris 234 k.

Markets: Monday, Tuesday, Friday, and Sunday, 7 to 9:30 A.M., Wednesday and Saturday, 7:30 to 11:30 A.M., Marché des Halles; Thursday and Sunday, 8 A.M. to 12:30 P.M., Place Velpeau.
Foire à l'Ail et au Basilic (garlic and basil fair): July 26.
Flea market: Wednesday and Saturday, 7 A.M. to 5 P.M., Place des Victoires.

If you happen to be in Tours on Wednesday or Saturday, catch the small but worthwhile flea market in the Place des Victoires, situated near the river and just a few blocks from the large indoor food market. You're likely to find a good selection of baskets, porcelain, and pottery. An early morning visit is recommended. Vieux Tours, the old restored section of town, is just a few blocks east. Note especially the antique shops lining Rue de la Scellerie and Rue de Cygne.

VILLAINES-LES-ROCHERS *(Indre-et-Loire)*

Azay-le-Rideau 5 k, Chinon 26 k, Tours 28 k.

POUR LA MAISON

LA VANNERIE DE VILLAINES-LES-ROCHERS
Villaines-les-Rochers, 37190 Azay-le-Rideau.
(47.45.43.03).
Open 9 A.M. to noon and 2 to 7 P.M. Monday through Saturday; 10 A.M. to noon and 2 to 7 P.M. Sunday and holidays Easter through September; 2 to 7 P.M. Sunday and holidays October to Easter. Closed Christmas and New Year's Day.
Will ship internationally.

The basket weavers of Villaines-les-Rochers.

Since 1849 village residents have operated a basket-weaving cooperative, which now employs almost ninety families. Even Balzac wrote glowingly about the local basketry. Not only do they design and weave a huge variety of wickerware, but they also grow, then dry, the sturdy willow reeds in this calm, secluded hamlet. If you drive through in the late spring, you'll find the roads lined with piles of golden reeds—willows that were picked during the winter months, then soaked in water (to make them pliable) until about May, when they were stripped and laid out to dry. Year-round, visitors are invited to watch the weavers at work in the sunlit studio, where locally grown and dried willows are transformed into everything from small bread-rising baskets lined with natural linen to huge baby carriages. The cooperative supplies many of France's bakers and pastry makers with wicker items. They make lovely cheese trays with glass inserts, sturdy and attractive shopping carts, and even baskets for hot-air ballooning.

VILLANDRY *(Indre-et-Loire)*

Azay-le-Rideau 10 k, Chinon 31 k, Paris 252 k, Saumur 52 k, Tours 20 k.

SPECIALITES REGIONALES

CHATEAU DE
    VILLANDRY
Villandry, 37300
    Joué-lès-Tours.
(47.50.02.09).
Garden open daily 9 A.M. to
    5 P.M. (*château* closed
    mid-November through
    mid-March).
Admission: 15 francs; 10
    francs for children under
    age 10 and for groups of
    more than 20.

SPECIALTY:
The kitchen garden.

This is one of the grandest, most exuberant gardens in France. After you have visited this formal fruit, vegetable, and flower garden that surrounds the sixteenth-century Château de Villandry, you'll want to go back home and plant, plant, plant. Six full-time gardeners tend to the flat, meticulously orchestrated spread of red chard, ornamental purple cabbage, and vermillion roses, and visitors are allowed to wander freely through the maze of mini gardens. The *château*—of less interest than the gardens—is also open for tours. The gardens are at their best in the months of August and September.

TARTE A LA CITROUILLE DE MILLANÇAY
PUMPKIN TART FROM MILLANÇAY

Until I lived in France, I never realized how much pumpkin the French consume: in sweet tarts topped with whole almonds, in soups mixed with tomatoes, in gratins blended with grated cheese, and in bread flecked with cornmeal. The bright fall and winter vegetable appears in many shapes and sizes, with meaty interiors that range from pale orange to a vibrant sunset red. In France, pumpkin is always sold by the slice, and each variety goes by a different name. You'll see it sold as courge, citrouille, potimarron, *and* potiron. *The recipe for this decorative almond-flavored pumpkin tart comes from Millançay, a village in the Sologne, where each fall they hold a* Fête à la Citrouille.

1 wedge fresh pumpkin (about 2 pounds, 1 kg)

1 cup (140 g) whole almonds

3 large eggs

⅓ cup (80 ml) *crème fraîche* (see Recipe Index) or heavy cream, preferably not ultra-pasteurized

¾ cup (165 g) firmly packed light brown sugar

1 tablespoon freshly squeezed lemon juice

Basic Short-Crust Pastry (see Recipe Index)

1. Preheat the oven to 425°F (220°C).

2. Remove the seeds and any strings from the pumpkin and cut into about 8 even pieces. Place the unpeeled pumpkin pieces in a steamer large enough to hold them. Cover and steam over boiling water until the pumpkin meat is tender, about 15 minutes. Drain the pumpkin and let cool until it can be handled. Then cut off the peel and discard it. Purée the pumpkin in a food processor or blender. You should have 2 cups (500 ml) purée. (The purée can be made in advance and refrigerated or frozen.)

3. Coarsely chop ½ cup (70 g) of the almonds in a food processor or blender. Add the pumpkin purée, eggs, *crème fraîche,* sugar, and lemon juice and mix well.

4. Roll out the dough to line a 10½-inch (27 cm) tart pan. Carefully transfer the dough to the pan. Pour the filling into the prepared dough and bake until a knife inserted in the center of the tart comes out clean, about 45 minutes.

5. While the tart is still warm, insert the remaining almonds, tips down, just inside the edge of the crust. Serve at room temperature, preferably within 2 or 3 hours of baking.

Yield: One 10½-inch (27 cm) tart.

CHEESES OF SOLOGNE AND THE LOIRE

1. SELLES-SUR-CHER: Fat discs of soft goat's-milk cheese, aged from ten days to three weeks or longer. The best Selles-sur-Cher is made of raw goat's milk and is elegantly smooth and light, with a faint flavor of hazelnuts, a pleasantly goaty aroma, a smooth, pure-white interior, and a mottled blue-gray rind. It is sometimes sprinkled with powdered charcoal, which turns the pure white rind to blue as the cheese ages. Excellent with the local Sauvignon *blanc.*

2. POULIGNY-SAINT-PIERRE: At its very best, this goat cheese— formed into proud, truncated pyramids—is one of the most refined and satisfying of all the cheeses available in France. From the rich perfumed milk of the familiar Alpine goats comes a very smooth-grained, ivory-white cheese with a mottled grayish rind, a cheese that's at once elegant and earthy. Pouligny-Saint-Pierre is made on small farms and in dairies, from whole goat's milk, both raw and pasteurized.

3. SAINTE-MAURE FERMIER: Shaped in the form of a soft, elongated cylinder, this very delicately flavored farm goat cheese, with its pleasantly goaty aroma, arrives at the market with a distinctive straw running through the center. The best Sainte-Maure—made with raw whole goat's milk—will be full-flavored, even-textured, with a mottled natural blue rind. Unfortunately, quantities of Sainte-Maure are made industrially of frozen goat's-milk curd, and may taste soapy.

4. CROTTIN DE CHAVIGNOL: One of the most popular of all France's goat cheeses, this small flattened ball appears in the market in many stages, from soft and fresh for grilling or for "curing" in oil and herbs, to very aged, hard, and brittle. *"Crottin"* literally translated means "horse dung," which is what a very dried and aged Crottin de Chavignol resembles. Delicious when well aged, chalky, and firm, with a local white Sancerre wine.

WINES OF SOLOGNE AND THE LOIRE

1. CHINON (CHARLES JO-GUET):
Of all the wines in my cellar, this is a favorite. The only problem is to forget about it and let it age, so that the spice, the mineral-like depth, of this serious Loire red has a chance to show its stuff! Another reputable name, and one you'll see often, is the house of Couly-Dutheil, particularly their well-made Clos d'Olive and Clos de l'Echo.

2. VOUVRAY SEC LE HAUT LIEU (DOMAINE HUET):
Vouvray is a white wine many of us ignore, and it's a shame, for a golden dry Vouvray—such as Huet's—is the perfect match for Loire river salmon. Also look for Vouvray by Prince Poniatowski and Gilles Champion.

3. BONNEZEAUX (CHATEAU DE FESLES):
Perfumed and sweet, this white plays some real tricks, blending sweet tones of honey with an apple tartness. As an aperitif, or with fruit desserts, this is a winner.

4. SAVENNIERES (CHATEAU D'EPIRE):
I find it hard to resist the apple-fruitiness of this great *chenin blanc*. Another trusted label you'll see quite often: Madame A. Joly's Château de la Roche aux Moines, Coulée de Serrant.

5. QUARTS DE CHAUME (DOMAINE BAUMARD):
A sweet, even luscious, white wine with delicate overtones of honey and apricots, the perfect drink to enjoy with a prized *tarte Tatin*. Production is very small, but the wine offers both richness and finesse.

6. SANCERRE CHAVIGNOL (VINCENT DELAPORTE):
A favorite dry flinty white with plenty of backbone, one that's a perfect match for the Loire's goat cheese, white river fish, salmon, and poultry. Note that there is also a Sancerre *rosé* (great with Chinese food), and in good years, a very light Sancerre *rouge*. Other popular names: Alphonse Mellot, Lucien Crochet, and Vacheron.

7. POUILLY FUME (DAGNUE-NEAU):
This dry white—known locally as *blanc fumé*—is a versatile wine, with a musty smokiness that makes it a perfect aperitif as well as a companion to local river fish. Also look for the most famous Pouilly Fumé of all, Château de Nozet's la Doucette, a dependable wine that manages to show up on the majority of wine lists in France.

Ile-de-France
ILE-DE-FRANCE

A toast from Cazaudehore.

Historically the Ile-de-France —the region that forms a 50-kilometer belt around the city of Paris, measuring from the cathedral of Notre Dame—has served as bread basket, market garden, hunting grounds, dairy to Paris. Although intensive urbanization has significantly transformed the rural landscape, reducing the number of *maraîchers,* or market gardeners, who supply the produce for the Parisian table, one can still depart from the capital in any direction and quickly find oneself driving through flat, golden fields of wheat and corn, through dense, green forests filled with deer and wild ducks, past farms and dairies supplying cream, poultry, and quantities of fruits and vegetables.

True, the famed *champignons de Paris,* which once grew in caves on the outskirts of Paris, now come mainly from the Loire, and the asparagus that made Argenteuil famous are more likely to have pushed through the soil of Provence, but one still finds quantities of watercress, beets, carrots, and cabbage carrying identity tags from the Ile-de-France.

Today numerous French dishes still bear the names of the towns and villages that were the source of many fine products, including cream from Chantilly, cherries from Montmorency, carrots from Crécy. Take one look at the various regional food festivals,

and you'll see that Arpajon is still proud of its beans, Montlhéry remains faithful to its tomatoes, Mantes-la-Jolie still celebrates the onion.

And despite the massive urban sprawl, one can still find oneself in the countryside in a matter of minutes, settled in at a table near the Fontainebleau forest in the charming village of Barbizon, home to the nineteenth-century Barbizon school painters such as Millet, Corot, and Théodore Rousseau; touring Marie-Antoinette's milk house at the *château* of Rambouillet; wandering through the incredible kitchens of the *château* of Vaux-le-Vicomte; or touring the marvelous produce markets of nearby Versailles.

WHEN YOU GO

Michelin Green Guide: *Environs de Paris.*

Getting there: All towns in the Ile-de-France are within an easy hour's drive from Paris. Alternatively, most addresses are accessible by train or RER, Paris's surburban train line, and then a short walk or taxi ride. Versailles is reached by taking the RER C-line to the Versailles–Rive Gauche station. Also, the weekly cultural events magazine, *Pariscope,* gives detailed instructions on getting to the most frequently visited spots by public transportation. *Pariscope* is available at most Paris newsstands.

Getting around: Michelin map 237 (Paris region).

Best time to visit: Because of its proximity to Paris, the Ile-de-France is active throughout the year, though it is at its prettiest from Easter through October.

MARKETS
(Liveliest markets are marked with an asterisk.)

Monday: Dreux, Egreville, *Méry-sur-Oise, Montlhéry.

Tuesday: Boussy-Saint-Antoine, Brie-Comte-Robert, Chartres, Chatou, Chennevières-sur-Marne, Clamart, Croissy-sur-Seine, Dreux, Enghien-les-Bains, Fontainebleau, Joinville-le-Pont, Jouy-en-Josas, Jouy-le-Châtel, Marly-le-Roi, Meudon, *Moret-sur-Loing, Poissy, La Roche-Guyon (in summer), *Rueil-Malmaison, Saint-Germain-en-Laye, Senlis, Versailles.

Wednesday: Beauvais, Bièvres, Bougival, Brou, Chantilly, Chartres, *Chatou, Clamart, Compiègne, *Coulommiers, Dourdan, Dreux, Maisons-Laffitte, Mantes-la-Jolie, Mennecy, Meudon, *Nangis, Rambouillet.

Thursday: Auvers-sur-Oise, Boussy-Saint-Antoine, Chatou, Enghien-les-Bains, Grigny, Joinville-le-Pont, Marcoussis, Milly-la-Forêt, Montfort-l'Amaury, Montlhéry, Poissy, Rambouillet, Versailles.

Friday: Arpajon, Brie-Comte-Robert, Chatou, *Chennevières-sur-Marne, Croissy-sur-Seine, Dreux, Fontainebleau, Illiers-Combray, Jouy-en-Josas, Jouy-le-Châtel, *Marly-le-Roi, Méréville, Méry-sur-Oise, Meudon, Moret-sur-Loing, Pierrefonds, Poissy, Rambouillet, La Roche-Guyon (in summer), Rueil-Malmaison, Saint-Germain-en-Laye, Senlis, Senonches, Versailles.

Saturday: *Beauvais, *Bièvres, Bougival, Champs-sur-Marne, *Chantilly, *Chartres, *Chatou, Clamart, Compiègne, Coulommiers, *Dourdan, Ecouen, *Enghien-les-Bains, Etampes, *Joinville-le-Pont, *Maisons-Laffitte, Mantes-la-Jolie, *Meaux, Mennecy, Meudon, Nangis, Poissy, Provins, *Rambouillet, La Roche-Guyon, *Rueil-Malmaison, Versailles.

Sunday: *Auvers-sur-Oise, Boussy-Saint-Antoine, Boutigny-sur-Essonne, Brie-Comte-Robert, Chatou, Clamart, Coulommiers, *Dreux, Fontainebleau, Grigny, *Joinville-le-Pont, *Marcoussis, Marly-le-Roi, *Meudon, *Poissy, Rambouillet, Saint-Germain-en-Laye, Saint-Mammès, Thoiry, Versailles.

FAIRS AND FESTIVALS

Last weekend in January in even years: *Fête de Saint-Paul* (wine festival), Provins.

Last week in February through the first week in March: *Foire au Jambon* (flea market), Chatou.

Sunday before Easter: *Foire aux Fromages* (cheese fair), Coulommiers.

May 1: *Fête du Muguet* (lily of the valley festival), Compiègne.

Third Sunday in June: *Fête de la Fraise* (strawberry festival), Marcoussis.

Mid-July: *Fête de la Moisson* (harvest festival), Guiry-en-Vexin.

Last Sunday in August: *Fête de la Moisson* (harvest festival), Provins.

Early September: *Fête de la Chasse* (hunt festival), Viarmes.

Second weekend in September: *Foire à la Tomate* (tomato fair), Montlhéry.

Third weekend in September: *Foire aux Haricots* (dried green bean fair), Arpajon.

Last two weeks in September: *Fête du Pâté à la Carmen* (traditional local festival), Montesson.

Mid-October: *Fête de la Pomme et du Cidre* (apple and cider festival), Saint-Augustin.

Second Sunday in November: *Salon de la Gastronomie* (gastronomic conference), Senlis.

First Wednesday in December: *Foire aux Oignons* (onion fair), Mantes-la-Jolie.

Second Monday in December: *Concours à la Volaille Grasse* (fattened poultry contest), Egreville.

On the terrace at l'Esturgeon.

BARBIZON *(Seine-et-Marne)*

Fontainebleau 10 k, Melun 11 k, Paris 55 k.

RESTAURANTS

HOSTELLERIE DU BAS-BREAU
22 Rue Grande, 77630 Barbizon.
(60.66.40.05).
Last orders taken at 2 P.M. and 10 P.M.
Closed January through mid-February.
Credit cards: AE, EC, V.
Terrace dining.
Private dining room for 80.
English spoken.
240- and 280-franc menus at lunch (weekdays only).
A la carte, 450 francs.

SPECIALTIES:
Gibier (wild game, generally October through February).

Before the last leaves fall and autumn turns to winter, I always make a point of spending at least a Sunday afternoon in Barbizon, the charming village that was home to Corot and Millet, the painters of sentimental landscapes of the Barbizon school. At the Bas-Bréau, the house where Robert Louis Stevenson lived and wrote, you can always count on a roaring fire, attentive service, and a marvelous selection of the freshest game from throughout Europe. Two dishes that I've most loved here include a *pâté chaud de grouse,* a rich, warm, and mildy gamey Scottish grouse pâté wrapped in pastry and bathed in clear brown sauce, and the *escalopes de foie gras chaud aux épinards,* slightly wilted warm spinach leaves topped with several quickly seared slices of *foie gras.* I've been less fond of the dessert soufflés—too sugary sweet.

AU GRAND VENEUR
63 Rue Gabriel-Séailles, 77630 Barbizon.
(60.66.40.44).
Last orders taken at 2 P.M. and 9:30 P.M. Closed Wednesday dinner, Thursday, and late July through August.
Credit cards: AE, DC, V.
Terrace dining.
Private dining room for 60.
About 350 francs.

SPECIALTIES:
Grillade (poultry, meat and game, grilled or roasted over an open fire). Game is generally available from October through February, and includes partridge, pheasant, venison, and wild boar.

I have friends who have driven out to Barbizon for lunch at Au Grand Veneur and not returned to Paris until well after dark. It's easy to see how time can lose all importance as one is seated in the huge hunting-lodge-style restaurant overlooking the Fontainebleau forest. The specialty here is *grillade*—meat, poultry, and game grilled or roasted in the gigantic fireplace that dominates the rustic dining room—and though there is more quantity than quality, I don't know anyone who ever had a bad time. Hope that the sun is shining, so afterwards you can take a ramble through the woods. Service here is very friendly, and children are welcome. (Directions: on the N7.)

CHANTILLY *(Oise)*

Compiègne 44 k, Meaux 48 k, Paris 50 k.

Market: Wednesday and Saturday, 8 A.M. to 12:30 P.M., Place Honère-Vallon.

RESTAURANT

LE RELAIS CONDE
42 Avenue du Maréchal-
Joffre, 60500 Chantilly.
(44.57.05.75).
Last orders taken at 2:30 P.M.
and 10 P.M.
Closed Monday and January.
Credit cards: AE, DC, EC, V.
Terrace dining.
Private dining room for 30.
English spoken.
150-franc menu. A la carte,
250 francs.

SPECIALTIES:
Goujonnettes de sole aux pâtes fraîches (sole with fresh pasta), *ris de veau* (sweetbreads), *foie gras maison* (fattened duck liver).

This warm, bright little restaurant is straight out of Hansel and Gretel. The dining room, installed in a former chapel, is decorated in shades of rose and pink, with high-backed upholstered chairs, a beamed vaulted ceiling, and a huge stone fireplace. The menu is varied and essentially classic, including grilled kidneys with mustard, sweetbreads with wild morel mushrooms, and a good selection of fish. Their best dish of all is the poached sole, served with fresh pasta in a light sauce of fish stock and cream.

MAINCY *(Seine-et-Marne)*

Fontainebleau 17 k, Melun 6 k, Paris 54 k.

SPECIALITES REGIONALES

**CHATEAU VAUX-LE-
VICOMTE**
77950 Maincy.
(60.66.97.09).
Open daily 10 A.M. to 6 P.M.
April through October; 2
P.M. to 5 P.M. Saturday and
Sunday only from
November through
March. Closed December
and January.
Admission: 38 francs for
adults, 32 francs for
children.

When in the area, make a detour to visit this superb *château,* one of the splendors of seventeenth-century France. I love the elaborate nineteenth-century kitchen—in use until 1956—which gives just a hint of the elaborate life and the style of cooking that was once the custom.

MONTFORT-L'AMAURY *(Yvelines)*

Paris 48 k, Rambouillet 19 k, Versailles 28 k.

Market: Thursday, 8 A.M. to 1 P.M., Place du Palais.

RESTAURANT

LES PREJUGES
18 Place Robert-Brault,
78490 Montfort-
l'Amaury.
(34.86.92.65).
Last orders taken at 2 P.M.
(2:30 P.M. in summer) and
10 P.M. (10:30 P.M. in
summer).
Closed Tuesday and January
through mid-February.
Credit cards: AE, DC, V.
Terrace dining.
Private dining rooms for 12
and 20.
English spoken.
180-, 250- (lunch only), and
350-franc menus. A la
carte, 450 francs.

SPECIALTIES:
Escalope de foie gras au gingembre
(foie gras with ginger),
pot-au-feu au foie gras
(pot-au-feu with *foie gras*),
saumon sauce au fumet d'huîtres
(salmon with oyster sauce),
gibier en saison (wild game in
season).

Les Préjugés is a dream of a romantic country restaurant, situated in a beautifully restored home with a carefully tended garden. Luxurious but far from cold, the dining room is filled with flowers and classical music, and the menu and wine list are intelligently conceived. I loved the unusual *pot-au-feu au foie gras* with rich duck liver that slowly melts into the rich broth, and their warm smoked salmon with a sauce of spicy Alsatian Gewürztraminer (see recipe, page 165). Desserts are imaginative and fresh: We sampled warm crêpes filled with raisins and almonds, and a lovely *sablé* cookie topped with slices of fresh mango and delicious vanilla ice cream. A red Bordeaux to try here, if it's still on the wine list, is Château Potensac, a dark, rich, and tannic Médoc that's generally a very good buy.

Marketing in Versailles.

POISSY *(Yvelines)*

Paris 38 k, Rambouillet 48 k, Saint-Germain-en-Laye 7 k.

Markets: Tuesday, Friday, and Sunday, 8:30 A.M. to 12:30 P.M., Place de la République; Thursday and Saturday, 8:30 A.M. to 12:30 P.M., Avenue Blanche-de-Castille.

RESTAURANT

L'ESTURGEON
6 Cours du 14-Juillet, 78300 Poissy.
(39.65.00.04).
Last orders taken at 2 P.M. and 9:30 P.M.
Closed Thursday and August.
Credit cards: AE, DC, V.
Enclosed terrace dining.
Private dining room for 12 to 15.
Some English spoken.
280 francs.

SPECIALTIES:
Coulibiac (salmon wrapped in fish mousse and puff pastry), *saumon à l'aneth* (salmon with dill), *bar beurre blanc* (striped bass with white butter sauce), *coquilles Saint-Jacques* (scallops), *filet de sandre* (filet of perch-like freshwater fish), *caneton aux cerises* (duck with cherries), *carré d'agneau gratin dauphin* (rack of lamb and scalloped potatoes), *tarte Tatin* (caramelized apple tart), *crêpes flambées* (flamed crêpes).

On the banks of the Seine.

Sturgeon, or *esturgeon,* isn't served at L'Esturgeon anymore, since the fat river fish no longer frequent the Seine. But they did once, and this old-fashioned waterside restaurant stands as a testament to a giant sturgeon plucked from the waters of Poissy on July 22, 1839. What they do serve at L'Esturgeon is a good *coulibiac* of salmon, a classic Russian dish one rarely finds in restaurants. The chef, Jean Soulat, prepares the *coulibiac* according to the recipe given to his father by a Russian chef in the 1930s, and it's been a specialty of the house ever since. This unusual dish of salmon wrapped in a firm fish mousse, then encased in puff pastry, is served with a classic beurre blanc, offering a nice marriage of buttery and tart, firm and supple, crunchy and moist. With it, order a simple green salad or the refreshing lobster salad, then finish up with an old-fashioned Vacherin, a huge block of meringue filled with chocolate ice cream and decorated with fresh whipped cream. On Sundays the dining room—actually an enclosed terrace overlooking the Seine—is filled with French families who turn lunch into a daylong affair, stretching out the hours with another cup of coffee or a Cognac.

SAUMON FUME TIEDE AU GEWURZTRAMINER LES PREJUGES
LES PREJUGES' WARM SMOKED SALMON WITH GEWURZTRAMINER

When I first eyed this dish on the menu at Les Préjugés, I knew I had to try it. I love the spicy Alsatian wine Gewürztraminer, and decided that the idea of marrying it with warm smoked salmon was pure genius. The addition of sautéed wild mushrooms (I like to use girolles *and* mousserons) *only makes it that much more special. Serve the dish, of course, with a glass or two of chilled Gewürztraminer.*

4 medium carrots, peeled cut into ½-inch (1 ½ cm) slices
1 tablespoon (½ ounce; 15 g) unsalted butter
1 teaspoon sugar
Salt and freshly ground black pepper to taste
14 ounces (400 g) mixed wild mushrooms, gently rinsed and patted dry
2 tablespoons virgin olive oil
2 cloves garlic, peeled but left whole
4 slices best-quality smoked salmon, each weighing about 3 ounces (95 grams)

Gewürztraminer sauce:
4 shallots, minced
3 tablespoons (1 ½ ounces; 45 g) unsalted butter
1 ⅓ cups (330 ml) Gewürztraminer
2 bay leaves
Grated zest (peel) of 1 lime
2 sprigs fresh dill, minced

1. Cook the carrots in boiling salted water until crisp-tender. Drain them, cool under cold running water, and drain again well. Sauté the carrot slices with 1 tablespoon butter, the sugar, and salt for 3 to 4 minutes. Taste for seasoning. Cover to keep warm.

2. If the mushrooms are large, cut them into manageable pieces. Heat the oil in a medium skillet over high heat until hot but not smoking. Add the mushrooms, garlic, salt, and pepper and sauté, stirring constantly, for 3 minutes. Remove the garlic cloves and taste for seasoning. Cover to keep warm.

3. Place 1 slice salmon on each of 4 ovenproof plates; fold the salmon if the piece is long. Divide the mushrooms and the carrots equally among the 4 plates.

4. Prepare the sauce: Place the shallots and 1 tablespoon of the butter in a small heavy saucepan and cook over low heat until translucent, 3 to 4 minutes. Pour in the Gewürztraminer, then add the bay leaves and lime zest. Heat the liquid to a boil and reduce to ½ cup (125 ml). Reduce the heat and whisk in the remaining 2 tablespoons butter until it is completely blended. Season to taste with salt and pepper. Cover the sauce to keep it warm.

5. While preparing the sauce, preheat the broiler.

6. Place the plates under the broiler and broil just long enough to barely cook the salmon and heat the dish through, about 1 minute. Whisk the dill into the sauce, taste for seasoning, then spoon the sauce over the salmon. Serve immediately with freshly toasted country bread.

Yield: 4 servings.

SAINT-GERMAIN-EN-LAYE *(Yvelines)*

Paris 17, Pontoise 20 k, Rambouillet 47, Versailles 23 k.

Market: Tuesday, Friday, and Sunday, 8 A.M. to 2 P.M., Place du Marché.

RESTAURANT

CAZAUDEHORE
1 Avenue Président-
 Kennedy, 78100
 Saint-Germain-en-Laye.
(34.51.93.80).
Last orders taken at 1:30 P.M.
 and 9:30 to 10 P.M.
Closed Monday.
Credit card: V.
Terrace dining.
Private dining room for 10
 to 30.
English spoken.
300 francs.

SPECIALTIES:
Basque; *foie de canard* (fattened
duck liver), *magret de canard*
(breast of fattened duck).

The bright flowered terrace of Cazaudehore, on the edge of the Saint-Germain forest in the historic little town of Saint-Germain-en-Laye, is ideal for a leisurely Sunday lunch. Energetic travelers may want to walk from the train station—it's a thirty-minute wander along the edge of the forest, full of songbirds and wildflowers. In addition to the terrace—one of the region's prettiest outdoor dining spots—there is a rustically elegant, well-appointed dining room, where service is accommodating and professional. Cazaudehore offers a few specialties of the Basque region, including *piperade* (here a blend of scrambled eggs mixed with peppers, country ham, and *chipolata* sausages), while the rest of the cuisine remains classic and *correct.* I loved their poached salmon set on a bed of freshly wilted spinach, as well as the lively Cassis sorbet served with elegant butter cookies.

SAINT-SYMPHORIEN-LE-CHATEAU *(Eure-et-Loir)*

Chartres 25 k, Dreux 60 k, Paris 68 k.

RESTAURANT

CHATEAU D'ESCLIMONT
2870 Saint-Symphorien-le-
 Château.
(37.31.15.15 or
 37.31.58.06).
Last orders taken at 2 P.M.
 and 9 P.M.
Open daily.
Credit card: V.
Private dining rooms for 10
 to 200.
English spoken.
225- and 410-franc menus.
 A la carte, 400 francs.

One cold but sunny winter Saturday my husband and I drove out to this enchanted castle just an hour's drive southwest of Paris. As we took our table by the window overlooking a romantic swan-filled lagoon, a helicopter set down and a young couple stepped out. Their expressions were decidedly blasé, as if to say, well, doesn't everyone helicopter their way to Saturday lunch? Château d'Esclimont is that kind of place, where you come to enjoy the scenery, to see and be seen, to share a few quiet, romantic hours at table. The setting is spectacular as you are bathed in old-fashioned splendor in this private *château* set in the midst of a forested park. The food, however, is the sort designed for timid palates (I've come to call it *goût du château*) and could stand some jazzing up. We did enjoy the little molds of fresh salmon filled with a salmony mousse and the generous wild hare stew, but generally the food sorely lacked flavor.

VERSAILLES *(Yvelines)*

Chartres 73 k, Fontainebleau 78 k, Paris 23 k.

Markets: Tuesday, Friday, and Sunday, 8 A.M. to noon, covered market, Place Notre Dame; Thursday, 8 A.M. to noon, open-air market, Place Saint-Louis. Flea market: Saturday and Sunday, 9 A.M. to 7 P.M., Passage de la Geôle near Place Notre Dame.

RESTAURANTS

ROTISSERIE DE LA BOULE D'OR
25 Rue du Maréchal-Foch, 78000 Versailles.
(39.50.22.97).
Last orders taken at 3 P.M. and 10 P.M.
Closed Sunday dinner and Monday.
Credit cards: AE, DC, EC, V.
English spoken.
145- (weekdays only) and 200-franc (weekends and holidays only) menus. 100-franc lunch menu Tuesday through Saturday. A la carte, 300 francs.

SPECIALTIES:
Authentic classic French dishes ranging from the eighteenth century to the present; specialties of the Jura; *agneau de lait* (milk-fed spring lamb, from mid-January to April.)

Where there's business, there's lunch.

Diners who want to remain historic to the core should visit La Boule d'Or, founded in 1674 and billed as the oldest inn in Versailles. Under the reign of Louis XIV, this was only one of 400 inns to be found in Versailles, and today it serves as a living culinary museum, offering dozens of thoroughly classic preparations, some dating back to 1383. I highly recommend La Boule d'Or for a Sunday lunch, when you can follow the lead of the well-heeled locals: doing a bit of marketing in the morning, spending a few hours at table, reserving the afternoon for the Versailles gardens.

The Cake of Kings,
The King of Cakes

Every January, pastry shop windows throughout France are filled with tempting golden *galettes des rois*, or kings' cakes, in celebration of the January 6 Feast of the Epiphany, the *fête des rois*. The finest of the round, delicate cakes are made of fine puff pastry and filled with a rich almond pastry cream called *frangipane*, and they have a tiny gold or porcelain charm hidden inside, often representing the infant Jesus. The cakes are always sold with a gold or silver paper crown, to be worn by the lucky person who gets the charm and is crowned "king for a day."

The *galette des rois* custom is said to date to the Romans, who chose a king for their festivals by drawing lots. It came into the Christian tradition in France around the fourteenth century, and the transfer is traced to a group of priests in eastern France who selected a chapel master each Epiphany. They would bake a coin in a loaf of bread and whoever got the coin in his piece of bread was chosen chapel master. Villagers picked up the custom, *gourmandise* intervened, and the bread was replaced by the butter-and-egg-rich brioche. Eventually the *galette des rois* custom spread throughout France. In the south it is still made with brioche, in the north with puff pastry.

The lore surrounding the tradition was enhanced in the sixteenth century, because of a dispute between bakers and pastry chefs. Each group wanted the exclusive right to make and sell the popular cake. The pastry chefs won, but to appease the bakers, King François I gave them the right to do something else. Always enterprising, the bread bakers continued making their trinket-filled bread at Epiphany, but instead of selling the bread, they gave it away. They placed a *fève*, or a dried fava bean, in each loaf. When the cake was cut, whoever found the *fève* in his slice was obliged to offer another *galette,* from the same baker, to someone else. In this way, bakers ensured popularity for themselves and they ultimately also gained the right to sell the *galette des rois.*

There are tales of some miserly *gourmandes* who swallowed the bean to avoid having to buy a *galette* for the crowd. But the bakers scored again: They began putting numerous beans in the *galette,* so that everyone would find a *fève* in his slice. The bean that counted was burned black, so there was always a king, or *roi de fête.* Once the king was crowned, the assembled revelers raised their glasses to proclaim *"Vive le roi! Le roi boit!"* (Long live the king! The king drinks!) as the king was obliged to down a huge glass of wine.

Families also celebrated the *fête des rois,* and in certain regions a slice was saved either for the Virgin Mary or for those who were absent. Families would then watch as the slice aged, as a sign of the absent family member's health: If the cake molded, the person was thought to be very ill. If the cake turned yellow, it was a bad omen indeed.

At the time of the French Revolution, in 1789, the *fête des rois* smacked too much of religion and was seen as anti-civic. So the festival continued as the *fête de bon voisinage,* or neighborliness holiday, and the Epiphany cakes became known as the *galette de l'égalité.* The porcelain baby Jesus was transformed into a *bonnet phrygien,* the red cap worn by Marianne, the symbol of the French Republic, as a symbol of liberty.

LE POTAGER DU ROY

1 Rue du Maréchal-Joffre,
78000 Versailles.
(39.50.35.34).
Last orders taken at 1:45 P.M.
and 9:45 P.M.
Closed Sunday and Monday.
Credit card: V.
Air-conditioned.
English spoken.
90- and 130-franc menus. A
la carte, 250 francs.

SPECIALTIES:
Seasonal; *poissons crus marinés*
(marinated raw fish).

Le Potager du Roy is one of Versailles' best dining bargains, and so it comes as no surprise to find the restaurant full at both lunch and dinner. The fare ranges from the most traditional—foie gras, filet of beef, *jarret de veau,* and *oeufs à la neige*— to more contemporary fare. Some dishes we sampled on the last visit included a light salad of marinated sardines served with a ramekin of tabouli; a cold fresh pasta salad in a creamy but light zucchini sauce; and a fine *charlotte d'aubergines* (eggplant charlotte filled with chunks of flavorful lamb). The orange and brown decor won't exactly cheer you up, but service is swift and friendly.

At the Brasserie du Théâtre.

BRASSERIE DU THEATRE

15 Rue des Réservoirs,
78000 Versailles.
(39.50.03.21).
Last orders taken at 3 P.M.
and 1:30 A.M.
Closed December 25.
Credit card: V
Terrace dining.
English spoken.
250 francs.

SPECIALTIES:
Choucroute (sauerkraut, various sausages, bacon, and pork, served with potatoes), grilled meats.

My first choice for lunch in Versailles is the lively Brasserie du Théâtre, a charmingly decorated turn-of-the-century spot featuring classic bistro fare: *choucroute* and *cassoulet,* salads of herring and *céleri rémoulade,* and a litany of daily specials that might include lamb with white beans or simple grilled sole. This neighborhood brasserie is billed as the Lipp of Versailles, and one can see why. The setting is right out of the movies, with a cast that includes a tall, handsome maître d'hôtel who resembles Roger Moore, and slim mustachioed waiters sporting white aprons that reach down to their toes. Travel posters, antique enamel advertising plaques, and autographed celebrity posters line the walls, while an enormous vase of bright fresh flowers welcomes you, as you enter the dining room.

The Versailles market.

SPECIALITES REGIONALES

POTAGER DU ROY
4 Rue Hardy, 78000
Versailles.
Open for sale of fruits and
vegetables Tuesday and
Friday 8:30 to 11:30 A.M.;
open for sale of
houseplants, flowers, and
herbs Monday through
Friday 8:30 to 11:30 A.M.
Guided tours (in French) of
the king's fruit, flower,
and vegetable gardens for
groups of 20 can be
arranged through the
Tourist Office, 7 Rue des
Réservoirs (39.50.36.22).

Anyone who has ever planted a carrot or a tulip, or watched pear or apple trees miraculously transform white flowers into ripe fruit, will love the Potager du Roy, the king's fruit, flower, and vegetable gardens adjacent to the Versailles *château*. From the looks of the marvelous enclosed gardens (open, unfortunately, only to groups, and by appointment), the court of Louis XIV ate rather well. Greenhouses provided royalty with asparagus in December, cauliflower in March, strawberries in April, and ripe melons each June. In warmer months fig trees grew in pots outside the gardener's lodgings, and the extensive orchards offered pears and apples for the royal table. Today the garden is attached to the national agricultural school, and features extensive greenhouses, plots of experimental flowers and vegetables, plus row after row of astonishing espaliered fruit trees, some with as many as six branches spreading out from the trunk. A few—with fat, gnarled trunks and branches—are more than a hundred years old.

CHEESES OF ILE-DE-FRANCE

1. FOUGERU: An Ile-de-France cow's-milk cheese, essentially the same as Coulommiers but aged with a decorative sprig of fern, or *fougère.*

2. FONTAINEBLEAU: A creamy, white, succulent dessert cheese—made of fresh cow's milk—sold in little white containers lined with cheesecloth. An elegant cheese, it's delicious with fresh strawberries, raspberries, and blueberries.

3. COULOMMIERS: Called "Brie's little brother" because it's about half the size of a Brie de Meaux, this bloomy, fat disc of cow's-milk cheese is a personal favorite, especially when it's well aged and tastes faintly of almonds. It takes a search, but you can still find farm-fresh versions at the cheese shops and market in the charming Ile-de-France village of Coulommiers. Note that the village hosts an annual international cheese fair on the Sunday before Easter.

Bourgogne
BURGUNDY

Chef Edith Remoissenet-Cordier, Le Petit Truc.

Burgundy is, above all, a region in which to feel at home. Town after town, sleepy village after sleepy village, familiar place names tumble past, making even uncommon ground seem friendly.

Mentally, I always divide Burgundy into two distinct areas: I think of the northern portion as gentle Burgundy, the flat to gently rolling land that takes off slowly and easily just an hour's drive south of Paris, passing through the limestone-rich hills of Chablis and ending at the doorstep of the Morvan, a rugged forest thick with oak, beech, and fir. To the south and east falls hearty Burgundy, the land of Charolais beef and lush green vineyards, the stretch of land that flows along the Saône from Dijon on south to Mâcon.

No matter where you wander, as you set foot in brand-name towns like Gevrey-Chambertin or Meursault, Dijon or Epoisses, there's a special sense of excitement, of being back with old friends. Whatever the size of the village, by the very power and prestige of the wines and foods that bear their names, you feel you are not just somewhere, but somewhere important.

The wine country of Burgundy is gift-wrapped France, the land of neat, well-kept parcels of vineyards, protected by decorative iron gates announcing the owner's presence and pride. It's the land

of clustered storybook hamlets, fine wines, deep purple, fragrant *crème de cassis,* of pungent hot mustard and an appealing array of gentle, refined goat's- and cow's-milk cheeses, ranging from the little-known monk's cheese from the Abbaye de Cîteaux to the dense and satisfying cylinder of pure goat's-milk Charolais.

From time to time, Burgundy disappoints. I have searched in vain for an edible version of *pochouse*—a stew that combines all the river fish of the region—always finding it too boney and too meager to count as a gastronomic treat. And I struck out all too often in my search for authentic regional food in small country bistros.

Yet Burgundy always wins me back, in the name of outstanding women like Simone Porcheret, the dedicated cheese merchant in Dijon, and Edith Remoissenet-Cordier of Le Petit Truc outside Beaune, a cook who runs the very sort of home-style restaurant I would love to have someday.

WHEN YOU GO

Michelin Green Guide: *Bourgogne.*

Getting there: Most spots in Burgundy are just a few hours' drive from Paris. Daily there are about ten TGV *(trains à grande vitesse),* or bullet trains, making the 1¾-hour journey between Paris's Gare de Lyon and Dijon and the 1½-hour journey from the Gare de Lyon to Le Creusot/Montceau-les-Mines. Cars can be rented at the train stations.

Getting around: Michelin maps 238 (Centre/Berry-Nivernais), 243 (Bourgogne/Franche-Comté), and 237 (Ile-de-France).

Best time to visit: Because of its popularity, its proximity to Paris, and its wealth of luxury restaurants, Burgundy is worth visiting year-round. The most beautiful months are from late May, when the vineyards begin leafing out, to harvest time, mid to late September.

MARKETS
(Liveliest markets are marked with an asterisk.)

Monday: Saint-Florentin, *Sens.

Tuesday: *Auxerre, Blanzy, Bléneau, Chalon-sur-Saône, Corbigny (second Tuesday of each month), Dijon, Gevrey-Chambertin, Marcigny, Prémery, Saint-Honoré-les-Bains, Villeneuve-sur-Yonne.

Wednesday: Autun, Chalon-sur-Saône, Charolles, Cosne-sur-Loire, Guérigny, Joigny, Noyers, Saint-Sauveur-en-Puisaye.

Thursday: Arnay-le-Duc, Avallon, Chagny, Châtillon-sur-Seine (second Thursday of each month), Donzy, Givry, Pougues-les-Eaux, *Saint-Honoré-les-Bains, Saulieu.

Friday: *Autun, *Auxerre, Auxonne, *Chalon-sur-Saône, Chauffailles, Decize, *Dijon, *Guérigny, Langres, Meursault, Montbard, Nuits-Saint-Georges, Paray-le-Monial, Pouilly-sur-Loire, Saint-Fargeau, Sens, *Villeneuve-sur-Yonne.

Saturday: Auxerre, *Avallon, *Beaune, Bourbon-Lancy, La Charité-sur-Loire, Château-Chinon, Châtillon-sur-Seine, Clamecy, Cluny, Dijon, *Donzy, *Joigny, Mâcon, Nevers, *Prémery, Saint-Honoré-les-Bains, *Saulieu, Seignelay, Tournus.

Sunday: Chablis, *Chagny, Chalon-sur-Saône, Cosne-sur-Loire, *Dijon.

FAIRS AND FESTIVALS

June 30: *Foire aux Cerises* (cherry fair), Escolives-Sainte-Camille.

First Sunday in August: *Fête de l'Andouillette et du Vin Blanc* (chitterling sausage and white wine festival), Clamecy.

Second Sunday in August: *Fête des Myrtilles* (blueberry festival), Glux-en-Glenne.

One Sunday afternoon in mid-August: *Fête de la Moisson* (harvest festival), Saint-Père-sous-Vézelay.

First week in September: *Festival International de Folklore et Fête de la Vigne* (international folklore and wine festival), Dijon.

September 14: *Foire aux Melons et aux Oignons* (melon and onion fair), Joigny.

Last Sunday in October: *Foire aux Marrons* (chestnut fair), Saint-Léger-sous-Beuvray.

First two weeks of November: *Foire Internationale Gastronomique* (international food fair), Dijon.

Summer fruits at the Dijon market.

ARNAY-LE-DUC *(Côte-d'Or)*

Autun 28 k, Beaune 34 k, Chagny 40 k, Dijon 57 k, Paris 287 k, Saulieu 28 k.

Market: Thursday, 8 A.M. to 1 P.M., Place de la Poste.

MUSEE

MAISON REGIONALE DES ARTS DE LA TABLE
15 Rue Saint-Jacques, 21230 Arnay-le-Duc.
(80.90.11.59).
Open from Easter through mid-October only, 10 A.M. to noon and 2 to 6 P.M. Closed Monday from Easter through May and from September through mid-October.
Admission: 10 francs; 5 francs per person for groups of 10 or more.

This compact, well-organized regional museum is dedicated to gastronomy in its many aspects. We visited as they were exploring the egg in all its forms—in folklore, religion, art, history, and in cooking, with careful, humorous displays of everything from wicker egg baskets to chicken cages, chocolate egg molds, and even unusual antique metal baskets for roasting eggs (yes, imagine!) over a wood-burning fire. They had organized collections of old and new eggbeaters, omelet pans, and hundreds of decorative egg cups. A folkloric tip: If you gather eggs on *Vendredi Saint* (Good Friday), they will never, ever spoil. As positive proof, the museum exhibited an egg collected on Good Friday in 1957, still intact and without a discernible odor (at least as it stood protected behind glass).

BEAUNE *(Côte-d'Or)*

Autun 48 k, Auxerre 131 k, Chalon-sur-Saône 30 k, Dijon 45 k, Paris 313 k.

Market: Saturday, 8 A.M. to 1 P.M., Place de la Halle.

RESTAURANT

LE PETIT TRUC
Place de l'Eglise, Vignoles, 21200 Beaune.
(80.22.01.76).
Last orders taken at 1 P.M. and 9 P.M.
Closed Monday, Tuesday, two weeks in February, and two weeks in August.
No credit cards.
Terrace dining in summer.
Reservations essential.
175-franc menu. A la carte, about 250 francs.

Le Petit Truc is one of those restaurants destined to breed controversy. Over the years, friends with palates I highly respect have returned from this country cottage dining room just outside Beaune with drastically different reports. "Inedible," glowered one. "Superlative," glowed another.

I seem to hit chef Edith Remoissenet-Cordier on her good days, for everything from the *salade paysanne au lard* (tender curly endive, delicious bacon cubes, sliced cooked potatoes, snipped fresh herbs) to the tasty, meaty *petit salé aux pommes de terre à la crème* (fresh salt pork with potatoes and cream)

SPECIALTIES:
Terrine de veau au Chablis
(terrine of veal with Chablis),
poulet au vinaigre (chicken with
vinegar), *tarte tiède au chocolat*
(warm chocolate cake).

was as good and as homey as one could hope.

It's hard not to fall in love with the decor: The tiny, tidy dining room—actually the front parlor of an old stone *presbytère,* or parsonage—boasts an enormous central hearth, and refectory tables are set with long table runners, lace doilies, fresh flowers, and shiny brass candlesticks. Add the church bells that chime in as you work your way through the meal, and this is about as quaint as you can get without being tacky. Be forewarned that the chef takes no more than twenty guests per meal. And don't bother coming unless you've phoned in advance, for you're very likely to be turned away.

(Directions: From Beaune take the D973 east toward Seurre. As soon as you cross the bridge over the *autoroute* just outside Beaune, look sharp: Take the first left—there is a minuscule "Petit Truc" sign at this corner—and go about 2 kilometers to Vignoles, which also is often spelled Vignolles. The restaurant does not have a sign, but you'll recognize it as the lovely parsonage next to the church.)

Contented cows, for Burgundian cheese.

CHARCUTERIE

ROGER BATTEAULT
4 Rue Monge, 21200
   Beaune.
(80.22.23.04).
Open 8 A.M. to 12:30 P.M.
   and 2:30 to 7 P.M.
   Tuesday through
   Saturday; 9 A.M. to noon
   Sunday in August and
   September. Closed
   Sunday off-season,
   Monday, and school
   holidays in February.

You can't travel to Burgundy without sampling *jambon persillé,* that delicious cold poached ham, cubed and layered with parsleyed gelatin. Try it here, served out of white porcelain crocks, along with their homemade dried pork sausage, *rosette artisanale.* The shop also stocks the top-of-the-line Fallot products: whole-grain and flavored mustards, vinegar, sherry wine vinegar, and capers. On Saturday mornings the line of customers stretches out from this tiny shop into the Rue Monge. It's right up the street from the open market.

SPECIALITES REGIONALES

FALLOT ET COMPAGNIE
31 Rue du Faubourg
  Bretonnière, 21200
  Beaune.
(80.22.10.02).
Open 8 to 11:30 A.M. and
  1:30 to 6 P.M. (5 P.M. on
  Friday). Closed Saturday,
  Sunday, and August.
Will ship internationally.

Paris Connection:
JARDIN EN L'ILE
8 Rue Jean-du-Bellay, 75004
  Paris.
(43.26.08.63).

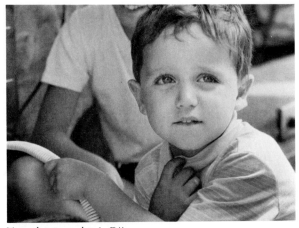

To market, to market, in Dijon.

S ome of the best—and hottest—mustard in France is made not in Dijon, but in Beaune, where you'll find a fine artisanal *moutarderie* located right in the center of town. (See "The Sauce with *un Goût du Diable*," page 188.)

BOUZE-LES-BEAUNE *(Côte-d'Or)*

Autun 55 k, Beaune 7 k, Dijon 46 k.

RESTAURANT

LA BOUZEROTTE
Bouze-lès-Beaune, 21200
  Beaune.
(80.26.01.37).
Last orders taken at 1:30 P.M.
  and 9 P.M.
Closed Monday, Tuesday,
  and August.
No credit cards.
About 100 francs.

S P E C I A L T I E S :
Simple home-cooked fare,
salads, omelets, and tarts.

A s you drive up to La Bouzerotte, a humble dining room set in the heart of Cassis and *framboise* country, you just might find the chef out in his roadside garden, picking a basket of greens for your lunch. Inside, the decor is serviceable at best, and the menu is a dream for those who crave the most basic French fare: a crispy salad showered with homemade croutons and sizzling *lardons* (here, of course, it's the *salade Bouzerotte*), a hefty omelet stuffed with thick slices of potatoes and *lardons,* both sautéed to a crispy brown (see recipe, following page), and a perfectly decent cheese tray that includes a fine local *chèvre.* For dessert the chef just might have prepared a fragrant raspberry tart (you'll know by the aroma and the flavor that the fruit was picked at its peak) or another fruit offering layered with sunset-orange apricots.

OMELETTE PAYSANNE LA BOUZEROTTE
LA BOUZEROTTE'S BACON, ONION, AND POTATO OMELET

My friend the wine merchant Kermit Lynch first took me to La Bouzerotte—a modest little restaurant by the side of the road—several years ago, when I was accompanying him on a wine-buying tour. After sampling wines all morning long, this unpretentious place really hit the spot, as did their earthy bacon, onion, and potato omelet.

4 ounces (125 g) slab bacon or side pork, rind removed, cut into 1 x ½-inch (4 x 2.5 cm) pieces

2 medium onions, coarsely chopped

2 tablespoons (1 ounce 30 g) unsalted butter

2 small potatoes peeled and thinly sliced

6 large eggs, gently beaten

1. Place the bacon and onion in a large (10- to 12-inch; 25 to 30 cm) nonstick skillet. Turn the heat to medium-high and cook, stirring frequently, until the bacon is crisp and the onions are cooked through.

2. Remove the onions and bacon from the pan and set aside.

3. Add the butter to the same skillet and heat over medium-high heat until the butter is hot but not smoking. Add the potatoes. Brown the potatoes evenly on one side, then turn and brown the other side. Spread them in a fairly even layer on the bottom of the pan.

4. Sprinkle the onions and bacon over the potatoes, without disturbing the arrangement of the potatoes. Then carefully pour the eggs evenly over the onions and bacon and tilt the pan from side to side to allow the eggs to run to the bottom. When the underside of the omelet begins to set, use a fork to lift the edges of the omelet and carefully fold the edges in toward the center. Invert a large plate on top of the omelet and turn the pan over onto the plate. Serve immediately, with plenty of toasted homemade bread.

Yield: 4 servings

CHAGNY *(Saône-et-Loire)*

Autun 43 k, Beaune 15 k, Chalon-sur-Saône 17 k, Paris 328 k.

Market: Thursday and Sunday, 8 A.M. to 1:30 P.M., Place de la Mairie, Rue du Bourg, Rue du Théâtre, Place du Théâtre.

RESTAURANT

LAMELOISE
36 Place d'Armes, 71150
  Chagny.
(85.87.08.85).
Last orders taken at 1:30 P.M.
  and 9:15 P.M.
Closed Wednesday,
  Thursday lunch, and the
  last week in December
  through the third week
  in January.
Credit card: V.
One air-conditioned dining
  room.
Private dining room for 25.
English spoken.
230- and 370-franc menus.
  A la carte, 450 francs.

S P E C I A L T I E S :
Ravioli d'escargots (snail-filled
ravioli), *pigeon de Bresse en vessie*
(Bresse pigeon poached in a
pig's bladder), *assiette du
chocolatier* (dish of assorted
chocolate desserts).

The ambience at Lameloise, a fifteenth-century house that's been enlarged bit by bit, is one of subdued sophistication, but it is not without humor. As you walk in the door, you're greeted by a bright, playful bowl of *trompe l'oeil* fruits and vegetables, created by the Lameloise chefs. The decor is both Burgundian—beamed ceilings, heavy upholstered chairs—and contemporary, lightened by flashes of white on the walls, the linens, even in the flowers carefully arranged at each table.

All this is in strong contrast to Jacques Lameloise, perhaps the most easy-going and modest grand chef in France. He likes to think of himself as a tradesman, a carpenter, a plumber, a mason, who succeeds by making his customers happy so they'll want to come back. He's not an intellectual and he says, self-critically, that he's probably read three books in his life, and those were cookbooks.

But Monsier Lameloise's cuisine shows a sophistication and understanding that far surpasses his self-image. Excellence and simplicity are his key attributes: a tiny wedge of *foie gras* simply sautéed, sprinkled with vinegar and a dose of fresh chives; plump *escargots* wrapped in pasta dough to form bite-size ravioli, cooked in a straightforward, garlic-infused bouillon. Langoustines, asparagus, and chervil bathed in just a *soupçon* of coral-colored cream. And the *pièce de résistance:* plump, moist pigeon breast thickly coated with finely minced truffles, served with just a bit of fragrant cooking juices. (All this does not mean there's not an occasional culinary flaw: At one meal, the *foie gras* was a bit stringy and the langoustines arrived slightly soggy.)

The Lameloise cheese tray is a tribute to Burgundy's wealth of cheeses: the Epoisses aged to a creamy richness, like none you'll find outside the region; and a superb *fromage blanc,* served with a touch of cream and sugar.

The wine list would make for a good night's reading, and wine service is equally impressive. Two wines highly recommended by Georges Pertuiset, named *Meilleur Sommelier de France* in 1980, are the Chassagne-Montrachet of Delagrange-Bachelet and the Volnay, Clos des Duc, Domaine Marquis d'Angerville. Other regional wines to look out for: François Jobart's Meursault; Domaine Leflaive's Chevalier Montrachet; Domaine Tollot-Beaut's Chorey-lès-Beaune; and Henri Jayer's Vosne-Romanée.

CHALON-SUR-SAONE *(Saône-et-Loire)*

Dijon 68 k, Mâcon 58 k, Paris 337 k.

Markets: Tuesday, 8 A.M. to noon, La Cité des Aubépins; Wednesday, 8 A.M. to noon, Les Prés Saint-Jean; Thursday, 8 A.M. to noon, La Cité du Stade; Friday and Sunday, 8 A.M. to noon, Place Saint-Vincent.

POUR LA MAISON

LES IMPITOYABLES
8 Impasse de la Tranchée,
   71108 Chalon-sur-Saône.
(85.48.17.81).
Open 9 A.M. to 5 P.M. Closed
   Saturday, Sunday,
   Monday, and August.

They call these huge and rather awkward-looking wine glasses *les impitoyables* because they take no pity on flawed wine. That is, these tall glasses with a wide base and a sharply narrowed rim are designed to show up the worst, and the best, qualities of a wine. The roomy bottom allows you to vigorously swirl your wine without fear of spilling, giving the wine plenty of breathing room, while the narrow opening helps retain the bouquet. I find them rather awkward to drink from (you really have to raise your glass and tilt your head way back for even just a sip), but they do impose a certain sense of discipline. Guzzlers need not apply!

DIJON *(Côte-d'Or)*

Auxerre 149 k, Beaune 45 k, Paris 312 k.

Market: Tuesday, Friday, and Saturday, 8 A.M. to 12:30 P.M., along the four
streets surrounding the covered market: Rue Bannelier, Rue Quentin, Rue
C.-Ramey, Rue Odebert.
Festival International de Folklore et Fête de Vigne (international folklore and wine
festival): first week in September.
Foire Internationale Gastronomique (international food fair): first two
weeks of November.

The lively city of Dijon offers an exceptional fruit and vegetable market,
located in a large covered market in the center of town. On the busiest day,
Friday, farmers come from the surrounding villages with their chickens and
mushrooms, fresh asparagus, and assorted vegetables.

RESTAURANT

**RESTAURANT
JEAN-PIERRE
BILLOUX**
14 Place Darcy, 21000
Dijon.
(80.30.11.00).
Last orders taken at 2 P.M.
and 9:30 P.M.
Closed Sunday dinner and
Monday.
Credit cards: AE, DC, V.
Terrace dining at lunch.
Air-conditioned.
Private dining room for 15.
English spoken.
200- and 335-franc menus.
A la carte, 300 francs.

SPECIALITES:
Change with the seasons.

Rue de la Liberté, Dijon.

In January 1986, the talented, mild-mannered
Jean-Pierre Billoux made a wise move. He gathered up his copper pots, his staff, and his wine
cellar and left the quiet Burgundian village of
Digoin for the brighter lights of Dijon. Monsieur
Billoux's new establishment manages to combine a
sense of luxury with a sense of familiarity. The
adjacent Hôtel de la Cloche serves as a fine (though
relatively expensive) base, and the choice of three
dining rooms means that even if you stay on a few
days, you can change scenery as you work your way
through his appealing menu.

At lunch, guests are seated in a large mirrored
and plant-filled dining room, while dinners are held
in a nicely appointed vaulted wine cellar just below.

On those days the sun chooses to shine, there's also a lovely enclosed garden for more informal meals.

Chef Billoux's cuisine is original, almost intellectual, but not the least bit contrived.

When I study a menu, there are certain ingredients—foods that I love—that jump out at me. If I spy lentils or red beans, anchovies, garlic, or anything that might even vaguely resemble a serious salad, I mentally begin to applaud.

In one way or another Billoux weaves all of these in, with remarkable success. The best dishes sampled here include a refreshing first-course salad of poached baby vegetables—the slimmest leeks, green beans, tiny carrots, cherry tomatoes, and asparagus bathed in a delicate vinaigrette; oven-baked salmon filets paired with a pleasantly assertive anchovy sauce; sweetbreads set on a bed of perfectly seasoned, creamy lentils; and an unusual sautéed scallops in a red wine sauce.

Though the food sounds fussy, it's not, for each dish seems to make a solid statement of its own. Also not to be missed are the chef's crusty homemade rolls and the exquisite cheese selection from the local cheese merchant Simone Porcheret. The accommodating service and the extensive wine list help to make this one of Burgundy's most appealing dining spots.

KIR

The sweet, fruity, and colorful combination of white wine and *crème de cassis* (black currant liqueur) has long been a traditional Burgundian aperitif, known simply as *vin blanc cassis*. But the drink took on added fame during the 1940s, when Dijon's mayor, canon Kir, lent his name to the popular drink. Legend holds that local Cassis sales were flagging, so the publicity-conscious mayor began serving Kir at all official city functions, a tradition that continues to this day. The classic recipe calls for one-third Cassis and two-thirds Burgundian white Aligoté, although most cafés and restaurants have lightened it up a bit, reducing the quantity of the more expensive Cassis to one quarter. Also popular is the *Kir royal,* Kir blended with Champagne.

PATISSERIE

MULOT ET PETITJEAN
13 Place Bossuet, 21000
Dijon.
also 16 Rue de la Liberté,
21000 Dijon.
(80.30.07.10).
Open daily 9 A.M. to noon
and 2 to 7 P.M.
Will ship internationally.

*P*ain d'épice, or spice bread, has long been a specialty of Dijon, and this is one of the spice bread landmarks. With their fetchingly old-fashioned packaging, Mulot et Petitjean's shops offer spice bread in every imaginable form: stuffed with jam, covered in chocolate, covered in a light sugar coating, mixed with nuts, plain, in loaves, in small cakes. Also a good source for both Maille and Fallot brand mustards, nougat, candied orange slices, and *crème de cassis.*

BOULANGERIE

AU PAIN D'AUTREFOIS
47 Rue du Bourg, 21000
Dijon.
(80.30.47.92).
Open 8 A.M. to 12:30 P.M.
and 3 to 7 P.M. Closed
Sunday, Monday, two
weeks in February, and
two weeks in July.

*A*fter marketing for cheese at Simone Porcheret's (see below), complete the picnic with a few loaves of bread from this decorative little shop. They offer breads flavored with raisins, nuts, cumin, and sesame, all baked in a wood-fired oven.

Simone Porcheret, a model cheese merchant.

FROMAGERIE

SIMONE PORCHERET
14 Rue Bannelier, 21000
Dijon.
(80.30.21.05).
Open 8 A.M. to 12:30 P.M.
and 3 to 7 P.M. Closed
Sunday, and Monday
afternoon.
Will ship in Europe.

*S*imone Porcheret's tidy cheese shop near Dijon's central market resembles a model cheese museum: wooden butter molds, pottery cheese-draining cups, butter churns, and decorated breads share the compact, fragrant space with the finest, most carefully aged cheeses of the region. The friendly, attractive Madame Porcheret offers an excellent Charolais, glows with pride over her Reblochon, seeks out goat cheese of every age and size, from creamy fresh to briefly aged, from *coulant,* or runny, to mottled and rock hard. She knows her business well, and when it comes to *affinage,* or the aging of cheese, she has a specific point of view: "I like my cheese to be well aged, but not too far gone or bitter," she explains. "If the cheese is overripe, you'll spoil our Burgundy wine." Her boutique is exceptionally fragrant, for it opens right into one of her cheese-aging *caves.*

CHARCUTERIE

**LA BOUCHERIE
NOUVELLE**
27 Rue Pasteur, 21000
Dijon.
(80.66.37.10).
Open 7:30 A.M. to 12:45 P.M.
and 3 to 7:45 P.M. Closed
Thursday afternoon,
Sunday, and August.

A worthy address, worth the detour, for their award-winning *jambon persillé* (cold poached ham, cubed and layered with parsleyed gelatin).

VIN, BIERE, ALCOOL

LA COUR AUX VINS
3 Rue Jeannin, 21000 Dijon.
(80.67.85.14).
Open 9 A.M. to 12:30 P.M.
and 2 to 7 P.M. Closed
Sunday, and Monday
morning. Open daily for
prearranged group wine
tastings.
Credit cards: AE, DC, V.
Will ship in France.

For those special wine-tasting glasses called *les impitoyables,* and Lucien Jacob's fine *crème de cassis* and *crème de framboise.*

POUR LA MAISON

ANDRE GRILLOT
4 Place François-Rude,
21000 Dijon.
(80.30.18.97).
Open 9 A.M. to noon and 2
to 7 P.M. Closed Sunday
and four weeks during
the year.

A funky little hardware shop specializing in *articles de cave et cadeaux* (wine cellar accessories and gifts): everything you need to make wine, or pretend you do, from wine labels, to corks, to small aging barrels for making your own vinegar.

The Grey-Poupon mustard shop.

SPECIALITES REGIONALES

GREY-POUPON
32 Rue de la Liberté, 21000
    Dijon.
(80.30.41.02).
Open 9:15 A.M. to noon and
    2:15 to 7 P.M. Closed
    Sunday and holidays.
Credit cards: EC, V.
International mail orders
    accepted December
    through May.

SPECIALTIES:
Mustards and antique
mustard jars.

Dijon is clearly the world mustard capital and it also has one of the few shops in the world devoted exclusively to mustard. The jewel-like Grey-Poupon boutique sells not only mustard but also beautiful hand-painted porcelain mustard jars, reproductions of the many museum-quality antique mustard pots that decorate the shop. The jars make excellent gifts and souvenirs and are pretty enough to make one want to begin a collection. (See "The Sauce with *un Goût du Diable,*" following page.)

SAISONS DES HALLES
26 Rue Odebert, 21000
    Dijon.
(80.30.45.98).
Open 6 A.M. to 12:30 P.M.
    and 3 to 7:30 P.M. Closed
    Monday.

SPECIALTY:
Primeurs (greengrocery).

Near the covered market, a superb greengrocer, with exquisitely fresh fruits and vegetables and lush herbs.

Dijon's lively covered market.

The Sauce with "un Goût du Diable"

"*A* *lexandre Dumas reported that in Paris, at 9 o'clock in the morning and 6 in the evening, the only people one met on the streets were children on their way to buy a centime's worth of mustard.*"

DIJON, APRIL 30—With an assertiveness and a pungency powerful enough to bring tears to the eyes, mustard is the king of French condiments. It's hard to imagine that this common household staple, a simple blend of ground mustard seeds and vinegar or slightly fermented wine, marketed in ordinary reusable supermarket tumblers, could have such a regal history.

King Louis XI, who often invited himself to supper on very short notice, always traveled with a jar of his private-blend mustard. The Dukes of Burgundy, ardent defenders of their local *moutarde de Dijon,* never left for battle without a supply. Even Pope John XXII—said to be passionately fond of mustard—appointed a private *moutardier,* or mustard maker, at the court in Avignon.

Mustard was such a gastronomic rage during the eighteenth and nineteenth centuries that one chronicler counted ninety-three varieties, including those flavored with nasturtiums, roses, anchovies, garlic, even truffles. Even back then it was a competitive market, requiring some clever salesmanship. One firm offered special mustards for men (they were the sturdy, pungent varieties) and special blends for women (delicate mustards better suited to the sensitive female palate).

Well into the nineteenth century, mustard was purchased fresh daily, like bread or coffee beans, from special mustard shops. Shoppers would bring their individual pots to be filled with a day's supply. Alexandre Dumas reported that in Paris, at 9 o'clock in the morning and 6 in the evening, the only people one met on the streets were children on their way to buy a centime's worth of mustard.

Today in Dijon, the mustard capital of the world, shoppers can still buy mustard the old-fashioned way at the Grey-Poupon boutique, which is decorated with dozens of colorful hand-painted mustard jars. The shop serves as a museum-like monument to the creamy-smooth, pale yellow condiment the French say has *un goût du diable,* a taste of the devil.

Dijon has long reigned as France's mustard capital, largely as a result of geography. In Gallo-Roman times, Dijon was along the spice route, and so the population became accustomed to heartily spiced foods. When the spice route shifted, the Dijonnais needed a substitute.

Wild mustard grew freely in the area, so the locals began to mix *verjus*—the acidic fermented juice of unripe grapes—with the dried grains of mustard, producing the whole-grain mustard we now call *moutarde à l'ancienne.* It was the *verjus* that distinguished Dijon mustard from all the rest.

Today those mustard fields have been replaced by a related crop, bright golden–flowered *colza,* used to produce rapeseed oil. French farmers have found it more lucrative to grow rapeseed than to grow mustard, and today the best mustard seeds are imported from Canada. And instead of *verjus,* either vinegar or slightly fermented wine is used.

While the town of Dijon gave its name to the popular *moutarde de Dijon* (and still produces about 70 percent of France's mustard), the name actually refers to the style of pungent, creamy-smooth mustard developed there. Legally, *moutarde de Dijon* can be made anywhere, and in fact some of the best French mustard is made nearby in Beaune, at the small artisanal *moutarderie* of Edmond Fallot. Here mustard is made the old-fashioned way in giant oak barrels painted a folkloric mustard yellow and trimmed in bold red: Dark brown mustard seeds are macerated with white wine vinegar (or with slightly fermented white wine), salt, and water, then ground to a paste with extra-hard flint stones.

For a sharp, smooth, creamy-yellow Dijon mustard, the hulls are sifted out by centrifuge. For a milder whole-grain mustard the hulls are left in. It's the light yellow flour inside the hull of the mustard grain that gives it the lovely color. But since this color fades as the mustard is exposed to air, a touch of golden turmeric is added to give it a bit of a boost.

What gives mustard its pungency? It's the volatile enzyme allyl senevol, which is released when the mustard seed is ground to a fine flour. Dark seeds— actually dark reddish brown—produce a pungent mustard, light seeds a mild one.

Fallot, which packages their mustard for a number of top French restaurants including Georges Blanc, Troisgros, and Tour d'Argent, also sells the same product to the Franprix supermarket chain in Paris. Their mustards can be found in specialty shops all over Beaune and Dijon, as well as at the Charles de Gaulle duty-free shops in Paris.

Roger Désarmenien, the Fallot company's friendly director, offers a few tips on mustard use: Mustard does not spoil, but once a jar is opened it begins to lose pungency, so buy mustard in small containers. If a pungent flavor is desired when cooking with mustard, open a fresh jar and add the mustard at the very last minute, for pungency fades as mustard is heated.

MUSEE

MUSEE DES BEAUX ARTS
Place de la Sainte-Chapelle,
    21000 Dijon.
(80.30.31.11).
Open 10 A.M. to 6 P.M. (10
    A.M. to 12:30 P.M. and 2 to
    6 P.M. Sunday). Closed
    Tuesday, holidays, and
    the first week in May.
Admission: About 8 francs;
    half price for groups of
    20 or more.

The ground floor of the museum houses one of the most incredible kitchens you're likely to encounter: the fifteenth-century cooking chambers of the original palace of the dukes of Burgundy, boasting six gigantic open chimneys.

*An after-lunch chat at
Le Petit Truc.*

ECHEVRONNE *(Côte-d'Or)*

Aloxe-Corton 5 k, Corgoloin 6 k, Dijon 35 k, Nuits-Saint-Georges 13 k.

VIGNERON

LUCIEN JACOB
Echevronne, 21420
    Savigny-lès-Beaune.
(80.21.52.15).
Open by appointment.
Will ship in Europe.

What makes an exceptional *crème de cassis?* Top-quality black currants (the *noir de Bourgogne* variety is preferred), careful harvesting, and just the right amount of sugar. The Jacob family, which also makes a Savigny wine, oversees 24 hectares (almost 60 acres) of black currants right outside of Beaune. They harvest the ripe fruit in July, macerate the berries with alcohol, then sweeten them lightly, to make a brilliant, fragrant drink for mixing with white wine or pouring over fresh peaches. *Crème de cassis* is a very delicate product, and the Jacobs advise that it should be consumed within a year of bottling. And once a bottle is opened, it should be refrigerated and consumed within a month.

EGRISELLES-LE-BOCAGE *(Yonne)*

Joigny 28 k, Villeneuve-sur-Yonne 11 k.

FROMAGER

JACQUES LANGLOIS
Les Régipaux,
  Egriselles-le-Bocage,
  89500 Villeneuve-
  sur-Yonne.
(86.86.01.48).
Open 10 A.M. to noon
  and 3 to 5 P.M. Closed
  Wednesday, and
  November through
  March.

Paris Connection:
  **FROMAGERIE
  MARIE-ANNE CANTIN**
12 Rue du Champ-de-Mars,
  75007 Paris.
(45.50.43.94).

Just an hour or so south of Paris lies the you'll-miss-it-if-you-blink hamlet of Les Régipaux, site of the Langlois family farm, where you'll find sixty fawn-colored Alpine goats and some of the simplest, freshest goat cheese around. Each day, working in tandem, Jacques and Claude Langlois transform some 150 liters (quarts) of fresh goat's milk into pure white, dimpled discs of goat cheese.

"Nothing could be simpler, and there's no secret. Know the acidity of your milk, and pay attention to cleanliness," explains Monsieur Langlois as he leads a tour of the *laiterie* (dairy).

His delicate cheese is cured for just three to four days, and once a week he carefully packs his bounty into a small truck and heads for Paris, where he delivers the fresh cheese to some twenty *fromageries* around town. Although the Langlois family is not set up for full-fledged tours, they are happy to welcome individual visitors, who may purchase the cheese directly from the farm.

EPOISSES *(Côte-d'Or)*

Joigny 85 k, Saulieu 36 k.

FROMAGER

FROMAGERIE BERTHAUT
Place Champ-de-Foire,
  21460 Epoisses.
(80.96.44.44).
Open 9 A.M. to noon and 3
  to 6 P.M. Closed Sunday.
Credit card: V.

**PARIS CONNECTION:
ALAIN DUBOIS**
80 Rue de Tocqueville,
  75017 Paris.
(42.27.11.38).

Epoisses is one of dozens of French villages with a reputation that's far grander than the place itself. This sleepy, modest town of just 600 inhabitants is known around the world for its moist and buttery cow's-milk cheese, a rust-colored disc that is aged slowly, washed daily with *marc de Bourgogne,* the raw and fiery regional *eau-de-vie.*

The Berthaut family makes a stunning and classic Epoisses, prepared from the fresh raw cow's milk of the region. Although Epoisses has been made in the village ever since the vegetarian Cistercian monks began preparing the cheese in the sixteenth century, production all but ceased between the two world wars as farmers went off to battle.

Local handmade production was resumed in 1946 when, at the urging of friends and family, Robert Berthaut began making the lively little cheese they all remembered from childhood. He worked from his own memory—as a youngster he used to watch while his aunt prepared and aged the cheese for the family's consumption—and before long his milk, his neighbor's milk, the entire village's milk, went toward the production of the newly revived Epoisses.

"Today our population is the same as it was centuries ago, and we make just about the same number of discs of cheese each day, as well, about 1,500," explains Monsieur Berthaut as he heads a tour of his spotless cheesemaking facility.

Curiously, though many cheesemakers have tried, the true and classic Epoisses cannot be made with pasteurized milk. It doesn't age properly, for the bacteria that gives the raw-milk cheese its flavor and life are killed off during pasteurization. The Berthaut family offers their mildly pungent Epoisses, aged for about five weeks in the *laiterie,* along with the younger fresh (and rather bland) Epoisses *blanc* and the cinder-covered Aisy Cendré.

GEVREY-CHAMBERTIN *(Côte-d'Or)*

Beaune 27 k, Dijon 12 k, Paris 313 k.

Market: Tuesday, 7:30 A.M. to noon, Place du Marché, Avenue de Nierstein.

RESTAURANT

LES MILLESIMES
25 Rue de l'Eglise, 21220
  Gevrey-Chambertin.
(80.51.84.24).
Last orders taken at 1:30 P.M.
  and 9 P.M.
Closed Wednesday lunch
  and Tuesday.

Wine, wine, more wine, and beautiful bread and cheese are served in a friendly atmosphere in this restaurant fashioned out of an authentic winemaking cellar in the center of this charming, active Burgundian village. I can't be as enthusiastic about the food, which seems like an afterthought: The grilled turbot certainly appeared

Credit cards: AE, DC, V.
Air-conditioned.
250-franc menu. A la carte,
about 400 francs.

SPECIALTIES:
Ris de veau braisés (braised veal
sweetbreads), *carré d'agneau
rôti* (crown roast of lamb),
galette de truffes et foie gras
(round flat cake of truffles
and *foie gras*).

baked, and tasted simply mushy and bland; the langoustine salad was only ordinary; the wild blueberry tart undercooked. But you'll swoon over the wine list (page after page of local Burgundies) and will certainly be enraptured by the cheese tray. Be sure to try the selections in this order, for best enjoyment: the mild Abbaye de Cîteaux, the spicy Langres, the beautifully aged Ami du Chambertin, and finally, the earthy Epoisses. Served with delicious bread, walnuts, and a smile! Do ask to visit the impeccable wine cellar.

FROMAGER

LAITERIE DE LA COTE
14 Rue de la Maladière,
   Brochon, 21220
   Gevrey-Chambertin.
   (80.52.45.55).
Open 8 A.M. to noon and
   3:30 to 6:30 P.M. Closed
   Wednesday and Sunday.

This unassuming little dairy/*épicerie* at the outskirts of Gevrey-Chambertin supplies nearly all of the restaurants and cheese shops in the area. Best bets here are Ami du Chambertin (a pleasant cow's-milk cheese that, like Epoisses, is washed with *marc de Bourgogne* as it ages), Saint-Vincent (also similar to Epoisses, but aged a bit longer, so it's stronger) and, of course, Epoisses.

*The community bread oven of
Fixey.*

SPECIALITES
REGIONALES

FOUR BANAL DE FIXEY

Along the side of the road in the tiny hamlet of Fixey (4 kilometers north of Gevrey-Chambertin via the D122), you'll find a beautifully restored community bread oven, known as a *four banal,* where just around the time of the grape harvest in early September, the local residents fire up the large brick oven and celebrate their harvest with a bread-baking *fête.*

JOIGNY *(Yonne)*

Auxerre 27 k, Dijon 168k, Paris 148 k.

Market: Wednesday and Saturday, 8 A.M. to noon, Place du Marché.
Foire aux Melons et aux Oignons (melon and onion fair): September 14.

RESTAURANT

LA COTE SAINT-JACQUES
14 Faubourg de Paris, 89300
  Joigny.
(86.62.09.70).
Last orders taken at 2 P.M.
  and 9:30 P.M.
Closed the last three weeks
  in January.
Credit cards: AE, DC, V.
English spoken.
About 500 francs.

SPECIALTIES:
Change with the seasons.

Ever since 1952, when Marie Lorain opened her solid brick boarding house along the Yonne river in northern Burgundy, La Côte Saint-Jacques has been a family affair. Little could she have imagined, however, that a few decades later her son, Michel, his wife, and their children would have transformed the eighteenth-century *maison bourgeoise* into one of France's most coveted hotel and restaurant complexes.

While Michel and his son, Jean-Michel, share duties in the kitchen, Michel's wife, Jacqueline, develops their growing wine *cave.* Their daughter, Catherine, handles accounting, and Jean-Michel's wife, Brigitte, directs the hotel and restaurant reception.

Like many father-and-son teams in the kitchen, Michel and Jean-Michel seem to have responsibilities clearly worked out. While the father's tastes run toward "quiet," unaggressive foods that don't attack the palate, son Jean-Michel enjoys creating more assertive combinations, such as his popular salmon with curry spices, and the simple, inspired, and colorful chilled gazpacho, topped with quickly roasted langoustines and little dollops of *crème de courgette* (see recipe, facing page).

The menu changes frequently, but if you have the chance, try Michel Lorain's superb *bar au beurre de truffes,* a rather sinfully elegant dish combining the freshest sea bass, oh-so-lightly cooked, with pure essence of truffle.

Jacqueline's wine cellar offers a generous selection of local Chablis, including one of her favorites, the Grand Cru Chablis "les Clos" from Domaine Pinson in Chablis.

Chocolate lovers are advised to save room for Jean-Michel's creation of three chocolate desserts on a single plate: He offers a scoop of chocolate ice cream, a chocolate layer cake (much like thin chocolate bars layered with chocolate mousse), and a chocolate soufflé, all served with a rich *crème anglaise*, or custard sauce.

LE GASPACHO DE CREVETTE A LA CREME DE COURGETTE
GAZPACHO WITH SHRIMP AND ZUCCHINI MOUSSE

This is the creation of chef Jean-Michel Lorain of La Côte Saint-Jacques in Joigny. I love the play of colors, textures, flavors in this dish. The acidity of the gazpacho, the creamy zucchini, and then the moist, salty shrimp or prawns make for a superb and unusual soup. Be sure that the soup is well chilled and served in chilled bowls, so that the hot shrimp will pose a nice contrast. If you can, grill the shellfish over an open fire—the smoky flavor will add another dimension.

Gazpacho:
1 clove garlic
5 medium tomatoes cored and quartered
1 small red bell pepper, stem and seeds removed, quartered
1 small cucumber, peeled, ends trimmed, quartered lengthwise
1 medium onion, peeled and quartered
2 tablespoons best-quality red wine vinegar
Salt and freshly ground pepper to taste

Zucchini mousse:
1 medium zucchini
¼ cup (60 ml) heavy cream, preferably not ultra-pasteurized

20 large prawns or shrimp (31 to 35 count per pound), peeled and deveined
1 tablespoon virgin olive oil

1. Prepare the gazpacho: Mince the garlic in a food processor. Add the remaining ingredients and process until thoroughly blended. Season with salt and pepper. The soup should be fairly thick. Refrigerate until just before serving. The soup should be served the day it is prepared.

2. Just before serving, prepare the zucchini mousse: Heat a small pot of water to a boil. Finely chop the zucchini in a food processor. Blanch the zucchini in the boiling water for several minutes, drain, rinse with cold water to stop the cooking, and pat dry. Whip the cream until stiff, then fold in the zucchini. Season to taste with salt and pepper.

3. Brush the prawns with oil and broil or grill just until they are opaque and still resilient but not too firm, about 2 minutes on each side.

4. To serve, ladle the gazpacho into 4 chilled shallow soup bowls. Arrange the prawns in a circle on top of the soup. Using a melon baller or pastry bag fitted with a large round tip, shape the zucchini mousse into balls and arrange them between the prawns. Serve immediately. If any zucchini mousse remains, pass it in a small bowl.

Yield: 4 servings.

ECOLE DE CUISINE

CHATEAU DU FEY
Villecien, 89300 Joigny.

Anne Willan, president and founder of Paris's respected La Varenne cooking school, has opened up the doors, and kitchens, of her graciously appointed seventeenth-century Château du Fey about 1½ hours south of Paris. Week-long sessions include practical cooking classes, excursions into the vineyards of Chablis, and dinners at two grand restaurants in the region: L'Espérance in Saint-Perè-sous-Vézelay and La Côte Saint-Jacques in Joigny. Additional excursions are possible for spouses who do not wish to attend cooking classes. Various food personalities also host classes during April and May. For more information, contact: La Varenne in Burgundy, P.O. 25574, Washington, D.C. 20007 (202-333-9077).

NUITS-SAINT-GEORGES *(Côte-d'Or)*

Beaune 17 k, Chalon-sur-Saône 45 k, Dijon 22 k.

Market: Friday, 8 A.M. to noon, Place de Verdun.

VIN, BIERE, ALCOOL

VEDRENNE
Rue Fagon, 21700
   Nuits-Saint-Georges.
(80.61.15.55).
Open 8:30 A.M. to 12:30 P.M.
   and 2:30 to 7 P.M. Closed
   Sunday and Monday.

This is the source of one of the best known and most respected brands of Burgundy's famous *crème de cassis* (black currant liqueur).

On the job, in Saint-Nicolas-lès-Cîteaux.

Saint-Leger-Vauban *(Yonne)*

Quarré-les-Tombes 10 k, Vézelay 34 k.

Fromager

**ABBAYE SAINTE-MARIE
DE LA PIERRE-
QUI-VIRE**
89830 Saint-Léger-Vauban.
(86.32.21.23).
Open daily 8 A.M. to noon
and 2 to 5 P.M.

Paris Connection:
ANDROUET
41 Rue d'Amsterdam, 75008
Paris.
(45.50.43.94).

A Cistercian monk and his cheese.

For years I've had this very romantic notion about the delicate white cow's-milk cheese known as Pierre-Qui-Vire. Was it the funny-sounding name—which translates as "the stone that moves"—that appealed, or the knowledge that this simple, artisanal cheese was made by a group of Benedictine monks sheltered in a rustic corner of the Morvan forest? The abbey is one of those lonely, hidden spots reached only with determination, via a winding road cut through the dense forest. In short, it's not on the way to anywhere. But if you're looking for a bucolic setting and fresh, tangy cheese made on the monks' compact, organically run farm, this is the place. The farm is not open to the public, so the cheesemaker, Brother Charles, won't be able to take you on a tour, but the cheese can be purchased (on the honor system) at the small public reception area near the abbey's bookstore, or *li-*

brairie. About six of the one hundred monks work the farm, tending to their herd of thirty six cows. From the fresh raw milk they produce a variety of very young, clean-tasting cheeses, some of them little *boulettes,* or balls, flecked with herbs. Since production is very small, the supply is quickly exhausted, so you might call ahead before making the journey.

Marc Meneau of L'Espérance greets his guests.

SAINT-NICOLAS-LES-CÎTEAUX *(Côte-d'Or)*

Dijon 27 k, Nuits-Saint-Georges 13 k, Seurre 20 k.

FROMAGER

ABBAYE DE CITEAUX
Saint-Nicolas-lès-Cîteaux, 21700 Nuits-Saint-Georges.
(80.61.11.53).
Open 9:30 A.M. to noon and 2:30 to 6 P.M. Monday through Saturday; 8:30 to 10:15 A.M. and 2:30 to 6 P.M. Sunday.

The creamy cow's-milk cheese made by the Cistercian monks in Cîteaux—just 23 kilometers (14 miles) south of Dijon—is definitely worth the detour. In truth, it's about the only way one ever gets to taste the Cîteaux cheese they've been making here since the turn of the century. Almost the entire production—which is aged for about two months and strongly resembles a well-aged Reblochon—is sold at the little shop at the Abbey. We were served by a chatty, gentle monk who reported his age as eighty-one. *"Je suis un vieux moine* (I am an old monk),'' he chuckled as he slowly wrapped up two discs of cheese in a bright blue and white wrapper. While you're there, pick up a tiny bit of their delicious, and not too sweet, honey-flavored hard candy. (Directions: From Dijon take route D966 in the direction of Seurre. The abbey is 4 kilometers east of Saint-Nicolas-lès-Cîteaux and is well marked.)

SAINT-PERE-SOUS-VEZELAY *(Yonne)*

Auxerre 54 k, Avallon 18 k, Paris 230 k, Vézelay 3 k.

Fête de la Moisson (harvest festival): one Sunday in August.

RESTAURANT

L'ESPERANCE
Saint-Père-sous-Vézelay,
89450 Vézelay.
(86.33.20.45).
Last orders taken at 2:30 P.M.
and 9:30 P.M.
Closed Wednesday lunch,
Tuesday, and the last
three weeks in January
through the first week in
February.
Credit cards: AE, DC, V.
Air-conditioned.
Private dining room for 20.
English spoken.
200-, 300-, and 400-franc
menus. A la carte, 550
francs.

SPECIALTIES:
Ambroisie de volaille au foie gras
(chicken with *foie gras*), *salmis
de pigeon à la Conti* (pigeon
stew), desserts.

In the kitchen with Marc Meneau.

Here in the foothills of the romantic ninth-century village of Vézelay, Marc and Françoise Meneau have turned a large private house into a bright and cozy garden restaurant and hotel, putting a very personal stamp on all that they touch.

Chef Meneau, a smiling, dedicated young man, has a lively, modern style of cooking. He is working toward simpler and simpler cuisine, a cuisine almost void of sauce but not of flavor. He enjoys offering palate surprises, such as an almost shocking, but remarkably pleasing, first course of green olives stuffed and also showered with black truffle shavings, and an equally original, though slightly more conventional, dish that combines slices of warm sautéed *foie gras* with a *galette de maïs,* or corn-based pancake.

Milk products come fresh from his cousin's farm right across the street, and his kitchen turns out a superb multi-grain bread each day (see recipe, following page). The dessert cart is such a chocolate lover's dream, you may have to pass up the superb fruit compote (see recipe, page 203), and the wine list is well annotated, offering a variety of wines from every region of France. I love the greenhouse-like dining room, and to me, at least, it's more appealing during the day than at dinner.

Pain aux Cinq Cereales Marc Meneau
MARC MENEAU'S FIVE-GRAIN BREAD

This dense, crusty, wholesome bread has become a staple in our house for toasting, snacking, and eating with cheese and salads. It's a variation on the bread that chef Marc Meneau serves at restaurant L'Espérance in Saint-Père-sous-Vézelay. In France, health food shops sell a five-grain mixture that includes flaked oats, wheat, barley, rice, and rye. Rye and rice flakes are not always easy to come by on their own, so I've adapted the recipe slightly. It is easy to make, and requires little kneading.

Starter:

2 cups (500 ml) lukewarm water

2½ teaspoons or 1 package active dry yeast

2 cups (280 g) unbleached all-purpose flour

Grain mixture:

1¼ cups (about 215 g) coarse yellow cornmeal or polenta

2 cups (about 200 g) barley flakes

2 cups (about 200 g) rolled oats (not the quick-cooking variety)

1 tablespoon salt

2 cups (500 ml) hot tap water

Flour mixture:

1⅔ cups (230 g) whole wheat flour

1 cup (140 g) unbleached all-purpose flour

2 teaspoons unsalted butter, for buttering the bread pans

1. Prepare the starter: Place the water, yeast, and flour in a large mixing bowl, and stir for 1 to 2 minutes (I like to count 100 turns). Cover with a cloth and let rise at room temperature for 1 hour.

2. Prepare the grain mixture: Place the cornmeal, barley flakes, rolled oats, salt, and water in a second large bowl, and stir until the water is completely absorbed. The mixture will be very mealy. Cover with a cloth and let soften at room temperature for 1 hour.

3. Stir down the starter, then add the grain mixture, and mix until thoroughly blended. Slowly add the whole wheat flour, mixing well after each addition. Add the all-purpose flour a little at a time, mixing well after each addition. The dough should be quite sticky, but not too stiff or dry. It will usually take the full cup of flour, but not more. Knead for 5 minutes, then cover with a cloth and let rise at room temperature until about doubled in bulk, about 2½ hours.

4. Punch the dough down, divide it into 2 equal pieces and shape them into loaves. Place the loaves in two buttered rectangular loaf pans, about 8 x 4 inches (23 x 12 cm). Cover with a cloth and let rise at room temperature until doubled in bulk, about 2 hours.

5. Preheat the oven to 375°F (190°C).

6. Bake the loaves until golden brown, about 50 minutes. For a crustier loaf, once baked, remove the bread from the pans and return to the oven for an additional 5 minutes. Remove from the oven and let cool thoroughly before slicing.

Yield: 2 loaves.

SAULIEU *(Côte-d'Or)*

Autun 41 k, Avallon 39 k, Beaune 76 k, Dijon 73 k, Paris 250 k.

Market: Thursday and Saturday, 8 A.M. to 1 P.M., Place Monge, in front of the post office (P.T.T.).

RESTAURANT

COTE D'OR
2 Rue Argentine, 21210 Saulieu.
(80.64.07.66).
Last orders taken at 2:30 P.M. and 10 P.M.
Closed mid-November through the first week in December, and the first two weeks in March.
Credit cards: AE, DC, V.
Private dining room for 25.
English spoken.
230-franc lunch menu; 260- and 380-franc dinner menus; 250-franc vegetarian tasting menu. A la carte, about 500 francs.

SPECIALTIES:
"Cuisine légère."

Over the years, I've had some very irregular experiences with Bernard Loiseau, as have many friends and readers. The biggest problem is that his *"cuisine légère"*—a very personal sort of cooking that calls for a minimum of butter and cream and depends essentially on brightly colored, vegetable-based sauces—is not easy to understand. In truth, it's not the sort of cooking we naturally warm up to (after a meal here, you're not inspired to race home and repeat his dishes), and I guess that as much as we are all concerned about leanness, thinness, lightness, we don't really go to grand restaurants to be restrained or deprived.

This said, I find myself applauding Loiseau's creative efforts, and since he's still quite young, his cuisine and point of view have plenty of time to reach maturity. Our last meal here did net some truly satisfying dishes, among them a platter of plump, gently fried frog's legs designed for picking up with your fingers and dipping in a delicate garlic purée; a cauliflower soup he calls *velouté de chou-fleur caramélisé;* and a delicious portion of the freshest *coquilles Saint-Jacques* in a delicate sauce infused with sea urchin roe. I sampled his vegetarian tasting menu, and as a former vegetarian and one thoroughly sympathetic to those who are, I felt the dishes were just a bit too repetitive to derive real satisfaction: The tiddlywinks-size discs of *céleri rave* (celery root), bathed in bright red beet sauce, didn't make me feel good, and healthy, just confused; and as I sampled the lovely combination of pencil-thin *poireaux* (leeks) with rounds of potatoes interlayered with fresh black truffles, I couldn't help thinking that something had been left out. The cheese tray was a bit embarrassing (an Epoisses that wasn't well aged, but chalky in the center; a local fresh goat cheese that was simply insipid; and a

Vacherin so bland it tasted as though it could have been made of skim milk). The wines remain quite untouchably priced, though I can recommend de Villaine's well-priced white Bourgogne Aligoté Bouzeron and Tollot-Beaut's beautifully balanced Corton Les Bressandes, which is expensive but offers an awful lot of pleasure per sip.

BOULANGERIE

BOULANGERIE DECHAUME
42 Rue du Marché, 21210 Saulieu.
(80.64.18.72).
Open 6 A.M. to 9 P.M. Closed Tuesday, mid-October through mid-November, and the last week in April through the first week in May.

Jean Dechaume and his wife, Odette, offer a fine sourdough country loaf, delicate rye bread, and the seldom-found regional *pain cordon,* a standard *pain de campagne* decorated with a thin strip of dough, or *cordon,* an addition that does not alter the flavor of the bread but does add a finishing touch.

FROMAGERIE

LAITERIE OVERNEY
6 Rue des Fours, 21210 Saulieu.
(80.64.07.88).
Open 8:30 A.M. to noon and 2 to 7 P.M. Closed Sunday and Monday.
Will ship in France.

Preserved fruits, Le Petit Truc.

The Overneys are rare *artisans:* Not only do they run their own cheese store, chock-a-block full of varieties from all over France, but they also make a number of very fine cheeses. Theirs are wonderful cheeses, including Epoisses (sold here at many stages of aging, from the young white version to one that's aged with *marc de Bourgogne*), the creamy, rich Brillat-Savarin, and a new creation, a cow's-milk cheese aged for five weeks, washed with the local white Chablis.

POIRES ET FIGUES CHAUDES A LA CANNELLE L'ESPERANCE
L'ESPERANCE'S COMPOTE OF PEARS AND FIGS WITH CINNAMON

I sampled this dessert the first time I visited the restaurant L'Espérance in Saint-Père-sous-Vézelay and can't imagine anyone who wouldn't love this combination of warm fruit and cold ice cream. The ripe fruit may break down during cooking, but the dish will still be delicious.

2 tablespoons (1 ounce; 30 g) unsalted butter

4 firm ripe pears, peeled, cut into eighths or sixteenths depending upon size, and cored

8 fresh figs, halved lengthwise

¼ cup (50 g) sugar

¼ cup (60 ml) water

2 sticks cinnamon

1 pint (.5 liter) vanilla ice cream

1. Melt the butter in a large skillet over medium-high heat. Add the pears, figs, and sugar and stir gently to coat the fruit with butter and sugar. Cook, shaking the pan gently, until the sugar begins to turn golden, just a few minutes. Add the water and cinnamon, reduce the heat to medium, and cook uncovered until the pears begin to soften, about 15 minutes. Shake the pan from time to time to keep the fruit from sticking to the pan. Discard the cinnamon. (The fruit can be prepared a few hours in advance and kept refrigerated. Reheat just before serving.)

2. To serve, place 4 warm fig halves in the center of each plate, surround them with pear slices, and top with a generous scoop of ice cream. Spoon any remaining sauce over the ice cream and serve immediately.

Yield: 4 servings.

Françoise Meneau at L'Espérance.

WINES OF BURGUNDY

1. VOSNE-ROMANEE (HENRI JAYER): Round, rich, and powerful, the reds of Henri Jayer are among the most respected Burgundies made today. Aged in oak, they're unfiltered, well-rounded wines that rarely disappoint. His wines show up often on the best wine lists.

2. NUITS SAINT-GEORGES LES CAILLES (ROBERT CHEVILLON): When I go down to my cellar I often count the remaining bottles of Robert Chevillon's Nuits Saint-Georges, ticking off special meals for which they're being saved. Spicy, rich, and generous reds, they're well worth keeping an eye out for.

3. CHABLIS GRAND CRU (FRANCOIS RAVENEAU): Many consider this the greatest wine in Chablis. Raveneau's wines are natural ones, aged in oak, with greater intensity than most Chablis, which tend to be thin and disappointing. Also look for the Chablis of Dauvissat.

4. ALIGOTE DE BOUZERONE (DE VILLAINE): Too many people think of Aligoté as a banal wine that begs for "improvement" by mixing it with Cassis for a Kir. Don't do that to de Villaine's lively white, with its pleasing hint of hazelnuts. It's almost always a good buy.

5. MEURSAULT (FRANCOIS JOBARD): François Jobard may be a shy and timid man, but he lets his wines speak for him: His Meursaults are clear, open, balanced, and seem to be nearly ageless. Also look for Michelot and Comte Lafon.

6. CHEVALIER MONTRACHET (LEFLAIVE): I first tasted Leflaive's elegant and powerful whites at the res-

taurant Taillevent in Paris, and now I never pass up the opportunity to sample his buttery, almondy wines. Also look for his Batard Montrachet and Puligny Montrachet.

7. POMMARD (DOMAINE LEJEUNE):
Domaine Lejeune offers powerful traditional wines: heady, concentrated, dark, and full-flavored, the kind of wine some call "rough and chewy." The Pommard is made the old-fashioned way: the grapes are not stemmed and undergo a long fermentation, making for a long-lasting wine full of rich color, flavor, and tannin.

8. BEAUNE CLOS DE MOUCHES (DROUHIN):
This is one of the "sure bet" wines I keep tucked away in my memory, for days when neither time nor temperament permit me to pore over a wine list. One of Joseph Drouhin's fin-

est efforts, this is a deep, spicy, tannic red. Also look for the Beaune of Domaine Tollot-Beaut.

9. VOLNAY CLOS DE LA BOUSSE D'OR (DOMAINE DE LA POUSSE D'OR):
Volnay is one of those wines that, by its very name, sounds rich. An elegant, silken red designed for celebrating special meals. The Clos de la Bousse d'Or from the Domaine de la Pousse d'Or can be rich, fruity, and outstanding. Look for the wines from Comte Lafon and Marquis D'Angerville.

10. CREME DE CASSIS (TRENEL & FILS):
One of the most trusted makers of fruity, almost heady, black currant liqueur, an essential ingredient in Dijon's prized aperitif known as Kir. Also keep an eye out for the Cassis from Jean-Michel Jacob.

CHEESES OF BURGUNDY

1. EPOISSES: A beautifully aged Epoisses is hard to find, but it is one of the world's rare cheese experiences. At its finest, the pungent Epoisses is so runny that it has to be served on a plate to suppress its exuberance. Named for a small Burgundian village, this disc of raw cow's-milk cheese is aged slowly, with daily washings of the local *eau-de-vie* known as *marc de Bourgogne*. Epoisses blanc is the same cheese, but in its bland and youthful state. Also look for the related Ami du Chambertin.

2. MONTRACHET: An elegant, re-fined cylinder of goat cheese, Montra-chet is prettily wrapped with a chestnut or grape leaf as it gently ages in cool, ventilated cellars. The best Montrachet, of raw goat's milk, will sport a bluish rind beneath the leaves, with a moist, firm, and delicate interior.

3. LANGRES: From the market town of Langres comes the funny-looking or-ange cheese that resembles a sunken crater. Similar to Epoisses but with a bit more spice, this soft, runny cow's-milk cheese is best *au lait cru,* made with the fresh raw cow's milk of the region. Look for Langres on the cheese tray at numer-ous restaurants in Burgundy.

4. CHAROLAIS: The Charolais area of Burgundy gives its name to one of France's most prized breeds of cattle as well as to a cheese, a tall, proud cylinder sometimes made of cow's milk, some-times of goat's milk, sometimes a mix of the two. My favorite is pure goat, both in its fresh form (when it is nutty, creamy, and spreadable) as well as aged (when the rind firms up and the smooth interior takes on an agreeably pro-nounced fresh goat's-milk flavor).

5. SOUMAINTRAIN: I fell in love with this creamy, supple cow's-milk cheese from the village of Soumaintrain when I first moved to France, and it's been a household staple ever since. Like the related Pierre-Qui-Vire and Saint-Florentin, this large flat disc has a fine texture, a nicely runny interior, and a golden yellow rind.

6. CHEVRE FRAIS: From spring to fall, when the goats are out and about feasting on fresh wildflowers, herbs, and grasses, a cheese lover could easily make this a "life survival" cheese. While *chèvre frais* (fresh *chèvre*) is a ge-neric cheese found all over France in a variety of sizes, some of the best ver-sions are thick cylinders made in Bur-gundy of raw goat's milk.

Lyon
LYONS

Madame Camille, at Café Bidon 5.

Gastronomically, Lyon is a city of contrasts. Moving from well-worn back-alley bistros to sparkling three-star temples, from smoke-filled train station eateries to sleek modern cafés, a visitor can ramble through France's second city sampling old France one moment, new France the next, spanning a handful of decades in a single day. In some ways, modern-day Lyon looks the way many of us imagine Paris of the 1930s, inspiring one recent visitor to announce: "The last time I saw Paris it was in Lyon."

Lyon, to be sure, offers its share of visually bothersome high-rises and there is a Love Burger fast-food shop firmly planted on the Place de Bellecour, but the city also offers a rich supply of cafés and bistros beaming with a character and an ambience that only time can buy. Many Lyonnais eating establishments have been slow to modernize, leaving us with a wealth of distinctively old-fashioned spots offering authentic regional fare. Prices, as well, appear attractively out-of-date.

When I go to Lyon, I like to forget about *amuse-gueules* and *petits fours,* starched linens and excessive culinary refinement. Rather, it's a place to roll up your sleeves, put on your walking shoes, turn your thoughts to no-frills eating, and enjoy. For here in Lyon, a big city

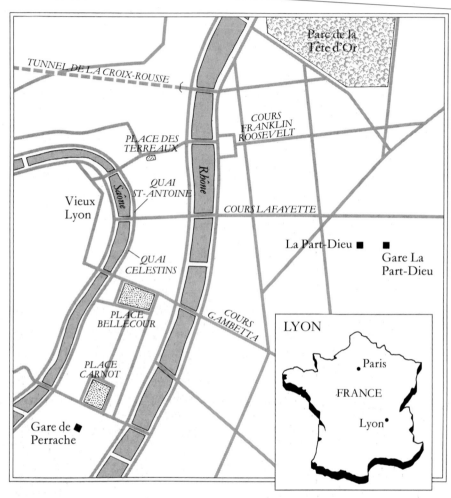

that bears the soul of a working-class village, home cooking from the heart is still in style. And despite mumblings to the contrary, there are still a handful of old-fashioned, traditional *mères lyonnaises* to feed you, scold you, tell you what you'll eat and what you won't.

The first thing to know about eating at some Lyonnais restaurants is that you may have to forego certain traditional dining customs. Like menus. Or choices. Or a change of silverware with each course. Don't be deterred. Pretend you're at your French grandmother's, and your palate and pocketbook will applaud you in the end. Picky eaters, don't bother to apply.

WHEN YOU GO

Michelin Green Guide: *Vallée du Rhône.*

Getting there: Air Inter offers about eight daily hour-long flights from Paris's Orly Ouest airport. The journey by train from Paris's Gare de Lyon takes 2 hours by TGV *(train à grande vitesse)*, or bullet train, or 5 hours by regular train to Lyon's downtown Perrache station or the Part-Dieu station at the edge of town. There are some twenty-four trains leaving daily. Cars can be rented at the airport and train stations.

Getting around: This is a good town for walking; most bookshops and kiosks sell detailed street maps.

Best time to visit: Lyon's a lively place year-round. But since the food's hearty, I prefer visiting during the cooler fall and winter months.

The Grand Café des Négociants, a Lyonnais tradition.

At the Grand Café des Négociants.

MARCHES

**MARCHE DU QUAI
SAINT-ANTOINE and
QUAI CELESTINS**
From the Pont
Alphonse-Juin to the
Pont Bonaparte, 69002
Lyon.
Open 8 A.M. to noon. Closed
Monday.

For a touch of country life in Lyon, wander along the Marché du Quai Saint-Antoine from Tuesday through Sunday, where you'll find local farmers selling their freshly harvested fruits and vegetables. Some regional specialties to look for: the bitter wintertime dandelion known both as *pissenlits* and as *groins d'âne; rattes de Grenoble,* bite-size white potatoes, perfect for stuffing with snails or caviar; a bright orange pumpkin known as *courge muscade;* and, in the springtime, fresh lake trout and miniature *goujons* for frying in oil.

LES HALLES DE LYON
102 Cours Lafayette, 69003
Lyon.
Open 7 A.M. to 12:30 P.M.
and 3 to 7 P.M. Tuesday
through Saturday; 7 A.M.
to 12:30 P.M. Sunday.
Closed Monday.

The city's largest market is instantly accessible to travelers: The huge and modern Les Halles is situated within the gigantic Part-Dieu complex, home of one of the train stations that service the high-speed TGV train from Paris and Marseille.

The market resembles a modern soulless shopping center, but open your eyes and you'll find some of the finest produce in all of France. Cheese merchants offer numerous specialties seldom seen outside the region (including the pungent Arômes à la Gène, or discs of cow's-milk cheese cured in vats of *marc,* then coated with the musty dried grape skins left over from winemaking); fishmongers feature fresh lake fish, including the *feret* and *omble chevalier* from Lake Annecy in the Savoie; while the *charcuteries* are festively decked out with row upon row of sausages, big and small, smoked and dried, from every region of France.

RESTAURANTS

BISTRO DE LYON
64 Rue Mercière, 69002
Lyon.
(78.37.00.62).
Last orders taken at 2:30 P.M.
and 1:30 A.M.
Open daily.
Credit card: V.
Terrace dining in summer.
Air-conditioned.
English spoken at dinner.
160 francs.

SPECIALTIES:
Saladier lyonnais (green salad
with a soft-cooked egg,
croutons, bacon, and herring),
salade de tomates et basilic
(tomato salad with basil),
saucisson chaud (hot sausage),
gras-double (tripe baked with
onions and white wine),
chariot de desserts (rolling
dessert cart).

This is *the* spot for late-night snacking and a look at the young and fashionable Lyonnais. The atmosphere is supercharged and you'll have to wait in line for fifteen minutes, or more, for borderline bistro fare; but the people-watching and the decor—Belle Epoque ceramic murals on the walls and ceiling, a giant antique wooden serving bar, and marble-top tables—make this museum-like bistro worth a detour. The bread is good, the Beaujolais drinkable, and the *chèvre* salad with cucumbers satisfying.

Lunchtime chatter at the Café des Fédérations.

CAFE DES FEDERATIONS
8 Rue du Major-Martin,
69001 Lyon.
(78.28.26.00).
Last orders taken at 2 P.M.
and 10 P.M.
Closed Saturday, Sunday, and
August.
Credit cards: AE, DC.
100-franc menu.

SPECIALTIES:
Charcuteries lyonnaises
(Lyonnais cold cuts, sausages,
terrines, pâtés), *tablier de
sapeur* (tripe that is marinated,
breaded, and grilled), *boudin
aux pommes* (pork blood
sausage with sautéed apples),
quenelles (fish dumplings),
andouille (cold smoked tripe
sausage), Saint-Marcellin
(runny cow's-milk cheese
disc).

This lively, funny, bustling place is the ultimate Lyonnais *bouchon:* gigantic sausages hang from the ceiling, sawdust protects the worn tile floor, local newspapers hang on a towel rack near the bar, the black wall telephone belongs in the PTT museum, and the daily menu is scratched out on a torn piece of cardboard that hangs in the window.

And the food is earthy and wonderful. Between bites, there's also the animated Françoise (a cheery, flippant blonde who can take care of herself, thank you) and the rather dapper *bistrotier,* slim and graying Raymond Fulchiron, whose chatter with the houseful of regulars makes for an amusing time.

For those unfamiliar with Lyonnais bistro etiquette, the Café des Fédérations might be considered an ideal training ground. Here diners do have the benefit of a written menu, but that's really just for show. Rather, Monsieur Fulchiron will pause at your table, tell you what he has that day for starters, and as the meal progresses he'll offer suggestions course by course.

The small café is packed with regulars sharing space on red-plastic-covered banquettes and everyone pours the house Beaujolais—a pleasant Morgon from winemaker André Gauthier—from the traditional *pot.*

On one visit, just minutes after we sat down, a huge stainless steel platter of moist, nicely seasoned *saucissons chauds de Lyon* arrived, accompanied by boiled potatoes and sprigs of watercress. Before we could make a dent in our portions of sliced pork sausages, a huge salad bowl appeared, filled with the seasonal cool-weather *pissenlits,* or dandelion greens, tossed with chunks of salty bacon and morsels of soft-cooked egg.

Along with traditional tripe offerings— *andouillettes,* or chitterling sausages, and *tablier de sapeur*—there was a mild and classic *blanquette de veau* and a platter of state-of-the-art *boudin aux pommes.* Any French housewife would have been proud to serve the *blanquette,* and the *boudin aux pommes* was about as good as that dish can be. The sausage was grilled to a crisp on the outside, moist and delicately seasoned on the inside. The piping hot sautéed apples (the chef uses the firm winter cooking apple known as *Canada Gris*) were a perfect, sweet foil for the earthy *boudin.*

Here, cheese is imperative. You'll eye the platters of weeping Saint-Marcellin, all at various stages of maturity, behind the bar as you enter.

Each day Monsieur Fulchiron also serves up a delicious fruit tart—most often pear or apple in a thick shortbread crust—which few diners manage to resist.

A smile from Françoise, a Lyonnais salute from Raymond Fulchiron.

LA GRILLE
106 Rue Sébastien-Gryphe,
    69007 Lyon.
(78.72.46.58).
Last orders taken at 1:45 P.M.
    and 9:15 P.M.
Closed Saturday, Sunday,
    holidays, and August.
No credit cards.
Two small private dining
    rooms.
96-franc menu. A la carte,
    150 francs.

S P E C I A L T I E S :
Foie de veau à la lyonnaise (veal
liver with onions), *sabodet*
(sausage of pork, beef, pig's
head and skin), *loup aux herbes*
(striped bass with herbs),
entrecôte (beef rib steak).

I think it would be hard not to have a good time at La Grille, where the food is simple and served with generosity. The entire Bernaud family—Marinette at the stove, husband Marcel and sons Joël and Pascal in the dining room—tends to their chalet-like bistro that serves as a living museum devoted to old-fashioned Lyonnais cuisine.

Marcel, with his barrel chest, white suspenders, and booming voice, clip-clops along in navy blue clogs, reveling in his role. *"Archicomplet! Archicomplet!"* (meaning there's not a prayer of securing a table) he roars at anyone who mistakenly wanders in, via the kitchen, without a reservation. Call ahead, and you'll be greeted with open arms and seated at one of thirty-five-odd places available. Strangers become regulars in a single meal, and whether you arrive with a raging hunger or just want to tide yourself over with a salad, an omelet, and a glass of wine, you'll be welcome.

Marinette, with a timid, bird-like voice, hides behind her casseroles, peeking out from time to time through the windows of glazed glass that separate the dining room from the compact kitchen.

Here one finds rustic *sabodets,* simmered for hours in Beaujolais and served with Marinette's delicate *pommes boulangère,* a wonderful potato gratin cooked slowly in chicken broth and a touch of white wine. The subtle potatoes are a perfect complement to the earthy, highly seasoned farm sausage that's served during the chilly winter months, just after the traditional slaughter of the pig.

There's the classic, abundant *saladier lyonnais* (see recipe, page 234)—today a colorful blend of *mâche,* rosy *trévise,* and green lettuce tossed with vinaigrette, a soft-cooked egg, and chunks of salty bacon, served with all-you-can-eat helpings of silken filets of herring and anchovy.

And of course La Grille offers a litany of homey fare, the dishes ladies like Marinette cook for their families: *ris de veau à la moutarde à l'ancienne* (sweetbreads with whole-grain mustard), mackerel marinated in white wine, sizzling snails, and *foie de veau,* or calf's liver, garnished with tiny onions.

Chocolate mousse lovers should save room for dessert: they set the entire bowl of dark, rich, and not-too-sweet mousse at your elbow and won't take it away until you ask them to.

Marinette works with one assistant, young Gilles Dodal, who turns out a splendid fruit tart: he tops fine, flaky pastry with a thin covering of applesauce, then adds, according to whim and season, slices of pears, apples, and plump prunes, either separately or in combination.

This is Marcel and Marinette's third Lyonnais restaurant in twenty-six years. They consider it their pre-retirement establishment—smaller, less taxing than those before. Over the years they've served everyone from Alain Delon to François Truffaut, and it seems they'll keep on going just as long as the phone goes on ringing.

LEON DE LYON
1 Rue Pleney, 69001 Lyon.
(78.28.11.33).
Last orders taken at 2 P.M. and 10 P.M.
Closed Sunday, Monday lunch, and between Christmas and New Year's holidays.
Credit card: V.
Air-conditioned.
Private dining rooms for 6, 12, and 25.
English spoken.
160-franc menu, not including service. A la carte, 350 francs.

SPECIALTIES:
Lyonnais classics and contemporary cuisine.

One restaurant that spans the ages with perfection is Léon de Lyon, perhaps the city's best-known traditional dining room, and one of the oldest.

Today, thirty-six-year-old Jean-Paul Lacombe runs the family restaurant with a flair and a sense of history that belies his age. "I don't want my restaurant to resemble any other in the world," says the cheery, outgoing chef. If Monsieur Lacombe were not cooking, he'd be an antiques dealer, and over the past several years he's gathered a remarkable collection of culinary artifacts—food-related oil paintings, advertising paraphernalia, amusing porcelain salt and pepper shakers, dozens of shiny copper molds—all of which are now artfully displayed in the restaurant's small dining rooms.

The charming two-story restaurant, squeezed into a narrow street situated near the open-air market along Quai Saint-Antoine, features both regional and modern fare, which means those who love hearty portions of earthy Lyonnais pork sausage, vinegared green lentils, and oil-bathed potatoes can dine side by side with those who prefer less traditional fare.

Léon de Lyon might in fact be dubbed a luxury bistro. Trim, friendly waiters are casually dressed in navy blue shirts and denim aprons, but their behavior and attention suggest that of a tuxedoed *maître d'hôtel*.

Monsieur Lacombe, his mother, and his sister work as a trio, offering a menu of remarkable balance and freshness. During the cool-weather months, many Lyonnais specialties seldom found outside the region—such as creamy gratins of *car-*

SALADE VERTE, COURONNE DE POMMES DE TERRE CROUSTILLANTES LEON DE LYON
LEON DE LYON'S GREEN SALAD WITH CRISP POTATO CROWN

Jean-Paul Lacombe is one of France's most talented young chefs, and this very simple and satisfying first-course salad is a testament to his ability to combine traditional and modern elements in cooking. Monsieur Lacombe calls it his answer to the favorite French green salad and pommes frites—a plain green salad topped with a very crispy, golden crown of thinly sliced potatoes. I love the way the silky, elegant texture of the tiny, flat-leafed greens plays against the rustic potato crown, which tastes like the best potato chip you've ever encountered. The breathtaking green and gold color contrast makes this one dish that is so beautiful, one almost hesitates to cut into it. Any available small leaf, flat salad green, such as spinach, watercress, lamb's lettuce, or arugula can be used here. The dish calls for a single, tame sort of green that will lie flat, allowing the potato crown to adorn the salad. Unruly greens such as curly endive just won't do, nor will a mix of greens.

3 tablespoons (1½ ounces; 45 g) unsalted butter

2 small, evenly shaped, oval potatoes

1 tablespoon best-quality red wine vinegar

Salt and freshly ground black pepper to taste

¼ cup (60 ml) virgin olive oil

1 quart (1 liter) densely packed tiny green leaf lettuce

1. Melt the butter. Using half the butter, brush a ring around the bottom of four 6-inch (15 cm) round baking dishes. Refrigerate until the butter is hardened, about 10 minutes.

2. Peel the potatoes and cut crosswise into paper-thin slices. Arrange the potato slices, overlapping, on each ring of hardened butter, pressing the slices down firmly. If necessary, make double layers to use up all the potato slices. Brush the slices with the remaining melted butter and refrigerate for 30 minutes.

3. Preheat the oven to 425°F (220°C).

4. Bake the potato rings until crisp and brown, about 15 minutes.

5. While the potatoes are baking, whisk together the vinegar, salt, and pepper in a large bowl. Add the oil and whisk until emulsified. Correct the seasoning. Add the greens and toss.

6. Divide the greens among 4 large plates, spreading the greens out and pressing them down to lie flat. Using a flexible spatula or knife, loosen the potatoes from the dishes. Very carefully turn each potato crown out onto a salad by quickly flipping the dish over the salad. Serve immediately.

Yield: 4 servings.

dons (celery-like edible thistle) and *crosnes* (subtly flavored Chinese artichokes)—appear on the menu, along with wild game and moist farm-fresh guinea hens. Come spring (usually from mid-March to mid-June), the chef offers an authentic *friture de goujons,* deep-fried miniature smelt-like lake fish that come fresh from local waters.

His modern fare is light and imaginative, including a salad of *mâche,* or lamb's lettuce, topped by a delicate crown of pan-fried potatoes (see recipe, page 215); cold spinach-wrapped oysters sauced with a touch of cream; tiny filets of *rouget,* or red mullet, served with an elegant sauce that contains the rich, full-flavored liver of this Mediterranean fish.

Whatever menu is chosen, diners should save room for the cheese course. The selection—from Renée Richard, the city's best-known cheese merchant—includes perfectly aged regional specialties, particularly the creamy golden cow's-milk Saint-Marcellin.

Wine lovers will enjoy the vast selection of Burgundies and some wines that are seldom seen on wine lists, including a white Beaujolais and an eight-year-old Moulin-à-Vent, considered the best and longest lived of the *cru* Beaujolais. Although neither wine is a gastronomic thriller, they're both fun to experience once in one's life. Do try the house *kir,* an unusual, and smooth, blend of Beaujolais and black currant liqueur.

Summertime, time for cafés.

CHEZ LILY ET GABY
76 Rue Mazenod, 69003
   Lyon.
(78.60.47.98).
Last orders taken at 1 P.M.
   and 9:30 P.M.
Closed Sunday lunch and
   Saturday from Pentecost
   through All Saints' Day;
   Saturday October
   through May; and
   August.
No credit cards.
Spanish spoken.
85-franc menu only at
   lunch, including wine,
   coffee, and service. A la
   carte at dinner, 125 francs.

Think of what 85 francs buys today in France: admission to two films...a quick telephone call to New York...a pound of Colombian coffee from Hédiard. Eighty-five francs can also buy lunch at Chez Lily et Gaby: maybe quiche or sausage for starters, perhaps the finest *gratin de pommes de terre*, or potato gratin, your palate has ever confronted (see recipe below), a pair of thick, juicy, pan-fried lamb chops, all the cheese you may desire, and an oversized *choux-chantilly*, a giant *choux* pastry filled with piped clouds of whipped fresh cream.

Lily, moving slowly and with a bit of hesitation, will size you up and decide what you ought to eat ("I have one slice of quiche left. It's for you," she decrees) while Gaby, his rectangular frame wrapped in a long blue apron, fills in the gaps, delivering baskets of bread, carafes of wine and water, making

---

GRATIN DAUPHINOIS CHEZ LILY ET GABY
CHEZ LILY ET GABY'S POTATO GRATIN

I have yet to find a person who does not love potato gratin. And I don't know many other classic dishes with so many variations. Maybe that's so gratin lovers can have a version for each day of the week. This recipe comes from Lyon's Chez Lily et Gaby, a bare-bones café-restaurant that is known for its potato gratin. When the cook, Lily Légroz, sent me the recipe she noted, "In effect, there's no real recipe, for, on one hand, everything depends on the cook's certain knack, on the other, on the quality of ingredients used." Need one say more?

1 clove garlic, peeled
   and halved
3 pounds (about 5; 1.5
   kg) Idaho Russet
   potatoes, peeled and
   very thinly sliced
3 cups (750 ml) milk
2 large eggs, lightly
   beaten
1½ teaspoons salt
Freshly ground black
   pepper to taste
1 cup (3 ounces; 100 g)
   grated Gruyère
   cheese
½ cup (125 g) *crème
   fraîche* (see Recipe
   Index) or heavy
   cream, preferably not
   ultra-pasteurized

1. Preheat the oven to 400°F (190°C).

2. Rub the inside of an oval porcelain gratin dish (about 14 x 9 x 2 inches or 35.5 x 23 x 5 cm) with the garlic. Arrange the potatoes in an even layer in the dish.

3. Mix the milk, eggs, and salt and pour over the potatoes. Sprinkle generously with pepper.

4. Bake, occasionally cutting the crust that forms on top and gently folding it into the potatoes, until the gratin is golden, about 55 minutes.

5. Remove the gratin dish from the oven, sprinkle with the grated cheese, then dab the gratin with *crème fraîche*. Return the dish to the oven and bake until the top is very crisp and golden, about 15 minutes.

Yield: 6 to 8 servings.

a special effort to chat with the female customers sprinkled about the compact dining room.

The decor is regulation 1950s: thick lace curtains, Formica-topped tables covered with paper cloths, walls scattered with dime-store art and menus of days past. Ask Gaby how long they've been there and he responds, "Ten years." Without missing a beat, Lily corrects him: "No-o-o, that's how long we've been living together. We've had the restaurant for eight years."

No matter. It seems they'll stay around a little longer, long enough for one to sample her famed *saucisson brioché* (sausage cooked in buttery, egg-enriched yeast bread), *poulet à la crème* (chicken in cream sauce), and to dive into seconds, maybe thirds, of the potato gratin French critics agree is the best in Lyon.

PAUL BOCUSE
50 Quai de la Plage, 69660
   Collonges-au-Mont-d'Or.
(78.22.01.40).
Telex: 375 382.
Last orders taken at 1:30 P.M.
   and 9:30 P.M.
Open daily.
Credit cards: AE, DC, V.
Air-conditioned.
Private dining rooms for 20
   and 50.
English spoken.
315-, 395-, 425-, and
   465-franc menus. A la
   carte, 560 to 650 francs.

S P E C I A L T I E S :
Soupe de truffes (truffle soup),
loup en croûte (striped bass in
pastry), *volaille en vessie*
(chicken poached in a pig's
bladder).

Restaurant Paul Bocuse might be called the Tour d'Argent of the French countryside. Thanks to his irrepressible ego and enormous energy, Monsieur Bocuse has the highest profile of any chef in the world, and his restaurant on the outskirts of Lyon is France's foremost international gastronomic shrine.

This means there will be tables of noisy tourists, light bulbs will be flashing between courses, and some diners may begin to wonder where the show ends and the meal begins. Whether or not the chef is there in person, he's there in spirit, in the cookbooks that line the sales boutique, in oversized portraits that fill the walls, in a full-color photo on the paper napkin ring.

But, one point that is often missed is that chef Bocuse offers the simplest, most down-to-earth regional food of any grand restaurant in France. If you're in the mood for unadorned roast farm chicken (turned to perfection on the giant fireplace that faces the dining room), scalloped potatoes, and a bit of Beaujolais, no one will turn up his nose. Bring your child along and he or she will be treated like royalty, ordering from the special menu for *"jeunes gourmands."*

Some of the dishes may be a bit too rich (the potato gratin is so creamy it would appear right at home on the dessert menu), and the enormity of the establishment may be turnoff to some, but when it comes to simplicity and gracious service, Bocuse cannot be faulted.

Paul Bocuse, in spirit.

CHEZ ROSE
4 Rue Rabelais, 69003 Lyon.
(78.60.57.25).
Last orders taken at 2 P.M.
and 9:30 P.M.
Closed Sunday, holidays, and August.
Credit card: V.
Air-conditioned.
Private dining rooms for 6, 8, and 16.
English spoken.
90-, 110-, and 140-franc menus. A la carte, 200 francs.

SPECIALTIES:
Lyonnais.

A fine family-run restaurant where father Marcel Astic runs the bar, son Gérard runs the kitchen, and mother Marie-Thérèse runs the whole show with a soft heart and an iron fist. Chez Rose has that no-nonsense decor (tile floors and clean yellow tablecloths) and seemingly disorganized, humorous bustle that puts diners instantly at ease. This is a trencherman's restaurant in a trencherman's town, the kind of place where many serious eaters intentionally dine alone so nothing will distract them from the matter at hand.

In typical Lyonnais fashion, when you order one dish at Chez Rose, another appears alongside, "just to taste." For a pittance you can plough through thick slices of meaty Lyonnais sausage, gargantuan *quenelles, coq au vin,* cheese, and dessert. If your appetite is less hearty, settle for a simple, respectably wintery *fricassée de poulet,* nourished with tomatoes, garlic, and wild *cèpes* mushrooms.

POULET A L'AIL CHEZ TANTE PAULETTE
CHEZ TANTE PAULETTE'S CHICKEN WITH GARLIC

I love the way the house smells as this dish—a garlic lover's delight—simmers away on the stove. Chicken with forty cloves of garlic is a rather traditional French dish, but I'd never sampled it in a restaurant before visiting Lyon's Chez Tante Paulette. I'm almost embarrassed to say that in one sitting, my friend and I polished off the entire platter. I like to think it was a small chicken! Actually, the quantity of garlic is not as formidable as it appears, for as the garlic cooks, it turns rather mild, absorbing the wine and Cognac essence. You'll enjoy the dish even more if you pick the golden brown cloves up with your fingers and suck out the soft, tender garlic. Do make an effort to find fresh, large, meaty cloves of garlic. And if you truly love garlic, don't limit yourself to forty cloves. The dish makes a very pretty presentation, a harmony of golden tones. Serve it with a simple green salad and a hearty red wine.

3 tablespoons virgin olive oil
1 tablespoon (½ ounce; 15 g) unsalted butter
1 chicken, 3 to 4 pounds (1.5 to 2 kg), cut into serving pieces, at room temperature
Salt and freshly ground black pepper to taste
About 40 large cloves garlic, unpeeled
1 cup (250 ml) dry white wine, such as Riesling
8 slices baguette
1 clove garlic, peeled
2 tablespoons Cognac
Chopped fresh parsley for garnish

1. Heat the oil and butter in a deep 12-inch (30 cm) skillet over high heat. (If you do not have a skillet large enough to hold all the chicken in a single layer, use 2 smaller skillets, dividing the chicken, oil, and butter in half for each pan.) Season the chicken liberally with salt and pepper. When the oil is hot but not smoking, add the chicken and brown on both sides until the skin turns an even golden brown, about 5 minutes each side. Carefully regulate the heat to avoid scorching the skin.

2. Reduce the heat to medium-high. Add the unpeeled garlic cloves, burying them under the chicken to make sure they settle in one layer at the bottom of the skillet. Sauté, shaking the pan frequently, until the garlic skins are lightly browned, about 10 minutes. Slowly add the wine to the skillet, shake the pan, scrape any browned bits off the bottom of the pan, and cook uncovered until the chicken is cooked through, about 10 minutes longer.

3. While the chicken is cooking, toast the bread on both sides. Cut the peeled clove of garlic in half. Rub both sides of the toast liberally with garlic.

4. Heat the Cognac in a very small pan over medium-high heat for 20 to 30 seconds. Ignite with a match and pour over the chicken, shaking the skillet quickly until the flames subside. Cook for an additional 2 to 3 minutes, shaking the pan.

5. To serve, place the toast on a warmed large platter, arrange the chicken and garlic on top, and pour the sauce over all. Garnish with parsley and serve immediately.

Yield: 4 servings.

CHEZ TANTE PAULETTE
2 Rue Chavanne, 69001
  Lyon.
(78.28.31.34).
Last orders taken at 2 P.M.
  and 9:30 P.M.
Closed Saturday night,
  Sunday, and two weeks in
  August.
No credit cards.
Private dining room for 10.
80-franc menu. A la carte,
  120 francs.

SPECIALTIES:
Poulet à l'ail (chicken with
garlic), *bouillabaisse de poulet*
(chicken stewed in olive oil
and Ricard, served with thick
spicy garlic sauce and
croutons), *pintade au choux*
(guinea hen with cabbage).

For years I imagined that somewhere out there, there was a lady running a restaurant that matched Paris's famed L'Ami Louis. I found it at Chez Tante Paulette, a matchbox-size restaurant hidden for the past four decades on a crooked street not far from Place des Terreaux.

The decor is pure, unadorned 1930s, with a copper bar squished into the entryway, a few tables on the main floor, and a first-floor dining room with tables framed by broad, arched windows.

The cook's name is Marie-Louise Auteli but she calls herself Paulette, and she might as well be dubbed the queen of garlic. If you think you've never had your fill of garlic, this is the place to seriously examine your tolerance and test your endurance. Call ahead, and specify that you want to order the *poulet à l'ail* (see recipe, facing page). You'll have to be two, and there's no use coming unless you're hungry.

Ask Paulette her age and she'll reply *"37 ans dans le désordre,"* which translates as a hearty 73. She's been slowed down a bit by a wintertime fall and a scraped, arthritic knee, but she still loves to spend spare moments sipping Pastis and smoking with patrons at the bar.

Her *poulet à l'ail* is worthy of an ode: nothing but tender farm chicken, cut into serving pieces, cooked with butter, oil, and at least forty whole cloves of unpeeled garlic. The dish cooks away, uncovered, and at the last minute she flames the

Smiles from Tante Paulette.

chicken with Cognac, then deglazes it with a bit of white wine. The sort of dish you need to make a hundred times to get it just right. She does.

Before this, she'll ply you with salad. Simple, freshly dressed greens showered with slices of raw garlic, chunks of salty bacon, and man-size croutons rubbed with still more garlic. You'll pour thin generic red wine out of thick, heavy-bottomed bottles, take seconds of the perfectly aged and pungent Saint-Marcellin (a cheese so creamy, so tender, it has to be served out of a bowl), and hope that Paulette had time to make dessert today, a very fine *quatre-quarts,* or pound cake, flavored with freshly cooked pears.

LA VOUTE (CHEZ LEA)
11 Place Antonin-Gourju, 69002 Lyon.
(78.42.01.33).
Last orders taken at 2 P.M. and 9:30 P.M.
Closed Sunday and three weeks in July.
Credit cards: AE, DC.
Air-conditioned.
Private dining rooms for 15 and 30.
English spoken.
80-, 100-, and 120-franc menus. A la carte, 130 francs.

SPECIALTIES:
Poulet au vieux vinaigre (chicken with vinegar), *saucisson chaud au mâcon* (hot sausage in wine), *tablier de sapeur* (tripe that is marinated, breaded, and grilled), *quenelle lyonnaise aux écrevisses* (fish dumpling with freshwater crayfish), *pommes paillasson* (pan-fried pancake of shoestring potatoes).

One of Lyon's most consistently heartwarming restaurants is Restaurant La Voûte (Chez Léa), situated just off the Place Bellecour along the Quai des Célestins. The formidable Léa, one of Lyon's infamous women chefs, sold the restaurant some years back, but the cooking is as good, or perhaps better than ever.

Young chef Philippe Rabatel serves up some of the most wonderful salads in town. There's the deliciously dressed *pissenlits* salad with fresh cubed croutons and soft-cooked egg, as well as an outstanding and simple mixed green salad showered with a mix of fresh herbs dressed with one of the world's most delicious vinaigrettes.

During the late winter and early spring (from about February to May) he serves roast *chevreau,* or spring goat, a seasonal treat that rarely appears on restaurant menus. The meat is chewy, moist, and delicate, and should appeal to anyone who enjoys wild, subtly pungent flavors. With it, there's a medley of choices: crispy *pommes paillassons,* the local macaroni gratin, as well as artichoke bottoms stuffed with a mushroom mousse.

Those who prefer more traditional fare will be delighted with the chef's superb *poulet au vinaigre de vin vieux:* great, tender local chicken bathed in top-quality red wine vinegars. (See recipe, facing page).

On one visit, the lovely looking apple tart had suffered from too many reheatings, but the rich multilayered chocolate cake was a perfect close.

POULET AU VIEUX VINAIGRE CHEZ LEA
CHEZ LEA'S CHICKEN WITH VINEGAR

There are days when even the simplest restaurant menu offers dishes more complex than your palate desires. At times like this, I hope the chef will offer a soothing classic such as this one. I recreated this recipe from my taste memory, following a very satisfying dinner at one of my favorite Lyon standbys, La Voûte (Chez Léa).

3 tablespoons virgin olive oil
1 tablespoon (½ ounce; 15 g) unsalted butter
1 chicken, 3 to 4 pounds (1.5 to 2 kg), cut into serving pieces, at room temperature
Salt and freshly ground black pepper to taste
4 shallots, finely minced
1 cup (250 ml) best-quality red wine vinegar
1 cup (250 ml) *crème fraîche* (see Recipe Index) or heavy cream, preferably not ultra-pasteurized
Chopped fresh parsley for garnish

1. Heat the oil and butter in a deep 12-inch (30 cm) skillet over medium-high heat. (If you do not have a skillet large enough to hold all the chicken in a single layer, use 2 smaller skillets, dividing the chicken, oil, and butter in half for each pan.) Season the chicken liberally with salt and pepper. When the oil is hot but not smoking, add the chicken and brown on both sides until the skin turns an even golden brown, cooking to desired doneness, about 12 minutes each side. Carefully regulate the heat to avoid scorching the skin.

2. Transfer the chicken to a serving platter, cover loosely with aluminum foil, and keep warm.

3. Add the shallots to the remaining oil and lightly brown over medium-high heat. Slowly add the vinegar to the skillet, then boil until reduced by half. Add the *crème fraîche* and cook until the mixture is well blended and nut-brown, about 4 minutes. Pour the sauce over the chicken, garnish with parsley, and serve immediately.

Yield: 4 servings.

CAFES

BIDON 5
44 Rue Mercière, 69002 Lyon.
(78.42.21.69).
Open 5 A.M. to 8 P.M. Closed Sunday afternoon and Monday.
English spoken when Madame Camille's nieces are there.

Madame Camille, the red-headed *patronne* of this spotless little *mâchon*, is as maternal and sweet as they come. She's the unofficial den mother to the local chefs, serving up friendly conversation along with early morning snacks, or *mâchons*. Sausage, wine, cheese, and bread are available throughout the day, but most people come just for a cup of coffee or the popular Burgundian white wine, *aligoté*. When chef Bocuse wanders in after completing his marketing along the nearby *quais*, he orders a cup of strong black *express* and a *citron pressé chaud*, a sort of warm unsweetened lemonade. Note the mural at the back of the room: It depicts the trans-Sahara auto race, in which the Bidon 5 was the name of a refueling stop along the route.

A summer break at Bidon 5.

CINTRA BAR
43 Rue de la Bourse, 69002
  Lyon.
(78.42.54.08).
Open 9 A.M. to 9:30 P.M.
  Closed Sunday and
  holidays.

A classy, classic English-style café, where a cast iron wood-burning stove warms the chic and moneyed crowd—women in furs, men in business suits—the sort of place to curl up with a glass of Cognac, finishing a novel, working the day's crossword puzzle, or catching up on the news.

CAFE GAMBS
4 Rue Président-Carnot,
  69002 Lyon.
(78.92.89.78).
Open 8 A.M. to 11 P.M. Closed
  Sunday and two weeks in
  August.
Credit cards: AE, DC, V.
Sidewalk terrace in summer.
English spoken.

Café Gambs is the newest and classiest café in town, a perfect contrast to spots such as Bidon 5 and Brasserie Georges. The modern, sleek, and spotless café opens at 8 A.M. for coffee (rich, black, some of the best in town) and is transformed into a full-scale restaurant at mealtime. The kind of place to linger, impeccably dressed and perfectly coiffed, reading the latest copies of *Elle* and *Vogue*. Do make a visit to admire the ultramodern bathroom, with a sloping slab of marble that doubles as a sink.

BRASSERIE GEORGES
30 Cours Verdun, 69002
  Lyon.
(78.37.15.78).
Open 7 A.M. to midnight.
  Closed May Day.

One French critic suggests that Brasserie Georges, tucked away behind the modernized Perrache station, has all the ambience of a train station waiting room, with waiters who seem to come straight from a Balzac novel.

Everything about this cavernous, neon-lit place, open since 1836, is big. The ceilings are so high, four tall men could stand on one another's shoulders and not hit the top. There must be room for 400 customers, at least. A great place to observe the locals, ranging from groups of old ladies seated in a circle, chatting away as they sip their herb tea, to a cigar-puffing loner who resembles a French Groucho Marx. Note the fabulous restored Alsatian ceiling murals, depicting various harvest and festival scenes.

GRAND CAFE DES NEGOCIANTS
1 Place Francisque-Régaud, 69002 Lyon.
(78.42.50.05).
Open 7 A.M. to 1 A.M. Closed Sunday.
Credit card: V.
Sidewalk terrace.
Piano bar.

More French cities should have places like the Grand Café des Négociants. Throughout the day, this spacious, bustling 110-year-old spot serves as a traditional café, offering hot and cold drinks and snacks. Come nighttime, a pianist steps up to the shiny black grand piano in the window and plays away as customers settle into the café's fresh and refreshing *plateau de fruits de mer,* which includes briny oysters, raw mussels, crab, sea urchins, periwinkles, and shrimp. Hope that this is one of the days they've bought their rye bread from Marius Petit, one of the city's better bakers.

VAL D'ISERE
64 Rue Bonnel, 69003 Lyon.
(78.71.09.39).
Open 7 A.M. to 8 P.M. Closed Sunday and July.

Arrive about 9 on any given morning and you'll find all the city's chefs huddled around a table, sharing their morning coffee as they take a break from their rounds at the market down the street. It's great to watch the dean of them all, Paul Bocuse, hold court as waiters and colleagues pay just homage. I love the way they all call him *Paul-l-l-l-e-e-e.*

SALON DE THE

SALTER'S TEA SHOP
24 Rue Saint-Jean, 69005
   Lyon.
(78.92.91.73).
Open noon to 10 P.M.
   Tuesday through
   Saturday; noon to 2:30
   P.M. Sunday. Closed
   Monday and August.

A funky English tea salon, where you'll find a great pot of brewed tea served out of lovely antique china, which you can also buy in the shop. Salter's reminds me of an old-fashioned front parlor, where ladies gather for gossip, hot tea, and sugary desserts. A fine spot to stop while wandering about Lyon's old town.

PATISSERIE

**LA MICHE AU VIEUX
   FOUR**
153 Avenue de Saxe, 69003
   Lyon.
(78.62.35.55).
Open 7:30 A.M. to 12:30 P.M.
   and 3 to 7:15 P.M. Closed
   Sunday.

The shop's wood-fired oven produces a marvelously dense and delicious walnut bread and a superb *galette de montagne au beurre,* a regional bread tart with the thinnest of crusts, topped with lemon, sugar, and cream and baked to a buttery, deep golden brown. (See recipe for *Galette Bressane,* page 245). The bread and onion tart is less exciting. Note the counter: It's an old *pétrain,* or bread kneading trough.

BOULANGERIES

L. MANO
92 Grande Rue de la
   Guillotière, 69007 Lyon.
(78.69.25.47).
Open 7 A.M. to 7:30 P.M.
   Tuesday through
   Saturday; 7 A.M. to noon
   Sunday. Closed Sunday
   afternoon, Monday, one
   week in January, and two
   weeks in the summer.

A bread lover's paradise for discovering new taste sensations: The *pain d'algues*—a truly unusual pale green seaweed bread—is wonderful. I can just imagine trying to make it with a bunch of freshly harvested seaweed! Monsieur Luc Mano's bread, baked Friday, Saturday, and Sunday, has a good, fresh seaweed flavor, rather fragrant, quite subtle. Also delicious is the *pain de campagne au levain,* not as sour as the seaweed bread, but dense and flavorful, with a great crust.

M. PETIT
9 Rue Lanterne, 69001
   Lyon.
(78.28.36.69).
Open 6:30 A.M. to 8 P.M.
   Irregular hours in the
   summer. Closed Sunday.

Marius and Simone Petit are a terrific pair: He tends to the ovens, baking the locally popular *couronnes,* marvelous crown-shaped loaves of sourdough bread, while she cheerfully manages their little shop, situated on a narrow old street not far from the Place des Terreaux. Try also Monsieur Petit's superb rye bread, served from time to time at the Grand Café des Négociants, and his unusual *Pain aux Oignons* (see recipe, page 228). From January to mid-March people come from all over Lyon to sample his crisp and delicate *bugnes,* a flat doughnut-like pastry that's a regional treat.

A little night music at the Grand Café des Négociants.

FROMAGERIES

LA BERGERIE
108 Rue Bossuet, 69006
  Lyon.
(78.24.84.04).
Open 8:30 A.M. to 12:30 P.M.
  and 3:30 to 7:30 P.M.
  Closed Sunday and three
  weeks in August.

A wonderfully friendly cheese shop: Just follow their advice on what's good and in season and you won't be disappointed. We sampled a marvelous Abondance (a firm, nutty cow's-milk cheese) from the Savoie, and it had that incredibly fresh farmyard taste, with the flavor of rich raw milk.

ELENORE MARECHALE
Les Halles de Lyon, 102
  Cours Lafayette, 69003
  Lyon.
(78.62.36.77).
Open 7 A.M. to 12:30 P.M.
  and 3 to 7 P.M. Tuesday
  through Sunday
  morning. Closed Sunday
  afternoon and Monday.

A beautiful selection of cheeses from all over France, displayed like little jewels in lovely wicker baskets. Note especially the unusual assortment of cheeses from the island of Corsica.

RENEE RICHARD
Les Halles de Lyon, 102
  Cours Lafayette, 69003
  Lyon.
(78.62.30.78).
Open 7 A.M. to 12:30 P.M.
  and 3 to 7 P.M. Tuesday
  through Sunday
  morning. Closed Sunday
  afternoon and Monday.

Flamboyant Renée Richard is one of Lyon's best-known culinary characters, highly respected for her selection of well-aged cheeses from all over France. Along with her highly competent daughter, also named Renée, she supplies cheese to many of the best restaurants throughout France. Must tries: the pungent, creamy Saint-Marcellin; well-aged versions of both French and Swiss Vacherin; the high-mountain Reblochon. They will be happy to pack cheese for traveling.

PAIN AUX OIGNONS MARIUS PETIT
MARIUS PETIT'S ONION BREAD

Marius Petit is one of Lyon's finest bakers, and he offers a delicious assortment of what the French call pains de fantaisie. *He bakes large, hearty loaves as well as tiny rolls flavored with onions, with walnuts, or with black olives. Monsieur Petit, who has been baking bread in Lyon since the 1940s, began offering the* fantaisie *breads as a way to offer some competition to industrial bakeries. He likes to eat his onion bread with* choucroute, *the traditional Alsatian blend of sauerkraut and sausages. I like it toasted, with goat cheese and a glass of white wine.*

2 cups (500 ml) lukewarm water

2½ teaspoons or 1 package dry yeast

4 to 4½ cups (560 to 680 g) unbleached all-purpose flour

1½ teaspoons salt

2 tablespoons virgin olive oil

5 medium onions, sliced into thin rounds

1. Combine the water, yeast, and 1 cup (140 g) flour in a mixing bowl or the bowl of a heavy-duty mixer. Let sit for 5 minutes to proof the yeast.

2. Add the salt, then begin stirring in the remaining flour, cup by cup, until the dough is too stiff to stir. Place the dough on a lightly floured surface and begin kneading, adding additional flour if the dough is too sticky. It should be fairly soft and not too firm. Knead until the dough is smooth and satiny, about 10 minutes. (The dough can also be mixed and kneaded in a heavy-duty mixer fitted with a dough hook.)

3. Place the dough in a bowl, cover, and let rise at room temperature until doubled in bulk, about 1 hour.

4. Meanwhile, prepare the onion mixture. Heat the oil in a large skillet over medium-low heat. Add the onions, stir until they are thoroughly coated with oil, and cook covered, stirring occasionally, for 20 minutes. The onions should be tender, thickened, and light golden. Remove from the heat and let cool.

5. Preheat the oven to 425°F (220°C).

6. Punch the dough down and carefully knead the cooled onion mixture into the dough, making sure the onions are evenly distributed. Shape the dough into a ball. Place a floured large kitchen towel in a shallow round bowl or basket and place the dough in the towel. Fold the towel over the dough, covering it loosely. Let rise again until doubled in bulk, about 1 hour.

7. Turn the loaf upside down onto a flour-dusted baking sheet or preheated baking stone. Slash the bread several times with a razor blade, so it can expand regularly during baking. Bake until golden brown, 45 to 50 minutes.

Yield: 1 loaf.

CHARCUTERIES

BOBOSSE (RENE BESSON)
66 Rue Bonnel, 69003 Lyon.
(78.62.66.10).
Open 7A.M. to noon. Closed
Sunday and Monday.
European mail orders
accepted.

Paris Connection:
**BOUCHERIE
LAMARTINE**
172 Avenue Victor Hugo,
Paris 16.
(47.27.82.29).

REYNON
13 Rue des Archers, 69002
Lyon.
(78.37.39.08).
Open 8:30 A.M. to 12:30 P.M.
and 3 to 7:30 P.M. Closed
Sunday, Monday, the last
three weeks in July, and
one week in February.
French mail orders
accepted.

Lyon's number one address for *charcuterie,* known for its rich blood sausage, or *boudin,* headcheese, and the delicious—though not to everyone's taste—*sabodet,* a strong and earthy sausage made up of pork, beef, pig's head and skin.

Lyon is a sausage lover's town, and one of its oldest, most traditional *charcuteries* is Reynon, situated not far from the Place Bellecour. All sorts of specialties—fresh truffle-and-morel-studded pork sausage for simmering in white wine, dried *rosettes* for picnics and snacking—are arranged along the windows of this family-run shop. There's also earthy *sabodet* for cooking in Beaujolais, and delicate hand-formed *quenelles,* the fluffy pike dumplings that are a Lyonnais favorite.

A SINFUL STORY

Butter, eggs, and sugar are a sinful trio, but today we don't exactly risk excommunication when we indulge. This wasn't always so.

In 1873, during the season of Lent, the souls of innumerable Lyonnais pastry cooks and doughnut lovers hung in the balance as an archbishop decided their fate. It seems that the original unpalatable flour-and-water doughnut or *bugne,* had been tampered with: Enterprising *bugne* makers, flouting the church's penitential Lenten diet rules, had turned the austere dough into a light, frivolously buttery pastry, and their customers were grabbing them up. Faced with excommunicating so many parishioners, the archbishop chose leniency.

Today *bugnes* remain a traditional pre-Easter treat in and around Lyon. But watch out, for when they're not prepared by skillful hands, they turn into lead sinkers, punishing contemporarary sweet tooths for the excesses of their fathers.

Chocolates with the Master's Touch

"If, like the Japanese, the French conferred the title of 'national treasure' upon living artists and artisans, then Maurice Bernachon would be a candidate."

LYON, FEBRUARY 7—Bernachon chocolates are so rich and intense that one is required to savor them, morsel by morsel, much like a well-aged, finely constructed Bordeaux that calls for pensive sipping, not guzzling.

A visit to their pristine chocolate-colored shop along Lyon's fashionable Cours Franklin-Roosevelt is an overwhelmingly sensory experience. The chocolates are displayed like rare gems, with the care and the flair that the French instinctively bestow upon all they value and respect. And the aroma, a heady mingling of bitter chocolate, sweet butter, caramelized sugar, vanilla, and roasted nuts is so overpowering that even the strongest among us soon weaken.

If, like the Japanese, the French conferred the title of "national treasure" upon living artists and artisans, then Maurice Bernachon would be a candidate.

But what distinguishes Bernachon chocolates from the hundreds of others around the world? Quite simply, it is the Bernachon dedication to perfection, a dedication that others have lost, or perhaps never knew. The Bernachons, who run one of the world's few remaining made-from-scratch chocolate shops, insist upon quality ingredients. They enjoy comparing the art of chocolate making to winemaking.

"But instead of grapes, you've got beans, and everything hinges on the quality of those beans: the soil in which they are grown, their care, their blending," explains young Jean-Jacques, Maurice's outgoing son, as he conducts a tour of the fragrant Bernachon *atelier.*

While the majority of chocolate makers are content to buy factory-produced fondant or *couverture,* the basic "dough" of the chocolate art, the Bernachons continue to oversee the process from start to finish, using the finest and freshest ingredients in their classic *crème-fraîche*-filled truffles and the forty-odd other varieties of handmade Bernachon chocolates, candies, cakes, and pastries.

They begin with top-quality *fèves* from Venezuela, Ecuador, Trinidad, and Madagascar: cocoa beans that account for a small percentage of the world's production, beans prized for their richness, their distinctive nutty flavor. The Bernachons use slender, pungent vanilla beans from Réunion, arrange for cocoa butter from the Netherlands, secure pistachios from Sicily, walnuts from the Dauphiné, hazelnuts from the Piedmont in Italy, and search out both sweet and bitter almonds from Provence as well as the hillsides of Spain. The butter, of course, is the superior sweet French *beurre des Charentes;* the cream is pure Lyonnais.

Before the chocolates reach the newly remodeled Bernachon boutique they will pass through the hands of perhaps a dozen employees, who go about their business in a maze-like series of bright little rooms that trail off behind the shop.

Everything begins with the beans. By the time they reach Lyon, they have already fermented in the open air in their country of origin, to partially rid them of their natural astringency. Just a bit larger than a coffee bean, they are still pale tan, a bit moist, barely fragrant, and unbelievably bitter.

Jean-Jacques roasts the beans, still in their thin shell, for twenty to thirty min-

utes, checking them every two or three minutes. The beans darken to a rich chocolate brown as they roast, shedding their moisture. The outer shell begins to fall
away, forming nibs that resemble chocolate chips. Even though at this point the
beans remain bitterly, inedibly acidic, the fresh, intoxicating aroma of pure bitter
chocolate has begun to waft through the air. The beans contain about 50 percent
pure cocoa butter, a natural vegetable fat, and 50 percent "meat," the half that
goes on to become cocoa.

The shells are sifted away and discarded, and now it's time to blend, to balance, to, as Maurice likes to say, "pull out our special recipe."

The assertive Venezuelan beans are blended with more delicate, subtler
beans from Trinidad and Madagascar, then with sugar, vanilla, and a supplemen-
tary dose of costly cocoa butter, added to improve the texture and gloss of the final
product. Together, the ingredients are passed slowly through steel rollers that look
like an old-fashioned clothes wringer—a process called *broyage*. The chocolate
emerges in paper-thin sheets, crackly and dry.

At last we have a blend that tastes of chocolate. But now it must be smoothed
out, undergoing a process known as *conchage:* For three days the mixture is
warmed to the melting point, then rocked back and forth ten to twelve hours a day
under the constant supervision of the Bernachon staff.

"Here you see why this is a dying art," notes Maurice. "No one wants to
bother with all this any more. They can substitute cheap synthetic butters for expensive cocoa butter, and can add soy lecithin and skip the *conchage* altogether."

Later, the thick and shiny brown liquid is poured into large stainless-steel
vats to cool overnight, and at last work can begin on the variety of chocolate preparations. Cooled chocolate is formed into blocks, to be wrapped, stored, and taken
from aging rooms as needed to prepare the chocolates, cakes, and pastries sold in
the retail shop.

Jean-Jacques leads his visitors through the series of tiny workshops, passing a
man energetically beating a blend of sugar and almonds in a giant copper bowl.
He adjusts his little white cap, lowers the flame, and takes a deep whiff of the fragrant praline.

Maurice surveys his band of young workers and notes the inevitable changes
that accompany the passage of time: "It used to be that kids would come here and
work for several years, in hopes of learning the art and one day opening their own
shops. Now they come, work a bit, and decide the business is not very glamorous,
does not give them enough free time, and they leave. The apprentice system is all
but dead."

The company, with a total of forty-nine employees, is still run much like
French family enterprises of days past. Many of the young girls working in the
boutique and the chocolate-making *atelier* live in dormitories above the shop and
take their meals in the company dining room. The Bernachons even employ a full-
time cook, so the employees are spared the time and expense of eating out.

Later, Maurice walks into his ultra-modern office, strewn with computers and
printers, and chuckles at the contrast. "Fortunately they haven't yet invented a
computer that can make chocolates like ours," he remarks, taking a bite of a
palet d'or, a blend of bitter chocolate and cream, dipped in bitter chocolate.

Consistently self-critical, his smile shifts to a minor frown. "They're too fresh.
They need a day to ripen. They'll taste a lot better tomorrow."

LE SUCCÈS DE BERNACHON
BERNACHON'S NUT MERINGUE CAKE WITH
CHOCOLATE CREAM

When I can't have the real thing—fresh Bernachon chocolates—I happily settle for a home-made chocolate cake of the sort one finds in the Bernachon shop in Lyon. Le Succès is a classic French meringue with a quantity of nuts added to give it a cake-like texture. This Bernachon version is filled and frosted with a rich chocolate cream and should be prepared the day before it is to be served, if possible.

Chocolate cream:
2 cups (500 ml) *crème fraîche* (see Recipe Index) or heavy cream, preferably not ultra-pasteurized.
10½ ounces (300 g) extra-bittersweet chocolate (preferably Lindt or Tobler brand), chopped in small pieces.

Cake:
1¼ cups (180 g) whole unblanched almonds
1 cup minus 1 tablespoon (180 g) sugar
Butter and flour for the baking sheets
6 large egg whites
2 tablespoons unsweetened cocoa powder, sifted, for garnish

1. Prepare the chocolate cream: Bring the *crème fraîche* to a boil in a medium saucepan over medium-high heat. As soon as it begins to boil, remove it from the heat and add the chocolate, piece by piece, stirring until all the chocolate is completely melted. Set the chocolate cream aside to cool, then refrigerate covered for at least 3 hours.

2. Prepare the cake: Place the almonds and all but 2 tablespoons of the sugar in the bowl of a food processor and process to a medium-fine powder.

3. Preheat the oven to 350°F (175°C).

4. Butter and flour 2 baking sheets, marking an 8-inch (20 cm) circle on each.

5. Beat the egg whites until stiff but not dry, slowly adding the remaining sugar as the whites begin to stiffen. The mixture should be very stiff. Fold in the powdered almond mixture.

6. Using a pastry bag fitted with a large plain tip, pipe the cake batter onto the prepared baking sheets in two 7-inch (18 cm) circles, starting in the center and spiraling outward. Bake for 15 minutes, or just until the cakes begin to brown.

7. Remove the cakes from the oven, loosen them from the pan, and allow them to cool completely before transferring them to a work surface.

8. Assemble the cake: Be certain that the chocolate cream is soft enough to spread. (To soften the chocolate cream, reheat it gently). Place one cake layer on a serving platter, smooth side up. Spread it with half the chocolate cream. Place the second layer on top, and frost the top and the sides. Refrigerate for 12 hours.

9. Remove the cake from the refrigerator 30 minutes before serving. Dust with the cocoa powder and serve.

Yield: 10 to 12 servings.

CHOCOLATERIE

BERNACHON
42 Cours Franklin-
Roosevelt, 69006 Lyon.
(78.24.37.98).
Open 8 A.M. to 7 P.M. Tuesday
through Saturday and 8
A.M. to 5 P.M. Sunday.
Closed Monday.
International mail orders
accepted.

Edible jewels from Maurice Bernachon.

Maurice and Jean-Jacques Bernachon make the best chocolate in the world, and it would be a shame to visit Lyon without sampling at least one morsel of their rich, deep, dark chocolate. Their newly enlarged shop, in the fashionable 6th arrondissement, is like a museum devoted to chocolate. Nothing but the finest fresh cocoa beans from Venezuela and Ecuador go into their chocolates. Do try the bittersweet *palets d'or,* the best of all their confections.

VIN, BIERE, ALCOOL

MALLEVAL
11 Rue Emile-Zola, 69002
Lyon.
(78.42.02.07).
Open 2 to 7 P.M. Monday,
8:30 A.M. to noon and 2
to 7 P.M. Tuesday through
Saturday. Closed Monday
morning and Sunday.
International mail orders
accepted.

A fabulously elegant wine and liquor shop, with an extensive selection. Note in particular the delicious *eaux-de-vie* from Jean Danflou.

SALADIER LYONNAIS
DANDELION GREENS WITH BACON, CROUTONS, EGG, HERRING, AND ANCHOVIES

Lyon has its version of the salade niçoise, *and this is it. Like the Niçois regional salad, one sees numerous versions. I've seen the* saladier lyonnais *served with croutons or without, with bacon or without, with as well as without herring and anchovies. Most often, a whole egg—cooked longer than a soft-cooked egg, shorter than a hard-cooked one—appears alongside. If dandelion greens are not available, use curly endive, or a mix of greens, such as lamb's lettuce and trévise. Do make an effort to find the best-quality oil-cured herring and anchovies. The salad makes a very satisfying meal on its own, served with a glass of red wine. Beaujolais, of course.*

4 large eggs, at room temperature

4 slices country-style bread, preferably homemade

2 cloves garlic, halved

6 ounces (170 g) slab bacon or side pork, rind removed, cut into 1½ x 1-inch (4 x 2.5 cm) pieces

Dressing:

2 tablespoons best-quality red wine vinegar

1½ teaspoons imported Dijon mustard

Salt and freshly ground black pepper to taste

5 tablespoons virgin olive oil

6 cups (1.5 liters) dandelion greens, curly endive, or mixed greens, rinsed, dried, and torn into pieces

Handful mixed fresh herbs, preferably chervil, tarragon, parsley, minced

8 oil-cured herring fillets (optional)

8 oil-cured anchovy fillets (optional)

1. Arrange the eggs in a single layer in a saucepan and fill with ½ inch (1.25 cm) cold water. Cook, uncovered, over medium-high heat until the first large bubbles rise steadily from the bottom of the pan. Reduce the heat so the water continues to simmer very gently but never boils. Simmer 6 minutes. Pour off the hot water and stop the cooking by filling the pan with cold water. When the eggs are cool, peel them.

2. Toast the bread under the broiler, watching carefully so the bread does not burn. While still warm, rub both sides generously with the garlic. Cut into 1 x ½-inch (2.5 x 1.25 cm) pieces.

3. Place the bacon in a large skillet. Adding no additional fat, cook, stirring frequently, over medium-high heat until crisp. Drain the bacon on paper towels and set aside. Discard the fat.

4. Prepare the dressing: Whisk the vinegar, mustard, salt, and pepper together in a small bowl. Add the oil and whisk until emulsified.

5. Combine the greens, herbs, croutons, and bacon in a large salad bowl. Add the dressing and toss until well mixed. Check the seasoning.

6. Divide the dressed salad among 4 large salad plates. Place a whole egg at the side of each salad.

7. Arrange the herring and anchovies, if using, in a serving dish and pass as a side dish to be eaten with the salad.

Yield: 4 servings.

CHEESES OF LYON

1. RIGOTTE DE CONDRIEU: Named for the Rhône valley wine village of Condrieu—which produces one of France's rarest white wines—this tiny cylinder of cow's-milk cheese is aged in dry cellars for just a week or two, emerging with a pleasingly delicate, lactic flavor. Rigotte's reddish-orange bloom is a result of a sprinkling of annatto, the yellowish-red pulp surrounding the seeds of the annatto tree.

2. AROME A LA GENE: *Arôme* is the generic name given to a variety of the cheeses of the Lyon area—including Rigotte, Saint-Marcellin, Pélardon, and Picodon—that have been steeped in *gêne*, or *marc*, the dried grape skins that are left after grapes are pressed for wine. The best versions have a tangy, lactic flavor and a faint aroma of alcohol, and may be made of cow's milk, goat's milk, or a mixture of the two.

3. SAINT-MARCELLIN: Once made on farms of raw goat's milk, this popular cheese of the Lyon region is now made from cow's milk and formed into a flat, solid disc. Almost all Saint-Marcellin—named for the village of Saint-Marcellin, in the Savoie—is made in small commercial dairies, some of which turn out a marvelously smooth and creamy cheese, found fresh and white; mildly aged, when the rind begins to turn a mottled yellowish orange; and at its well-aged best, when it is so runny, it must be served on plate.

WINE OF LYON

FLEURIE (FERRAUD): When it comes to Beaujolais, there is the good, the bad, and the indifferent. The Pierre Ferraud label is a trusted one, known for elegant violet wines of distinction.

Jura/Rhône-Alpes
JURA/RHONE-ALPS

Paul Koeberlé of Villars-les-Dombes.

The Jura/Rhône-Alpes—a vast expanse of land stretching from the Rhône valley on the west to the Jura mountains to the east, encircling the Savoie and the land of Bresse, the walnut groves of Grenoble and the steep, steep vineyards that straddle the wide, roving Rhône—was my land of discovery. I think that it was here, as I moved through the world of village bread ovens and farmhouse Morbier, Bresse poultry farmers and small-town sausage makers, that my eyes were truly opened to the wealth of rural France. Time and again, I was stirred, gladdened, and gratified by the people I met, who opened their doors, and thus their lives, to talk about traditions which they refuse to let die. There were serendipitous times when single interviews stretched into daylong affairs and I found myself not on the road at lunchtime as planned, but at table with cheesemakers, talking of milk cooperatives and the proper breeding of bulls.

But just as I witnessed the continuation of tradition, I watched as others constructed myths so folks could keep their dreams. No one wanted to talk about those regional French specialties—the frog's legs and snails, fresh morel mushrooms and crayfish—no longer found in abundance in France's fields, forests, and streams. Instead, frog's legs come from Yugoslavia and crayfish from Turkey,

morels from Italy and live snails from Greece, and are served as
authentic specimen of France's gastronomic heritage.

Later, as I reviewed the recipes I had gathered, I realized that
the Jura and the Rhône-Alpes had made an indelible impression,
for cream and sugar Bressane tarts and smoky Morteau sausages

are now part of my family's repertoire, and I cannot sample a slice of nutty Beaufort without wondering whether the milk came from Jules Roux-Daigue's contented cows.

WHEN YOU GO

Michelin Green Guides: *Jura/Franche-Comté, Alpes/Savoie-Dauphiné, Vallée du Rhône/Vivarais-Lyonnais.*

Getting there: Air Inter offers about eight 1-hour flights daily to Lyon, leaving from Paris's Orly Ouest airport. The journey by train takes 2 hours by TGV *(train à grande vitesse),* or bullet train, or 5 hours by regular train to Lyon's downtown Perrache station or the Part-Dieu station at the edge of town.

There are also about seven TGV making the 2-hour journey daily between Paris and Dole, while four TGV travel to Bourg-en-Bresse in 2 hours. There are ten TGV making the 3½-hour journey to Grenoble and the 3-hour journey to Valence.

All trains leave from Paris's Gare de Lyon. Cars can be rented at the airport and train stations.

Getting around: Michelin maps 243 (Bourgogne/Franche-Comté) and 244 (Rhône-Alpes).

Best time to visit: Like much of France, the prettiest time of year runs from Easter through October, though with the excellent hiking and cross-country ski trails in the Jura mountain area and downhill skiing in the Alps, the region is popular during the winter months as well.

MARKETS
(Liveliest markets are marked with an asterisk.)

Monday: Besançon, Bessenay (June and July), La Clusaz, Oyonnax, Poligny, Poncin, Saint-Etienne, Seyssel.

Tuesday: *Annecy, Arbois, Belfort, Besançon, Bessenay (June and July), Divonne-les-Bains, Dole, *Evian-les-Bains, Gray, Grenoble, Lure, Montbéliard, Morteau, *Roanne, Romans-sur-Isère, Saint-Etienne, Valence, Villars-les-Dombes.

Wednesday: Aix-les-Bains, *Ambérieu-en-Bugey, Audincourt, *Belfort, Besançon, Bessenay (June and July), *Bourg-en-Bresse, Grenoble, Maîche, Meximieux, Montbéliard, Saint-Etienne, Valdoie.

Thursday: Aime, Annecy, Baume-les-Dames, Belfort, Besançon, Bessenay (June and July), Dole, Grenoble, *Lons-le-Saunier, *Pontarlier, Saint-Claude, Saint-Etienne, Salins-les-Bains, Thonon-les-Bains, Valence, Vésoul, Vonnas.

Friday: Ambérieu-en-Bugey, Annecy, *Arbois, Belfort, Besançon, Bessenay (June and July), *Divonne-les-Bains, Evian-les-Bains, *Gray, *Grenoble, Megève, Oyonnax, Poligny, Port-sur-Saône, *Roanne, Romans-sur-Isère, Saint-Etienne.

Saturday: *Aix-les-Bains, Ambérieu-en-Bugey, *Annecy, *Audincourt, Belfort, Belley, Besançon, Bessenay (June and July), Bourg-en-Bresse, Chamonix, Champagnole, *Dole, Ferney-Voltaire, Gex, *Grenoble, Lons-le-Saunier, *Maîche, Mandeure, *Montbéliard, Morez, *Morteau, Nantua, *Oyonnax, Pontarlier, Roanne, Romans-sur-Isère, Ronchamp, Le Russey, Saint-Claude, Saint-Etienne, Salins-les-Bains, Thônes, Valdoie, Valence.

Sunday: Annecy, *Belfort, Bessenay (June and July), *Grenoble, Roanne, Romans-sur-Isère, Saint-Etienne, Villard-de-Lans.

FAIRS AND FESTIVALS

Late January and early February: *Semaines Gastronomiques* (gastronomy weeks), Les Arcs.

One week in March: *Semaine Régionale de la Cuisine* (regional cooking week), Les Arcs.

Sunday before Easter: *Fête du Vieux Four* (bread baking festival), Catton-Grammont.

Easter Sunday: *Fête du Vieux Four* (bread baking festival), Vongnes.

Mother's Day: *Fête du Vieux Four* (bread baking festival), Marignieu.

Sunday and Monday of Pentecost: *Fête des Gentianes* (gentian festival), Le Russey.

Third Sunday in May: *Fête du Fromage* (cheese festival), Chambost-Allières.

Fourth Sunday in May in even years: *Fête des Bigarreaux* (cherry festival), Bessenay.

First or second Sunday in June: *Fête du Vieux Four* (bread baking festival), Parves.

June 13: *Fête du Vieux Four* (bread baking festival), Belmont.

June 24: *Fête du Vieux Four* (bread baking festival), Fougerolles.

July: *Fête des Moissons* (harvest festival), Fressinières.

First Sunday in July: *Fête des Cerises* (cherry festival), Fougerolles.

Weekend before July 14: *Fête des Brimbelles* (blueberry festival), Giromagny.

Third Sunday in July: *Fête du Vieux Four* (bread baking festival), Saint-Champ.

July 22: *Fête de la Vigne et du Vin* (wine festival), Arbois.

July 27: *Fête de l'Olivier* (olive festival), Les Vans.

Last weekend in July: *Fête du Comté* (Comté cheese festival), Poligny; *Fête des Airelles* (cranberry festival), Duerne.

First two weeks in August: *Fête du Reblochon* (Reblochon cheese festival), La Clusaz.

First Sunday in August: *Fête du Vieux Four* (bread baking festival), Crest-Voland; *Fête de l'Alpage* (alpine festival), Le Grand-Bornand.

Mid-August: *Fête de l'Alpage* (alpine festival), Les Gets; *Fête des Myrtilles* (blueberry festival), Sauvain.

Second Sunday in August: *Journées des Produits Régionaux* (regional specialties days), Morteau.

Sunday after August 15: *Fête du Pain* (bread baking festival), Cordon.

Third Sunday in August: *Fête des Alpages* (alpine festival), Châtel; *Fête de la Cancoillotte* (Cancoillotte cheese festival), Loulans-les-Forges.

August 29: *Fête et Foire aux Oignons* (onion festival and fair), Tournon-sur-Rhône.

Last weekend in August: *Fête de la Bière* (beer festival), Morvillars.

Last Sunday in August: *Fête de la Batteuse* (traditional gastronomic and folklore festival), Meys.

First weekend in September: *Fête du Poulet et Agriculture* (chicken and agriculture festival), Saint-Trivier-de-Courtes.

Second Sunday in September: *Fête du Miel* (honey festival), Chambost-Allières.

Three days around September 13: *Foire de Beaucroissant* (traditional local fair), Beaucroissant.

Mid-September: *Foire du Vin et de la Gastronomie* (wine and gastronomy fair), Belfort.

Third Sunday in September: *Fête du Vieux Four* (bread baking festival), Flaxieu.

Last Sunday in September: *Foire au Boudin* (blood sausage festival), Curis-au-Mont-d'Or.

First Sunday in October: *Fête du Vin Cuit* (pear and apple jam festival), Saint-Trivier-de-Courtes.

Late October/early November: *Salon de la Gastronomie et des Produits Régionaux* (gastronomy and regional specialties fair), Bourg-en-Bresse.

November 11: *Journée de la Pomme* (apple day), Pélussin.

Next to last weekend in November: *Salon de la Gastronomie* (gastronomy fair), Le Coteau.

Next to last or last weekend in November: *Foire au Miel* (honey fair), Saint-Cyr-au-Mont-d'Or.

December 8: *Rôtie Monstre de Châtaignes* (chestnut-roasting festival), Annonay.

Third Sunday in December: *Les Trois Glorieuses* (poultry contest and exhibit), Bourg-en-Bresse.

AIME *(Savoie)*

Albertville 38 k, Bourg-Saint-Maurice 13k, Chambéry 85 k,
Moûtiers 11 k, Paris 612 k.

Market: Thursday, 8 A.M. to noon, Place de l'Eglise.

FROMAGER-AFFINEUR

**COOPERATIVE AFFINAGE
BEAUFORT**
Avenue de Tarentaise, 73210
Aime.
(79.55.61.68).
Open 9 A.M. to noon and
2:30 to 6:30 P.M. Closed
Sunday afternoon and
Wednesday.
Will ship in France.

*The Beaufort-making process
begins.*

Beaufort is among the noblest of French cheeses,
a rustic cow's-milk cheese fragrant with mountain herbs and flowers, aged patiently for up to two
years in the cooperative aging rooms of the region.
This cooperative offers some of the finest Beaufort
available: Be sure to ask for an aged Beaufort *d'été*
or Beaufort *d'alpage,* an assurance that the cheese
was made in the mountains of raw cow's milk
during the best milking period, from mid-June to
the end of September, when the cows wander about
the pasture feasting on mountain flowers, herbs,
and grasses.

AMBERIEU-EN-BUGEY *(Ain)*

Bourg-en-Bresse 30 k, Lyon 53 k, Paris 457 k.

Markets: Wednesday and Saturday, 8 A.M. to noon, Place du Champ-de-Mars; Friday, 8 A.M. to noon, Place de la Gare.

BOULANGERIE

JACQUES GRATTARD
30 Rue Amédée-Bonnet,
01500 Ambérieu-
en-Bugey.
(74.38.01.89).
Open 7:30 A.M. to 12:30 P.M.
and 2 to 7:30 P.M. Closed
Monday, two weeks in
February, and four weeks
in September and
October.

One Sunday morning I was driving past this village bakery when I saw a man coming out of the shop with one of the most beautiful loaves of country bread I'd ever seen. I immediately stopped, parked the car, and headed into what appeared to be a very ordinary-looking shop, where they make a very extraordinary bread. We snacked on the crusty sourdough loaf for the better part of the week. How I wish I could say I found hundreds of loaves such as this on my tour of France, authentic sourdough bread so flavorful you can make a meal of it. Monsieur Grattard bakes only a few dozen loaves of *pain de campagne au levain* each day, so arrive early, when they're still warm from the wood-fired oven.

ANNECY *(Haute-Savoie)*

Genève 43 k, Lyon 137 k, Paris 533 k.

Markets: Tuesday, Friday, and Sunday, 8 A.M. to noon, Rue Sainte-Claire; Thursday, 8 A.M. to noon, Avenue de France; Saturday, 8 A.M. to noon, Boulevard Taine.

Do not pass through the region without a visit to the Rue Sainte-Claire market which winds through the streets of old Annecy, certainly one of the most beautiful and charming towns in all of France. Go especially during the summer months, when the city is at its floral best and you can wander through the narrow streets and sip coffee at the cafés along the Thiou river, which runs through the center of town. At the market you'll find an outstanding selection of local sausages as well as cheeses, including perfectly aged Reblochon, two-year-old Beaufort *d'alpage,* and one of the most beautiful Saint-Marcellins I've ever seen. The little Saint-Marcellin had that golden exterior, that creamy, runny interior, the look of a cheese that seems to be crying out, "Buy me now, I'm ready!"

The summer glory of Annecy.

ARBOIS *(Jura)*

Dole 35 k, Lons-le-Saunier 38 k.

Market: Tuesday and Friday, 8:30 A.M. to noon, Place du Champ-de-Mars.
Fête de la Vigne et du Vin (wine festival): July 22.

BISTRO A VIN

LA FINETTE
22 Avenue Pasteur, 39600
    Arbois.
(84.66.06.78).
Last orders taken at 10 P.M.
Open daily.
Credit card: V.
Air-conditioned.
Private dining rooms can be
    arranged.
Some English spoken in
    season.
45- to 120-franc menus. A la
    carte, about 100 francs.

La Finette is a lively village wine bar/restaurant, offering the local Arbois white, red, and rosé wines from a number of producers. But since La Finette is owned by Henri Maire, the king of Arbois winemakers, the respectable Maire wines dominate. With any of the wines, try the local pork sausage served with a warming platter of red lentils, or the filling cheese fondue. Around November, La Finette serves baskets of fresh walnuts to eat with the rare *vin de paille,* the straw-colored wine aged for at least six years, then bottled, to live eternally.

FROMAGERIE

**COOPERATIVE LAITIERE
    ET FROMAGERE**
Rue des Fossés, 39600
    Arbois.
(84.66.09.71).
Open daily 7 A.M. to noon
    and 5:30 to 8 P.M.

One of many spots in the Jura where you can watch the cheesemaking process, and you can purchase the fine local Comté cheese as well.

GALETTE BRESSANE
CREAM AND SUGAR TART FROM BRESSE

This tart—so obvious, so delicious, it's hard to believe it's so easy—can be found in just about every pastry shop in the area of Bourg-en-Bresse. This recipe comes from the village pastry shop in Villars-les-Dombes, where the Koeberlé family has been tending the stove for three genera-tions. They use a brioche dough for the base. Whenever local residents bake bread in the com-munity ovens, they make a cream and sugar tart for the day's dessert, using leftover bread dough. In the nearby medieval village of Pérouges, a similar tart is prepared with a butter and sugar topping, and lemon zest is kneaded into the dough. Whether one uses brioche or bread dough is a matter of personal taste. I prefer the bread dough—it's more rustic.

Grated zest (peel) of 1
lemon
1 pound (500 g) Basic
Bread Dough made
through second rise
(see Recipe Index)
½ cup (125 ml) *crème
fraîche* (see Recipe
Index) or sour cream
½ cup (100 g) sugar

1. Preheat the oven to 450°F (230°C).

2. Knead the lemon zest into the bread dough. Roll out the dough to fit a 10½-inch (27 cm) tart pan and carefully transfer the dough to the pan.

3. Spread the *crème fraîche* evenly onto the bread dough right to the edge. Sprinkle with the sugar.

4. Bake until the tart is puffed and golden brown, about 25 minutes. Remove from the oven, let sit for about 3 minutes (so the cream and sugar soldify and the tart is easier to cut), and serve.

Yield: one 10½-inch (27 cm) tart.

Making Comté in the Jura.

BOURG-EN-BRESSE *(Ain)*

Annecy 119 k, Chambéry 110 k, Lyon 62 k, Paris 413 k, Roanne 118 k.

Market: Wednesday and Saturday, 8:30 A.M. to noon, Champ de Foire.
Salon de la Gastronomie et des Produits Régionaux (gastronomy and regional specialties fair): late October/early November.
Les Trois Glorieuses (poultry contest and exhibit): third Sunday in November.

RESTAURANT

LE FRANCAIS
7 Avenue Alsace-Lorraine,
    01000 Bourg-en-Bresse.
(74.22.55.14).
Last orders taken at 2 P.M.
    and 10 P.M.
Closed Saturday dinner,
    Sunday, August, and
    Christmas week.
Credit cards: AE, V.
Terrace dining.
English spoken.
70-, 100-, and 130-franc
    menus. A la carte, 150
    francs.

S P E C I A L T I E S :
Grenouilles (frog's legs), *volaille
à la crème et morilles* (chicken
with cream and morels),
quenelles (fish dumplings),
fish.

One of those wonderfully faded gastronomic monuments, this small-town restaurant/café is just the sort of authentic local place I love to find when traveling. There's a solid, shirt-sleeves clientele (businessmen settle in with the newspaper, Bresse chicken, and a bottle of Burgundy), and the food is refreshing, unfussy, familiar. For a pittance you can enjoy all the salad you can eat, delicious roast *poulet de Bresse,* potato gratin, and a decent local cheese tray.

CHOCOLATERIE

La Finette, Arbois.

CHOCOLATERIE MONET
14 Rue Bichat, 01000
    Bourg-en-Bresse.
(74.23.47.42).
Open 9 A.M. to noon and 2
    to 7 P.M. Closed Sunday
    and Monday.
Credit card: V.
Will ship internationally.

This spotless gem of a shop is a must for chocolate lovers: Young Jean-Claude Charpentier is one of the few chocolate makers in France to make his own *couverture,* roasting and blending cocoa beans and working them into a smooth, rich chocolate base. Try especially the chocolate-covered *pâte d'amandes au gingembre* (almond paste flavored with ginger), and anything with his incredible fruit *ganache,* a filling that blends rich chocolate with pure fruit pulp.

CHAMPAGNOLE *(Jura)*

Dole 60 k, Genève 89 k, Lons-le-Saunier 34 k, Paris 426 k.

Market: Saturday, 8 A.M. to noon, Place Camille-Prost.

CHARCUTERIE

RELAIS DE FUME
18 Avenue de la République,
  39300 Champagnole.
(84.52.00.91).
Open 7 A.M. to noon and 2
  to 7 P.M. Closed Sunday
  afternoon, Monday, and
  September.
Credit card: V.
Will ship in France.

This shop is a sausage lover's dream, with its wonderful selection of local products including *saucisson sec* (dried pork sausage), *saucisse de Morteau* (smoked pork sausage), and meat terrines. Most items are vacuum-packaged for longer keeping and sanitation. Although the plastic packaging takes away a bit from the folklore, it's a great idea for travelers and picnickers.

TARTE A L'OIGNON DE CATTON-GRAMMONT
ONION TART FROM CATTON-GRAMMONT

One sunny Sunday afternoon in early May we were touring the old-fashioned community bread ovens near Bourg-en-Bresse. Spotting a poster for a bread tart festival being held that very day in the village of Catton-Grammont, we raced there as fast as humanly possible, arriving just as the tarts—baked in large rectangular metal pans and loaded onto an old wooden door to cool—were coming out of the oven. We stayed a while to chat with the village "bakers" and sample the local white Bugey wine. I think about that afternoon each time I make this tart.

3 tablespoons (1½
  ounces; 45 g)
  unsalted butter
5 medium onions,
  sliced into thin
  rounds
1 pound (500 g) Basic
  Bread Dough (see
  Recipe Index)
1 large egg
2 tablespoons *crème
  fraîche* (see Recipe
  Index) or sour cream
¼ cup (30 g) walnuts,
  finely ground
1 tablespoon walnut oil
Salt and freshly ground
  black pepper to taste

1. Preheat the oven to 450°F (230°C).

2. Melt the butter in a large skillet over medium-low heat. Add the onions, stir until they are thoroughly coated with butter, and cook covered, stirring occasionally, for 20 minutes. The onions should be tender, thickened, and light golden. Remove from the heat and let cool for 5 minutes.

3. Roll out the bread dough to fit a 10½-inch (27 cm) tart pan and carefully transfer the dough to the pan.

4. Stir the egg, *crème fraîche*, walnuts, and walnut oil into the onions. Season with salt and pepper. Spread the mixture evenly onto the bread dough right to the edge.

5. Bake until the tart is puffed and golden brown, about 25 minutes. Serve immediately.

Yield: One 10½-inch (27 cm) tart.

Pampered Poultry, Poulet de Bresse

"*Raised on tiny, tranquil farms, the poultry of Bresse enjoy a pampered barnyard life for more than three months, running free, digging up worms, dining on insects and cracked corn from nearby fields.*"

LOUHANS, SEPTEMBER 20—When the French speak of them, they say *poulet,* then pause briefly, with reverence, before completing the phrase, *de Bresse.* For in a country where lineage and signature labels count for everything, *poulet de Bresse* is the unrivaled king of chickens, the chicken of kings, venerated equally by French farm wives and three-star chefs.

Here in France's barnyard, a land of fertile plains and sunbathed hills, the soil and climate combine to create an ideal environment for the elite Bresse breed of French poultry, distinguished by their coral-red combs, snowy white feathers, and brilliant blue legs.

Unlike the assembly-line birds that appear in supermarkets precut and plastic-wrapped, the famed free-running poultry of Bresse are hand-raised, corn-fattened, and delivered to market with certified lineage. The bird, which takes its name from the Bresse region in which it has been raised for centuries, is sold wearing a red, white, and blue badge with the name of the bird's producer and a silver leg band bearing the grower's identify number.

Each year France produces 1 billion chickens, but only 1 million of them have the right to bear the Bresse label. Raised on tiny, tranquil farms, the poultry of Bresse enjoy a pampered barnyard life for more than three months, running free, digging up worms, dining on insects and cracked corn from nearby fields. They drink the clear water of streams fed by the snowy peaks of the Jura mountains to the north and live out the final fifteen days in a *salle de finition* (finishing room) in a small barn, where the plump become plumper on a diet of whole milk and white corn. All these elements combine to create a rich, moist, subtly flavored 2-kilo (4-pound) bird, plump but virtually fat-free, with fine white skin and firm but tender, truly milky white meat. (By comparison, the French industrial chicken—of Cornish, not French, lineage—spends six to eight weeks confined and crowded indoors, living off a high-fat diet of commercial feed, growth hormones, and antibiotics. The result is a small, spongy, watery bird, with a flavor so undeveloped it is nearly nonexistent.)

The Bresse legend goes back centuries, and everyone from King Henry IV to Brillat-Savarin has raved of the purity of the region's poultry. But it is only since 1957 that the birds of Bresse have rated an official government pedigree, actually an *appellation* such as the French confer on their best wines. Before that time, any poultry in the region could be sold as Bresse poultry, regardless of breed, diet, age, and growing conditions.

Today the criteria are strictly controlled by a government committee headed by chef Georges Blanc, which ensures that the poultry's breeding, diet, and finishing all follow the letter of the law. The Interprofessional Committee of Bresse Poultry even selects the farmers who are permitted to use the Bresse name on their poultry.

Robert Gauthier, who has been raising *poulet de Bresse* since 1963, is typical of these select few. By choice as well as by law, his commercial agriculture is limited to Bresse chickens and, for holidays, turkeys.

The Gauthier farm fits the postcard image of agriculture in days long past. Farm life is unhurried, and one quickly surmises that the atmosphere of calm and tranquility, not just the diet, has something to do with the succulent richness of the bird.

Though he is limited to raising 450 birds in each flock, for each Bresse chicken he takes to market Monsieur Gauthier is paid three times the price he would receive for the less-favored industrial bird. Some of his neighbors raise *poularde de Bresse,* female birds that go to market at five months, weighing more than 2 kilos (5 pounds). Others raise flocks of Bresse *chapons,* the castrated male birds that live six months and spend the final month in finishing rooms dining on corn and milk. These capons, highly prized at holiday time, sell for as much as 800 francs, if you can put your hands on one.

The distinctive blue legs of the Bresse breed serve to protect the farmer as well as the consumer. But fraud is not easy to detect. Since restaurants obviously don't serve up Bresse birds with labels and appendages, all one can do is take the management's word when *poulet de Bresse* appears on the menu. Fraud involving chickens purportedly from Bresse is said to be uncommon, although about half a dozen incidents are discovered each year. Besides fines of up to 2,500 francs, merchants and restaurateurs are subject to public humiliation. Notices of fraud are posted in the markets or restaurants, and the public is also informed through advertisements in local newspapers. However, outside of France the committee has no jurisdiction, and Bresse poultry is exported throughout Europe, including Switzerland, Germany, England, and the Netherlands.

What about the authenticity of all those Bresse pigeons appearing time and again on French menus? That's another story. "If a pigeon happens to land in the Bresse region, and he's caught there, he becomes a Bresse pigeon," laughs one spokesman, who explains that though the birds appear in the markets with the official tricolored label, they are wild, not domesticated, and certainly not raised by any specific standards.

CHAPELLE-DES-BOIS *(Doubs)*

Morbier 13 k, Mouthe 19 k.

FROMAGER

ANTOINETTE BURRI
Combe-des-Cives,
  Chapelle-des-Bois, 25240
  Mouthe.
(81.69.22.06).
Open daily, 8 A.M. to noon to
  watch the cheesemaking,
  to 7 P.M. to buy cheese.

For authentic farm Morbier, the funny-looking cow's-milk cheese with the black stripe down the center, stop in at Madame Burri's side-of-the-road farm stand (see "Morbier, With a Dash of Ash," page 252).

CHAUX-DES-CROTENAY *(Jura)*

Champagnole 14 k.

FROMAGER

GILBERT BANDERIER
Chaux-des-Crotenay, 39150
  Saint-Laurent-en-
  Grandvaux.
(84.51.51.75).
Open 7 A.M. to 12:30 P.M.
  and 2 to 8 P.M. Closed
  Sunday afternoon.

A good address to know, along the *Route de Comté,* where you can watch a variety of local cheeses being made in this small cooperative. Try especially their Comté, Morbier, Vacherin, and Raclette. They also produce a small amount of raw butter.

CHEZERY-FORENS *(Ain)*

Bourg-en-Bresse 88 k, Gex 40 k, Paris 498 k.

FROMAGER

FROMAGERIE DE
  L'ABBAYE
01410 Chézery-Forens.
(50.56.91.67).
Open daily 7 A.M. to noon
  and 7 to 8 P.M.

Although the delicate, sweet, blue-veined cow's-milk cheese known as Bleu de Gex has been made in France for more than 450 years, today only five dairies make the cheese. André and Suzanne Gros, who have been making Bleu de Gex for more than thirty years, make about forty-five wheels a day, aging them in their small artisanal dairy for about one month. I recommend the longer-aged cheese as it has more punch.

Antoinette Burri, "Madame Morbier."

CHINDRIEUX *(Savoie)*

Bourg-en-Bresse 92 k, Chambéry 33 k, Paris 506 k.

RESTAURANT

RELAIS DE CHAUTAGNE
73310 Chindrieux.
(79.54.20.27).
Last orders taken at 1:30 P.M.
   and 9 P.M. (6 P.M.
   off-season).
Closed Monday (except July
   and August), and
   December 27 through
   mid-February.
Air-conditioned.
Private dining rooms for 20
   and 45.
70-, 95-, and 125-franc
   menus. A la carte, 100
   francs.

SPECIALTIES:
Fritures du lac (small fried lake
fish, served from April to
December), *cuisses de grenouille
à la provençale* (frog's legs
sautéed in garlic and olive
oil).

One of the great food and wine marriages of this region is white Savoie wine and a *friture,* a platter of piping hot, tiny batter-fried lake fish. Today it's almost impossible to find an authentic *friture* anywhere in France. Too often the fish are not even local, they've been frozen—and perhaps even cooked in rancid oil, making for a lethal dish.

Whenever I'm in lake country in France, I search for the perfect platter of tiny fried fish. Well, I think I found *friture* heaven at Relais de Chautagne, a roadside bar and restaurant in the village of Chindrieux.

The restaurant's loaded with local color: It's the meeting place for local businessmen and families, as well as the groups of hang gliders you'll see floating down from the nearby mountains. Even the voice of Edith Piaf came bursting from the radio behind the bar as we dug into the *friture.* The fish are netted each morning in the nearby Lac du Bourget, where the catch varies from *perchette* to *goujon,* depending on the season. The *perchettes* we sampled were fresh, crisp, tender, light, and not the least bit oily. The best sign of all: They were thoroughly digestible. The *friture* goes nicely with the house Roussette de Savoie (from Ambroise Bollard in nearby Brison-Saint-Innocent).

Morbier, With a Dash of Ash

"*M*other and son work quietly in tandem, pressing the fresh cheese into large wooden molds as the whey sloshes about, dripping off the sloping wooden worktable. A sweet lactic aroma mingles with the smoke, and windows fog with steam."

COMBE-DES-CIVES, JANUARY 15—It's known, most commonly, as that funny French cheese with the black streak running through the center. It's called Morbier, and the most authentic version can be found about 11 kilometers (7 miles) northeast of the tiny Jura mountain village that gives its name to this supple, mildly tangy cow's milk cheese.

Follow a narrow, gently winding road—flanked by spectacular ski and hiking trails—traveling just beyond the hamlet of Chapelle-des-Bois, population 165. Here, in a cluster of farms known as Combe-des-Cives, live the last two makers of authentic Morbier, both of whom sell their cheese, butter, and milk from roadside barns. One woman and one man, longtime neighbors, make their raw-milk cheese in the old-fashioned way, that is, in a giant copper caldron warmed by a fire of high-mountain spruce and fir.

It's barely 8 A.M., yet Antoinette Burri, mother of eleven, has been up and about since 5:45. To greet visitors, she ascends from the cool and humid aging cellar beneath the smoky red-and-white-tiled cheesemaking room. Since before dawn, she's been tending to her seventy-five wheels of Morbier aging on planks of damp fir. Each 5-kilo (10-pound) cheese will be cured for about three months, during which time it will require a daily turning and a light "washing" with coarse sea salt.

In the adjacent barn her husband, accompanied by a chatty family dog and a radio, goes about milking the brown and white spotted Montbéliard cows, which produce a favored, richly flavored milk. Today's milking will yield about 100 liters (100 quarts), enough to make just two wheels of Madame Burri's distinct, tangy, and mildly salty farm cheese.

Her shiny copper caldron—looking much like a giant egg-white bowl— swings from a black iron rod attached to a giant chimney. In proper farm fashion, everything here seems to serve a dual purpose: The chimney is filled with home-made pork sausages and home-cured hams that profit from the daily infusion of smoke.

A wheat-colored mass of curds now fills the caldron: Madame Burri has warmed the skimmed milk from last night's milking (the cream will go to make butter), the whole milk from this morning's milking, then added rennet.

Working by the light of a single bare bulb, enveloped in her floor-length apron, she continues in a rhythmical, methodical fashion, and as ashes swirl about the room, the fire pops and crackles.

Taking in hand a flexible metal band, she cuts the curds into soft, wobbly cubes. Then, clutching a giant metal whisk, she stirs, and stirs and stirs some more, for a good twenty minutes as the fire slowly burns, heating the milky contents to a tepid 37 degrees (98.6°F).

Dipping her thick, stubby hands into the steaming mass, she squeezes the curds, releasing the cloudy whey. "We're ready," she announces, and, like clockwork, her burly young son, Bernard, arrives to assist.

He works rapidly, tying a giant cloth around his neck, bib fashion, and rolling the other end around the flexible metal band. He slips the cloth into the caldron and retrieves a sack of curds, dripping with whey.

Mother and son work quietly in tandem, pressing the fresh cheese into large wooden molds as the whey sloshes about, dripping off the sloping wooden worktable. A sweet lactic aroma mingles with the smoke, and windows fog with steam. As soon as the molds are roughly half full, Bernard looks up.

"Now you'll see the secret of the black streak," he volunteers.

He washes his hands with the whey, presses his palms against the outside of the blackened caldron, and transfers the fir and spruce ash to the curds settling in the molds.

The history of the black streak goes back to the early nineteenth century, when Morbier was made in two steps, not one as today. Then, the milk was cooked twice daily, following each milking. To protect the evening curds that half-filled the molds, the farmers covered the exposed end with ash. The next morning, they completed the cheese making process, pressing, then aging the Morbier just as it is done today.

Although Morbier was traditionally prepared on independent farms in autumn and winter, when the quantity of milk is reduced, today it can be found year round, on farms and in cooperative dairies scattered about the region. While other cheesemakers follow the same process as Madame Burri, their copper caldrons are warmed electrically.

Today Morbier leads two lives—one as an earthy-flavored, authentic raw-milk mountain cheese prepared and aged for a full three months, the other as a bland and banal industrial cheese, prepared from pasteurized milk.

In searching for authentic Morbier, look for a pale golden cheese with bubbly holes and a few cracks and fissures. The cheese is best eaten in very thin slices, with the rose-gray rind removed, and accompanined by a slice of fresh country bread and a glass of local red or white Arbois wine.

When visiting the Jura mountain region of France, travelers can stop in at any of the 380 small artisanal *fruitières,* or cheesemaking cooperatives, to watch the cheesemaking process and to sample and buy cheese, cream, butter, and sometimes yogurt. They are easy to find, for in the Jura it's hard to drive more than a few miles without seeing a *Route de Comté* sign pointing the way to the nearest *fruitière.* The cooperatives operate 365 days a year, and generally are open from 9 A.M. to noon and 6 to 8 P.M. The best Morbier will be found in the region close to the town of Morbier. Madame Burri's roadside shop can be reached by taking route D18 north of Morbier (about 56 kilometers, or 35 miles, northwest of Geneva) to Les Mortes, then continuing on route D46 to Chapelle-des-Bois and Combe-des-Cives.

COURCHEVEL 1850 *(Savoie)*

Chambéry 97 k, Moûtiers 24 k, Paris 621 k.

SPECIALITES REGIONALES

CHEZ MA COUSINE
73120 Courchevel 1850.
(79.08.21.68).
Open 10 A.M. to 1 P.M. and 4 to 8 P.M. Closed Tuesday afternoon, Wednesday morning, and May through mid-December.
Will ship in France.

This marvelous little shop in the center of one of France's most famous ski villages offers more than thirty kinds of local sausage plus the high-mountain summer Beaufort from one of my favorite cheesemakers, Jules Roux-Daigue.

FOURCATIER-ET-MAISON-NEUVE *(Doubs)*

Champagnole 45 k, Morteau 57 k.

FERME-AUBERGE

LE POELE
Fourcatier-et-Maison-Neuve, 25370 Les Hôpitaux-Neufs.
(81.49.90.99).
Last orders taken at 9 P.M., or 10 P.M. for fondue.
Open daily during French school holidays. Closed Tuesday in July and August; Tuesday and Wednesday September to June.
No credit cards.
Terrace dining.
English spoken.
65 francs.

SPECIALTIES:
Truite au serpolet (trout with wild thyme), *saucisse de montagne grillée aux herbes* (mountain sausage grilled with herbs), *jambon fumé gratiné* (gratin of smoked ham).

Marketing in Bourg-en-Bresse.

In this restored farm dating from the fourteenth century, the Sembely family opens their home to guests, to sample the cured hams that are smoked over juniper and pine in the giant smoking room known locally as a *tuyé*. Try their fondue made with local Comté cheese and crisp white wine, and their grilled mountain sausage and delicious home-fried potatoes, all served with fresh crusty bread from a local baker.

IGUERANDE *(Saône-et-Loire)*

Charolles 46 k, La Clayette 27 k, Paray-le-Monial 37 k.

SPECIALITES REGIONALES

JEAN LEBLANC
71340 Iguerande.
(85.84.07.83).
Open 8:30 A.M. to 7 P.M.
 Closed Sunday.
Will ship internationally.

Rhône valley peaches, anyone?

Jean Leblanc is the hazelnut- and walnut-oil maker to France's great chefs. If you've tired of rancid nut oils, try Leblanc's. It's among the freshest, and the best. (Directions: Opposite the post office in Iguerande.)

METABIEF *(Doubs)*

Champagnole 45 k, Morteau 51 k.

FROMAGER

SANCEY RICHARD
Métabief, 25370 Les
 Hôpitaux-Neufs.
(81.49.12.71).
Open 10 A.M. to noon and 4
 to 6 P.M. Closed Sunday.

Try to visit this *fromagerie* between September and March, when you can watch the band of young cheesemakers prepare the luscious Vacherin Mont d'Or, one of the creamiest, boldest, and most pungent of French cheeses. Here the cheese is made from the fresh raw milk of Montbéliard cows that graze at an altitude of at least 700 meters, nurtured on the freshest herbs in the cleanest air. The cheese is distinguished by its cratered, bloomy orange crust, banded with a strip of pine; it is aged in a distinctive pine box. During the winter months, the dairy's Mont d'Or is sold on the premises, along with Comté, Morbier, yogurt, and *fromage blanc*.

MORTEAU *(Doubs)*

Belfort 89 k, Besançon 67 k, Montbéliard 71 k, Paris 477 k.

Market: Tuesday and Saturday, 8:30 A.M. to noon, Place de l'Hôtel-de-Ville.
Journée des Produits Régionaux (regional specialties day): second Sunday in
August.

CHARCUTERIE

ADRIEN BOUHERET
26 Rue Fauche, 25500
  Morteau.
(81.67.10.39).
Open 7:30 A.M. to noon and
  2:30 to 7 P.M. Closed
  Thursday afternoon and
  Sunday.

Adrien Bouheret is one of those rare village sausage makers, a fourth-generation *charcutier* who prepares and smokes his delicious Morteau sausages and hams right on the premises. Prepared with the finest local pork shoulder and sea salt, Monsieur Bouheret's firm, lightly smoked *Jésus de Morteau* has become a personal favorite, especially when it's cooked with small new potatoes in dry white wine (see recipe, page 271). During the winter months try his *saucisse de choux,* seasoned with ham, cabbage, and cumin.

Hams and sausages of the Jura.

SPECIALITES REGIONALES

LA FRUITIERE
40 Grande-Rue, 25500
  Morteau.
(81.67.07.05).
Open 8 A.M. to noon and 2
  to 7 P.M. Closed Sunday,
  and Monday morning.
Credit card: V.
Will ship in France.

This shop captures the Jura—a wonderfully fragrant boutique filled with smoked sausages, well-ripened cheeses, honeys, and wild morel mushrooms.

ORDONNAZ *(Ain)*

Ambérieu-en-Bugey 31 k, Lyon 84 k.

FERME-AUBERGE

FERME AUBERGE RENE LARACINE
01510 Ordonnaz.
(74.36.42.38).
Last orders taken at 1 P.M. and 8 P.M.
Closed mid-December to mid-January.
No credit cards.
Terrace dining.
Private dining room for 28.
Fixed menu only: 43-franc menu at dinner, 65-franc menu at lunch (about 80 francs including wine and service).

SPECIALTIES:
Gratin dauphinois (potato gratin), *jambon de pays* (local ham), *fromage blanc à la crème* (fresh white cheese with cream from the farm), *tarte à la crème* (sugar and cream tart).

Whether or not a restaurant is worth a detour depends upon what you're after. It also depends on the nature of the detour. If you would like to sample a remarkable farm-cooked Savoyard meal—local salt-cured ham, bread baked in the community's bread oven, the best-ever potato gratin made with home-grown potatoes cooked in milk and cream fresh from the cow, guinea hen served with mounds of fresh mushrooms—then the drive to the Ferme Auberge René Laracine will be considered not a detour, but a delight. When the bill arrives, diners are doubly delighted, for a multi-course meal will cost no more than 80 francs per person.

You can reach the sleepy cluster of buildings known as Ordonnaz by taking *départementale* road 32 northwest from the town of Belley, traveling along a long, winding, steep mountain drive, passing—in the spring and early summer—an endless variety of fanciful wildflowers. The *ferme-auberge* is easy to spot: Look for the official *Chambre d'Hôte* sign by the side of the road.

This is a seasonal *auberge*, best for early to late summer touring, when many guests take off for a hike into the woods (a national hiking trail, GR 59, passes through Ordonnaz) before or after one of Michéle Laracine's copious meals, which are served on a pleasant little terrace in the warmer months.

If you arrive on Friday or Saturday morning, you might find Madame Laracine firing up the local bread oven. She's one of the last in Ordonnaz to use the arched stone oven, baking about ten loaves each week, along with twenty *tartes au sucre,* round brioche tarts covered with cream and sugar.

Her typical multi-course meal will include, necessarily, products from the farm, but those in search of lighter fare can drive up for a simple salad, an omelet, a glass of wine.

MARJOLAINE PERE BISE
PERE BISE'S MULTI-LAYERED CHOCOLATE CAKE

This is, unquestionably, one of the most stunning desserts I know. Although the instructions appear rather formidable, the preparation can actually be spread over several days, then the cake is assembled the day before serving. I first sampled it at the Auberge du Père Bise in Talloires several years ago and worked through the recipe nine times before coming up with this version.

Praline powder:
Vegetable oil for the
   baking sheet
1 cup (140 g) whole
   almonds
1 cup (140 g)
   confectioners' sugar

Chocolate cream:
2 cups (500 ml) *crème
   fraîche* (see Recipe
   Index) or sour cream
15 ounces (425 g)
   bittersweet
   chocolate, preferably
   Lindt or Tobler,
   broken into pieces

Pastry cream:
8 large egg yolks
1 cup (200 g)
   granulated sugar
½ cup (70 g)
   unbleached all-
   purpose flour
2½ cups (625 ml) milk
1¼ cups (10 ounces;
   300 g) unsalted
   butter

Cake:
1 cup (130 g) hazelnuts
¾ cup (150 g)
   granulated sugar
10 large egg whites
¼ cup (35 g)
   unbleached all-
   purpose flour

1. Prepare the praline powder: Preheat the oven to 300°F (150°C). Oil a baking sheet with a light vegetable oil. Spread the almonds on another baking sheet and bake until fragrant and light brown, about 10 minutes. Let cool.

2. Combine the nuts and sugar in a heavy-bottomed saucepan. Cook, stirring constantly, over medium heat until the sugar begins to melt. The mixture will go through several stages from a dry blend to one where the sugar forms little bubbles the size of peas. Continue cooking, stirring constantly so all of the sugar clinging to the almonds melts, until the mixture is dark brown and syrupy and the nuts make a popping sound. The whole process will take about 5 minutes.

3. Quickly pour the mixture onto the oiled baking sheet. The mixture will harden to give almond brittle. When the praline is cool, break it into pieces. Grind it to a fine powder in a food processor or blender. (Praline can be made weeks in advance and refrigerated or frozen in an airtight container.)

4. Prepare the chocolate cream: Heat the *crème fraîche* to a boil in a medium saucepan. Remove from the heat and whisk in the chocolate, piece by piece, until it is completely melted and blended. Let sit until cool and thick. It should have the consistency of a thick, but spreadable, frosting.

5. Prepare the pastry cream: Using a whisk or electric mixer, beat the egg yolks and sugar in a mixing bowl until thick and lemon-colored. Gently whisk in the flour. Heat the milk to a boil in a large heavy-bottomed saucepan. Whisk one third of the hot milk into the egg yolk mixture, then pour the egg mixture into the remaining milk. Boil, stirring constantly, over medium-high heat until thickened, about 2 minutes. Transfer to a bowl and let cool.

6. Beat the butter until soft and creamy. When the pastry cream is completely cool, whisk in the softened butter.

Rum cream:

2 cups (500 ml) Pastry
  Cream
1 tablespoon vanilla
  extract
1 tablespoon rum

Praline cream:

2 cups (500 ml) Pastry
  Cream
2 cups (280 g) Praline
  Powder

7. Prepare the cake: Preheat the oven to 300°F (150°C). Heavily butter 2 jelly-roll pans, about 14 x 10 x 1 inches (35.5 x 25.5 x 2.5 cm). Line them with parchment paper, and butter and flour the paper.

8. Spread the hazelnuts on a baking sheet and bake until fragrant and light brown, about 10 minutes. Remove from the oven and rub the warm nuts in a cotton dish towel to remove as much skin as possible. Cool, then grind them with ¼ cup (50 g) of the sugar in a food processor or blender.

9. Using a whisk or electric mixer, beat the egg whites until they begin to stiffen. Gradually beat in the remaining sugar and continue to beat until stiff but not dry. Fold in the flour and the hazelnut mixture. Spread the batter evenly in the prepared pans. Bake until the cakes are thoroughly browned, 25 to 30 minutes.

10. Remove the cakes from the oven and invert them onto racks to cool, paper side up. Cover the cakes with a damp towel for several minutes, then remove the parchment paper while the cakes are still warm. Let cool completely. Cut each cake lengthwise in half.

11. At least 24 hours but no more than 3 days before serving, assemble the *marjolaine:* Divide the pastry cream in half. For the rum cream, blend the vanilla extract and rum into one portion of the pastry cream. For the praline cream, blend the praline powder into the remaining pastry cream. (Mix the praline cream just before assembling the cake, for the flavor will fade if mixed in advance.) The chocolate and pastry creams should be chilled, but spreadable.

12. Place one cake layer on a large rectangular serving platter. Spread half the chocolate cream on the cake. Refrigerate until firm, about 10 minutes. Cover the chocolate cream with a second cake layer. Spread with all the rum cream and refrigerate until firm, about 15 minutes. Top the rum cream with the third cake layer. Spread with all the praline cream and refrigerate until firm, about 15 minutes. Top the praline cream with the fourth cake layer. Frost the top and sides of the cake with the remaining chocolate cream. Refrigerate uncovered for 15 minutes, then cover with plastic wrap. Refrigerate 1 to 3 days before serving.

13. To serve, let the cake warm at room temperature for 15 minutes, then cut into thin slices.

Yield: 16 to 20 servings.

PÉROUGES *(Ain)*

Bourg-en-Bresse 37 k, Lyon 39 k.

SALON DE THE

**HOSTELLERIE DU VIEUX
   PEROUGES**
Place du Tilleul, Pérouges,
   01800 Meximieux.
(74.61.00.88).
Open 2 to 6 P.M. Closed
   Wednesday and
   Thursday February
   through November;
   closed Sunday in
   December and January;
   and an unspecified
   period in November and
   December.

Pérouges is a restored historic artists' village with a touch of Disneyland, and the Hostellerie du Vieux Pérouges plays a proper role: waitresses in costumes, bare wooden tables, windowsills decked out with geranium-filled boxes. The day we stopped, the famous *galette de Pérouges* (a cream- and sugar-topped puff pastry tart) was a bit disappointing—the pastry was tough and the topping quite skimpy. But go, for history's sake, and wear flat-heeled shoes for wandering about the rough cobblestone streets of this postcard village. Just outside the restaurant, note the giant linden tree, an *arbre de liberté,* planted during the eighteenth century to celebrate the Revolution and freedom.

PLASNE *(Jura)*

Dole 37 k, Lons-le-Saunier 28 k, Paris 403 k, Poligny 1 k.

FROMAGER

FROMAGERIE DE PLASNE
Plasne, 39800 Poligny.
(84.37.14.03).
Open daily, 6 A.M. to
   12:30 P.M.

Since the age of sixteen, Gabriel Guyot has risen before 6 each morning to begin his 365-day-a-year job as Comté cheesemaker. Now assisted by his wife, Monique, Monsieur Guyot is cheesemaker for a cooperative of fifteen farmers, all of whom deliver their fresh cow's milk each morning, to be turned into giant 45-kilo (99-pound) wheels of fruity, nut-like Comté. Visits to watch the Comté-making process can be arranged by appointment; simply call ahead.

POLIGNY *(Jura)*

Dole 37 k, Lons-le-Saunier 28 k, Paris 403 k.

Market: Monday and Friday, 8 A.M. to noon, Place Nationale.
Fête du Comté (Comté cheese festival): last weekend in July.

FROMAGERIE

ARNAUD FRERES
15 Place Nationale, 39800
  Poligny.
(84.37.13.50).
Open 8 A.M. to 12:30 P.M.
  and 2:30 to 7 P.M. Closed
  Sunday, and Tuesday
  afternoon.
Credit card: V.
Will ship in France.

Great one-stop shopping for the cheese, wine, and sausages of the Jura. Special cheeses include Comté, Morbier, Bleu de Gex, and in winter months, Vacherin du Mont-d'Or.

Comté, aged with care.

AFFINEUR

ARNAUD FRERES
Avenue de la Gare, 39800
  Poligny.
(84.37.14.23).
Open 7 A.M. to noon and
  1:30 to 6:30 P.M. Closed
  Saturday.

If you'd like to see how the giant wheels of Comté cheese are salted and turned as they are stored and aged for up to six months, then call ahead to visit one of the area's most trusted cheese agers. Cheese may also be purchased here.

MUSEE

MAISON DU COMTE
Avenue de la Résistance,
  39800 Poligny.
(84.37.23.51).
Open daily 9 A.M. to noon
  and 2 to 6 P.M. July
  through mid-August.
  Open by appointment
  off-season.
Admission: 6 francs for
  adults, 4 francs for
  children.

Open since July 1985, this museum is devoted to the history of Comté cheesemaking and includes exhibits of old cheesemaking equipment, a photo display, and a twenty-minute slide show. The museum can arrange visits to Comté cheesemaking cooperatives.

ROANNE *(Loire)*

Lyon 86 k, Paris 390 k.

Selected markets: Tuesday and Friday, 7:30 A.M. to 12:30 P.M., Hôtel-de-Ville and Place du Marché.

RESTAURANT

RESTAURANT
  TROISGROS
Place de la Gare, 42300
  Roanne.
(77.71.66.97).
Last orders taken at 1:30 P.M.
  and 9:30 P.M.
Closed Tuesday, Wednesday
  lunch, January, and two
  weeks in August.
Credit cards: AE, DC, EC, V.
Terrace dining.
Private dining room for 18.
English spoken.
210-, 325-, and 390-franc
  menus. A la carte, 500
  francs.

S P E C I A L T I E S :
Escalope de saumon à l'oseille
(salmon with sorrel sauce), *le
grand dessert* (large rolling
dessert cart).

One warm July day I took the slow train from Lyon to this abandoned patch of France to have lunch in the restaurant on the Place de la Gare. I sat with the locals, who came in twos and in extended families, with their dogs and their children. There were almost no businessmen, and most people seemed to be there for a special occasion, the children playing with toy trucks and trains during the slow, extended meal hour. They ordered the foods the French find essential for festivities and there was a veritable parade of plates and platters filled with Scotch salmon and *foie gras* from the Landes, Bresse pigeon and sauced Breton lobster. The lean and cheery, yet proper, *sommelier* served mostly the local house wines—for white, a pleasant Saint-Véran, for red, an affordable Beaujolais—and the only language I heard was French. The scene is not the usual picture at one of France's top-rated restaurants, but at Troisgros, one of the homiest of France's "grand" restaurants, this is the way it is.

Restaurant Troisgros, still a straightforward, finely tuned family place, goes on with a natural day-to-day rhythm depite the loss of one member of its supporting cast, Jean Troisgros, in 1983. Jean's brother and partner, Pierre, now works in tandem with his son, Michel, and together the two have gone about creating the sort of French food that would have been taboo not many years ago.

Despite the classic French family atmosphere of the restaurant, which sits across from a drab village train station, the food served here is among the most international to be found in France. As the Troisgros chefs travel around the world, they search out ingredients that are not traditionally French, creating a cuisine that both respects and reinterprets the classics. So what you're likely to find now is irreproachably fresh and full-flavored Bresse pigeon sauced with a refined and delicate zucchini chutney (see recipe below); delicate and feathery *rouleaux de crabe* (a fine interpretation of an oriental egg roll) encased in colorful zucchini blossoms; and in a new twist to a classic nursery dish, vanilla custard flavored with an infusion of jasmin tea and topped off with a lime-puckery meringue.

If this bothers traditionalists, there is no need to worry. You can walk in anytime and order a simple grilled sole, the apricot tart was perfect enough to put any grandmother to shame, and if all else fails, the most popular dish in the house is the one that's been the specialty for nigh on three decades, the indefatigable salmon with sorrel.

CHUTNEY DE COURGETTES PIERRE ET MICHEL TROISGROS
PIERRE AND MICHEL TROISGROS' ZUCCHINI CHUTNEY

This wonderfully versatile and lively vegetable accompaniment signifies the sorts of changes taking place in French cuisine today. A few years ago, a grand French restaurant would not have dared to offer a dish with the very British name of chutney. The spicy black peppercorns and snips of fresh ginger would have only worsened the case. Thank goodness things have loosened up a bit, with the Troisgros family leading the pack. They serve this dish in all seasons, sometimes accompanying grilled lamb, at other times, roasted pigeon.

2 lemons
3 medium zucchini,
   peeled and cut into
   1-inch (2.5 cm)
   pieces
2 medium onions,
   thinly sliced
¾ cup (185 ml) dry
   white wine, such as
   Riesling
2 teaspoons sugar
24 whole black
   peppercorns,
   crushed
1 walnut-size nugget
   fresh ginger, minced
Salt to taste

1. Cut all the peel and white pith from the lemons and discard. Cut the lemons into thin slices and discard the seeds.

2. Combine all the ingredients in a small saucepan and cook, covered, over medium heat for 1 hour. Stir the mixture from time to time to make sure it does not burn. The chutney should have the consistency of marmalade.

3. Serve as an accompaniment to grilled meats, fish, or roast poultry. The chutney is good served warm or cold.

Yield: 4 servings.

ROMANS-SUR-ISERE *(Drôme)*

Grenoble 81 k, Paris 562 k, Saint-Etienne 93 k, Valence 18 k.

Market: Tuesday, Friday, and Sunday, 8 A.M. to noon, Place Maurice Faure.

PATISSERIE

PIERRE MOURIER
39 Rue Jacquemart, 26100
Romans-sur-Isère.
(75.02.32.29).
Open 6:30 A.M. to 7:30 P.M.
Closed Monday.

In the days when everyone in the area baked his own bread, the housewives would save a handful, or *poignée,* of dough, form it into a crown, and bake it in the oven as a treat for the children. Little by little, butter was added to the dough, then eggs, then sugar, and the *pogne* was born. Later, commercial bakers began making the regional specialty at Easter time. The town of Romans-sur-Isère is considered the *pogne* capital of France, and baker Pierre Mourier makes one of the best I know. His version, flavored with orange-flower water, is available year round.

LES ROUSSES *(Jura)*

Genève 47 k, Gex 30 k, Paris 469 k, Saint-Claude 33 k.

FROMAGER

**COOPERATIVE
FROMAGERE LES
ROUSSES**
137 Rue Pasteur, 39220 Les
Rousses.
(84.60.02.73).
Open 8 A.M. to noon and
3 to 7:30 P.M. Closed
Sunday afternoon.

If you're the early morning sort, arise at 5 to see cheese in the making at this steaming little dairy. In the center of a popular ski resort, it is a cooperative run by ten local farmers who combine their milk to make delicious raw-milk Comté, Morbier, and Raclette, and also their own *crème fraîche, fromage blanc,* and yogurt. Twice each week, they even make a small batch of raw butter, churned the old-fashioned way, in a wooden barrel.

SAINT-ETIENNE *(Loire)*

Lyon 63 k, Paris 516 k, Valence 92 k.

Markets: Monday, Wednesday, Friday, and Saturday, 7 A.M. to 1 P.M., Place Jacquard; Tuesday and Sunday, 7 A.M. to 1 P.M., Place Carnot; Tuesday, Thursday, and Sunday, 7 A.M. to 1 P.M., Place Bellevue.

RESTAURANT

**GABRIELLE ET PIERRE
    GAGNAIRE**
3 Rue Georges-Teissier,
    42000 Saint-Etienne.
(77.37.57.93).
Last orders taken at 2 P.M.
    and 9:30 P.M.
Closed Sunday, Monday, one
    week in February, three
    weeks in August, and the
    week before Christmas.
Credit cards: AE, DC, V.
Private dining room for 12.
English spoken.
170-, 280-, and 400-franc
    menus. A la carte, 400
    francs.

SPECIALTIES:
Change with the seasons.

If not so long ago someone had told me I'd drive all the way to the dreary industrial city of Saint-Etienne for a single meal, I'd have said "No way!" But several meals later I can wholeheartedly say that Gabrielle and Pierre Gagnaire's is worth a detour. Everything about the lean, fair-haired Gagnaire and his outgoing, down-to-earth wife, Gabrielle, is refreshingly original, even unorthodox. The California-inspired decor, the complex combinations of food, even the organization of his kitchen, suggest that the Gagnaires have a confident vision of how their restaurant ought to be run. They seem to realize that today's public craves exotic, spicy dishes, served by a chef with a personal, almost intellectual approach to food. It's as if diners sit at the table and say, "Surprise us, give us something new, but please don't ignore all those familiar foods in tried and true combinations." So Gagnaire offers *brandade* and mashed potatoes, plenty of game in winter, local river fish in summer, and innumerable gratins. He even makes potato chips, and an astonishingly rich chocolate soufflé so creamy he calls it a soup.

You take a look at some of the complex descriptions on the menu and wonder how the palate will respond. But then you sample the tempura of the freshest Breton langoustines, delicately fried, served with just a glaze of cinnamon-infused *beurre blanc;* or a stacked "hero" sandwich of sweetbreads, *foie gras,* and breast of pigeon, served with a *confit* of shallots, a clump of warm sweet and sour cabbage, and you say, "Of course."

If most other chefs tried to do what Pierre Gagnaire does, they would fall flat. But he succeeds for the simple reason that his food wakes up tired palates.

A word of caution: At the Gagnaires' the written menu should be considered just a blueprint for what is to come. Chef Gagnaire's cooking is totally spontaneous, and he rarely makes the same dish twice, so the garnishes and finishes on your plate may differ dramatically from the menu description.

The Bread Oven Tradition

The tradition of the community bread oven is strongest in the Rhône valley, particularly in the Bugey, a vineyard-rich area found midway between the Beaujolais and the Savoie. With the growth of the modern-day *boulangerie* many community ovens fell into disuse during the 1950s, but until then, a single oven could easily serve a village of 400 inhabitants. Now many ovens remain idle, except for annual bread baking festivals (see page 240).

Following is a self-guided tour of the area, which can easily be completed in a few hours. Begin in Nivollet-Montgriffon, about 32 kilometers (20 miles) southeast of Bourg-en-Bresse (use Michelin map 244).

MONTGRIFFON: A bit out of the way, but architecturally worth a detour. This village of 25 residents has restored one of the most beautiful ovens in the Bugey. Note the back of the oven, with its unusual beehive shape, and the giant *arbre de liberté*, a linden tree planted to celebrate the French Revolution.

BELMONT: An arched bakehouse.

OUCHE: An ivy-covered bakehouse, one of the tidiest on the tour. Note the neat bundles, or fagots, of vine cuttings stacked in the corner.

CEYZERIEU: A bakehouse with a flagstone floor, arched door, and a classic lean-to washhouse alongside.

CATTON-GRAMMONT: Each Palm Sunday, the village women prepare hundreds of gigantic rectangular sourdough tarts. The men take the sizzling onion or apple tarts from the oven, pile them on an old wooden door, then sell them for about 10 francs a slice. Villagers and visitors crowd the local vintner's stand with a glass of Roussette or Mondeuse wine in one hand and a slice of onion tart in the other, debating the architectural merits of their local bread ovens.

VONGNES: Not just a bread oven, but also vineyards and Alain Nambotin's bakery-café. He'll be happy to sell a loaf of bread baked in the brick-lined oven he built himself.

FLAXIEU: The home of Maurice and Paule Bal, and of Camille Crussy, who makes an award-winning *vin de Bugey*.

MARIGNIEU: A bakehouse.

SAINT-CHAMP: Another bread oven. Along the road from Chemillieu, note the grape vines that double as roadside fences.

PARVES: The little oven sits alone by the side of the road. Inside, you'll find an old-fashioned pegboard, one system villagers used to assign baking days.

SORBIER: Southeast of Parves along the D107, and not on the Michelin map, Sorbier's beautifully restored oven, with climbing roses at the entrance, is one of the most photographed ovens on the tour. Note the variegated gray and yellow stone, the fine detail of the steplike roof, and the assortment of baking equipment, including a wooden *pelle* for shuffling bread in and out of the oven.

CHEMILLIEU: Chickens wander between the bakehouse (dated 1825) and the washhouse across the street.

SAINT-LAURENT-EN-GRANDVAUX (*Jura*)

Champagnole 22 k, Lons-le-Saunier 46 k, Paris 448 k.

SPECIALITES REGIONALES

MICHEL REBOUILLAT
La Savine, 39150
   Saint-Laurent-en-
   Grandvaux.
(84.60.82.78).
Open daily 8 A.M. to 7 P.M.
Credit card: V.
Will ship in France.

Agreat regional specialty shop in the Jura, offering the best of the area's *charcuterie*, including delicious smoked hams as well as home-smoked trout.

TALLOIRES (*Haute-Savoie*)

Albertville 33 k, Annecy 13 k, Paris 545 k.

RESTAURANT

AUBERGE DU PERE BISE
Talloires, 74290
   Veyrier-du-Lac.
(50.60.72.01).
Last orders taken at 2 P.M.
   and 9 P.M.
Closed Tuesday mid-
   October through early
   May, Wednesday lunch
   late April through early
   May, and mid-
   December through
   January.
Credit cards: AE, DC, EC, V.
Private dining room for 25.
English spoken.
300-, 400-, and 500-franc
   menus. A la carte, 500 to
   700 francs.

S P E C I A L T I E S :
Truite saumonée façon François
(marinated salmon trout with
a ginger-flecked mayonnaise),
blanquette de homard breton
(stew of Breton lobster),
poularde de Bresse (prized
poultry from Bresse).

Going a bit against the flow of popular opinion, I remained a fan of Père Bise long after many formerly faithful diners had broken allegiance. For me, this cottage-like restaurant set along the banks of the magical Lake Annecy in the Savoie was and still is one of the most romantic dining spots in France. But at my last dinner there, I felt as though I were visiting an old friend who'd gotten paunchy and let himself go, who'd simply lost touch with reality. It was as though they had locked the kitchen door sometime around 1954 and had not let anyone out. There was, simply, no excitement there, and the food was, figuratively and in reality, tired and stale. The biggest jolt of all was the famed *marjolaine*, the incredibly rich, superbly delicious chocolate layer cake I consider the ultimate dessert of all time (see recipe, page 258). When the dessert cart rolled around, I was presented with a dried-out leftover "heel" of cake, the last slice of *marjolaine* made who knows when. Still, loving the spot as much as I do, I know I'll return, and hope that they've unlocked the doors to the kitchen and let in the new day's sun.

Bon Comme le Bon Pain

"*M*adame Bal is in sight now, rolling a handmade cart stacked precariously with the leavened loaves. Over her floral print apron she has wrapped another long white apron that reaches down to her toes. And in her hand she grasps a scratched green Tupperware bowl that holds a fragrant mixture of chopped onions, walnuts, and their home-pressed walnut oil, topping for a single precious tart."

FLAXIEU, MARCH 13—Maurice Bal dusts a speck of flour from his thick woolen beret and with broad rhythmic motions sweeps large, crackling rounds of sourdough bread from the wood-fired oven. Working side by side with his wife, Paule, the pair proceed quickly, nervously, arranging the dozen fragrant and thick-crusted loaves to cool along stone benches spread with golden straw. Wasting no motion, they refill the brick-lined oven with rustic bread tarts, tarts showered at the final moment with onions, apples, moist sugared plums, even hand-cracked walnuts.

It's 9 A.M. on a drizzly, gray day in the Bugey, a remote patch of southeastern France in the *département* of the Ain. This is the first time since the Bals rose in the dark at 5 that morning that they've had a chance to exhale, to smile, to chat about their lives and the bread rituals of this quiet region at the edge of the Savoie.

Here in Flaxieu—population, 10 families—the Bals are the last to carry on the warming tradition of the community bread oven, a tradition found in many areas of France, but predominantly in the regions bordering Switzerland. Since 1940—save for a few war years when they had no wheat—the two have quietly maintained the rite that was part of their childhood, part of the lives of generations of Frenchmen before them.

Until the turn of the century, few rural French communities could support a baker, so villagers gathered together to construct a single large bakehouse, or *four banal,* designed for community use. These one-of-a-kind compact structures—the size of a tool shed and fashioned of rough gray stone—were inevitably placed in the center of the village, with the large oven built into one narrow end. Most often, the community washhouse, or *lavoir,* was conveniently attached to the bakehouse in lean-to fashion, so village women could tend to the family's laundry as they waited for their breads and tarts to bake. After each baking, or *fournée,* the soft, gentle heat that remained would serve to dry the season's crop of apples, pears, or walnuts.

While many of the Bugey's bakehouses have been allowed to tumble into piles of rocks, some of the better architectural specimens have been lovingly restored and now shine with carefully reconditioned roofs of glistening gray slate. In several communities, annual bread festivals serve as fund-raising events (see The Bread Oven Tradition, page 266.)

In Flaxieu, the Bals fire up the community oven for their personal baking every three weeks, give or take a day. Following tradition, Madame Bal, as housewife, is in charge of the dough. Monsieur Bal, as man of the house, tends to the oven, filling it the night before with tidy bundles of *sarments de vigne,* last season's clippings from the same vines that supply them with Jacquère and Chardonnay grapes for making their likable white *vin de Bugey.*

Even after decades of baking bread together, there's ample tension in the air. The rosy-cheeked Monsieur Bal, who has a permanent mischievous gleam in his dark eyes, rambles back and forth from the bakehouse to the farm kitchen, fretting as he nudges Madame Bal along. He's fearful that her bread won't be ready when the oven's hot enough for baking. She's apprehensive: With all his chattering, the oven won't be hot enough to accept her dough, rising in thick straw baskets now stacked like minor still lifes all about the country kitchen.

Nowadays the dough is kneaded in her trusty postwar electrified wooden mixer, a barrel-like contraption the size of compact washing machine. But Madame Bal recalls, with not a whisper of nostalgia, the days she kneaded the mixture by hand for hours, working the soupy, glutinous dough in her giant wooden kneading trough.

The bread, as ever, is made with white flour. But following customs that date back to childhood days, she'll sprinkle the cloth-lined baskets with rye and bran just before she plops the spongy masses in to rise. Her small wrinkled hands are covered with mittens of dough as she shuttles back and forth across the cluttered room.

While Madame Bal readies the dough, Monsieur Bal heads straight out to the bakehouse, a three-minute walk from the farm. In the days when everyone in the community still baked his own bread, Monsieur Bal would find the oven still warm from his neighbor's baking the previous day. But now the oven boasts a good three-week chill and needs a long, slow firing to heat it to the intensity necessary to bake the bread and tarts. Today it will take more than three hours. He feeds the fire as the blaze rages inside the arched oven, smoke billowing out the oven door, across the bakehouse, and out the chimney perched atop the entrance.

When the flames have dwindled to fiery red coals and the bricks lining the top of the vaulted oven have turned a pure, even white, it's time to bake. Using a long-handled metal scraper, Monsieur Bal pushes the cinders to the back of the oven, saving some to pile near the door, to guard against drafts as he bakes.

He checks to see that Madame Bal is on her way, then picks up a makeshift boxwood broom, dips it into the nearby well, and begins to swab out the inside of the oven. This practice serves a dual purpose: to clean any ash from the floor of the oven, and to provide the necessary burst of steam that will send the loaves on their way.

Madame Bal is in sight now, rolling a handmade cart stacked precariously with the leavened loaves. Over her floral print apron she has wrapped another long white apron that reaches down to her toes. And in her hand she grasps a scratched green Tupperware bowl that holds a fragrant mixture of chopped onions, walnuts, and their home-pressed walnut oil, topping for a single tart.

Monsieur Bal places the loaves close together so that as they rise, the sides will touch. The baked loaves will have to be pulled apart after they're taken from the oven. In France, loaves that touch like this are said to "kiss," and they bring good luck. The Bals say not a word to one another, yet an observer senses a slow shared heave of satisfaction as the short, agile pair pose outside the community oven of Flaxieu, celebrating, yet again, another successful *fournée*.

VALENCE *(Drôme)*

Grenoble 99 k, Lyon 99 k, Paris 560 k.

Markets: Tuesday, 6 A.M. to noon, Place Saint-Jean; Thursday and Saturday, 6 A.M. to noon, Place des Clercs.

RESTAURANT

JACQUES PIC
285 Avenue Victor-Hugo,
   26000 Valence.
(75.44.15.32).
Last orders taken at 1:30 P.M.
   and 9:30 P.M.
Closed Sunday dinner,
   Wednesday, ten days in
   February, three weeks in
   April, and August.
Credit cards: AE, DC.
Terrace dining.
Air-conditioned.
Private dining room for 20.
English spoken.
380- and 450-franc menus.
   A la carte, 500 francs.

S P E C I A L T I E S :
Blanc de turbot aux morilles
(turbot with morel
mushrooms), *homard rôti aux
truffes* (roast lobster with
truffles), *nougat glacé* (frozen
nougat).

Jacques Pic's restaurant, across from the Talbot garage in the rather dull town of Valence, remains one of the most provincial of France's "grand" restaurants. Sure, you'll see a table or two of Japanese businessmen, an occasional American, German, or Swiss, but basically Jacques Pic's place is for the locals, the place they go for a *fête,* to celebrate birthdays, anniversaries, or simply the good fortune to be living at this time, in this place. I love the restaurant's homey quality, and even manage to tolerate the rather heavy *bourgeois* decor. My last meal here was a veritable feast, including a superlative first course that combined the freshest fat local asparagus bathed in warm *hollandaise* with a smothering of caviar. The play of hot, cold, salt, and butter was a magnificent treat. Equally satisfying were the *blanc de turbot aux morilles,* served like a sandwich of ocean-fresh turbot filled with local wild morel mushrooms; and the creamy *nougat glacé,* a frozen nougat dessert I find better than ice cream any day (see recipe, page 275). Monsieur Pic's wine list reads like a regional wine bible: You won't go wrong with either Georges Vernay's white Condrieu or the Chave family's red Hermitage. Herb tea lovers take note: Pic offers magnificent teas made with freshly picked herbs, including a soothing *verveine menthe,* or minted verbena.

VILLARS-LES-DOMBES *(Ain)*

Bourg-en-Bresse 28 k, Lyon 34 k, Paris 433 k.

Market: Tuesday, 8:30 A.M. to noon, Place de la Mairie.

PATISSERIE

PAUL KOEBERLE
Rue du Commerce, 01330
  Villars-les-Dombes.
(74.98.03.76).
Open 8 A.M. to noon and 2
  to 7 P.M. Closed Monday,
  and late January through
  mid-February.

Robust, cheery, outgoing Paul Koeberlé makes one of the best bread tarts in the region, a feathery brioche dough topped with a blend of cream and sugar. He calls his a *galette des Dombes;* elsewhere, with certain variations in topping and dough, it's known as a *galette bressane* (see recipe, page 245) and *galette de Pérouges.*

LE JESUS DE MORTEAU AU VIN BLANC
SMOKED PORK SAUSAGES COOKED IN WHITE WINE

This is one of the simplest, most satisfying recipes I know. It was offered to me by Adrien Bouheret, a third-generation sausage maker from the village of Morteau. This fine blend of firm, smoked pork sausage and potatoes is a marvelous fall and winter dish that can be prepared quickly and makes a perfect supper when served with a green salad and perhaps a side dish of lentils. In place of the Jura sausage—which is often laced with a bit of cumin—use any top-quality smoked sausage. As to the origin of the name, Jésus, *there's great disagreement. The most likely story suggests that the* Jésus *earned its name because it was always made from the best meat and was traditionally served at the midnight meal on Christmas Eve. Serve with a dry white wine, such as Riesling.*

1 tablespoon (½ ounce;
    15 g) unsalted butter
1 pound (500 g) fresh
    smoked pork sausage
    or about 4
    individual farmer's
    sausages
1 pound (4 to 5; 500 g)
    small new potatoes,
    rinsed but not peeled
1 medium onion,
    coarsely chopped
2 cloves garlic
1 bottle (750 ml) dry
    white wine, such as
    Riesling
1 tablespoon tomato
    paste
1 branch fresh thyme or
    ¼ teaspoon dried
1 bay leaf
Small handful of fresh
    parsley, minced

1. Melt the butter in a medium saucepan over medium heat. Add the sausage and slowly brown on all sides. Do not pierce them. Add the remaining ingredients (reserving half the parsley for garnish), stir, and heat to a boil. Immediately reduce the heat and cover, leaving the lid slightly ajar. Simmer for about 1 hour. Check the potatoes occasionally to be sure they do not overcook. If necessary, transfer them to a heatproof dish and keep covered in a low oven.

2. When the sausages are cooked, transfer them to a heatproof dish with the potatoes.

3. Strain the cooking liquid and return it to the saucepan. Cook over high heat until slightly thickened, about 5 minutes.

4. To serve, cut the sausages into thick slices, arrange on warmed dinner plates or on a serving platter with the whole potatoes, and ladle the sauce over all. Sprinkle with the reserved parsley and serve immediately.

Yield: 4 servings.

GOURMANDISE GLACEE AUX FRUITS ROUGES GEORGES BLANC
GEORGES BLANC'S MERINGUE, RED BERRY, AND SORBET DESSERT

This dessert—the meringue cake featured on the cover—is like the spirit of summer with its bright, fresh berries and feather-light meringue. Georges Blanc uses red currants in place of the raspberries, but it is wonderful with raspberries and strawberries, or a mixture of both.

Meringue:
Butter and flour for the
    baking sheets
5 large egg whites
Pinch of salt
½ cup plus 3
    tablespoons (145 g)
    granulated sugar
1 cup (140 g)
    confectioners' sugar,
    sifted

Pastry cream:
1 cup (250 ml) milk
1 vanilla bean, cut in
    half lengthwise
3 large egg yolks
½ cup (100 g) sugar
1 tablespoon all-
    purpose flour

Coulis:
½ pound (250 g)
    raspberries
½ cup (70 g)
    confectioners' sugar
    or to taste
Juice of 1 lemon or to
    taste

1 pound (500 g) small,
    fresh strawberries,
    rinsed and hulled
1 pint best-quality
    raspberry sorbet

1. Preheat the oven to 250°F (120 C). Butter and flour 2 baking sheets.

2. Prepare the meringue: In a large bowl beat the egg whites with the salt until they are stiff but not dry. Add the 3 tablespoons of granulated sugar and continue beating until the egg whites are glossy and hold a peak. Lightly fold in the remaining granulated sugar and the confectioners' sugar until thoroughly incorporated.

3. Fill a pastry bag fitted with a plain round tip with the meringue mixture and pipe out twelve 4-inch circles on the baking sheets, leaving about ½ inch between circles. Gently even out the tops of the meringue circles with a small spatula so they are flat. Bake the meringues until firm to the touch and pale gold, about 1 hour. Remove from the oven and let cool.

4. Prepare the pastry cream: Place the milk and the vanilla bean in a medium saucepan and bring to a boil over medium-high heat. Remove the pan from the heat, cover, and steam for 5 minutes. Remove the vanilla bean. Combine the egg yolks and the sugar in a medium bowl and whisk until thick and pale yellow. Whisk in the flour, then the milk. Return the mixture to the saucepan and bring to a boil over medium heat, stirring constantly. Allow it to boil for 2 minutes, remove from the heat, transfer to a bowl, and set aside to cool.

5. Prepare the coulis: Purée the raspberries in a food processor or food mill. Add the confectioners' sugar and the lemon juice to suit your taste.

6. Whisk the cooled pastry cream so it is spreadable, then divide it among 6 of the cooled meringue rounds, spreading it evenly to the edge of each meringue. Carefully cover the pastry cream with strawberries. Spread the sorbet evenly over the remaining meringue rounds, to within ⅛ inch of the edges. Quickly top the sorbet rounds with the pastry cream rounds. Pour the coulis around each of the pastries. Serve immediately.

Yield: 6 servings.

VONGNES *(Ain)*

Flaxieu 2 k, Ouche 7 k.

Fête du Vieux Four (bread baking festival): Easter Sunday.

BOULANGERIE-BAR

ALAIN NAMBOTIN
Vongnes, 01350 Culoz.
(79.87.93.20).
Closed Monday, Tuesday,
 Wednesday, and the
 month of February.
The bakery is open 2 to 7
 P.M. Thursday, 7 A.M. to 8
 P.M. Friday, and 7 A.M. to
 noon Saturday in
 summer. The bar is open
 Friday and Saturday
 nights until midnight.

This unusual combination of bakery and café allows you to sample Alain Nambotin's bread (baked in the bread oven he built himself) as well as the local specialty, *diots,* pork sausages cooked in red wine. (Monsieur Nambotin also takes his bread to the Belley market Saturday morning.)

VONNAS *(Ain)*

Bourg-en-Bresse 24 k, Lyon 66 k, Mâcon 19 k, Paris 412 k.

Market: Thursday, 8 A.M. to noon, Place Ferdinand and Place du Marché.

RESTAURANT

**GEORGES BLANC (La Mère
 Blanc)**
01540 Vonnas.
(74.50.00.10).
Last orders taken at 2 P.M.
 and 9:30 P.M.
Closed Wednesday,
 Thursday lunch, and
 after New Year's through
 the first week in
 February.
Credit cards: AE, DC, V.
Terrace dining.
Private dining room for 30.
English spoken.
260- and 390-franc menus.
 A la carte, 500 francs.

Georges Blanc, in Vonnas.

Georges Blanc, the boyish fourth-generation chef who took over from his mother back in 1973, runs one of France's more controversial "grand" restaurants. Over the years, he's transformed a simple family restaurant in this village of 250 into a luxury hotel-restaurant complete with

SPECIALTIES:
*Cuisine moderne et cuisine de
tradition régionale* (modern and
regional traditional cooking).

swimming pool and helicopter pad, for those who have to eat and run. Many diners are turned off by the fanfare, yet I've always found his food a fine blend of modern and traditional, and I certainly have nothing against dining in a beautiful flower-filled environment. I guess I'm a traditionalist at heart, so when I go to Georges Blanc's I still enjoy the foods that made La Mère Blanc famous, like frog's legs and snails, and plump Bresse chicken. I've loved his *salade tiède de cuisses de grenouilles à la ciboulette,* prepared with fresh frog's legs, touches of butter and shallots, cream and lemon juice, and sprinkled liberally with chives and fresh tarragon, and the hearty *cassolette d'escargots,* giant snails served with a sauce of cream, garlic, shallots, and butter, laced with fresh wild mushrooms and diced fresh tomatoes. Chef Blanc began his culinary career specializing in pastry, and so naturally he pays more attention to desserts than the average chef: His chocolate offerings get a special mention, especially his chocolate mousse, rich chocolate cakes, and fine chocolate truffles. (For a sample of his light and colorful *gourmandise glacée aux fruits rouges*—the dessert pictured on the cover—see recipe, page 272).

FRENCH GROUND HOG'S DAY

Some say it's a legend, some say it's a custom of days past, but everyone, from the mayor's office of La Chapelle-en-Valgaudemar (population 184) to the tourist office of the Hautes-Alpes, can tell you about the tradition of the omelet festival in Les Andrieux. By all accounts, this tiny Alpine hamlet, shielded from the sun a whopping 100 days of the year, annually celebrated the sun's return with a major festival. In the dark morning of February 10 (or 11 or 12, depending on who's telling), the festivities began at home as the inhabitants of Les Andrieux busily cracked eggs for their golden omelets. At 10 A.M. the villagers gathered in the town square to dance and offer their omelets to the sun. At noon, without fail, the sun appeared, and the villagers returned home in the daylight to feast on their sun-kissed omelets.

NOUGAT GLACE JACQUES PIC
JACQUES PIC'S FROZEN NOUGAT

Surprisingly, desserts are often the part of the meal I can take or leave. But not this one. Perhaps it's my fondness for the soft, creamy white nougat candy from Montélimar that makes me love the homemade frozen version. As far as I'm concerned, this dish is better than any homemade ice cream, and a touch more elegant. I first sampled it at Jacques Pic's in Valence and have seen it in numerous restaurants throughout Provence and the Côte-d'Azur. It's a terrific summer dessert and one that can be made a day ahead. It's worthwhile making the effort to find a candy shop that sells good-quality candied fruit, rather than using the tasteless commercial variety.

⅓ cup (45 g) whole almonds
⅓ cup (45 g) hazelnuts
1 vanilla bean, split
4 large eggs, lightly beaten
4 tablespoons (2 ounces; 60 g) unsalted butter, at room temperature
½ cup (100 g) sugar
4 ounces (125 g) candied fruits, preferably orange peel and cherries, coarsely chopped
2 cups (500 ml) heavy cream, preferably not ultra-pasteurized

1. Preheat the oven to 300°F (150°C).

2. Spread the almonds and hazelnuts separately on 2 small baking sheets and roast them until they are fragrant and lightly browned, about 10 minutes. Remove the nuts from the oven. Let the almonds cool, but rub the warm hazelnuts in a cotton dish towel to remove as much skin as possible. Set aside to cool.

3. Scrape the small seeds from the split vanilla bean. Place the vanilla seeds, eggs, butter, and sugar in a medium saucepan. Cook, stirring constantly, over medium heat just until the eggs begin to set. They will resemble creamy scrambled eggs, but do not be alarmed. Remove the pan from the heat and immediately transfer the mixture to a large mixing bowl to cool. When the mixture has cooled, stir in the whole nuts and candied fruits. Set aside.

4. Whip the cream in a second large mixing bowl until stiff, then stir it into the fruit and nut mixture.

5. Pour the mixture into a nonstick, straight-sided, 8 x 4-inch (25 x 12 cm) rectangular loaf pan, or a regular loaf pan lined with parchment paper. Cover with plastic wrap and freeze until thoroughly set, about 4 hours.

6. To serve, unmold the nougat, cut into even slices, and place on chilled dessert plates.

Yield: 8 servings.

WINES OF JURA/RHONE-ALPS

1. VIN DE SAVOIE CHIGNIN (QUENARD):

This is the sort of wine that wine writers often toss off as "amusing," but I'd never laugh at Raymond Quénard's Chignin-Bergeron, an elegant white made from the *roussanne* grape, the same grape that goes into the white Hermitage.

2. VIN DE PAILLE:

A sweet, almost syrupy, intense dessert wine, this expensive oddity, made from grapes dried on straw mats, is worth sampling with toast and a slice of rich fresh foie gras.

3. VIN JAUNE (ROLET):

This sherry-like white from the Jura is my favorite wine for drinking with a fruity, well-aged Comté cheese. The best known is Château-Chalon.

4. HERMITAGE (CHAVE):

My wine cellar is heavy on Chave's Hermitage, both red and white, and it's a wine you'll see often on wine lists all over the country. His rich, long-lived, elegant wines, made just north of Valence, are always a good buy and rarely disappoint.

5. CORNAS (CLAPE):

August Clape is the best-known winemaker of Cornas, a northern Rhône wine that is brightly colored, intensely fruity, tannic, and satisfying. Often overlooked on wine lists and generally well priced.

6. COTE-ROTIE (ROSTAING):

As refined and elegant as it's big and spicy, the Côte-Rôtie of René Rostaing is one of my favorite wines, one that marries beautifully with full-flavored game dishes and roasts.

7. COTE-ROTIE (GUIGAL):

Is there a wine more sought after by connoisseurs and collectors? Many chefs and *sommeliers* feel that the power of the Guigal name is a bit overblown, but his wines do appear on wine lists all over France, and are perfect with wintery *daubes* and grilled meats.

CHEESES OF JURA/RHONE-ALPS

1. BEAUFORT: Of the hundreds of cheeses made in France, Beaufort is one of my personal favorites. The best is made in high-mountain chalets during the summer, then aged up to two years in large humid aging rooms. Made with raw whole cow's milk, Beaufort is formed into giant concave wheels weighing up to 60 kilos (132 pounds). Beaufort has a pleasantly grainy texture, much like a well-aged Italian Parmesan. The flavor is fruity, nutty, almost buttery, and carries with it the fragrance of wild mountain flowers. When buying Beaufort, don't look for holes (it has very few), and don't be alarmed if you see small horizontal cracks running through it. That's normal.

2. TOMME DE SAVOIE: Throughout the Savoie, one sees dozens of different *tommes,* fat discs of both cow's- and goat's-milk cheese with bumpy gray to light yellow rinds. The fat content of the cheese will vary, from 0 to 45 percent, depending upon whether it was made with whole or skimmed milk. Many *tommes* are seasoned with herbs or black pepper. They are sold under a variety of names, most commonly Tomme de Savoie.

3. TAMIE: Also known as Trappiste de Tamié, this thick disc of cow's-milk cheese is made in the Trappist monastery in Tamié, in the Savoie. A tender, elastic cheese, it is distinguished by its bright blue and white paper wrapper and is similar to Reblochon.

4. REBLOCHON: An ancient cheese, known since the fourteenth century, mild and creamy Reblochon is made from raw whole cow's milk and formed into flattened discs. The best, with a rosy orange rind covered with an ivory white bloom, is unctuous and supple, with a rather pronounced mustiness, tasting faintly of hazelnuts. It's made both on farms and in small dairies, and aged in cold cellars for four to five weeks. Try it with a Roussette de Savoie, the fruity white wine of the Savoie.

Provence
PROVENCE

At La Beaugravière in Mondragon: the Julliens, and a single truffle.

The wind comes up quickly—at first seemingly out of nowhere, then distinctly from the north. You're driving calmly along one of the winding roads of northern Provence, gazing at purple carpets of lavender to the left, giant sunflowers to the right, regimented rows of green, green grapevines in the distance, when the *mistral,* a ferocious force of nature, threatens to toss your car into the next lane. Soon you find yourself commiserating with Madame de Sévigné, who hated the pesky *mistral,* the furious Provençal gust she described as "that bitter, freezing wind which cuts one's being to the quick."

Fortunately the *mistral,* which funnels through the narrow Rhône valley from the Massif Central to the Mediterranean, is all there is to dislike about this enchanted land, a region that stretches from Montélimar in the north all the way down to Marseille.

One can spend some splendid days touring here, beginning the trip somewhere around Montélimar, zigzagging through stretches of the Drôme and the Vaucluse, slipping on down to the Bouches-du-Rhône, traipsing about sleepy hilltop villages, sampling local wines and goat cheeses, tasting the region's famed lamb and guinea fowl, touring markets, wine *caves,* and castles, and ending on a cool, windy note with an early morning drive to the summit of Mont Ventoux. In the summer in particular, everywhere you look there are posters for wine festivals, flea markets, and gastronomic *fêtes,* allowing for a bit of serendipitous shopping and celebration.

One never needs an excuse to return to Provence, the region of France that's my unequivocal favorite. How could one not embrace a land that gives us first-of-season asparagus, fruity olive oil, meaty black olives, and the prized, so rare, black truffle?

So take a gentle trip, avoiding the irritation of the *autoroute,* and search out the quiet, scenic *départemental* roads outlined in green on the Michelin map. Spend mornings combing the markets that move about the region on a regular schedule, shopping for a picnic lunch to fill the midday calm. Afternoons are for touring villages on foot, peeking inside old churches and weekend houses under renovation, or for following a self-arranged *route de vin* for tasting the incredible variety of wines that come from the fertile valley stretching to the east of the Rhône.

You'll see that some towns, like Mirabel-aux-Baronnies, south of the olive center of Nyons, are so small that cars passing through almost knock over the café tables that spill onto the narrow main street. Others like twelfth-century Crestet (population 269) and Séguret (population 687), seem to be designed for the impatient traveler. You can "do" such towns on foot in a leisurely ten- or fifteen-minute jaunt, wandering up and down the narrow steps that lead to a fantasy world of ancient stone houses.

These are the villages of beautiful views, scenic walks, and tranquility, where nearly every home boasts a cypress tree to the north, a Provençal welcome sign that also serves as a natural windbreak, and where every town big enough to support a café also has an alley-like stretch of ground for *boules,* the bowling-like game that is still played for hours on end by old men in worn navy bérets.

You'll see quickly how Provençal markets have a character and accent all their own, offering a fascinating glimpse into the region's culture and customs. Village to village, the scene changes little as merchants make their weekly rounds.

If this is Vaison-la-Romaine, it must be Tuesday. Garlands of bright purple garlic catch the eye, while the heady aromas of perfumed Cavaillon melons, fragrant *muscat de Hambourg* grapes, and tiny violet-hued figs mingle in the warm summer air.

A wiry young merchant, microphone in hand, hawks no-iron sheets, while a farmer from the Ardèche, across the Rhône, offers wild *mousseron* mushrooms by the gram, tossing in verbal recipes with every sale. Nearby, shoppers line up at the knife-sharpener's cart to put their kitchen tools in order, and a lean blonde sells fresh *croissants* from a van equipped with its own oven.

Meanwhile, a clever housewife well into her sixties has just discovered the secret to securing the freshest eggs in the market: *"Bonjour, jeune homme,"* she addresses a barrel-chested farmer about her own age. They shake hands, exchange winks, then from behind a stall laden with fresh-picked herbs, leeks, lettuce, and clay pots filled with multicolored geraniums, he clandestinely extracts a wicker basket, and glancing around to see that no one is looking, pulls out a half-dozen eggs wrapped carefully in yesterday's edition of *Le Provençal.*

The farm chèvre *of Provence.*

WHEN YOU GO

Michelin Green Guides: *Provence* and *French Riviera/Côte-d'Azur* (both available in English).

Getting there: Air Inter offers about a dozen 1½-hour flights daily from Paris to Marseille, leaving from Roissy (Charles-de-Gaulle) and Orly Ouest airports. About five daily TGV *(trains à grande vitesse)*, or bullet trains, make the 4¾-hour journey from Paris's Gare de Lyon to Marseille, with most trains making stops in Valence (3 hours), Montélimar (3¼ hours), and Avignon (3¾ hours). Cars may be rented at the airport and train stations.

Getting around: Michelin map 245 (Provence/Côte-d'Azur).

Best time to visit: Provence is lovely throughout the year, although of course the summer months are best. May can be rainy, it begins to warm up in June, and July and August are the busiest and most popular months, when the long, hot days and endless festivals make this one of the best places to be in the summertime. Fall is also a fine, and calmer, time to visit, as the weather's still warm, the days still long.

Required reading: There are numerous good books on Provence, the best of which include Laurence Wylie's classic *Village in the Vaucluse,* a warm and human social history of a Provençal village; Mireille Johnston's *The Cuisine of the Sun* for some good contemporary recipes; and Pierre Deux's *French Country* for a look at contemporary Provençal life.

MARKETS
(Liveliest markets are marked with an asterisk.)

Monday: *Aix-en-Provence *Bollène, *Cavaillon, Châteaurenard-Provence, *Fontvieille.

Tuesday: *Aix-en-Provence, Avignon, Châteaurenard-Provence, La Ciotat, *Crest, Gordes, Grignan, Tarascon, *Vaison-la-Romaine, Vitrolles.

Wednesday: *Arles, Avignon, Barbentane, Buis-les-Baronnies, Cassis, Châteaurenard-Provence, Courthézon, Crest, Die, Malaucène, Montélimar, Roussillon, *Saint-Rémy-de-Provence, *Salon-de-Provence, *Valréas, Violès.

Thursday: *Aix-en-Provence, Avignon, Beaucaire, Bourdeaux, Châteaurenard-Provence, Dieulefit, L'Isle-sur-la-Sorgue, Martigues, Maussane-les-Alpilles, Montélimar, Noves, *Nyons, *Orange, Vitrolles.

Friday: *Aix-en-Provence, Avignon, Bonnieux, *Carpentras, *Cassis, Châteauneuf-du-Pape, Châteaurenard-Provence, Fontvieille, Lambesc, Pierrelatte, Saint-Martin-de-Crau, Salon-de-Provence, Suze-la-Rousse, *Vitrolles.

Saturday: *Aix-en-Provence, *Apt, *Arles, *Avignon, Châteaurenard-Provence, *Crest, *Die, Montélimar, Saint-Rémy-de-Provence, Salon-de-Provence, Valréas.

Sunday: *Aix-en-Provence, *Avignon, *Beaucaire, Courthézon, *L'Isle-sur-la-Sorgue, *Martigues, Saillans, Salon-de-Provence, Sarrians, *Vitrolles.

FAIRS AND FESTIVALS

Sunday nearest May 16: *Fête de la Saint-Gens,* Monteux-le-Baucet.

Three weeks in June: *Foire à l'Ail et aux Taraïettes* (garlic and terra-cotta pottery fair), Marseille.

Last weekend in June: *Fête de la Tarasque,* Tarascon.

Last Sunday in June: *Fête du Papagaï* (parrot festival), Bollène.

Beginning of July: *Fête du Costume,* Arles.

Weekend before July 14: *Foire du Tilleul, de la Lavande, et de l'Olivier* (linden blossom, lavender, and olive fair), Buis-les-Baronnies.

July 8 to 14: *Foire à l'Ail et aux Produits du Terroir* (garlic and regional specialties fair), Cabriès.

Second Saturday in July: *Fête du Vin* (wine festival), Visan.

A few days around July 14: *Fête du Vin* (wine festival), Vacqueyras.

Third week in July: *Fête du Picodon* (Picodon festival/goat cheese competition), Saoû.

Fourth Sunday in July: *Fête du Vin* (wine festival), Cairanne.

Last week in July and first week in August: *Concours de Pêche au Thon* (tuna fishing competition), Fos-sur-Mer.

Third week in August: *Festival Provençal,* Séguret.

First weekend in September: *Fête d'Automne* (autumn festival), Courthézon.

Olives, pickles, salads galore.

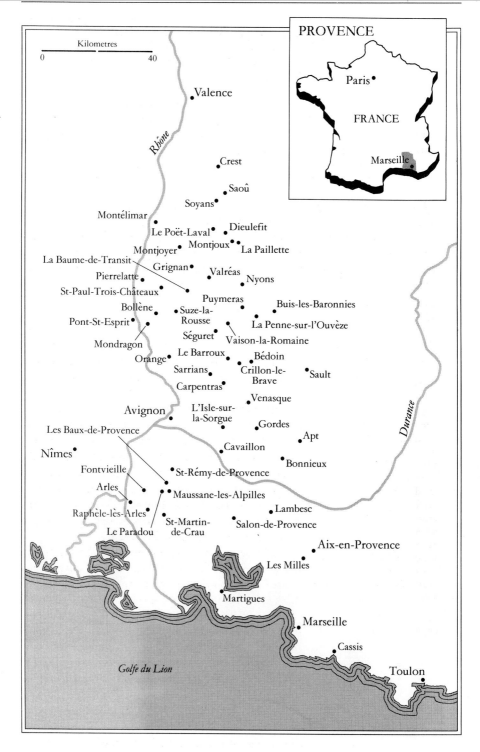

PROVENCE

Kilometres

0   40

Valence

Rhône

Crest

Saoû

Soyans

Montélimar

Le Poët-Laval   Dieulefit

Montjoyer   Montjoux   La Paillette

La Baume-de-Transit   Grignan

Pierrelatte   Valréas   Nyons

St-Paul-Trois-Châteaux   Puymeras

Bollène   Suze-la-   Buis-les-Baronnies
           Rousse

Pont-St-Esprit   La Penne-sur-l'Ouvèze

Mondragon   Séguret   Vaison-la-Romaine

Orange   Le Barroux   Bédoin

Sarrians   Crillon-le-   Sault
            Brave

Carpentras   Venasque

Avignon   L'Isle-sur-   Gordes
           la-Sorgue

Les Baux-de-Provence   Apt

Nîmes   Cavaillon

Fontvieille   Bonnieux

Arles   St-Rémy-de-Provence

Raphèle-lès-Arles   Maussane-les-Alpilles

Le Paradou   St-Martin-   Lambesc
              de-Crau   Salon-de-Provence

Aix-en-Provence

Les Milles

Martigues

Marseille

Cassis

Golfe du Lion   Toulon

Durance

PROVENCE

Paris

FRANCE

Marseille

AIX-EN-PROVENCE *(Bouches-du-Rhône)*

Avignon 80 k, Marseille 31 k, Nice 175 k, Nîmes 105 k, Paris 756 k, Toulon 81 k.

Markets: Daily, 8 A.M. to noon, Place Richelme; Tuesday, Thursday, and Saturday, 8 A.M. to noon, Place des Prêcheurs.
Flea market: Tuesday, Thursday, and Saturday, 8 A.M. to noon (open longer hours the week before Christmas; closed Christmas Day), Place de Verdun, next to the Place des Prêcheurs food market.

When you are in Aix, don't limit yourself to the cafés along the Cours Mirabeau. Get out around town: Wander through the narrow passageways to summertime markets selling tiny fist-size Cavaillon melons; elongated, banana-shaped onions known as *échalotes-bananes;* giant zucchini blossoms; baby red peppers; and baskets full of first-of-season *tilleul*—the dried leaves of the local linden tree—sold here by the hecto (100 grams).

RESTAURANTS

AUBERGE D'AILLANE
Route de Robole, 13290 Les Milles.
(42.24.24.49).
Last orders taken at 3 P.M. (and 11 P.M. in July).
Open for lunch only, Monday through Friday (except during the month of July). In July, open for lunch and dinner Monday through Friday and for dinner only on Saturday. Closed Sunday and August.
Credit card: V.
Terrace dining in July.
English spoken.
70- to 200-franc menus. A la carte, 100 francs.

SPECIALTIES:
Provençal.

Sometimes career changes are born not of desire, but of necessity. Such is the case of Fernand and Marcelle Curto, now proprietors of one of France's most unusual restaurants.

Twenty-one years ago the Curtos and their eight children began to assemble their dream house, bit by bit, in the middle of wheat fields and vineyards just minutes from Aix-en-Provence. Six years later the face of the land changed, and an industrial park had sprung up. Adjacent farms and homes were bulldozed, but the Curto family decided that the home that they had built, salvaged tile by salvaged tile, must be saved.

Marcelle, as the mother of eight, knew all about cooking for a crowd, and Fernand had worked as a maître d'hôtel in Aix-en-Provence. The children were eager to pitch in. So they made a deal with the factories that had become their neighbors: We'll transform our house into a restaurant for your employees, if we get to keep the house.

Today the Curto family shares a multitude of careers. Three attractive daughters wait tables at lunch while each pursues a different art career during off-hours. The parents share the cooking. As tiny Marcelle modestly explains, "Fernand handles all the big pots and makes the bread. I just sort of

AN AUGUST DICTUM

*Pluio d'aous
Duono d'ooulovi eme de
mous.*

*Rain in August
brings olives and wine.*

putter along after him . . ."

The regal multistory Provençal home stands as a green sanctuary in the center of a characterless industrial park. A double row of trees shades the airy, garden-like dining room, where tables are set along a wall of huge arched windows looking out onto a flower-filled patio.

The guests—mostly groups of businessmen in short-sleeved shirts—dine to classical music and pour their wine out of two-liter glass jugs as they're cheerfully served by Monique, Patricia, and Brigitte, all dressed fetchingly in white blouses, black wrap-around apron-skirts, black fishnet stockings, and high platform sandals. Not the ambience of your average factory canteen.

The daughters set a relaxed, welcoming mood as they arrive first with the menu and a bowl of appetizers (a tasty salad of chick-peas, spring onions, and black olives in vinaigrette), then slice the giant *miche* of bread that Papa made that morning.

The food here is modest, rustic Provençal home cooking, with a menu that consists of peppery *socca* (pan-fried chick-pea batter, the size of a dinner plate, cooked like an ultra-light, crinkled crêpe); a satisfactory beef *daube* served with a meltingly soft side dish of cooked potatoes, zucchini, and carrots; or *gigot d'agneau,* moist, flavorful leg of lamb sliced into thin strips. And Marcelle's apple tart is a delight: The puff pastry dough is rough, a bit too thick, but deliciously, unquestionably, homemade. (Directions: Take the *autoroute* south from Aix-en-Provence and exit at Les Milles.

A PROVENCAL CUSTOM

Traditionally, in Provence all children were brought into the world at home, with midwives in attendance. As neighbors, friends, and family came to visit the new mother and infant, they carried with them a morsel of bread, an egg, salt, and a match, so the child would grow up *bon comme le pain, plein comme un oeuf, sage comme le sel, et droit comme une allumette* (as good as bread, as filled out as an egg, as wise as salt, and as straight as a match.)

Follow the signs to the *zone industrielle,* bearing left at a fork in the road, passing the village of Les Milles. Exit at the sign to Bouc-en-Belair. Double back under the *autoroute* bridge, make a right, and follow the road around to the left. Turn right at the first crossroad, continue about ½ kilometer [¼ mile], and just before the first traffic circle you will see a clump of trees and a wrought iron gate on the right, with the *auberge*—unmarked—hidden behind the trees.)

LE CLOS DE LA VIOLETTE

10 Avenue de la Violette, 13100 Aix-en-Provence. (42.23.30.71).
Last orders taken at 1:30 P.M. and 9:30 P.M.
Closed Monday lunch, Sunday, mid-February through the first week in March, and the first two weeks in August.
Credit cards: AE, V.
Terrace dining.
Private dining room for 10.
English spoken.
300-franc menu. A la carte, about 350 francs.

SPECIALTIES:
Change with the seasons.

Even *cuisine moderne* has its place in Provence, and one of the newer stars on the local horizon is Jean-Marc Banzo, who moved from the center of Aix-en-Provence (where he was chef at the Henri IV) to the edge of town, where he and his wife have installed themselves in a lovely large home they call Le Clos de la Violette.

There's something a bit tentative about the service and the setting, but the food is lively, creative, and agreeable. If the *barigoule d'artichaut en terrine* is on the menu that day, sample this sublime terrine of thick, whole artichoke bottoms layered one atop the other, served with a superb red pepper *coulis.* Another delicious creation is his *croûte de la brousse en persillade,* a dish that combines fresh local goat cheese, tons of herbs, and flavorful *palourdes,* or clams. The dish ends up tasting remarkably like pizza, only the elements are organized in a different manner. With the meal, sample the lovely white Cassis Domaine du Paternel, from the fishing village just outside Marseille. Save room for dessert, an incredible mint soufflé infused with a generous dose of lively fresh mint.

CAFE

LES DEUX GARCONS

53 Cours Mirabeau, 13100 Aix-en-Provence. (42.26.00.51).
Open daily 6 A.M. to 1 A.M.
Credit cards: AE, V.
Sidewalk terrace.

If I had the time to linger at just one café in all of France, I'd choose Les Deux Garçons. Go, take along a good book of short stories, and while away the afternoon in the shade of the plane trees set in double rows along one of Provence's loveliest avenues. And don't forget to peek inside to admire the old-fashioned interior.

Le Melon de Cavaillon

"*I have never eaten fresher, more flavorful or more palatable melons than those of my annuity*," *Dumas later wrote, adding that he hoped that the people of Cavaillon would always find his books as charming as he found their melons.*"

CAVAILLON, JUNE 9—November 15, 1864, was a historic day for Alexandre Dumas *père,* as well as for the famously fragrant and juicy Provençal fruit known the world over as *melon de Cavaillon.*

On that date the prolific French writer made a deal with the municipal government of this market-garden city along the Durance river: In exchange for donating 194 volumes of his work to the local library, Dumas received a lifetime annual gift of a dozen fresh Cavaillon melons.

"I have never eaten fresher, more flavorful or more palatable melons than those of my annuity," Dumas later wrote, adding that he hoped that the people of Cavaillon would always find his books as charming as he found their melons.

The arrangement came about after a librarian wrote asking Dumas to send two or three of his favorite works. Since Dumas was equally fond of all his writings, he sent the lot, then requested that they toss in the melon annuity to sweeten the deal.

The annuity ended shortly after his death in 1870, but a few years ago a French academician convinced the mayor of Cavaillon to reinstitute the agreement and send the prized melons to Dumas' descendants.

Cavaillon actually can thank François I for its success with melons. For it was he who visited the city in 1537 and authorized local farmers to redirect the water from the Durance, allowing them to irrigate the land that until then could support only cereal crops. Thus Provence became one of the first agricultural areas in France to profit from irrigation, and it quickly claimed the fast-growing, sun-loving melon—which was actually grown in the area in prehistoric times—as its own. Today more than half of the 200,000 tons of melons grown annually in

BOULANGERIES

LA BOULANGERIE DU COIN
4 Rue Boulegon, 13100 Aix-en-Provence.
(42.21.49.69).
and **LA BOULANGERIE,**
18 Rue Gaston-de-Saporta, 13100 Aix-en-Provence.
(42.23.18.63).
Open 7 A.M. to 1 P.M. and 4 to 8:30 P.M. Wednesday, Friday, and Sunday; 7 A.M. to 8:30 P.M. Tuesday, Thursday, and Saturday. Closed Monday.

This is one of the funniest little bread shops I know, advertising forty-one different varieties, including a rye and barley loaf they call *petit Irlandais,* a whole wheat bread with onions, a green olive bread, and a *baguette paysanne*—one of the most delicious *baguettes* I've ever tasted, with great crust and a dense interior loaded with coarsely ground rye and wheat. Also, a whole series of lacy, fantasy-shaped *fougasses,* ladder-shaped flat breads flavored with olives, with tomatoes, or with cracklings. Like a bistro, they even have a revolving list of daily specials: If there is anchovy bread, it must be Tuesday.

France come from the Cavaillon region, which offers the proper soil, the intense heat, and the blasting sun necessary to support a melon culture.

As history would have it, the small sunset-orange-fleshed melon we know today bears little resemblance to the fruit that brought Cavaillon its early fame. The melon of earlier times was as big as a rugby ball, with a thick dark green skin and rose-colored flesh. Over the years the melon got smaller and changed colors, and the varieties diminished from some five hundred to the handful grown today.

The French court particularly loved melons: Louis XIV grew seven varieties, and on at least one occasion Catherine de Medici suffered indigestion after overindulging in the sugary fruit. In 1727, Louis XV's wife, a noted gourmand, reportedly became extremely ill after eating an excess of chilled melons. (That wasn't, however, Marie Leszcynska's first gastronomic indiscretion. The previous autumn she lost consciousness after consuming some fifteen dozen oysters.)

The most popular variety of French melon grown today is the Charentais, a variety which is, in fact, the fruit we know today as *melon de Cavaillon*. With its yellowish green, slightly ribbed skin and brilliant orange flesh, it falls into the category of netted, or nutmeg, melons.

Melons profit from an extremely long growing season in France. In a good year, the initial crop arrives in the Cavaillon market the first week of April, fetching a wholesale price of a whopping 140 francs per kilo. But even those willing to pay the opening price are, most likely, disappointed. The early melons, largely grown under plastic sheeting with a little artificial heat, simply can't offer the same overpowering fragrance, the densely fruity flavor, that one finds in the *plein champ*, or open field, melons that appear from early July to mid-September, when they can be found all over Provence's markets priced at around 3 francs per kilo.

For maximum enjoyment, a melon should be consumed just slightly chilled (one poet delighted in the fact that melon charmed the throat and cooled the belly). A ripe melon should actually seem a bit heavy for its size, and ought to be slightly soft at the stem end, gloriously fragrant at the blossom end. Unripe melons should be stored at room temperature until properly soft and fragrant. Once ripe, melons will remain even-flavored and succulent if carefully chilled.

LE GIBASSIER
46 Rue Espariat, 13100
Aix-en-Provence.
(42.27.53.54).
Open 2 A.M. to 1 P.M. and 2 to 8 P.M. Closed Sunday and mid-July through mid-August.

A good address to know if you happen to be wandering around Provence in the middle of the night, in need of a bread fix. Even during daylight hours this *boulangerie*, run by Joachim Piantino, offers some seldom seen regional breads, including a good *pain d'Aix* (variously shaped sourdough loaves, sometimes like a sunflower, other times a chain-like loaf of four linked rounds) and the local *gibassier*, also known as *pompe à l'huile d'olive*, a flat sweet bread flecked with lemon rind and flavored with olive oil.

JEAN RICHARD
46 Rue du Puits Neuf, 13100
Aix-en-Provence.
(42.23.34.63).
Open 5 A.M. to 1 P.M. and 4
to 7 P.M. Closed Sunday
and Monday.

The best of many wonderful breads sampled in Aix. Try to get there on Tuesdays and Fridays at 5 P.M. when their double-mounded *pain d'Aix* comes out of the oven. When we asked Monsieur Richard about his version of this regional bread, he said, with great apologies, that it most nearly resembled *"une paire de seins"* (a pair of breasts). The rest of the time, you won't go wrong settling for the thin and crispy *baguettes* known as *ficelles*. They're also known for their olive-oil-flavored *gibassiers*.

FROMAGERIE

GERARD PAUL
9 Rue Marseillais, 13100
Aix-en Provence.
(42.23.16.84).
Open 8 A.M. to 12:30 P.M.
and 4 to 7 P.M. Closed
Sunday and Monday.

Wander into this spotless boutique and begin your cheesemaker's *tour de France:* Note the well-aged Beaufort *d'alpage* (made with summer mountain milk), sheep's cheese from the Pays Basque, a fine-looking Saint-Nectaire, and a good selection of local goat cheeses. A great place to stock up for a picnic lunch.

CONFISERIE

A LA REINE JEANNE
32 Cours Mirabeau, 13100
Aix-en-Provence.
(42.26.02.33).
Open 8 A.M. to 12:30 P.M.
and 2 to 7 P.M. Closed
Sunday.
Credit cards: AE, DC, V.
Will ship internationally.

This is one of the prettiest shops along the Cours Mirabeau, and entering it is like stepping back about 125 years. Provence is full of all sorts of historical sweets, and one of the most ubiquitous is the diamond-shaped almond paste candy known as *calissons,* the most famous of which comes from Aix. Historically, the major almond market in Provence took place in Aix, so it made sense that someone would develop a way to preserve them. They grind the almonds, mix them with the local candied melon, and turn all this into a paste. The paste is shaped into little diamonds, which are set on a thin sheet of edible rice paper and covered with white sugar frosting. The end result, to my mind, is much ado about nothing (they're really just too sweet, the almond flavor gets buried in the process, and unless you read the ingredients label, you'd never know there were melons in there), but they do remain a rather pretty little touch of regional folklore.

Golden fields of sunflowers.

POUR LA MAISON

GALERIES TROPEZIENNES
31–33 Rue Mignet, 13100
Aix-en-Provence.
(42.96.20.85).
Open 8:30 A.M. to 12:30 P.M.
and 2:30 to 7 P.M. Closed
Monday.
Credit cards: EC, V.
Will ship internationally.

A luxury bazaar, offering a wide range of beautiful and beautifully designed objects, including kitchenware, linens, lingerie, and both men's and women's casual clothing.

MAISON UGHETTI
14 Avenue Pasteur, 13100
Aix-en-Provence.
(42.23.28.32).
Open 8 A.M. to noon and 2
to 7 P.M. Closed Sunday.
Will ship internationally.

An unusual hardware store for exceptional and sturdy handmade tools, for gardening and building.

APT *(Vaucluse)*

Aix-en-Provence 55 k, Avignon 52 k, Carpentras 49 k, Paris 730 k.

Market: Saturday, 7 A.M. to noon, Cours Lauze-de-Perret.

POUR LA MAISON

ATELIER BERNARD
Jean Faucon
12 Avenue de la Libération,
84400 Apt.
(90.74.15.31).
Open 8 A.M. to noon and 2
to 6:30 P.M. Closed
Sunday, Monday, and two
weeks in January.
Credit cards: V.
Will ship internationally.

One of the most respected names in Provençal pottery, a generations-old shop where each lovely plate, cup, and saucer is still made by hand. All items are made to order, and though there is always a wait, it's well worth it. I'm particularly fond of Jean Faucon's simple ochre plates, for they're a pure touch of Provence.

ARLES *(Bouches-du-Rhône)*

Aix-en-Provence 76 k, Avignon 37 k, Cavaillon 44 k, Marseille 95 k,
Nîmes 30 k, Paris 727 k.

Market: Wednesday, 7:30 A.M. to 12:30 P.M., Boulevard Emile-Combes;
Saturday, 7:30 A.M. to 12:30 P.M., Boulevard des Lices.
Fête du Costume: beginning of July.

I love the Arles market, perhaps because Arles is so different from the rest of
Provence. Although it's a good-size city—population 50,000—the people
here seem to have a very definite, small-city sense of self, so as you wander
through markets that wind around the city, you'll certainly strike up lively and
unusual conversations. The market offers an abundance of cheeses, sausages,
and lively characters, so go, and profit from all three.

RESTAURANT

LOU MARQUES
Hôtel Jules César, Boulevard
   des Lices, 13200 Arles.
   (90.93.43.20).
Last orders taken at 1:30 P.M.
   and 9:30 P.M.
Closed November through
   the first three weeks in
   December.
Credit cards: AE, DC, EC, V.
Terrace dining.
Private dining room for 40.
English spoken.
250-franc menu. A la carte,
   300 francs.

S P E C I A L T I E S :
*Mousse de rascasse au pistil de
safran* (scorpion fish with
saffron mousse).

I'm not sure whether I attract dramatic sunsets
   or just spend an awful lot of time dining on
terraces in the summertime in Provence, but I shall
never forget one evening in June when we sat and
watched the golden sun set, the crescent moon rise,
and a black sky burst forth with stars as we sipped
Château Simone rosé, dove into chef Michel Picq's
deliciously fresh monkfish and vegetable soup
known as *baudroie* (see recipe, facing page), and
feasted on poached rayfish topped with the vibrant
raïto, a warm Provençal sauce that blends red wine,
herbs, olives, and capers (see recipe, page 295).
Service can be on the slow and haughty side, but I
wouldn't let that stop me from returning.

FROMAGERS

LACHAFRANIERE
At the market, Wednesday,
   along the Boulevard
   Emile-Combes near Place
   Voltaire; Saturday, on the
   Boulevard des Lices, on
   the food side, across the
   street from the *monument
   aux morts* (war memorial).

A beautiful selection of unusual and original
   cheeses made on a cooperative farm: Try especially the dried *chèvre* flavored with ground black
pepper and thyme.

BAUDROIE LOU MARQUES
RESTAURANT LOU MARQUES' MONKFISH SOUP

All I have to do is look at this list of ingredients and I can taste summer in Provence. Unlike the more complicated Provençal fish soups—bouillabaisse and bourride—this is a very simple soup, in which the local Mediterranean monkfish is the star. If you have access to good fresh monkfish, you've got it made. The recipe comes from one of the most famous restaurants in Arles, the Lou Marques. Baudroie, by the way, is the Provençal name for monkfish.

2 navel oranges
3 medium potatoes, peeled and very thinly sliced
3 medium onions, very thinly sliced
16 small mushroom caps
2 cloves garlic, very thinly sliced
3 fresh artichoke bottoms, quartered
2 medium tomatoes, peeled, cored, seeded, and coarsely chopped
1 large sprig fresh thyme
2 bay leaves
3 tablespoons extra-virgin olive oil
2 quarts (2 liters) water
2 pounds (1 kg) very fresh monkfish, membrane removed and cut into ½-inch (1.5 cm) crosswise slices
Salt and freshly ground black pepper to taste
Small handful of flat-leaf parsley, minced

Garnish:
4 slices country-style bread, preferably homemade
1 clove garlic, halved
1 tablespoon extra-virgin olive oil

1. Carefully cut the zest (the colored part of the peel) from each orange, being sure not to get any of the white pith. Leave the zest in large pieces, for it will be removed before serving the soup.

2. Combine the orange zest, potatoes, onions, mushrooms, garlic, artichokes, tomatoes, thyme, bay leaves, and 2 tablespoons of the oil in a large, heavy-bottomed soup pot. Add the water and heat to a boil over high heat. Boil rapidly for 15 minutes. Add the monkfish and cook 5 minutes longer, carefully skimming the soup as the fish cooks.

3. Preheat the broiler.

4. As the fish cooks, prepare the garnish: Rub the bread on both sides with garlic and brush with oil. Toast the bread on both sides under the broiler.

5. Remove the bay leaves and orange zest from the soup and season it with salt and pepper.

6. To serve, divide the vegetables and fish evenly among 4 warmed soup bowls and ladle the broth over all. Sprinkle with parsley and the remaining 1 tablespoon oil. Serve with the grilled garlic bread.

Yield: 4 servings.

MONSIEUR BLEUZE
At the market, Wednesday, on the corner of Rue Jean-d'Alembert and Boulevard Emile-Combes; Saturday, on the Boulevard des Lices in front of the Vaux-hall café.

This chatty, outgoing merchant is always willing to slice off samples for customers to taste. Do try the delightfully creamy Tomme de Camargue (also sometimes called Tomme Arlésienne) sprinkled with summer savory (a rare blend of goat's milk and cow's milk), as well as his superb sausages, including *saucisson d'Arles* (here a blend of nicely seasoned beef, pork, and donkey), and a spicy *saucisson camarguais* (here a blend of bull and wild boar, tomato sauce, and paprika).

POUR LA MAISON

TERRAILLES ET FAIENCES DU MIDI
15 Rue Tour du Fabre, 13200 Arles.
(90.93.02.37).
Open 9:30 A.M. to noon and 2 to 6:30 P.M. Closed Monday and February.

This dusty shop in the center of town is part museum, part potter's studio, part pottery shop. There's a lovely collection of antique Provençal pottery (most of it not for sale) and a good assortment of contemporary pottery and tableware, colorful green or ochre omelet plates, bowls, and *daubières*—pots for making *daube provençale*.

A variety of chèvres, *a variety of styles.*

MUSEE

MUSEON ARLATEN
Rue de la République, 13200 Arles.
(90.96.08.23).
Open 9 A.M. (10 A.M. in June) to noon and 2 to 5 P.M. (6 P.M. in April, May, and October; 7 P.M. in June and July). Closed Monday from October through May.
Admission: 6 francs for adults, 4 francs for children and students.

Arles is just different from the rest of Provence, a city with its own particular personality. You'll understand it a bit better once you've wandered through this musty but amusing museum full of local costumes, all sorts of artifacts donated by the local hero, poet Frédéric Mistral (who founded the museum with the winnings from his Nobel prize for literature), as well as some charming folkloric room settings depicting life in old Arles.

RAITO
RED WINE SAUCE WITH HERBS, OLIVES, AND CAPERS

This wonderful sauce combines all of the best ingredients of Provence: sturdy red wine, plump cloves of garlic, ripe red tomatoes, black olives, and capers. Traditionally raïto, which must be eaten hot, is served as an accompaniment to grilled fish, but I also love it as a sauce for pasta. I first came across it in Arles, while dining on the terrace of the restaurant Lou Marques. The chef, Michel Picq, served the raïto with rayfish, or skate, and it was superb. While the traditional recipe calls for mixing the olives and capers with wine sauce, chef Picq spread the sauce on a warm plate, covered it with the baked fish, then spooned the hot olive and caper condiment on top of the rayfish, making for a beautiful presentation and a delicious dish. After a friend tested this recipe, she wrote back saying, "This dish makes me want to wear espadrilles, a white straw hat, and my blue-and-white-striped French sundress."

3 tablespoons virgin olive oil

2 onions, minced

2 cloves

1 bottle (750 ml) red wine, preferably Côtes-du-Rhône

2 cups (500 ml) water

5 medium tomatoes, quartered

4 cloves garlic, peeled and halved

Handful of mixed fresh herbs, preferably thyme, rosemary, tarragon, and flat-leaf parsley

Salt and freshly ground black pepper to taste

Condiment:

1 teaspoon virgin olive oil

1 cup (250 ml) oil-cured black olives, preferably from Nyons, pitted and chopped

⅓ cup (80 ml) capers, drained

1. Heat the oil in a deep, heavy-bottomed saucepan over medium-high heat. Add the onions and cook until lightly browned. Add the cloves, wine, water, tomatoes, garlic, and herbs. Cook over high heat until the sauce is quite thick and there is very little liquid left, 1 to 1½ hours. Pass through a food mill or a fine-mesh sieve and season with salt and pepper. (The sauce can be made ahead and reheated.)

2. Prepare the condiment: Heat the oil in a small saucepan over medium-high heat. Add the olives and capers and cook until soft and thoroughly heated through.

3. To serve, reheat the wine sauce, add the condiment, and spoon over hot pasta, grilled fish, chicken, or meat.

Yield: 4 servings.

AVIGNON *(Vaucluse)*

Aix-en-Provence 80 k, Arles 37 k, Marseille 100 k, Nîmes 43 k,
Paris 686 k, Valence 126 k.

Markets: Tuesday through Saturday, 8 A.M. to noon, covered market, Place Pie;
Saturday and Sunday, 8 A.M. to noon, open-air market,
Porte Magnanen ramparts.

RESTAURANTS

LA FOURCHETTE II
17 Rue Racine, 84000
   Avignon.
(90.85.20.93).
Last orders taken at 2 P.M.
   and 9:30 P.M.
Closed Saturday, Sunday, two
   weeks in January, and
   two weeks in June.
No credit cards.
Air-conditioned.
English spoken.
85-franc menu. A la carte,
   150 francs.

SPECIALTIES:
Sardines fraîches marinées
(marinated sardines); *daube de*
boeuf à l'avignonnaise (beef
stewed in red wine); *fricassée de*
pintade aux nouilles fraîches
(guinea hen with fresh
noodles).

For refreshing and updated bistro-style food with a Provençal touch, try La Fourchette II, a casual, inexpensive spot near the center of Avignon. Offerings include a beautiful platter of fresh sardines marinated in tarragon and lemon; a vegetable terrine with spinach cream; beef stew, or *daube,* with a macaroni gratin; and a fricassee of *pintade,* or guinea fowl, with fresh noodles. With all this there is a fine new-vintage Châteauneuf-du-Pape by the carafe. The decor is a bit on the cute side, and service may be a bit slow, but this is a good spot to know about when you're not in the mood for a lengthy multi-course meal.

HIELY
5 Rue de la République,
   84000 Avignon.
(90.86.17.07).
Last orders taken at 1:15 P.M.
   and 9:15 P.M.
Closed Monday, Tuesday, the
   last week in December
   through mid-January,
   and the last two weeks in
   June.
Credit cards: AE, V.
Air-conditioned.
English spoken.
350 francs.

SPECIALTIES:
Gratin de moules aux épinards

Traditionally Hiély is considered one of Provence's finest regional restaurants, and although as a regular client I've experienced some extremely variable food over the years, I do keep going back. On some visits the food just comes off as heavy, too rich with cream. But on others it evokes the fresh, airy feel of Provence. Land at Hiély on a good day—as I did on my last visit—and you're likely to find an appealing assortment of authentically regional fare, including deliciously delicate grilled lamb from the hills around Les Baux (served with a warming gratin of crisp, paper-thin potatoes), a satisfying *gratin de moules aux épinards;* local young rabbit, or *lapereau,* stuffed with its

(gratin of mussels and spinach); *râble de lapereau farci de son foie, sauce poivrade* (rabbit with liver stuffing in a peppery sauce); *mousseline de brochet* (pike mousseline), *ragoût de homard* (lobster stew).

flavorful liver and served with a peppery *sauce poivrade;* and a platter of fresh pasta sprinkled with *palourdes* (clams) and delicate strips of sole, bathed in a red pepper *coulis*. There's also a marvelous selection of local *chèvres* and a dessert cart that will melt the will of the most disciplined among us. There's an extraordinary Vacherin which they smother with chocolate sauce, marvelous bread pudding, and an endless procession of fruit-flavored sorbets. Hiély also boasts one of the best wine lists of the region, including an expertly chosen assortment of full-bodied Châteauneuf-du-Pape, silken, rich Hermitage, and heady Côte-Rôtie. Among these, best bets include Domaine Tempier's Bandol and the black-cherry-colored Châteauneuf-du-Pape from Vieux Télégraphe. The welcome here is always warm, and service, generally, comes with a smile.

BOULANGERIE

A. SOLAZ
49 Rue Joseph-Vernet,
   84000 Avignon.
(90.86.62.87).
Open 6:30 A.M. to 7:30 P.M.
   Closed Saturday
   afternoon and Sunday.

For a generous assortment of regional breads, including *pain aux noix* (walnut bread) and *pain aux olives* (olive bread).

POUR LA MAISON

JAFFIER PARSI
42 Rue des Fourbisseurs and
   39 Place de la Principale,
   84000 Avignon.
(90.86.08.85).
Open 8:45 A.M. to noon and
   2 to 7 P.M. Closed Sunday,
   Monday morning,
   August, and one week in
   February.

I call this place a toy store for cooks, much like the famous Dehillerin cookware shop in Paris. I could spend hours just wandering up and down the narrow aisles, dreaming about a new copper sauce-pan, an olivewood salad bowl, a new cookbook. The shop has everything the cook might need—and more, including electric oyster openers!

LE BARROUX *(Vaucluse)*

Carpentras 12 k, Vaison-la-Romaine 16 k.

BOULANGERIE

**MONASTERE SAINTE-
MADELEINE**
Le Barroux, 84339 Caromb.
(90.62.56.31).
Open for bread 8 to 9:15
A.M., 11 to 11:45 A.M.,
and 2:30 to 5:15 P.M.
Wednesday afternoon,
Thursday (*miche,* or large
round loaf, only),
Saturday, and Sunday
(*miche, pain aux olives,* or
olive bread, and
demi-seigle aux noix, or
half-rye with walnuts).
Closed six days of the
year.

One summer Sunday I was sampling wine at a tasting center in the village of Gigondas and was offered a slice of delicious walnut bread. I was certain someone had imported a loaf of Lionel Poilâne's world-famous bread from Paris. No, insisted the friendly face behind the table, it came from the monastery in Le Barroux. Monk bread? Sure enough, the following week we drove up to the monastery to see, and to sample. Also try their *pain d'olives* (olive bread) and *croque-moines* (honey and almond cookies).

AN UNCOMMON BAKER

The Provençal storyteller Marcel Pagnol wrote lovingly and humorously about the lives of the everyday people of the Midi. One of his tales, *"La Femme du Boulanger,"* or "The Baker's Wife," recounts the story of a middle-aged village baker whose beautiful wife leaves him for a local shepherd. The baker is so heartbroken, he no longer has the energy to continue with the work that is also his passion, bread baking. The townspeople, deprived of their daily nourishment, plot to win her back, along with their bread. For the return of his wife, the baker promises his friends a tender reward:

I will make you bread like you have never seen. I will knead each batch half an hour longer, and with the sticks and twigs for heating the oven, I will mix rosemary.
And while the bread is baking, I won't sleep the way bakers usually do; instead I will open the oven door every five minutes and I won't let the bread out of my sight. I will make you a bread so good that it will be food for the gods. ...And each day, in addition to the bread I normally make, I'll knead 5 kilos for the poor....And in each loaf that I make for you, there will be friendship and thanks.

LA BAUME-DE-TRANSIT *(Drôme)*

Orange 27 k, Pierrelatte 17 k, Saint-Paul-Trois-Châteaux 9 k.

FERME-AUBERGE

**FERME-AUBERGE
   DOMAINE DE
   SAINT-LUC**
La Baume-de-Transit, 26790
   Saint-Paul-Trois-Châteaux.
   (75.98.11.51).
Open for dinner only, to
   guests staying at the
   farm.
Five rooms; 12 guests
   maximum.
Closed Sunday.
No credit cards.
Terrace dining.
About 100 francs.

SPECIALTIES:
Pintadeau à la purée d'ail
(young guinea hen with garlic
purée), *ratatouille* (cooked dish
of eggplant, zucchini, onions,
tomatoes, peppers, garlic, and
olive oil), *purée de pêche* (peach
purée).

A few years ago Eliane and Ludovic Cornillon fell in love with a rundown eighteenth-century farm. They restored it, added bedrooms and baths, filled the gardens with herbs, flowers, and vegetables, and finally decided to take in paying guests. You can dine in the courtyard beneath an aging olive tree, sampling some delicious homemade Provençal fare: their own house rosé and meaty olives from Nyons; a fresh green bean salad showered with basil, a touch of cream, and olives; a perfectly roasted guinea hen and a sizzling *gratin provençal*. The gratin, made up of layers of sliced tomatoes and potatoes, is infused with local herbs, garlic, and olive oil. Madame Cornillon offers fresh goat cheese, known as *tomme de chèvre*, and scouts out local markets for fresh fruits that she turns into light and appealing desserts. If you visit in the spring, you're likely to sample the family's home-grown asparagus, while in the summertime the *auberge* is famous for its *soupe au pistou*, a vegetable soup touched with a hint of basil and garlic. More often than not, guests leave with a few bottles of the Cornillons' Château du Tricastin red and rosé wines, which have won medals at agricultural fairs in Paris and Montélimar.

A BREAD SUPERSTITION

Never turn a loaf of
bread upside down, or
witches will come to
dance upon it.

Goat cheese for sale.

LES BAUX-DE-PROVENCE *(Bouches-du-Rhône)*

Arles 19 k, Avignon 31 k, Marseille 86 k, Nîmes 44 k, Paris 716 k,
Saint-Rémy-de-Provence 10 k, Salon-de-Provence 32 k.

RESTAURANTS

**OUSTAU DE
  BAUMANIERE**
Les Baux-de-Provence,
  13520 Maussane-les-
  Alpilles.
(90.54.33.07).
Last orders taken at 2 P.M.
  and 9 P.M.
Closed Thursday lunch and
  Wednesday November
  through March, and
  mid-January through
  February.
Credit cards: AE, EC, V.
Terrace dining.
English spoken.
395- and 485-franc menus.
  A la carte, 600 francs.

S P E C I A L T I E S :
Agneau d'Alpilles (lamb from
the hills around Les Baux),
rouget au basilic (red mullet
with basil).

For decades, travelers have been making gastronomic pilgrimages to Les Baux-de-Provence, the
tiny village that is home to this luxurious, internationally renowned restaurant. This is the place
where couples and families, friends and lovers, have
clinked Champagne glasses and consumed quantities of Alpilles lamb, eggplant gratin, local goat
cheese, and sturdy Provençal red wine as they
celebrated birthdays, anniversaries, and good fortune on the sun-blessed terrace beside the pool.

Yet despite it all, there are disappointing signs.
Some of the staff could not be more attentive, but
others are merely going through the motions, having lost interest a long time ago. Food can vary from
dull—the Alpilles lamb should be among the best
in the world, but here it's often simply bland—to
gastronomically exciting. I truly love the vibrant
flavors of their eggplant gratin (see recipe, following page) and the finely seasoned *terrine d'aubergines
sauce poivrons doux,* chunks of lamb enveloped in
thinly sliced eggplant, served warm with a lively red
pepper sauce (see recipe, page 304).

And on those days when all falls into place,
there is a true generosity about Baumanière: If an
individual orders a rack of lamb for two, he may be
charged for only one serving. If several diners order
different side vegetable courses, everyone will be
offered a sample of each.

Despite the annoying flaws, I don't know of
any more romantic dining spot in Provence, and it's
still the place that springs to mind when it comes
time to stage a gastronomic celebration. So I go,
clink glasses, and cross fingers.

If you go, take advantage of the good regional
wines on the list. Try Château Simone's Palette, a
tiny appelation south of Aix producing one of
Provence's best wines (it's a lively white—more
than just for quaffing: one that makes you sit up

and take notice), then a red Châteauneuf-du-Pape from Beaucastel, and make it as old a bottle as you can afford.

GRATIN D'AUBERGINES BAUMANIERE
BAUMANIERE'S EGGPLANT GRATIN

Gratins of any sort are satisfying. There's something about a crispy, bubbly crust that is universally appealing. This is a version of the gratin served at the famous restaurant Oustaù de Baumanière in Les Baux-de-Provence. I sampled the gratin the first time I dined there, and I know I asked for seconds more than once. This method of browning the eggplant—in the oven, rather than in a frying pan—allows you to control the amount of oil used, making for a lighter dish. The only caution is to watch the eggplant slices and remove them as soon as they begin to turn brown.

2 medium eggplants (about 2 pounds; 1 kg)
3 tablespoons virgin olive oil
3 cups (750 ml) Basic Tomato Sauce (see Recipe Index)
Handful of mixed fresh herbs, preferably basil, chervil, thyme, and flat-leaf parsley, minced
Salt and freshly ground black pepper to taste

1. Preheat the oven to 450°F (230°C).

2. Peel and cut the eggplant crosswise into slices ⅛ inch (3 mm) thick. Using a pastry brush, coat both sides of the eggplant slices with oil and place them on an oiled baking sheet. Bake the eggplant until the bottom is light brown, 5 to 10 minutes. Turn and bake until light brown on the other side, about 5 minutes longer. Check the eggplant frequently and remove the slices as they brown.

3. Cover the bottom of a shallow 5-cup (1.25 liter) porcelain gratin dish with a thin layer of the tomato sauce. Sprinkle with some of the minced herbs and cover with a layer of eggplant. Season lightly with salt and pepper. Continue in this manner until all the ingredients are used, ending with a layer of tomato sauce.

4. Bake until crispy and bubbly, about 30 minutes. Serve warm or at room temperature.

Yield: 4 servings.

LA RIBOTO DE TAVEN
Les Baux-de-Provence,
   13520 Maussane-les-
   Alpilles.
(90.97.34.23).
Last orders taken at 2 P.M.
   and 9:15 P.M. (9:30 P.M. in
   July and August).
Closed Sunday dinner
   October through May,
   Monday, and the last
   three weeks in January
   through the first three
   weeks in February.
Credit cards: AE, DC, V.
Terrace dining.
Private dining room for 35.
English spoken.
230-franc menu. A la carte,
   280 francs.

SPECIALTIES:
According to the seasons; *nage
fine d'huîtres et de moules*
(oysters and mussels served in
their poaching liquid), *agneau
des Alpilles* (lamb from the hills
around Les Baux), game.

Provence has its share of romantic dining spots, but few can equal La Riboto de Taven, an intimate, cottage-like stone farmhouse nestled secretively, mysteriously, in the hills of Les Baux.

The dining room is rustic but elegant, with bare stone walls, black and white checkerboard tile floors, peach-tone tablecloths, and classic Provençal farm chairs, and the fare is pleasingly regional. If there's been rain, you'll find the superb local wild mushrooms known as *mousserons,* while year round there's the superb Alpilles lamb and the restaurant's own home-cured black olives, some of the meatiest, most carefully seasoned you'll find in the region. Cheese lovers should take note here, for La Riboto de Taven has tracked down a rare *tomme de Camargue,* a firm, full-flavored, creamy cheese that combines both goat's and sheep's milk. Sprinkled generously with sprigs of wild rosemary, this is a lively cheese with well-developed flavor, a bit tame and wild at the same time. The cheese tray also offers the seldom seen Banon *vrai,* the real goat's-milk cheese made near Banon in the Alpes-de-Haute-Provence, where the cheese is traditionally dipped in *eau-de-vie,* then aged in dried chestnut leaves. With the meal, sample the Châteauneuf-du-Pape *blanc,* or the pleasing house red.

Dessert offerings include a superb regionally popular *nougat glacé* (a rich vanilla ice cream preparation filled with top-quality candied fruits) and a refreshing orange compote.

POUR LA MAISON

LA MAISON DE MARION
Les Baux-de-Provence,
   13520 Maussane-les-
   Alpilles.
(90.97.34.49).
Open daily Easter through
   November, and during
   the Christmas holidays,
   10 A.M. to 1 P.M. and 2 to
   7 P.M. From December to
   Easter open Saturday and
   Sunday only, 10 A.M. to 1
   P.M. and 2 to 6 P.M.
Credit cards: AE, DC, V.
Will ship in France.

A charming boutique that offers a small but well-chosen selection of locally handmade baskets, some of them woven of pine bark and decorated with whole cones. At Christmastime there's also a lovely selection of decorative woven ornaments.

BEDOIN *(Vaucluse)*

Avignon 39 k, Carpentras 15 k, Nyons 38 k, Sault 35 k,
Vaison-la-Romaine 22 k.

RESTAURANT

L'OUSTAOU D'ANAIS
Route de Carpentras, 84410
Bédoin.
(90.65.67.43).
Last orders taken at 1:30 P.M.
and 9 P.M. (9:30 P.M. in
July and August). Closed
Monday and Tuesday
except holidays, one
week in June, and the
last week in September
through October.
Credit cards: AE, V.
Private dining room for 80.
140-franc menu. A la carte,
140 francs.

SPECIALTIES:
Game, *gratin de picodon à la
sarriette* (gratin of goat cheese
in cream with summer
savory), *gratin de pieds de porc
aux truffes* (gratin of pig's feet
and truffles).

Yannick Daubert, the owner of this modern
pink stucco Provençal *mas,* or farmhouse, just
north of Carpentras, works to offer traditional
regional dishes you won't find on every menu, and
she has succeeded royally. The decor here is just a
bit too cute for my taste, but the food makes up for
it. Who could complain about a steaming hot *terrine
d'aubergines,* a *sauté* of local lamb infused with fresh
rosemary, a hearty gratin of pig's feet and truffles,
or a piquant gratin of tangy Picodon goat cheese? I
can close my eyes and almost taste the vibrant
cheese gratin, a piping hot blend of beautifully aged
Picodon covered lightly with cream and summer
savory, the rosemary-like herb that goes by many
names including *sarriette, poivre d'ain,* and *poebre
d'ain.* It's like a Provençal fondue, really, eaten by
dipping slices of bread into the creamy mass. If
you're lucky that day, the bread will come from the
village bakery at nearby Crillon-le-Brave. Even after
all this, the rolling cheese and dessert trays are hard
to resist: a little wicker basket of fresh *sarriette* rests
amid a regional cheese assortment, and desserts
include a variety of homemade sherbets served
from stoneware crocks. Service is friendly, chatty,
and efficient.

BOULANGERIE

**BOULANGERIE
VIENNOISERIE**
Crillon-le-Brave, 84410
Bédoin.
(90.65.68.30).
Open 7:30 A.M. to 12:30 P.M.
and 3:30 to 9 P.M. Closed
Monday and Tuesday.

Baker Didier Suran recently rebuilt a beautiful
ancient wood-fired oven, in which he bakes
some marvelous regional breads, including *pain aux
raisins* (raisin bread), *pain à l'anis* (aniseed bread),
fancifully shaped *fougasses,* and a good *pain au levain*
(sourdough bread). This tiny restored village is
worth a detour, as is a visit to Monsieur Suran's
lovely bakeshop.

CHARLOTTE D'AGNEAU AU COULIS DE POIVRONS ROUGES BAUMANIERE
BAUMANIERE'S LAMB CHARLOTTE WITH RED PEPPER SAUCE

I've seen this lamb charlotte served all over France, but it seems to belong most fittingly to Provence. This is a variation on the version served at Oustaù de Baumanière in Les Baux-de-Provence. It makes for a most colorful presentation, especially if you happen to have an ochre-colored platter. On visuals alone, it will transport you to Provence. It may be served warm or at room temperature.

Red pepper sauce:
4 red bell peppers (about 1 pound; 500 g)
2 tablespoons virgin olive oil
½ cup (125 ml) *crème fraîche* (see Recipe Index) or heavy cream, preferably not ultra-pasteurized
Pinch of salt

Tomato sauce (or use 1 cup Basic Tomato Sauce, see Recipe Index):
1 tablespoon virgin olive oil
5 medium tomatoes, peeled, seeded, and coarsely chopped
1 medium onion, finely chopped
1 clove garlic
Salt and freshly ground black pepper to taste

Lamb:
1½ pounds (750 g) boned leg of lamb, fat and tendons removed (your butcher will do this for you)

1. Prepare the red pepper sauce: Cut the peppers in half, remove the stems and seeds, and cut them into very thin strips. Heat the oil in a medium skillet over medium heat. Add the peppers and cook, stirring frequently, until tender, about 30 minutes. Place the peppers with the pan juices in a food processor or blender and purée. Add the crème fraîche and purée again. Season with the salt. This makes a rustic purée. If you want a finer sauce, press it through a food mill or fine-mesh sieve. (This can be prepared several hours in advance and refrigerated. Let warm to room temperature before serving.)

2. Prepare the tomato sauce: Combine the oil, tomatoes, onion, and garlic in a large saucepan. Cook, stirring frequently, over medium-high heat until reduced to a thick sauce, about 20 minutes. Season with salt and pepper. (This can be prepared several hours in advance and refrigerated.)

3. Prepare the lamb: Cut the lamb into 1-inch (2.5 cm) cubes. Heat the oil in a large skillet over medium-high heat. Add the lamb and brown on all sides. Reduce the heat, stir in the herbs, garlic, and tomato sauce and cook, stirring frequently, until the ingredients are heated through, 5 to 8 minutes. Season with salt and pepper.

4. Preheat the oven to 450°F (230°C).

5. Prepare the eggplant: Peel and cut the eggplant lengthwise into slices ⅛ inch (3 mm) thick. Using a pastry brush, coat both sides of the eggplant slices with olive oil and place them on an oiled baking sheet. Bake the eggplant until the bottoms are light brown, 5 to 10 minutes. Turn and bake until light brown on the other side, about 5 minutes longer. Check the eggplant frequently and remove the slices as they brown.

2 tablespoons olive oil
Handful of mixed fresh
herbs, preferably
basil, thyme, chervil,
oregano, and flat-leaf
parsley, minced
3 cloves garlic, minced

Eggplant:
2 medium eggplants
(about 2 pounds;
1 kg)
3 to 4 tablespoons
virgin olive oil

6. Line a 5-cup (1.25 liter) charlotte mold or soufflé dish with the eggplant slices: Arrange them in a fan-like fashion, allowing the slices to overlap and placing the narrowest ends in the center of the mold and the wide ends over the edge. If there is any leftover eggplant, chop it coarsely and add it to the lamb mixture.

7. Fill the mold with the lamb mixture and cover the lamb with the overhanging eggplant. Cover the dish securely with aluminum foil. Bake until heated through, about 30 minutes. Remove from the oven and let sit for a few minutes. If serving at room temperature, this can be prepared several hours in advance.

8. If serving the dish warm, gently heat the red pepper sauce. Carefully unmold the charlotte into the center of a large shallow platter. Spoon the sauce around the charlotte and serve immediately. If serving the charlotte at room temperature, serve the sauce at room temperature as well.

Yield: 8 servings.

BONNIEUX *(Vaucluse)*

Aix-en-Provence 48 k, Apt 13 k, Avignon 47 k, Carpentras 43 k, Cavaillon 26 k, Paris 725 k.

Market: Friday, 8 A.M. to noon, Place du Terrail.

PÂTISSERIE

HENRI TOMAS
7–9 Rue de la République,
84480 Bonnieux.
(90.75.85.52).
Open 7 A.M. to 12:45 P.M.
and 3 to 7:30 P.M. Closed
Monday September
through June, one week
in October, and two
weeks in February.

The French have a saying, *Faute de grives on mange des merles* (If you can't eat thrush, eat blackbirds). Likewise, if you can't find a bakery when walking out of the Musée de la Boulangerie, a pastry shop will do. When I left the museum I wandered right into Henri Tomas's shop across the street and fell in love with his *galette provençale,* a sweet pastry tartlet flavored with grated orange zest and filled with praline and almond cream. When we called to discuss listing him in the book, his excited response was: "I'll even show the American ladies how to make pastry. I love America!"

MUSEE

MUSEE DE LA BOULANGERIE
12 Rue de la République, 84480 Bonnieux.
(90.75.88.34).
Open 10 A.M. to noon and 3 to 6:30 P.M. Closed Tuesday from June through August; open weekends only September through May; closed January and February.
Admission: 5 francs.

As a bread fanatic, I'd probably travel halfway around the world to anything named "bread museum," and this one should not disappoint fellow bread lovers. In 1983 this traditional village *boulangerie*—with a wood-fired stone oven dated 1844—was lovingly and carefully converted into a fine mini-museum that pays homage to the strong, though dying, bread tradition in France. Visitors can step inside the *gloriette,* the room in which the baker kneaded his bread, examine the *panouche,* the instrument used for cleaning the brick oven floor, learn about *pain de l'égalité* (after the French Revolution, it was decreed that only one kind of bread could be made, one of three parts wheat flour and one part rye flour), and examine the fine display of bread-baking paraphernalia and historic documents relating to bread throughout history.

The pizza truck, a modern Provençal specialty.

ECOLE DE CUISINE

NATHALIE WAAG
La Sara, Route du Pont-Julien, 84480 Bonnieux.
(90.75.86.63).
Open May to October.

Since 1983 Nathalie Waag has sponsored her "Eight Days in Provence" cooking and food vacation at La Sara, an old farmhouse nestled among oak trees, fields of lavender, and vineyards in the foothills of Bonnieux. She takes only four guests at a time, and together they tour local outdoor fruit and vegetable markets, visit vineyards, and take excursions to goat farms, olive oil mills, and the nearby towns of Aix-en-Provence and Avignon. The program is free-form: Lunch is usually a picnic in a local café, while at dinnertime guests are invited to cook along with Madame Waag, or just watch, or just eat!

CARPENTRAS *(Vaucluse)*

Avignon 24 k, Orange 23 k, Paris 678 k, Vaison-la-Romaine 28 k.

Market: Friday, 8 A.M. to noon, Allée Jean-Jaurès and throughout the center of town.

O n Friday mornings throughout the year, but particularly in summertime, Carpentras becomes one mammoth street fair as local market gardeners, farmers, and cheesemakers crowd the streets with their fresh, fresh fare. There's a flea market as well, so keep your eye out for antique linens and pottery.

SPECIALITES REGIONALES

FRANCIS LIARDET
At the market, Friday, from
    Easter through
    September, Place Verdun.

F or a wonderful selection of locally grown herbs including the vibrant purple hyssop and pungent summer savory, or *sarriette,* and the rarely found home-grown fresh green lentils.

CASSIS *(Bouches-du-Rhône)*

Aix-en-Provence 46 k, Marseille 23 k, Paris 803 k, Toulon 44 k.

Market: Wednesday and Friday, 8 A.M. to 1 P.M., near the post office (P.T.T.).

RESTAURANT

CHEZ GILBERT
Quai Baux, 13260 Cassis.
(42.01.71.36).
Last orders taken at 1:45 P.M.
    and 10 P.M.
Closed December through
    February; Sunday dinner
    and Tuesday off-season;
    Tuesday lunch in July
    and August.
Credit cards: AE, DC, V.
Terrace dining.
Private dining room for 30.
140-franc menu. A la carte,
    230 francs.

SPECIALTIES:
Seafood; *ratatouille* (cooked
dish of eggplant, zucchini,
onions, tomatoes, peppers,
garlic, and olive oil).

O n certain warm, sun-kissed days in summer, I close my eyes and dream about the *ratatouille* at Chez Gilbert, a casual café-restaurant overlooking the fishermen's wharf of this tiny coastal village. I remember the first time I visited Chez Gilbert, years ago—I must have consumed a pound of cured black olives and an equal amount of their famous *ratatouille,* which is cooked slowly and long, so those chunks of fresh vegetables are almost transformed into a thick, rich jam. I've tried to re-create it many times at home, but it's almost just as well I have failed, for it keeps me coming back, to sip Domaine du Paternel's refreshing white Cassis, to feast on whatever fish is fresh that day (even as you dine, fishermen's wives will wander in to peddle the daily catch to the chef), and, of course, to dive into a bowlful of soothing *ratatouille.*

DIEULEFIT *(Drôme)*

Crest 37 k, Montélimar 27 k, Nyons 31 k, Orange 58 k, Paris 633 k, Valence 72 k.

Market: Friday, 8 A.M. to noon, Place de l'Hôtel-de-l'Hôpital, also called Place du Champ-de-Mars.

POUR LA MAISON

POTERIE DE HAUTE PROVENCE
Route de Nyons, 26220
Dieulefit.
(75.46.42.10).
Open 8 A.M. to noon and
1:30 to 6 P.M. (8 P.M.
mid-June through
September). Closed
Saturday and Sunday
October through
mid-June.
Will ship internationally.

Agreat spot to pick up authentic regional contemporary pottery, including fanciful glazed pots decorated with sprigs of lavender, clusters of grapes, daisies, or baskets of wildflowers. Their square plates, with hand-painted watercolor scenes of nearby villages and mountains, make a perfect plate setting for cheese or dessert.

FONTVIEILLE *(Bouches-du-Rhône)*

Arles 10 k, Avignon 30 k, Marseille 92 k, Paris 724 k,
Saint-Rémy-de-Provence 18 k.

Market: Friday, 7:30 A.M. to noon, between the church and the town hall.

RESTAURANT

LA REGALIDO
13990 Fontvieille.
(90.97.60.22).
Last orders taken at 1:30 P.M.
and 9:30 P.M.
Closed Tuesday lunch,
Monday, and mid-
December through
January.
Credit cards: AE, DC, V.
Terrace dining.
Private dining room for 20.
English spoken.
190- to 350-franc menus. A
la carte, 250 francs.

Throughout the region, abandoned stone olive oil mills have been transformed into antiques shops, restaurants, boutiques, even homes, but few are quite as stunning as that of the *auberge* La Regalido in the quiet village of Fontvieille. The old arched mill has been tastefully and simply transformed into an elegant dining room that looks out onto a joyously unrestrained Provençal garden. Brilliant purple delphiniums, fragrant, slender wisps of lavender, and vigorous pink roses form an exuberant backdrop as diners settle in for drinks on the terrace before dinner, for coffee and chocolates after.

The menu here is refreshingly local, including

a lightened variation of a traditional Provençal *gratin de moules* (here served as a clump of wilted fresh spinach blended with hollandaise, topped with mussels and a touch more of sauce, then quickly broiled—see recipe, following page); a generous *tranche de gigot,* or slice of oven-roasted leg of lamb, served with whole cloves of roasted garlic and more meaty black olives. Unfortunately, on one visit their preparation of duck with local green olives suffered from overcooking. With the lamb, sample the Beaucastel Châteauneuf-du-Pape—one of, if not *the,* finest Châteauneufs around.

The rolling dessert cart is impressive, and includes a seasonal cherry *clafoutis,* or custard, a cool, mousse-like *gâteau aux fraises,* or strawberry cake, and a rich chocolate dessert that includes layers of meringue and chocolate mousse.

Onions are a noble vegetable in France, figuring as importantly in the French language as in the cuisine (the French produce some 145,000 tons each year, most of them cultivated in Provence, and import more than 1.5 million tons, largely from Italy, the Netherlands, and England). Like the bite of their fumes, their use tends to be insulting.

If someone gets a bit nosy, you tell them to *"occupe-toi de tes oignons,"* or "mind your own business." Someone who dresses in multiple layers of clothing is said to be *"vêtu comme un oignon,"* while those who wait in line, whether to get into the theater or to kiss the bride at a wedding, are said to be *"en rang d'oignon."*

If someone creates a scene in France, it is called *"un spectacle aux petits oignons."* On the kinder side, if you make something with particular care, you will be complimented for making it *"aux petits oignons."*

The French method for cutting onions without raising a tear? Stick a large ball of white bread on the end of the knife you use to cut the onions. Another method is to freeze the onion for a few minutes first, then as you cut it, be sure not to tear the base of the onion, source of the lacrimonious vapors. Finally, if you find raw onions difficult to digest, quickly blanch them first, or soak them in olive oil for several days.

GRATIN DE MOULES AUX EPINARDS LA REGALIDO
LA REGALIDO'S MUSSEL AND SPINACH GRATIN

Mussels and spinach are a marvelous combination, especially when they're bound with a tangy hollandaise sauce and quickly passed under the broiler. This recipe from La Regalido in Font-vieille makes for a colorful, flavorful first course that might be followed by a roast leg of lamb and a potato gratin.

2 pounds (1 kg) mussels
½ cup (125 ml) dry
   white wine
2 pounds (1 kg) fresh
   spinach, stemmed,
   rinsed, and dried
Salt and freshly ground
   black pepper to taste
Freshly grated nutmeg

Hollandaise:
3 large egg yolks
2 tablespoons mussel
   cooking liquid
½ cup (4 ounces;
   125 g) unsalted
   butter, at room
   temperature
¼ teaspoon salt
1 teaspoon freshly
   squeezed lemon juice

1. Thoroughly scrub the mussels and rinse with several changes of water. Beard the mussels.

2. Combine the mussels and wine in a large deep saucepan and heat to a boil over high heat. Cover and cook just until the mussels open, about 5 minutes. Do not overcook. Remove from the heat and strain through several thicknesses of cheesecloth, reserving the liquid. Discard any mussels that do not open.

3. Let the mussels sit until cool enough to handle, then remove them from their shells and set aside.

4. Heat a large pot of salted water to a rolling boil. Add the spinach and cook just until soft, 1 to 2 minutes. The spinach should remain a bright, vivid green. Immediately drain the spinach and rinse it thoroughly in cold water to set the color. Drain thoroughly, squeezing out any excess liquid. Coarsely chop the spinach, season with salt, pepper, and freshly grated nutmeg, and set aside.

5. Prepare the hollandaise: Place the egg yolks and mussel cooking liquid in the top of a double boiler and whisk over hot but not boiling water until fluffy.

6. Add a few spoonfuls of butter to the mixture and whisk constantly until the butter has melted and the sauce begins to thicken. Be certain that the water in the bottom of the boiler remains hot but not boiling. Continue adding the butter, bit by bit, whisking constantly. Add the salt and lemon juice. Taste and adjust the seasoning if necessary.

7. Preheat the broiler.

8. Add 2 tablespoons hollandaise to the spinach and toss. Divide the spinach among four 6-inch (15 cm) round baking dishes and flatten it into a smooth bed. Arrange the mussels evenly over the spinach, then spoon the remaining hollandaise over the mussels.

9. Broil just until the top is crisp and brown. Serve immediately.

Yield: 4 servings.

Pélardon of Provence.

POUR LA MAISON

MARCEL FOUQUE
Maison de Saint-Michel,
    159 Route du Nord,
    13990 Fontvieille.
(90.97.74.61).
Open 10 A.M. to noon and 3
    to 8 P.M. Closed Monday.
Will ship internationally.

A nice spot for browsing, and for learning, before or after a meal. Monsieur Fouque specializes in seventeenth-, eighteenth-, and nineteenth-century furniture, *faïence,* and paintings, all with a fine Provençal accent.

GORDES *(Vaucluse)*

Apt 20 k, Avignon 38 k, Carpentras 34 k, Cavaillon 17 k, Paris 716 k.

Market: Tuesday, 8 A.M. to 1 P.M., Place du Château.

RESTAURANT

LES BORIES
Route de Sénanque, 84220
    Gordes.
(90.72.00.51).
Last orders taken at 1:30 P.M.
    and 9 P.M.
Closed Sunday, Monday, and
    Tuesday dinners,
    Wednesday, and
    December.
No credit cards.
Terrace dining.
Private dining room for 10,
    25, or 30.
Some English spoken.
350 francs.

S P E C I A L T I E S :
Truffes (truffles), *agneau*
(lamb), *poissons méditérranéens*
(Mediterranean fish); in
winter, game.

L es Bories, a tiny stone *auberge* with a crisp, intimate dining room, is one of the most charming and thoroughly regional restaurants in Provence. Once you're installed beneath the fig and olive trees on a sunny afternoon, with a carafe of young, golden Châteauneuf-du-Pape, you'll surely decide there's nowhere else on earth you'd rather be. Chef Gabriel Rousselet's menu is strictly seasonal: In the summertime, you'll find Mediterranean mussels nicely paired with the locally popular *blettes,* or Swiss chard, while indoors in the winter he offers diners a well-chosen assortment of wild game grilled over an open fire, including tiny *grives* (thrush), *perdreau* (partridge), *lièvre* (wild hare), *faisan* (pheasant), *chevreuil* (venison), and *sanglier* (wild boar). With the game, try the stunning Château de Fonsalette, a vibrant red that is one of the best Côtes-du-Rhône wines made today. Later, wander through the remarkable stone village of Gordes.

MUSEE

VILLAGE DES BORIES
84220 Gordes.
(90.72.03.48).
Open daily 9 A.M. to sunset.
Admission: About 11 francs
for adults, half-price for
those under age 18.

Another gold mine for those passionate about old-fashioned bread-baking techniques. This fascinating reconstructed village—built along the lines of mortarless stone houses believed to have been there during the seventeenth and eighteenth centuries—is made up of some twenty unusual *pierre-seche* structures, or *bories,* grouped around a beautiful communal bread oven set in a courtyard surrounded by olive trees. Also note the reconstructed Provençal kitchen.

GRIGNAN *(Drôme)*

Crest 47 k, Montélimar 28 k, Nyons 23 k, Orange 44 k, Paris 632 k, Pont-Saint-Esprit 37 k, Valence 71 k.

Market: Tuesday, 8 A.M. to noon, Place du Mail.

POUR LA MAISON

POTERIE DU CHATEAU
Rue Montant-au-Château,
26320 Grignan.
(75.46.57.26).
Open 9 A.M. to noon and 3
to 7 P.M. Closed Monday
and October.
Will ship internationally.

After touring the *château,* wander down the narrow street to browse about this small local pottery shop. Their glazed white china, decorated with delicate red and green flowers, has a pleasant Provençal air. Also a nice selection of *mazagrans* (tall, handleless, sturdy pottery coffee cups) and tiny espresso cups.

MUSEE

CHATEAU DE GRIGNAN
26320 Grignan.
(75.46.51.56).
Open 9:30 to 11:30 A.M. and
2:30 to 5:30 P.M. Closed
Wednesday morning,
Tuesday, and November.
Admission: About 9 francs
for adults, 5 francs for
children and per person
for groups of more than
20.

Anyone who's ever enjoyed the seventeenth-century letters of Madame de Sévigné—many of them full of curious gastronomic tales—will want to visit the *château* owned by her son-in-law and beloved daughter, Françoise-Marguerite. Madame de Sévigné visited here often, enjoying the thyme-and-marjoram-infused partridge, the breathless view, the nightingales. In the center of town, be sure to look for the charming statue of this remarkable woman.

L'ISLE-SUR-LA-SORGUE *(Vaucluse)*

Apt 32 k, Avignon 23 k, Carpentras 17 k, Orange 41 k,
Paris 697 k.

Markets: Thursday and Sunday, 8 A.M. to 12:30 P.M., Place de l'Eglise, and also
along the river Sorgue on Sunday.
Flea market: Sunday, 9 A.M. to sunset (longer hours at Easter and August 15),
Avenue des 4-Otages.

Don't pass through the region without spending a Sunday morning in L'Isle-sur-la-Sorgue, where the open-air food market features the best of the local produce (including great olives and goat cheese) and where the open-air flea market (with indoor markets scattered all over town—just keep on walking and wandering) offers an incredible selection of used and not-so-used wares. (Be forewarned that because the village is crowded on Sundays, many of the cafés do not serve food.)

RESTAURANT

MAS DE CURE BOURSE
Route de Caumont, D25,
  Cure Bourse, 84800
  L'Isle-sur-la-Sorgue.
(90.38.16.58).
Last orders taken at 1:30 P.M.
  and 9:30 P.M.
Closed Monday off-season
  and Sunday dinner.
Credit cards: AE, DC, EC, V.
Terrace dining.
Private dining rooms for 6
  and 60.
English spoken.
88- to 208-franc menus. A la
  carte, about 200 francs.

SPECIALTIES:
Seasonal, Provençal home
cooking.

A real find in an area of Provence where restaurant pickings are rather slim. This cozy restored *mas,* or farmhouse, is a lovely spot to try for Sunday lunch, before or after visiting the flea market along the Sorgue river in town. Chef Françoise Donzé is one of France's most talented female chefs, offering good home cooking with a modern Provençal twist. She's as energetic, lively, and personal as her cuisine. Some of the best dishes I've sampled here include a soothing *caviar d'aubergines* (cold eggplant purée); a salad of fresh tuna; chicken smothered in the freshest *pleurottes,* or delicate wild mushrooms; and a delicious *gâteau de poire au caramel,* a dessert that resembles the pineapple upside-down cake of my childhood. In the summertime, guests dine on a casual terrace. Portions here are large, prices remarkably low.

POUR LA MAISON

**TERRAILLES ET FAIENCES
  DU MIDI**
At the market, Sunday, near
  the post office (P.T.T.)

For a lovely assortment of contemporary Provençal pottery based on traditional colors and designs: pots and tableware, colorful green or ochre omelet plates, bowls, and *daubières,* or pots for making *daube provençale.* When in Arles, visit their shop in the center of town (see page 294).

MAS DE CUREBOURG
Route d'Apt, 84800
  L'Isle-sur-la-Sorgue.
(90.20.30.06 or
  90.20.37.85).
Open 9 A.M. to noon and
  2 to 7 P.M. Saturday and
  Sunday from November
  through February; 9 A.M.
  to 7 P.M. daily the rest of
  the year.
Will ship internationally.

My favorite antiques shop in all of Provence—a museum, really—with an ever-changing assortment of local wares, from baskets to china, tableware to furniture. (Directions: 6 kilometers south of L'Isle-sur-la-Sorgue via the N100.)

VINCENT MIT L'ANE
Route d'Apt, 84800
  L'Isle-sur-la-Sorgue.
(90.20.63.15).
Open daily (Saturday and
  Sunday only off-season),
  10 A.M. to noon and 3 to
  7 P.M.
Will ship in Europe.

The sort of antiques shop you can poke around in for a good while: You'll see everything from china to pottery, garden furniture to huge antique sinks. (Directions: 1 kilometer south of L'Isle-sur-la-Sorgue via the N100.)

A TASTE OF PROVENCE

La Taste is a chain of regional gourmet shops offering a wide variety of locally made items, including olive oils, olives, herbs, vinegars, cookbooks, posters, dried flowers, and wines.

Standard hours are 9 A.M. to 12:30 P.M. and 2 to 7 P.M. Most shops are closed Sunday and one month in January or February.

Credit card: V.

Will ship in France.

AIX-EN-PROVENCE
66 Rue Boulegon.

APT
15 Quai Léon-Sagy.

ARLES
24 Boulevard des
  Lices.

AVIGNON
50–52 Rue de la
  Balance.

**LES BAUX-DE-
PROVENCE**
2 Rue de l'Eglise.

CARPENTRAS
28 Rue des Halles.

CAVAILLON
15 Place aux Herbes.

GORDES
Place du Château.

NYONS
21 Place de la
  Libération.

LAMBESC *(Bouches-du-Rhône)*

Aix-en-Provence 21 k, Apt 38 k, Cavaillon 30 k, Paris 730 k.

Market: Friday, 8 A.M. to noon, Place des Etats-Généraux.

RESTAURANT

MOULIN DE TANTE
   YVONNE
Rue Benjamin-Raspail,
   13410 Lambesc.
(42.28.02.46).
Last orders taken at 2 P.M.
   and 9 P.M.
Officially closed Tuesday
   through Thursday,
   August, and February.
   But call anyway—they
   might feel like having
   guests.
No credit cards.
Private dining room for 20.
250 francs.

SPECIALTIES:
"Fantaisie de la cuisinière"
(specialties according to the
chef's whim), *gibier* (game),
soupe de poissons (fish soup),
canard en terrine (duck terrine),
poissons de petits bateaux (fish
caught on small fishing
boats).

Dining at the Moulin de Tante Yvonne is a bit like dining in a Provençal museum, or in a temple devoted to authentic Provençal cooking. Just north of Aix-en-Provence, in a carefully restored fifteenth-century olive oil mill in the center of the village of Lambesc, Tante Yvonne serves up a medley of homey local fare, including an incredibly flavorful beef *daube* (the kind of stew that's so tender, you can eat it with a spoon), in an atmosphere that's thoroughly appealing.

The mill—which boasts vaulted stone walls and an enormous fireplace flanked by overstuffed arm chairs—is decorated with copper pots and Provençal figurines known as *santons,* and traditional costumes made of brightly colored fabrics.

Even though Tante Yvonne—Yvonne Soliva—is in her eighties, she finds time to tour the region in search of the best it has to offer. She shares her discoveries at the table, including the delicious olive oil from the cooperative at Maussane-les-Alpilles, near Les Baux, and the sturdy red wine from the village of Visan, near Vaison-la-Romaine.

MARSEILLE *(Bouches-du-Rhône)*

Aix-en-Provence 31 k, Avignon 100 k, Nice 187 k, Nîmes 125 k,
Paris 776 k, Toulon 64 k.

Market: Daily, 8 A.M. to 1 P.M., Place Castellane.
Retail fish market: Daily 8 A.M. to noon, Quai des Belges.
Wholesale fish market: Daily, midnight to 5 A.M., Port de Saumaty, 13016
Marseille. (Directions: from the center of town, take the Quai du Port, *direction
la Joliette,* and follow the *quais* to Port de Saumatry).
Flea market: Sunday, 7:30 A.M. to 1 P.M., Place du Capitane Gèze,
13014 Marseille.
Foire à l'Ail et aux Taraïettes (garlic and terra-cotta pottery fair):
three weeks in June.

RESTAURANTS

MAURICE BRUN
(Aux Mets de Provence)
18 Quai Rive-Neuve, 13007
  Marseille.
(91.33.35.38).
Last orders taken at 1:30 P.M.
  and 9 P.M.
Closed Sunday, Monday, and
  holidays.
Credit card: DC.
Single 330-franc menu,
  including wine and
  service.

SPECIALTIES:
Single menu of regional
specialties.

Envision an authentic Provençal meal. It would be based on fruity olives and this season's oil; fresh grilled Mediterranean fish; perhaps a well-seasoned *daube;* with tomatoes, artichokes, and grilled game or poultry weaving their way into the meal. There must be goat cheese (preferably a young, fresh *chèvre* fragrant with herbs), and for dessert, pillows of white nougat bursting with chunks of grilled almonds, candied fruits, and pale green pistachios. For wine, a dry white Cassis, full of finesse; a sturdy red Bandol, rich with the *mourvèdre* grape, and with dessert, a glass of sweet muscat-fragrant Beaumes-de-Venise. This is basically the meal that has been served, lunch and dinner, since 1936 at Maurice Brun, a cozy family-run restaurant with the atmosphere of a Provençal museum, overlooking Marseille's Vieux Port. Maurice Brun's menu has aged remarkably well, and even those well versed in the cooking of Provence are likely to pick up a tip or two. But be warned that this gastronomic education will take some time: set aside a good three hours to wend your way through the Provençal feast.

The summer scent of melons.

**RESTAURANT VIEUX
  PORT NEW-YORK**
7 Quai des Belges, 13001
  Marseille.
(91.33.60.98).
Last orders taken at 2:30 P.M.
  and 11 P.M.
Open daily.
Credit cards: AE, DC, V.
Air-conditioned.
English spoken.
Private dining room for 60.
About 160 francs.

SPECIALTIES:
Fish.

A bustling brasserie right along the old port. The food here is thoroughly local—there's delicious *mérou,* like a very mild cod, baked with tomatoes, onions, and black olives; as well as the purely regional *poutargue.* Service is super-friendly, and there's a fine outdoor café for people-watching on a warm summer day.

MUSEES

MUSEE DU VIEUX MARSEILLE
Maison Diamantée, 2 Rue de la Prison, 13002 Marseille.
(91.55.10.19).
Open 10 A.M. to noon and 2 to 6:30 P.M. Closed Wednesday morning, Tuesday, and holidays.
Admission: 3 francs. Free on Sunday mornings.

Devoted to the city's rich past, the Museum of Old Marseille pays particular attention to everyday life in the eighteenth and nineteenth centuries, and includes entire rooms devoted to Provençal furniture, traditional costumes, domestic utensils, nativity scenes, as well as *santons*, the Provençal clay figurines.

MUSEE DES ARTS ET TRADITIONS
5 Place des Héros, 13013 Marseille.
(91.68.14.38).
Open Saturday, Sunday, Monday, and Wednesday, 2 to 6 P.M. in winter and 3 to 7 P.M. in summer.
Admission: 5 francs.

A museum devoted to daily life in Provence, housed in the elegant Château Gombert. Displays include costumes from Marseille and Arles, and pottery from Marseille, Moustiers, and Montpellier.

MAUSSANE-LES-ALPILLES *(Bouches-du-Rhône)*

Arles 19 k, Marseille 92 k, Paris 716 k, Saint-Rémy-de-Provence 10 k, Salon-de-Provence 28 k.

Market: Thursday, 8 A.M. to 12:30 P.M., Place Laugier-de-Monblan.

SPECIALITES REGIONALES

COOPERATIVE OLEICOLE DE LA VALLEE DES BAUX
Rue Charloun, 13520 Maussane-les-Alpilles.
(90.97.32.37).
Open 8 A.M. to noon and 2 to 6 P.M. Monday through Saturday from November through January; Tuesday and Saturday from February through October.
Will ship in Europe.

This is the source of the earthy, fragrant virgin olive oil that wins all the agricultural awards, and one of my current favorites. A visit to this wonderful old stone mill is like taking a trip back in time. If you can get there between late November and early spring, pick up a bucket full of *olives cassées*, the smooth fresh green olives cured in a rich fennel-infused brine. During the same period, you'll also find these Vallée des Baux olives at the open-air markets in the region.

MONDRAGON *(Vaucluse)*

Bollène 6 k, Orange 16 k.

RESTAURANT

LA BEAUGRAVIERE
Route Nationale 7, 84430
  Mondragon.
(90.40.82.54).
Last orders taken at 2 P.M.
  and 9 P.M.
Closed Sunday dinner and
  the last two weeks in
  September.
Credit card: V.
Terrace dining.
English spoken.
45- to 195-franc menus. A la
  carte, 150 to 300 francs.
SPECIALTIES:
Tous les plats à base de truffe (all
dishes with truffles).

Chef Guy Jullien and a monster truffle.

Just south of Montélimar, within the city limits of the village of Mondragon, is one of my favorite restaurants in all of Provence, a modest place called La Beaugravière. Here chef Guy Jullien has created a menu and wine list that carefully, lovingly integrate the bounty of the local soil: the Rhône wines, truffles, rabbit, and lamb. I love spending winter Sundays dining in front of their roaring fire, summer evenings beneath the giant maple tree that spreads out over the patio.

I first visited La Beaugravière in the winter of 1984, on a tip that Monsieur Jullien had a fabulous collection of local Rhône wines. He does indeed, but he also makes one of the most memorable truffle omelets you'll ever encounter. This truffle omelet isn't filled with specks of truffles, but with whole chunks, so big they crunch when you bite into them.

Other excellent regional specialties include fresh-killed farm rabbit, simply roasted and served with a generous helping of whole roasted garlic; and delicate roast lamb from the herb-filled hillsides of the nearby Drôme.

One could spend hours poring over chef Jullien's extensive wine list, but I'd recommend any of the Rhône greats, such as Raymond Trollat's Saint Joseph and Gérard Chave's red and white Hermitage.

MONTÉLIMAR *(Drôme)*

Avignon 82 k, Aix-en-Provence 152 k, Nîmes 106 k, Paris 606 k.

Markets: Wednesday and Saturday, 8 A.M. to noon, Place du Marché;
Thursday, 8 A.M. to noon, Place Saint-James.

CONFISERIE

CHABERT ET GUILLOT
1 Rue André-Ducatez,
26200 Montélimar.
(75.01.47.22).
Open daily 8 A.M. to 6 P.M.
Closed in July.
Tours can be arranged by
appointment.
Credit cards: AE, V.
Will ship internationally.

Chabert et Guillot, with its main shop right across from the train station, makes some 3 tons of nougat each day, all of it by hand: Almonds and powdered egg whites, honey, sugar, and vanilla are all heated in giant unlined copper kettles for a good hour and a half, the mixture constantly turned by muscular male workers. When the heavy, aromatic paste is properly blended and heated, they heave the nougat onto rectangular slabs, then push, shove, roll it into shape. Thin sheets of rice paper are rolled over the huge slabs of nougat, which is then cut, dried, and wrapped, ready to be sold as a grand *souvenir de Provence.*

A TASTE OF HONEY

Montélimar and its nougat always remind me of the old Atlantic City and its taffy: this harmlessly tacky city is not much more than one long string of motels, hotels, and nougat stands, most of which sprang up along the old National 7, the original route from Paris to Nice. Although nougat has been synonymous with Montélimar since the early eighteenth century, it was the snack-happy motorist who brought it true twentieth-century fame. Until the turn of the century, this honey-sweetened chewy-candy was essentially a regional, seasonal treat, made—at home or in pastry shops—for the holidays. Both *nougat blanc,* or white nougat, and *nougat noir,* black nougat, are part of the Provençal *treize desserts* served before attending midnight mass on Christmas Eve. Old recipes suggest that the original nougat (much like today's *nougat noir*) was a blend of equal parts of honey and almonds, similar to a praline; contemporary cookbooks offer instructions for a very appetizing *nougat blanc* that combines lavender honey, pistachios, almonds, vanilla, and egg whites.

Back to the Soil

"*W*as *it the wine that tasted so fruity and alive, or was it the August sun and the freedom of driving through Provence amid the rolling hills of lavender that made it seem so special?*"

LA PENNE-SUR-OUVEZE, AUGUST 15—The first time I sampled Paul Tardieu's robust natural wine, I was seated in his rose-filled garden in Provence on a blazing summer Saturday.

My husband and I were on our way to a casual picnic, with a basket full of crusty country bread spread with homemade *rillettes,* a few juicy Cavaillon melons, and a bottle of Vinsobres red. We'd heard from a friend that there was this French businessman turned organic farmer who was making a little red wine worth checking out. I was a bit skeptical: I'd sampled some of France's *vin biodynamic* and had not been impressed.

After spending an hour or two in the sizzling noonday sun, sampling the two recent vintages of Monsieur Tardieu's young, spicy, and vigorous wine along with his meaty Nyons olives and delicate olive oil, his lavender-scented honey, and some earthy goat cheese from a nearby farm, we almost never made it to the picnic. We chatted with Paul Tardieu and his mother, Rose, played with the half-dozen cats wandering about, and left an order for several cases of wine, a few liters of oil, a dozen jars of olives, some honey, and a few pots of irresistibly good homemade apricot preserves.

As we drove off, I wondered if we hadn't been a bit impetuous. Was it the wine that tasted so fruity and alive, or was it the August sun and the freedom of driving through Provence amid the rolling hills of lavender that made it seem so special? At home in Paris, would this wonderful little wine taste like so much mouthwash?

We needn't have worried. In no time Domaine de la Gautière, which then cost us a big 9 francs a bottle, was adopted as our "house red." I gave a lot of the wine and olives away as gifts, and it seemed that every three months we'd be out of wine or olives or both and I'd have to call Rose to send a fresh supply via the French railroad.

We found ourselves returning summer after summer to renew the friendship in person and to sample Monsieur Tardieu's changing vintages, often before they were bottled.

Paul Tardieu's story is a familiar one. He studied agriculture and all his life dreamed of owning a farm, on which he'd raise bees and make his own wine from grapes grown without chemicals or insecticides. His wife, Georgette, thought of the simple, naturally cured olives of her youth in Provence and wished to re-create the honest flavor that has been lost now that so many olives are cured and preserved with chemicals.

But instead of going into farming Monsieur Tardieu went into business in Avignon, importing and exporting fruits and vegetables. Still, his dream would not die, and in 1973, soon after his fortieth birthday, he found a stretch of mountainous land for sale in northern Provence.

The land had changed hands three times during the previous five years. And though much of it consisted of woods that had been all but abandoned, there were some olive and fruit trees, the clay- and lime-rich soil was excellent for grapes, and there was the potential of renting more olive groves as well as fields of lavender for raising bees.

First Monsieur Tardieu set about clearing 22 hectares (54 acres) of land for grapes, and he sought the assistance of the local agricultural agent. "I followed his advice to the letter," says the robust farmer, sporting a rugged farmer's brand of tan and a wide, warm smile.

Vines went in in 1975. He planted 50 percent *grenache* grapes, to give his wine strength and fruitiness. Thirty-five percent of the vineyard was given over to *syrah*, the same variety used in much of the nearby Rhône valley and a grape that adds robustness and bouquet and gives the wine its fine purple color. Finally, the agent recommended that the remaining 15 percent be planted with *cinsault* grapes, to lighten the wine and give it balance, to add warmth and fullness.

Monsieur Tardieu's first vintage, in 1979, was all he had hoped for: "I was looking for a dark, rich, fruity taste," he says, and that is what he had achieved.

The next vintage was, in some ways, an experimental year, with a portion blended exactly as in the 1979 vintage and a portion blended with a good deal more *cinsault*. The difference was remarkable: The version blended with a large portion of *cinsault,* as much as 50 percent, was light and drinkable but lacked the Tardieu signature, the solid robustness and complexity he seeks to achieve. All later vintages have followed the agricultural agent's earliest recommendations and after a full year's aging, are ready for bottling each November.

The winemaker's production, and the amount of soil given over to vines, have grown slowly but steadily. From a small production of less than 1,200 cases in 1979, he now bottles about 8,000 cases each year, with nearly 16 hectares (40 acres) in production.

Domaine de la Gautière has much in common with Beaujolais, in that it's fruity and best drunk young and chilled. At the same time, because of the complexity of the blending and the extra year's aging before bottling, it offers some of the hearty strength of a Côte-du-Rhône.

Paul Tardieu's toughest problem, he says today, is fighting progress. That is, he doesn't believe much in it, finding that simple, old-fashioned winemaking methods work for him. Because he does so little to the wine, even eliminating the final filtering, a bit of sediment remains at the bottom of the bottle. The wine is best decanted, or at least left to stand upright for a few hours, before serving.

Paris Connection: Wine, olives, olive oil, and honey from Domaine de la Gautière can be found at SOLEIL DE PROVENCE, 6 Rue du Cherche-Midi, 75006 Paris. Telephone: 45.48.12.02.

MONTJOUX *(Drôme)*

Dieulefit 6 k, Montélimar 33k.

RESTAURANT

RESTAURANT MIELLE
La Paillette, Montjoux,
26220 Dieulefit.
(75.46.40.09).
Last orders taken at 1 P.M.
and 8 P.M. (Easter through
August).
Closed October, and dinner
September until Easter.
Credit card: V.
70-franc menu. A la carte,
100 francs.

SPECIALTIES:
Truffle omelets, lamb, trout,
Picodon (tangy goat cheese).

Restaurant Mielle is a simple, no-frills village restaurant, full of blue-collar workers and French couples on vacation with their dogs. There is only one copy of the handwritten menu—I guess the regulars know it by heart—so if you need to consult it, the waitress will have to pull it out of the glass case in the window.

Along with a truly piquant Picodon on the cheese platter, there are two items not to miss here: the tender, creamy truffle omelet filled with authentic chunks of local black truffles, and superbly fresh *truite meunière,* from a nearby farm, cooked simply and quickly in butter. With the symphony of regional specialties, order a fresh green salad and a bottle of Côtes-sur-Rhône—the red from the cooperative in Vinsobres is just fine. (Directions: From Dieulefit take the D538 4 kilometers east, toward Montjoux. Take the D130 east 2 kilometers to La Paillette.)

MONTJOYER *(Drôme)*

Grignan 13 k, Montélimar 17 k, Valréas 22 k.

EAUX-DE-VIE

DISTILLERIE
D'AIGUEBELLE
Monastère d'Aiguebelle,
Montjoyer, 26230
Grignan.
(75.98.52.33).
Open 8 A.M. to noon and 2
to 6 P.M. Closed Saturday,
Sunday, and the last two
weeks in August.
Will ship in France.

A tasting panel of French wine and spirits specialists rated the Aiguebelle monastery's *eau-de-vie de poire* (pear brandy) one of the best in France. It is beautifully fragrant, and it doesn't hit you over the head with that overbearing, penetrating jolt of alcohol that makes you gasp. There's something sort of romantic and old-fashioned about driving through the woods to a monastery to stock your liquor cabinet. We always keep a bottle on hand and lovingly refer to it as "the monks' *poire."*

NYONS *(Drôme)*

Orange 42 k, Vaison-la-Romaine 16 k, Valréas 14 k.

Market: Thursday, 8 A.M. to noon, Place des Arcades, Place de la Libération, Place Buffaven.
Les Olivades (olive festival): second Sunday in July.
Fête de l'Alicoque (festival to celebrate the new crop of olives and oil): end of January or beginning of February, depending on the olive harvest.

I f you're in Provence on Thursday, the Nyons market is a must: In the fall and winter months, look for the wild-mushroom man who sets up his stand at the southwestern end of the market along the Place de la Libération, near the tourist office. A good market for local cheeses, olives, and the modern Provençal specialty, pizza freshly baked in a wood-fired oven built into the middle of a panel truck!

POUR LA MAISON

LA SCOURTINERIE
36 La Maladrerie, 26110 Nyons.
(75.26.33.52).
Open 9 A.M. to noon and 2:30 to 7 P.M.

S *courtins* are the sturdy round woven mats tradi-tionally used when pressing olives for oil. They also make terrific door mats, especially for a coun-try house.

Saint-Félicien—earthy, well aged.

SPECIALITES REGIONALES

COOPERATIVE AGRICOLE DU NYONSAIS
Place Olivier-de-Serres, 26110 Nyons.
(75.26.03.44).
Open 8:30 A.M. to noon and 2 to 6 P.M. Monday through Friday; 3 to 6 P.M. Saturday and Sunday.
Credit card: V.
Will ship in Europe.

SPECIALTIES:
Olives et huile d'olives (olives and olive oil).

F or award-winning extra-virgin olive oil, meaty cured black olives, honey, and Côtes-du-Rhône wines.

J. RAMADE
Avenue Paul-Laurens, 26110
   Nyons.
(75.26.08.18).
Open 9 A.M. to noon and 2
   to 7 P.M. Closed Sunday.

SPECIALTIES:
Huiles divers (various cooking
oils).

For olive oil, *tapenade* (here, a blend of black olives and olive oil), *anchoïade* (purée of anchovies, olive oil, and vinegar), walnut oil, and hazelnut oil.

Le Paradou *(Bouches-du-Rhône)*

Arles 16 k, Maussane-les-Alpilles 3 k.

Restaurant

LE BISTRO DU PARADOU
Avenue de la Vallée-des-
   Baux, 13125 Le Paradou.
(90.97.32.70).
Last orders taken at 1:30 P.M.
   and 9 P.M.
Closed Sunday and two
   weeks in February.
Credit card: EC.
Private dining room for 60.
English spoken.
73-franc menu Monday
   through Friday, 100-franc
   menu Saturday.

Jean-Louis Pons, Le Bistro du Paradou.

SPECIALTIES:
Thursday: *pot-au-feu* (beef
simmered with vegetables).
Friday: *aïoli* (here, boiled
snails, assorted vegetables,
and salt cod, served with a
garlic mayonnaise). Saturday:
gigot d'agneau rôti aux herbes
(roast leg of lamb with herbs).
Winter: *daube* (meat stew with
olives), *coq au vin* (mature
male chicken stewed in red
wine), *pigeon aux gousses d'ail*
(pigeon with garlic), *gratin
d'aubergines* (eggplant gratin),
gratin de pommes de terre (potato
gratin).

The world has plenty of bankers, but not many *bistrotiers* like lean, cheery, and outgoing Jean-Louis Pons. Make a reservation for lunch, look for the white house with royal blue shutters along the D17 heading west from Maussane-les-Alpilles, and plan to settle into a fine regional meal at an authentic country café.

Jean-Louis, son of a bistro owner, originally worked as a banker in Arles, then later became director of an industrial bakery. One day he bought a weekend house in Le Paradou, and soon he decided to give up city life altogether.

That was in 1984, and ever since, he and his wife, Mireille, have tended this most democratic bistro, the sort of spot that appeals to grandmothers and firemen, families with small children, businessmen, and travelers. There's only one price, one wine (the local co-op red), and one daily menu.

While Jean-Louis single-handedly waits tables, his wife prepares the daily *plat du jour*. You take a seat in the long stone-walled dining room and Jean-Louis serves whatever Provençal specialty they're offering that day: *lapin à l'ail nouveau* (rabbit with fresh garlic), *gratin d'aubergines, gigot d'agneau,* and *gratin de pommes de terre* are just a few.

Here you'll find an authoritative selection of local goat cheeses, including an exceptionally well-aged Banon wrapped in dried chestnut leaves; a creamy little-known cheese called *gaudre,* from nearby Fontvieille; and a very fresh goat cheese sprinkled with the marvelous extra-virgin olive oil pressed at the cooperative in neighboring Maussane-les-Alpilles.

For dessert there's fresh fruit, perhaps one of Jean-Louis' tarts, and if you're lucky, one of the regulars will offer to buy you a cup of coffee as a rite of initiation. The scene is a happy-go-lucky one, as everyone seems to know everyone else, with a lot of table-hopping, a lot of kidding. Despite this, strangers, even foreigners, will be made to feel right at home.

"We have no tourists here, only friends," explains Jean-Louis, who has been known to stay up well into the night helping a group of Americans perfect their game of *boules,* Provence's favorite outdoor pastime.

Throughout the afternoon, locals wander in to sip Pastis at the tiled bar, to read the stack of newspapers kept next to the peanut dispenser, and to josh with Jean-Louis, who gives the regulars a good-natured rough time.

Later, just as the room begins to clear out, one 250-pound regular asks the question everyone else has on his mind: "What's for lunch tomorrow?"

POUR LA MAISON

L'ANTIQUAIRE DU
    PARADOU
Le Paradou, 13520
    Maussane-les-Alpilles.
(90.54.32.33).
Open 10:30 A.M. to noon
    and 2:30 to 6 P.M. Closed
    Sunday.
Will ship internationally.

A beautiful old olive mill has been restored and transformed into a museum-like antiques shop, filled with charming regional furnishings and decorative items.

Picodon: Milk from the Poor Man's Cow

"*T*he locals talk of days not so long ago when infants were raised on goat's milk and when breakfast consisted of pain de campagne spread with fresh-churned goat's butter, and café au lait was made, necessarily, with steaming goat's milk."

SAOU, JUNE 19—This is a rugged, mountainous corner of the world, a rather lost patch of northern Provence, where purple plots of lavender embellish the Kodachrome landscape of blue skies, parched fields, and terra-cotta roofs.

In the summer months, as you drive along the steep and winding roads of the region called the Drôme, crossing the streams the French call rivers, you are likely to be slowed up by a passing herd of goats, roaming about in search of the tasty herbs and mountain wildflowers that will make fragrant and rich their highly prized milk.

For this is *chèvre* land, a land where, historically, each and every farmer, no matter how impoverished, owned at least one "poor man's cow." The locals talk of days not so long ago when infants were raised on goat's milk and when breakfast consisted of *pain de campagne* spread with fresh-churned goat's butter, and *café au lait* was made, necessarily, with steaming goat's milk.

When and if there was any milk left over, the farm wives made cheese, and when the goats stopped producing milk during the cooler months, families reached into terra-cotta pots stashed away in the wine cellar and dug out Picodon, tiny discs of cheese they'd stashed away for meager months. Before they hid the cheese away, they'd wash it several times in homemade *gnole*, or brandy, set it out to dry, then put it away to age and harden, to help them get through the long, damp days of winter.

Today this traditional mountain cheese of the Drôme and Ardèche *départements* is enjoying a solid rebirth. Picodon—usually found as a flat disc weighing no more than 100 grams (3½ ounces)—is one of the latest French cheeses to obtain its *Appelation d'Origine Contrôlée* (AOC), meaning that its history and tradition is being protected, that its method and territory of fabrication have been strictly defined and limited.

Ideally, the AOC label should mean better cheese. But in the minds of Solange and Emile Magnet, cheesemakers who campaigned for twenty-three years to obtain the AOC (finally granted in 1983), the fight may not have been worth it.

"We had to make a lot of concessions," said Monsieur Magnet, shrugging as he sipped from a bottle of Pelforth beer on the front porch of his farm, a porch properly decorated with a colorful poster depicting all of France's AOC cheeses.

To obtain the AOC, the cheesemakers had to agree to expand the geographic limits of Picodon cheesemaking beyond their little corner of the Drôme. They also, regrettably, gave in to pressure from larger producers and agreed upon a shorter aging time.

While the Picodon of olden times was aged for months, the contemporary version can go to market at the tender age of twelve days. In other words, the hard, piquant, pungent disc the locals still consider the authentic Picodon resembles not at all the fresh, mild, faintly fragrant little goat cheese that looks much like any young *chèvre* found all over France. Now, instead of a single authentic

Picodon there are, indeed, many that can legally claim the label.

Many of the local farm cheesemakers are disheartened; they feel that when the cheese is sold at twelve days, it is bland and totally lacking in character. As Monsieur Magnet insists, the cheese needs at least *un petit mois* (a little month) for its characteristic flavor to develop.

The situation, of course, is not unique to Picodon cheesemakers, for today the same scenario is being replayed all over France. Everywhere, locals want their cheese to taste just as it did in the old days, and that usually means stronger rather than milder. At the same time, Parisian merchants try to convince farmers to produce a cheese that will please their own clientele, whose tastes lean toward lighter, blander cheeses, those aged for just hours or days, not weeks or months.

To complicate matters further, today's local tastes change drastically from village to village. According to Michèle Tariot, a Saoû (pronounced "soo") cheesemaker who sells her Picodon at the markets in nearby Crest and Saillans, tastes change by the kilometer.

"When I go to Crest, I know I'll sell more creamy cheese, while in Saillans, fifteen kilometers away, the older the cheese, the better they love it," says Madame Tariot, a buxom young blond with a winning smile.

Like many of their neighbors in the Drôme, Michèle and Guy Tariot gave up raising pigs for goats several years ago, as the national appetite for goat cheese grew and local banks decided that, agriculturally at least, the economic future of the region lay in goat cheese and the sparkling white wine known as Clairette de Die.

"But if you see people making goat cheese, it's not necessarily out of a love of cheesemaking," explained one farmer. "It's because people can't make a living selling goat milk to a co-op, but they can by making their own goat cheese and selling it at the local markets."

To appeal to local as well as national tastes, most farmers, like the Tariots and the Magnets, go to market with several varieties of Picodon. Young cheese, one to two days old, is sold as *tomme de chèvre*, while those eight to ten days old are called *tomme fraîche*. The aged Picodon, made in the traditional manner and set to age in glazed earthenware jars, is sold as *picodon méthode Dieulefit*.

Throughout the region, you will also see another wildly fragrant specialty known as *foudjou*. Madame Tariot makes and sells her own version, a blend of leftover cheese—usually what's remaining at the bottom of the previous batch of *foudjou* blended with Roquefort, *fromage blanc*, hot peppers, and *gnole*. It's a wonderful, spreadable cheese, pungent enough to make your eyes water.

Cheese made on the Tariot and Magnet farms can be purchased at the farm (see page 333) or at the several outdoor food markets.

What does one look for in buying authentic Picodon? Unfortunately there is no sure-fire indicator, but after sampling dozens upon dozens of farm-made goat cheeses all over France, I've found one consistent theme: The best young *chèvre* is usually the purest white, clean and fresh-looking, nicely formed and firm enough to stand up on its own. If you are looking for a strong Picodon, you'll usually be in luck if the cheese merchant labels his *fromage fort, fromage affiné*, or *méthode Dieulefit*. You'll often see these tiny discs sold by weight, wrapped tightly in packages of a dozen or so. It seems as though they would keep indefinitely, though I've never managed to keep them very long to find out.

AU MAS SAINT-ROCH
13125 Le Paradou.
(90.97.31.23).
Open 8 A.M. to 7 P.M.
Will ship internationally.

Another shop that could well serve as a Provençal museum, offering furnishings from the Middle Ages to the nineteenth century, along with paintings, bric-a-brac, and more contemporary garden furniture.

LA PENNE-SUR-L'OUVEZE *(Drôme)*

Buis-les-Baronnies 5 k, Carpentras 37 k.

SPECIALITES REGIONALES

DOMAINE DE LA
   GAUTIERE
La Penne-sur-l'Ouvèze,
   26170 Buis-les-
   Baronnies.
(75.28.09.58).
Open 8 A.M. to noon and 2
   to 5:30 P.M. Closed
   Saturday and Sunday.
Will ship internationally.

Georgette Tardieu, at Domaine de la Gautière.

For fabulous olives, exquisite local honey, organic dried apricots, olive oil, *tapenade* (here a pure black olive spread), herbs, and excellent Domaine de la Gautière red and rosé wines. (See "Back to the Soil," page 320.)

LE POËT-LAVAL *(Drôme)*

Crest 42 k, Dieulefit 5 k, Nyons 36 k, Paris 638 k.

RESTAURANT

LES HOSPITALIERS
Le Poët-Laval, 26160 La
   Bégude-de-Mazenc.
(75.46.22.32).
Last orders taken at 2 P.M.
   and 9 P.M.
Closed mid-November
   through February.
Credit cards: AE, DC, EC, V.
Terrace dining.
Private dining room for 25.
English spoken.
200-franc menu. A la carte,
   300 francs.

Just north of Dieulefit (meaning "God made it") lies Le Poët-Laval, a minuscule medieval village that's been carefully restored. Here, Les Hospitaliers—with heated pool, summer terrace, and both an elegant and a casual dining room—is an ideal resting spot. The chef offers some appealing, authentic regional fare. Try the locally popular *caillettes* (little patties of ground Swiss chard, herbs, spinach, and a touch of pork wrapped in caul fat, served warm), the *pintade aux lentilles* (here, a tender *confit* of guinea hen served with green lentils), or the *pot-au-feu d'agneau* (moist cubes of choice local lamb

SPECIALTIES:
Change with the season;
Provençal.

set on a bed of Swiss chard, onions, carrots, and leeks). There are also crunchy fresh *baguettes,* a generous cheese platter, and a solid regional wine list. The Domaine Saint-Sauveur, a red from the village of Aubignan, marries perfectly with the cuisine.

PUYMERAS *(Vaucluse)*

Buis-les-Baronnies 17 k, Nyons 18 k, Vaison-la-Romaine 7 k.

SPECIALITES REGIONALES

PLANTIN
Le Saffre, Puyméras, 84110
   Vaison-la-Romaine.
(90.46.41.44).
Open April to mid-
   September only, 8 A.M. to
   noon and 2 to 5 P.M.
   Closed Saturday and
   Sunday.

SPECIALTY:
Truffes (truffles).

One of the last remaining truffle *conserveries* in the region, offering preserved black truffles as well as *morilles* (wild morel mushrooms) preserved in truffle juice.

RAPHELE-LES-ARLES *(Bouches-du-Rhône)*

Arles 10 k, Saint-Martin-de-Crau 5 k, Salon-de-Provence 32 k.

SPECIALITES REGIONALES

MOULIN LA CRAVENCO
Route d'Eyguières,
   Raphèle-lès-Arles, 13200
   Arles.
(90.96.50.82).
Open 8 A.M. to noon and 2
   to 6 P.M. Closed Saturday
   afternoon, Sunday, and
   holidays.
Will ship in France.

SPECIALTIES:
Olives et huile d'olives (olives
and olive oil).

When it comes to olives and olive oil, so much comes down to personal taste preferences. I truly love the olive products from this corner of Provence, especially their *olives vertes cassées* (fresh green olives in a fennel-infused brine) and *picholines du pays* (fresh *picholine* green olives in brine), available only from late November until supplies run out a month or so later. Their extra-virgin oil has a fresh, lively, fruity flavor—I love to mix it with a touch of sherry vinegar for tossed green salads.

SAINT-MARTIN-DE-CRAU *(Bouches-du-Rhône)*

Arles 17 k, Marseille 79 k, Martigues 40 k, Paris 726 k,
Saint-Rémy-de-Provence 23 k, Salon-de-Provence 24 k.

Market: Friday, 8 A.M. to noon, Place du Marché.

CHARCUTERIE

J. MOUSSET
Route Nationale, 13310
  Saint-Martin-de-Crau.
(90.47.30.40).
Open 7:30 A.M. to 12:15 P.M.
  and 3:30 to 7:30 P.M.
  Closed Sunday afternoon,
  Monday, two weeks in
  February, and three
  weeks in September.
Credit card: V.
Will ship in France.

So much sausage today is industrially made, loaded with fillers and chunks of fat that get stuck in the spaces between your teeth, that most of us have just about given up trying to find a handsome, rosy, well-made sausage that's nicely seasoned, not indigestible, perfect for slicing and layering on a buttered *baguette*. Well, you'll find it here, the *saucisson d'Arles,* a top-quality dried sausage that blends pork, beef, and gentle seasoning.

SAINT-PAUL-TROIS-CHATEAUX *(Drôme)*

Montélimar 25 k, Orange 20 k, Suze-la-Rousse 10 k.

MUSEE

**MAISON DE LA TRUFFE
  ET DU TRICASTIN**
Rue de la République,
  26130 Saint-Paul-
  Trois-Châteaux.
(75.96.61.29).
Open 9:30 A.M. (10 A.M. on
  Sunday) to noon and
  2:30 to 6 P.M. Closed
  Monday morning.
Admission: 12 francs for
  adults, 6 francs for
  children under age 13,
  free for children under
  age 5, 10 francs for
  adults and 5 francs for
  children in groups of 10
  or more.
Will ship in France.

A new mini-museum inside the village tourist office, where visitors can learn a bit about truffle plantations and the truffle's growth and care, and buy preserved truffles as well as the regional Tricastan wines.

SAINT-REMY-DE-PROVENCE *(Bouches-du-Rhône)*

Arles 25 k, Avignon 21 k, Marseille 91 k, Nîmes 42 k, Paris 706 k, Salon-de-Provence 37 k.

Market: Wednesday, 6 to 11 A.M., Place de la Mairie, Place de la République, Rue Lafayette; Saturday, 6 to 11 A.M., Rue Lafayette.

POUR LA MAISON

BROCANTE DU PARAGE
19 Boulevard Gambetta and
10 Rue du Parage, 13210
Saint-Rémy-de-Provence.
(90.92.25.11).
From Easter through
October, open 10:30 A.M.
to noon and 3 to 7:30
P.M.; closed Thursday
morning and Monday.
From November to
Easter, open only 3 to
7:30 P.M. Saturday and
10:30 A.M. to noon and 3
to 7:30 P.M. Sunday.

A dusty little shop that's chock-a-block full of old glassware, linens, china, and decorative postcards from every region of France.

MADE IN PROVENCE

Nothing typifies Provence like the decorative Souleiado fabrics, the bright cotton prints based on eighteenth- and nineteenth-century folkloric designs. Today these popular fabrics appear as table linens and lamp shades, umbrellas and notebook covers, summery sundresses and dainty coin purses. The following is a list of selected Souleiado shops in the region.

Standard hours are 9:30 A.M. to 12:30 P.M. and 2 to 7 P.M. Most shops are closed Monday morning and two weeks in August.

Credit cards: AE, DC, EC, V.

Will ship internationally.

AIGUES-MORTES
16 Rue Jean-Jaurès.

GORDES
Place du Monument.

AIX-EN-PROVENCE
Place des Tanneurs.

MARSEILLE
101 Rue Paradis.

APT
47 Rue Saint-Pierre.

SAINT-REMY-DE-PROVENCE
2 Avenue de la Résistance.

ARLES
4 Boulevard des Lices.

AVIGNON
5 Rue Joseph-Vernet.

VAISON-LA-ROMAINE
2 Cours J.H.-Fabre.

SPECIALITES REGIONALES

MAISON LILAMAND ET FILS
Route d'Avignon, 13210 Saint-Rémy-de-Provence. (90.92.11.08).
Open 8 A.M. to noon and 2 to 6 P.M. Closed Saturday and Sunday.
Will ship internationally.

SPECIALTY:
Fruits confits (candied fruits).

The best address I know for authentic hand-preserved candied fruits, or *fruits confits*. For more than eighty years this small family firm has carefully purchased, then preserved, the finest fruits of the region, including the rare *rosé de Provence* apricots, figs from Brignolles, plums from Tarascon, and peaches from the outskirts of Nîmes.

FRUITS CONFITS
Candied Fruit

Glistening like colorful precious jewels, almost too pretty to eat, the *fruits confits* of Provence are one of the region's oldest and best-known confections. Throughout the year you'll see the windows of the finest pastry shops filled with still lifes of candied preserved fruit, including whole sparkling melons, brilliant clementines, and sunset-orange apricots. Today, of course, it is hard to imagine why anyone would want to go to great efforts to replace a fruit's thoroughly natural juice with pure sugar. But try to transport yourself back to the days when candying was the sole way of preserving the color and form of summer's bounty for year-round enjoyment.

Today the best handmade *fruits confits* (there is a great deal made industrially) are prepared in the traditional manner. Each fruit is cooked separately in a sugar syrup—that is, apricots with apricots, melons with melons—sometimes going through eight or nine cookings in unlined copper basins. After each cooking the fruit is transferred, to cool, into heavy round terra-cotta bowls. With each cooking more sugar is added, and the syrup gets progressively more concentrated. The repeated slow cookings and long coolings allow the fruit to hold its natural shape and ensure that the fruit juice is thoroughly replaced by the sugar water. The fruit can be stored indefinitely in the syrup, then just before it is sold it is drained, brushed with sugar syrup, and left to dry before packaging.

Today, 70 percent of the *fruits confits* made in France—largely around Apt and Saint-Rémy in Provence and in Nice and along the Côte-d'Azur—is sold between Christmas and New Year's, when a basket of shiny preserved fruit remains a popular holiday gift.

SAOU (Drôme)

Crest 13 k, Dieulefit 23 k.

Fête du Picodon (Picodon festival/goat cheese competition): one Sunday in July.

FROMAGERS

PICODON DE FLOREAL
Guy and Michèle Tariot,
26400 Saoû.
(75.76.03.70).
No particular hours; call
first to be certain
someone will be there to
greet you.
Closed October to Easter.
Will ship in France.

For excellent farm-made goat cheese, known locally as Picodon (see "Milk from the Poor Man's Cow," page 326). (Directions: From Saoû, take the D538 east for 1 kilometer. Look for the *Ferme de Floréal* sign on the left.)

**PICODON DE ROCHE
    COLOMBE**
Emile and Solange Magnet,
Soyans, 26400 Crest.
(75.76.00.46 or
    75.76.03.17).
No particular hours; call
first to be certain
someone will be there to
greet you.
Closed December through
February.
Will ship in France.

Another source for excellent Picodon. (Directions: From Saoû, take the D538 west to the D136. Continue along the D136 for 300 meters in the direction of Soyans. Turn left off the D136 at the farm, at the base of the Roche Colombe mountain.)

SARRIANS (Vaucluse)

Carpentras 8 k, Orange 15 k.

Market: Sunday, 8 A.M. to noon, Place Jean-Jaurès.

BOULANGERIE

MARIUS DUMAS
Porte d'Amont, 84260
    Sarrians.
(90.65.42.15).
Open 5 A.M. to 7 P.M. Closed
    Sunday and the last week
    in July through August.

It really is worth rolling out of bed early some morning to beat a path to the door of Marius Dumas' authentically Provençal bakery. (You'll know you're at the right spot when you see the pile of wood stacked in front of the door.) Monsieur Dumas is outgoing, chatty, passionate, and off-the-wall nuts about bread, and he loves to invite visitors into his bread-baking room to admire the 300-year-old wood-fired oven. Give him half a chance and he'll drag out his scrapbook from his trip to Japan, where he helped the Japanese learn French bread-baking techniques. If you're lucky, you'll arrive the second his chewy, satisfying *fougasse aux grattelons* (webbed bread with cracklings) comes out of the oven. I can't say that cracklings are the best thing to put into an empty stomach, but they sure did the trick early one Saturday in July.

His other specialty is *pain Beaucaire,* one of those regional breads that have all but disappeared. The bread is made much like puff pastry, only with bread dough, and it is turned and folded, rolled, then baked. It seems like an awful lot of effort, but when it is sampled warm, fresh from the oven, it's a real bread-lover's treat.

SÉGURET *(Vaucluse)*

Carpentras 23 k, Vaison-la-Romaine 10 k.

RESTAURANT

LA TABLE DU COMTAT
Séguret, 84110
  Vaison-la-Romaine.
(90.46.91.49).
Last orders taken at 2 P.M.
  and 9 P.M.
Closed Tuesday dinner,
  Wednesday (except
  during July, August,
  Easter, and Christmas),
  the last two weeks in
  November, and February.
Credit cards: AE, DC, EC, V.
Air-conditioned.
Private dining room for 12.
English spoken.
175-, 220-, and 300-franc
  menus. A la carte, 300
  francs.

SPECIALTIES:
Filet de rouget à la crème de
romarin et foie gras (tiny red
mullet filets in a cream of
rosemary and *foie gras*).

This restaurant has one of the most stunning panoramic views in all of Provence, overlooking the sharp-crested pine- and oak-covered peaks known as the Dentelles de Montmirail. On a summer evening as the sun sets, painting the sky a million brilliant shades of red and orange, La Table du Comtat can't be beat. Unfortunately, I can't be as enthusiastic about the food, which is *correct,* though frustratingly ambitious. But I go anyway, for the view, for the roast lamb seasoned with herbs and garlic, for the cheese tray (which usually includes a remarkable Picodon), and for the wine list, which includes some old-vintage Châteauneuf-du-Pape and a range of Côtes-du-Rhône.

SUZE-LA-ROUSSE *(Drôme)*

Bollène 7 k, Orange 17 k, Paris 642 k, Valence 80 k.

Market: Friday 8 A.M. to 12:30 P.M., Place du Champ-de-Mars.

ECOLE DE VIN

UNIVERSITE DU VIN
Château de Suze, 26130
  Suze-la-Rousse.
(Château, 75.04.81.44;
  school, 75.04.86.09).
Guided tours at 2:30, 3:30,
  4:30, and 5:30 P.M. Closed
  Tuesday and November.
Admission: About 9 francs
  for adults, 5 francs for
  children under age 15,
  and 5 francs per person
  for groups of 20 or more.

This imposing medieval *château* perched on a hilltop serves as a learning center for wine, as a setting for summer concerts, and can also be toured simply as a *château*. Visitors to the wine university—which itself is open by appointment only—can take a quick preliminary tour of the extensive library of wine books and publications, watch an audiovisual display explaining, in English, the activities of the school, and take a look at the up-to-date tasting rooms and the modern laboratory where wines, particularly those from the region, are analyzed by the school's chemists. English-language tours can be arranged, and the wine library is open to the public by appointment. Classes, taught in French and English, include the history of wine and its commercialization, as well as offering a series of wine-tasting weekends that include visits to the Rhône valley vineyards.

Café chatter on a Provençal morning.

VAISON-LA-ROMAINE *(Vaucluse)*

Avignon 47 k, Carpentras 28 k, Montélimar 65 k, Paris 669 k.

Market: Tuesday, 8 A.M. to noon, Avenue Jules-Ferry, Grande-Rue, and throughout the center of town.

Do not go to Provence without passing through this lively little village, really three towns in one: the restored Roman village, the active, contemporary center, and the medieval *haute ville* at the southern edge of town. Try to make it on a Tuesday morning, when the roving market winds through the streets, swelling the population and transforming all into one electric festival. On a winter market-day morning around 10, peek into the Bar Moderne on Avenue Jules-Ferry, where you may find farmers and brokers haggling over the price of freshly unearthed, fragrant black truffles.

FROMAGERIE

LOU CANESTEOU
10 Rue Raspail, 84110
    Vaison-la-Romaine.
(90.36.31.30).
Open 8 A.M. to 1 P.M. and
    3:30 to 7:30 P.M. Closed
    Sunday, and Monday
    afternoon. (In winter,
    closed also on Tuesday
    afternoon.)

Nicole Dejoux, at Lou Canesteou.

Bubbly, red-headed Nicole Dejoux is a model shopkeeper and a woman who's passionate about her work, which is to buy and then age the best cheeses she can find. She says that when she opened in the late 1970s there was barely a cheese shop in the area, and even supermarkets sold only industrially made cheeses. Over the years she has carefully built up her local contacts, and now she offers an exceptional regional assortment, including very fresh, creamy white goat cheese from nearby Valréas; very piquant Picodon; flat, dried, and pungent discs of Pélardon; good runny Saint-Marcellin; as well as a variety of raw-milk cheeses from all over France. She has good judgment on wine, too, and stocks some fine local reds. Try especially the Gigondas and Vacqueyras Domaine "La Garrigue," both gutsy unfiltered reds typical of the best Côtes-du-Rhônes.

Asparagus may be the most revered vegetable in France, and the French are fiercely loyal to its cultivation—the first asparagus beds were recorded in the fourteenth century. Nearly half the asparagus grown in the European Common Market, some 100,000 tons, comes from Provence, Languedoc, and the Loire regions. Tiny shoots of greenhouse-grown asparagus begin to appear in the markets in February, but the most plentiful season runs from early April through June. Asparagus—fat or slim, white, green, or purple—are often sold bundled in bright paper wrappers. The most-admired green varieties are cultivated in the Provençal village of Villelaure, while the prized white varieties are grown in the swampy Sologne. The rare purple-tipped asparagus—those most often seen as decoration on antique *barbotine* plates—appear in markets in Nice and Cannes during the month of June.

Often served swaddled in a white linen napkin on a silver tray, asparagus is eaten with the fingers, stalk by precious stalk, usually with a simple butter or hollandaise sauce. This wasn't always the case: The vogue once was to eat asparagus with oil, though certain gastronomes remained faithful to simple melted butter. The honor of good Frenchmen was divided over the issue. As the story goes, during the eighteenth century, the French author Bernard le Bovier de Fontenelle, a devotee of oil, invited the Abbot of Terrasson, a butter loyalist, to dinner. As a proper host, he planned to serve half the asparagus with butter, and half with oil. But just before sitting down at the table, the abbot fell ill and fainted. Fontenelle rushed breathlessly to the kitchen and ordered the chefs to change the asparagus order to *"toute à l'huile maintenant, toute à l'huile!"*

SPECIALITES REGIONALES

ANDRE AUGIER ET FILS
Route d'Orange, 84110
　Vaison-la-Romaine.
(90.36.03.21).
Open 9 A.M. to noon and 2
　to 6 P.M.
Will ship in Europe.

For preserved local black truffles and award-winning honey, particularly their lavender-scented *miel de lavande.*

AU COIN GOURMAND
14 Rue de Maquis, 84110
　Vaison-la-Romaine.
(90.36.30.04).
Open 7:30 A.M. to 1 P.M. and
　3:30 to 8 P.M. Closed
　Sunday afternoon.
Credit card: V.

A first-class specialty shop, offering a beautiful selection of local goat's- and cow's-milk cheeses, including delicious Picodon at various stages of aging and creamy Saint-Marcellin. Also a well-chosen assortment of regional wines, olives from nearby Nyons, local preserved black truffles, and specialty products from Paris's Fauchon.

VALREAS *(Vaucluse)*

Grignan 9 k, Nyons 14 k, Vaison-la-Romaine 30 k.

Markets: Wednesday, 8 A.M. to noon, Places de la Mairie and de la Poste;
Saturday, 8 A.M. to noon, war memorial.

SPECIALITES REGIONALES

REVOUL
84600 Valréas
(90.35.01.26).
Open 8 A.M. to noon and 2
　to 6 P.M. Closed Saturday
　afternoon from May
　through September.

S P E C I A L T Y :
Truffes (truffles).

One of the few remaining *conserveries* for preserved local truffles. (Directions: across the street from the wine cooperative.)

Picodon, Picodon, Picodon for sale.

VENASQUE *(Vaucluse)*

Apt 33 k, Avignon 35 k, Carpentras 12 k, Cavaillon 32 k, Orange 35 k, Paris 705 k.

POUR LA MAISON

ATELIER DE FAIENCE
Place de la Fontaine, 84210
Venasque.
(90.66.07.92).
Open daily 10 A.M. to 7 P.M.
from Easter through
September; by
appointment the rest of
the year.
Credit card: V.

I love to collect—and to give as gifts—potter Etienne Viard's charming and playful hand-painted *faïence*. His bright little boutique in the center of the village is filled with an incredible assortment of fanciful contemporary blue-and-white ceramics, ranging from huge salad bowls to plates, mugs, and candlesticks.

France, which produces nearly 2 million tons of apples each year, is the largest exporter of apples in the world and one of the world's major consumers as well. The French buy about 13 kilos (29 pounds) of apples per capita per year, two-thirds of which are Golden Delicious, or *"les goldens."* As elsewhere in the world, many of the old-fashioned varieties have disappeared from the marketplace. In 1978 a group called the *"Croqueurs de Pommes"* (the Apple Eaters) was established to bring back some of the older, more flavorful varieties and to encourage the establishment of new, flavorful hybrids. Some other apples to look for in the marketplace are Reinettes, Reine de Reinettes, Belle de Booskoop, Starkcrimson, and Melrose. Apples are transformed into wonderful delicacies that range from the caramelized upside-down apple tart known as *tarte Tatin* to a simple compote served with buttery cookies and jam.

It is said in France that if you eat an apple first thing in the morning it develops the memory, and if you eat one last thing at night it helps you sleep. The French enjoy the image of apples as much as their sweet, crisp bite. If you faint in France you are said to *"tomber dans les pommes."* A very nice person is considered to be *"aux pommes,"* a small child is said to be *"haut comme trois pommes,"* and a rosy tomato is called a *"pomme d'amour,"* or apple of love. A *"pomme de discorde"* is a topic of disagreement, and a gift for a close friend is *"pour ma pomme."*

WINES OF PROVENCE

1. CHATEAU DE FONSALETTE: I was first introduced to this vibrant, intense red at the restaurant La Beaugravière in Mondragon. It is chef Guy Jullien's favorite wine: He drinks it, he cooks with it, he encourages everyone else to love it.

2. DOMAINE TEMPIER BANDOL: One of my very favorite wines— a big, spicy red—Domaine Tempier's Bandol bottles the herbaceous zest of Provence. It's found on wine lists all over France and is almost always a very good buy.

3. CHATEAU SIMONE PALETTE: Another wine of Provence that deserves to be much better known, Palette is a tiny *appellation* from vineyards just south of Aix-en-Provence, where they make reds, whites, and rosés. Château Simone's firm and elegant white is a favorite.

4. MUSCAT DE BEAUMES-DE-VENISE (DOMAINE DES BERNARDINS): One of those made-in-heaven marriages is a sip of Beaumes-de-Venise and fruity Cavaillon melon. This sweet, powerful, fruity wine is also delicious as an aperitif and with *foie gras* and fruit tarts.

5. COTES-DU-RHONE (RABASSE-CHARAVIN): You won't see this wine much outside the region, for the reds of the charming perched Provençal village of Cairanne are just beginning to be discovered. They're rich, black-cherry-like, mouth-filling wines, and those of Rabasse-Charavin are among the best.

6. GIGONDAS (FARAUD): Georges Faraud makes one of the finest, most traditional Gigondas, an unfiltered red designed for drinking with wild game, grilled meats, and cheese.

7. CHATEAUNEUF-DU-PAPE (BEAUCASTEL ROUGE): If your wine memory is short and you want a sure-fire winner that's also a remarkably good value, then remember the intense, fruity, Châteauneuf-du-Pape. Beaucastel's wine is spicy, concentrated, and long lived, and always a good buy. Other growers to look for: Vieux Télégraphe, Château Rayas, and Château Fortia.

8. CHATEAUNEUF-DU-PAPE (VIEUX TELEGRAPHE BLANC): White Châteauneuf-du-Pape is rare (less than 5 percent of the production is white), yet much of it manages to find its way into restaurant cellars. A racy, aromatic, nonacidic wine, it is perfect with fish and shellfish, especially langoustines, scallops, and turbot.

CHEESES OF PROVENCE

1. PICODON: At its best, this marvelous goat's-milk cheese from the mountainous area of northern Provence is firm, aromatic, and agreeably piquant. Often several discs of firm white Picodon are wrapped together and sold by weight.

2. LOU PEVRE: A lactic, earthy little disc of goat's-milk cheese, Lou Pevre is a piquant delight, rolled in grains of coarsely cracked black pepper.

3. POIVRE D'AIN: Poivre d'Ain, a tiny solid disc of goat's-milk cheese, takes its name from the local word for wild savory, the herb that is pressed into this fresh, fragrant Banon cheese. Historically Poivre d'Ain was made on individual farms, although there are also versions made in commercial dairies, where the cheese is prepared with goat's milk or a mixture of cow's and goat's milk.

4. PELARDON: Pélardon is the generic name for a variety of firm white goat's-milk cheeses still made on farms in many regions of France, and found in markets throughout Provence.

5. BANON: Traditionally, this cheese—which takes its name from the village of Banon, in the Alps of Provence—was a goat's- or sheep's-milk cheese made on individual farms. The cheese was wrapped in brown dried chestnut leaves and tied with raffia, then marinated in *eau-de-vie* and stored in clay jars for up to a year, turning more pungent and aromatic with age. Today, Banon is made on farms and in commercial dairies, and one sees many versions. The two most common are the very white, young, yeasty Banon *frais* (sold both unwrapped and wrapped, usually in fresh green chestnut leaves), and the Banon *vrai,* an earthy, pungent, firmly aged version wrapped in dried chestnut leaves and tied with raffia. Today the cheese is made of goat's, sheep's, and cow's milk, alone or in combination. The best, and the rarest, is the aged pure-goat's-milk version, wrapped in dried leaves. White Banon is also rolled in dried summer savory and called Banon au Poivre d'Ain, or simply Poivre d'Ain.

Alpes/Côte-d'Azur
ALPS/COTE-D'AZUR

Serge Philippin and Adrien Sordello, Restaurant du Bacon outside Antibes.

Stretching from the Mediterranean shores all the way to the Alps, this sun-filled corner of France is a sweet land, scented with lavender, dotted with gnarled olive trees and hillside villages with fountain-filled squares. It is perhaps the only place in France where when it rains—ever so rarely—people run joyously into the streets and thank the heavens. Encompassing the glitz, glamour, and gastronomy of Nice, Cannes, and Saint-Tropez with the calm unspoiled fabric of the Alpes de Haute-Provence in the north, this region seems to corner the market on blue skies: In the summer months the area welcomes nearly 1,800 hours of sunshine, while Paris gets by with less than 1,300.

We approached the Alpes de Haute-Provence from the west on our first visit, beginning the journey on a stunningly beautiful day near the end of June. I had decided beforehand that the trip should officially begin on the peak of Mont Ventoux, for there, from the mountain that dominates all of Provence, one could survey the scenery and villages that lay ahead: Sault, Forcalquier, Banon, and Sisteron.

We soared up the mountain, taking the hairpin turns with ease, gladdened by the sight of infant wildflowers preparing to bloom. The sky was cloudless, and it looked as though a Mediterranean scorcher lay ahead. The descent was swift, and just before reaching the village of Sault, we passed a field covered with a stunning patch of the deepest purple flowers I'd ever seen. A special variety of lavender, perhaps? No, it was hyssop, a fragrant mint-like thistle, beautiful in bloom, one of the multitide of herbal medicines that the French guarantee cure everything. (It's also marvelous in the kitchen: fine for slipping into salads, showering over pasta, or blending with apricots for a flavorful tart).

Although the plan was to head on to the town of Banon—in hopes of finding, at its source, the pungent and creamy goat's-milk cheese wrapped in dried chestnut leaves—we stopped briefly in the hilltop village of Sault, for there was a market in progress.

The scene could have taken place a century ago. In front of a helter-skelter *quincaillerie,* or hardware store, stood a lean, bearded man hawking snake oil. No, not really snake oil, but an orange salt sure to pacify corns, eye problems, bad circulation, varicose veins, and even warts. Nearby, a handful of farmers had set up card tables and were selling home-grown strawberries, peas, and herbs that grow on that stretch of land tumbling down from Ventoux.

We went on like this for days, perched village to perched village, town to town, market day to market day, absorbing the spirit and personality of a quiet land. This is an area where one can casually drift from place to place, without specific plan, and have a fine time simply observing the festivity of day-to-day life.

In Sisteron (an impressive village set in tiers against the side of rugged hills) we endured the hour-long march up to the thirteenth-century citadel, soon rewarded by the view of the Durance river.

We chatted with an eclectic mix of local residents—with a couple who raise pigeons for a living, with bakers, restaurateurs, farmers, a man who has been pressing olive oil since 1936, and even a couple who have dedicated themselves to tracking down the method for fabricating the authentic local Banon cheese—dipped in *eau-de-vie,* then wrapped in dried chestnut leaves and gently aged for a full year.

It occurred to me that what is most striking about the people of this area is their easy acceptance of daily life, their ability to gain pleasure from the simplest acts. One Monday morning in the Forcalquier market I studied a slender, dark-haired girl as she chose

a melon. Slowly she lifted melon after melon to her nostrils, inhaling, concentrating on selecting the sweetest, ripest, the most perfect of fruit. Time was not the question; excellence was.

Here there is a special way of looking out at the world. Jean Giono, a local poet, said it most beautifully in his *Rondeur des Jours:* "All civilized people see the day beginning at dawn or a little after or a long time after or whatever time their work begins; this they lengthen according to their work, during what they call 'all day long'; and end it when they close their eyes. It is they who say the days are long. On the contrary, the days are round."

WHEN YOU GO

Michelin Green Guide: *French Riviera/Côte-d'Azur* (available in English).

Getting there: Air Inter offers about a dozen 1½-hour flights daily from Paris to Marseille, leaving from both Roissy (Charles-de-Gaulle) and Orly Ouest airports. There are also about a dozen 1¼-hour Air Inter flights daily to Nice, leaving from the two Paris airports.

    About five daily TGV *(trains à grande vitesse),* or bullet trains, travel from Paris to Marseille in 4¾ hours. There are at least six TGV making the 8-hour journey every day from Paris to Nice, while six more make the 7-hour journey from Paris to Cannes. One TGV goes from Paris to Digne each day; the trip is 7 hours. There are overnight trains to Nice, Cannes, and Digne. All trains leave from Paris's Gare de Lyon. Cars may be rented at the airports and train stations.

Getting around: Michelin map 245 (Provence/Côte-d'Azur).

Best time to visit: This warm, sunny vacationland is wonderful throughout the year, though of course the months from June through August are the most popular, as well as the most crowded. The locals—the lucky ones who live here year round —look forward to the fall, winter, and spring months, when the Alpes/Côte-d'Azur belongs to them. Note that some establishments are closed from late fall into early spring.

MARKETS
(Liveliest markets are marked with an asterisk.)

Monday: Beausoleil, *Forcalquier, Menton, Toulon.

Tuesday: *Antibes, Bandol, *Banon, Barjols, Beausoleil, Cannes, Colmars-les-Alpes, Cotignac, Fayence, Grasse, Lorgues, Menton, Mouans-Sartoux, *Nice, *Roquebrune-sur-Argens, Saint-Tropez, Toulon, Vence.

Wednesday: Antibes, Aups, Barcelonnette, *Beausoleil, Bormes-les-Mimosas, Brignoles, Cagnes-sur-Mer, Cannes, Castellane, Cogolin, Digne, Draguignan, Grasse, Menton, *Nice, Riez, *Sanary-sur-Mer, *Sault, *Sisteron, Tende, Toulon, Vallauris, Villefranche-sur-Mer.

Thursday: *Antibes, Barjols, Beausoleil, Cannes, Digne, Fayence, Gonfaron, Grasse, Le Lavandou, Menton, *Mouans-Sartoux, *Nice, Saint-Jeannet, Sospel, Toulon.

Friday: Beausoleil, *Cagnes-sur-Mer, Cannes, *Colmars-les-Alpes, Flassans-sur-Issole, Grasse, Menton, *Nice, Roquebrune-sur-Argens, Saint-Etienne-de-Tinée, Solliès-Toucas, Toulon, Valbonne, *Vence, Villefranche-sur-Mer.

Saturday: *Antibes, *Aups, *Barcelonnette, *Barjols, *Beausoleil, *Brignoles, *Cannes, *Castellane, *Digne, *Draguignan, *Fayence, Grasse, Manosque, *Menton, *Nice, *Riez, *Saint-Tropez, *Sisteron, *Toulon.

Sunday: Antibes, *Cannes, Menton, *Nice, Saint-Etienne-de-Tinée, Toulon, *Vallauris.

FAIRS AND FESTIVALS

January 16 (Saint Marcel's Day): *Fête des Tripettes* (traditional local festival), Barjols.

Mardi Gras: *Fête du Citron* (lemon festival), Menton.

Beginning of April: *Foire aux Vins* (wine fair), Brignoles.

First two weekends in May: *Fête des Mais* (May festival), Nice.

June 8: *Procession aux Limaces* (traditional local festival), Bouyon.

Last Sunday in June or first Sunday in July: *Fête de la Saint-Pierre* (Saint Peter's Day festival), Menton.

One day in July: *Foire de l'Olive* (olive fair), Draguignan.

First two weeks in August: *Festival de Haute-Provence,* Forcalquier.

First Sunday in August: *Corso de la Lavande* (lavender parade), Digne; *Jasminades* (jasmin festival), Grasse; *Foire aux Vins* (wine fair), Vidauban.

First Sunday following August 6: *Fête du Raisin* (grape festival), Fréjus.

Around August 24: *Foire à l'Ail* (garlic fair), Hyères.

Last Sunday in August or first Sunday in September: *Foire Provençale et Fête des Vendanges* (Provençal fair and grape harvest festival), Cogolin.

First Sunday in September: *Fête des Baguettes* (traditional local festival), Peille.

First or second Sunday in November: *Fête des Châtaignes* (chestnut festival), Isola.

Café time on the Côte-d'Azur.

ANTIBES *(Alpes-Maritimes)*

Aix-en-Provence 158 k, Cannes 11 k, Nice 23 k, Paris 916 k.

Market: Tuesday through Sunday, 9 A.M. to noon, Cours Massséna.

RESTAURANT

RESTAURANT DE BACON
Boulevard de Bacon, 06600
  Cap d'Antibes.
(93.61.50.02).
Last orders taken at 2 P.M.
  and 9:30 P.M. (10:30 P.M.
  in July and August).
Closed Sunday dinner,
  Monday, and mid-
  November through
  January.
Credit cards: DC, V.
Terrace dining.
Air-conditioned.
English spoken.
250- and 350-franc menus
  at lunch only. A la carte,
  about 500 francs.

SPECIALTIES:
Bouillabaisse (Mediterranean
fish and shellfish soup),
assorted local fish and
shellfish.

A chef's greatest challenge is to secure the finest, freshest ingedients, treat them simply and with utmost respect, then present the food in an atmosphere that's warm, welcoming, appealing. If it were a simple task to succeed at all this, we'd be deluged with great restaurants. But luckily for us, there are restaurateurs who do understand these concepts, who suppress the human desire to improve upon nature.

The Sordello brothers—proprietors of the family-run Restaurant de Bacon—know that there's really no improving on nature, especially when you're talking about fish just a few hours out of the water. To secure the freshest local catch the brothers head out to the fish markets each morning—Adrien takes Cannes, Etienne takes Antibes—then return around 10 A.M. to plan the day's menu with their chef, Serge Philippin.

On a good day you'll find the rare *cigale de mer,* or sea cricket, big as a lobster; tiny rose-colored *rouget* for grilling with fresh herbs from the nearby countryside; and an entire procession of strange-sounding Mediterranean fish (like *corb* and *sar, marbre* and *denti*) that will be grilled with fennel or steamed with basil, poached with a medley of vegetables or simply baked in parchment.

Just as diners begin to arrive for lunch on Bacon's shaded terrace overlooking the glistening blue waters of the Baie des Anges and the old town of Antibes, the collection of fresh whole fish is arranged like a brilliant still life on a huge rectangular platter. Following personal whim and individual mood, diners select their fish, then decide whether they'd like it grilled, poached, baked, or steamed.

First-course offerings are simple and sublime. There's a salad of mixed greens, or *mesclum,* tossed with garlic croutons, and a stunningly fresh and full-flavored raw fish salad, prepared with the monster *mérou* when we sampled it, sprinkled with fresh lemon juice and a mixture of herbs.

But the real star is the baked Saint-Pierre, a preparation that helps one understand that perfect simplicity is a rare luxury. The whole fish is doused with extra-virgin olive oil, lemon juice, sliced lemons, fresh tarragon, and small cubes of tomato, wrapped in parchment, then baked in a very hot oven for about twenty-five minutes. At the table, the Saint-Pierre is carefully boned and presented with all the fragrant cooking juices (see recipe, following page). With the Saint-Pierre, sample the delicious Bellet white, from the hills beyond Nice.

Bacon's desserts are equally appealing, and include a rich and extravagant *nougat glacé au coulis de framboises* (frozen fruit-and-nut-filled nougat with raspberry sauce) and a fresh raspberry tart.

BANON *(Alpes-de-Haute-Provence)*

Forcalquier 25 k, Sault 29 k.

Market: Tuesday, 7 A.M. to 12:30 P.M., next to the post office, on the *boules* court (Place de la République).

Banon, population 850, was ready for us as we drove up the hill: Its fountains and wrought iron balconies, blue-shuttered shops, and church tower topped with a decorative wrought iron campanile set the scene. There at the edge of town we saw a dog, walking along with a sense of purpose, a baguette clenched firmly in his mouth. I instantly imagined that somewhere in Banon a little old lady was wondering what was taking him so long in town.

Also there, in the tiny open-air market crammed into the Place de la République, under the shade of an aging chestnut tree, farm ladies were selling creamy white discs of young Banon, offering the traditional sprig of fresh *sarriette,* or summer savory, to serve alongside.

I photographed one chubby, large-breasted woman who had protected her handmade goat cheese from insects with a blanket of antique lace. "Everyone wants to buy the lace," she said shyly. "They're disappointed when I tell them all I have to sell is *chèvre.*"

There was of course, the decorative, spider-web-like local bread called *fougasse,* and spilling out of wooden crates we saw live chickens, pigeons, and baby chicks. Parked in the square in Banon we also saw the world's largest pizza truck, one the size of a double-width trailer home, outfitted with a wood-fired oven for baking crisp pizzas and a rotisserie for roasting farm-fresh chickens.

POISSON EN PAPILLOTE RESTAURANT DE BACON
RESTAURANT BACON'S FISH BAKED IN PARCHMENT

Fish en papillote *is one of the most abused fish preparations. Too often the fish is not fresh, or it's overcooked, or, just as bad, it is cooked in an aluminum foil pouch, which to me will always resemble a doggy bag and nothing else. So, when Adrien Sordello, of the lovely family restaurant Bacon, in Cap d'Antibes, suggested I sample his* Saint-Pierre en Papillote *I was a bit leery. Boy, was I surprised when the waiter snipped open the crinkly, steaming package to find fragrant, shimmeringly fresh John Dory mingled with local herbs, virgin olive oil, tasty tomatoes, and a touch of lemon. I've tried this dish with a variety of whole fish and find that cooking times are not as critical as one might suspect. Just be sure the fish is fresh and the olive oil is the best you can find.*

1 whole John Dory, Alaska snapper, or red snapper, 3 to 4 pounds (1.5 to 2 kg), dressed

Salt and freshly ground black pepper to taste

2 medium tomatoes, peeled, cored, seeded, and coarsely chopped

1 lemon, thinly sliced

2 tablespoons freshly squeezed lemon juice

¼ cup (60 ml) extra-virgin olive oil

Handful of mixed fresh herbs, preferably tarragon, chives, marjoram, chervil, and flat-leaf parsley, minced

1. Preheat the oven to 450°F (230°C).

2. Place the whole fish at one end of a large sheet of baking parchment (about 24 x 16 inches or 61 x 41 cm). Season the fish inside and out with salt and pepper, then sprinkle with the remaining ingredients. Carefully fold the other half of the paper over the fish, closing it like a book. To seal the package, double fold the 3 open edges and secure each side with 4 or 5 staples.

3. Place the package on a large baking sheet and bake for 20 minutes.

4. Remove the package from the oven and cut it open with scissors. Let the fish sit for about 3 minutes to allow the flesh to firm up enough to fillet. To serve, fillet the fish and divide it among 4 warmed dinner plates. Pour several spoonfuls of sauce over each portion and serve immediately.

Yield: 4 servings.

BIOT *(Alpes-Maritimes)*

Antibes 8 k, Grasse 18 k, Nice 22 k,
Paris 924 k, Vence 19 k.

CAFE

CAFE DE LA POSTE
24 Rue Saint-Sébastien,
06410 Biot.
(93.65.19.32).
Open 7 A.M. until the last
customer leaves. Closed
Wednesday.

This place is a classic: Trendy Parisians, wide-eyed tourists, and hard-core locals all make themselves right at home in this turn-of-the-century village café complete with zinc bar. Come in out of the blinding sun and settle down with a *citron pressé*, made with freshly squeezed lemon juice.

POUR LA MAISON

FENOUIL
Golfe de Biot, 06410 Biot.
(93.65.09.46).
Open daily 11 A.M. to sunset
from Easter through
October only.
Will ship internationally.

A veritable museum of beautiful, colorful antique *barbotine* pottery, including a collection of more than 3,000 asparagus plates in 80 different models; also silver asparagus tongs and lamb chop holders. I could spend hours in this shop, making wish lists to last a lifetime.

**BOUTIQUE DE LA
VERRERIE DE BIOT**
3 bis Rue Saint-Sébastien,
06410 Biot.
(93.65.01.06).
Open Monday through
Saturday 10 A.M. to noon
and 2:30 to 6:30 P.M.,
Sunday 2:30 to 6:30 P.M.
Will ship internationally.
and **VERRERIE DE BIOT**
Chemin des Combes, 06410
Biot.
(93.65.03.00).
Open Monday through
Saturday 8 A.M. to 6 P.M.
(8 P.M. June through
September); Sunday
10:30 A.M. to 1 P.M. and
2:30 to 6:30 P.M. (10 A.M.
to 1 P.M. and 3 to 7 P.M.
June through
September).
Credit cards: AE, V.
Will ship internationally.

What began in 1956 as a small glass-blowing enterprise has grown into a major local industry and now includes an entire line of thick, hand-blown bubbled glassware, colorful ceramic pottery (some designs more tasteful than others), and matching linens. At the factory (Verrerie de Biot) on the edge of town, visitors are invited to watch the glassblowers at work.

Robert and Gilbert Auda, market-garden farmers outside Nice.

MUSEE

**MUSEE D'HISTOIRE
  LOCALE**
6 Place de la Chapelle,
  06410 Biot.
(93.65.11.79).
Open 2:30 to 6 P.M.
  Thursday, Saturday, and
  Sunday. Closed
  November through
  mid-December.
Admission: 3 francs.

Set aside ten minutes to wander through this charming museum of local history, complete with its nineteenth-century *Biotoise* kitchen full of glazed pottery and with a traditional open hearth, and a small but fascinating collection of costumed figures dressed in nineteenth-century everyday clothing.

CANNES *(Alpes-Maritimes)*

Aix-en-Provence 146 k, Marseille 158 k, Nice 32 k, Paris 901 k,
Toulon 123 k.

Markets: Tuesday through Sunday (daily June through September), 7 A.M. to 12:30 P.M.: covered market (Marché Forville), between Rues Docteur-Gazagnaire and Louis-Blanc; open-air market, Place du Commandant-Maria; open-air market, Place Gambetta.

On one visit to Cannes, I spent a morning in the Forville fruit, vegetable, and fish market, shopping with Adrien Sordello, one of the owners of Restaurant de Bacon in Cap d'Antibes (see page 348).

"Fish...fish...I dream about fish all night," laughs the lean and lanky Monsieur Sordello. He has come, as he does every morning, to select the fish that will be served in his restaurant that day.

To the untrained eye, the assortment carefully set out by a handful of fishermen's wives looks rather insignificant. It's high season but there are no more than a dozen tables, most offering what looks like a rather motley collection: a *rascasse* here, a *mulet* there.

"It's the rarity that sets the price here," says Monsieur Sordello as he unfolds a wad of 500-franc bills. The catch from the Baie de Cannes and the nearby Iles de Lérins is a quality one, but a small one. There aren't more than twenty or thirty boats that roam these waters, and on a successful outing a single fisherman will net no more than 20 kilos (about 45 pounds) of Saint-Pierre, plus perhaps an assortment of *rouget* and *merlan.*

Quickly one sees why Sordello, dressed like an international tourist in plaid bermuda shorts and a yellow Lacoste shirt, is so excited. Many of the fish are so fresh, they flip-flop right off the table.

The presentations here may appear primitive, but they get the job done. Each table is covered with thick plastic sheets filled with crushed ice, keeping the fish cool but not touching the ice.

"Look at this *mérou*," says Sordello, cradling a huge, delicate-fleshed Mediterranean monster. "It's never touched ice, it never will." Ice, he explains, may keep the fish looking fresh, but it'll thin out the flavor in the end.

Sordello bounces from table to table, chatting, teasing, arguing, and selecting his purchases fish by fish—three or four mean-spirited-looking *rascasses* from one table, four or five glistening Saint-Pierres from another. He scoops up 30 kilos (65 pounds) of assorted Mediterranean fish for the day's fish soup, grabs the head of a monkfish for making fish stock, then moves on to buy one fisherman's entire catch of Saint-Pierre.

The process eats up Sordello's entire morning, for the fishermen straggle in from 7 until well past 10, and the restaurateur wants to be the first to examine their catch.

RESTAURANT

LA MERE BESSON
13 Rue des Frères-
  Pradignac, 06400
  Cannes.
(93.39.59.24 and
  93.38.94.01).
Last orders taken at 1 P.M.
  and 10 P.M. (11 P.M. June
  through September).
Closed for lunch in July and
  August, and Sunday
  except holidays.
Credit cards: AE, EC, V.
Sidewalk dining in the warm
  months.
English spoken.
200 francs.

SPECIALTIES:
Monday, *estouffade à la
provençale* (beef stew with
onions, garlic, carrots, and
orange zest); Tuesday, *aïado*
(roasted stuffed lamb
shoulder); Wednesday, *piech*
(boiled veal brisket stuffed
with vegetables, rice, ham,
and herbs); Thursday, *lapereau
farci aux herbes de Provence*
(saddle of rabbit stuffed with
veal, liver, and herbs, and
baked with wine); Friday, *aïoli*
(here, boiled vegetables, salt
cod, mussels, and squid with
a garlic mayonnaise sauce);
Saturday, *osso bucco* (sautéed
veal braised with tomatoes).

How can you go wrong with a place that serves beef stew on Monday, lamb with garlic on Tuesday, rabbit with Provençal herbs on Thursday, and, of course, *aïoli* on Friday? That's La Mère Besson, a Cannes standby for decades, a casual spot for taking the whole family, situated on a peaceful street a short stroll from the port.

Everything here will remind you of Provence, including the delicious *lou mesclum* and the dependable *salade niçoise* (here tiny Niçois olives, anchovies, celery, mixed greens, red and green peppers, and chunks of tuna, topped with a marvelous blend of basil and oil).

The *lottes niçoise* (monkfish as small as the palm of a hand) are perfectly pan-fried, then covered with a satisfying sauce of tomatoes and olives, and the fine *estouffade à la provençale* is served with ribbed Italian pasta and a sprinkling of Parmesan. With the meal, sample one of the best wines Provence has to offer, the Bandol from Domaine Tempier.

BISTRO A VIN

L'ETAGERE
22 Rue Victor-Cousin,
   06400 Cannes.
(93.38.27.17).
Last orders taken at 11 P.M.
   (midnight in summer).
Closed for lunch, Sunday,
   and the school holidays
   between Christmas and
   New Year's.
Credit cards: AE, DC, V.
Sidewalk dining in the warm
   months.
Private dining room for 20.
English spoken (*"suffisamment
   pour faire plaisir"*).
150 francs.

SALON DE THE

ROHR
63 Rue d'Antibes, 06400
   Cannes.
(93.39.04.01).
and 47 La Croisette, 06400
   Cannes.
(93.38.07.69).
Open daily 8:30 A.M. to
   12:30 P.M. (1 P.M. Sunday
   and holidays) and 3
   (4 Sunday and holidays)
   to 7 P.M.
Will ship internationally.

BOULANGERIE

LA PALINE
108 Rue d'Antibes, 06400
   Cannes.
(93.38.50.00).
Open 7:30 A.M. to 1 P.M. and
   3:30 to 7:30 P.M. Closed
   Sunday.

Ice cream, for taking to the country.

This lively wine bar hidden on a small street right behind the Grand Hotel is devoted to good times, to the wines of Provence (the outgoing owner, Harika, offers some 130 choices), and to pure, uncomplicated regional foods. Some products of note: homemade bread, salads with creamy, farm-fresh *tomme de chèvre* (goat cheese), lamb grilled over a wood fire, and delicious homemade fruit desserts. Try the superbly fresh peaches marinated in red wine and blackberry liqueur.

One morning, after a long sunrise run along the beach, I sat on the terrace of the La Croisette shop and indulged in one of Rohr's flaky croissants and a bracing cup of strong black coffee. What a great way to wake up!

An unusual combination of bakery and butcher shop, where they offer one of the most delicious and incredible breads I've ever tasted in France. Around 4 each afternoon, a huge, long country loaf comes from the oven, and shoppers line up to buy the flavorful sourdough bread by the slice. The owner, Jean Pigaglio, kindly welcomes visitors to see his ancient wood-fired oven set below the street. Also try the homemade *gressini,* or bread sticks.

FROMAGERIES

CREMERIE AGNESE
114 Rue d'Antibes, 06400
Cannes.
(93.38.53.66).
Open 7:30 A.M. to 12:30 P.M.
and 3:30 to 7:30 P.M.
Closed Sunday, Monday
afternoon, and the last
week in November
through the first week in
December.

A tiny helter-skelter cheese shop run by two of the most passionate cheese mavens around: Adrien and Marguerite Agnese travel all over France in search of the best farm cheeses available. They also offer some well-aged Camembert, Pont l'Evêque, Reblochon, and Cabécou.

LA FERME SAVOYARDE
22 Rue Meynadier, 06400
Cannes.
(93.39.63.68).
Open Tuesday through
Saturday 7 A.M. to 12:30
P.M. (1 P.M. April through
August) and 3:30 to 7:30
P.M. Closed Sunday
(except Sunday morning
April through August),
Monday, and the second
week in November
through mid-December.

The best-known cheese store on the Côte d'Azur, a spotless, fragrant shop where you'll find hundreds of mildly aged French cheeses. The local taste here is for mild cheeses, so don't come looking for older cracked and crinkly versions. But their young, fresh goat cheeses are exceptional and the boutique itself is a model of cleanliness and clarity. I think it would be hard to leave empty-handed. I'm not terribly fond of their fabricated cheeses: Brie with truffles and goat cheese with olives is just too forced for my taste. (While you're there, do take the time to wander down Rue Meynadier, a pedestrian street filled with appealing food boutiques. Note especially all the pasta and ravioli shops.)

CONFISERIES

BRUNO
50 Rue d'Antibes, 06400
Cannes.
(93.39.26.63).
Open 8:30 A.M. to 12:30 P.M.
and 2:30 to 7:30 P.M.
Closed Sunday.
Credit cards: AE, DC.
Will ship internationally.

Candy shop or jewelry store? It's hard to tell from the window, where the bowls filled with glistening candied melons lure you inside. I fell in love with their *gelée de fruits,* bite-size candies made of pure fruit pulp and molded in the shape of the fruit. The pulp is very gently sweetened, so the candies retain a vibrant, pure-fruit flavor.

MAIFFRET
31 Rue d'Antibes, 06400
Cannes.
(93.39.08.29).
Open daily 9 A.M. to 7:30 P.M.
Credit card: V.
Will ship internationally.

A gem of a candy shop, specializing in irresistible *manon* (a blend of almond paste, butter, and walnuts covered in white chocolate) and deliciously runny caramels, known as *caramels liquides.* Visitors are welcome to watch chocolates being made between 4 and 6 P.M. Tuesday through Saturday.

SPECIALITES REGIONALES

CHEZ CANNOLIVE
16 Rue Vénizelos, 06400
   Cannes.
(93.39.08.19).
Open 8 A.M. to noon and
   2:30 to 7 P.M. Closed
   Sunday, Monday
   morning, and the last
   three weeks in January.
Credit cards; EC, V.
Will ship in Europe.

LIBRAIRIE

**CANNES ENGLISH
   BOOKSHOP**
10 Rue Jean-de-Riouffe,
   06400 Cannes.
(93.99.40.08).
Open 9:30 A.M. to 7 P.M.
   Closed between 1 and 2
   P.M. in winter, and
   Sunday.

MADE IN FRANCE

Nothing typifies the south of France like the decorative Souleiado fabrics, the bright cotton prints based on eighteenth- and nineteenth-century folkloric designs. Today these popular floral, paisley, and geometric print fabrics appear as table linens and lamp shades, umbrellas and notebook covers, summery sundresses and dainty coin purses. The following is a list of selected Soleiado shops in the region.

   Standard hours are 9:30 A.M. to 12:30 P.M. and 2 to 7 P.M. Most shops are closed Monday morning and two weeks in August.
   Credit cards: AE, DC, EC, V.
   Will ship internationally.

CANNES
Le Gray-d'Albion, 17 La Croisette.

LE LAVANDOU
21 Avenue des Commandos-d'Afrique.

SAINT-TROPEZ
Avenue Foch.

SANARY-SUR-MER
1 Place de la Liberté.

For excellent salt-cured anchovies from Collioure, olive oil (sold the old-fashioned way, out of giant barrels), honey, *santons,* Provençal fabrics.

A lovely little shop with a good selection of cookbooks and travel books, in English of course. A place to know about when you've run out of things to read.

CHATEAU-ARNOUX *(Alpes-de-Haute-Provence)*

Digne 25 k, Forcalquier 30 k, Manosque 39 k, Paris 717 k, Sault 74 k, Sisteron 14 k.

RESTAURANT

LA BONNE ETAPE
04160 Château-Arnoux.
(92.64.00.09).
Last orders taken at 2 P.M. and 9 P.M.
Closed Sunday dinner, Monday off-season, and January (after New Year's) through mid-February.
Credit cards: AE, DC, EC, V.
Air-conditioned.
Private dining rooms for 10 and 20.
English spoken.
180-, 290-, and 330-franc menus. A la carte, 300 francs.

SPECIALTIES:
In summer, *fleurs de courgette farcies aux légumes* (zucchini blossoms stuffed with vegetables), *daube d'agneau en gelée* (lamb stew in aspic), *agneau de Sisteron* (lamb from the nearby Sisteron hills), *caneton au miel de lavande et citron* (duck with lavender honey and lemon). In winter, *mousseline de gibier à plumes au genièvre* (mousseline of wild fowl with juniper berries), *colvert au coriandre* (mallard duck with coriander), *marcassin poêlé aux pignons de pin et raisins* (wild boar with pine nuts and raisins).

I remember my first meal at La Bonne Etape as if it were yesterday. Rarely had I encountered flavors and aromas so vibrantly fresh that they all but flew off the plate! The olive oil, the vegetable-stuffed zucchini blossoms, the local pigeon, the incredible aged Banon goat cheese, were all revelations. I've returned again and again to this quietly elegant eighteenth-century *relais de poste* (stagecoach stop) and am rarely disappointed by the foods that Pierre and Jany Gleize, father and son, bring to the table. Tender zucchini blossoms—picked just as the sun is setting—are filled with a brilliant blend of garlic, mint, and zucchini (see recipe, following page). Herbs and vegetables, like mushrooms, zucchini, tomatoes, and thyme, are blended into a brightly colored layered omelet (see recipe, page 360). The roast pigeon, raised on a nearby farm, is among the best I've ever sampled, and the fresh cod spread with *tapenade* (a rich blend of oil-cured olives and capers) is a main dish I think I could sample every night of the week. Ask them to make up a simple green salad, and you'll find a wondrous mix of greens from Pierre's garden, including the mildly peppery, slightly crunchy green *pourpier,* or purslane. The rolling cheese cart offers a fine assortment of local goat cheeses, including the Banon that Pierre ages for a good six months, sprinkling the discs with brandy and wrapping them in dried chestnut leaves. Desserts vary with the seasons, but one can usually depend upon the unusual *tarte au citron et au chocolat* (see recipe, page 363), a marvelous blend of puckery lemon and bitter chocolate spread atop a lemon-flecked pastry shell. The wine list offers some good regional buys, including the red, white, and rosé Palette from Château Simone, the Cassis from Domaine du Paternel, and Domaine Tempier's luscious Bandol.

FLEURS DE COURGETTES FARCIES SAUCE POMME D'AMOUR LA BONNE ETAPE

LA BONNE ETAPE'S STUFFED ZUCCHINI BLOSSOMS WITH TOMATO SAUCE

Who could imagine that a blend of zucchini, mint, and garlic could be so divine? Each summer evening a local farmer arrives at La Bonne Etape in Château-Arnoux with a basketful of freshly gathered zucchini blossoms. He prefers the male zucchini flower, because it is larger, and advises they be picked either late in the morning when the dew has dried or after sundown. If you do not have access to zucchini blossoms, bake the seasoned zucchini in individual ramekins, then serve with the fragrant, flavorful tomato sauce. Pomme d'amour—*or love apple—is an old-fashioned name for the tomato.*

Tomato sauce:
5 medium tomatoes
2 tablespoons virgin
   olive oil
1 clove garlic, minced
1 lemon, peel and all
   white pith removed,
   then seeded and
   finely chopped
1 teaspoon coriander
   seeds, crushed
Large handful of fresh
   herbs, preferably
   basil, chervil, and
   flat-leaf parsley,
   minced
Salt and freshly ground
   black pepper to taste

Zucchini stuffing:
3 medium zucchini
1 tablespoon olive oil
4 cloves garlic, minced
3 tablespoons fresh
   bread crumbs
1 large egg
Handful each of fresh
   mint leaves, fresh
   parsley, and fresh
   basil, minced

18 zucchini blossoms
1 cup (250 ml) chicken
   stock, preferably
   homemade

1. At least 12 hours before serving, prepare the tomato sauce: Peel, core, and seed the tomatoes, then coarsely chop them. Combine the tomatoes and remaining sauce ingredients. Allow the sauce to marinate at room temperature for at least 12 hours.

2. Preheat the oven to 350°F (175°C).

3. Prepare the zucchini stuffing: Trim the zucchini and finely chop it in a food processor. This may have to be done in several batches.

4. Heat the oil in a large skillet over medium-high heat. Add the zucchini and garlic and cook until almost all the liquid has evaporated, about 5 minutes. The mixture should be moist but not soggy. Remove from the heat and stir in the bread crumbs, egg, and herbs. Season with salt and pepper to taste.

5. Carefully remove the pistils from the zucchini blossoms, as they become bitter when cooked. Using a pastry tube or a very small spoon, fill the blossoms with the zucchini stuffing. Place the filled blossoms in a gratin dish and pour the chicken stock all around them. Cover the dish with aluminum foil and bake until heated through, about 15 minutes.

6. As the blossoms bake, gently heat the tomato sauce just until warm. To serve, place 3 cooked blossoms on each of 6 warmed dinner plates and spoon the tomato sauce over the top.

Yield: 6 servings.

COGOLIN *(Var)*

Hyères 42 k, Le Lavandou 31 k, Paris 870 k, Saint-Tropez 9 k,
Sainte-Maxime 13 k, Toulon 60 k.

Markets: Wednesday, 8 A.M. to 12:30 P.M., Place des Boules; Saturday, 8 A.M.
to 12:30 P.M., Place de l'Eglise.

RESTAURANT

LA FERME DU MAGNAN
83310 Cogolin.
(94.49.57.54).
Last orders taken at 1:30 P.M.
and 9:30 P.M. (10:30 P.M.
June through
September).
From June through
September, open for
dinner only, closed
Tuesday. From October
through May, open for
lunch and dinner Friday,
Saturday, Sunday, and
holidays. Closed
February.
No credit cards.
Terrace dining.
Four menus from 106 to 200
francs. A la carte, 200
francs.

SPECIALTIES:
Volailles (poultry raised on the
Magnan farm).

This is a wonderfully rustic spot to go with the family or a large group, for a very basic soup-to-nuts meal. This poultry farm, transformed into a restaurant at mealtime, reminds me of a suburban steak house where people go for a good feed and a good time. The poultry raised here is delicious, and some of the side dishes are not bad either. Try the grilled mussels (huge, plump *moules* grilled over a wood fire, so they've a marvelously smokey flavor), the rabbit with mustard (*lapin à la moutarde*), and *pintadeau,* or guinea fowl, cooked in red wine, mushrooms, and diced smoked bacon. Service is a bit haphazard, and desserts are nothing to write home about. (Directions: 4 kilometers west of Cogolin on the N98.)

Salads in France are incomparable. Sprightly mixtures of multi-colored and multi-textured leaves and flower blossoms dressed in wonderfully piquant or luxuriously smooth dressings, they can be the most subtle, the most amusing mixtures in a French meal. Salads are mixtures that translate to the language as well: If someone gets into a muddle and begins confusing facts, he'll be accused of creating *"une vraie salade."* If the same person persists with his jumbled facts or lies, he'll be told to quiet down, to *"cessez de nous raconter vos salades."* If there is little sympathy for confusion, there is at least some for salad merchants, for someone who attempts to convince others of an idea is said to *"vendre sa salade."*

OMELETTE FROIDE DE LEGUMES A LA TAPENADE LA BONNE ETAPE

LA BONNE ETAPE'S COLD VEGETABLE OMELET WITH OLIVE, ANCHOVY, AND CAPER SAUCE

This is a remarkable dish—remarkable for its flavor and its beauty—and one that I sampled on the first of many visits to restaurant La Bonne Etape in Château-Arnoux. Although the recipe may appear complicated, the dish is really not difficult to prepare. Fortunately the omelet— which more closely resembles a layered vegetable pâté—can be prepared ahead of time. I have simplified chef Jany Gleize's recipe, reducing his six layers to three. The vibrant red, yellow, and green set off by the jet black tapenade *make a stunning first course or luncheon dish.*

Tapenade:
¾ cup (100 g) oil-cured
     black olives,
     preferably from
     Nyons, pitted
1 can (2 ounces; 57 g)
     flat anchovy fillets,
     drained, soaked in
     water for several
     minutes, drained
     again, and patted
     dry
2 tablespoons capers,
     rinsed and drained

Tomato layer:
1 tablespoon virgin
     olive oil
4 shallots, minced
10 medium tomatoes
     (about 2 pounds;
     1 kg), cored and
     quartered
Several branches fresh
     oregano or 1
     teaspoon dried
Salt and freshly ground
     black pepper to taste

Zucchini layer:
½ teaspoon virgin olive
     oil
2 cloves garlic, minced
10 ounces (2 small;
     300 g) zucchini,
     trimmed and cut
     into large chunks

1. Prepare the *tapenade:* Place the olives, anchovies, and capers in a food processor or blender and process until smooth. Set aside. (The *tapenade* will keep indefinitely, well covered, in the refrigerator.)

2. Prepare the tomato layer: Heat the oil in a medium nonstick pan over low heat. Add the shallots and cook, stirring occasionally, until transparent. Coarsely chop the tomatoes in a food processor or by hand with a knife. Increase the heat to medium-high and add the tomatoes, oregano, salt, and pepper. (If using fresh oregano, mince it just before adding.) Cook uncovered, stirring occasionally, until almost all the liquid has evaporated, about 30 minutes. Check the seasoning. Remove from the heat and transfer to a small strainer to drain off any remaining liquid.

3. Prepare the zucchini layer: Heat the oil in a medium nonstick pan over low heat. Add the garlic and sauté just until softened, a minute or two. Finely chop the zucchini in a food processor or by hand with a knife. Increase the heat to medium-high and add the zucchini and salt and pepper to taste. Cook uncovered, stirring occasionally, until the zucchini is tender, about 5 minutes. Check the seasoning. Remove from the heat and transfer to a small strainer to drain off any remaining liquid.

4. Preheat the oven to 300°F (150°C).

5. For the first layer of the omelet, break 4 eggs into a bowl and whisk until the whites and yolks are blended. Add the tomato mixture and mix well. Pour the mixture into a medium nonstick pan and set over low heat. Using a whisk, continuously stir the eggs, making sure to scrape back into the pan any egg that flows up the edge of the pan. As the egg mixture cooks, season it with salt and pepper to taste. Cook just until the egg

12 large eggs

Herb layer:
Handful of mixed fresh
    herbs, preferably
    basil, thyme, and
    chervil, finely
    minced

Several tablespoons
    best-quality red wine
    vinegar

mixture is uniformly thick and smooth, being careful not to overcook them so they get lumpy or undercook them so they remain runny.

6. Transfer the egg and tomato mixture to a nonstick, straight-sided, 8½-inch (21.5 cm), rectangular loaf pan. Smooth the mixture with a spatula before beginning the next layer.

7. Cook the second layer in the same manner, using 4 eggs and the herbs. Add to the loaf pan, and smooth the top.

8. Cook the third layer in the same manner, using the last 4 eggs and the zucchini. Add to the pan, and smooth the top.

9. Cover the pan with foil and bake just until the omelet is set, about 20 minutes. Remove from the oven to cool to room temparature.

10. To serve, cut the omelet into 8 even slices. Place each slice in the center of a dinner plate, spoon a dollop of *tapenade* on either side of the omelet, and sprinkle the omelet with vinegar just as the dish is being served.

Yield: 8 servings.

FLASSANS-SUR-ISSOLE (Var)

Aix-en-Provence 62 k, Draguignon 45 k, Gonfaron 11 k, Le Luc 11 k,
Marseille 89 k.

Market: Friday, 8 A.M. to noon, Place de l'Eglise.

RESTAURANT

LA GRILLADE AU FEU DE BOIS
83340 Le Luc.
(94.69.71.20).
Last orders taken at 2 P.M.
  and 8:30 P.M. (9:30 P.M. in
  summer).
Credit cards: AE, DC, V.
Terrace dining.
Private dining room for 25.
English spoken.
130-franc menu. A la carte,
  200 francs.

SPECIALTIES:
Traditional Provençal cooking,
fish, and wild boletus
mushrooms.

Driving up the winding road that leads to this charming Provençal hotel-restaurant, you feel as though you're about to enter a secluded retreat. The only noise you'll hear is the birds. The young owners are friendly and casual, and instantly make you feel at home. In good weather you can dine on the terrace in the shade of fig trees, at cooler times there's the large, cozy dining room decorated with some nice antiques. The food is homey and traditionally Provençal, including grilled local lamb served with a potato gratin, delicious sardines stuffed with herbs and fresh cheese, and grilled red peppers layered with strips of anchovies. There's also an excellent local wine from a neighboring property, the deep red, tannic Commanderie de Peyrassol. (Directions: 4 kilometers west of Le Luc on the N7.)

Socca, *hot* socca, *at the market in Nice.*

TARTE AU CITRON ET AU CHOCOLAT LA BONNE ETAPE
LA BONNE ETAPE'S LEMON AND CHOCOLATE TART

I am quite certain that if you polled the world to determine dessert preferences, chocolate and lemon would come out on top. The chocolate layer on this unusual lemon tart—made popular at restaurant La Bonne Etape in Château-Arnoux—came about quite by accident. Chef Pierre Gleize found that the uncooked lemon topping would seep into the crust, making it soggy. So he separated the lemon and pastry with a layer of bittersweet chocolate and came up with this wonderful tart. Do assemble it just a few hours before serving. This dough is child's play and produces a flavorful, lemon-scented crust.

Pastry:
¾ cup (100 g)
    unbleached all-
    purpose flour
2 tablespoons (25 g)
    sugar
Pinch of salt
Grated zest (peel) of 1
    lemon
1 large egg
¼ cup (60 g) unsalted
    butter, cubed, at
    room temperature

3 ounces (90 g)
    bittersweet
    chocolate, preferably
    Lindt or Tobler

Lemon topping:
2 large eggs, separated
½ cup (100 g) sugar
Grated zest (peel) of 1
    lemon
2 tablespoons freshly
    squeezed lemon juice
Pinch of salt

1. Preheat the oven to 425°F (220°C).

2. Prepare the pastry: Place the flour, sugar, salt, and lemon zest in a food processor or medium mixing bowl. Blend thoroughly, then add the egg and butter and mix just until blended. The dough should have the consistency of a soft cookie dough. Press the dough into the bottom of a 10½-inch (27 cm) tart pan (preferably with a removable bottom), and smooth it out. Use the blunt side of a knife blade to form scalloped ridges around the edge of the dough. This is a flat tart with no sides.

3. Prick the dough with a fork, then bake just until the pastry begins to brown, about 10 minutes. Remove from the oven to cool.

4. About 2 hours before serving, prepare the chocolate layer: Melt the chocolate in a small saucepan over very low heat, stirring so it does not burn. Spread the chocolate evenly over the pastry. Let cool to set.

5. Prepare the lemon topping: Using an electric mixer or a whisk, beat the egg yolks and ¼ cup (50 g) sugar until lemon colored. Stir in the lemon zest and juice.

6. Beat the egg whites with a pinch of salt in another bowl until the whites begin to stiffen. Gradually beat in the remaining sugar, then continue to beat until stiff but not dry. Carefully fold the egg yolk mixture into the egg white mixture and spread evenly over the chocolate-covered pastry. Refrigerate up to 2 hours.

Yield: One 10½-inch (27 cm) tart.

FORCALQUIER *(Alpes-de-Haute-Provence)*

Aix-en-Provence 66 k, Apt 42 k, Digne 49 k, Manosque 23 k, Paris 772 k, Sisteron 44 k.

Market: Monday, 9 A.M. to noon, Place Bourquet, Place Martial-Sicard.

RESTAURANT

AUBERGE CHAREMBEAU
04300 Forcalquier.
(92.75.05.69).
Last orders taken at 1:30 P.M. and 8:30 P.M.
Closed Monday, and November through January.
No credit cards.
English spoken.
150 francs.
Restaurant open only to guests staying at the hotel.

This is one of the nicest country dining spots in the region, with a large, open dining room with a giant hearth. Service is casual and friendly, and guests feel so much at home that soon they're chatting with one another across the tables. This is home cooking Provence style, and the chef offers up a moist *daube provençale* (generous chunks of beef marinated, then cooked for hours in red wine and aromatic vegetables), a motherly cheese gratin, and a surprising *charlotte aux noix*—ladyfingers and finely chopped walnuts in a creamy bavarian mixture. Very nutty and deeply satisfying. (Directions: just east of Forcalquier on the N100.)

GOLFE-JUAN *(Alpes-Maritimes)*

Antibes 5 k, Cannes 6 k, Grasse 21 k, Nice 27 k, Paris 915 k.

RESTAURANT

TETOU
Boulevard des Frères-Roustau, 06220 Golfe-Juan.
(93.63.71.16).
Last orders taken at 2 P.M. and 10 P.M.
Closed Wednesday, mid-October through the third week in December, and three weeks in March.
No credit cards.
English spoken.
350 francs.

Quantities of bouillabaisse, *the specialty of Tétou.*

SPECIALTIES:
Bouillabaisse (Mediterranean
fish and shellfish soup),
langouste (spiny lobster), *poisson*
(fish).

Dining at Tétou—a family favorite since 1920—is like going to the beach but not having to put up with the sand, the crowds, the sticky heat. Instead, you install yourself in what's probably the classiest fish shack in the world, a bright and spotless restaurant along the Golfe-Juan beach. Go with an appetite, roll up your sleeves, and plan to spend a few hours getting acquainted with their *bouillabaisse,* an affair that's served in a procession of courses, beginning with a rich and full-flavored fish soup served with grilled toast and mounds of garlic-and-saffron-enriched mayonnaise, known as *rouille.* Once you've become familiar with the soup, the waitress arrives with platters of boiled potatoes, meaty monkfish, and luxurious langoustine. Then, just as you've had your fill, she arrives with another platter laden with fresh Mediterranean *rascasse* and *galinette,* urging you to go just one more round.

GONFARON *(Var)*

Brignoles 25 k, Draguignan 40 k, Nice 100 k.

Market: Thursday, 7:30 P.M. to noon, Place de la Victoire.

BOULANGERIE

L'HERMITAGE
83590 Gonfaron.
(94.78.31.66).
Open 6 A.M. to 8 P.M. Closed
    Saturday, Sunday, two
    weeks at Christmas, and
    the last two weeks in
    August.
Will ship in Europe.

You may not be inclined to drive all the way out to the country for a single loaf of exceptional sourdough bread, but if you want to witness a remarkable family baking affair, it may be worth the detour. In 1979 the Dufaye family began making natural sourdough bread for themselves, and soon the passion mushroomed into a thriving business. Their giant electric oven works fifteen to eighteen hours a day, baking their moist and crusty country loaves, all made with organic ingredients. I loved the rye and olive loaf best of all. Their distinctive award-winning breads can be found at health food stores around the area, including the Wednesday and Saturday markets in Saint-Tropez. (Directions: Turn off the road at the *gendarmerie,* or police station, toward the *"base de loisirs."* Go 3 kilometers until you see a sign for "L'Hermitage.")

GRASSE *(Alpes-Maritimes)*

Cannes 17 k, Digne 117 k, Draguignan 56 k, Nice 42 k, Paris 918 k.

Market: Tuesday through Saturday, 7 A.M. to noon, Place aux Aires.

FROMAGERIE

LA FROMAGERIE
5 Rue de l'Oratoire, 06130
   Grasse.
(93.36.61.23).
Open 7:30 A.M. to 12:30 P.M.
   and 3 (2:30 in winter) to
   7:15 P.M. Closed Sunday
   and Monday.

A model cheese shop tucked away along one of Grasse's most charming winding streets. Try especially the unusual assortment of *brebis de pays,* or local sheep's-milk cheese.

MOUGINS *(Alpes-Maritimes)*

Antibes 12 k, Cannes 7 k, Grasse 11 k, Nice 32 k, Paris 908 k, Vallauris 8 k.

RESTAURANTS

**L'ESTAMINET DES
   REMPARTS**
24 Rue Honoré-Henri,
   06250 Mougins-Village.
(93.90.05.36).
Last orders taken at 1:30 P.M.
   and 9 P.M.
Closed Monday dinner,
   Tuesday, and the last
   week in December
   through January.
No credit cards.
A small terrace for dining.

On hot summer days this is just the sort of place we all search out: a charming, authentic village café/bistro, with cooling stone walls and a cozy, welcoming atmosphere. This little spot is run by a single harried cook-owner named Georgette, and she offers the simplest tossed green salads, splendid tomato tarts, and a rich fig tart that tastes like homemade Fig Newtons. I love the decor—a bit of this, a bit of that, nicely chosen flea market finds, including beautiful pottery bowls and pitchers, many of which are put into use in the restaurant.

Cafés, for people-watching, for contemplation.

MOULIN DE MOUGINS
Quartier Notre-Dame-
   de-Vie, 06250 Mougins.
(93.75.78.24).
Last orders taken at 2 P.M.
   and 10 P.M.
Closed Thursday lunch,
   Monday, and the third
   week in November
   through the third week
   in March.
Credit cards: AE, DC, V.
Terrace dining.
Private dining room for 50.
English spoken.
430-france menu. A la carte,
   600 francs.

SPECIALTIES:
Seasonal Provençal specialties.

The friendly, outgoing, hard-working Roger Vergé has managed to do what few others have along the coast: he offers very classy yet authentically homey Provençal cooking in a dreamy, sophisticated setting made for romance. He and his wife, Denise, have a flair for combining luxury and simplicity, working toward perfection in the presentation of a single fresh orchid, in the freshest of peach juice blended with vintage Champagne. One very warm evening in July a group of us—all dressed in cool white summer dresses and suits—enjoyed one of the more elegant, satisfying, and extravagant meals of our lives: whole truffles tucked inside zucchini blossoms, perfect sautéed fresh *cèpes,* the tiniest violet-tinged asparagus, perfect Mediterranean *rouget* infused with the flavors of orange and fennel, lamb that tasted like lamb. And just before we got up to leave, we were presented with an astonishing flavor that is pure Provence, whole sprigs of just-picked purple lavender blossoms, dipped in a blend of egg whites and sugar. (Directions: southeast of Mougins on the D3.)

MOUSTIERS-SAINTE-MARIE *(Alpes-de-Haute-Provence)*

Aix-en-Provence 86 k, Castellane 45 k, Digne 48 k, Draguignan 62 k, Manosque 50 k, Paris 820 k.

Market: Friday, 8 A.M. to 4 P.M., Place de l'Ecole.

POUR LA MAISON

ATELIER DE SEGRIES
04360 Moustiers-Sainte-
   Marie.
(92.74.66.69).
Open daily 10:30 A.M. to
   12:30 P.M. and 2 to 6 P.M.
   (7 P.M. in July and
   August).
Credit cards: AE, EC, V.
Will ship internationally.

Paris Connection:
ATELIER DE SEGRIES
31 Rue de Tournon, 75006
   Paris.
(46.34.62.56).

The tiny village of Moustiers—population 602—is rightly famed for its milky-white-glazed hand-painted *faïence,* or pottery, made there since 1679. The best (and most expensive) pottery comes from l'Atelier de Ségriès, which offers a wide choice of patterns, including those embellished with delicate Provençal wildflowers.

NICE *(Alpes-Maritimes)*

Cannes 32 k, Marseille 187 k, Paris 931 k,

Markets: Tuesday through Sunday, 7 A.M. to 1:30 P.M., Cours Saleya, Place
Pierre-Gauthier, Place du Général-de-Gaulle.
Fish market: Tuesday through Saturday, 5 A.M. to noon, Place Saint-François.
Flower market: Tuesday through Sunday, 7 A.M. to 5 P.M. (1:30 P.M. on Sunday),
Cours Saleya.
Market street: Rue Pairolière in the old section of town—cheeses, dried fruits,
cakes, fish, pasta, *porchetta.*
Flea market: Tuesday through Sunday, 8 A.M. to sunset, Boulevard Risso.

Neither the overheated *autoroutes* nor the crowds of the Côte-d'Azur can
begin to diminish the charm, authenticity, and enjoyment of this city's
famous open-air market stretched out along the Cours Saleya.

Stash your car in the underground parking lot beneath the marketplace, go
it on foot, and plan to make your tour at least a morning long, or if there's a
luxury of time, make it a day. You'll see things and taste things you won't find
elsewhere in France, you won't spend much money, and you will understand
how a single French city can still manage to support a style of food all its own.

Sheltered from the morning sun, the fruits and vegetables at one of the
country's freshest, liveliest food markets are protected by a still life of faded
striped umbrellas: The colors, the textures, the variety, will visually overwhelm.

Perfect specimens of golden-brown *cèpes,* covered with damp, dark earth,
are arranged with ultimate care on a bed of vine leaves set inside a worn wicker
basket. Nearby, *cocos blancs,* the fresh white beans encased in the palest of green
pods, are piled in sturdy wooden crates, ready to play their essential role in the
great Provençal soup known as *pistou.* Peppers, shiny red, green, and yellow,
await the frying pan, while tables are piled high with braids of plump garlic
called *violets de Provence,* with red onions, yellow onions, shallots, and the tiny
white bell-shaped onions the French call *grelots.* At another stand, golden-orange
zucchini blossoms, attached to firm, miniature zucchini, seem to be still alive,
opening slowly, ready to sing an aria to shoppers who pass by. White fist-size
boxes are filled to the brim with raspberries, black currants, and red currants,
still covered with droplets of morning dew.

Until well into June, you will see the rare *asperges violettes,* firm slim
asparagus that slowly fade, tip to stem, from the deepest of purples to the most
delicate of ivories, a sort of Technicolor that adds everything, and yet really
nothing at all, to one's gastronomic enjoyment. There are green string beans
mottled with purplish black, known both as *pélandrons* and *haricots gris,* thumb-
size gooseberries, and half a dozen kinds of potatoes.

And there is *socca. Socca* is to Nice as chicken is to Bresse, as sausage is to
Arles, as olives are to Nyons. *Socca* is a delicious, hot Provençal sort of crêpe
made with a thin, thin batter of chickpea flour, baked on flat round pans the

size of a tractor wheel. About every fifteen minutes throughout the market day, sizzling hot *socca* the color of a brilliant sunset is delivered to the Cours Saleya market from a hole-in-the-wall shop just a few blocks away.

The *socca,* along with *pissaladière* (a Niçois pizza topped with onions, anchovies, and black olives), arrives at Chez Thérèse's market stand, transported on the back of a customized bicycle. The delivery boy barely has time to unload the hot metal pans before customers swarm about. "Eat it while it's hot, it's no good cold," a local enthusiast shouts to a pair of first-timers.

If time permits, head off from the market down the streets of old Nice— along Rue de la Boucherie, passing the fish market at Place Saint-François, and up Rue Pairolière—long, winding alleyways lined with *charcuteries* boasting colorful whole stuffed pigs, or *porchetta,* with shops displaying ravioli and a dozen kinds of pastas, with dance studios and cheap clothing stores and restaurants advertising, in modest lettering, *"cuisine de famille."*

RESTAURANTS

L'ANE ROUGE
7 Quai des Deux-
   Emmanuel, 06000 Nice.
(93.89.49.63).
Last orders taken at 1:30 P.M.
   and 9:30 P.M.
Closed Saturday, Sunday,
   holidays, and the second
   week in July through
   August.
Credit card: AE, DC, V.
Terrace dining.
English spoken.
400 francs.

SPECIALTIES:
Moules farcies (stuffed mussels);
bourride provençale (creamy
garlic fish soup); assorted
Mediterranean fish and
shellfish.

Like *bouillabaisse,* a good *bourride* is hard to find, even on home ground. They're both expensive dishes to prepare, and long in the making. Perhaps because of the copious nature of the dish and the fanfare that accompanies its service, most diners sit in awe, forgetting to pass judgment on the quality of the ingredients or the execution.

The best restaurant-prepared *bourride* I've ever sampled was found at L'Ane Rouge, an elegant little restaurant set along the port of Nice off the road to Monaco.

The specialties of Nice: hot socca, *hot pizza.*

~~Here the *bourride*—a creamy fish soup pre-~~ pared with monkfish, sea bass, and John Dory—is served with proper fanfare, as part of a fine menu that also includes stuffed mussels, grilled lobster, and a variety of fish and shellfish preparations.

Place your order and the waiter will arrive with a large pink *serviette de bourride,* a ceremonial linen bib, and the classic *bourride* accompaniments, including tiny rounds of grilled toast, bowls of grated Gruyère, garlicky *aïoli* and sunset-orange *rouille,* vibrant sauces to flavor the feast to come.

Next, a giant white tureen appears, and the waiter carefully spoons out a bowl of creamy liquid, a rich blend of fish stock, garlic, and egg yolks. This is your first course, for lacing with *aïoli,* soaking your bread, sprinkling with grated cheese. Before you've had a chance to make a dent in the soup, the waiter arrives with a platter of assorted fish, for spooning, chunk by chunk, into the filling liquid. (Don't even consider ordering *bourride* unless your appetite is hearty and your stomach is empty.)

One can quibble about some of the elements of L'Ane Rouge's *bourride* (the sauces could be more assertive, the toast less stale), but the fact is, you're not likely to find better unless you make it yourself. The perfect wine to accompany all this is the local Bellet *blanc,* a light and agreeable wine of some finesse, seldom found outside the region.

LA BARALE
39 Rue Beaumont, 06000 Nice.
(93.89.17.94).
Last orders taken at 9 P.M.
Open for dinner only.
   Closed Sunday, Monday, and August.
No credit cards.
Air-conditioned.
Private dining room for 80.
A single 170-franc menu, wine and service included.

SPECIALTIES:
Niçois.

No other restaurant in Nice captures the flavor of traditional Niçois home cooking like La Barale, a funky tavern-like place presided over by the wiry, energetic octogenarian Catherine-Hélène Barale.

La Barale, with its nightly sing-alongs and assembly-line food, is like a tourist restaurant designed to please the locals, which it does. The whole place is an antique stage set: red checked curtains at the windows, old stone walls lined with a collection of antique bric-a-brac that must have taken a lifetime to assemble. There's a bevy of middle-aged waitresses flying through their chores by rote, clip-clopping along the patchwork-tiled floors in floppy slippers. The house German shepherd holds court, trying to trip anyone who gets in his way, occasionally succeeding.

The menu here is set: Everyone eats the same thing at the same time, night in and night out. The food, on the whole, lacks spontaneity and freshness, but there is a certain appealing robustness that keeps us all coming back.

Dinner begins with a very good *pissaladière,* the pizza-like specialty, with a fine, flaky crust covered with onions cooked to a purée and strewn with Niçois olives. Maize-colored *socca* comes next, hot and hearty portions of that crunchy blend of chickpea flour, olive oil, water, and salt. If you down it quickly and then appear a bit antsy, the waitress will offer seconds, serving you directly from the thin, flat pan in which the *socca* is cooked to a delicious scorch.

An uninspired *salade niçoise* follows, but ignore that to save room for the fine *ravioli niçoise,* rough, thick pockets of pasta filled with beef, pork, Swiss chard, and cheese. Next come giant platters of *lou piech* (veal poached and stuffed with eggs, chard, and cheese), served with dandelion greens.

But the best part of the meal is the *tourte de blettes,* a thin double-crusted tart filled with chard, pine nuts, and raisins, then sprinkled with a coating of sugar. It's a most pleasant dessert.

By the time you've hit the dessert, which also includes generous bowls of fresh oranges and apples, the well-oiled crowd has begun its nightly singalong. Pamphlets are passed out so that the uninitiated can join in.

LA MERENDA
4 Rue de la Terrasse, 06000 Nice.
(No telephone.)
Last orders taken at 1:30 P.M. and 9:30 P.M.
Closed Saturday dinner, Sunday, Monday, February, and August.
No credit cards.
English spoken.
About 150 francs.

Perhaps the finest and most authentic bistro in all of Nice is La Mérenda, located just steps from the Cours Saleya market. This is a tiny spot—it seats no more than twenty-four on bare wooden stools. There's no special decor, no telephone, no television, just authentic Niçois fare prepared in a postage-stamp-size kitchen that opens right into the dining room.

The menu, written on a chalkboard that's carted from table to table, will hit you like a welcome shot of sunshine: There's pizza and superb stuffed sardines, pasta smothered in the basil and garlic sauce known as *pistou,* and a marvelously

SPECIALTIES:
Niçois: *pâtes au pistou* (fresh
pasta with basil, garlic, and
olive oil), *daube* (beef stew),
sardines farcies (stuffed
sardines), *stockfish* (here a
blend of dried haddock,
tomatoes, potatoes, olives,
and pesto).

fresh salad of *mesclum*—a blend of eight dainty
greens—showered with Nice's finest olive oil, from
the *moulin* of Ludovic Alziari.

Their batter-dipped and deep-fried zucchini
blossoms are incredible (yes, just like eating a
flower, light and delicious), and this is one place in
the world to find an authentically prepared *stockfish,*
a blend of dried (but not salted) haddock, tomatoes,
potatoes, tiny Niçois olives, and a dab of pesto. It
bears all the olfactory charm of an already overripe
cheese left in a locked car in the summer heat, but
the taste is actually rather tame and quite appealing. If you're not known here and do decide to
order *stockfish,* one of Nice's favorite preparations,
you'll need to pass a test. You'll have to get up from
your stool, step into the kitchen, taste a sample with
a slice of bread, then give the go-ahead before they
proceed. If you say it's good, you've passed the test,
and the tall, lean chef will shake your hand.

Later, sample the young goat cheese sprinkled
with thyme and olive oil, and hope that the Cours
Saleya market has provided some dewy fresh berries
to offer the perfect ending to an already rather
perfect Provençal meal.

BAR RENE SOCCA
2 Rue Miralhétti, 06000
    Nice.
(93.62.37.81).
Last orders taken at 8 P.M.
Closed Monday, the last
    week in October through
    the first week in
    November, and the last
    three weeks in May.
Pedestrian-street dining.
50 francs.

SPECIALTIES:
Niçois; *pissaladière* (onion,
olive, and anchovy tart),
sardines farcies (stuffed
sardines), *socca* (chickpea
tart).

At the very end of Rue Pairolière you'll find René
Socca, Nice's king of *socca.* Here everything
from fried stuffed zucchini blossoms to classic
pizza, as well as *socca,* is sold from an ever-busy
sidewalk carry-out window. Get on line, don't forget
to take an extra napkin, and call out for a slice of
socca: For about 8 francs, they'll scrape a generous
portion of the golden, sizzling crêpe onto a plain
paper plate. You can take your place on one of the
stools scattered along the pedestrian walkway, then
order up a glass or a carafe of thin Provençal rosé.

BOULANGERIES

ESPUNO
22 Rue Vernier, 06000 Nice.
(93.88.83.33).
Open 7 A.M. to 12:45 P.M.
and 3:30 to 8 P.M. Closed
Sunday, Monday, two
weeks in February, and
three weeks in August.

LE FOUR A BOIS
35 Rue Droite, 06300 Nice.
(93.80.50.67).
Open 7 A.M. to 1 P.M. and
3:30 to 8 P.M. Closed
Sunday afternoon and
Monday.

SPECIALITES REGIONALES

ALLEES DE LA COTE D'AZUR
1 Rue Saint-François-
de-Paule, 06000 Nice.
(93.85.87.30).
Open 7:30 A.M. to 7 P.M.
Closed Sunday afternoon,
Monday, and October.

HENRI AUER
7 Rue Saint-François-
de-Paule, 06300 Nice.
(93.85.77.98).
Open 8 A.M. to 12:30 P.M.
and 2:30 to 7:30 P.M.
Closed Monday morning.
Credit card: V.
Will ship internationally.

You won't believe the variety of breads at Espuno and Le Four à Bois—thirty in all. The bakers, André Espuno and his sons, even offer a bread menu! Their dense, full-flavored olive bread is my favorite, but there are also loaves, big and small, flavored with thyme, garlic, onions, or Roquefort; walnut bread; and of course the flat lace-like Provençal specialty, *fougasse*.

Thierry and Jean-Jacques Auer, candy kings of Nice.

One of the most surprising—and most unusual—foods I've ever eaten are *capons* (which means "tiny" in the local dialect), deliciously sweet and intensely fruity dried figs wrapped in fig leaves and tied with raffia. You'll find them at this strange little store that sells a mix of hardware, candies, and postcards.

A lovely spot to stop for tea, coffee, dessert, and to pick up a package of *fruits confits,* or candied fruits, to take home. Try especially their remarkable *confiture de clementines confites,* a rich jam prepared with candied clementines. Breakfast will never be the same again!

What Is This Thing Called Mesclum?

"*However mesclum is grown, no matter its composition, the idea is to present a multi-colored, multi-textured salad with a subtle contrast of flavors, ranging from feathery and delicate to pungent and assertive.*"

CARROS, JULY 27—Some say *mesclum*. Others say *mesclun*. Some insist that this fashionable Provençal salad is a blend of a dozen different greens, all sown, grown, and picked together. Jean and Yvonne Tabo, *maraîchers,* or market gardeners, who were among the first to grow *mesclum* commercially in France, insist otherwise.

Yvonne Tabo is categorical: It's called *mesclum*. It's a blend of nine different tender greens (except in winter, when the number grows to ten), each grown in a separate row, then tossed together in approximately equal proportions as they're picked. And if you want each of the greens to have the right texture and flavor, you pick them very small and very young.

The Tabos, who live in Carros, the herb- and vegetable-growing region just north of Nice, switched from selling vegetables to growing them about ten years ago. They settled on *mesclum* because at the time no one was growing this tradition-ally Niçois salad mixture commercially. Today their lettuce is savored not just in France, but from Copenhagen to London, Berlin to Toronto, where it is flown three times each week, year round, from the Nice airport nearby.

The Tabos' *mesclum,* grown in impeccably neat rows in a series of low open-sided greenhouses, includes both red- and green-tipped oak-leaf lettuce, rocket, ro-maine, chervil, both a slightly curly white endive and a firmer, very curly green va-riety, escarole, and a very bitter variety of dandelion. In the wintertime they add a few rows of colorful red treviso, the firm and bitter green that takes its name from the Italian town of Treviso.

"For some reason, when we grow treviso here in the summertime the leaves won't turn red, and it doesn't taste the same," explains Madame Tabo.

The salad is picked early in the morning, and only the youngest, tenderest shoots are selected. The greens are plunged, all together, directly into a water bath, then drained and packed gently for market, carefully arranged in sturdy wooden crates.

No one seems absolutely sure about the history of *mesclum*. Some historians suggest the salad blend came across the border to Nice from the Ligurian region of Italy before Nice was reunited with France in 1860. Once in Nice, the salad be-came known as *mesclun* in French, *mesclum* in the Niçois dialect called *nissarde*.

The Tabos and others in the region remember that their parents and grand-parents always grew a blend of greens in the family *potager,* or vegetable garden, then mixed them with all the wild and domestic herbs that grow so naturally and profusely in the area.

During the late 1940s, as restaurants proliferated along the Côte-d'Azur, *mes-clum* grew in popularity and also became better known outside of Provence. Today *maraîchers* like the Tabos have plenty of company here north of Nice, where the terraced hillsides are covered with row upon row of greenhouses, shelters for the tons of herbs, lettuces, tomatoes, and zucchini blossoms that are grown in the hot, humid climate year round.

However *mesclum* is grown, no matter its composition, the idea is to present a multi-colored, multi-textured salad with a subtle contrast of flavors, ranging from feathery and delicate to pungent and assertive. A home-composed *mesclum* salad might include peppery nasturtium blossoms, firm-leafed *pourpier* (purslane), *mâche* (lamb's lettuce), *senneson* (chickweed), and parsley, as well as a few leaves of basil, summer savory, and lavender-tipped hyssop.

Purists, such as the Tabos, insist that neither vegetables, croutons, nor cheese should be added to this already complex mixture, and that the salad should be tossed by hand after sprinkling it with a thoroughly uncomplicated vinaigrette consisting of nothing but virgin olive oil, homemade red wine vinegar, salt, pepper, and perhaps a touch of Dijon mustard.

The colorful salad appears as both *mesclum* and *mesclun* on menus throughout the area, and also shows up in the outdoor fruit and vegetable markets throughout the region. The best place to find *mesclum* is in Nice's Cours Saleya market, which is held every morning but Monday, when it is replaced by an active and popular flea market.

Commercially blended *mesclum* seeds, usually a mixture of five or six greens, can be purchased at seed shops and in markets throughout France. The various seeds can also be purchased in individual packets. One of the better seed companies is Vilmorin, with a shop at 4 Quai Mégisserie, 75001 Paris (42.33.61.62).

A bird's-eye view of the market in Nice.

Ludovic Alziari in his shop.

ALZIARI

14 Rue Saint-
  François-de-Paule, 06300
  Nice.
(93.85.76.92).
The olive oil mill, 332–334
  Boulevard de la
  Madeleine, 06000 Nice.
(93.44.45.12).
Both boutique and mill
  open 8:15 A.M. to 12:30
  P.M. and 2:15 to 9:30 P.M.
  Closed Sunday, Monday,
  and the second week in
  November through the
  first week in December.
Will ship internationally.

S P E C I A L T Y:
Huile d'olives (olive oil).

Ludovic Alziari presses one of my favorite olive oils, light and mildly fruity, packaged in a decorative bright blue tin that you'll keep as a souvenir. This shop is a classic, full of the good tastes and scents of Provence: olive oil, tiny cured Niçois olives, the flavorful green *olives vertes picholines de Provence,* olive oil soap, and lavender honey.

OPIO *(Alpes-Maritimes)*

Cannes 22 k, Grasse 7 k, Mougins 15 k, Vallauris 23 k.

SPECIALITES REGIONALES

HUILERIE DE LA BRAGUE
2 Route de Châteauneuf,
  06650 Opio.
(93.77.23.03).
Open 8:30 A.M. to noon and
  2 to 6 P.M. Closed Sunday,
  and mid-October
  through mid-November.
Credit card: V.
Will ship internationally.

A sort of one-stop shop for the specialties of Provence, this olive oil mill offers first-class oil, olives, olivewood bowls, Provençal linens and clothing, you name it.

PEILLON *(Alpes-Maritimes)*

Contes 13 k, L'Escarène 13 k, Menton 33 k, Nice 19 k, Paris 954 k,
Sospel 35 k.

RESTAURANT

**AUBERGE DE LA
MADONE**
Peillon-Village, 06440
L'Escarène.
(93.79.91.1 /).
Last orders taken at 2 P.M.
and 9 P.M..
Closed Wednesday, and
mid-October to
mid-December.
No credit cards.
Terrace dining.
Private dining room for 10
to 30.
English spoken.
Menus from 80 to 160
francs. A la carte, 250
francs including wine
and service.

SPECIALTIES:
*Salade de primeurs au fromage
blanc* (mixed greens and
vegetable salad with fresh
cheese); *daube de boeuf à
l'orange et aux cèpes* (Provençal
beef stew with orange zest and
wild mushrooms); *carré
d'agneau au thym* (rack of lamb
with thyme).

Settled in at this quiet, old-fashioned country *auberge,* you would never imagine you were just a few kilometers from the bustle of Nice. From the olive-tree-shaded terrace of the Auberge de la Madone, you look out on the village of Peillon, one of the most spectacular hillside villages in the Nice hinterlands. You'll feel as though you're far, far from modern civilization—until, of course, the food arrives, good home-style regional fare prepared with care and love. The menu varies according to the seasons, and the waiter may play a role in your choice (they don't always have everything that's on the menu that day), but I doubt you'll be disappointed. We loved the *lapin à la grand-mère,* moist sautéed rabbit served with *ratatouille* and a fine gratin of potatoes, zucchini, and red peppers; and the *pintade aux pêches,* roasted guinea fowl served with perfect poached peaches. Also try the delicious local goat cheese in oil and the sturdy local red wine. Both the wine and the olive oil, from the local mill, can be purchased at the *auberge.*

A summer scene, Saint-Tropez.

SAINT-TROPEZ *(Var)*

Aix-en-Provence 120 k, Brignoles 63 k, Cannes 75 k, Draguignan 50 k, Paris 878 k, Toulon 69 k.

Market: Tuesday and Saturday, 8 A.M. to 12:30 P.M., Place des Lices.

RESTAURANT

MAS DE CHASTELAS
Domaine Bertaud, 83990
  Saint-Tropez.
(94.56.09.11).
Last orders taken at 2:30 P.M.
  (lunch reserved for hotel
  clients only) and 11 P.M.
Open daily. Closed October
  through March.
Credit cards: AE, DC, EC, V.
Terrace and poolside dining.
Private dining room for 30.
English spoken.
A single 240-franc menu.

S P E C I A L T I E S :
Regional fish and a table of
desserts de Paulette.

Oh how I long to return to this intimate, restrained, romantic little spot, a pale pink stucco restored *magnanerie,* or silkworm-rearing house, just outside of Saint-Tropez. Settle into white wicker chairs at poolside and sip Champagne and nibble delicious thyme-flecked black olives as you select your evening's meal from the tempting, but limited, menu. Later, as you move on to the jasmin-scented, romantically lit veranda for a fine regional feast, you'll find you can't take your eyes off the symphony of desserts set out on a long table—we counted eight kinds of fruit tarts, including strawberry, wild strawberry, apricot, apple, lemon, peach, raspberry, and a pear *clafoutis.* Making an effort to save room for what's to come, you'll dive into a fresh, fresh salad of lamb marinated in a zingy mint vinaigrette; filets of tiny *rouget,* or red mullet, flavored with pitted black olives, fresh fava beans, squash, and a sprinkling of chervil; as well as a fine stewed chicken served with a spectacular *timbale*-size gratin that combines zucchini with a goat cheese custard. (Directions: 3 kilometers west of Saint-Tropez on the Route de Gassin.)

CAFES

CAFE DES ARTS
Place des Lices, 83990
  Saint-Tropez.
(94.97.02.25).
Open 8:30 A.M. to 8:30 P.M.
  September through June
  (to 4 A.M. in July and
  August).

Do not go to Saint-Tropez without wandering over to the classy Café des Arts, one of the liveliest spots in town, where you can linger on the sycamore-tree-shaded terrace to watch French celebrities play *boules.* Summer Saturday mornings are particularly active, when the outdoor market—featuring food, clothing, as well as a pretty good flea market—takes over the square.

SENEQUIER
Quai Jean-Jaurès, 83990
    Saint-Tropez.
(94.97.00.90).
Open daily, 8 A.M. to
    midnight.

Sitting at the most famous café in Saint-Tropez is sort of like sitting on Paris's Saint-Germain-des-Prés, but instead of watching people stroll by, you admire some of the most beautiful, and coddled, boats in the world. A rare touch of summertime magic.

PATISSERIE

SENEQUIER
4 Place aux Herbes, 83990
    Saint-Tropez.
(94.97.00.90).
Open 8 A.M. to 12:30 P.M.
    and 2:30 to 8 P.M. Closed
    mid-November to
    mid-December.
Will ship internationally.

Do not leave Saint-Tropez without sampling Senequier's famous *nougat blanc,* some of the freshest, most homemade-tasting I've ever sampled. Their soft, not-too-sweet confection is filled with the soothing flavors of honey, chunks of almonds, and whole green pistachios. It's no wonder they've been winning medals for it since 1889. I tried to get them to part with the recipe, but to no avail. I was told, kindly, it was "Topppp Secrette."

Café des Arts, Saint-Tropez.

POUR LA MAISON

**GALERIES
    TROPEZIENNES**
56 Rue Gambetta, 83990
    Saint-Tropez.
(94.97.02.21).
Open 9:30 A.M. to 12:30 P.M.
    and 1:30 to 7:30 P.M.
    Closed Sunday and
    Monday from November
    through February.
Credit cards: AE, DC, EC, V.
Will ship internationally.

A luxury bazaar, offering a wide range of beautiful and beautifully designed objects, including kitchenware, linens, lingerie, and both men's and women's casual clothing.

SISTERON (Alpes-de-Haute-Provence)

Barcelonnette 97 k, Digne 39 k, Gap 48 k, Paris 703 k.

Market: Wednesday and Saturday, 8 A.M. to 1 P.M., Place du Docteur-Robert
(also called Place de l'Horloge).
Fair: Second Saturday of each month.

BOULANGERIE

R. BERNAUDON
37 Rue Droite, 04200
Sisteron.
(92.61.12.33).
Open 6 A.M. to 1 P.M. and
2:30 to 7:30 P.M. Closed
Sunday, Monday
(October through May),
and June.

Try to visit Sisteron on market day, when farmers gather around the beautiful Place de l'Horloge, then wander over to Monsieur Bernaudon's bakery to sample the wonderful *fougasse à l'anchois,* like a puff pastry pizza covered with salty anchovies.

CONFISERIE

CANTEPERDRIX
Place de la République,
04200 Sisteron.
(92.61.08.41).
Open 9 A.M. to noon and 2
to 7 P.M. daily.
Will ship internationally.

In pastry shops all over France, you'll find Canteperdrix's delicious almond paste candies known as *calissons.* I find theirs tastier than the better-known version from Aix-en-Provence, for they're just a bit more almondy. Try also their nougat, the Provençal candy of egg white, honey, and nuts.

VALLAURIS (Alpes-Maritimes)

Antibes 8 k, Cannes 6 k, Grasse 18 k, Nice 31 k, Paris 915 k.

Market: Wednesday and Sunday, 8 A.M. to noon, Avenue de Cannes.

POUR LA MAISON

FOUCARD JOURDAN
65 bis Avenue Georges-
Clémenceau, 06220
Vallauris. (93.63.74.92).
Open 10 A.M. to noon and
3 to 5:30 P.M. September
through June; 9 A.M. to
7:30 P.M. July and August.
Closed Sunday.
Credit cards: AE, EC, V.
Will ship internationally.

Vallauris is one giant pottery shop, and this is one of the most tasteful shops in town, featuring traditional Provençal pottery, clay cookware, baskets, glassware, and local fabrics.

VILLENEUVE-LOUBET *(Alpes-Maritimes)*

Antibes 12 k, Cannes 23 k, Grasse 23 k, Nice 16 k,
Paris 923 k, Vence 12 k.

MUSEE

**MUSEE DE L'ART
CULINAIRE**
06270 Villeneuve-Loubet
(Village).
(93.20.80.51).
Open 2 to 6 P.M. Closed
Sunday, Monday, and
November.
Admission: 10 francs for
adults, 5 francs for
students and groups of
20 or more.

Next time you visit Nice, set aside a few minutes to visit this very personal museum set up in the birthplace of Auguste Escoffier, one of the most influential French chefs in the history of cooking. The charming museum is crammed with all sorts of cooking gadgets (he was crazy about roasting foods over an open fire, and even invented various cooking paraphernalia) and old menus, and you're sure to learn all sorts of odd facts. Monsieur Escoffier's wife was so embarrassed by the fact that she had married a lowly cook that when he published cookbooks, she added poems to elevate the level of their contents! We also discovered that around 1892 in London the chef invented the dish *pêche Melba* for the singer Nelly Melba. As the story goes, she was so passionate about ice cream that she overindulged from time to time. Also, all that cold was bad for her vocal chords. The chef managed to create a "lightened" dessert that would help her to reduce the quantity of ice cream she consumed as well as warm up the dish a bit, by combining poached peaches, a touch of ice cream, and a raspberry sauce. Monsieur Escoffier traveled a good deal, and in one photo we find him posing with a group of mushroom growers in Pennsylvania.

Senequier, Saint-Tropez.

SALADE NICOISE

This is my personal version of salade niçoise. *The secret of success is simple: Use the best, freshest ingredients available (in particular, don't skimp on the quality of the oil or the vinegar), and be sure to carefully layer all the ingredients in a very large, rather shallow bowl. The ingredients can be layered in advance and dressed and tossed thoroughly at the very last minute. It's certainly a meal all on its own.*

Vinaigrette:

3 cloves garlic, finely minced

¼ cup (60 ml) best-quality red wine vinegar

Salt and freshly ground black pepper to taste

½ cup (125 ml) extra-virgin olive oil

Salad:

1 pound (4 to 5; 500 g) small potatoes

1 pound (500 grams) young green beans, trimmed

1 can flat anchovy fillets (2 ounces; 57 g)

6 scallions or small white onions

1 red bell pepper, seeded

4 hard-cooked eggs

5 medium tomatoes

1 can (6½ ounces; 195 g) water-packed albacore tuna

1 quart (1 liter) loosely packed crisp lettuce, such as romaine or curly endive, rinsed and dried

½ cup (125 ml) whole oil-cured black olives

Handful of mixed fresh herbs, preferably flat-leaf parsley, chervil, tarragon, and rosemary, finely minced

1. Prepare the vinaigrette: Whisk the garlic, vinegar, salt, and pepper together in a small bowl. Add the oil and whisk until emulsified.

2. Prepare the salad: Boil the potatoes until just soft. Drain and set aside to cool. Blanch the green beans and rinse under cold water to stop the cooking. Drain and set aside. Drain the anchovies, soak them in water for several minutes, then drain again, and pat dry.

3. Thinly slice into rounds the potatoes, scallions, bell pepper, and peeled eggs.

4. Cut the green beans into bite-size pieces and the tomatoes into wedges. Flake the tuna.

5. Layer the salad ingredients in a large, shallow bowl in this order: the greens, potatoes, beans, scallions, pepper, tomatoes, tuna, olives, eggs, anchovies, and herbs. At the table, add the vinaigrette and toss gently but thoroughly. Serve immediately.

Yield: 8 servings.

Languedoc
LANGUEDOC

A fisherman repairs his nets in Port-Vendres.

The Languedoc is the land of sunshine and espadrilles, peaches and red cherries, fresh-cured anchovies and meaty Bouzigues mussels. Bordered by the Pays Catalan to the west and the marshy Camargue to the east, the Languedoc encompasses a myriad of cultures, each with its own special Mediterranean accent. The cuisine here, not surprisingly, favors the fruits of the sea, yet certain dishes—such as the earthy Catalan snail feast known as *cargolade* and the heady Camarguais *gardiane,* a stew of bull meat, red wine, and black olives—help give the Languedoc a uniquely rustic regional flair. Add to this the tiny piquant goat cheese Pélardon and the world-famous Roquefort blue, and all you need is a bottle of wine (perhaps a velvety red Collioure) to complete the scene.

Of all the regions in France, the Languedoc poses some of the most dramatic contrasts. I fell in love with the Catalan villages of Céret and Collioure, and with the city of Perpignan, with its vast canals bordered with bright, pastel-flowered oleanders. But with equal passion I loathed the region's crowded *autoroutes,* the vast parks of campers, the seedy seaport of Sète, and the series of newly fashioned summer resort towns along the coast, towns like La Grande-Motte, with its abrasive pyramid-shaped structures.

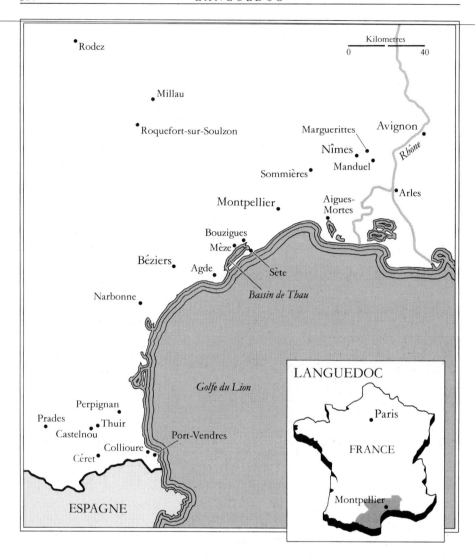

Wherever you go, anticipate contrasts, such as I experienced one evening during my last visit to the ancient village of Aigues-Mortes. After feasting on *gardiane* and goat cheese, I went for a walk in the moonlight and soon found myself seated in stadium, watching the region's favorite summer sport, *taureau piscine*. It's a strange "game," in which amateur bullfighters try to lure a raging bull into a makeshift swimming pool, then risk their lives by standing in the pool with the bull. Any place where they serve you bull, and then suggest you watch one be made a fool of, surely has a strange sense of humor!

WHEN YOU GO

Michelin Green Guides: *Provence* (available in English), *Pyrénées/Roussillon,* and *Gorges du Tarn.*

Getting there: Air Inter offers three daily 1-hour flights to Perpignan, leaving from either Paris's Orly Ouest airport or from the Roissy (Charles-de-Gaulle) airport. There are also at least five TGV *(trains à grande vitesse),* or bullet trains, making the 5-hour journey between Paris's Gare de Lyon and Montpellier, stopping at Nîmes 30 minutes before Montpellier. Cars can be rented at the airport and train stations.

Getting around: Michelin map 240 (Languedoc/Roussillon).

Best time to visit: Roads, villages, and markets can become hopelessly crowded during July and August weekends. In June, September, and early October, one can still take advantage of long days and the warmth of the sun, without the crowds.

MARKETS
(Liveliest markets are marked with an asterisk.)

Monday: Alès, Béziers, Bourg-Madame, Castelnaudary, Elne, Montpellier, Perpignan, Sète.

Tuesday: Béziers, Carcassonne, Couiza, Cuxac-d'Aude, Fabrezan, Ganges, *Leucate, Montpellier, Nîmes, Perpignan, *Roquebrun, Saint-Jean-du-Gard, Villefranche-de-Conflent.

Wednesday: Aigues-Mortes, *Bagnols-sur-Cèze, Collioure, Cuxac-d'Aude, Elne, Ille-sur-Têt, Manduel, Montpellier, Perpignan, Quillan, *Sète.

Thursday: *Agde, Anduze, Banyuls-sur-Mer, Beaucaire, Béziers, Carcassonne, Cuxac-d'Aude, *Fabrezan, *Frontignan, Mèze, Montpellier, *Narbonne, Perpignan, Saint-Gilles, Tuchan.

Friday: *Béziers, Cuxac-d'Aude, *Elne, Fabrezan, *Ganges, Ille-sur-Têt, Leucate, Limoux, Montpellier, *Nîmes, Perpignan, Remoulins, *Roquebrun, Sète.

Saturday: Banyuls-sur-Cèze, *Carcassonne, *Céret, Cuxac-d'Aude, *Frontignan, Lodève, Montpellier, Perpignan, Pézenas, Pont-Saint-Esprit, Port-Vendres, Quillan, Sommières, Thuir, Uzès.

Sunday: Aigues-Mortes, Banyuls-sur-Mer, Beaucaire, Collioure, Frontignan, Narbonne, *Perpignan, *Saint-Gilles.

FAIRS AND FESTIVALS

Pentecost: *Fête de la Féria* (bull festival), Nîmes.

First Friday in July: *Foire à l'Ail Rose* (pink garlic fair), Lautrec.

First Sunday in July: *Fête de la Mer* (fishermen's festival), Palavas-les-Flots.

The week starting July 21: *Foire de Beaucaire* (bull festival), Beaucaire.

AIGUES-MORTES *(Gard)*

Arles 47 k, Montpellier 29 k, Nîmes 41 k, Paris 749 k.

Market: Wednesday and Sunday, 7:30 A.M. to noon, just outside the walls of the town.

Arrive at the market in Aigues-Mortes early on a summer morning, before the heat pounds down and while the beachcombers are still in bed! In mid-July the air smells of melons, *hirondelles* (swallows) flutter around the striking crenelated ramparts of this thirteenth-century fortified town, and the locals go about their daily business, buying melons so ripe they've split open, along with mounds of fragrant local peaches and apricots.

RESTAURANT

LA CAMARGUE
19 Rue de la République,
    30220 Aigues-Mortes.
(66.53.86.88).
Last orders taken at 10 P.M.
Closed for lunch except
    Sunday. Closed Monday
    off-season, and the first
    week in January through
    the first week in
    February.
Credit cards: AE, DC, V.
Terrace dining.
90- and 132-franc menus. A
    la carte, 200 francs.

SPECIALTIES:
Tellines (tiny clams), *violets*
(soft, iodine-strong shellfish),
gardiane (here, a stew of bull
and black olives).

Preparing the fire, La Camargue.

Don't go to Aigues-Mortes without stopping for dinner at this friendly, casual family restaurant, where regional fare is served under spreading fig trees festooned with bright red and green lights. In the warmer months the mood is set by the giant open-air grill, the friendly waiters, and tables full of families out to have a very good time.

    This fine regional landmark is the place to go when you're very, very hungry, for courses arrive in rapid succession. Everyone begins with *crudités,* huge baskets of raw vegetables for dipping into bowls of vinaigrette, for munching with thick slices of country bread grilled over the open fire. Next there may be *tellines* (bowls of tiny clams the size of a fingernail, sautéed in olive oil with plenty of garlic), omelets blended with *violets* (an unusual, iodine-strong, soft-shelled sea creature), as well as grilled lamb chops served with bowls of *pommes de terre sous la cendre* (potatoes cooked in fiery ash). The brave will order the *gardiane,* served with the nutty local rice, *riz de Camargue.*

There will be platters of local goat cheese, bowls of fresh fruit, and bottles of refreshing *gris de gris,* the local low-alcohol rosé-style wine. Later, around dessert time, a group of gypsy guitar players arrive to serenade the happy crowd.

BOUZIGUES *(Hérault)*

Agde 20 k, Montpellier 34 k, Paris 789 k, Sète 18 k.

RESTAURANT

LA COTE BLEUE
34140 Bouzigues.
(67.78.30.87).
Last orders taken at 2 P.M.
and 9:30 P.M.
Closed Sunday dinner and
Monday July through
August, Tuesday dinner
and Wednesday
September through June,
February, and the third
week of October.
Credit cards: EC, V.
Terrace dining.
Private dining room for 16.
English spoken.
About 200 francs.

SPECIALTIES:
Fish and shellfish.

I love this large, bright, and casual family fish restaurant that overlooks the glistening mussel and oyster beds in the saltwater lagoon known as the Bassin de Thau. One Sunday afternoon in July we sat on the shaded veranda, sharing you-can't-get-any-fresher platters of fish and shellfish, including the flat oysters from Bouzigues (iodine-rich and delicious), tiny clams, sweet crab, langoustines, chewy *bulots* and *buccins* (we call them whelks), and, of course, local mussels. The *moules de Bouzigues* are meaty and large and ideal for eating on the half shell. Even those who aren't particularly fond of raw mussels ought to try these.

Other specialties include the *rillettes de Thau,* a compact, lemon-scented fish terrine blending herbs, smoked salmon, and an assortment of rockfish (see recipe, following page), mussels stuffed with sausage and simmered in tomato sauce, and the rare, tiny *cigales de mer,* or sea crickets, tender crayfish-like creatures served, most simply, grilled.

RILLETTES DE THAU LA COTE BLEUE
LA COTE BLEUE'S RILLETTES DE THAU

One hot summer afternoon we were driving out of the Mediterranean seaport of Sète and left the crowded highway in hopes of finding a less-traveled route. Quite by accident, we happened upon La Côte Bleue, a bright family fish restaurant overlooking the picturesque mussel and oyster beds in the Bassin de Thau, a large saltwater lagoon. Having just eaten lunch elsewhere, we settled for coffee on La Côte Bleue's terrace. But as the week went on, I could not get the restaurant out of my mind. So the schedule was rearranged to work in a meal there before leaving the region. La Côte Bleue did not disappoint. That Sunday afternoon in July, we sampled the rillettes—actually a mosaic-like fish terrine—as a first course. The rich terrine, which should be served in thin slices, has a remarkably fresh and lemony tang, and the smoked salmon adds color and gives depth to the flavor. Chef Olivier Lombard uses a variety of local rockfish, such as rouget grondin, rascasse, and rouget barbet. Any firm white-fleshed fish can be used, such as red snapper, rock cod, striped bass, or sea bass. Serve with a chilled white wine or a fresh rosé.

Salt
1 whole red snapper or
    rock cod, dressed
    (3 to 4 pounds; 1.5
    to 2 kg), or 1 pound
    10 ounces (750 g)
    rockfish fillets
1 ½ cups (12 ounces;
    360 g) unsalted
    butter, at room
    temperature
3 large egg yolks
2 tablespoons virgin
    olive oil
⅓ cup (80 ml) freshly
    squeezed lemon juice
Handful of fresh chives,
    minced
3 ½ ounces (100 g)
    smoked salmon,
    coarsely chopped
Freshly ground black
    pepper to taste

1. Measure enough water into a fish poacher or large pot to cover the fish. Add 1 tablespoon salt for each 2 quarts (2 liters) of water. Heat to a boil, then reduce the heat to medium. Add the fish and poach, adjusting the heat to keep the liquid just below a boil, until the flesh flakes readily and turns opaque instead of translucent. This should take about 10 minutes for a whole fish, 5 to 6 minutes for fillets. Drain the fish and set aside to cool. Discard the cooking liquid.

2. Using a food processor or electric mixer, process or mix the butter until soft and smooth. Add the egg yolks, oil, lemon juice, and chives one ingredient at a time, blending well after each addition.

3. Fillet the poached fish, discarding the skin and bones, then break the fillets into ½-inch (1 cm) pieces. You should have about 4 cups (1000 ml) loosely packed fish.

4. Using a wooden spoon, carefully but thoroughly fold the fish and smoked salmon into the butter mixture, making sure the fish is well coated with the butter mixture. Season with salt and pepper.

5. Spoon the mixture into a large loaf pan, about 10 x 4 inches (25.5 x 10 cm). Smooth the top and cover securely. Refrigerate until firm, about 6 hours. This dish should be eaten within a day or two of preparation.

6. To serve, cut into thin slices and serve with toast and lemon wedges.

Yield: 12 to 14 servings

MUSEE

**MUSEE DE LA
CONCHYLICULTURE**
4 Rue Saint-Nicolas, 34140
Bouzigues.
(67.78.30.12).
Open daily 10 A.M. to noon
and 2 to 7 P.M.
Admission: 10 francs for
adults, 7 francs for
children under age 11,
7 francs per person for
adult groups.

This tiny museum is devoted to fishing activities along the Bassin de Thau, where shellfish have been cultivated since Hellenic times. Since World War II fishing has become an even more important industry here, and today some 900 workers are supported by *conchyliculture,* the breeding of oysters and mussels. The museum offers a fascinating display of all the paraphernalia used to raise those prized mollusks, as well as an excellent videocassette explaining (in French) the miscellaneous fishery activities in the area, including a discussion of the new attempts to raise shrimp in the lagoon's constantly moving waters.

CASTELNOU *(Pyrénées-Orientales)*

Céret 29 k, Paris 926 k, Perpignan 19 k, Prades 37 k.

RESTAURANT

L'HOSTAL
Castelnou, 66300 Thuir.
(68.53.45.42).
Last orders taken at 2 P.M.
and 9 P.M. September
through June (10 P.M. in
July and August).
Closed Monday, Wednesday
dinner, and January
through March.
No credit cards.
Terrace dining in July and
August.
English spoken in July and
August.
80- to 150-franc menus. A la
carte, 80 to 200 francs.

SPECIALTIES:
Cargolade (Catalan mixed grill
of snails, sausage, and lamb
chops), *poulet à la catalane*
(chicken with tomatoes and
peppers), *boules de Picoulat*
(meatballs served with cooked
white beans).

Some people call the hillside Catalan village of Castelnou a Saint-Paul-de-Vence without the crowds. That's stretching it a bit, but this northern Pyrénées artists' village southwest of Perpignan makes for a perfect weekend ramble—the steep medieval walled town of 159 inhabitants invites wandering through its narrow streets, with an obligatory stop at the small, family-run L'Hostal.

This is a simple, rustic restaurant, with a spacious terrace offering a spectacular view of the Roussillon, and a homey Catalan-inspired interior. On weekends, when remote spots like this are at their lively best, the restaurant takes on a festive air, its tables filled with local French families out for a special meal.

This is certainly one of the few restaurants in France to offer the regional Catalan feast known as *cargolade,* a super-copious mixed grill that includes the hearty local (not imported) fresh (not canned) snails, plump grilled pork sausages, and lamb chops. Here, as at many local summer festivals, the fragrant *cargolade* is cooked outdoors on a huge brick grill over quick-burning vine clippings, or *sarments de vigne.* Guests are welcome to join in the festivities, if only as onlookers. The tiny snails, known as *petits gris,* are stuffed with a blend of bread, herbs, oil, vinegar, and garlic, then cooked on a round custom-made wire grill. They arrive at your table sizzling away, to be plucked from the shells and dipped into a garlicky *aïoli.* The mixed grill, known here as *cargolade monstre,* goes well with a simple and refreshing *salade catalane,* a blend of greens, anchovies from nearby Collioure, peppers, and tomatoes. Another local specialty is *boules de Picoulat,* nicely seasoned meatballs served with cooked white beans.

Service is efficient and friendly, and the price of the *cargolade* (which must be ordered in advance) includes all the local red wine you can drink.

Before or after your meal, take the time to wander down to the foot of the village to visit the charming Eglise de Fontcouverte, which is surrounded by an intriguing cemetery set under an enormous live oak.

On the streets of Aigues-Mortes.

Moules de Bouzigues

"*L*ike a stark, exotic Japanese painting that says it all in a few strokes, Bouzigues says it all with a few sticks sprouting from the water."

BOUZIGUES, JULY 21—This is the kind of place that could be called a brand-name town, like Camembert or Cognac—places with gastronomic reputations that surpass their touristic worth.

Bouzigues—as in *moules de Bouzigues*—might well bill itself as the mussel capital of France. This Languedoc village at the northern tip of the Bassin de Thau cultivates one third of France's mussel crop, a crop that totals more than 80,000 tons each year.

In contrast to the nearby Mediterranean port of Sète, with its overcrowded streets, bleak quayside restaurants, and oil refineries, Bouzigues—population 904—is calm, clean, and beautiful. A romantic, moody sort of beautiful, with a gray-blue saltwater lagoon that fades gently into the sandy blue haze of the sky, and vineyards that crowd right up to the water's edge. Like a stark, exotic Japanese painting that says it all in a few strokes, Bouzigues says it all with a few sticks sprouting from the water.

As you drive along the N113 just east of town, row after orderly row of stilt-like frames jut out from the lagoon. If you did not know they were raising mussels and oysters out there, you would be confused, for the brownish-gray frames resemble strange stationary rafts. They appear at once inaccessible and abandoned. But it is from these frames that France's biggest, darkest, fleshiest mussels—clinging to hundreds of nets and sticks attached to cords hanging down into the shallow lagoon—are brought to maturity.

Unlike the smaller Atlantic coast *moules de bouchot,* which grow clinging to fat oak poles driven into the sediment of shallow coastal beds, Bouzigues mussels grow in suspension. Hanging on tight with the bundles of tough, hair-like fibers we call the beard, the mussel clings to wooden sticks or metal rods dangling in the water. Some mussels also grow encased in nets several meters long, nets that expand month after month as the blue-bearded bivalves grow, producing bright orange, succulent meat encased in violet-tinged, blackish shells.

As the mussels hang in suspension, they profit from the lagoon's slow-moving current, enhanced by the wind, ensuring a steady supply of food in the form of plankton. As they capture their food, they filter water at a rapid pace; some mussels filter at the rate of 57 liters (15 gallons) a day. Every few months, the nets and poles are thinned, and the younger mussels are put back into the water.

They grow slowly, very slowly. By the time the mussel is ready for the table, it's about to celebrate its first birthday.

Up and down the coastline along this scenic portion of the N113, there are roadside oyster and mussel stands; there is also a pleasant beach in the lively nearby town of Mèze. But the best place for sampling the *moules de Bouzigues* is at La Côte Bleue, a modest modern motel and restaurant with a marvelous terrace overlooking the glistening mussel and oyster beds (see page 387).

CERET *(Pyrénées-Orientales)*

Paris 936 k, Perpignan 31 k, Port-Vendres 36 k, Prades 55 k.

Market: Saturday, 7 A.M. to noon, Place de la Liberté and Place des Tilleuls.

Don't miss the lively Saturday morning open-air market set beneath rows of gigantic sycamore trees. This village was a favorite of Pablo Picasso and friends, and the cafés clustered around the main squares offer a perfect vantage point for observing the local culture. Here, you'll find stands of homemade whole wheat bread, gorgeous cherries and apricots, and folkloric red cotton espadrilles. And if you'd like to snack, try the local *chichi*—fried Catalan doughnuts filled with cream and rolled in granulated sugar, made to order on the spot.

POUR LA MAISON

MADAME JANINE BONAY-AGREMON
6 Boulevard Jean-Jaurès, 66400 Céret.
(68.87.00.73).
Open 8:45 A.M. to noon and 2:30 to 7 P.M. Closed Sunday afternoon, Monday, and one week in August.
International mail orders accepted.

Live snails in Perpignan.

A classic regional shop offering a wide selection of brightly colored, folkloric Catalan fabrics and linens.

COLLIOURE *(Pyrénées-Orientales)*

Céret 32 k, Paris 931 k, Perpignan 27 k, Port-Vendres 4 k, Prades 64 k.

Market: Wednesday and Sunday, 8 A.M. to noon, Place du Maréchal-Leclerc.

RESTAURANT

HOSTELLERIE LA FREGATE
24 Quai de l'Amirauté, 66190 Collioure.
(68.82.06.05).
Last orders taken at 2 P.M. and 10 P.M.
Unfixed closing days.
Credit card: V.

Some of my fondest memories of my tours about France go back to a summer day in this charming medieval village, a day that included a late-afternoon hike along the cliffed and rugged shoreline, dinner under the white canopy of La Frégate, and an after-dinner wander through the town, watching the locals play at France's favorite outdoor sport, *boules*.

Terrace dining.
English spoken.
150-franc menu. A la carte,
  250 francs.

SPECIALTIES:
Change with the seasons;
regional.

As restaurants go, the food at La Frégate is no big deal, and service can be slow and annoying, but we did enjoy the delicately marinated fresh anchovies, the grilled *calamar,* or squid, sprinkled with parsley and olive oil, and the seldom seen and appealing local Collioure wine, a deep, rich, velvety red. For dessert, try the memorably rich and creamy *crème catalane* (see recipe below).

CREME CATALANE
LEMON, VANILLA, AND FENNEL-SEED CUSTARD

I first sampled this rich and luxurious dessert one warm summer evening on the terrace of the restaurant La Frégate, in the charming Catalan village of Collioure. The fennel, vanilla, and lemon flavorings make a vibrant blend that stimulates and soothes the palate, leaving one feeling magically satisfied.

2 cups (250 ml) heavy
  cream, preferably not
  ultra-pasteurized
⅓ cup (80 ml) milk
1 tablespoon fennel
  seeds, crushed in
  mortar with pestle
1 vanilla bean
3 large egg yolks
⅓ cup (65 g) sugar
Grated zest (peel) of 1
  lemon

1. Scald the cream and milk with the fennel seeds in a medium saucepan over high heat. Remove from the heat, cover, and let infuse for 30 minutes.

2. Preheat the oven to 300°F (150°C).

3. Cut the vanilla bean lengthwise in half and, with the aid of a small spoon, scrape out all the small seeds.

4. Blend the vanilla seeds, egg yolks, sugar, and lemon zest thoroughly in a small bowl. Strain the cream mixture and gradually whisk it into the egg yolk mixture.

5. Pour the flavored cream into six 6-inch (15 cm) round baking dishes. Bake just until the mixture begins to tremble in the middle, about 30 minutes.

6. Refrigerate at least 1 hour or up to 24 hours. Remove from the refrigerator 5 minutes before serving.

Yield: 6 servings.

POUR LA MAISON

LA CASA CATALANA
Quai de l'Amirauté, 66190
Collioure.
(68.82.09.74).
Open daily 10 A.M. to noon
and 3 to 7 P.M. April
through September,
before the Christmas
season, and holidays;
open irregular hours
off-season. Closed
Monday off-season.
Credit card: V.
French mail orders for fabric
accepted.

SPECIALITES REGIONALES

SOCIETE ROQUE
2 bis Rue des Treilles, 66190
Collioure.
(68.82.04.99).
Open 8 A.M. to noon and
1:30 to 6:30 P.M. Monday
through Friday; 10 A.M.
to noon and 2:30 to 6:30
P.M. Saturday, Sunday, and
holidays.
No credit cards.

A fine regional shop offering handmade Catalan pottery, colorful espadrilles, aprons, and various local crafts.

Catch of the day, Port-Vendres.

This is the best source I know for *anchois au sel* (salt-cured anchovies) and *anchois à l'huile* (oil-cured anchovies), still prepared in the old-fashioned way. (See "Le Vrai Anchois de Collioure," page 396.)

MANDUEL *(Gard)*

Arles 24 k, Marguerittes 8 k, Nîmes 11 k.

Market: Wednesday, 8 A.M. to noon, Cours Jean-Jaurès.

FROMAGER

LECOCQ
Chemin de Garons, 30129
Manduel.
(66.20.26.11).
Open 10 A.M. to noon and
3 to 6 P.M. Closed
Wednesday and Friday.

Yvonne and Michel Lecocq gave up busy careers in Paris to move back to their roots. Now they, their children, their grandchildren, and twenty-five goats are living happily ever after in a modern suburban development just outside of Nîmes. Their deliciously fresh-flavored, beautifully aged discs of firm Pélardon goat cheese have won medals. The

Lecocqs also offered us a fine tip on storing cheese for the winter: Traditionally, farmers stashed their Pélardons away in glass jars, covering them with a mixture of olive oil and *eau-de-vie*. Technically the *eau-de-vie* was added as a sort of antifreeze, to keep the oil from solidifying, but I imagine it also adds a nice kick to this venerable country cheese! (Directions: From Manduel take the road to Bouillargues 1 kilometer until you reach a fork. Take the road to the left; it's 500 meters to the farm.)

PERPIGNAN *(Pyrénées-Orientales)*

Béziers 93 k, Montpellier 152 k, Paris 907 k.

Market: Daily, 7 A.M. to 12:30 P.M., Place de la République and Place Cassanyes.
Flea market: Sunday, 7 A.M. to 1 P.M., Terrain Boure in the Parc des Expositions along the Têt river.

POUR LA MAISON

THERESE NEPY
9 Place de la République, 66000 Perpignan.
(68.34.47.65).
Open 7:30 A.M. to 12:30 P.M. daily and 3 to 7 P.M. Saturday.

One of the few places in France you'll see live *escargots*, sold along with an unusual collection of hardware and groceries, ranging from specially made grills for cooking those snails (or whatever else you wish) over an open fire to colorful strings of hot dried red peppers.

ROQUEFORT-SUR-SOULZON *(Aveyron)*

Montpellier 115 k, Paris 665 k, Rodez 82 k.

FROMAGER

ROQUEFORT SOCIETE
12250 Roquefort-sur-Soulzon.
(65.60.23.05).
Open daily (except during Christmas week) from 9 to 11 A.M. and 2 to 5 P.M.

It's in the *caves* of Roquefort-sur-Soulzon that all the Roquefort in the world is aged. Visitors may tour the model aging cellar of Roquefort's major cheesemaker, Société. During the months of July and August, an English-speaking guide is on hand. Visitors are advised to bring sweaters or warm clothing. (See "Roquefort: Myth and Mystery," page 399.)

Le Vrai Anchois de Collioure

"The anchovy business is a tough business. One would think that simple gambling would be easier on the nerves, and just as profitable."

PORT-VENDRES, JULY 19—The sangria-colored Catalan sun rose over the docks just as the sardine and anchovy boats began rolling in. As he was every morning from March to October, Guy Roque was there precisely at 7 to greet the anchovy fishermen when they returned from their eleven-hour journey into the Mediterranean.

As the tattered blue boats approached the harbor minutes from the French-Spanish border, Monsieur Roque—who owns the major anchovy-curing business in nearby Collioure—stopped conversation in mid-sentence. There was resigned despair in his voice.

"No anchovies today. See, they're bypassing the docks. They didn't catch a thing..." and his voice trailed off. This year he's talking of a *rupture totale,* that is, last year's stock is nearly depleted and replacements are very slow in coming.

The anchovy business is a tough business. One would think that simple gambling would be easier on the nerves, and just as profitable. But for French anchovy fishermen like Jean-Claude Siauvaud, who has contracted to sell his entire catch to Roque, it's a way of life, and from his point of view, one that suits him just fine, thank you.

"In a good year, we'll bring in 200 tons. A bad year, 30. On a good night's fishing, my boat can haul in 50 tons, easily. Yesterday I returned with nearly 4 tons; today, nothing," he says, just off the boat, a few days' growth of beard shading his tanned face.

The gamble is this: You can go out from this port, travel an hour or so into the Mediterranean, and fish for sardines. You're all but guaranteed to come back with a boat laden with silvery, fat, beautiful fish. If a lot of other fishermen didn't go out that night, you'll get 2 francs per kilo for your catch. If a lot of men decide to fish along with you, you may not be able to sell the sardines you bring in.

With anchovies, it's different. Everyone wants them. They'll pay 8, maybe 10, francs per kilo, wholesale. Anchovies are smaller and more delicate than sardines, they cure well, they've been deemed precious since the days of the Greeks and Romans. But, of course, the catch is more risky.

The anchovies, say the fishermen, are there. The problem—as with every crop that man has ever tried to cultivate or capture—is the weather.

"Last night, there were anchovies everywhere," explained Monsieur Siauvaud over an early-morning cup of coffee at the fishermen's bar. "But the water was too turbulent to bring them in. What we'd earn on the anchovies we'd have to spend replacing our nets."

So the story goes. Every night at 9, he and his crew of twelve set off in his oak-framed boat—built in Casablanca in 1961—and travel for four hours into the sea until they reach anchovy territory. They fish *au lampero,* with a light that attracts and gathers the anchovies in one place. If the seas are calm, no problem. They contentedly haul in their anchovy-filled nets, then begin the four-hour journey back to Port-Vendres.

But often the seas are turbulent. The nets would be destroyed, putting the men's livelihood in jeopardy. So on those nights, most nights, they return with an empty boat, hungry, tired, and yet ready to go out again the next evening for another try at the jackpot. It's no surprise that fifteen years ago, twenty-five or so boats set out from Port-Vendres each evening. Now there are eight.

Back in the adjacent village of Collioure, the traditional anchovy capital, the anchovy curing, packing, and selling goes on in the Roque *atelier*. This is a most artisanal factory where a handful of local women sit in an upstairs loft—tiled appropriately in sea blue—and filet anchovies onto absorbent brown paper or pack canning jars with whole salted fish, chatting about the weather, gossiping, smiling as they go along.

Beneath them, in humid cool cellars, rests last year's catch. The day the small blue-tinged fish are taken from the waters, they are packed in coarse sea salt and layered in large steel barrels. The anchovies rest there anywhere from four days to a month, depending on when someone has time to deal with them. As the anchovies cure and age, they form their own brine, and soon they float in a heady, salty, marine-fragrant mixture.

After a first curing, the heads are taken off by hand and the anchovies are eviscerated. The fish are returned to the barrels with a new batch of salt, where they should ripen for at least three months, but will cure just fine for up to one year.

Later, as time permits, they're fileted and cured in olive oil or in vinegar, or left whole and cured yet again with a sprinkling of salt. The Catalan anchovies are shipped all over France and sold in open-air markets along with olives, but are really best purchased on the spot, at Roque's little retail shop along the entrance to the enchanting port city of Collioure, a twenty-minute drive from Perpignan.

What to look for in a well-cured anchovy? When the tiny Mediterranean fish is caught, its flesh is pure white. As the salt cures and ages the flesh, it turns a fine rosy red, much like a well-cured ham. The best cured anchovies are purchased whole, packed in salt. At home they can be rinsed off, soaked in cold water for about fifteen minutes, then fileted, to be used in salads, pizzas, in combination with roasted red peppers, or as a stuffing for roasted potatoes.

Of course in Collioure—the ancient anchovy port, which was replaced in the 1960s by Port-Vendres as fishing methods changed—anchovies are found everywhere. Most restaurants offer a variety of preparations, including starter salads of salt-cured anchovies sprinkled with sherry vinegar and served, necessarily, with a few chopped hard-cooked eggs, or fresh anchovies sprinkled with olive oil and herbs.

Paris Connection: Roque brand anchovies are often in stock at Lepic sur Mer, 10 Rue Lepic, 75018 Paris (46.06.15.18).

SOMMIERES (Gard)

Aigues-Mortes 28 k, Montpellier 28 k, Nîmes 28 k, Paris 737 k.

Market: Saturday, 8 A.M. to 12:30 P.M., Place du Marché.

RESTAURANT

ENCLOS MONTGRANIER
30250 Sommières.
(66.80.92.00).
Last orders taken at 1:45 P.M.
and 9:30 P.M.
Closed Sunday dinner,
Monday except in July
and August, and
mid-November through
mid-March.
Credit cards: AE, EC.
Terrace dining.
Private dining rooms for 16
and 30.
English spoken.
90- through 340-franc
menus. A la carte, 300
francs.

SPECIALTIES:
Seasonal and regional.

One of those lost-in-the-country gems that deserves to be better known. This unusual and elegantly restored stone farmhouse offers so many of the qualities I look for in a restaurant—excellent regional food, a tasteful and beautiful setting, a good selection of regional wines, and superb, friendly service. On a summer evening it's hard to beat sitting out on the carefully though simply appointed terrace of Enclos Montgranier as the golden sun is setting. The menu changes according to the season, but one's likely to find variations such as fresh Cavaillon melon served with home-smoked tuna; a *fricassée* of wild *girolles* mushrooms, sprinkled with garlic and herbs; tender rabbit and *ratatouille;* or delicious local lamb served with grilled tomatoes and zucchini. Another plus: The mix-and-match menu offers unlimited options. If you feel like having two first courses, or three, no one's going to put up a fuss. And do try the Faugères, a robust, little-known local red wine. (Directions: 3 kilometers south of Sommières on the D12.)

ROUGE COMME UNE CERISE
Red Like a Cherry

Sometime around May 1, 1922, a proud group of farmers from the Catalan village of Céret decided to send their first-of-season cherries to the president of the republic, Alexandre Millerand. The patriotic gesture has turned into a successful attention-getting scheme for the village, which to this day is linked with the sweet, red, early maturing Saint-Georges variety of cherry—the last of the fruit trees to blossom, the first to mature. Each year, without fail, the president of France is the first to sample Céret's cherry crop.

Roquefort: Myth and Mystery

"The growing loaves of cheese . . . are stacked on their rounded edges and lined up so the cool breeze can circulate around them for two to three weeks, enough time for the mold to pulse on through the veins."

ROQUEFORT-SUR-SOULZON, OCTOBER 24—It's merely a matter of weeks before this remote limestone village, with its red-tiled roofs and steep, narrow roadways, comes to life again. The normal year-round population of 900 will swell to 2,000 when the workers return—as they do for seven months of each year—to make the fragrant blue cheese that's brought Roquefort fame and recognition around the world.

Soon the flocks of sturdy Lacaune sheep will offer their rich, creamy milk, the shepherds will gather their cheesemaking tools, and the *affineurs* will continue the rhythmical cycle of aging, transforming the young white cylinders of whole ewe's milk into the prized bluish-green-veined Roquefort.

Soon the relentlessly chilly, humid, open maze of limestone cellars that lurk some eleven stories deep beneath the village will carry on their mysterious work, as pencillium spores float invisibly through the drafty air, clinging to water-soaked rocks, to stairwells, to the thick slabs of oak that line the natural *caves.*

By now, the unusual band of local bakers have begun fashioning their bizarre outsize 10-kilo (22-pound) loaves of dense rye bread, the bread that will be cooked in a scorchingly hot oven (so that the outside forms a thick black crust, capturing the moisture inside), then be left to mold away for two or three months in these same gray rock *caves.*

And when the rye bread has taken on the proper rot, the center will have sprouted a powdery gray-green mass of penicillium spores, spores to be dried, pounded, strained, then carefully sprinkled over the cheese, like salt or pepper, when it's still in the curd stage.

Of course the world being what it is today, only a certain percentage of Roquefort is really made this way. Often that penicillium mold is a liquid created in a laboratory, not a folkloric little green powder that holds the mystery and the secret of what is France's third favorite cheese, following closely on the heels of Camembert and *chèvre.*

And not every drop of milk comes from the 800,000 sheep that make their home on the pastureland that hugs this southwestern village, a good hour's drive north of Montpellier. A small, though constantly declining, percentage of that milk may legally come from sheep raised in the Pyrénées and Corsica.

There is, no doubt, a great deal of myth and mystery attached to Roquefort.

Each year, some 17,000 tons of Roquefort are aged in these windy *caves,* and that is the only cheese in the world that has the right to bear the name "Roquefort." By law, it must be made from whole, raw (never pasteurized, never frozen) ewe's milk coming from Lacaune sheep raised in eight southern departments of France, as well as Corsica. Some 80 percent of that cheese is made industrially—that is, by machine.

Eleven companies have the right to make Roquefort. Société Roquefort and its affiliates (including the labels Papillon and Maria Grimal) make about 80 per-

cent of that cheese, while a handful of artisanal cheesemakers play a compara-
tively minor role, each making about 700 tons of Roquefort annually (names to
look for include Gabriel Coulet, Carles, Constans-Crouzat, Bon Berger).

One of the best artisanal cheesemakers is Gabriel Coulet, a house run by two
fourth-generation-Roquefort brothers, André and Pierre Laur.

Working with about two hundred area farmers, they make all their Roquefort
by hand. Their farmers raise only the Lacaune breed of sheep—silly-looking animals with triangular-shaped heads and ears that stick straight out, a bit like
propellers—prized not only for the quantity and quality of their milk, but also for
their meat (after supplying us with the milk for Roquefort cheese for seven years,
they provide us with mutton for our table). Over the past few decades, breeding
and selection have doubled the amount of Roquefort they can make: Twenty years
ago, the average sheep gave about 80 liters of milk per year, only enough to make
seven whole 2.5-kilogram (5-pound) wheels of Roquefort. Now, if all goes well,
each sheep produces a whopping 170 liters.

The sheep give milk from December until July, and so this is the only season
in which Roquefort is made. The Laur brothers' cheesemaking process begins at
the farm, where the raw morning and evening milk is strained through cotton
mesh, then heated to a tepid 30°C (86°F). Natural animal rennet is added, and
in about two hours, the milk has curdled.

The cheesemaker cuts the curds into cubes and then, working with his bare
hands, transfers the cottage-cheese-like mass into perforated molds, sprinkling,
then massaging in, that famous rye bread mold, known scientifically as *penicillium
roqueforti.*

The cheese rests in the molds in a chilled room for three or four days, then is
turned three times daily, to make sure the cool air circulates as the excess whey
drains off, ensuring the beginning of a nice, even aging.

Later the cheese is unmolded, then salted with sea salt from Narbonne, three
days on one side, two days on the other, again with the hope that the salt will
"take" slowly and evenly.

At about ten days of age, these pale ivory cylinders are transported to the
Gabriel Coulet cellars in the center of town, where they'll be punched full of holes
from end to end to create a sort of aerating chimney—to help the live cheese
breathe, to stimulate the growth of that famed blue-green mold.

Now it's time for the famous *caves*—which remain a steady 8° or 9°C (45°F)
year round, with a constant 95 percent humidity—to do their work. The growing
loaves of cheese (at this stage, they really are called *pains*) are stacked on their
rounded edges and lined up so the cool breeze can circulate around them for two
to three weeks, enough time for the mold to pulse on through the veins.

Then, to slow down—but not halt—the molding process, each cylinder is
meticulously enveloped in a thick, malleable sheet of pure tin (not aluminum foil),
ensuring that for the next few months, the cheese will age, blue, and grow, but oh
so slowly.

The tin-wrapped cheese is sent off to cold-storage rooms around the village,
where it will rest for anywhere from a minimum of three months to a year or
more, when it will be unwrapped, checked for quality, then wrapped in foil bearing the official red sheep seal, certifying that it's authentic Roquefort.

So what's the difference, really, between a handmade and a machine-made

Roquefort, and what are the visual clues? Visually, an artisanal Roquefort is a pale ivory white. (Yellowed cheese is a sign that liquid penicillium was used, not, as some might assume, a sign that the milk is richer.) In a good handmade cheese the rather aggressive blue-green veins should spread almost all the way out to the edge of the cheese. (In most machine-made versions, the veins are a palish green and are clustered around the center of the cheese.)

Because the artisanal cheese is formed and pressed by hand, the curds are compacted, and they retain a bit of moisture as the cheese ages, making for a cheese with a cleaner, less crumbly cut. (The curds of the industrial version almost turn to a purée, resulting in a drier cheese, one that crumbles and falls apart when it is cut.)

Then there's the question of salt, nature's miracle preservative. Generally, cheese mixed with rye mold is less fragile (along with the natural mold, you get all the good protective bacteria), so the cheese needs less preserving, thus less salting.

Quite simply, Roquefort should smell, not stink. The aroma should be fresh, lactic, and pleasing. On the palate, the cheese should taste fresh, alive, clean, with a luxurious texture. It should be soft and moist enough to spread easily. It's natural for Roquefort to sweat a bit, suggesting that it's retained the proper quantity of liquid. Dried-out cheese tends to get bitter and acrid. Roquefort should be stored in the refrigerator, wrapped in aluminum foil, then in plastic wrap, to retain its moisture. For maximum enjoyment, allow the wrapped cheese to sit at room temperature for two or three hours before serving.

What to drink with Roquefort? While the cheesemakers themselves suggest a light local red, such as Faugères, one of the world's great food and wine marriages is a pairing of an *artisanal* Roquefort and a golden Sauternes.

Paris Connection: Gabriel Coulet cheese is sold at most fine cheese shops, including Androuët, 41 rue d'Amsterdam, 75008 Paris (48.74.26.90), and Ferme Saint Hubert, 21 Rue Vignon, 75001 Paris (47.42.79.20).

Of boats and ports, the Languedoc.

WINE OF LANGUEDOC

COLLIOURE (DOMAINE MAS BLANC): A velvety red from grapes grown on the steeply terraced vineyards near the Spanish border, this very small *appellation* takes its name from the charming port of Collioure, once the anchovy capital of France. In the Languedoc, also keep an eye out for the robust red Faugères and the dry white Picpoul de Pinet, a perfect mate for the fresh fish and shellfish served all along the coast.

CHEESES OF LANGUEDOC

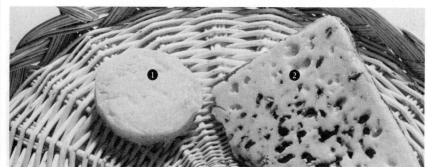

1. CABECOU: This small round goat's-milk cheese from the southwest (also made with sheep's milk or a mixture of goat's and cow's milk) is a traditional farm cheese found in a variety of forms, from very young, soft, and smooth to firm, dry, nutty, and aromatic. Also known as Rocamadour.

2. ROQUEFORT: Perhaps the world's best-known cheese, the velvety blue-veined Roquefort is made only from raw sheep's milk and is aged in the vast maze of underground rock caves in the village of Roquefort-sur-Soulzon. The cheese is made between December and July, when the Lacaune breed of sheep give milk. The best Roquefort is made by hand, and once aged, turns a pale ivory white.

Auvergne
AUVERGNE

Chef Michel Bras, in Laguiole.

The profile of the Auvergne is a rugged one, for this is a remote, volcanic, mountainous land of green valleys and deep, rambling streams, steep-roofed gray stone houses and narrow, winding country roads. It's most often described as *rude,* which means rough, hard, arduous. Where else on earth would there be a restaurant named Le Bout du Monde, literally "the end of the world"?

Gastronomically, this translates into a cuisine designed for enormous country appetites, a peasant diet that revolves around mountain hams and sausages, aged country cheese, giant rounds of rye bread, and rib-sticking fare such as *aligot,* an unctuous blend of mashed potatoes, garlic, and *tomme,* the fresh curds used in making Cantal cheese; and *pounti,* a dense pork loaf containing Swiss chard, prunes, eggs, milk, and herbs. The streams and rivers provide an abundance of fresh salmon trout as well as the prized firm-fleshed *omble chevalier,* while the forests supply tables all over France with sweet wild blueberries, wild morel mushrooms, and the delicate parasol mushroom known as *cocherelle.* And from the town of Le Puy come the famous green lentils—the tiny bean-like *lentilles de Puy*—that are cooked and served with sausages and salt pork, or sliced smoked ham, or are used to thicken hearty soups.

And while the Auvergnat wines are not well known outside the region, you're likely to find some pleasant surprises, including the light, refreshing white Saint-Pourçain and the meaty Chanturgue, an explosive red that goes well with the hearty cuisine.

As remote as the Auvergne is, it is far from run-down, and with a population density of 28 inhabitants per square kilometer (the Paris region clocks in at 20,000 per kilometer), it is, indeed, the place to go to get away from it all, to spend days exploring villages and gathering picnic fare from small town markets.

The Auvergne is a region of country villages, many of them storybook sites, such as the *plus beau village* of Tournemire—a hamlet situated between Salers and Aurillac—where one can easily spend an hour exploring the restored Auvergnat homes with their slate-gray roofs and stone bread ovens, their tidy vegetable gardens bordered by a raging mountain stream.

When you go, do not miss Salers and Saint-Nectaire—two villages that have given their names to the Auvergne's most famous cheeses—or Besse-en-Chandesse, a charming medieval village filled with huge gray houses built of stones formed from volcanic rocks.

WHEN YOU GO

Michelin Green Guides: *Auvergne, Vallée du Rhône/Vivarais-Lyonnais.*

Getting there: Air Inter offers about three hour-long flights daily to Clermont-Ferrand, leaving from Paris's Orly Ouest airport. The same journey by train, leaving from the Gare de Lyon, takes 4 hours; there are about four trains daily. Cars can be rented at the airport and train station.

Getting around: Michelin map 239 (Auvergne/Limousin).

Best time to visit: The rugged, mountainous Auvergne is an active region year round, for in spring, summer, and fall it's great for touring by car, while during the winter months it is popular with French families for downhill skiing. Gastronomically, September is best, when the Auvergne is abundant with wild mushrooms and chestnuts. Note that many restaurants close for six to eight months of the year.

MARKETS
(Liveliest markets are marked with an asterisk.)

Monday: Besse-en-Chandesse, Billom, Clermont-Ferrand.

Tuesday: Châtelguyon, Clermont-Ferrand, Condat, Massiac (every other week), *Le Monastier-sur-Gazeille, *Royat, *Vic-sur-Cère.

Wednesday: Allègre, Aurillac, *Clermont-Ferrand, Egliseneuve-d'Entraigues, Laguiole, Murol, Salers.

Thursday: Ambert, Clermont-Ferrand, Mauriac (second and fourth Thursday of the month), Maurs, Yssingeaux.

Friday: Champeix, Châtelguyon, *Clermont-Ferrand, Le Mont-Dore, Murat, Saugues, Vertaizon, Vic-sur-Cère.

Saturday: *Aurillac, Brioude, *Clermont-Ferrand, *Laguiole, Olliergues, Le Puy, Riom, Riom-ès-Montagnes, Royat, Saint-Flour.

Sunday: Le Monastier-sur-Gazeille, Saint-Nectaire (June through September).

FAIRS AND FESTIVALS

June 5: *Fête de la Cerise* (cherry festival), Vieillevie.

Second Sunday in June: *Fête aux Fraises* (strawberry festival), Saint-Geniez-d'Olt.

June 25: *Saint-Eloi des Fraises* (food festival), Thiers.

First Saturday in August: *Fête du Pain* (bread baking festival), Auzeral.

Thursday after the first Sunday in August: *Foire à la Bouffe* (food fair), Saint-Chély-d'Apcher.

Next to last Sunday in August: *Fête Votive de Saint-Barthélémy* (Saint Bartholomew's Day festival), Najac.

Sunday closest to August 20: *Fête du Pain* (bread baking festival), Olliergues.

Last weekend in August: *Foire des Vins* (wine fair), Saint-Pourçain-sur-Sioule.

September 14: *Foire du Pré* (traditional fair), Thiers.

First weekend in October: *Journées de la Fourme* (Montbrison cheese days), Montbrison.

October 6 and 27: *Foire aux Cèpes* (wild boletus mushroom fair), Saugues.

Third Sunday in October: *Fête de la Châtaigne et du Cidre* (chestnut and cider festival), Quézac.

First Saturday in November: *Foire aux Cèpes* (wild mushroom fair), Saint-Bonnet-le-Froid.

November 12: *Foire de la Saint-Martin* (Saint Martin's Day fair), Allègre.

December 1: *Saint-Eloi des Goges* (food festival), Thiers.

Last weekend in February: *Foire des Vins* (wine fair), Saint-Pourçain-sur-Sioule.

AMBERT *(Puy-de-Dôme)*

La Chaise-Dieu 33 k, Clermont-Ferrand 89 k, Paris 434 k, Le Puy 72 k, Saint-Anthème 22 k, Vichy 92 k.

Market: Thursday, 8 A.M. to noon, Place Saint-Jean, Place du Pontel, Place Charles-de-Gaulle, Rue du Château.

BOULANGERIE

JOSEPH MEY
4 Route de Lyon, 63600 Ambert.
(73.82.01.41).
Open 9 A.M. to 12:30 P.M. and 2:30 to 7 P.M. Tuesday through Saturday; 9 A.M. to noon Sunday.

A good address for picnickers: Monsieur Mey offers a variety of hearty breads, including *pain de seigle à l'ancienne* (old-fashioned rye bread) and *pain bis,* a whole wheat loaf we sampled still warm from the oven. Great for pairing with Michel Abonnenc's farm Saint-Nectaire.

FROMAGERIE

MICHEL ABONNENC
4 Place Pompe, 63600 Ambert.
(73.82.11.19).
Open 8 A.M. to 12:30 P.M. and 2:30 to 7 P.M. Tuesday through Saturday; 9 A.M. to noon Sunday.
Will ship in France.

One of those wonderfully friendly little shops, with a small but excellent assortment of authentic—and rare—well-aged farm Saint-Nectaire, the local Fourme d'Ambert, Cantal, and various mountain cheeses.

Scenic beauty of the Auvergne.

AURILLAC *(Cantal)*

Clermont-Ferrand 167 k, Paris 567 k, Salers 46 k,
Vic-sur-Cère 19 k.

Market: Wednesday and Saturday, 5 A.M. to noon, Place de l'Hôtel-de-Ville.
Cheese market: Saturday, 7 A.M. to 12:30 P.M., Place des Tocks, next to the
préfecture de police.

PATISSERIE

J. C. CRUCHANDEAU
21 Rue Victor-Hugo, 15000
  Aurillac.
(71.48.13.11).
Open 6:30 A.M. to 7 P.M.
  Closed Monday and the
  last week in June through
  mid-July.

A wonderful local pastry shop selling delicious *crêpes jambon,* or country-ham-filled crêpes, perfect for eating out of hand as a snack or for stashing away for a picnic. Also try their raisin bread with rye, and their homemade jams.

BOULANGERIES

BOULANGERIE BARCELO
12 Rue des Frères, 15000
  Aurillac.
(71.48.61.32).
Open 6:30 A.M. to 12:30 P.M.
  and 2:15 to 7:15 P.M.
  Closed Sunday and four
  weeks during the year.

Wow! Working round the clock, the owners of this pint-size bakery turn out giant 2-kilo (4-pound) loaves of rye bread they ship all over the world, including, they say, California.

L'EPI CANTALIEN
10 Rue du Buis, 15000
  Aurillac.
(71.48.46.95).
Open 7 A.M. to 12:30 P.M.
  and 3 to 7 P.M. Closed
  Monday.

An old-fashioned *épicerie,* where they sell a beautiful *tarte encalat,* or local cheesecake, and giant rounds of country *pain de seigle.* The shop is right across the street from the Saturday morning cheese market.

FROMAGERIE

CREMERIE LEROUX
15 Rue Emile-Duclaux,15000
  Aurillac. (71.48.28.89).
Open 8 A.M. to noon and 2
  to 7 P.M. Tuesday through
  Sunday; 8 A.M. to noon
  Monday.

This is an impeccable boutique with shiny white tile walls, pink scallop-shell decoration along the ceiling, marble counters, and striking black, white, and blue tile floors. The beautiful farm cheeses include Salers, Saint-Nectaire, and fresh Cantal curds.

BESSE-EN-CHANDESSE *(Puy-de-Dôme)*

Chambon-sur-Lac 11 k, Clermont-Ferrand 51 k, Paris 440 k,
Saint-Nectaire 17 k.

Market: Monday, 9 A.M. to 4 P.M., in all the squares in town.

RESTAURANT

LES MOUFLONS
Route de Super Besse, 63610
  Besse-en-Chandesse.
(73.79.51.31).
Last orders taken at 1:30 P.M.
  and 8:30 P.M.
Open June through
  September.
Credit cards: AE, V.
68- to 135-franc menus. A la
  carte, about 250 francs.

SPECIALTIES:
Salade de lapereau au serpolet
(rabbit salad with wild
thyme); *saumon aux
champignons sylvestres* (salmon
with wild mushrooms).

Besse-en-Chandesse is one of the prettiest villages in the Auvergne, a picture-postcard town filled with appealing cheese boutiques and pastry shops offering mouth-watering European blueberry *tartes aux myrtilles.* One of the better dining and lodging spots in the area is Les Mouflons, which translates literally as "the wild sheep." This large, modern, and rather cold hotel-restaurant at the edge of town was not exactly what I'd expected from the name, but it was nice to wake up to clanging cowbells and dramatic sunrises. The cuisine here is a bit on the sleepy side, though we did enjoy the vibrant orange-colored local salmon trout served with sautéed mushrooms; turbot with wild *cèpes;* and a fine rabbit salad. Try especially the local Chanturgue red: It's an invigorating wine.

CHAMBON-SUR-LAC *(Puy-de-Dôme)*

Clermont-Ferrand 37 k, Issoire 32 k, Le Mont-Dore 19 k, Paris 425 k.

FROMAGER

DOMAINE BERLAIRE
Chambon-sur-Lac, 63790
  Murol.
(73.88.60.75).
Cheesemaking
  demonstration begins at
  6:30 P.M. and lasts 45
  minutes. Closed Sunday.

It's not often that one's invited to watch a farm wife make cheese, but for the past twenty years Madame Rigaud—whose farm is spectacularly situated—has opened her little cheesemaking room to visitors, who chat, ask questions, keep her company, as each afternoon she transforms her milk into about thirty flat, creamy discs of Saint-Nectaire *fermier.* Her cheese is earthy and young and may not appeal to all palates (though I loved it). (Directions: From Chambon-sur-Lac take the D996 3 kilometers northwest. Take the fork to the right after Bressoulleile. There is a sign to the farm.)

CLERMONT-FERRAND *(Puy-de-Dôme)*

Aurillac 164 k, Paris 338 k, Saint-Etienne 146 k.

Market: Monday through Saturday, 9 A.M. to 5 P.M., Place Saint-Pierre.

RESTAURANT

RESTAURANT JEAN-YVES
   BATH
Place Saint-Pierre, 63000
   Clermont-Ferrand.
(opening September 1987).
Last orders taken at 2 P.M.
   and 10 P.M.
Closed Sunday, holidays, and
   mid-July through August.
Credit cards: AE, V.
Terrace dining.
Private dining room for 30.
English spoken.
150-franc menu (lunch
   only). A la carte, 280
   francs.

SPECIALTIES:
Salade de poisson vinaigrette aux
truffes (baked fish salad with
truffle vinaigrette).

Jean-Yves Bath is unquestionably one of the best young chefs in the Auvergne, succeeding where so many others fail, as he combines updated regional fare with his own contemporary, seasonal inspirations. Chef Bath has moved his restaurant from a restored *bergerie,* or vaulted stone sheep barn, outside of town to the newly renovated Place Saint-Pierre, which will no doubt offer him some much-needed exposure. He appears to be a super-dedicated chef, insisting on making just about everything, including his own chocolates as well as an assortment of homemade herbal liqueurs and wines. Some of my favorite Bath dishes include an eye-opening salad of baked salmon set atop a bed of greens dressed with a truffle vinaigrette (see recipe, facing page); salmon served with the local green *lentilles de Puy,* and a stunning warm fresh fig tart served with lavender sorbet.

EGLISENEUVE-D'ENTRAIGUES *(Puy-de-Dôme)*

Besse-en-Chandesse 17 k, Clermont-Ferrand 67 k, Condat 11 k, Paris 457 k.

Market: Wednesday, 8 A.M. to 12:30 P.M.

MUSEE

LA MAISON DES
   FROMAGES
Place Forail, 63850
   Egliseneuve-d'Entraigues.
(73.71.93.69).
Open daily 10 A.M. to 6 P.M.
   mid-June through
   September. Closed
   October through
   mid-June.
Admission: 11 francs for
   adults, 5 francs for
   children.

A modest yet fascinating regional museum designed to explain the history and process of Auvergnat cheesemaking. Here you'll see how they make Fourme d'Ambert, Bleu d'Auvergne, and Saint-Nectaire, as well as Cantal. There's a slide show (in French), as well as a chance to sample the local cheese and wine. Note especially all the antique cheesemaking paraphernalia that decorates this old Auvergnat sloped-roof structure.

SALADE DE SAUMON VINAIGRETTE AUX TRUFFES JEAN-YVES BATH
JEAN-YVES BATH'S SALMON SALAD WITH TRUFFLE VINAIGRETTE

This is a beautiful, elegant salad, and one I can see making with all sorts of fresh fish. I've come to call it "baked salad," for that's just what it is. Thin slices of salmon are set atop a bed of dressed greens and are then baked in a very hot oven. It's amazing how quickly the fish bakes (usually in less than 2 minutes), and how that baking instantly merges the flavors of the vinaigrette, the greens, the fish. Chef Jean-Yves Bath is a very creative cook, and I'll always be grateful to him for this recipe, as well as the inspiration to perk up a salad with a touch of orange zest!

Vinaigrette:
2 teaspoons best-quality
    red wine vinegar
2 teaspoons best-quality
    sherry wine vinegar
Salt and freshly ground
    black pepper to taste
⅓ cup (80 ml) extra-
    virgin olive oil
1 preserved small black
    truffle, cut into
    julienne strips
    (optional)

4 small handfuls
    (5 ounces; 150 g)
    mixed salad greens,
    rinsed and dried
Grated zest (peel) of
    1 orange
1 shallot, minced
Small handful of fresh
    parsley leaves
2 small tomatoes,
    peeled, cored,
    seeded, and cut into
    small dice
8 ounces (250 g)
    salmon fillet, cut
    diagonally into 12
    slices
Small handful of fresh
    chives, snipped into
    1½-inch (4 cm)
    pieces

1. Preheat the oven to 500°F (250°C).

2. Prepare the vinaigrette: Whisk the vinegars, salt, and pepper together in a small bowl, then blend in the oil. Add the truffle, if using, and let sit.

3. Tear the greens into bite-size pieces. Toss the greens, orange zest, shallot, parsley, and all but 2 teaspoons of the vinaigrette together in a large bowl. Divide the greens among 4 large ovenproof plates; spread the greens out and press them down to make a flat bed.

4. Toss the tomatoes with the remaining vinaigrette and season with salt and pepper. Set aside.

5. Sprinkle the salmon slices liberally on both sides with salt and pepper. Arrange 3 slices of salmon on top of the greens on each plate.

6. Place the plates in the oven and bake just until the salmon is barely cooked through, about 2 minutes. Sprinkle with the chives and tomatoes and serve immediately with toasted country bread.

Yield: 4 servings.

LAGUIOLE *(Aveyron)*

Aurillac 82 k, Chaudes-Aigues 32 k, Espalion 24 k, Paris 552 k, Rodez 56 k, Saint-Flour 64 k.

Market: Wednesday and Saturday, 8 A.M. to 12:30 P.M., Place de la Mairie.

RESTAURANT

MICHEL BRAS
12210 Laguiole.
(65.44.32.24).
Last orders taken at 1:30 P.M. and 9 P.M.
Open April through mid-October. Closed Sunday dinner and Monday (except in July and August, when closed only Monday lunch).
Credit cards: AE, V.
English spoken.
100- to 310-franc menus. A la carte, about 350 francs.

SPECIALTIES:
Sauté de queues d'écrevisses (sauté of crayfish tails), *filet de lapin aux truffes* (rabbit with truffles), *aligot* (mashed potatoes with garlic and the fresh curds used in making Cantal cheese, served with country sausage).

This dreary, unremarkable village that's a long way from anywhere has taken France by storm, thanks to the highly publicized and innovative cooking of the shy young Michel Bras, who studied cooking not with Troisgros or Bocuse, but with his mom. I can't say I am ready to agree with others who find Monsieur Bras one of the top young chefs in France, but I certainly am willing to watch him grow. As you approach the dull brown modernized exterior of this village hotel-restaurant, you haven't a clue as to what you'll find inside: The dining room is a spectacularly restored cheese-aging *cave,* a vaulted stone affair that's been tastefully and warmly decorated in shades of brown and gray, with an inviting skylight at the far end. Chef Bras offers a finely orchestrated menu that combines pure regional country fare (I think I could live on his *aligot*) with many imaginative offerings. The famed first-course wild mushroom tart was a disappointment, arriving dried out and oversalted, though I loved his idea of sprinkling wild *cèpe* mushrooms with a touch of grated walnuts. A better bet was the earthy rabbit preparation, moist boned rabbit and superb sautéed rabbit kidneys set on a bed of wilted spinach and sprinkled with finely chopped truffles. The cheese course is a must here: Try the delicious local farm cheese that's half goat's, half cow's milk, tasting much like a fine Saint-Marcellin, as well as the local Laguiole and farm Saint-Nectaire, for sampling with plenty of their deliciously crusty rye bread.

LENTILLES VERTES DU PUY AUX SAUCISSES FUMEES
SMOKED PORK SAUSAGES WITH GREEN LENTILS FROM PUY

Come October, market stands all over the south of France boast of "Lentilles Vertes du Puy, Nouvelle Recolte." That means it's time to think about preparing this earthy combination of fresh smoked sausages and seasoned lentils, the kind of dish that seems custom-tailored to late Saturday lunches in front of the fire, accompanied by a glass, or two, of chilled and fruity new-season Beaujolais.

1 tablespoon (½ ounce; 15 g) unsalted butter

1 pound (500 g) fresh smoked pork sausage or 4 individual farmer's sausages

1 branch fresh thyme or ¼ teaspoon dried

2 bay leaves

8 cloves garlic, halved

2 medium onions, coarsely chopped

½ pound (250 g) green lentils, preferably dark green from Puy

1 bottle (750 ml) dry white wine, such as Riesling

Dressing:

2 tablespoons best-quality sherry wine vinegar

¼ cup (60 ml) extra-virgin olive oil

1 tablespoon imported Dijon mustard

Salt and freshly ground black pepper to taste

Small handful of fresh parsley, minced

Small bunch of fresh chives, minced

1. Melt the butter in a large saucepan over medium-high heat. Add the sausage and brown on all sides, being careful not to pierce it. Add thyme, bay leaves, garlic, onions, lentils, and wine, stir, and heat to boiling. Immediately reduce the heat and cover. Simmer, stirring occasionally, about 1 hour. Sample the lentils occasionally and cook just until they lose their crunchy firmness. If the wine is absorbed before the lentils are done, add more.

2. Transfer the sausage to a warmed platter and cover with aluminum foil to keep warm.

3. Prepare the dressing: Blend the vinegar, oil, and mustard, and pour the dressing over the warmed lentils. Toss to coat. Season generously with salt and pepper.

4. To serve, cut the sausage into thick slices and return it to the platter. Spoon the seasoned lentils around the sausage. Sprinkle with the parsley and chives and serve immediately with plenty of spicy Dijon mustard.

Yield: 4 servings.

MONTSALVY *(Cantal)*

Aurillac 35 k, Conques 35 k, Entraygues 14 k, Paris 600 k.

RESTAURANT

AUBERGE FLEURIE
15120 Montsalvy.
(71.49.20.02).
Last orders taken at 12:30
  P.M. and 7:30 P.M. (8 P.M.
  in summer).
Closed mid-November to
  mid-March.
Credit cards: AE, DC, EC, V.
Private dining room for 35.
Menus translated into
  English.
40-, 60-, and 90-franc
  menus. A la carte, about
  150 francs.

SPECIALTIES:
Choux farcis (stuffed cabbage),
pintade aux morilles (guinea
hen with morels), *omelette aux
cèpes* (wild mushroom omelet),
truite aux petits lardons (trout
with bacon), *crêpes au jambon*
(ham crêpes), *potée auvergnate*
(cabbage, pork, and bean
stew).

A classic, friendly village inn, with a motherly chef/owner who is happy to prepare whatever your heart desires, from the simplest of wild *cèpe* omelets to a leafy green salad with tomatoes and one of those zingy vinaigrettes only French grandmothers seem to have mastered. This is a cheery, old-fashioned place, filled with an international clientele who quickly make friends by chatting across tables, comparing travel notes.

SAINT-FLOUR *(Cantal)*

Aurillac 76 k, Espalion 80 k, Marvejols 68 k, Paris 489 k.

Market: Saturday, 8 A.M. to noon, throughout the town.

CAFE

**GRAND HOTEL DES
  VOYAGEURS**
25-27 Rue du Collège,
  15100 Saint-Flour.
(71.60.34.44).
Open April through
  mid-October 11:30 A.M.
  (7:30 A.M. in July and
  August) to 1 A.M.

A beautiful old-fashioned café and *salon de thé* with a window filled with appealing fruit tarts.

Good friends, good times.

BOULANGERIE

CHRISTIAN DANIAS
12 Rue du Collège, 15100
  Saint-Flour.
(71.60.03.53).
Open 6:30 A.M. to 8 P.M.
  Closed Monday,
  September, and October.

One of the dozen or so best breads I sampled in France: extraordinary rye *baguettes,* giant round rye loaves (called *tourtes*), and truly one of the finest rye breads with raisins I have ever tasted. Their *tarte aux myrtilles* (European blueberry tart) looked exquisite.

FROMAGERIE

SALVAT-TRUYOL
53 Rue des Lacs, 15100
  Saint-Flour.
(71.60.08.20).
Open 8 A.M. to 12:30 P.M.
  and 2 to 7:30 P.M. Closed
  Monday.
Will ship in France.

A fine regional cheese shop, for sampling Cantal at various stages of aging, superb Laguiole, farm Saint-Nectaire, and Fourme d'Ambert.

SPECIALITES REGIONALES

**AUX PRODUITS
  D'AUVERGNE**
Cours Spy-des-Ternes,
  15100 Saint-Flour.
(71.60.31.87).
Open 9 A.M. to noon and 3
  to 7 P.M.; 10 A.M. to noon
  Sunday. Closed Sunday
  afternoon.

A fascinating *épicerie,* full of regional specialties, including dried mushrooms *(cèpes, girolles, morels),* various fruit brandies *(eaux-de-vie-de-prune, myrtille, framboise),* local *lentilles de Puy,* and various dried sausages and hams.

Rugged Mountain Cantal

"*T*" *he prized Salers breed of cows, renowned for milk that tastes of mountain flowers, is slowly being phased out. Their milk may be rich, but they don't give enough of it to satisfy a dairy industry bent on industrialization.*"

SALERS, SEPTEMBER 18—Here in the rugged, misted mountains of the Auvergne, summer has turned the corner into fall as the annual rite of *trans-humance* signals the close of another cheesemaking season. The sturdy, mahogany-colored Salers cows have nibbled the once-lush mountain pastures to a stubble—there's barely a stem of wild fennel or golden gentian to be found—which means it's time they descend to the valleys to sit out the winter.

Their quiet, blue-eyed master, Raymond Dutrery, has just completed his thirty-fifth year as a cheesemaker, a craft in which he takes justifiable pride. No matter that he rises each morning at 5 to get to the mountains by 6, where—with two assistants and a single donkey—he works well into the night tending to a herd of forty-four, milking each cow by hand twice a day, instantly transforming their milk into the rustic, earthy mountain Cantal cheese known as Salers.

A few hours with Monsieur Dutrery explains why almost no one does it this way anymore; why handmade Salers has given way to blander, standardized, assembly-line Cantal; why the prized Salers breed of cows, renowned for a milk that tastes of mountain flowers, is slowly being phased out. Their milk may be rich, but they don't give enough of it to satisfy a dairy industry bent on industrial-ization.

Here in the mountains near the medieval hill town of Salers, life centers on the isolated *buron,* a tidy two-story gray stone shepherd's hut where the cheese is made and where the two workers live from early May to late September, the only time one can legally make the 10- to 40-kilogram (22- to 88-pound) wheels of a cheese that's been known in this region for the past two thousand years.

The *buron* is not wired for electricity; heat comes from the stone fireplace,

SALERS *(Cantal)*

Aurillac 49 k, Brive-la-Gaillarde 102 k, Mauriac 19 k, Murat 43 k, Paris 505 k.

Market: Wednesday, 8 A.M. to noon, Place Tissandier-d'Escous.

FROMAGER

SYNDICAT D'INITIATIVE
Place Tissandier-d'Escous,
15410 Salers.
(71.40.70.68).

From May to October, individuals may arrange for visits to stone Auvergnat cheesemaking huts, known as *burons* (see "Rugged Mountain Can-tal," above).

and water from nearby streams. Yet there is a rich and enviable natural rhythm to this mountain life: Faces are void of tension, and the bucolic cling-clang of cow-bells serves as a sort of rural symphony.

"This isn't a craft for folks in a hurry. It takes an hour for milk to curdle," he remarks. "Salers is the only cheese I ever eat. Snacks. After dinner. For breakfast," he says matter-of-factly.

When the milk has curdled, he reaches up in the rafters and pulls down a wooden instrument that resembles a sawed-off ski pole. He gently plunges the pole into the curds, moving it evenly through the concentrating mass. Then he takes up a wooden paddle—an ecclesiastical-looking instrument with a cross punched out of the center—and dips it into the broken curds. He stirs, and stirs, working until all the heavy mass sinks to the bottom of the barrel.

Monsieur Dutrery dips a bucket into the barrel and begins to collect the whey. Quickly, his youthful assistant—communicating with gestures, not words—pours the whey into a hand-cranked cream separator, and exerting every muscle in his well-developed arms, he churns and churns until the whey pours out in a rapid stream, the cream trickles out drop by drop.

Meanwhile, the cheesemaker has poured the aromatic curds into a sloping wooden cloth-draped press. The press, resembling a giant waffle iron, serves to force out any recalcitrant whey. Soon the loose curds are transformed into a solid rectangular block, which will be pressed and cut, and pressed and cut some more, and all night long it will drip, drip, drip, until not a drop of whey remains.

The next morning, he'll cut the compacted block into slices, pass the slices through a machine that looks like a giant parsley grater, salt the newly formed curds, then press them into huge cylindrical wooden molds. Days will pass, and when the cheese is firm enough and strong enough to stand up on its own, he'll transfer the white cylinders to the cool, humid cellar adjacent to the parlor. There the cheese will rest for months, attended to day by day, as the wheels are turned and brushed, then salted, and massaged with whey until finally the crust turns golden, the color of freshly harvested wheat. If all has gone well, the cheese will exude a fruity, lactic odor. It will taste of mountain flowers.

THIEZAC *(Cantal)*

Aurillac 26 k, Clermont-Ferrand 249 k, Paris 527 k.

FROMAGER

AU BURON
Salilhes, 15450 Thiézac.
(71.47.52.16).
Open 9 A.M. to noon and 2 to 6 P.M. Closed Sunday afternoon.

François and Catherine Verdier are a wonderfully resourceful young couple who make their own Cantal, which they sell out of a tiny roadside shop at their farm. They're happy to have visitors watch them make their earthy, full-flavored cow's-milk cheese. (Directions: Salilhes is 3 kilometers northeast of Vic-sur-Cère, via the N122. There is a sign to the farm.)

CHEESES OF AUVERGNE

1. BLEU D'AUVERGNE: One could call Bleu d'Auvergne a "cow's-milk Roquefort," for traditionally both use the dried penicillium spores of molded rye bread to "blue" the cheese. Today this cylinder of blue-veined mountain cheese is made year round in farms and dairies, using raw as well as pasteurized milk. The veins of a good Bleu d'Auvergne should be evenly distributed and spread almost all the way out to the edge of the cheese. The flavor should be sharp and engaging. Watch out for excessive saltiness.

2. CANTAL-LAGUIOLE: This pale straw-colored cheese that tastes of mountain herbs and flowers—gentian, fennel, and thyme—is made from the raw milk of cows grazing about the pastures of Aubrac, at an altitude of 800 to 1,400 meters (2,600 to 4,600 feet). Traditionally Laguiole (pronounced *lie-yull*) is made only from

May to September, in the *burons,* small stone huts in the mountains, where the cows and the shepherds live during the prime milking period. The cylinders of firm lactic cheese may weigh up to 50 kilos (110 pounds) and are aged in the *burons* for a minimum of four months. In local markets, one finds very earthy, sharp varieties aged up to two years. Related cheeses: Cantal, Salers, aged Cheddars.

3. BLEU DES CAUSSES: Like Bleu d'Auvergne, Bleu des Causses is made of whole cow's milk, raw or pasteurized, but it's much lighter veined and finer grained. Legally, the cheese must be aged at least seventy days, but it is best when aged for three to six months. A firm, strong, and fatty cheese, Bleu des Causses is often used in cooking—added to omelets, pasta, or potatoes.

4. FOURME D'AMBERT: One of France's greatest cheeses—as a blue cheese, many connoisseurs consider it superior to Roquefort—this tall cylinder of blue-veined cow's-milk cheese takes its name from the Auvergnat village of Ambert. Legally, Fourme d'Ambert must be aged at least forty days, but the finest remains in humid cellars from four to five months. Buttery and unctuous, Fourme d'Ambert has a soft, almost fruity flavor, a gray to orange rind, with a faintly musty aroma of the cellar in which it was aged. Related to Fourme de Montbrison.

5. SALERS: Also known as Cantal Salers, these huge cylinders made of raw cow's milk appear in a variety of sizes, from 10 kilos (22 pounds) up to 40 kilos (88 pounds). Legally, Salers may be made in only a specific area of the Auvergne, from the milk of cows grazing at an altitude of 700 to 1,000 meters (2,300 to 3,300 feet). The best is made by hand from May to September, in mountain cabins known as *burons*. Related cheeses: all Cantals and aged Cheddars.

6. SAINT-NECTAIRE: A rugged mountain cheese that now suffers from banalization—most are not aged long enough to bring out their best qualities—the finest Saint-Nectaire is made on farms, of raw cow's milk. These farm cheeses are sold with a distinguishing elliptical green stamp. Versions made in dairies carry a rectangular green stamp. A good Saint-Nectaire will be a flat disc with a dimpled yellow to rust-colored rind, a supple straw-colored interior, and an aroma of wild mushrooms, a taste of grilled hazelnuts.

WINE OF AUVERGNE

SAINT POURCAIN BLANC (PETILLAT): I first discovered this wine at the restaurant Ambassade d'Auvergne in Paris, where the red goes so perfectly with the hearty Auvergnat fare. In the Auvergne, keep an eye out for wines that seldom leave the region, including Chanturgue—at its best a powerful red full of berry fruitiness.

Gascogne, Toulouse, et Quercy
GASCONY, TOULOUSE, AND QUERCY

Christine and Michel Guérard, Eugénie-les-Bains.

France still has regions where one can drive for hours and not meet another vehicle. That is true of Gascony and the Quercy, with its gently rolling hills in a range of muted tones, where the only signs of life are, as often as not, a few waddling white geese or a stray gray cat.

This is an agricultural area, and its farm families partake of solid peasant food that is rustic, abundant, and strongly influenced by the Arabs, who for nearly 800 years held substantial portions of Spain just beyond the Pyrénées, leaving traces of their presence in all phases of the culture. One sees it in native dishes like the *tourtière,* which is a not-too-distant cousin of *baklava,* and in the *cassoulet,* a blend of beans and sausages and preserved meat that, it has been suggested, is simply an adaptation of the Arab fava bean and mutton stew.

The fertile soil easily provides the essentials for the well-furnished southwestern table: corn-fed geese and ducks to be preserved as *confits* and to supply the liver for *foie gras,* prunes for

preserving in *eau-de-vie,* wild mushrooms and truffles for holiday meals, and grapes for the table as well as for the coarse red *vin du pays.* I love this quiet, gentle region most of all in the fall, when the rich and colorful abundance of autumn harvest is evident everywhere and farmers' markets are laden with freshly picked *cèpe* mushrooms, brilliant red-skinned pumpkins, and moist and meaty first-of-the-season walnuts.

In the country, roadside stands offer *cèpes* for a mere 60 francs a kilo (housewives pay three times that in Paris markets), plump fowl populate the neatly kept farmyards, and slender corncribs are filled to overflowing with a late fall harvest of rich golden feed.

WHEN YOU GO

Michelin Green Guides: *Pyrénées/Aquitaine* and *Périgord/Quercy.*

Getting there: Air Inter offers about three 1-hour flights to Toulouse daily, leaving from Paris's Orly Ouest airport. The same journey by train from the Gare d'Austerlitz takes about 7 hours; there are at least seven trains daily. Cars can be rented at the airport and train station.

Getting around: Michelin maps 234 (Aquitaine) and 235 (Midi-Pyrénées).

Best time to visit: May and June, and September and October. Since the food here tends to be hearty, I prefer to avoid the region during the hot months of July and August.

MARKETS
(Liveliest markets are marked with an asterisk.)

Monday: Mauvezin, Mirande, Samatan.

Tuesday: Aire-sur-l'Adour, Albi (second and fourth Tuesday of each month), Aurignac, *Casteljaloux, Castres, Colomiers, Fleurance, Marmande, Mont-de-Marsan, Muret, Toulouse.

Wednesday: *Castres, *Condom, Gimont, Hagetmau, Peyrehorade, Toulouse, Valence-d'Agen.

Thursday: Auch, Castelsarrasin, Castres, Colomiers, Eauze, Marmande, Mézin, Plaisance, Saint-Clar, Saint-Gaudens, Toulouse.

Friday: Castres, Gaillac, Lautrec, Monflanquin, Riscle, *Toulouse, Verdun-sur-Garonne, Vic-Fézensac.

Saturday: Albi, Auch, Beaumont-de-Lomagne, Casteljaloux, *Castres, *Colomiers, Condom, Cordes, Grenade, *Marmande, Moissac, Mont-de-Marsan, Montauban, *Muret, Nérac, Tournon-d'Agenais (July, August, September), Toulouse.

Sunday: *Mézin, *Moissac, Toulouse.

SPECIALTY MARKETS

Note: The various regional marchés au gras *and* marchés aux foies gras *include the sale of both the fattened poultry (variously duck and goose) and their livers.*

Monday: Caussade (*foie gras*—December through February), Mauvezin (*ail,* or garlic—first or second Monday, July through December), Samatan (*foie gras*—9:45 to 10:45 A.M., November through March).

Tuesday: Fleurance (*foie gras*—10 to 11 A.M., November through January or February, depending on the weather), Valence-d'Agen (*foie gras*—November through January).

Wednesday: Montauban (*foie gras*—November 11 through mid-March).

Thursday: Eauze (*foie gras*—9 to 10 A.M., November through January or February), Castelsarrasin (*foie gras*—December through February), Saint-Clar (*ail,* or garlic—10 to 11 A.M., second Thursday in July through the first days of January).

Friday: Riscle (*foie gras*—November through March), Vic-Fézensac (*foie gras*—November through February).

FAIRS AND FESTIVALS

Second Monday after Mardi Gras: *Foire au Gras* (fair of fattened poultry and their livers), Agen.

First Monday after Easter: *Omelette Géante* (giant omelet festival), Bessières.

Last week in May: *Foire Nationale d'Agen et du Lot et Garonne,* Agen.

End of June: *Fête du Boeuf* (roast beef festival), Montauban.

July 13 and 14: *Festival de la Gastronomie Lot et Garonnaise,* Villefranche-du-Queyran.

Bastille Day (July 14): *Journées Gastronomiques,* Hagetmau; *Foire aux Fromages de Chèvres* (goats'-milk cheese fair), Plaisance.

Sunday in mid-July: *Fête du Grand Fauconnier* (festival of the falconer), Cordes.

Second Sunday in August: *Fête du Melon* (melon festival), Lectoure.

Mid-August: *Election du Roi des Menteurs* (king of the liars contest), Moncrabeau.

Monday after August 15: *Fête de l'Ail* (garlic fair), Mauvezin.

One week in September: *Fête du Chasselas* (grape festival), Moissac.

Saturday preceding the first Monday after September 15 (or September 22 if the 15th is a Monday): *Foire de la Prune* (plum fair), Agen.

October: *Fête du Chasselas et des Vendanges* (grape harvest festival), Prayssas.

AIRE-SUR-L'ADOUR *(Landes)*

Auch 82 k, Condom 67 k, Dax 76 k, Mont-de-Marsan 31 k, Orthez 59 k, Paris 721 k, Pau 49 k, Tarbes 69 k.

Market: Tuesday, 8 A.M. to 5 P.M., Place de l'Hôtel-de-Ville.

RESTAURANT

DOMAINE DE BASSIBE
Ségos, 32400 Riscle.
(62.09.46.71 and
  62.09.43.55).
Last orders taken at 2 P.M.
  and 9:30 P.M.
Closed November until
  Easter.
Credit cards: AE, DC, V.
Private dining rooms for 15
  and 30.
English spoken.
170- and 210-franc menus.
  A la carte, 300 francs.

S P E C I A L T I E S :
Soupe en croûte aux cèpes
(pastry-topped soup with wild
mushrooms), *escalope de foie de
canard aux poires* (sliced duck
foie gras with pears).

This is the sort of Relais et Châteaux spot to go to enjoy the quiet of the country and to be pampered. The restaurant is light, bright, and airy, located in its own building adjacent to the pool and hotel. The raised hearth and white-painted beamed ceilings give the place both a homey and a modern air, and the food is modest and appealing. Try the fragrant *soupe en croûte aux cèpes* and the special *boeuf de Bazas à la ficelle,* boiled local beef on a string, served with mounds of plain boiled vegetables, the perfect, delicate dish for those who—for the moment at least—prefer to shy away from richer fare. (Directions: From Aire-sur-l'Adour, take the N134 south 9 kilometers. Make a left onto the D260. The restaurant is marked.)

AUCH *(Gers)*

Agen 71 k, Lourdes 92 k, Montauban 86 k, Paris 768 k, Tarbes 73 k.

Markets: Thursday, 8:30 A.M. to noon, Avenue Hoche; Saturday, 9:30 A.M. to 6 P.M., Place de la République.
Flea market: second Saturday of the month, 8 A.M. to 12:30 P.M. and 2 to 8 P.M., Place Jean-David.

RESTAURANT

HOTEL DE FRANCE
Place de la Libération,
  32000 Auch.
(62.05.00.44).
Last orders taken at 1:30 P.M.
  and 9:30 P.M.
Closed Sunday dinner,
  Monday, and January.

One wonders where Gascon cooking would be without André Daguin, unquestionably the biggest booster of France's hearty southwestern cuisine. The outgoing and boyishly handsome chef travels about the world promoting his region's specialties, including Armagnac, *foie gras,* and *confit,* and thus has become a sort of idol among south-

Credit cards: AE, DC, V.
Air-conditioned.
Private dining rooms for 10
and up to 90.
English spoken.
250- and 375-franc menus.
A la carte, 400 francs.

SPECIALTIES:
Foie gras, confit (goose, duck,
or pork cooked and preserved
in its fat).

western housewives, who are proud to see him popularize the simple dishes they have cooked for generations in farm kitchens all over this sparsely populated region. So this is the place to come to feast on *foie gras* (in not one but dozens of forms, with truffle juice and oysters, with seaweed, with capers, even with quince), on lentil soup with a *confit* of gizzards, on roast pigeon accompanied by an unforgettable *confit* of garlic. Unfortunately, the meals I've had at the Hôtel de France over the years have not been totally consistent, and there is obvious and sometimes annoying favoritism toward guests who are known, with a lack of attention toward those who are merely passing through.

EUGENIE-LES-BAINS *(Landes)*

Aire-sur-l'Adour 14 k, Dax 69 k, Mont-de-Marsan 26 k, Orthez 53 k,
Paris 731 k, Pau 53 k.

RESTAURANT

LES PRES D'EUGENIE
Eugénie-les-Bains, 40320
Geaune.
(58.51.19.01).
Last orders taken at 1:30 P.M.
(or 2 P.M. with a
reservation) and 9:30 P.M.
(10 P.M. in summer).
Closed December through
February.
Credit cards: AE, DC.
Private dining room for 14.
English spoken.
360- and 380-franc menus,
not including wine and
service. A la carte, 600
francs.

SPECIALTIES:
Changing seasonal menu,
including *cuisine minceur,* or
spa cuisine.

Does the perfect French country inn exist? Perfection is, of course, relative, but given the choice, I'd head straight for Eugénie-les-Bains every time, for Michel and Christine Guérard's enchanting inn combines a rare sense of comfort, country warmth, and a sincere form of elegance. Over the years I've returned time and again to eagerly sample the renowned spa cuisine known as *cuisine minceur,* relishing the more clearly embellished version known as *gourmande,* enjoying breakfast trays decorated with bright flowers and fresh-from-the-garden herb teas. I love the way Christine Guérard has filled every bit of space on the sprawling estate with personal touches: old oil paintings, collections of baskets and ceramic spice jars, little antique tables, and plenty of palm trees and fountains. I hold the same admiration for Michel Guérard's style of cooking, which features the sorts of foods I crave most. He's generous with herbs and salads fresh from his neatly kept garden out back. Fish, shellfish, and game are grilled over the huge open fireplace in his kitchen, always cooked with their skin or shells intact, guarding flavor and texture.

The roots of Guérard's cuisine are a mix of country and city, and while the local Armagnac, farm-fresh chicken, and *foie gras* dominate the menu, there are also black truffles, lobster, scallops, and fresh salmon to round the meal out with a fine dose of luxury. (Note that *cuisine minceur* meals are served by reservation only and at an earlier seating than *gourmande* meals, and only to guests of the hotel.)

LUPPE-VIOLLES *(Gers)*

Aire-sur-l'Adour 11 k, Auch 70 k, Mont-de-Marsan 37 k.

RESTAURANT

LE RELAIS DE L'ARMAGNAC
Luppé-Violles, 32110 Nogaro.
(62.08.95.22).
Last orders taken at 2 P.M. and 9 P.M.
Closed Sunday dinner, Monday, and January.
Credit cards: AE, V.
Private dining rooms for 8 and 24.
English spoken.
65-, 130-, 180-, and 230-franc menus. A la carte, 200 francs.

SPECIALTIES:
Change with the seasons; *pigeonneau désossé et farci à ma façon* (stuffed pigeon), *filet de sole au beurre rouge et aux morilles* (sole with red butter sauce and morels), *filets mignons de veau aux cèpes* (veal with wild mushrooms).

This little village restaurant by the side of the road is as cute as a dollhouse, all decked out in flowery and feminine pinks and whites. The food here lacks polish, but Marie-Martine Duffour's cooking is sincere, and the overall experience is good enough to make me want to return. Her very best dish is the *demoiselles assaisonnées,* duck served as strips of *"filet mignon"* (the narrow, delicate strip of meat lying at the back of the breast meat) quickly marinated in sherry vinegar, then at the last minute dressed with a blend of shallots, green peppercorns, oil, and salt. The seasoning was perfect, just delicate enough to add some pizzazz but not so overwhelming one couldn't enjoy the meaty richness of the silken-textured duck. Another winner is the *papillote de coeurs d'oies aux cerises.* Before you turn your nose up at the thought of an entire main course of goose hearts, try this version: beautifully textured, meaty, rich, and satisfying, the goose hearts are cooked sealed (unfortunately in foil) with a fragrant blend of whole-grain mustard, orange-flower water, and cherries. It's a gutsy dish, designed for hearty southwestern appetites. Less successful was the *magret de canard* (a fattened duck breast), which arrived overcooked, dried out, tasting as though it had been reheated. This is definitely a haven for Armagnac lovers: An entire dining table is set out with an astonishing assortment of Armagnacs, all brands, all ages, all sizes, all prices.

MONCAUT *(Lot-et-Garonne)*

Agen 11 k, Nérac 20 k.

EAUX-DE-VIE

SAINT-GAYRAND
Moncaut, 47310 Laplume.
(53.97.13.83).
Open daily 9 A.M. to 5 P.M.
Will ship to most countries.

When in the area, do make a little detour to this small artisanal distillery, where they offer a wide selection of fine fruit brandies, many of which have won endless praise and awards from *sommeliers* around France. I first sampled Saint-Gayrand's unusually fragrant *eau-de-vie-de-muscat* (a delicate grape brandy) in a Paris restaurant, then tracked them down when I found my way to Agen. I was delighted also by their marvelously fruity *eau-de-vie-de-prunes* (plum brandy), as well as their prunes marinated in plum brandy, a delicious topping for vanilla or prune ice cream. (Directions: From Agen, take the D656 south to Roquefort. Go through Roquefort, and when you reach a fork in the road continue on the D656. Three kilometers from the fork you will reach Pléchac. After another 800 meters there will be a sign for the "Domaine de Pouzergues," which is also the Domaine de Serguillon [Saint-Gayrand].)

PLAISANCE *(Gers)*

Aire-sur-l'Adour 30 k, Auch 55 k, Condom 64 k, Paris 701 k, Pau 65 k, Tarbes 44 k.

Market: Thursday, 9 A.M. to 5 P.M., Place du 11-Novembre.
Foire aux Fromages de Chèvre (goat cheese fair): Bastille Day (July 14).

RESTAURANT

RIPA-ALTA
3 Place de l'Eglise, 32160
  Plaisance.
(62.69.30.43).
Last orders taken at 2 P.M.
  and 10 P.M.
Open daily June through
  September. Closed
  Sunday dinner and
  Monday October through

Simple, basic, and purely regional, this is the place to go to sample some of the southwest's earthiest fare. The plain, old-fashioned, dark-wood dining room will take you back to the 1930s, as will the very reasonable prices. Roll up your sleeves and dig into the raw oysters and warm sausages (what a great marriage of hot and cold, a fine contrast of textures and forthright flavors), the goose hearts

May, and November.
Credit cards: AE, DC, EC, V.
Private dining room for 30.
English spoken.
66-, 125-, and 230-franc
menus. A la carte, 200
francs.

SPECIALTIES:
Foie gras au Juraçon (*foie gras*
with southwestern wine),
feuilleté de ris d'agneau aux cèpes
(lamb sweetbreads and wild
mushrooms in puff pastry).

blended with fragrant wild *cèpe* mushrooms, and the classic—though far from ordinary—*confit*. I think I died just a little bit—of joy—when I tasted chef Maurice Coscuella's duck *confit* and white beans, as rich and wonderful as that dish can be, with long-simmered beans full of rich duck flavor. For dessert, do not ignore the fresh and flaky *croustade aux pruneaux* (pastry filled with apples and prunes in Armagnac) and the unforgettably intense prune ice cream.

POUDENAS *(Lot-et-Garonne)*

Agen 47 k, Aire-sur-l'Adour 62 k, Condom 19 k, Nérac 17 k, Paris 666 k.

RESTAURANT

LA BELLE GASCONNE
Poudenas, 47170 Mézin.
(53.65.71.58).
Last orders taken at 2 P.M.
and 9:30 P.M.
Closed Sunday dinner,
Monday, the first two
weeks in December, and
the two weeks after
January 1.
Credit cards: AE, DC, V.
English spoken.
98-, 150-, and 220-franc
menus. A la carte, 220
francs.

SPECIALTIES:
Foie gras frais de canard (duck
foie gras), *civet de canard au sang*
(duck stew), *gâteau au chocolat*
(chocolate cake).

The place to go to profit from the abundance of Gascony is the tiny village of Poudenas, home to the outgoing, dedicated Marie-Claude and Richard Gracia, owners of La Belle Gasconne.

Madame Gracia is one of France's leading women chefs, a bubbly, red-haired dynamo who shows us what real Gascon home cooking should taste like: If the food doesn't come from her garden, or from that of her neighbors, she doesn't serve it. And she's not there just to feed bodies, but spirits as well.

So there are rich lobes of fresh *foie gras*, seared and served atop a bed of thick, fresh noodles (see recipe, following page); a homey and satisfying *tourte* filled with soft, sweet leeks and autumn *cèpes*, wrapped in fine, thin pastry; a salad of tender roast quail, dressed with her own puckery melon vinegar; and a *civet de canard*, a rustic, unadorned duck stew so moist, so tender, so clearly homemade, you'll most certainly beg for seconds.

Madame Gracia, like her mother, grandmother, and great-grandmother before her, has dedicated her life to feeding the public, and she does so with particular grace and spirit. The Gracias' small, cozy restaurant—alive with classical music, garden flowers, and an outgoing local clientele—has been fashioned out of an old miller's residence. Soon they hope to have completed work on the companion mill across the street: The new dining room will offer a glassed-in view of the picture-book village, with its ancient stone bridge and the rushing stream below, and upstairs, rooms will provide much-needed lodging for travelers.

MACARONADE LA BELLE GASCONNE
FOIE GRAS AND WILD MUSHROOM PASTA LA BELLE GASCONNE

One of my favorite ways to eat warm foie gras *is cubed, then tossed with warm fresh pasta. This version, a variation on the* macaronade *served at the charming La Belle Gasconne in Poudenas, is rich with morels, which take on a powerful wild mushroom flavor when they're reduced with fresh cream. You get a lot of flavor mileage out of this dish, for even though you use rather small quantities of* foie gras *and morels, the rich essence of each really comes through. For a real feast, a black truffle may be shaved over the pasta just as it is being tossed.*

2 ounces (60 g) dried morels
2 cups (500 ml) hot tap water
2 cups (500 ml) crème fraîche (see Recipe Index) or heavy cream, preferably not ultra-pasteurized
2 tablespoons extra-virgin olive oil
1 pound (500 g) small mushrooms, caps thinly sliced, stems reserved for another dish
Salt and freshly ground black pepper to taste
10 ounces (300 g) fresh tagliatelle
3 ounces (125 g) *foie gras,* cut into small cubes
1 small black truffle (optional)

1. Soak the morels in the hot water for 15 minutes and drain them, reserving the liquid. Strain the liquid to remove any sand. Add it with the morels to a medium saucepan and bring to a boil over medium-high heat. Reduce the liquid until about ½ cup remains, then add the *crème fraîche* and cook until the mushrooms have absorbed half the cream. This should take about 15 minutes. Keep the mixture warm over low heat.

2. Heat the olive oil in a large skillet over medium-high heat. Add the sliced mushrooms and sauté just until they begin to soften, about 5 minutes. Add them to the morels and season the sauce to taste with salt and pepper.

3. Bring a large pot of salted water to a boil and cook the pasta just until it is done, about 5 minutes. Drain it and return it to the pot. Add the mushroom mixture and the *foie gras* and toss gently until all the ingredients are thoroughly mixed. Divide the mixture among 4 warmed dinner plates and, if using the truffle, shave equal amounts over each serving. Serve immediately.

Yield: 4 servings.

PUYMIROL *(Lot-et-Garonne)*

Agen 17 k, Moissac 43 k, Paris 642 k, Villeneuve-sur-Lot 30 k.

RESTAURANT

L'AUBERGADE
52 Rue Royale, 47270
   Puymirol.
(53.95.31.46).
Last orders taken at 2 P.M.
   and 9 P.M.
Open daily July and August.
   Closed Monday
   mid-April through
   October, Sunday dinner
   and Monday November
   through mid-April.
Credit cards: AE, DC, V.
Terrace dining in summer.
Private dining rooms for 10,
   20, and 50.
English spoken.
120-franc menu weekday
   lunch only; 240- and
   380-franc menus. A la
   carte, 350 francs.

SPECIALTIES:
*Lasagne de homard au persil
simple* (lobster lasagne with
parsley), *terrine de poireaux à la
vinaigrette et julienne de truffes*
(leek terrine with truffles),
truite de mer et sa peau croustillée
(sea trout), *pigeonneau aux épices*
(pigeon with spices), *larme de
chocolat au Banyuls* (chocolate
teardrop filled with chocolate
mousse and cherries),
*millefeuille de nougatines glacées
au pralin* (napoleon of frozen
layers of praline).

Maryse and Michel Trama, at L'Aubergade.

Michel and Maryse Trama's quiet country restaurant known as L'Aubergade is one of the finer tables in France today. Since 1979 the couple has labored to transform this medieval residence of the counts of Toulouse into a warm, welcoming spot to enjoy Michel's exquisite cuisine.

Amazingly, Trama has no professional chef's training, and one says "amazing" because his food is so elegant, refined, and perfect, you can't believe he has not spent decades at the stove.

While his menu is not obviously regional—you don't come here for grilled goose hearts or *cassoulet*—you'll find fine local duck, pigeon, rabbit, and capon, as well as a larder full of seasonal game, wild mushrooms, and local vegetables.

Try his vibrant salad of pistachio-studded wild duck sausage, served in hearty slices layered atop a thick bed of firm-cooked potatoes, circling a well-dressed salad of mixed colorful greens. Better yet, consider the unusual and successful combination of fresh cod (here called *morue*), surrounded by mounds of the freshest, finest *cèpes* I've tasted in years. The delicacy of the cod and the glorious freshness of the mushrooms are brought together with a vibrant sauce blending shallots and vinegar and a good dose of reduced mushroom stock.

Wild-game lovers will love the unadorned *col vert au citron vert,* simple roast mallard duck—very gamey, very rosy—served with a clump of wilted spinach.

Desserts are equally appealing: His humorous *larme de chocolat* consists of a "teardrop" of rich bitter chocolate filled with a chocolate mousse-like confection, with cherry surprises buried within.

Like many of France's more ambitious and creative young chefs, Trama's food is bold and aggressive. Truffle and mushroom sauces really taste of truffles and mushrooms, vinaigrettes are assertively acidic; but best of all, his dishes have a polish, a finished quality that even the most elegant of foods generally lack. It's as if he labors toward a specific refinement and elegance, and just as a dish reaches that stage, he pushes it just one step further.

SALADE DE JAMBON DE PAYS GRILLE A L' ECHALOTE
GRILLED COUNTRY HAM SALAD WITH SHALLOTS

It is difficult to understand why this simple and satisfying recipe is not yet a classic. It's a warming country dish from the city of Agen, where the locals prefer the prized échalote grise *(the French shallot, admired for its role as an aromatic garnish) to the more common onion. The sliced shallots are marinated for several hours to soften and sweeten them, adding a fine, mellow flavor to the warm grilled ham.*

8 shallots, sliced into thin rounds
½ cup (125 ml) extra-virgin olive oil
8 very thin slices unsmoked ham, such as prosciutto
¼ cup (60 ml) best-quality red wine vinegar
Handful of fresh chives, minced
Salt and freshly ground black pepper to taste
1 head curly endive or escarole, rinsed, dried, leaves separated

1. Marinate the shallots in the oil at room temperature up to 24 hours.

2. Just before serving the salad, grill the ham slices under a broiler, over a charcoal fire, or on a ridged cast-iron griddle just until the edges begin to brown, about 15 seconds each side.

3. Place the grilled ham in a salad bowl. Cover the ham with the shallots and oil, sprinkle with the vinegar, chives, salt, and pepper, and toss. Cover the bowl and let sit for 5 minutes to allow the ham to absorb the sauce.

4. Remove the ham from the bowl, add the greens, and toss well. Divide the dressed salad among 4 plates and top each salad with 2 slices of ham. Serve immediately.

Yield: 4 servings.

TOULOUSE *(Haute-Garonne)*

Agen 76 k, Bordeaux 244 k, Montauban 52 k, Paris 705 k, Samatan 50 k.

Markets: Tuesday through Sunday, 9 A.M. to 1 P.M., covered markets, Place des Carmes and Place Victor-Hugo; Tuesday through Sunday, 9 A.M. to 1 P.M., open-air market, Boulevard de Strasbourg; Wednesday, 9 A.M. to 5 P.M., open-air market, Place du Capitole.
Flea market: Sunday, 8 A.M. to 1 P.M., Place Saint-Sernin.

RESTAURANTS

DARROZE
19 Rue Castellane, 31000 Toulouse.
(61.62.34.70).
Last orders taken at 1:30 P.M. and 9:30 P.M.
Closed Saturday lunch and Sunday.
Credit cards: AE, DC, V.
Air-conditioned.
225- and 280-franc menus. A la carte, 250 francs.

SPECIALTIES:
Change with the seasons; fish and game in season.

Darroze is a restaurant of contrast and seeming contradictions: The decor is as dull, modern, and somber as the food is lively, exciting, and well seasoned. So take my advice and go for the food, which could well serve as a model of southwestern cooking. Mounds of wild *cèpe* mushrooms smothered in garlic; a classic, beautiful *pipérade* (here served as scrambled eggs mixed with green and red peppers, tomatoes, and onions, topped with a flavorful slice of ham); and a truly harmonious dish that combines pinkish-rare *noisettes* of venison, a peppery blueberry condiment, and a dark, rich, gamey sauce—all make for a truly memorable meal in a city that's well worth the detour.

VANEL
22 Rue Maurice-Fontvieille, 31000 Toulouse.
(61.21.51.82).
Last orders taken at 1:30 P.M. and 9:45 P.M.
Closed Sunday, Monday lunch, and August.
Credit cards: AE, EC.
Air-conditioned.
English spoken.
350 francs.

SPECIALTIES:
Change daily.

If you want to dine with the most fashionable crowd in Toulouse, then go to Vanel. It's always spirit-lifting to be part of the crowd that feels at home, that's happy to be there, where the service is personal and friendly. And the food—though a bit disappointing—would still put this large, spacious restaurant on my list of places I'd be sure to return to. Like the food at many successful restaurants in France, Lucien Vanel's cuisine seems to straddle the line between country and city fare, and the end result looks prettier than it tastes. In many cases, just a touch more seasoning in the kitchen would solve the problem. The dishes we did enjoy here include a classic, full-flavored, and satisfying *civet de lièvre* (wild hare stew) served with a touch of rabbit sausage, a lovely poached pear, and chestnuts; and a marvelous dessert of poached pears gratinéed with almond butter, served with fresh almond macaroons. Less satisfying were the lamb with white beans and the assortment of beautiful but largely bland salads. The wine list is worth a trip all on its own—it's extensive, nicely annotated, and well priced. If they have it that day, try the Prieuré-de-Saint-Jean-de-Bébian, a vibrant red Coteaux-du-Languedoc. Vanel also offers a lovely coffee and tea menu, and serves delicious herbal teas, or infusions, brewed from fresh herbs.

CAFES

BIBENT
5 Place du Capitole, 31000 Toulouse.
(61.23.89.03).
Open 8 A.M. to 12:30 A.M. Closed Sunday.
Credit cards: AE, DC, V.
Sidewalk terrace.

One of those wonderful dressed-up Belle Epoque cafés, with high ceilings and thick ornamentation along the walls, and waiters in black vests and ties. Try to ignore the rock music and the smoke, and settle into a wicker chair along the terrace to admire the wide open space of the Place du Capitole and the Toulouse Opera nearby. At mealtime they offer platters of raw and cooked shellfish.

GRAND CAFE FLORIDA
12 Place du Capitole, 31000 Toulouse.
(61.21.49.92 or 61.21.87.59).
Open daily 7:30 A.M. to 2 A.M.
Sidewalk terrace.

Another grand café, rather tastefully redone to imitate its turn-of-the-century counterparts, with cozy red velvet banquettes, wicker chairs, a long bar, and giant mirrors.

The southwest of France, especially the area north of Toulouse, is plum country. Here the succulent plums—known in French as *prunes* in both the fresh and the dried state—are transformed into succulent dried fruits, smothered in batter and baked in a sweet comforting dessert, or cut in two and carefully arranged on a delicate crusted tart. They may count for a lot in the cuisine of France, but if someone says they've worked for *"des prunes,"* it means they've worked for nothing. However, if you're asked to do a favor and it's just too much, respond *"Des prunes!"* and you won't be asked again.

FROMAGERIES

LA PASTORALE
10 Place des Carmes, 31000
  Toulouse.
(61.55.49.66).
Open 9 A.M. to 12:30 P.M.
  and 3:30 to 7:15 P.M.
  Closed Sunday, Monday,
  and July or August.

A pleasant little cheese shop right outside the Carmes covered market: not a huge selection, but what there is, is well chosen, well aged.

XAVIER
6 Place Victor-Hugo, 31000
  Toulouse.
(61.21.53.26).
Open 8:15 A.M. to 12:30 P.M.
  and 3:30 to 7:15 P.M.
  Closed Sunday, Monday
  morning, and July or
  August.
Will ship in France.

O ne of those country-cottage cheese shops, filled with a fragrant selection of more than 250 different, tastefully displayed, well-aged cheeses (from all over France and elsewhere), a boutique decorated with new and antique cheesemaking and aging paraphernalia.

CONFISERIE

CONFISERIE OLIVIER
27 Rue Lafayette, 31000
  Toulouse.
(61.23.21.87).
Open 9 A.M. to 12:30 P.M.
  and 1:30 to 7 P.M. Closed
  Sunday.
Credit cards: AE, V.
Will ship in France.

S P E C I A L T Y:
Violettes de Toulouse (candied violets).

T he place in town to find the famous glistening, delicate—and rather tasteless—candied violets of Toulouse, a specialty once celebrated as a medication to soothe sore throats and stomachs. The little purple candies are pretty for decorating cakes and pastries, and the colorfully decorated gift boxes make fine souvenirs. Historically, the idea of candying violets and other flowers originated in Toulouse around the 1880s, when it was also fashionable to garnish green salads with fresh violets. So much for the newness of *nouvelle cuisine*!

SPECIALITES REGIONALES

SAMARAN
At the Victor-Hugo market,
  stand 139–140, Tuesday
  through Sunday.
(61.21.26.91).

S P E C I A L T Y:
Fresh local poultry.

W hen wandering through the Victor-Hugo market, do stop here to admire the selection of freshest local poultry, and pick up some beautifully cured *jambon de magret* (duck breast cured like ham), perfect picnic or traveling fare.

GERARD CUQ
At the Carmes market, stand
20, Tuesday through
Sunday.
(61.53.73.37).

SPECIALTY:
Fresh local poultry.

Another poultry specialist, offering an astonishing selection of local poultry, along with duck *confit,* duck carcasses, you name it. You'll see here that nothing, but nothing, goes to waste on these animals!

LES VIGNES *(Tarn-et-Garonne)*

Bourg-de-Visa 2 k, Brassac 4 k, Moissac 24 k, Puymirol 21 k.

SPECIALITES REGIONALES

ANDRE POCHAT
Agence de Voyages
Midi-Pyrénées, Les Vignes,
82190 Bourg-de-Visa.
(63.94.24.30).

SPECIALTY:
Week-end à la Ferme (farm
weekend).

The friendly, outgoing, well-organized André Pochat arranges traditional cooking weeks and weekends with local farm women, where students learn to prepare country soups, stews, stuffed chicken *(galantine de poule),* as well as the region's famous *cassoulet,* a rich blend of beans, sausages, and meats (see "A Farmhouse Kitchen, A Cozy Classroom," facing page). Free time is set aside for visiting wine cellars and for Armagnac tastings. Students stay in Monsieur and Madame Pochat's beautifully restored seventeenth-century manor house, situated amidst the calm and greenery of the Quercy countryside. Courses can be translated into English, on request.

Jeanne-Marie Mourière in her kitchen.

A Farmhouse Kitchen, A Cozy Classroom

"*Madame Mourière cooks with an understanding born of decades at the stove, and her food, like the best of what the southwest has to offer, is hearty without being heavy.*"

BRASSAC, JULY 4—It is nearly noon in the farmhouse kitchen of Jeanne-Marie Mourière. A plump chicken is browning in the brick oven and a *clafoutis* cools on the windowsill, but Madame Mourière's thoughts are not on today's lunch.

"Now let's get the beans going for tomorrow's *cassoulet*," she says as she moves methodically across the kitchen that she has ruled for fifty of her seventy-five years. She drops a few spoonfuls of goose fat onto the beans that are just beginning to bubble on the stove. Looking mildly guilty, like a child who has taken one too many cookies, she says defensively, "It's to nourish the beans."

Here in this whisper of a town, Madame Mourière and her husband, Jean-Marie, typify the Quercy culinary tradition. Their children are grown and scattered and their flock of geese was sold off long ago, but for Madame Mourière the habit of cooking for a small, eager horde continues, so from time to time she opens her kitchen to those who share her passion for the food of Quercy.

While she bustles about between stove and table, her husband is always at hand to refill glasses with wine. Like most couples who have been married for half a century, their manner toward each other is humorously, habitually impatient. She sends him out for half a dozen eggs; he absentmindedly comes back with twice that many. He wanders out to the garden to gather sorrel and is not seen for half an hour. "For fifty years I've never been right," he says with a resignation that is obviously no longer bothersome.

Madame Mourière cooks with an understanding born of decades at the stove, and her food, like the best of what the southwest has to offer, is hearty without being heavy. She is known throughout the region for her spectacular farm dishes: stuffed goose neck encased in a buttery brioche, a remarkably digestible *cassoulet,* her own *confit* of goose, and her *tourtière,* which appears regularly at local weddings and feasts, fresh from her brick bread oven on the back porch. This feather-light local pastry, known elsewhere as *pastis* or *croustade,* is a multi-layered construction of transparently thin strudel dough filled with apples and prunes from nearby Agen and sprinkled with sugar and generous doses of Armagnac from the Gascon region to the south.

Like every cook in the southwest, Madame Mourière has fixed opinions about the proper *cassoulet,* which for her must be neither greasy nor unreasonably complicated. "*Cassoulets* are often ruined by adding too many ingredients," she says. "If you have a good *confit d'oie,* why add mutton? It will only overwhelm the dish." Her *cassoulet* is made of beans and *confit,* Toulouse sausage, and tomatoes.

Madame Mourière works methodically, chatting freely in *patois.* By week's end she has flown with ease through meals that would tire women half her age, cooking always in glazed clay pots to keep things soft, in wood-fired brick ovens to impart a smoky richness. She offers thick country apple pies, and a lean pork and veal terrine laced with Armagnac and green olives, parsley, and thyme. And with each meal, she serves a wholesome green salad, dressed with the homemade vinegar that steeps in the old clay jug resting atop her kitchen counter.

ARMAGNACS OF GASCONY, TOULOUSE, AND QUERCY

Armagnac is sometimes called "the other brandy," to distinguish it from Cognac. While differences between the two are largely a matter of style, Armagnac is more earthy and rustic. And like Cognac, Armagnac still boasts a number of worthy small producers, as well as some trusted *négociants*. Names to look for include a variety of *château*-bottled brandies selected by Francis Darroze, the Château de Lassalle from Baronne de Pampelonne, and Laberdolive.

Pays Basque
BASQUE COUNTRY

Leeks and fresh eggs at the Bayonne night market.

Anytime I want to transport myself back to the Pays Basque, I just close my eyes and see before me a clear, bright, Technicolor flourish of red, white, and green—straightforward colors that appear and reappear in festive espadrilles and red woolen berets, in newly painted shutters on gleaming white lime-washed houses, in table linens, on flags, in posters, almost everywhere one goes in this proud, mountainous area of France that hugs the border with Spain.

I see, too, the blue-on-blue fishing village of Saint-Jean-de-Luz, the green, green pastures of the Pyrénées, and the flocks of woolly white sheep, branded with splotches of red paint, waddling through villages as the early hour haze gives way to vibrant blue skies.

Of all the varied regions of France, the Basque country is the most visually harmonious, one of the most clearly defined, and one of the most frankly foreign. Is it all those unusual Basque words—like *larunbat* (Saturday) or *itsaso* (ocean)—that stop us short, or is it quite simply the fact that the culture we see is neither the familiar French nor the expected Spanish, but purely, simply Basque?

To get along here, the locals need to be trilingual, speaking Basque at home while needing both French and Spanish for business. Many road and shop signs appear in both Basque and

French, and some menus even offer multilingual translations.

Stretching from the port city of Saint-Jean-de-Luz on the Golfe de Gascogne to the rugged Pyrénées mountains to the east, the French side of the Basque country is made up of many small, accessible inland villages filled with folkloric whitewashed houses, homes built with their backs to the sea, their front doors facing the morning sun.

It is a land of fishermen and farmers, shepherds and winemakers, a land that reflects a single, unified culture but one that is open to worlds not its own. While in other regions of France people peek suspiciously from behind closed, curtained windows, here in the Pays Basque the windows and shutters remain wide open, and people smile warmly at passersby.

I first visited this favored land on an Indian summer Saturday in late September. Arriving in the spotless, animated city of Bayonne well before lunchtime, I quickly found myself caught up in weekend festivities.

The covered market was swarming with customers sampling bite-size portions of black cherry-filled *gâteau basque,* while butchers hawked first-of-the-season *palombes,* or wild pigeons, birds that would be roasted that evening in wood-fired ovens in the countryside. I counted at least a dozen different versions of golden sheep's-milk cheese, known as *brebis,* admired the rows of authentic Bayonne hams rubbed with spicy red pepper (for color as well as to preserve the meat), and managed *not* to indulge in a late-morning snack of the famous *tourtière landaise,* a local sort of strudel filled with apples and prunes and laced with Armagnac.

Nearby, mustachioed men in berets lined up along the Marengo bridge, fishing poles in hand, hoping to catch the baby bass that swim through from the narrow river Nive into the wide Adour. At the same time, a band of strolling musicians wandered past, and like Pied Pipers, they were followed happily through the streets by local merrymakers. The musicians, all male, played ancient instruments that resembled flutes, tiny drums, and tambourines. I knew immediately that I was going to love the Pays Basque, for here daily life itself was a celebration.

And so the days went on like this: markets, touring, long chats with shepherds and tuna fishermen, winemakers, bakers, and distillers of fruity *eaux-de-vie.* Our rental car soon took on the

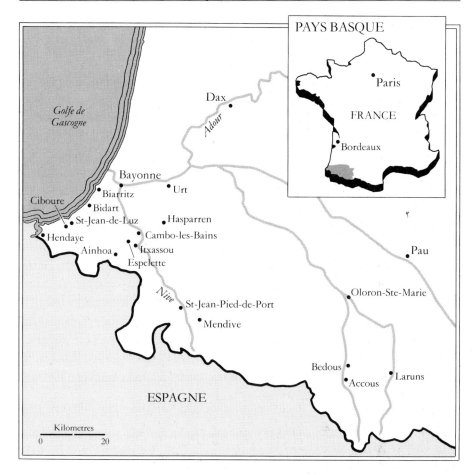

fermenting aroma of aging *brebis,* as we found we could not resist taking home samples of each golden wheel of cheese that caught our eye. Bread and cake crumbs tumbled to the floor as we gave up resisting midday snacks of cornbread and *gâteau basque* from the fifty-year-old Moulin de Bassilour outside Biarritz.

We drove from port cities to inland villages and back again, through a rolling landscape dotted with characteristic long, low farmhouses. We fell in love with Ainhoa, the most idyllic Basque village of all, storybook beautiful and loaded with natural, unforced charm. Walking down the streets of this placid town—population 543—one soon understands that nowhere in France is man's love of his home more evident than in the Pays Basque. In Ainhoa, and in many other villages, each house tenderly bears a title, much the way we assign names to cottages or country houses. On some, the crimson lintels are even inscribed with a message, perhaps the names of the man and woman of the house, the date of their marriage, even the date of the death of a treasured family member. In fact, one resident explained that often people are called by their house name rather than their proper name. One house name seen most often: *Etxe-Eder,* Basque for "beautiful house."

We drove through Espelette (the hot-pepper capital of France), where garlands of fiery red peppers dry outside the farmhouses, and spent hours in the minuscule town of Saint-Jean-Pied-de-Port, where the Monday market is an all-day affair, with live cattle and dozens of farmers selling produce and cheese at makeshift tables.

We wondered about all those huge trucks passing through this little town and learned, from a multitude of sources, that the main street of Saint-Jean-Pied-de-Port is still part of the smugglers' trail between France and Spain (they used to smuggle lace; now it's horses and calves). As one resident explained, rather tongue-in-cheek, Basque families were always large, so the eldest son became a priest, the eldest daughter a nun, the third child went to America, the fourth took over the family farm, and all that was left for the fifth was to set up life as a smuggler!

We had not much time, but we packed in so many activities that we felt we'd had a rich, rewarding month. One morning in the resort-like fishing village of Saint-Jean-de-Luz, we eagerly awakened at sunrise to greet the tuna boats that roll into the bright blue port, then later feasted on that freshly caught *thon blanc,* or grilled white tuna, at Arrantzaleak, the fisherman's shack across the way.

Strolling the pedestrian walkways of this popular resort town, we stumbled on shop after shop of candies and sweets and decided that Saint-Jean-de-Luz should be dubbed the sweet-tooth capital of France.

Later that day, as we set about to return to Paris, we knew we'd be back again soon to this character-filled land, and that next time, we'd get across the border into Spain, to see the rest of the magic world of the Pays Basque.

WHEN YOU GO

Michelin Green Guide: *Pyrénées/Aquitaine.*

Getting there: Air Inter offers at least three daily one-hour flights to Biarritz, leaving from either Paris's Orly Ouest airport or from the Roissy (Charles-de-Gaulle) airport. There are also comfortable overnight trains making the daily 780-kilometer (485-mile) journey between the Gare d'Austerlitz and Biarritz. Cars can be rented at the airport and train station.

Getting around: Michelin map 234 (Aquitaine).

Best time to visit: The most beautiful months are May and October.

Required Reading: Adam Nicolson's *Long Walks in France* details several walks through the region, and offers some splendid photography as well. For another look at the Basque country, the *Aquitaine* volume of the Larousse/Reader's Digest series entitled *Pays et Gens* (available in most major bookstores in France) offers a warm and colorful look at daily life in this part of France.

MARKETS

(Liveliest markets are marked with an asterisk.)

Monday: Bayonne, Biarritz, Pau, *Saint-Jean-Pied-de-Port.

Tuesday: Bayonne, Biarritz, Pau, Saint-Jean-de-Luz.

Wednesday: Bayonne, Biarritz, Hendaye, *Pau.

Thursday: *Bayonne, Biarritz, Pau.

Friday: Bayonne, Biarritz, Oloron-Sainte-Marie, *Pau, Saint-Jean-de-Luz, Saint-Palais.

Saturday: *Bayonne, *Biarritz, Hendaye, Laruns, Pau.

Sunday: Biarritz (in summer).

FAIRS AND FESTIVALS

The three days preceding Easter: *Foire aux Jambons* (ham fair), Bayonne.

One day in June: *Fête des Cerises* (black cherry festival), Itxassou.

One Thursday in July and two Thursdays in August: *Foire aux Fromages* (cheese fair), Saint-Jean-Pied-de-Port.

Around July 4: *Fête du Thon* (tuna festival), Saint-Jean-de-Luz.

September: *Foire aux Fromages* (cheese fair), Saint-Jean-Pied-de-Port.

First weekend in October: *Foire aux Fromages* (cheese fair), Laruns.

Last weekend in October: *Fête du Piment* (pepper festival), Espelette.

ACCOUS *(Pyrénées-Atlantiques)*

Bedous 3 k, Oloron-Sainte-Marie 27 k, Pau 50 k.

FROMAGER

LES FERMIERS
    BASCO-BEARNAIS
64490 Accous.
(59.34.76.06).
Open 8 A.M. to noon and 2
    to 6 P.M. Closed Saturday
    and Sunday.

Founded in 1982, this active farmers' cooperative, with about sixty members, now offers a fine variety of high-quality whole raw-milk cheeses, including those of pure sheep's milk and pure cow's milk, along with a *fromage mixte,* a less intensely flavored cheese made with a blend of sheep's and cow's milk. The cheese is made on independent farms in the prized Aspe valley, then brought to the co-op for aging and shipping. The cheese, sold under the label *Pyrénées Fermier de la Vallée d'Aspe,* is marketed throughout Europe and can readily be found in shops all over France. A personal favorite is the rich, deep-flavored, pure sheep's-milk cheese, sold generally as *pur brebis fermier, au lait cru entier.*

AINHOA *(Pyrénées-Atlantiques)*

Bayonne 26 k, Cambo-les-Bains 11 k, Paris 798 k, Saint-Jean-de-Luz 23 k.

RESTAURANT

ITHURRIA
Ainhoa, 64250
    Cambo-les-Bains.
(59.29.92.11).
Last orders taken at 2 P.M.
    and 9 P.M.
Closed Tuesday dinner,
    Wednesday, and
    mid-November through
    mid-March.
Credit cards: AE, DC, V.
 Private dining rooms for 30
    and 100.
120- and 190-franc menus.
 A la carte, 220 francs.

SPECIALTIES:
Darne de louvine beurre blanc
(striped bass filet with a
white-wine butter sauce).

A charming and folkloric local gathering spot set in the center of the most picturesque village in the Basque region. The food in this cozy restaurant—decorated with beamed ceilings and some fine local antiques—tends to elegance rather than rusticity, though diners can be assured of delicious local lamb, fresh grilled *louvine* from the port at Saint-Jean-de-Luz, and piquant red peppers stuffed with a garlicky, peppery purée of salt cod, their version of *piment farci de morue.* The *gâteau basque* was nothing to write home about, but there's a pleasing pear sorbet and a nicely aged sheep's-milk *brebis du pays.* On a warm day, there's a thirst-quenching house Rioja rosé, a wine that marries well with the local cuisine.

From farm to market, along the bridges of Bayonne.

FOLKLORIQUE

ARTS POPULAIRES
Maison Kantorenia,
Ainhoa, 64250
   Cambo-les-Bains.
(59.29.90.16).
Open daily 10 A.M. to 7:30
   P.M. July, August, and the
   first two weeks in
   September (closed
   Monday, first two weeks
   in September). Open 3 to
   7:30 P.M. mid-September
   through June; closed
   Monday.
Credit card: V.

A lovely local crafts shop for the huge, sturdy, blue shepherds' umbrellas, hand-woven baskets, and thick Pyrénées wool for knitting handmade sweaters.

BAYONNE *(Pyrénées-Atlantiques)*

Biarritz 7 k, Bordeaux 183 k, Paris 771 k.

Markets: Monday through Saturday, 7 A.M. to 12:30 P.M., modern covered market, Quai de la Nive.
Tuesday, Thursday, and Saturday, 2:30 to 8:30 A.M., open-air market, Marengo and Pannecau bridges.
Foire aux Jambons (ham fair): the three days preceding Easter.

In Bayonne, during the early morning hours, farmers set up the *marché première main* (wholesale market) and sell to restaurateurs and housewives until around 8:30 A.M., when they move to the modern covered market, and boost their prices!

RESTAURANT

EUSKALDUNA
61 Rue Pannecau, 64100
　Bayonne.
(59.59.28.02).
Last orders taken at 2 P.M.
　and 9:30 P.M.
Open for lunch Tuesday
　through Friday and
　Sunday; open for lunch
　and dinner Saturday.
　Closed Monday, two
　weeks in October, and
　two weeks in May.
No credit cards.
About 125 francs.

SPECIALTIES:
Omelette aux piments (pepper
omelet), *haricots rouges* (a
Basque *cassoulet* of red beans,
sausages, peppers, pork, and
blood sausage), *soupe de poissons*
(fish soup), *moules vinaigrette*
(mussels in vinaigrette),
chipirons à l'encre (sliced squid
in squid ink sauce), *thon frais
aux oignons et aux piments* (fresh
tuna with onions and peppers),
gâteau au chocolat et aux noix
(chocolate and walnut cake).

Chef Aroxxa Aguirre, of Euskalduna.

What may well be the finest pepper omelet in France is found at one of the region's most authentic and charming bistros, Euskalduna—which is Basque for "Basque." This is not only a friendly, relaxed place but a pretty one as well: Blue and white gingham curtains and tablecloths give it a homey air, as do the copper pots, old Ricard carafes, and local posters. From the dining room, diners can see clearly into the kitchen—decorated with a collection of antique blue and white china—from which the young blond chef, Aroxxa Aguirre, runs the restaurant almost single-handedly. Madame Aguirre, now into her thirties, began waiting tables here at the age of thirteen, when her mother did all the cooking. Now this outgoing Basque woman handles the affair all on her own, serving up a medley of hearty local specialties, a range of foods that varies with the seasons.

The pepper omelet—delicious not only for its fresh, mild green *piments* but also for its incredibly fresh farm eggs—is served from June through October, when the green peppers are replaced by salt cod or fresh *cèpes*. During other seasons, the eggs are mixed with potatoes or fresh onions and cooked just until set, with a nice, slightly runny interior.

Other dishes to try at Euskalduna include fresh white tuna from Saint-Jean-de-Luz, smothered in soft, sweet onions cooked with a touch of vinegar and topped with more of those fabulous green peppers (see recipe, facing page); and *chipirons à l'encre,* tooth-tender squid sliced into loops and cooked long and slowly in the black squid ink.

THON FRAIS AUX OIGNONS ET AUX PIMENTS EUSKALDUNA
EUSKALDUNA'S FRESH TUNA WITH ONIONS AND MILD CHILES

I've come to call this dish "tuna Euskalduna" because it's one of the specialties at Bayonne's cheery little bistro by the same name. In typical Basque style, chef Aguirre serves tuna with onions topped with the mildly hot local green peppers called piments d'Espelette. *Here the onions serve as a vegetable, rather than a garnish, so don't be surprised by their quantity. The general rule of thumb is to use, by weight, about 1½ times onions to tuna. The onions are cooked with a touch of vinegar and cayenne, giving the dish a nice punch.*

6 tablespoons virgin olive oil

2 pounds (1 kg) onions, sliced into very thin rounds

¼ cup (60 ml) distilled white vinegar

½ teaspoon salt, plus additional to taste

¼ teaspoon ground cayenne pepper, plus additional to taste

6 cloves garlic, lightly crushed

4 fresh white tuna, yellowfin, or bonito steaks (each about 6 ounces; 180 g), skin removed

1 cup dry white wine or water, approximately

4 small mildly hot green chiles (such as serrano) or 2 hot green chiles

1. Preheat the oven to 450°F (230°C).

2. Heat 4 tablespoons oil in a large heavy-bottomed casserole over medium-high heat. Add the onions, reduce the heat to medium-low, and stir until they are thoroughly coated with oil. Cook covered, stirring occasionally, for 10 minutes. Add the vinegar, ½ teaspoon salt, and ¼ teaspoon cayenne. Cook covered until the onions are very soft, about 10 minutes longer.

3. While the onions are cooking, prepare the tuna: Heat the remaining 2 tablespoons oil in a heavy-bottomed skillet over medium-high heat. Add the garlic and cook just until lightly browned, about 2 minutes. Add the fish and brown on one side, 2 to 3 minutes. Turn, season the cooked side lightly with salt and cayenne pepper, and brown the other side. Turn the fish and season the second side lightly with salt and cayenne pepper. Place the fish in a single layer in a casserole. Discard the garlic in the skillet but set the skillet with oil aside to cook the chiles later.

4. Cover the tuna with the onions and add enough wine to half cover the fish and onions. Cover and bake until the tuna is cooked through, about 40 minutes.

5. A few minutes before the tuna and onions are ready, seed the chiles and slice them into ⅛-inch (3.5 mm) strips, removing the white ribs on the inside. (When preparing chiles, be sure to wear rubber gloves to protect your hands.) Heat the oil in the skillet you set aside over medium-high heat. Add the chiles and quickly sauté 1 to 2 minutes. The peppers should remain firm and bright green.

6. Remove the fish from the casserole and discard any bones. Place the fish on 4 warmed dinner plates. Spoon the onions over the fish and top with the peppers. Serve immediately.

Yield: 4 servings.

SALON DE THE

CHOCOLAT CAZENAVE
19 Rue Port-Neuf, 64100
  Bayonne.
(59.59.03.16).
Open 9 A.M. to noon and 2
  to 7 P.M. Closed Sunday,
  Monday (except during
  school holidays), and
  October.
International mail orders
  accepted.

A welcome to the land of gâteaux
basques.

D on't leave Bayonne before stopping at Cazenave, an elegant, old-fashioned sidewalk tea
salon sheltered beneath the expansive old city arcades. One Indian summer Saturday we sat on
dainty wicker chairs to sip chocolate and people-
watch, marveling at how elegantly everyone was
dressed (almost, to a person, all in white), admiring
a table of six little girls dressed in frilly, pristine
white frocks, out for chocolate with their grandmothers. Eyes opened wide as the cups of steaming
hot chocolate arrived, chocolate so frothy that the
foam rose above the rim of the cup like a proud
soufflé. The filter coffee (the real thing) and tea
service is fit for a queen: Your order arrives on a
fine pink and white china tray, laid out with an
array of matching china. A wonderful, forgotten
world of fussy elegance, to relax, to enjoy.

PATISSERIES

J. ARRASTIA
In the modern covered
  market, Saturday, on the
  Quai de la Nive.
Open 7 A.M. to 1 P.M.

F or delicious homemade *gâteau basque,* both the
black cherry and the pastry cream variety. Perfect for sampling on the spot, or to save for a picnic
lunch.

LABORDE
66 Rue d'Espagne, 64100
  Bayonne.
(59.59.20.86).
Open 2 to 7:30 P.M. Monday;
  7:45 A.M. to 12:30 P.M.
  and 2 to 7:30 P.M.
  Tuesday through
  Saturday; 7 A.M. to 1 P.M.
  and 3:30 to 7:30 P.M.
  Sunday.

LE MOULIN DE BASSILOUR
In the modern covered
  market, Monday through
  Saturday, on the Quai de
  la Nive.
Open 7 A.M. to 1 P.M. Closed
  Sunday and the second
  week in October through
  the third week in
  November.

An array of breads, Le Moulin de Bassilour.

BOULANGERIE

LE FOUR A BOIS
Boulangerie Francis Hubert,
6 Rue Pannecau, 64100
  Bayonne.
(59.59.36.97).
Open 6 A.M. to 1:30 P.M. and
  3 to 8 P.M. Closed Sunday,
  two weeks in February,
  and three weeks in
  July–August.

A spotless, beautifully decorated shop, full of local sweet specialties, including chocolates and *gâteau basque.*

Sweets and chocolate at Cazenave.

A little outlet for my very favorite *pastiza,* or *gâteau basque:* Try especially their chewy black cherry jam–filled version (see recipe, following page).

A great little bakery where you can watch them bake bread in the wood-fired oven that opens into the shop. Try the crusty *pain aux noix* (walnut bread) and delicious *pain paillé* (country loaf).

Gateau Basque
BASQUE CAKE

In the Basque region, one can barely walk by a pastry shop without coming face-to-face with the gâteau basque, a wonderful dessert that combines a cookie-like dough with rich black cherry preserves. Traditionally, the cake was made with the dark black cherries of the region, but since tho e are hard to find these days, many local cooks replace the cherries with pastry cream, a far less satisfying substitute. This recipe comes from the shop that I think makes the finest gâteau basque in France, the Moulin de Bassilour near Biarritz. In testing, we found the best brand of preserves to use was Amore from Italy.

Pastry:

2 cups (280 g) all-purpose flour (do not use unbleached)

¾ cup plus 2 tablespoons (7 ounces; 200 g) unsalted butter, cubed, at room temperature

1 large egg

2 large egg yolks

1¼ cups (175 g) confectioners' sugar

Grated zest (peel) of 1 lemon

Pinch of salt

Filling:

¾ cup (235 g) best-quality black cherry preserves or jam, preferably Amore

1 large egg yolk, lightly beaten

1. Prepare the pastry: Place the flour in a large shallow bowl and make a well in the center. Add the butter, egg, egg yolks, sugar, lemon zest, and salt to the well and mix them thoroughly together with your fingers. Gradually work in the flour, using your fingers and working quickly. The dough should be soft and supple, almost like a soft cookie dough. Divide the dough into 2 unequal portions of about one third and two thirds. Flatten the dough into thick discs, wrap with waxed paper, and refrigerate at least 1 hour.

2. Preheat the oven to 375°F (190°C).

3. Place the larger portion of dough between 2 sheets of waxed paper that have been sprinkled with flour. Carefully roll out the dough to a 12-inch (30.5 cm) circle, remove the top sheet of waxed paper, and transfer the dough to a 10½-inch (27 cm) springform pan. Bring the edge partway up the side of the pan, so it covers the seam.

4. Spoon the preserves evenly over the dough to within 1 inch (3 cm) of the side of the pan. In the same manner as the first portion, carefully roll out the remaining dough to a 10½-inch (27 cm) circle and carefully place it on top of the jam. Fold the edge of the bottom pastry over the top and press down on it gently to seal it. Do not be concerned if the edges are slightly uneven. These imperfections melt away in baking. Brush the top with the egg yolk.

5. Bake until the pastry is cooked through and the top is a very deep golden brown, about 50 minutes. Run a knife around the edge of the cake to loosen it. Let cool completely. Remove side of pan and serve at room temperature.

Yield: One 10½-inch (27 cm) cake.

FROMAGERIE

LA FROMAGERIE
71 Rue d'Espagne, 64100
  Bayonne.
(59.59.26.04).
Open 7 A.M. to 12:30 P.M.
  and 3:30 to 7:30 P.M.
  Closed Sunday and
  Monday off-season.
French mail orders
  accepted.

A fine little shop specializing in local farm cheese. I counted eight different varieties of *brebis,* the rich and dense cheese of pure sheep's milk.

CHOCOLATERIE

DARANATZ
15 Rue Port-Neuf, 64100
  Bayonne.
(59.59.03.55).
Open 9 A.M. to 12:15 P.M.
  and 2 to 7:15 P.M. Closed
  Sunday and the first two
  weeks in February.

The place to go in Bayonne if you're looking for *touron* (marzipan loaf) or chocolates.

A country kitchen, the Musée Basque.

POUR LA MAISON

BERROGAIN
Carrefour des Cinq-Cantons,
  64100 Bayonne.
(59.59.16.18).
Open 9 A.M. to noon and
  2:30 to 7 P.M. Monday,
  Tuesday, and Wednesday;
  9 A.M. to noon and 2 to 7
  P.M. Thursday, Friday, and
  Saturday. Closed Sunday.
Credit card: V.

A lovely, elegant shop where you can spend hours examining the wide assortment of colorful Basque linens. Selections range from traditionally rustic and folkloric sets in red, white, and blue to more elegant pure-cotton pieces.

MUSEE

MUSEE BASQUE
1 Rue Marengo, 64100
   Bayonne.
(59.59.08.98).
Open 9:30 A.M. to 12:30 P.M.
   and 2:30 to 6:30 P.M. July
   through September; 10
   A.M. to noon October
   through June. Closed
   Sunday and holidays.
Admission: 6 francs for
   adults, 4 francs for
   groups of 10, 2 francs for
   students and military
   personnel, free for
   children under 7.

A traditional hearth, the Musée Basque.

One of France's finest folklore museums, just off the Marengo bridge. A visit is essential for anyone who wants to truly understand daily Basque life, both past and present.

This spotless gem is built like a small Basque village, with a special chocolate-making room with all the necessary utensils; an espadrilles-maker's shop; and many tasteful rooms decorated with blue and white gingham curtains, blue and white polka-dot pitchers and soup tureens, even bedrooms decorated with pale blue and white–striped linens.

Upstairs you'll find the Basque equivalent of the sportsman's hall of fame, a colorful display of *pelote* paraphernalia, *pelote* being a form of handball, played on the courts one sees in every Basque village no matter how small. (The courts usually stand right next to the town church, and in some tiny villages, the court is literally set in the center of town, and too bad for you if you'd like to drive on through while a game is in progress.) The museum display features antique playing uniforms, a series of balls signed by famous players of the past, as well as an extensive collection of rackets, gloves, and trophies.

The only display that set me back a bit was a strange room filled with rather menacing-looking black iron cages. It seems that from the year 1215 until the Revolution, women of questionable character (I wonder who turned them in?) were locked in these cages, paraded about in public, then plunged into the Nive river as punishment for their aberrant behavior!

BIARRITZ *(Pyrénées-Atlantiques)*

Bayonne 7 k, Bordeaux 194 k, Paris 780 k.

Market: Monday through Saturday (daily in July and August), 8 A.M. to 1:30 P.M., Rue Victor-Hugo.

SALON DE THE

MIREMONT
1 bis Place Georges-
    Clémenceau, 64200
    Biarritz.
(59.24.01.38).
Open daily 9 A.M. to 12:45
    P.M. and 3 to 7:30 P.M.

A rather dusty, down-at-the-heels tea salon, with a breathtaking view of the Atlantic Ocean and Biarritz's imposing casino. Sit amid the mirrored walls and Louis XVI furniture and sip their inspired hot chocolate, which comes with a separate bowl of whipped cream, served with a little roll of chocolate standing upright in the center.

PATISSERIE

PARIES
27 Place Georges-
    Clémenceau,
    64200 Biarritz.
(59.22.07.52).
Open 9:30 A.M. to 12:30 P.M.
    and 2:30 to 7 P.M. Closed
    Sunday except in the
    summer.

For the best caramels you can imagine, as well as chocolate truffles and a delicious almond paste.

BOULANGERIE/ PATISSERIE

**LE MOULIN DE
    BASSILOUR**
64210 Bidart.
(59.41.94.49).
Open 8 A.M. to 8 P.M. Closed
    the second week in
    October through the
    third week in November.

A rare spot, worth getting lost for! We arrived at 11:30 one fall morning, welcomed by the mingling aromas of sautéed garlic (Madame was cooking lunch) and fresh-milled corn. Their spectacular rounds of golden *méture* (corn bread; see recipe, following page) were just about to come from the oven as Henri Amati, the baker who married the miller's daughter, came to greet us. All around, crust crackled in the clean, cool air as sounds of the millstream rushed in through wide-open windows. This is not your traditional bakery but rather a working flour mill with a series of ovens, and lots of long wooden tables for cooling the corn bread, coarse wheat bread, their unusual *miche* (a sweet anise-flavored cake-like bread), and their real specialty, *veritable pastiza,* or real *gâteau basque* (see recipe, page 450). Directions: Go north on the N10 from Saint-Jean-de-Luz toward Biarritz. In Bidart, just after the Atherbea Restaurant on the right, turn right onto the D455 in the direction of Arbonne.

PAIN DE MAIS MOULIN DE BASSILOUR
CORN BREAD FROM THE MILL OF BASSILOUR

For years I had been searching for a yeast-risen corn bread that has that great corn taste, golden corn color, and good texture. I found it at the Moulin de Bassilour, a centuries-old corn and wheat mill not far from Biarritz. Since 1934, baker Henri Amati has been making this bread with a blend of their freshly milled corn and wheat. He bakes the loaves in small round pans, but traditional rectangular loaf pans will do as well. This is a no-knead bread, and the light dough will be more like a batter than a standard bread dough. It's great toasted.

Starter:
2 cups (500 ml) lukewarm water
2½ teaspoons or 1 package active dry yeast
2 cups (280 g) unbleached all-purpose flour

Corn mixture:
3 cups (450 g) coarse yellow cornmeal
1 tablespoon salt
2 cups (500 ml) hot tap water

2 teaspoons unsalted butter, for buttering the bread pans

1. Prepare the starter: Place the water, yeast, and flour in a large mixing bowl, and stir for 1 to 2 minutes. (I like to count 100 turns.) Cover with a cloth and let rise at room temperature for 1 hour.

2. Prepare the corn mixture: Place the cornmeal, salt, and water in another large bowl, and stir until the water is completely absorbed. Cover with a cloth and let soften at room temperature for 1 hour.

3. Stir down the starter, then stir in the cornmeal mixture, and mix until thoroughly blended. The dough will be liquidy and batter-like. Cover with a cloth and let rise at room temperature for about 2 hours. The dough will be bubbly, and will rise slightly.

4. Stir down the dough and pour or spoon it into two well-buttered round baking pans, measuring about 7½ x 2 inches (19 x 5 cm), filling them about three-quarters full. The bread also can be baked in two rectangular loaf pans, measuring about 9 x 4 inches (23 x 10 cm). They, too, should be about three-quarters full. Cover with a cloth and let rise at room temperature for about 2 hours. The dough will rise slightly.

5. Preheat the oven to 425°F (220°C).

6. Bake the loaves until golden brown, 50 to 60 minutes. Remove from the pans and cool thoroughly on a rack before slicing. For a crustier loaf, once baked, remove the bread from the pans and return to the oven for an additional 5 minutes.

Yield: 2 loaves.

A miller's break, Le Moulin de Bassilour.

FROMAGERIE

MILLE ET UN FROMAGES
8 Avenue Victor-Hugo,
    64200 Biarritz.
(59.24.67.88).
Open 8 A.M. to 1 P.M. and
    3:30 to 7:45 P.M. Closed
    Sunday.

CHOCOLATERIE

DARANATZ
12 Avenue Maréchal-Foch,
    64200 Biarritz.
(59.24.21.91).
Open 9 A.M. to 12:30 P.M.
    and 2:30 to 7:30 P.M.
    Closed Sunday and two
    to three weeks in
    February.

SPECIALITES REGIONALES

AROSTEGUY
5 Avenue Victor-Hugo,
    64200 Biarritz.
(59.24.00.52).
Open 9 A.M. to 1 P.M. and
    3:30 to 8 P.M. Monday
    through Saturday; 11 A.M.
    to 1 P.M. Sunday.
Credit cards: AE, V.

Perhaps not really 1,001 cheeses, but an extensive selection nonetheless. A place to begin gathering a picnic lunch, including cheese, *foie gras,* and smoked salmon. Also one of the few places you'll find *brebis fermier croûte brulée,* fresh local sheep's-milk cheese with a slightly burnt, or grilled, crust.

The place to go in Biarritz if you're looking for *touron* (marzipan loaf), chocolates, or pastries.

Grains ready to be ground, Le Moulin de Bassilour.

A specialty shop offering 350 kinds of spirits, 125 kinds of whiskey, 140 spices, 70 teas, plus salmon and caviar. Look for the exceptional *eau-de-vie de poire* (pear brandy) Etienne Brana.

ESPELETTE *(Pyrénées-Atlantiques)*

Bayonne 20 k, Biarritz 23 k, Cambo-les-Bains 6 k. Saint-Jean-de-Luz 25 k.

Live lamb market: Wednesday.
Fête du Piment (pepper festival) last weekend in October.

RESTAURANTS

EUZKADI
Espelette, 64250
    Cambo-les-Bains.
(59.29.91.88).
Last orders taken at 2 P.M.
    and 9 P.M.
Closed Monday, Tuesday
    from mid-September
    through mid-June; one
    week in February, and
    mid-November through
    mid-December.
Credit card: V.
Four menus from 50 to 120
    francs. A la carte, 120
    francs.

S P E C I A L T I E S :
Pipérade basquaise (soft
scrambled eggs with
tomatoes, green Espelette
peppers, onions, garlic), *axoa*
(chopped veal sautéed with
onions and green Espelette
peppers and seasoned with
spicy ground red Espelette
pepper), *tripoxa* (calf's blood
sausage served with spicy red
Espelette peppers), *pot-au-feu*
(beef simmered with
vegetables), and *poule au riz*
(poached chicken and rice).

A moonlight market, along Bayonne's river Nive.

The vine-covered Euzkadi is one of the best places to celebrate the local *piments d'Espelette*. The long family-style dining room has been fashioned out of a traditional Basque house in the center of the village. This is where the locals come to *fête* and to feast, especially on Wednesday, when everyone gathers for the live lamb trading, and of course for the noon meal on Sunday. Here chef André Darraïdou serves a memorable *pipérade au jambon,* a fine fresh pepper omelet, and *tripoxa,* an unusual veal blood sausage served with a mildly spicy dark tomato sauce.

During the early fall and winter months, the specialty to try is *salmis de palombes,* a dense, full-flavored stew prepared with local wild pigeon, red wine, and vegetables. This is a mild dish, good for those who are not fond of strong, gamey flavors.

Euzkadi's daily specials include Saturday's *saucisse confite aux choux* and Sunday's *pot-au-feu grand-mère.* Wine choices range from the Irouléguy (a local wine I find dull) to the substantial Spanish Rioja.

LE RELAIS DU LABOURD
Route de Souraïde,
  Espelette, 64250 Cambo-
  les-Bains.
(59.29.90.70).
Last orders taken at 2:30 P.M.
  and 10 P.M.
October through June: open
  for lunch only, closed
  Wednesday. July through
  September: open for
  lunch and dinner, closed
  Sunday dinner and
  Monday.
Credit cards: AE, DC, V.
Terrace dining.
Private dining rooms for 50
  and 250.
120 francs.

SPECIALTIES:
Magret de canard (breast of
fattened duck), *agneau
chilindron* (sauté of lamb with
potatoes and garlic).

This big traditional whitewashed Basque farmhouse offers simple, homey, local fare. I loved the hot meaty *cèpes,* showered with cloves of whole garlic, snippets of minced garlic, and a generous garnish of parsley, and the giant lamb chops, equally enhanced with garlic (though one could do without the bread crumbs on the potato gratin). Desserts are on the bland side, and the wine list needs a boost, but still a good family spot for a leisurely Sunday lunch. (Directions: Just outside Espelette, off the D918 in the direction of Saint-Jean-de-Luz.)

*Traditional pottery, the Musée
Basque.*

HASPARREN *(Pyrénées-Atlantiques)*

Bayonne 24 k, Cambo-les-Bains 10 k, Paris 779 k,
Saint-Jean-Pied-de-Port 33 k.

FROMAGERIE

ABBAYE DE BELLOC
Urt, 64240 Hasparren.
(59.29.65.55).
Open daily 8 A.M. to noon
  and 1:30 to 6:30 P.M.

Guests are invited to visit this large modern monastery where the Benedictine monks make a very popular sheep's-milk cheese, a *brebis* sold under the label Abbaye de Belloc.

SAINT-JEAN-DE-LUZ *(Pyrénées-Atlantiques)*

Bayonne 21 k, Biarritz 15 k, Paris 793 k.

Market: Tuesday and Friday, 7:30 A.M. to 12:30 P.M., Boulevard Victor-Hugo.
Tuna auction: 7 A.M. daily, at the port.
Fête du Thon (tuna festival): around July 4.
Fête du Horo (fish soup festival): first or second Sunday in September.

S aint-Jean-de-Luz has an authentic farmers' market, and one of the liveliest in the region, where you'll see wicker baskets full of figs and quince, obviously freshly picked that morning; so many varieties of peppers that you'll lose count; dozens of little stands offering homemade breads and pastries; and clusters of farm wives selling colorful golden wheels of homemade cheese.

RESTAURANT

ARRANTZALEAK
Avenue Jean-Poulou,
　Ciboure, 64500
　Saint-Jean-de-Luz.
(59.47.10.75).
Last orders taken at 2 P.M.
　and 10 P.M..
Closed Monday dinner and
　Tuesday October through
　June; Monday July
　through September, and
　mid-December through
　mid-January.
Credit cards: AE, DC.
About 100 francs.

S P E C I A L T I E S :
Fish and seafood.

A s one travels about in search of the simple, the authentic, the good buys with a personality, one becomes resigned to this unavoidable fact: The best things in life are hard to find.

This fisherman's shack/makeshift restaurant in the village of Ciboure, adjacent to the port of Saint-Jean-de-Luz, is that sort of place. Bridges, *quais,* and one-way streets all plot against drivers unfamiliar with the territory, but Arrantzaleak is worth getting lost for, if only to sample the freshly grilled *thon blanc,* the delicate white albacore tuna served from June through September. This is a no-frills restaurant, furnished with bright blue wooden benches and oilcloth table coverings, with the inevitable buoys and fishnets dangling from the ceiling. But prepare yourself for a minor feast. While you wait for your food, waiters offer bowls full of freshly simmered *bigorneaux* (periwinkles), which diners fish out of the shell with a common stickpin. If the local *louvine* is on the menu that day, try this delicate, snowy white fish, a relative of *bar,* or striped bass. The fish, fresh from the Golfe de Gascogne (the Bay of Biscay), is grilled over the giant open fireplace that dominates the restaurant, then boned and served with a sprinkling of sliced garlic chips, freshly ground black pepper, parsley, and a light vinaigrette.

PATISSERIES

MAISON ADAM
6 Place Louis-XIV and
49 Rue Gambetta, 64500
  Saint-Jean-de-Luz.
(59.26.03.54).
Open 7:45 A.M. to 12:30 P.M.
  and 2 to 7:30 P.M. Closed
  Monday off-season and
  mid-January through
  mid-February.

Many an afternoon, as groans of hunger break the silence of my office, my thoughts turn to the moist, chewy, magnificent *macarons aux amandes* (almond macaroons) from Adam. The best in the world perhaps!

J. ARRASTIA
In the covered market,
  Tuesday and Friday,
  Boulevard Victor-Hugo.

For delicious homemade *gâteau basque,* both the black cherry and the pastry cream variety. Perfect for sampling on the spot, or to save for a picnic lunch.

**LE MOULIN DE
  BASSILOUR**
In the covered market,
  Tuesday and Friday,
  Boulevard Victor-Hugo.
Closed the second week in
  October through the
  third week in November.

Another outlet of Bassilour, where they make my favorite version of *pastiza,* or *gâteau basque:* Try especially the chewy black cherry jam–filled version (see recipe, page 450).

Basque breads and cakes.

PARIES
9 Rue Gambetta, 64500
  Saint-Jean-de-Luz.
(59.26.01.46).
Open daily 6 A.M. to 6 P.M. in
  summer and 7 A.M. to
  8 P.M. in winter.
Credit card: V.

After tasting the fresh, smooth, seductive caramels from Pariès, you'll say, "Oh, that's what caramels are supposed to taste like!" Also note their chocolate truffles (they call them Othello) and their delicious *pâte d'amande* (almond paste). Be sure to walk down Rue Tourasse, where a huge picture window opens into the Pariès chocolate "factory," allowing visitors to enjoy, firsthand, the art of candy making.

Le Piment d'Espelette

"*The* piment d'Espelette *is an elegant chile with a rich, almost sweet piquancy, a heat that doesn't attack the throat or the back of the palate but offers a pleasant, lingering tingling on the middle of the tongue.*"

ESPELETTE, SEPTEMBER 27—Anywhere else in France, the garlands of fiery red peppers would look out of place. But in this picturesque Basque village, too small to rate its own postal code, strings of peppers are perfectly at home, drying outside whitewashed farmhouses, decorating restaurant hearths and butcher-shop windows, even serving as the subject of an annual hot pepper festival on the final weekend of October.

All over the Pays Basque, the *piment d'Espelette* shows up fresh as well as dried, green as well as red. It's ground and chopped, pickled and stuffed, and appears in just about every dish that takes to bold seasoning.

Traditionally, the young and barely piquant green peppers go fresh and whole into omelets or are chopped to season the famous vegetable and egg mixture known as *pipérade*. Mature, hot red peppers are dried and ground and used in place of ground black pepper.

In one famous Basque preparation—*jambon de Bayonne*—the ground dried pepper serves two purposes: Rubbed into the bone of the ham as it cures, the pepper acts as a preservative. When rubbed on the exterior, the rosy red color gives the ham a festive look and adds, if only slightly, to the final flavor of the meat.

The *piment d'Espelette* is slender, 7.5 to 10 centimeters (3 to 4 inches) long, and hot, but not ultra-hot. Rather, it's an elegant chile with a rich, almost sweet piquancy, a heat that doesn't attack the throat or the back of the palate but offers a pleasant, lingering tingling on the middle of the tongue. By comparison, the paralyzing cayenne pepper is about three times hotter.

Hot peppers have thrived in the Pays Basque since the days of the conquistadors, perhaps even since 1493, when Columbus returned from Haiti and introduced hot peppers to Europe. Although the hazy, humid Basque climate is hardly suited to this tropical plant, *piment* has played such an important role in Basque culture that farmers have managed to breed more than a dozen different varieties.

Some scientists suggest that the reason people crave hot peppers is that the brain secretes endorphins, a natural opiate, in response to a burning tongue, thereby providing the pleasant euphoria that follows a spicy meal.

FROMAGERIE

DUPIN
41 Rue Gambetta, 64500
   Saint-Jean-de-Luz.
(59.26.00.85).
Open 7:30 A.M. to 12:45 P.M.
   and 3 to 7:30 P.M. Closed
   Sunday.

A marvelous selection of regional cheeses, as well as the excellent *eaux-de-vie*—both the *poire* (pear) and *framboise* (raspberry) brandy—of Etienne Brana.

Whatever good feeling the chile provides, its cultivation also demands tremendous manpower. Until 1983 there was no organized Basque pepper industry. Individual farmers grew the peppers and dried and ground them for their own consumption, selling any excess to spice merchants from as nearby as Bayonne, as far away as Marseille.

A few years back, local restaurateurs and merchants noticed that each September, fewer and fewer houses were decorated with the familiar festoons of drying red peppers; fewer farmers were willing to devote the long hours to harvesting, stringing, drying, and grinding that generally kept the family occupied from early September to first frost.

To save the *piment d'Espelette,* farmers formed a cooperative called Biperra, Basque for *piment,* or hot pepper. It was through the cooperative that the dozen varieties developed by farmers were discovered, since every farmer saved his seeds from year to year.

"Out of those twelve, we've selected the four varieties we find the best," explained Léon Darraïdou, the cooperative's marketing director. They treat pepper varieties the way winemakers treat grape varieties, looking for the complex blend that produces a ground pepper most typical of the region.

Annually, fifty farmers supply the cooperative with about 40 tons of peppers. These will be turned into powder or purée, pickled whole in vinegar, and even blended with tomatoes and other spices for a Basque ketchup known as *ketchupade.*

One of the best places to sample the *piment d'Espelette* is at the village's vine-covered restaurant, Euzkadi, where one can also purchase Biperra products to take home (see page 456).

Paris Connection: Biperra products are available at Fauchon, 26 Place de la Madeleine, 75008 Paris (47.42.60.11). And the Comptoir Alinentaire Landais et Basco Bearnais, 52 Rue Montmartre, 75002 Paris (42.36.93.41).

POUR LA MAISON

MAISON CANDAU
11 Rue Gambetta, 64500
  Saint-Jean-de-Luz.
(59.26.10.99).
Open 10 A.M. to 12:30 P.M.
  and 3 to 7:30 P.M. Closed
  Sunday and Monday.
Credit cards: EC, V.

For a fine selection of woven cotton Basque linens, placemats, napkins, and tablecloths.

FRIP' OU NET'
21 Rue Loquin, 64500
    Saint-Jean-de-Luz.
    (59.26.92.89).
In summer open daily 10
    A.M. to 12:30 P.M. and 3 to
    7:30 P.M. In winter open
    11 A.M. to 12:30 P.M. and
    3 to 7 P.M. Closed Sunday,
    Monday morning, and
    October.

IPARRALDE
2 Rue Gambetta, 64500
    Saint-Jean-de-Luz.
    (59.26.30.09).
In winter open daily 9:30
    A.M. to 12:30 P.M. and
    2:30 to 7:30 P.M.; in
    summer 9:30 A.M. to
    midnight.
Credit cards: AE, DC, V.
International mail orders
    accepted.

SOULEIADO
51 Rue Saint-Jacques, 64500
    Saint-Jean-de-Luz.
    (59.51.05.24).
Open 10 A.M. to noon and
    3 to 7 P.M.
Credit cards: AE, DC, V.

A little gem of a boutique, filled with lovely, lacy, antique Basque linens, as well as a large selection of antique clothing.

Traditional cookware, the Musée Basque.

For Basque linens and wonderful handmade espadrilles in folkloric colors and styles.

One of the prettiest Souleiado shops in all of France: a touch of Provence with a Basque accent, as well as some of the loveliest, sturdiest espadrilles around.

SAINT-JEAN-PIED-DE-PORT *(Pyrénées-Atlantiques)*

Bayonne 52 k, Dax 86 k, Paris 823 k, Pau 98 k.

Market: Monday, 9 A.M. to 5 P.M. (7 P.M. in July and August),
in the center of town.
Foire aux fromages (cheese fair): one Thursday in July and two Thursdays in
August (dates vary).

This folkloric village of fewer than 2,000 inhabitants literally bursts at the seams on Mondays, when local farm ladies come bearing wicker baskets filled with farm cheese, eggs, peppers, and vegetables. They sell their produce while the men, donning traditional *bérets Basques,* take to the cafés to catch up on a week's worth of gossip.

RESTAURANTS

CHALET PEDRO
Mendive, 64220
  Saint-Jean-Pied-de-Port.
(59.37.02.52).
Open daily June through
  November 11; weekends
  and during ski season.
No credit cards.
90-franc menu; à la carte,
  about 100 francs.

SPECIALTIES:
Fresh trout, *jambon de pays*
(country ham), *omelette aux
cèpes* (wild mushroom omelet).

On the spectacular drive up the mountain to this modest little chalet (just follow the signs to the Iraty ski slopes), you'll pass brambled fences, peach-colored *pelote* courts, flocks of sheep, stack after stack of ferns (used locally as bedding for cattle), and numerous farms selling homemade sheep's cheese.

Chalet Pedro—which caters to hikers, skiers, and construction workers, as well as hungry travelers—is an honest mountain chalet, where the trout comes jumping from the adjacent stream, fresh wild *cèpes* are served as a copious side dish (like French fries—can you imagine), and the *cèpe* and garlic omelet makes you realize that there are few foods as luxurious, as simple, as sublime. Service is impossibly slow, and the waitress may be the one to decide what you'll eat that day, so don't bother if you're in a hurry or feeling cranky. The chef-owner raises his own trout and makes his own wonderful sheep's-milk cheese, cures his own country ham, and prepares homemade *gâteau basque,* all of which can be consumed on the spot or purchased to take with you. In warmer months, tables move out onto the grass for picnic-style meals under the pine trees.

LOTTE A LA BASQUAISE
MONKFISH WITH ONIONS, TOMATOES, AND GREEN CHILES

Few dishes are more patriotically Basque than this dish of red tomatoes, green peppers, and white onions, garlic, and monkfish, which mimic the red, white, and green Basque colors one sees everywhere in the region. In the fall months, the fresh green peppers with a rather gentle piquantness are found everywhere in the markets, along with braids of garlic, and portions of lotte, or monkfish. Green bell peppers can easily be substituted for the hot peppers. This dish is wonderful as well the next day, served chilled as a salad.

6 tablespoons plus 1 teaspoon virgin olive oil
4 medium onions, coarsely chopped
10 medium tomatoes, peeled, cored, seeded, and coarsely chopped
Salt and freshly ground black pepper to taste
Pinch of sugar
4 small mildly hot green chiles (such as serrano) or 2 green bell peppers
20 cloves garlic, peeled and cut crosswise into thin slices
2 pounds (1 kg) monkfish, membrane removed, cut crosswise into 8 thick slices

1. Place 3 tablespoons of the oil and the onions in a large skillet. Stir over low heat until the onions are thoroughly coated with oil, then cover and cook, shaking the pan frequently, for 30 minutes. The onions should be soft, tender, and pale golden.

2. Add the tomatoes, salt, pepper, and sugar to the onions, increase the heat to medium, and cook uncovered until the tomatoes are softened but still in whole pieces, about 15 minutes. Set aside.

3. If using chiles, put on rubber gloves to protect your hands. Cut the tops from the chiles, slice lengthwise in half, and remove all of the seeds. Cut the chiles into very thin slices. If using bell peppers, seed them and slice into thin strips. Heat 1 teaspoon of the oil in a small skillet over medium-high heat until hot but not smoking. Add the chiles or peppers and sauté them quickly until they begin to turn golden at the edges, 1 to 2 minutes. They should remain bright green. Remove from the heat and set aside.

4. Heat the remaining 3 tablespoons oil in a large skillet over medium-high heat until hot but not smoking. Add the garlic and sauté quickly. Add the monkfish and cook until it is opaque and still resilient, not soft or overly tough, about 6 minutes on each side. Season the fish with salt and pepper after it has been turned. Do not be concerned that the monkfish gives off a great deal of liquid.

5. To serve, reheat the tomato sauce and divide it equally among 4 warmed dinner plates. Place the monkfish and garlic on top of the sauce, then garnish with the chiles or peppers.

Yield: 4 servings.

LES PYRENEES
19 Place du Général-de-
  Gaulle, 64220
  Saint-Jean-Pied-de-Port.
  (59.37.01.01).
Last orders taken at 2 P.M.
  and 9 P.M.
Closed four weeks in
  November/December/
  January, Monday night
  from November to
  March, and Tuesday from
  mid-September through
  June, except holidays
  that fall on Tuesday.
Credit cards: AE, V.
Private dining rooms for 30
  and 40.
120-, 170-, 220-, and
  280-franc menu. A la
  carte, 350 francs.

SPECIALTIES:
Foie gras aux pommes (foie gras
with apples), *saumon frais grillé*
de l'Adoubs (grilled salmon),
assiette des grands desserts au
chocolat (dish of chocolate
desserts).

CHARCUTERIE

CHARCUTERIE J.
  AGUIRRE
Place du Général-de-Gaulle,
  64220 Saint-Jean-Pied-
  de-Port.
(59.37.03.58).
Open 8 A.M. to 12:30 P.M.
  and 2 to 7:30 P.M.
  Monday through
  Saturday; 9 A.M. to noon
  and 3 to 7 P.M. Sunday.
French mail orders
  accepted.

You can't say you've been to the Pays Basque until you've visited the charming, diminutive village of Saint-Jean-Pied-de-Port, and Les Pyrénées is definitely the place to dine in town. The food is on the fussy side, and service can be a bit stiff, but you're sure to find some good regional fare on the menu. Try especially the rustic *garbure aux choux* (here, a fine soup of white beans, leeks, carrots, potatoes, and duck *confit*) and the refreshing, wholesome *lotte à la basquaise* (see recipe, facing page), a local version of monkfish smothered in tomatoes, onions, garlic, and slightly piquant chile peppers.

Bayonne merchants take time for a chat.

A little food stand in the center of the village, offering a variety of preserved regional specialties, including ham, cheese, canned meats, and dried ground *piment d'Espelette.*

EAUX-DE-VIE

ETIENNE BRANA
23 Rue du 11-Novembre,
  64220 Saint-Jean-
  Pied-de-Port.
(59.37.00.44).
Open 8 A.M. to noon and 2
  to 7 P.M. Closed Saturday
  afternoon, Sunday, and
  January or February.
French mail orders
  accepted.

This is no faceless factory but rather a small, traditional affair, with the entire Brana family involved, from growing the fine pear William's for their superb *eau-de-vie de poire* to the careful distilling, and aging in oak casks, of their delicious *eau-de-vie de prune,* or plum brandy. The plum brandy is aged a full five to six years, making for a very refined, lovely oak-colored *eau-de-vie.*

POUR LA MAISON

MAISON CANDAU
Rue Eglise, 64220 Saint-
  Jean-Pied-de-Port.
(59.37.00.03).
Open 9:30 A.M. to noon and
  2 to 7 P.M. Monday
  through Saturday; 10 A.M.
  to 12:30 P.M. and 3 to
  6 P.M. Sunday.
French mail orders
  accepted.
Credit card: V.

For Basque linens as well as regional fabric by the yard, Basque wool jackets, blankets, bathrobes.

CHEESE OF PAYS BASQUE

L' Ossau-Iraty-Brebis-Pyrénées: A big name for such a simple, but sublime, sheep's-milk cheese. This thick convex wheel weighing from 2 to 7 kilos (4½ to 15½ pounds) is made on farms and in commercial dairies, in the mountainous area of the Basque region. Formerly, much of the sheep's milk from the Pyrénées was used to make Roquefort, but today that milk goes into a variety of sheep's-milk and mixed sheep's- and cow's-milk cheeses, varying in color, texture, size, and taste, depending upon where they were made and how they were aged. The best are firm and fragrant, with a distinctively rich and earthy flavor.

La Dordogne
THE DORDOGNE

René Neuville, baker of Terrasson-la-Villedieu.

The Dordogne, a serene and luscious green stretch of land in southwestern France, is remarkably easy to love. With a panoramic landscape that's both familiar enough to make one feel at home and exotic enough to know that one is not, the Dordogne promises all the elements that make for pleasurable traveling. It's a visually harmonious place, draped in a soft, romantic haze much of the year as sunlight filters through the poplars and weeping willows that hug the banks of the Dordogne and its tributary, the Vézère, two rivers that cut through a region often called by its ancient name, the Périgord.

Here one can dine in a farmhouse one night, lunch in a *château* or converted mill the next, pause for a coffee or *citron pressé* in any number of diminutive villages perched along the route, then sleep the night away to the soothing whir of a rushing stream. Between meals, there are historic and prehistoric sites to visit, as elegant feudal castles and carefully tended prehistoric caves appear every few minutes, testaments to the Dordogne's rich and varied past.

A tidy region that is aware of tourism but not obsessed by it, the Dordogne has long been favored by French and British travelers, many of whom have established summer homes in restored mills, farmhouses, and *châteaux*. But only recently has the Dordogne begun to attract Americans in numbers. Perhaps it has been slow because it lacks a Michelin three-star restaurant, a lure that determines many a traveler's journey in France. Or perhaps it is simply that for so many years it has been overshadowed by the sunshine of Provence, the wine roads of Burgundy, the beaches of Brittany, and the glamour of the Côte-d'Azur.

No matter, for given even a week's time, it would be difficult for anyone to fully absorb the treasures of the Dordogne, a land caught in the British-French tug of war during the thirteenth, fourteenth, and fifteenth centuries, when decisive battles were fought along the Dordogne river during the Hundred Years' War. Today the region is decidedly, solidly French, but the longtime British interest means that English is almost a second language here, easing the way for the traveler.

Most everything worth seeing in the Dordogne is easily accessible, and driving here is infinitely pleasurable. Villages are clustered close together, and while roads may be narrow and winding, they're rarely very crowded.

The Dordogne is a rich agricultural land, and from the country roads one views the small farms where families raise geese and ducks for their famed fatted livers, where corn, tobacco, and walnuts are major crops, and where rushing streams still manage to run a collection of mills for pressing fragrant walnut oil, for grinding feed corn, and from time to time, for milling wheat for the region's consistently spectacular country bread.

Gastronomically, the Dordogne offers a surfeit of good things. Along with the classic favorites of silken *foie gras,* fragrant black truffles, and hearty *confits* of preserved duck and goose, there are firm and pungent discs of pure goat cheese known as Cabécou (pronounced kha-bee-coo), the clear and fragrant *eau-de-vie de prune* distilled from fresh-picked purple plums in the early fall, tangy green sorrel in the spring and early summer, fresh, meaty walnuts, and an abundance of wild mushrooms come autumn.

Some of the Dordogne's wines have been known since the Middle Ages but are just returning to fashion, such as Bergerac, with its light, fruity, low-alcohol red and crisp dry white. Even better than Bergerac is the little-known Pécharmant, a rich, purply wine that's right at home with a platter of *charcuterie,* with game or red meats. Monbazillac, from the vineyards growing along the

Dordogne's left bank, is also making a strong comeback. It's a fine sweet white wine worth seeking out, especially for drinking very cold with *foie gras* or with fruit-based desserts.

The Dordogne also remains a history lover's paradise, boasting numerous prehistoric caves and rock shelters, including the Font-de-Gaume cave in Les Eyzies-de-Tayac, the village where skeletons of Cro-Magnon man were found in 1868.

As well, there are canoes to rent for a paddle about the deep bends of the Dordogne river, and biking and hiking trails for touring back roads in search of ancient stone dovecotes or lovingly restored bread ovens. In Sorges, travelers can take a mile-long self-guided walking tour of half a dozen truffle plantations, where the rare black Périgord truffle grows in forests rich with scrub oaks and hazelnut trees. The adventuresome might spend a weekend on an active Périgord farm, helping to preserve the winter's supply of *foie gras,* pork sausages, and salt-cured hams.

And then there are the villages. Thank goodness someone cared enough to retain the history and charm of places like Domme, La Roque-Gageac, Collonges-la-Rouge, Beynac, and Monpazier, each of which is one of the *"Plus Beaux Villages de France,"* a designation honoring fewer than a hundred villages throughout the country, all of them historic and active restored rural spots—not ghost towns that survive strictly on tourism. They're all impeccable, neatly ordered towns that beam with civic pride. Even the telephone booths are built not of metal, but of sturdy wood, so as not to blemish the rustic landscape.

Some of the "Most Beautiful Villages"—like Domme, a *bastide,* or fortified walled town, and unquestionably the prettiest of all of the Dordogne villages—boast an active outdoor market, a fine hotel, and a restaurant, while others—like La Roque-Gageac, nestled beneath dramatic limestone cliffs along a gentle curl in the Dordogne river—seem destined to star as quintessential *citron pressé* towns, the ideal spot for sipping a lemonade and taking time to count one's blessings.

In the remarkably beautiful village of Collonges-la-Rouge (population 305), the red sandstone houses offer a sharp contrast to the rolling green hills, neatly ordered walnut groves, and vineyards. Monpazier, a thirteenth-century *bastide,* is one of the best-preserved villages in the region. Best seen in full sunlight, this military

fortress, built by King Edward the First of England in 1284, is a shining ochre stone monument to the past. The town is laid out in a strict, formulated rectangle, with an impressive series of stone arches leading into the central market square.

Inevitably, a first visit to the Dordogne inspires a second. The traveler who has once savored spring's early morning light or marveled at the long, extended days of summer will surely be moved to return again, to sample firsthand the excitement of a fresh winter truffle, to partake in the fall walnut harvest, or to welcome spring by paddling down a bucolic stretch of the river.

WHEN YOU GO

Michelin Green Guide: *Périgord/Quercy.*

Getting there: The Dordogne is about an 8-hour drive from Paris. There are also regular Air Inter (1-hour) flights and express trains (about 5 hours) from Paris to Bordeaux, where you can rent a car for the 2-hour drive into the region. Trains from Paris also serve many of the Dordogne's cities, including Périgueux (with a change in Limoges) and Brive-la-Gaillarde (direct).

Getting around: Michelin maps 239 (Auvergne/Limousin), 235 (Midi-Pyrénées), and 233 (Poitou/Charentes).

Best time to visit: May and June, and September and October. July and August are usually hot and beautiful, but at times insufferably crowded as well.

MARKETS
(Liveliest markets are marked with an asterisk.)

Monday: Les Eyzies-de-Tayac (Easter through September), Hautefort (first Monday of the month), Saint-Cyprien (second Monday of the month), Souillac.

Tuesday: Bretenoux, Brive-la-Gaillarde, Gourdon, Puy-l'Evêque, Saint-Céré.

Wednesday: Bergerac, Cahors, Figeac (fourth Wednesday of the month), Hautefort, Martel, Montcuq (second Wednesday of the month), *Montignac, Périgueux, Saint-Céré (first and third Wednesday of the month), Sarlat-la-Canéda, Souillac.

Thursday: Brive-la-Gaillarde, Domme, Gramat (second and fourth Thursday of the month), Terrasson-la-Villedieu.

Friday: *Brantôme, Sorges (in summer only), *Souillac.

Saturday: *Bergerac, *Bretenoux, *Brive-la-Gaillarde, *Cahors, Figeac (second Saturday of the month), *Gourdon, *Martel, Montignac, Nontron, *Périgueux, *Saint-Céré, *Sarlat-la-Canéda, Thiviers, Villefranche-du-Périgord.

Sunday: Issigeac, *Saint-Cyprien.

FAIRS AND FESTIVALS

April: *Journées Gastronomiques de la Noix* (walnut festival), Martel.

June: *Journées Gastronomiques* (food festival), Martel.

First Sunday in August: *Fête de la Moisson* (harvest festival), Gourdon.

Beginning of August: *Foire des Produits Régionaux* (regional food fair), Caminel, near Fajoles.

Christmastime: *Foire au Foie Gras* (*foie gras* festival), Martel.

BRANTÔME *(Dordogne)*

Angoulême 58 k, Limoges 90 k, Paris 502 k, Périgueux 27 k.

Market: Friday, 9 A.M. to noon, Place du Marché.
Foie gras and truffle market: three or four consecutive Fridays around
Christmas, 9 A.M. to noon, Place du Marché.

When you are in the region on a Friday, the early morning fruit and vegetable market in Brantôme is a must. Here, in a storybook-like village set along the river Dronne, farmers and fishmongers, cheese merchants and shoe salesmen vie for space along the bridge, spilling out into side streets and stopping in the shadow of the famous Brantôme abbey, founded by Charlemagne in 769. Today in the market you'll find cheesemakers offering creamy white cow's-milk cheese gift-wrapped in sheer white paper, the sort of cheese many farm women still make at home on a daily basis. There's also an earthy *tomme de vache,* with its wrinkled, pale gray skin, and a delicately flavored, ochre-skinned *fromage* Echourgnac (also known as *trappe*) from the neighboring Trappist monastery. Trout are abundant in the area's meandering streams, and in markets all over the Dordogne, independent fishmongers can be found selling live trout from tanks set in the back of a truck or station wagon.

RESTAURANT

LE MOULIN DU ROC
24530 Champagnac-
    de-Belair.
(53.54.80.36).
Last orders taken at 2 P.M.
    and 10 P.M.
Closed Tuesday, Wednesday
    lunch, mid-November
    through mid-December,
    and mid-January through
    mid-February.
Credit cards: AE, DC, EC, V.
Terrace dining.
Private dining room for 20.
English spoken.
190- and 250-franc menus.
    A la carte, 350 to 450
    francs.

SPECIALTIES:
*Foie gras chaud en feuille de
choux* (warm *foie gras* in
cabbage leaves), *confit de
canard à l'oseille* (preserved
duck with sorrel).

Lucien and Solange Gardillou, Le Moulin du Roc.

This converted walnut oil mill brims with a haphazard sort of charm as the chef, Solange Gardillou, and her husband, Lucien, play out their roles as host and hostess to the international variety of pilgrims who have made this their headquarters in the Dordogne. It is a thoroughly romantic spot—during the warmer months, guests dine on the terrace overlooking the river Dronne, shaded by a thick growth of bamboo—and the menu provides a balance of traditional and modern fare. Madame Gardillou's cooking lacks polish, but some dishes are highly recommended: The delicately smoked salmon trout arrives with a sprinkling of fragrant walnut oil, and the grilled *confit d'oie* is accompanied by a superb sorrel purée and a shower of raw shredded sorrel. The duck sausage *(saucisson de canard)* and the bland *pintade* (guinea fowl) in mustard sauce were far less successful. (Directions: Follow the D78 and D83 6 kilometers northeast of Brantôme.)

SPECIALITES REGIONALES

DEBORD
Rochevideau, 24530
   Champagnac-de-Belair.
(53.54.81.42).
Open 8 P.M. to 6 P.M. Closed
   Sunday, and December
   through March.

S P E C I A L T Y:
Huile de noix (walnut oil).

After sampling the exquisite walnut oil at Le Moulin du Roc, the only solution is to go to the source and pick up a bottle to take home. As one approaches the 700-year-old mill alongside a narrow stream, there is the aroma of freshly roasted walnuts. Anything that smells this good has to taste great, and indeed it is among the best and freshest walnuts oils available in France. Years ago, there were ten walnut oil mills within the 13-kilometer stretch from Brantôme to Saint-Jean-de-Côle. Now, only Marcel Debord's mill remains. The oil is still pressed in the simplest, old-fashioned way: Shelled walnuts are ground, heated in a caldron over a wood fire to help release the oil, then pressed. The Debords also press oil for neighbors who arrive throughout the season with their own shelled walnuts. On a good day, Debord presses about 200 liters (quarts), using about 5 kilograms (10 pounds) of walnuts in the shell for each liter. When purchasing oil, most clients bring their own containers, but if you forget, they'll dig into their cellar and come up with something. We trekked home with a Suze bottle sparkling with liquid gold! If you are traveling, I would advise bringing a plastic mineral water bottle with a screw-on cap. And be sure to refrigerate the oil as soon as you get it home, to keep it fresh-tasting for up to a year. (Directions: From Brantôme take the D78 east; it's the first farm on the left just before the hamlet of Rochevideau. No sign.)

CABRERETS *(Lot)*

Cahors 33 k, Figeac 44 k, Gourdon 44 k, Paris 593 k, Saint-Céré 64 k, Villefranche-de-Rouergue 42 k.

RESTAURANT

LA PESCALERIE
46330 Cabrerets.
(65.31.22.55).
Last orders taken at 1 P.M. and 9 P.M.
Closed November through March.
Credit cards: AE, DC, V.
Terrace dining.
English spoken.
90-franc menu without wine. A la carte, 300 francs.

SPECIALTIES:
Change with the season; dishes with *foie gras, confit* (preserved duck and goose), *truffes* (truffles).

Quiet times at La Pescalerie.

One of my most pleasant dining discoveries in years is La Pescalerie. Its bucolic, natural setting and its carefully prepared cuisine make it a spot I'd go back to tomorrow without hesitation. Plump farm chickens peck around in the grass as you drive up to this tastefully restored eighteenth-century stone residence, ringed with terraces and thriving flower, fruit, and vegetable gardens. The owner, Roger Belcour, leads a double life: By day he's a surgeon in Cahors, by night he is the attentive host. I knew the dinner would be good when I

If someone says with a sly wink that they're going to *"aller aux fraises,"* it means they're going to walk in the woods with a gallant companion. *"Sucrer les fraises"* is said of an elderly person who is afraid and may be shaking, or who is senile.

passed the sparkling blue-and-white-tiled kitchen and heard the chef cheerily whistling as he worked.

A meal here is as satisfying as the ambience: Try the *salade au cou d'oie* (garden greens topped with warm slices of grilled stuffed goose neck) and the perfectly moist farmhouse chicken, roasted with a hint of sage. You will not be able to resist the sourdough bread, and the cheese tray is a lesson in regional simplicity—they offer only three well-made selections: a rare, well-aged Saint-Nectaire, a young Cabécou goat cheese, and a tangy Cantal.

If there's room for dessert, sample the delicate fruit *tartelettes* or the rustic and pungent homemade lime sorbet, laced with fresh mint and flecks of lime and orange zest. There are not more than a handful of tables, so do reserve in advance.

Confiture de Vieux Garcon
BACHELOR'S CONFITURE

I love the name for this country fruit mixture, and enjoy being able to snitch bits of fruit from a huge glass jar late at night as we did while sitting around the fire with our friends Dany and Guy Dubois, farmers in the Dordogne. In French, a vieux garçon is a rather hopeless bachelor, and I can just picture a group of old men cheering themselves up with their evening confiture. This blend of seasonal fruit soaked in vodka or clear eau-de-vie and sugar should mellow for at least two months for maximum flavor. It's a wonderful instant dessert to have on hand, for sampling as is or serving over ice cream or custard.

2 pounds (1 kg) any combination mixed fresh fruits, such as peaches, plums, apricots, prunes, pears, apples, figs, strawberries, raspberries, cherries, grapes, and currants
1 bottle (750 ml) vodka, plus additional if needed
2 pounds (1 kg) sugar
1 large lemon, very thinly sliced

1. Prepare the fruit: Peel and pit the peaches, and cut into eighths. Pit the plums, apricots, and prunes and cut into sixths. Halve and core the pears and apples, and cut into eighths. Halve the figs. Leave the remaining fruit whole.

2. Pour the vodka into a large glass jar with a lid. Add the sugar and stir to dissolve. Add the fruit and lemon slices. Pour in additional vodka if needed to cover the fruit completely. Let stand in a cool dry place at least 2 months, stirring occasionally and adding more vodka, fruit, sugar, and lemon as desired to replenish the supply.

Yield: 2 pounds (1 kg).

LA DORNAC *(Dordogne)*

Brive-la-Gaillarde 20 k, Cahors 108 k, Larche 8 k, Paris 549 k,
Sarlat-la-Canéda 36 k, Terrasson-la-Villedieu 10 k.

SPECIALITES REGIONALES

DANY and GUY DUBOIS
La Dornac, 24120
   Terrasson-la-Villedieu.
(53.51.04.24).
Foie gras weekends all year
long. Pig weekends
November through April.

SPECIALTY:
Week-end à la Ferme (farm
weekend).

The best address I know for excellent homemade *foie gras d'oie* (goose *foie gras*), as well as numerous pork products (everything from ham to headcheese). Farm products are sold daily, but it is best to call first to be certain someone is there to greet you. The friendly, outgoing Dubois family also offers intensive hands-on farm weekends, where you can make your own *foie gras* and preserve your own geese, or even a whole pig, to take home. (Directions: From Brive-la-Gaillarde take the N89 west to Larche, then take the D60 5 kilometers in the direction of Sarlat. At Chavagnac turn right toward La Dornac. In La Dornac drive to La Cassagne; here there are signs to the farm.) (See "Down on the Weekend Farm," page 485).

Geese on the Dubois farm.

LES EYZIES-DE-TAYAC *(Dordogne)*

Brive-la-Gaillarde 62 k, Paris 532 k, Périgueux 45 k, Sarlat-la-Canéda 21 k.

Market: Monday, Easter through September, 8 A.M. to 5 P.M., along the main street.

RESTAURANT

CRO-MAGNON
24620 Les Eyzies-de-Tayac.
(53.06.97.06).
Last orders taken at 2 P.M.
  and 9 P.M.
Closed mid-October to
  mid-April.
Credit cards: AE, DC, EC, V.
Terrace dining.
English spoken.
110- to 300-franc menus. A
  la carte, 300 francs.

SPECIALTIES:
Foie gras maison (homemade fatted duck or goose liver), *pigeonneau au verjus* (pigeon with a sauce made of unripe grapes, or grapes left on the vine after harvest), *confit d'oie à l'oseille* (preserved goose with sorrel).

I really fell in love with this old-fashioned vine-covered restaurant that, in appearance at least, seems to have changed little since the 1950s: The oak-beamed ceilings, the bright orange walls, and the giant fireplace all give the place a homey, cozy air. But the food is perfectly up-to-date, with some nice regional touches. We loved the *confit d'oie à l'oseille,* a dish that is at least three times lighter than it sounds, and the satisfying *daube de mouton,* which I know I could sample once a week, it's so full of flavor (see recipe, following page). The cheese tray is nicely presented and includes a lovely fresh cow's-milk cheese served with fresh walnuts and a local Cabécou goat's-milk cheese. For dessert, try their truly exquisite *tarte Tatin.*

GRAMAT *(Lot)*

Brive-la-Gaillarde 57 k, Cahors 56 k, Figeac 37 k, Gourdon 39 k, Paris 549 k, Saint-Céré 20 k.

Market: Second and fourth Thursday of the month, 9 A.M. to 5 P.M., Place de la Halle.

EAUX-DE-VIE

MAISON VIGOUROUS
9 Place de la République,
  46500 Gramat.
(65.38.70.30).
Open 8 A.M. to noon and 2
  to 7 P.M. Closed Sunday.
Will ship in France.

Maison Vigourous' golden, aged *eau-de-vie de prunes "du Vieux Pigeonnier"* from the Ségala distillery has a stunning freshness about it, with scents of intensely fragrant ripe plums mingling with the earthiness of plum stones. It's among the finest plum brandies I've found in France.

DAUBE DE MOUTON RESTAURANT CRO-MAGNON
RESTAURANT CRO-MAGNON'S MUTTON AND
BLACK OLIVE STEW

I first sampled this satisfying daube *one cool evening in May at the charmingly old-fashioned restaurant Cro-Magnon in Les-Eyzies-de-Tayac and decided then and there that my guests would be sampling it soon. I love lamb, black olives, red wine, and garlic, so why not combine them into a delicious stew? The quantity of wine used in the dish may seem excessive, but somehow, as it cooks down, it is transformed into a lovely, lusty sauce rich with the fragrance of olives and lamb.*

2 bottles (750 ml each) red wine, preferably Gigondas

3½ pounds (about 1.5 kg) lamb or mutton shoulder, cut into 4-inch (10 cm) chunks, with fat carefully removed (a butcher can do this for you)

Salt and freshly ground black pepper to taste

¼ cup (60 ml) virgin olive oil

2 medium onions, coarsely chopped

1 carrot, peeled and coarsely chopped

Bouquet garni: several leaves basil, 2 sprigs each parsley and thyme, 1 small leek, rinsed clean of sand, and 2 celery ribs, all tied with kitchen string

1 whole head garlic, cloves peeled and halved

8 ounces (250 g) imported French black olives, preferably from Nyons

Small handful of fresh basil, minced

1. The day before serving the *daube,* heat the wine to a boil in a large saucepan and let boil for 2 to 3 minutes. Set aside to cool.

2. Season the lamb with salt and pepper. Heat the oil in a large enameled casserole over medium-high heat. Add the lamb in batches without crowding and brown on all sides. Using a slotted spoon, remove it from the casserole.

3. Add the onions and carrot to the casserole and sauté until soft but not browned. Pour off any fat in the casserole, then add the browned lamb, bouquet garni, and garlic and mix well. Cook, stirring continually, until the garlic is browned, about 5 minutes. Add the wine and olives stir until thoroughly combined, and remove from the heat. Refrigerate overnight.

4. The next day, skim the sauce carefully to remove all trace of impurities or fat. Heat the *daube* to a simmer and continue to simmer gently, stirring occasionally, until the lamb is very tender, about 2 hours.

5. To serve, discard the bouquet garni and taste the sauce for seasoning. Spoon over buttered noodles and sprinkle some of the basil over each serving.

Yield: 6 servings.

MONTFORT *(Dordogne)*

Brive-la-Gaillarde 58 k, Gourdon 20 k, Paris 534 k, Sarlat-la-Canéda 10 k, Vitrac 3 k.

RESTAURANT

LA FERME
Caudon-de-Vitrac, 24200
   Montfort-Caudon.
(53.28.33.35).
Last orders taken at 1 P.M.
   and 8:30 P.M.
Closed Monday and
   October.
No credit cards.
Private dining room for 30.
Some English spoken.
Four menus, 55 to 120
   francs. A la carte, 180
   francs.

SPECIALTIES:
Soupe paysanne du Périgord (rye
bread soup), *confit de canard*
(preserved duck), grilled
meats.

A typical Dordogne farm scene.

There are few restaurants as authentic and generous as La Ferme, a rustic restored farmhouse that's filled with bric-a-brac and the sounds of good times. The 55-franc menu is not to be believed: You'll be invited to weave your way through tureens of hearty rye bread soup, slices of country ham, jars full of goose *rillettes,* thick grilled lamb chops, cheese, and all the deep red Cahors you can wisely consume. Not to mention basket after basket full of crusty country bread. The owner, Maurice Escalier, is a rather humorous curmudgeon. "Don't eat too much bread," he cautions one bread lover. "Eat your soup," he admonishes a slow but appreciative eater. He seems to fit perfectly into the scene of La Ferme. There is a limited menu (including good grilled meats, rather dry omelets, and acceptable *pommes sarladaise*), but the thick and satisfying rye bread soup is not to be missed: Long-simmered white beans, carrots, and potatoes are poured over day-old rye bread, and each diner is offered his personal tureen, for those obligatory seconds (see recipe, page 482). (Directions: From Sarlat take the road for Bergerac as far as Vitrac. Here take the Souillac road 1 kilometer, where there is a large house with a sign for La Fagne-Caudon. Make a right here and follow this road to the restaurant.)

ROCAMADOUR *(Lot)*

Brive-la-Gaillarde 55 k, Cahors 59 k, Figeac 46 k, Gourdon 36 k, Paris 545 k,
Saint-Céré 29 k, Sarlat-la-Canéda 66 k.

FROMAGER

FERME JEAN LACOSTE
Les Alix, 46500 Gramat.
(65.33.62.66).
Open daily 9 A.M. to 7 P.M.
Closed in January or
    February if there is no
    milk.
Will ship in France.

At this old stone farmhouse with fading white shutters, the friendly farm wife, Marcelle Lacoste, still milks her seventy goats by hand. As long as she can remember, she's been making the local specialty, Cabécou, delicate discs that she ages for just two weeks in her cool, humid cellar. What sets Cabécou apart from other goat cheeses is the way the cheese is made: Once the curds and whey are separated, the drained curds are actually kneaded by hand before being pressed into molds, resulting in a firmer, drier, denser cheese. It's hard to believe it when you look at the miniature discs—about the size of a silver dollar—but it takes half a liter (a full pint) of milk to make a single Cabécou. Locally, the cheese is also known as Lou Cabécou. (Directions: From Rocamadour take the road toward Mayrignac-le-Francal. The Lacoste farm, which is marked, is the second farm after the hamlet of Les Alix.)

SAINT-CIRQ-LAPOPIE *(Lot)*

Cahors 33 k, Figeac 45 k, Paris 607 k, Villefranche-de-Rouergue 36 k.

SPECIALITES
REGIONALES

CHRISTIAN DESTIEN
Saint-Cirq-Lapopie, 46330
    Cabrerets.
Flexible hours, open only
    during the summer
    months.

SPECIALTY:
Poterie (pottery).

A source for truly appealing sun-colored pottery, yellow and green omelet plates, as well as elegant contemporary oxblood-red plates and vases.

SAINT-CYPRIEN *(Dordogne)*

Beynac 10 k, Paris 539 k, Périgueux 54 k, Souillac 51 k.

Market: Sunday and the second Monday of the month, 9 A.M. to 1 P.M.,
Place Gambetta.

SPECIALITES REGIONALES

AUGUSTE CYPRIEN
Place de l'Eglise, 24220
   Saint-Cyprien.
(53.29.25.12).
Open June through
   September only, 9 A.M. to
   noon and 2 to 6 P.M.
   Closed Saturday and
   Sunday.
Will ship in France.

Saint-Cirq-Lapopie.

The southwestern connection for the famous
Petrossian specialty shop in Paris. Here they
make their own *foie gras* and *confit* and offer a variety
of luxury products—such as preserved truffles and
Sauternes—presented in a gracefully restored shop
in the center of this captivating village.

SAINTE-NATHALENE *(Dordogne)*

Gourdon 26 k, Paris 555 k, Périgueux 75 k, Sarlat-la-Canéda 9 k,
Souillac 21 k.

SPECIALITES REGIONALES

**HUILERIE DU MOULIN
   DE LA TOUR**
Sainte-Nathalène, 24200
   Sarlat-la-Canéda.
(53.59.22.08).
Open daily 9 A.M. to 12:30
   P.M. and 2 to 7 P.M.
Will ship in France.

The most famous, but to my mind not the best,
walnut oil mill in the region. Still, the oil is
probably fresher than you'll find in most markets,
and half the price. At the same time you'll have a
chance to see an authentic working walnut oil mill,
one of the last in France. (Directions: 9 kilometers
northeast of Sarlat, via the D47. There are signs to
the mill).

SOUPE PAYSANNE DU PERIGORD LA FERME
LA FERME'S RYE BREAD SOUP

Don't turn your nose up at this simple peasant soup. It's one of the least expensive dishes I know, and one of the more filling and satisfying, especially on a cold winter day. When restaurateur Maurice Escalier sent me this recipe, his last instructions were: "Laisser mijoter jusqu'à midi (Let it cook just until noon)," which is what they do at his rustic restaurant, La Ferme, outside of Sarlat. If you happen to have a loaf of wonderful homemade rye bread, all the better. And if you wish to add a touch of garlic, some thyme, and a bay leaf to this original peasant version, there is no reason not to. Like most soups, this is even better the next day.

1 pound (500 g) dried white Northern beans

1 pound (about 2 medium; 500 g) potatoes, peeled and thinly sliced

8 ounces (250 g) carrots, peeled and thinly sliced

8 ounces (250 g) leeks, well rinsed, dried, and thinly sliced

1 tablespoon duck fat or butter

Salt and freshly ground black pepper to taste

12 very thin slices day-old rye bread

1. One day before serving the soup, soak the beans in plenty of cold water.

2. Three hours before serving the soup, drain the beans. Heat 5 quarts (5 liters) water to a boil in a large soup pot. Add the drained beans, the potatoes, carrots, leeks, duck fat, salt, and pepper. Return to a boil, then reduce the heat and barely simmer the soup, partially covered, for 3 hours. Taste and adjust the seasonings.

3. To serve, put a slice of rye bread in each warmed soup bowl, ladle the soup over the bread, and season with pepper.

Yield: 12 servings.

SARLAT-LA-CANEDA *(Dordogne)*

Bergerac 74 k, Brive-la-Gaillarde 51 k, Cahors 61 k, Paris 539 k, Périgueux 66 k.

Market: Wednesday, 9 A.M. to noon, Place de la Mairie; Saturday, 9 A.M. to 5 P.M., Place de la Mairie.

On market days, especially in the fall and winter months, Sarlat is at its captivating best, a lively spot that serves as the main commercial center for many of the Dordogne's farmers, who bring their walnuts and *foie gras,* fatted geese and ducks, and sometimes black truffles to the active Saturday market. Even if time is limited, don't omit Sarlat from the itinerary, for its mellow yellow stone Renaissance buildings, roofed in sturdy gray stone, and its steep and narrow cobblestone streets are among the most beautiful and best preserved in all the Périgord.

BOULANGERIE

B. PAULIAC
Madrazes, 24200 Sarlat.
(53.59.37.13).
Open 7:30 A.M. to 12:30 P.M.
and 4 to 7:30 P.M. Closed
Monday.

After you sample the rye bread soup at La Ferme nearby, you'll want to get your own loaf of Pauliac's magnificent crusty rye, made only on Wednesdays. Their sourdough *pain de seigle* is so good you can almost eat it in two courses, first the chewy crust, then the softer interior, the *mie*. This *boulangerie* looks like an afterthought: It is actually located in the front room of a house on the outskirts of Sarlat. (Directions: From Sarlat take the road for Gourdon-Souillac; the bakery is on the right and there is a *Chambres à Louer*, or "Rooms for Rent," sign in front.)

SORGES *(Dordogne)*

Brantôme 25 k, Limoges 77 k, Nontron 45 k, Paris 470 k, Périgueux 24 k, Thiviers 13 k, Uzerche 174 k.

Market: In summer, Friday, 9 A.M. to noon, along the main street.

MUSEE

**ECOMUSSEE DE LA
TRUFFE**
24420 Sorges.
(53.05.90.11).
Open 2 P.M. to 5 P.M. (10 A.M.
to noon and 2 to 5 P.M. in
July and August). Closed
Tuesday.
Admission: 11 francs for
adults, 6 francs for
children.

A mini-museum devoted to the famed black Périgord truffle, the precious mushroom that is rapidly disappearing from this region. The museum presents an exhibit on truffle growing and culture and, by appointment, will organize hikes through nearby truffle plantations.

TERRASSON-LA-VILLEDIEU *(Dordogne)*

Brive-la-Gaillarde 21 k, Paris 510 k, Périgueux 52 k, Sarlat-la-Canéda 42 k.

Market: Thursday, 9 A.M. to noon, Quai du 4-Septembre.

BOULANGERIE

RENE NEUVILLE
Terrasson, 24120
  Terrasson-la-Villedieu.
(53.51.68.40).
Open 9 A.M. to noon and 2
  to 7 P.M. Closed Monday
  and Wednesday.

René Neuville is a very special sort of baker: He seems to bake his giant crusty country loaves out of sheer energetic passion. Wander in around 4 or 5 in the afternoon and half the community will have joined him there in his makeshift garage/ *boulangerie.* They come, they visit, and they chat as they wait for the country loaves to come tumbling from his giant wood-fired oven.

STRAWBERRIES

The French have a blatant love affair with strawberries that dates back centuries. The Parisian socialite Thérèse Tallien, wife of the eighteenth-century revolutionary Jean Lambert Tallien, took baths in strawberry juice to keep her skin soft and smooth. It took 10 kilos (more than 20 pounds) of berries to properly embellish each bath.

Bathing in strawberries may be going too far, but who does not love a plump strawberry fresh from the plant, the sun's heat still radiating from its juice-filled flesh? Whether it's a tiny *fraise des bois,* or wild strawberry, that explodes with flowery perfume in your mouth, or the more subtly flavored domestic strawberry, they're served to perfection in France, with a light dusting of sugar or a dollop of tart *crème fraîche.*

In France there are two basic types of strawberries: small ones derived from tiny wild berries, of which the best known is called *fraise des quatre-saisons,* and larger ones that originally came from the southern United States.

Down on the Weekend Farm

"*D*uring the next four days of intensive labor we would learn all one could wish to know about preserving a 150-kilo (300-pound) pig, raised on the Dubois farm on a rich diet of beets, corn, and barley."

LA DORNAC, OCTOBER 28—Dany Dubois opened wide the doors to her rambling contemporary French farmhouse and called to her noontime arrivals: "You're just in time for lunch. Come on in and make yourselves at home."

French fries were sizzling on the stove, steaks were ready to pan-fry, terrines of pork and goose *rillettes* and pork pâté were arranged on the long table, and the thirty-seven-year-old Périgord farm wife was busy cutting thick slices of crusty country bread.

A few minutes later her lanky husband, Guy, wandered in from the barn and began uncorking bottles of rough homemade red wine. In the pasture next door, a calf was about to be born. Down in the valley hunters were stalking *palombes,* or wood pigeons.

For the next seventy-two hours there was barely a moment of calm at the Dubois farm, which is set on a green hill in the Dordogne. We were the first farm weekend guests of the year, here for *Les Journées du Cochon* (see page 476). During the next four days of intensive labor we would learn all one could wish to know about preserving a 150-kilo (300-pound) pig, raised on the Dubois farm on a rich diet of beets, corn, and barley. On Sunday noon, we'd leave with many pounds of *boudin noir,* or blood sausage, and dozens of glass jars with gelatinous headcheese, rich *pâté de foie de porc, rillettes,* and *confit.*

The ham—wrapped tightly in muslin and seasoned with salt, mounds of freshly ground black pepper, and bay leaves from the garden—would remain at the farm, ready to be picked up months later. We left two giant hams resting under fresh wood cinders in a giant wooden keg, where they would age for six weeks before being hung to dry and cure, emerging as *jambon cru,* ready for cutting into paper-thin slices for lunches and snacking.

On the Dubois family farm, only sugar, coffee, butter, and bread are purchased. Everything else served to guests has been raised and preserved right on their farm. That includes the fresh and fragrant walnut oil for dressing greens from the garden, the wild *cèpe* mushrooms that appear in a hearty first-course omelet, the beefy *magret d'oie* (breast of fatted goose, pan-fried and served with a rich green peppercorn sauce), and even the variety of ciders and fruit wines—peach, orange and apple—that appear as aperitifs. At breakfast, fresh cow's milk is poured into giant cups for the coffee, and after dinner everyone sits around the fireplace, cracking this season's crop of meaty walnuts and playing parlor games.

Dany and Guy Dubois are typical of many French couples who have opened their homes to guests for a working weekend on the farm; they also offer *foie gras* weekends in preserving the more than 1,000 geese they force-feed each year. Their weekends do not offer formal cooking lessons, but rather an opportunity for intimate contact with the French countryside and its traditions. Guests become a part of the family, and this means they may end up sweeping floors or helping to move a herd of cattle from one field to another on a sunny afternoon.

FOUR EASY PHRASES

What to do when you are at table having a wonderful time and are offered more, but can't possibly take another bite? Here are four easy phrases that will allow you to exit gracefully:

Non merci, c'était parfait.
(No thanks, it was perfect.)

Vraiment non, mais c'était délicieux.
(Really no, but it was delicious.)

Non merci, j'ai très bien mangé, je n'ai vraiment plus faim.
(No thank you, I've eaten very well, I'm just not hungry anymore.)

Non merci, je ne pourrais pas avaler une seule bouchée de plus.
(No thank you, I couldn't swallow one more bite)

Rye bread, Sarlat-la-Canéda.

Bordeaux et La Côte de l'Atlantique
BORDEAUX AND THE ATLANTIC COAST

A La Tupiña welcome in Bordeaux.

From Arcachon to La Rochelle, Cognac to Poitiers, this is a wholesome, gifted land, a flat and luminous region that supplies France with delicate green-hued oysters, smooth amber-colored brandy, the creamiest, most fragrant sweet butter, as well as fine wines that are among the most prestigious in all the world. Here we have a cuisine that is at once earthy and elegant, one that finds its roots in the vineyards, on the beaches, in the harbors—traditional fare that puts to creative use the wealth of the ingredients most readily at hand.

It was in the city of Bordeaux that I first sampled the ingenious and delicious combination of fresh oysters, spicy sausages, and white wine, a dish known as *huîtres à la charentaise*. A cool oyster is downed first, then you take a bite of sausage, then wash it all down with chilled wine. Today, oysters and sausages are found in cafés and restaurants throughout the region, and I love the dish best with really spicy sausages and a golden white Graves.

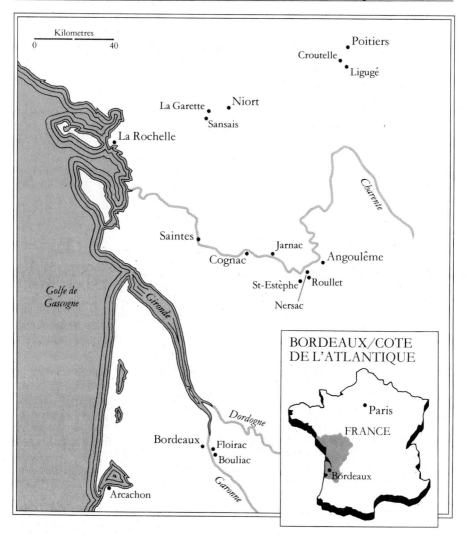

Along the coast and inland toward the swampy area known as the Poitou-Charentes, cooks use quantities of garlic; tiny sprigs of gentle winter garlic appear on the tables in January, served most often with roast *chevreau,* or goat, a moist and subtle local delicacy.

Those who love mussels will be delighted to see them appear in every guise, as *éclade,* a favorite picnic dish of mussels grilled beneath a bed of pine needles, as well as *mouclade,* a golden creamy soup flavored with saffron or curry, particularly delicious when spiked with a touch of Cognac just before it's served.

Eels and land snails—uncommon fare, no matter where you

may be—are served in the most elegant of forms. The tiny spaghetti-like eels known as *pibales* appear for just a few weeks from mid-January to March, when they're cooked in garlic and oil and served piping hot. The snails, known here as both *lumas* and *cagouilles* (it seems that every other restaurant between Bordeaux and Poitou calls itself La Cagouille), are served in a variety of ways—stuffed with garlic butter, in tomatoes and red wine, and with the local sweet wine, *pineau des Charentes.*

But the most unusual regional specialty of all is white beans: not just any kind of white bean but the creamy white, almost nutty *mojette,* served fresh as well as dried, most often with slices of delicious fresh ham that tastes the way I think fresh ham should, that is, like pork on its way to being ham.

For travelers, this is a region that cries out to be explored. Though I find Bordeaux a rather stuffy, characterless town—too snooty *bourgeois* for those of us who are not part of the clan—it does work as a gateway to a part of France that is open to new gastronomic discovery.

WHEN YOU GO

Michelin Green Guides: *Poitou/Vendée/Charentes* and *Pyrénées/Aquitaine.*

Getting there: Air Inter offers about seven 1-hour flights daily from Paris to Bordeaux, leaving from either Orly Ouest airport or from the Roissy (Charles-de-Gaulle) airport. The same journey by train (leaving from the Paris Austerlitz train station) takes about 4 hours; there are at least ten trains daily. TAT airline flies to La Rochelle from Orly Ouest about twice a day Monday through Friday; the flight takes about 1 ½ hours. There are also at least five trains daily making the 5-hour trip from the Paris Austerlitz station to La Rochelle. Cars can be rented at the airports and train stations.

Getting around: Michelin maps 232 (Pays de Loire), 233 (Poitou/Charentes), and 234 (Aquitaine).

Best time to visit: The area is at its most beautiful from May to September, but to sample many of its gastronomic specialties, such as *pibales* (baby eels) and *chevreau à l'ail vert* (goat with young green garlic shoots), you'll have to plan a visit in late January or February.

MARKETS

(Liveliest markets are marked with an asterisk.)

Monday: Arcachon, Bordeaux, Chalais, Lencloître (first Monday of the month), Meschers, La Roche-Posay, La Rochelle, Les Sables-d'Olonne.

Tuesday: Angoulême, Arcachon, Bordeaux, *Bressuire, *Challans, Civray (first Tuesday of the month), Cognac, l'Ile-d'Yeu (mid-May to mid-September), *Jarnac, Lezay, Marennes, Meschers, *Mont-de-Marsan, Poitiers, *La Roche-Posay, Rochefort, La Rochelle, Royan, Les Sables-d'Olonne, Saint-Gilles-Croix-de-Vie, Saintes.

Wednesday: Angoulême, *Arcachon, Blaye, Bordeaux, Bourcefranc-le-Chapus, Le Château-d'Oléron, Fontenay-le-Comte, Gujan-Mestras, Jarnac, Luçon, *Meschers, Parthenay, Poitiers, Pons, La Roche-Posay, *La Rochelle, Royan, *Saint-Gilles-Croix-de-Vie, Saintes.

Thursday: Angoulême, Arcachon, Bordeaux, Le Château-d'Oléron, Jarnac, Marennes, Meschers, *La Mothe-Saint-Héray, *Niort, Poitiers, La Roche-Posay, Rochefort, La Rochelle, Royan, Les Sables-d'Olonne, Saint-Gilles-Croix-de-Vie, Saint-Macaire, Saintes.

Friday: Angoulême, Arcachon, Bordeaux, Challans, Le Château-d'Oléron, Civray, Cognac, *Jarnac, Meschers, Noirmoutier-en-l'Ile, La Roche-Posay, La Rochelle, Royan, Les Sables-d'Olonne, Saintes.

Saturday: *Angoulême, *Arcachon, *Blaye, *Bordeaux, Bressuire, Le Château-d'Oléron, *Chauvigny, *Cognac, *Confolens, *Fontenay-le-Comte, Jarnac, *Lencloître, Luçon, *Marennes, *Meschers, Niort, Pauillac, *Poitiers, Pons, La Roche-Posay, *Rochefort, *La Rochelle, *Royan, Les Sables-d'Olonne, *Saint-Gilles-Croix-de-Vie, Saint-Savinien, Sainte-Foy-la-Grande, *Saintes.

Sunday: *Angoulême, Arcachon, Barsac, *Bourcefranc-le-Chapus, *Le Château-d'Oléron, Jarnac, Meschers, Poitiers, La Roche-Posay, La Rochelle, Royan, Les Sables-d'Olonne, Saint-Emilion, Saint-Gilles-Croix-de-Vie, *Saintes.

FAIRS AND FESTIVALS

Thursday before Mardi Gras: *Foire des Boeufs Gras* (fattened-beef festival), Bazas.

Last Sunday in April: *Journée Gastronomique* (food fair), Lezay.

One Sunday in June: *Fête de la Cagouille* (land-snail festival), Angoulême.

Third weekend in July: *Fête de l'Huître* (oyster festival), Andernos-les-Bains.

Three days near the end of August: *Foire aux Melons* (melon fair), Saint-Georges-des-Coteaux.

One weekend in August: *Foire aux Huîtres* (oyster fair), Gujan-Mestras.

One Sunday in August or September: *Fête du Goret* (roast pig festival), Ranton.

Fourth Monday in October: *Foire aux Marrons* (chestnut fair), Chevanceaux.

ANGOULÊME *(Charente)*

Bordeaux 116 k, Niort 112 k, Paris 450 k.

Markets: Tuesday through Sunday, 7 A.M. to 12:30 P.M., covered market, Place des Halles; Saturday, 7 A.M. to 12:30 P.M., open-air market, Place Victor-Hugo. *Fête de la Cagouille* (land snail festival): one Sunday in June.

RESTAURANT

AUBERGE DU PONT DE LA MEURE
Route Hiersac, Nersac, 16440 Roullet-Saint-Estèphe.
(45.90.60.48).
Last orders taken at 2 P.M. and 9 P.M.
Closed Friday dinner, Saturday, and August.
Credit cards: AE, DC, V.
Private dining rooms for 6 to 10 and 25.
85- and 130-franc menus. A la carte, 160 francs.

S P E C I A L T I E S :
Anguille aux poireaux (eel with leeks); *chevreau à l'aillet* (young goat with garlic); *salade de cresson aux foies de volaille* (watercress and chicken liver salad).

The menu at this combination café-bar-restaurant set right alongside the Charente river should get an award for regionalism: superbly fresh watercress salad showered with cubes of crisply cooked chicken livers, local eel stewed to tenderness in slivers of leeks, and a platter of deliciously succulent and meaty goat showered with tiny shoots of young garlic—a curious and marvelous local specialty that marries young goat with the mild winter garlic, a flavor that resembles white spring onions. Unfortunately the setting is drab, the welcome is cold, and the bored waiters seem to be thinking "We don't care that you've come." So be forewarned, try to go on a sunny day when you can sit at a table overlooking the river, order up a bottle of chilled local red Gamay du Haut Poitou, and enjoy. (Directions: 5 kilometers southwest of Angoulême via the D699.)

BORDEAUX *(Gironde)*

Angoulême 116 k, Cognac 119 k, Niort 183, Paris 579 k, La Rochelle 187 k, Toulouse 244 k.

Markets: Monday through Saturday, 7 A.M. to 1 P.M., covered markets, Cours Victor-Hugo, Place des Grands-Hommes, Place du Marché des Chartrons, Place de Lerme; Wednesday, 7 A.M. to 1 P.M., Place Stehelin.
Flea markets: daily, Quartier Saint-Michel; Saturday, Sunday, and Monday, Place Meyard, at the foot of the Eglise Saint-Michel, at the Quais de la Monnaie, de la Grave, and Salinières; Saturday morning, Esplanade des Quinconces; Sunday and holidays, Place Saint-Pierre. Antiques shops are centered around the Quartier Notre-Dame.

RESTAURANTS

LE CHAPON FIN
5 Rue de Montesquieu,
    33000 Bordeaux.
(56.79.10.10).
Last orders taken at 2:15 P.M.
    and 9:30 P.M.
Closed Sunday, Monday,
    school holidays in
    February, and the last
    three weeks in July.
Credit cards: AE, DC, V.
English spoken.
Private dining room for 10
    to 40.
180- (lunch only), 265-, and
    290-franc menus. A la
    carte, 350 francs.

SPECIALTIES:
Regional specialties that
change with the seasons,
including fish and shellfish,
wild game, *pibales* (baby eels,
mid-January to March only),
lamproie à la bordelaise
(lamprey eel stew), *bisque de
palombes aux marrons* (wild
pigeon and chestnut soup),
tarte fine aux pommes (apple
tart).

I'm very fond of Francis Garcia, a Spanish-born chef who moved to the Bordeaux region in the 1950s when he was just a child. He has had solid training, appears passionate as well as wise, and what's more, his food has a vibrancy, a sense of personality, and a clarity that I find lacking in many of France's movie-star chefs. Monsieur Garcia's food is not for wimpy palates, but those who enjoy flavors that pack a wallop will love his *bisque de palombes aux marrons,* a thick and meaty soup filled with chunks of roasted wild pigeon and crunchy chestnuts; the *lamproie à la bordelaise,* the rich local lamprey eel and red wine stew; and the more delicate and elegant *soupe d'huîtres au cresson,* a soothing cream-and-wine-based soup filled with slivers of carrots and leeks, plump local oysters, and a refreshing *chiffonade* of finely shredded watercress with a touch of saffron (see recipe, facing page). If you visit Bordeaux between mid-January and the end of February, you'll hit *pibale* season, and if the tiny spaghetti-like river eels are in the market, Garcia will be sure to offer up piping hot bowls of sizzling *pibales,* bathed in olive oil and an abundance of garlic. My sole objection to the chef Garcia's cooking is his heavy hand with the salt shaker.

Butter figures in the French language almost as much as it does in the cuisine. If you manage to get some financial help that makes life go more easily, you'll say *"Ça met du beurre dans les épinards."* When an affair goes very smoothly, without problems, it goes *"comme dans du beurre."* Someone is said to *"faire son beurre"* when he makes a lot of money in a reasonably honest way. But for every good side there is a bad one: If something counts for little it is said to *"compter pour du beurre,"* and a person who is not too terribly intelligent is said to have not yet *"découvert le fil à couper le beurre."* Meanwhile, if you drink too much, you're likely to become *"beurré,"* get into a fight, and end up with a black eye, or an *"oeil au beurre noir."*

CHEZ PHILIPPE
1 Place du Parlement, 33000
  Bordeaux.
(56.81.83.15).
Last orders taken at 1:30 P.M.
  and 10:30 P.M.
Closed Sunday, Monday, and
  August.
Credit cards: AE, DC, V.
Terrace dining.
Air-conditioned.
Private dining room for 12.
160-franc menu (lunch
  only). A la carte, 350
  francs.

SPECIALTIES:
Fresh fish and shellfish.

Ask anyone in Bordeaux to name the best fish restaurant in town and they're likely to say Chez Philippe. This is a casual, lively, friendly spot, with tables that tumble out onto the terrace in fine weather. Inside, quarters are a bit cozy and cluttered, but service is discreet and professional. The dishes I've most enjoyed here include the superbly fresh grilled *rougets,* or rich tiny red mullet, and the delightful sautéed *chipirons,* good-size squid cooked ever so quickly in a sizzling hot pan and sprinkled at the last minute with minced garlic and parsley. Most guests rave about the chocolate mousse, which I found a bit too fluffy for my palate.

SOUPE D'HUITRES AU CRESSON FRANCIS GARCIA
FRANCIS GARCIA'S OYSTER AND WATERCRESS SOUP

Bordeaux chef Francis Garcia calls this deliciously light and fresh-tasting blend of oysters, leeks, carrots, and watercress his soupe à la minute, *or instant soup. Once the oysters are opened and you have chopped and blanched the vegetables, the soup can be made in just a minute. When I sampled the dish at chef Garcia's, I was convinced that it had been enriched with egg yolks. But no, it was the delicate touch of saffron that fooled my eye as well as my palate. The soup, with its fresh green, gold, and orange colors, reminds me of springtime.*

1 dozen large oysters,
  with their liquor
2 medium leeks, well
  rinsed and dried
2 carrots, peeled
Large handful of
  watercress, washed,
  dried, and stemmed
1 cup (250 ml) *crème
  fraîche* (see Recipe
  Index) or heavy
  cream, preferably not
  ultra-pasteurized
1 cup (250 ml) dry
  white wine, such as a
  white Graves
¼ teaspoon powdered
  saffron
Salt and freshly ground
  white pepper to taste

1. Remove the oysters from their liquid and set aside. Strain the liquid through three thicknesses of cheesecloth and set aside.

2. Cut the leeks and the carrots into 2-inch-long pieces, then cut those into *julienne* (fine) strips. Cut the watercress leaves into a *chiffonnade:* Stack the leaves on top of one another, and using a long chef's knife, cut the watercress into very fine strips.

3. Place the *crème fraîche* and white wine in a medium saucepan and bring to a boil over high heat. Boil just until the mixture has thickened slightly, about 3 minutes. Reduce the heat to medium low and add the oyster liquid and the saffron and stir well. Add the vegetables and stir until they are heated through. Season to taste with salt and white pepper.

4. Just before serving, arrange 3 oysters in the bottom of each of 4 heated soup bowls. Cover with the soup and serve immediately.

Yield: 4 servings.

SAINT-JAMES
3 Place Camille-Hosteins,
    Bouliac, 33270 Floirac.
(56.20.52.19).
Last orders taken at 2 P.M.
    and 10 P.M.
Credit cards: AE, DC, V.
Terrace dining.
Private dining room for 10
    to 20.
120- and 330-franc menus.
    A la carte, 500 to 600
    francs.

SPECIALTIES:
Salade d'huîtres au caviar
(oyster and caviar salad),
agneau de Pauillac
(southwestern lamb), *civet de
canard à la cuillère* (duck stew).

There are times, after a meal that promises a good deal and delivers much less, when you just want to take the chef out back and shake him up a bit. This is the way I felt the last time I lunched at Saint-James, a bright, elegant Relais et Châteaux hotel/restaurant in a lovely wooded setting just outside Bordeaux. Chef Jean-Marie Amat's menu was so enticing—tender local Pauillac lamb with garlic sauce; oysters and caviar; a salad of pigeon and truffles; a delicate duck stew with pasta; a *crème brûlée* flavored with honey and saffron—that I was already looking forward to the next visit. This was indeed a place to go and be thoroughly relaxed and content, seated in front of a roaring fire, awaiting a feast of flavors, aromas, and colors. Then came the food, lovely to look at, beautifully presented, but dish after dish seemed to share one common trait: no taste. Truly, it was as if someone had injected a needle into each preparation and extracted all the flavor. The promised garlic sauce had not a hint of that magical, pungent seasoning. The duck stew was so bland it made one want to cry. The long-anticipated *crème* tasted of cornstarch. It was neither the first nor the last time I have found such discordance in a "grand" French restaurant. Is it that real flavor offends? That refined food must be void of character to meet popular notions of taste? There are no simple answers, except to encourage chefs to stop walking around in the emperor's new clothes and bring flavors back to elegant French food. (Directions: 9 kilometers southeast of Bordeaux via the D10.)

*Open grilling at La Tupiña,
Bordeaux.*

LA TUPINA

6 Rue Porte-de-la-Monnaie,
33000 Bordeaux.
(56.91.56.37).
Last orders taken at 2 P.M.
and 11 P.M.
Closed Sunday and holidays.
Credit card: V.
Private dining room for 20.
250 francs.

SPECIALTIES:
Southwestern: *boeuf du Bazas*
(local beef), *agneau du Pauillac*
(local lamb), *magret grillé*
(grilled fattened duck breast),
brochette de coeurs de canard
(grilled duck hearts), *mignons
de canard vinaigrette à l'échalote*
(duck tenderloins in shallot
vinaigrette), *foie gras frais cuit
au four* (oven-roasted fattened
duck liver).

La Tupiña is my kind of bistro, offering food that's cooked over a roaring fire, service that's casual yet professional, and a crowd that's there for feasting and good times. The compact, spotless La Tupiña is decorated with colorful red, white, and blue Basque linens, the walls are lined with more bottles of Cognac than one could consume in many lifetimes, and the wine list offers a wealth of fine Bordeaux. I return again and again, to sample dishes such as the marvelously fresh oven-roasted *pétoncles,* or tiny scallops; *macaronade,* a rich, full-flavored blend of wild and domestic mushrooms and chunks of *foie gras* smothered in fresh pasta; charcoal-grilled *magret;* and a refreshing *mignons de canard.* I'm not terribly fond of chef Jean-Pierre Xiradakis's layered potato cake; it always seems underseasoned and undercooked. And some of the food may suffer from oversalting.

CAFES

BAR DES GRANDS
   HOMMES
10 Place des Grands-
   Hommes, 33000
   Bordeaux.
(56.81.18.26).
Open 7 A.M. to 9:30 P.M.
   Closed Sunday and
   holidays.

After touring the lively covered market on the trendy Place des Grands-Hommes, linger over a *grand crème* and the morning news at this minuscule old-fashioned café with its lovely Belle Epoque facade.

BRASSERIE DE NOAILLES
12 Allées de Tourny, 33000
   Bordeaux.
(56.81.94.45).
Open 9 A.M. to 11:30 P.M.
   Closed Wednesday and
   three weeks in July.

An old-fashioned 1930s-style café-brasserie in the center of town, a nice place to go after the theater to down platters of briny oysters with hot spicy sausages—the local specialty that's known as *huîtres à la charentaise*—with a few glasses of crisp white wine.

SALON DE THE/
POUR LA MAISON

LE PETIT DROUOT
39 Rue des Remparts, 33000
   Bordeaux.
(56.81.00.22).
Open 11 A.M. to 7 P.M. Closed
   Sunday and Monday.
Credit card: V.

Such a wonderful idea—why haven't more people thought of it? This combination tea shop, antiques shop, and gift shop allows you to sit sipping a cup of *express* while you decide whether to buy the decorative asparagus platter, the hand-embroidered antique shawl, or the Art Deco light fixture.

CONFISERIE

CADIOT-BADIE
26 Allées de Tourny, 33000
    Bordeaux.
(56.44.24.22).
Open 8:30 A.M. to 12:30 P.M.
    and 2 to 7 P.M. Closed
    Sunday and holidays.

A beautifully fussy, frilly, old-fashioned candy shop, offering cherry-flavored hard candies in a decorative blue and red tin, deliciously almondy macaroons from Michel Poupin in nearby Saint-Emilion, as well as a lovely assortment of handmade chocolates.

FROMAGERIE

JEAN D'ALOS
4 Rue de Montesquieu,
    33000 Bordeaux.
(56.44.29.66).
Open 8:30 A.M. to 12:45 P.M.
    and 3:30 to 7:15 P.M.
    Closed Monday morning.
Will ship in Europe.

I dream of cheese shops such as this: spotless, folkloric, enticing. Cheese-ager Jean d'Alos is passionate about cheese and treats his assortment of more than 150 farm and raw-milk cheeses as jewels, which they are. Try especially the Beaufort *d'alpage* (a cow's-milk cheese from the Savoie, made during the prime summer milking period), the Brebis des Pyrénées (the gutsy sheep's-milk cheese from the Pays Basque), a Rigotte (cow's-milk cheese from near Lyon) so well aged and runny that it's served in a cup.

VIN ET ALCOOL

LA VINOTHEQUE
8 Cours du 30-Juillet, 33000
    Bordeaux.
(56.52.32.05).
Open 9:15 A.M. to 7:15 P.M.
    Closed Sunday.
Will ship internationally.

This warehouse-size shop is like a candy store for wine lovers, offering a selection of more than 200 different Bordeaux wines. Prices are high, but even if you don't buy, it's great fun to just wander through the aisles, examining labels, dreaming on, mentally building a model wine cellar. Here you'll also find a wealth of wine paraphernalia.

L emons are imported into France from all over the world, and their wonderful tang flavors everything from sorbets to soups. The French have pulled a handful of expressions from the 115,000 tons of yellow fruit that grace market stands each year: If you torture your mind for a new idea, you might begin to *"se presser le citron,"* while if you exploit someone, you're likely to *"presser quelqu'un comme un citron."* And if you're hit on the head, you're said to *"recevoir un coup sur le citron."*

Café time in Bordeaux.

LIBRAIRIE

LIBRAIRIE MOLLAT
9-15 Rue Vital-Carles,
   33000 Bordeaux.
(56.44.84.87).
Open 9 A.M. to noon and
   2 to 6:45 P.M. Closed
   Sunday, and Monday
   morning.
Credit card: V.

Mollat is one of the most impressive bookstores I've ever seen, a huge complex of shops offering a veritable library of books on every subject. Their gastronomy section (virtually all in French) is a treasure trove of seldom-seen books on regional French cooking, while the neighboring wine section offers a good assortment of British and French wine books, many of which never make it to America. For the food and wine books, enter at No. 13 Rue Vital-Carles.

POUR LA MAISON

HUMBERT
38 Cours Victor-Hugo,
   33000 Bordeaux.
(56.91.70.05).
Open 9 A.M. to noon and 3
   to 6:30 P.M. Closed
   Saturday afternoon and
   Sunday.
Will ship internationally.

A helter-skelter sort of shop, offering everything you'll need to make wine, plus an assortment of grape harvesters' baskets (they're rustic and decorative, great for storing magazines or dried flowers) and wooden aging barrels (essential for making top-quality vinegar).

COGNAC *(Charente)*

Angoulême 44 k, Bordeaux 119 k, Niort 83 k, Paris 479 k, Poitiers 128 k.

Market: Tuesday, Friday, and Saturday, 8 A.M. to 12:30 P.M., Boulevard Denfert-Rochereau.

VIN ET ALCOOL

LA COGNATHEQUE
10 Place Jean-Monnet,
  16100 Cognac.
(45.82.43.31).
Open 10 A.M. to 1 P.M. and
  2 to 6:45 P.M. Closed
  Sunday.
Will ship in Europe.

This boutique near the city's main square offers perhaps the most extensive selection of Cognacs you'll find under one roof. It's also the place to find the beautiful and unusual cobalt blue tasting glasses used by professional Cognac tasters.

MUSEE

MUSEE MUNICIPAL
40 Boulevard Denfert-
  Rochereau, 16100
  Cognac.
(45.32.07.25).
Open 10 A.M. to noon and
  2 to 6 P.M. June through
  mid-September; 2 to
  5 P.M. mid-September
  through May. Closed
  Tuesday and holidays.

A tidy, tiny regional museum devoted to the folklife of the Cognac region, including a small but fascinating display of local hand-painted pottery, glassware, and carafes; a reconstructed winemaker's cottage dating from 1875; a selection of regional bonnets and headgear; as well as an extensive exhibition devoted to the art and craft of Cognac making. The Cognac exhibit includes a model *alambic* used for distilling Cognac, and a room devoted to Cognac-related posters and advertising materials.

JARNAC *(Charente)*

Angoulême 27 k, Cognac 12 k, Saintes 45 k.

Market: Tuesday through Sunday, 7:30 A.M. to 1 P.M., Rue du Chêne-Vert.

VIN ET ALCOOL

COGNAC DELAMAIN
7 Rue Jacques-et-
  Robert-Delamain, 16200
  Jarnac.
(45.81.08.24).

There's one Cognac upon which most experts agree, and that's Delamain, a very refined and elegant Cognac of exceptional smoothness. Unlike most of the brand-name Cognacs, which are aged for a mere four to six years, the Delamain brandy is aged for at least twenty-five years in used oak barrels that have lost their harsh tannin, allowing Delamain to produce a smoother, more mellow Cognac. Alain Braastad-Delamain continues the family business in the charming town of Jarnac, where—by appointment—visitors are welcome to tour the aging rooms in the shadow of the beautiful Eglise Saint-Pierre. Cognacs of various ages can be purchased here, and visitors may "taste" the way the experts do, that is, by sniffing, not sipping.

NIORT *(Deux-Sèvres)*

Angoulême 108 k, Bordeaux 183 k, Paris 406 k, Poitiers 74 k,
La Rochelle 63 k.

Market: Thursday and Saturday, 8:30 A.M. to 6 P.M., Place des Halles.

RESTAURANT

**LES MANGEUX DU
 LUMAS**
La Garette, 79270 Sansais.
(49.35.93.42).
Last orders taken at 2 P.M.
and 9 P.M.
Closed Monday dinner,
Tuesday, the first two
weeks in January, and
one week in February.
Open daily July and
August.
Credit cards: AE, V.
Terrace dining.
Private dining room for 60.
English spoken.
50- to 100-franc menus. A la
carte, 150 francs.

SPECIALTIES:
Jambon grillé aux mojettes
(grilled ham with white
beans), *lumas à la crème, au
beurre, au pineau des Charentes*
(various land-snail
preparations), *poulet fermier
sauté aux écrevisses* (sautéed
farm chicken with crayfish).

This bright and tidy old-fashioned restaurant hidden in the swamps, or *marais,* of the enchanting canal-filled area known as the Marais-Poitevin offers an authentic selection of regional specialties. *"Les Mangeux du Lumas"* means "the snail eaters": The deliciously tender tiny *petits gris* land snails, known as *lumas,* are a favorite local treat, prepared in three different ways—bathed in cream, in butter, and in the local aperitif known as *pineau des Charentes.* It's also the spot to enjoy the huge white dried beans known as *mojettes:* Here they're offered in two versions, in a salad blending warm beans and sautéed *gésiers,* or duck gizzards, and as a side dish to the moist and tender, very delicately salted local ham. (Directions: 13 kilometers southwest of Niort via the N11 and D1.)

POITIERS *(Vienne)*

Niort 74 k, Paris 334 k.

Market: Tuesday, Thursday, and Saturday, 6 A.M. to 3 P.M., Place du Marché.

RESTAURANT

PIERRE BENOIST
Croutelle, 86240 Ligugé.
(49.57.11.52).
Last orders taken at 2:15 P.M.
and 9:30 P.M.
Closed Sunday dinner,
Monday, the school
holidays in February, and
the last week in July
through the first week in
August.
Credit cards: DC, EC, V.
Private dining room for 20.
English spoken.
140-franc menu. A la carte,
about 275 francs.

SPECIALTIES:
Coquilles Saint-Jacques au
Vouvray (scallops with Vouvray
wine sauce, October to
April), *huîtres chaudes à l'émincé*
de poireaux (warm oysters with
leeks, October to April), *cul de*
chevreau à l'ail vert (young goat
with young garlic shoots,
February to April).

I highly recommend this cheery provincial farm-house overlooking the Poitevin hills to anyone who loves food with clear, vibrant flavors. After dining in so many restaurants offering a bland and staid sort of copycat cuisine, chef Pierre Benoist's food is pleasantly refreshing. His *salade de langouste* was just that: a sparkling fresh green salad flecked with pea-size rounds of avocado and huge, moist chunks of rock lobster meat. I know that years from now I will still be dreaming of chef Benoist's *fondant de lapereau au romarin,* one of the most perfect rabbit dishes I've ever sampled. The rabbit arrives plump and moist, adorned with succulent sautéed kidneys, the rich *foie-gras*-like rabbit liver sliced into rounds, all set upon a bed of buttery artichokes. Combined, the flavors create an ideal marriage, all tied to-gether with the heady wild fragrance of rosemary. I was less enthused about the flavors of the beautiful *consommé en gelée aux queues de langoustines et crème de poivrons,* a chilled gelatinous soup that would have been exceptional save for the overbearing, and dulling, flavor of green peppers. Desserts are excel-lent, including a satisfying *chaud-froid de poires à la glace au miel* (warm glazed pear slices served with a rich honey ice cream). For a change, sample the refined sparkling Vouvray *pétillant* with the meal. Also note that this is goat cheese country, and chef Benoist offers a wide selection of the delicate local *chèvre.*

MOUCLADE
CREAMY MUSSEL SOUP

On one trip to the Poitou-Charentes I found a small paperback cookbook with more than 200 mussel recipes, including more than 20 different versions of mouclade, *the creamy mussel soup served throughout the region. While each recipe includes mussels, butter, cream, and egg yolks, some versions are seasoned with curry powder, others with saffron, and still others include the local Cognac, or the sweet aperitif* pineau des Charentes. *This version is my favorite, a bit lighter than some and delicately seasoned with saffron, a flavor I find less aggressive than curry powder.* Mouclade *has quickly become a favorite in our home, where I often serve it with angel-hair pasta—delicious. Traditionally, the soup is served in individual bowls, with several layers of neatly arranged mussels set on the half shell, and topped with the creamy broth. At home, I prefer to present the mussels on one very large white platter, for it makes an elegant, enticing presentation, especially when the mussels are covered with the fragrant, golden soup.*

3 pounds (about 1.5 kg) fresh mussels

1 ½ cups (375 ml) dry white wine, such as Riesling

½ cup (125 ml) *crème fraîche* (see Recipe Index) or heavy cream

2 large egg yolks

¼ teaspoon saffron

2 tablespoons (1 ounce; 30 g) unsalted butter

2 shallots, very finely minced

2 tablespoons freshly squeezed lemon juice

1. Preheat the oven to 225°F (105°C).

2. Thoroughly scrub the mussels and rinse with several changes of water. Beard the mussels. (Do not beard the mussels in advance, or they will die and spoil.)

3. Combine the mussels and wine in a 6-quart (6 liter) Dutch oven, and heat to a boil over high heat. Cover and cook just until the mussels open, about 5 minutes. Do not overcook. Remove from the heat and strain through several thicknesses of cheesecloth, reserving the liquid. Discard any mussels that do not open.

4. Leaving the cooked mussels in their shell, remove the top shell and discard. Arrange the mussels on a very large ovenproof serving platter, in several layers if necessary. Cover loosely with aluminum foil and place in the oven to keep warm.

5. In a small bowl whisk together the *crème fraîche,* the egg yolks, and the saffron, and reserve.

6. Melt the butter in a medium saucepan over medium-high heat and sauté the shallots just until they soften and begin to turn translucent, about 5 minutes. Add the lemon juice and the mussel cooking liquid, and reduce the heat to very low. Whisk in the *crème fraîche* mixture, being careful that it does not curdle. Adjust seasoning, adding more lemon juice or saffron to taste, and continue cooking for about 5 minutes. The soup should be fairly thin and broth-like.

7. Pour the soup over the mussels and serve immediately, with finger bowls.

Yield: 4 servings.

LA ROCHELLE (Charente-Maritime)

Angoulême 141 k, Bordeaux 187 k, Niort 63 k, Paris 468 k.

Market: Daily, 8 A.M. to 1 P.M., Place du Marché.

RESTAURANT

RICHARD COUTANCEAU
Plage de la Concurrence,
    17000 La Rochelle.
(46.41.48.19).
Closed Sunday dinner and
    Monday.
Last orders taken at 1:30 P.M.
    and 9:30 P.M.
Credit cards: AE, DC, V.
160- and 330-franc menus.
    A la carte, 350 to 400
    francs.

SPECIALTIES:
Mouclade rochelaise (curried
mussel soup, fall and winter
only), ravioli de langoustines
(ravioli of spiny lobster),
salade de goujonnettes de sole et
langoustines (salad of sole and
spiny lobster), blanc de turbot et
bigorneaux à la crème de curry
(turbot with periwinkles and
curried cream).

Chef Richard Coutanceau is a young and ambitious La Rochelle native clearly on the rise. His big, bright, and beautiful restaurant overlooks the La Rochelle beaches, offering a cuisine inspired by the abundance of fresh local fish and shellfish. Each morning his father visits the local criée, or fish auction, to select the best of the day's catch. While the young chef's cooking style could use further refinement (I found the sauces heavy and repetitive), I wouldn't let that stop me from reserving a table. In season—during the fall and winter months—sample the mouclade rochelaise, here a very rich and classic version of the elegant local mussel soup, flavored with cream and curry (see recipe, page 491); and year-round try the salade de goujonnettes de sole et langoustines, a first-course salad that is filling enough to make a meal. Also worth sampling is his giant ravioli de langoustines, which arrives as delicate, paper-thin sheets of pasta surrounding giant, fresh, and meaty chunks of feather-light spiny lobster.

TOUS LES JOURS? PAS EXACTEMENT!
(Every Day? Well, Not Exactly!)

When checking shop or restaurant closing days and hours, beware of the four seemingly encouraging words Ouvert Tous les Jours, literally translated as "open every day," seven days out of seven. In reality, "open every day" more often means open every day of the normal working week, Monday through Friday, not Saturday, not Sunday, not holidays, and not school vacations. To avoid disappointment, ask specifically whether the shop will be open the day you plan to visit.

Buttering Up

B eautiful golden butter remains a cornerstone of the French diet: From the buttery *croissant* to the battery of butter-enriched sauces, the sweet and creamy spread serves as a building block of French cuisine. Throughout the nation, pastry shop windows boast of the butter cakes and pastries within—*"toute au pur beurre"*—while restaurant menus advertise *"La cuisine est fait entièrement au beurre,"* both suggesting that oils and margarines are second-rate substitutes.

Historically, the cuisine in the north of France—where most of the butter is produced—has been based on butter and cream; the south—rich with olives for fruity oil—depended largely on oil for cooking. Elsewhere, goose, duck, and pig fat reign supreme.

The Normans were among the first French butter *gourmands,* so much so that during the fifteenth century they were given a special dispensation by the church to eat butter during Lent, when animal fats were normally banned. During that period, taxes collected from the sale of butter built a tower of the Rouen cathedral that is still called the *"la tour de beurre."*

Still, until the sixteenth century, the Flemish were mocked by the rest of the French for being "butter eaters," but by the seventeenth and eighteenth centuries butter had become a food of distinction throughout France. Even Marie-Antoinette had her own private little dairy at the Trianon Palace in Versailles, where she supervised the making of butter.

Today France produces 10 percent of the world's butter, and each Frenchman consumes about 20 kilos (more than 40 pounds) annually. Breton butter, unlike the sweet butter produced elsewhere in France, is traditionally lightly salted. Local Breton sea salt was orginally added as a perservative, but today the flavor is highly prized in the region, where pastries such as *kouign-amann* taste pleasantly of rich, delicately salted butter.

The finest sweet French butter comes from the Poitou-Charentes, the only region with an *appellation d'origine controlée* (AOC), or pedigree, for its butter. Any butter labeled "Beurre Charentes-Poitou," "Beurre des Charentes," or "Beurre des Deux-Sèvres" guarantees high quality and a mild, slightly nutty flavor.

The Poitou-Charentes became a butter-producing region quite by accident: When the region's vines were destroyed by phylloxera in the 1870s, the vineyards were transformed into pastureland and turned over to Norman cows that produced creamy, top-quality milk. A plucky dairyman was so pleased with his product that he brought three huge mounds of butter up to Paris to sell, and won the hearts and palates of the gastronomes in the capital city. Today nearly 80 percent of the milk in the Poitou-Charentes goes into making butter (compared to 20 percent elsewhere in France), and the finest cheese shops still feature golden mounds of Charentes butter, which is cut into thick slabs for cooking or table use.

Today almost all French butter is made from pasteurized milk, though in the springtime one finds small quantities of Norman and Breton raw cream dairy butter in the market, generally sold in foil packets for better preservation, rather than *à la motte* (in mounds). Don't confuse *beurre cru,* or raw cream butter, with *beurre du cru,* the butters given the *appellation d'origine contrôlée,* which are always made from pasteurized cream.

WINES OF BORDEAUX AND THE ATLANTIC COAST

Of the hundreds of excellent wines found in the Bordeaux region, here are just a few personal favorites. Some of them are not terribly famous but are worth getting to know:

1. CHATEAU POTENSAC (MEDOC): A classy full-bodied and tannic Médoc made by the owners of Léoville-Las Cases. A red Bordeaux that's a real sleeper and generally an exceptional buy.

2. CHATEAU LANESSAN (HAUT MEDOC): A robust, fruity, distinguished red, very close to the *commune* of Saint-Julien. Generally a very good value.

3. CHATEAU CANTEMERLE (HAUT MEDOC): A newly restored vineyard, this is beginning to make waves. The 1982 and 1983 vintages are wines to look out for.

4. CHATEAU MONTROSE (SAINT-ESTEPHE): Over the years, Château Montrose has been a wine that offers consistent pleasure. To me it epitomizes the elegance and stability of a grand Bordeaux.

5. CHATEAU DOISY-DAENE (BARSAC): I remember well the first time I sampled the crisp, dry white Château Doisy-Daëne in a Paris fish restaurant. It's since become a standby,

a vibrant, inexpensive wine that's a sheer delight. The same estate produces a fine sweet Barsac.

6. CHATEAU SAINT-PIERRE-SEVAISTRE (SAINT-JULIEN): Years ago a young *sommelier* introduced me to this robust, almost rustic, little-known Saint-Julien, and I've enjoyed it on numerous occasions. A wine to watch. In 1982 the name was shortened to Château Saint-Pierre.

7. CHATEAU DUCRU-BEAU-CALLIOU (SAINT-JULIEN): What the British call a classic claret—an outstanding, consistent red. Wine writer Robert Parker says, "Growing old is not such a bad prospect knowing that wines of this majesty are awaiting my consumption." I concur.

8. SAUTERNES (CHATEAU RAYMOND LAFON): We all know Château d'Yquem, one of the world's most famous, and justifiably most expensive, wines. But when budgets demand a more reasonably priced wine, think of this sweet, rich, fruity Sauternes. Your palate will thank you.

French/English Food Glossary

For many diners, the restaurant menu can present a confusing and intimidating barrier to the pleasures of dining out. The French language, of course, is no help with so many sound-alike words. It is so easy to confuse *tourteau* (crab) with *tortue* (turtle), *ail* (garlic) with *aile* (a poultry wing), *chevreau* (young goat) with *chevreuil* (venison).

The variety of fish and shellfish found in France's waters can be equally confusing, particularly when one is faced with a multitude of regional or local names given to each species. The large, meaty monkfish, for example, might be called *baudroie, lotte,* or *gigot de mer,* depending upon the region or the whim of the chef.

In preparing this glossary, I have tried to limit the list to contemporary terms, making this a practical guide for today's traveler in France. Translations are generally offered for those dishes, foods, and phrases one is most likely to encounter on menus, in markets, and in shops. I have also added regional expressions or terms one might not find explained elsewhere.

A

A point: cooked medium rare.

Abat(s): organ meat(s).

Abati(s): giblet(s) of poultry or game fowl.

Abondance: firm thick wheel of cow's-milk cheese from the Savoie, a *département* in the Alps.

Abricot: apricot.

Acajou: cashew nut.

Achatine: land snail, or *escargot,* imported from China and Indonesia; less prized than other varieties.

Addition: bill.

Affinage: process of aging cheese.

Affiné: aged, as with cheese.

Agneau (de lait): lamb (young, milk-fed).

Agneau chilindron: sauté of lamb with potatoes and garlic, specialty of the Basque country.

Agneau de Paulliac: breed of lamb from the southwest.

Agnelet: baby milk-fed lamb.

Agnelle: ewe lamb.

Agrume(s): citrus fruit(s).

Aïado: roast lamb shoulder stuffed with parsley, chervil, and garlic.

Aiglefin, aigrefin, églefin: small fresh haddock, a type of cod.

Aïgo bouido: garlic soup, served with oil, over slices of bread; a specialty of Provence.

Aïgo saou: "water-salt" in Provençal; a fish soup that includes, of course, water and salt, plus a mixture of small white fish, onions, potatoes, tomatoes, garlic, herbs, and olive oil; specialty of Provence.

Aigre: bitter, sour.

Aigre-doux: sweet and sour.

Aigrelette, sauce: a sour or tart sauce.

Aiguillette: a long, thin slice of poultry, meat, or fish. Also, top part of beef rump.

Ail: garlic.

Aile: wing of poultry or game bird.

Aile et cuisse: used to describe white breast meat *(aile)* and dark thigh meat *(cuisse),* usually of chicken.

Aillade: garlic sauce; also, dishes based on garlic.

Aillé: with garlic.

Aillet: shoot of mild winter baby garlic, a specialty of the Poitou-Charentes region along the Atlantic coast.

Aïoli, ailloli: garlic mayonnaise. Also, salt cod, hard-cooked eggs, boiled snails, and vegetables served with garlic mayonnaise; specialty of Provence.

Airelle: wild cranberry.

Aisy cendré: thick disc of cow's-milk cheese, washed with *eau-de-vie* and patted with wood ashes; also called *cendre d'aisy;* a specialty of Burgundy.

Albuféra: béchamel sauce with sweet peppers.

Algue(s): edible seaweed.

Aligot: mashed potatoes with *tomme* (the fresh curds used in making Cantal cheese) and garlic; specialty of the Auvergne.

Alisier, alizier: eau-de-vie with the taste of bitter almonds, made with the wild red serviceberries that grow in the forests of Alsace.

Allumette: "match"; puff pastry strips; also fried matchstick potatoes.

Alose: shad, a spring river fish plentiful in the Loire and Gironde rivers.

Alouette: lark.

Aloyau: loin area of beef; beef sirloin, butcher's cut that includes the rump and *contre-filet.*

Alsacienne, à l': in the style of Alsace, often including sauerkraut, sausage, or *foie gras.*

Amande: almond.

Amande de mer: smooth-shelled shellfish, like a small clam, with a sweet, almost hazelnut flavor.

Amandine: with almonds.

Ambroisie: ambrosia.

Amer: bitter; as in unsweetened chocolate.

Américaine, Amoricaine: sauce of white wine, Cognac, tomatoes, and butter.

Ami du Chambertin: "friend of Chambertin wine"; moist and buttery short cylinder of cow's-milk cheese with a rust-colored rind, made near the village of Gevrey-Chambertin in Burgundy. Similar to *Epoisses* cheese.

Amourette(s): spinal bone marrow of calf or ox.

Amuse-bouche or amuse-gueule: "amuse the mouth"; appetizer.

Ananas: pineapple.

Anchoïade: sauce that is a blend of olive oil, anchovies, and garlic, usually served with raw vegetables; specialty of Provence; also, paste of anchovies and garlic, spread on toast.

Anchois (de Collioure): anchovy (prized salt-cured anchovy from Collioure, a port town near the Spanish border of the Languedoc), fished in the Atlantic and the Mediterranean.

Ancienne, à l': in the old style.

Andouille: large smoked chitterling (tripe) sausage, usually served cold.

Andouillette: small chitterling (tripe) sausage, usually served grilled.

Aneth: dill.

Ange à cheval: "angel on horseback"; grilled bacon-wrapped oyster.

Anglaise, à l': English style, plainly cooked.

Anguille: eel.

Anis: anise or aniseed.

Anis étoilé: star anise.

AOC: see *Appellation d'origine contrôlée.*

Apéritif: a before-dinner drink that stimulates the appetite, usually somewhat sweet or mildly bitter.

Appellation d'origine contrôlée (AOC): specific definition of a particular cheese, butter, fruit, wine, or poultry—once passed down from generation to generation, now recognized by law—regulating the animal breed or variety of fruit, the zone of production, production techniques, composition of the product, its physical characteristics, and its specific attributes.

Arachide (huile d'; pâté d'): peanut (oil; butter).

Araignée de mer: spider crab.

Arc en ciel (truite): rainbow (trout).

Ardennaise, à l': in the style of the Ardennes, a *département* in northern France; generally a dish with juniper berries.

Ardi gasna: Basque name for sheep's-milk cheese.

Arête: fish bone.

Arlésienne, à l': in the style

of Arles, a town in Provence; with tomatoes, onions, eggplant, potatoes, rice, and sometimes olives.

Armagnac: brandy from the Armagnac area of southwestern France.

Aromate: aromatic herb, vegetable, or flavoring.

Arômes à la gêne: generic name for a variety of tangy, lactic cheeses of the Lyon area that have been steeped in *gêne,* or dry *marc,* the dried grape skins left after grapes are pressed for wine. Can be of cow's milk, goat's milk, or a mixture.

Arosé(e): sprinkled, basted, moistened with liquid.

Arpajon: a town in the Ile-de-France, dried bean capital of France; a dish containing dried beans.

Artichaut (violet): artichoke (small purple).

Artichaut à la Barigoule: in simplest form, artichokes cooked with mushrooms and oil; also, artichoke stuffed with ham, onion, and garlic, browned in oil with onions and bacon, then cooked in water or white wine; specialty of Provence.

Asperge (violette): asparagus (purple-tipped asparagus, a specialty of the Côte-d'Azur).

Assaisonné: seasoned; seasoned with.

Assiette anglaise: assorted cold meats, usually served as a first course.

Assiette de pêcheur: assorted fish platter.

Assorti(e): assorted.

Aubergine: eggplant.

Aulx: plural of *ail* (garlic).

Aumônière: "beggar's purse"; thin crêpe, filled and tied like a bundle.

Aurore: tomato and cream sauce.

Auvergnat(e): in the style of the Auvergne; often with cabbage, sausage, and bacon.

Aveline: hazelnut or filbert, better known as *noisette.*

Avocat: avocado.

Avoine: oat.

Axoa: a dish of ground veal, onions, and the local fresh chiles, *piment d'Espelette;* specialty of the Basque region.

Azyme, pain: unleavened bread; matzo.

B

Badiane: star anise.

Baeckeoffe, baekaoffa, backenoff: "baker's oven"; stew of wine, beef, lamb, pork, potatoes, and onions; specialty of Alsace.

Bagna caudà: sauce of anchovies, olive oil, and garlic, for dipping raw vegetables; specialty of Nice.

Baguette: "wand"; classic long, thin loaf of bread.

Baguette au levain or *à l'ancienne:* sourdough *baguette.*

Baie: berry.

Baie rose: pink peppercorn.

Baigné: bathed.

Ballotine: usually poultry, boned, stuffed, and rolled.

Banane: banana.

Banon: village in the Alps of Provence, source of dried chestnut leaves traditionally used to wrap goat cheese, which was washed with *eau-de-vie* and aged for several months; today, refers to various goat's-milk cheese or mixed goat-and-cow's-milk cheese

from the region, sometimes wrapped in fresh green or dried brown chestnut leaves and tied with raffia.

Bar: ocean fish, known as *loup* on the Mediterranean coast, *louvine* or *loubine* in the southwest, and *barreau* in Brittany; similar to sea bass.

Barbouillade: stuffed eggplant, or an eggplant stew; also, a combination of beans and artichokes.

Barbue: brill, a flatfish related to turbot, found in the Atlantic and the Mediterranean.

Barder: to cover poultry or meat with strips of uncured bacon, to add moisture while cooking.

Baron: hindquarters of lamb, including both legs.

Barquette: "small boat"; pastry shaped like a small boat.

Basilic: basil.

Basquaise, à la: Basque style; usually with ham or tomatoes or red peppers.

Bâtarde, pain: "bastard bread"; traditional long, thin white loaf, larger than a *baguette.*

Batavia: salad green, a broad, flat-leafed lettuce.

Bâton: small white wand of bread, smaller than a *baguette.*

Bâtonnet: garnish of vegetables cut into small sticks.

Baudroie: in Provence, the name for monkfish or anglerfish, the large, firm-fleshed ocean fish also known as *lotte* and *gigot de mer;* also a specialty of Provence, a fish soup that includes potatoes, onions, fresh mushrooms, garlic, fresh or dried orange zest, artichokes, tomatoes, and herbs.

Bavaroise: cold dessert; a rich custard made with cream and gelatin.

Bavette: skirt steak.

Baveuse: "drooling"; method of cooking an omelet so that it remains moist and juicy.

Béarnaise: tarragon-flavored sauce of egg yolks, butter, shallots, wine wine, vinegar, and herbs.

Béatille: "tidbit"; dish combining various organ meats.

Bécasse: small bird, a woodcock.

Bécassine: small bird, a snipe.

Béchamel: white sauce, made with butter, flour, and milk, usually flavored with onion, bay leaf, pepper, and nutmeg.

Beignet: fritter or doughnut.

Beignet de fleur de courgette: batter-fried zucchini blossom; native to Provence and the Mediterranean, now popular all over France.

Belle Hélène (poire): classic dessert of chilled poached fruit (pear), served on ice cream and topped with hot chocolate sauce.

Bellevue, en: classic presentation of whole fish, usually in aspic on a platter.

Belon: river in Brittany identified with a prized flat-shelled *(plate)* oyster.

Berawecka, bierewecke, bireweck, birewecka: dense, moist Christmas fruit bread stuffed with dried pears, figs, and nuts; specialty of Kaysersberg, a village in Alsace.

Bercy: fish stock–based sauce thickened with flour and butter and flavored with white wine and shallots.

Bergamot: name for both a variety of orange and of pear.

Berrichonne: garnish of braised cabbage, glazed baby onions, chestnuts, and lean bacon named for the old province of Berry.

Betterave: beet.

Beurre: butter.
  demi-sel: butter (lightly salted).
  blanc: classic reduced sauce of vinegar, white wine, shallots, and butter.
  cru: raw cream butter.
  des Charentes: finest French butter, from the region of Poitou-Charentes along the Atlantic coast.
  de Montpellier: classic butter sauce seasoned with olive oil, herbs, garlic, and anchovies.
  du cru: butter given the *appellation d'origine contrôlée* pedigree.
  Echiré: brand of the finest French butter, preferred by French chefs, with an AOC pedigree, from the region of Poitou-Charentes along the Atlantic coast.
  noir: sauce of browned butter, lemon juice or vinegar, parsley, and sometimes capers; traditionally served with *raie,* or skate.
  noisette: lightly browned butter.
  vierge: whipped butter sauce with salt, pepper, and lemon juice.

Bibelskäs, bibbelskäse: fresh cheese seasoned with

horseradish, herbs, and spices; specialty of Alsace.

Biche: female deer.

Bien cuit(e): cooked well done.

Bière (en bouteille, à la pression): beer (bottled, on tap).

Bifteck: steak.

Bigarade: orange sauce.

Biggareau: red firm-fleshed variety of cherry.

Bigorneau: periwinkle, tiny sea snail.

Bigoudène, à la: in the style of Bigouden, a province in Brittany; *(pommes)* baked slices of unpeeled potato; *(ragoût)* sausage stewed with bacon and potato.

Billy Bi, Billy By: cream of mussel soup, specialty of the Atlantic coast.

Biologique: organic.

Biscuit à la cuillère: ladyfinger.

Bistrotier: bistro owner.

Blanc (de poireau): white portion (of leek).

Blanc (de volaille): usually breast (of chicken).

Blanc-manger: chilled pudding of almond milk with gelatin.

Blanquette: classic mild stew of poached veal, lamb, chicken, or seafood, enriched with an egg and cream white sauce; supposedly a dish for convalescents.

Blé (noir): wheat (buckwheat).

Blette, bette: Swiss chard.

Bleu: "blue"; cooked rare, usually for steak. See also *Truite au bleu.*

Bleu d'Auvergne: a strong, firm and moist, flattened cylinder of blue-veined cheese made from cow's milk in the Auvergne, sold wrapped in foil; still

CRÈME FRAICHE

Crème fraîche, *which literally means fresh cream, is actually a rather mature cream with a nutty, slightly sour tang. The name goes back to the days before refrigeration, when naturally occurring bacteria soured the cream before it could be consumed. Parisians, especially, developed a taste for* crème fraîche, *for by the time fresh cream had been transported from the farms to the capital, it was certain to be sour. Today, of course, the cream is matured under controlled conditions.*

2 cups (500 ml) heavy cream (preferably not ultra-pasteurized)

2 tablespoons cultured buttermilk

1. Thoroughly mix the cream and buttermilk in a medium bowl. Cover loosely with plastic wrap and let stand at room temperature until fairly thick, or overnight. (If using ultra-pasteurized cream, the mixture may take several hours longer to thicken.)

2. Cover tightly and refrigerate at least 4 hours to thicken it even more. The cream may be stored for several days, as the tangy flavor continues to develop.

Yield: 2 cups (500 ml).

---

made on some farms.

Bleu de Bresse: a cylinder of mild blue-veined cow's-milk cheese from the Bresse area in the Rhône-Alps region; industrially made.

Bleu de Gex: thick, savory, blue-veined disc of cow's-milk cheese from the Jura; made in only a handful of small dairies in the *département* of the Ain.

Bleu des Causses: a firm, pungent, flat cylinder of blue-veined cow's-milk cheese, cured in cellars similar to those used in making Roquefort.

Blini: small thick pancake, usually eaten with caviar.

Boeuf à la ficelle: beef tied with string and poached in broth.

Boeuf à la mode: beef marinated and braised in red wine, served with carrots, mushrooms, onions, and turnips.

Boeuf gros sel: boiled beef, served with vegetables and coarse salt.

Bohémienne, à la: gypsy style; with rice, tomatoes, onions, sweet peppers, and paprika, in various combinations.

Boisson (non) comprise: drink (not) included.

Bolet: type of wild boletus mushroom. See *Cèpe.*

Bombe: molded, layered ice cream dessert.

Bonbon: candy or sweet.

Bon-chrétien: "good Christian"; a variety of pear, also known as *poire William's.*

Bondon: small cylinder of

delicately flavored, mushroomy cow's-milk cheese made in the Neufchâtel area in Normandy.

Bonite: a tuna, or oceanic bonito.

Bonne femme (cuisine): meat garnish of bacon, potatoes, mushrooms, and onions; fish garnish of shallots, parsley, mushrooms, and potatoes; or white wine sauce with shallots, mushrooms, and lemon juice; (home-style cooking).

Bordelaise: Bordeaux style; also refers to a brown sauce of shallots, red wine, and bone marrow.

Bouchée: "tiny mouthful"; may refer to a bite-size pastry or to a *vol-au-vent.*

Bouchoteur: mussel fisherman; a dish containing mussels.

Boudin: technically a meat sausage, but generically any sausage-shaped mixture.

Boudin blanc: white sausage of veal, chicken, or pork.

Boudin noir: pork blood sausage.

Bouillabaisse: popular Mediterranean fish soup, most closely identified with Marseille, ideally prepared with the freshest local fish, preferably rockfish. Traditionally might include dozens of different fish, but today generally includes the specifically local *rascasse* (scorpion fish), Saint-Pierre (John Dory), *fiéla* (conger eel), *galinette* (gurnard or *grondin*), *vive* (weever), and *baudroie* (monkfish) cooked in a broth of water, olive oil, onions, garlic, tomatoes, parsley, and saffron. The fish is served separately from the broth, which is poured over garlic-rubbed toast, and seasoned with *rouille* which is stirred into the broth. Varied additions include boiled potatoes, orange peel, fennel, and shellfish. Expensive shellfish are often added in restaurant versions, but this practice is considered inauthentic.

Bouilliture: eel stew with red wine and prunes; specialty of the Poitou-Charentes on the Atlantic coast.

Bouillon: stock or broth.

Boulangère, à la: in the style of the "baker's wife"; meat or poultry baked or braised with onions and potatoes.

Boule: "ball"; a large round loaf of white bread, also known as a *miche*.

Boule de Picoulat: meatball from Languedoc, combining beef, pork, garlic, and eggs, traditionally served with cooked white beans.

Boulette d'Avesnes: pepper-and-tarragon-flavored cheese, made from visually defective *Maroilles*, formed into a cone, and colored red with paprika; named for Avesnes, a village in the North.

Bouquet: large reddish shrimp (see also *Crevette rose*).

Bouquet garni: typically fresh whole parsley, bay leaf, and thyme tied together with string and tucked into stews; the package is removed prior to serving.

Bouquetière: garnished with bouquets of vegetables.

Bourdaloue: hot poached fruit, sometimes wrapped in pastry, often served with vanilla custard; often pear.

Bourgeoise, à la: with carrots, onions, braised lettuce, celery, and bacon.

Bourguignonne, à la: Burgundy style; often with red wine, onions, mushrooms, and bacon.

Bouribot: spicy red-wine duck stew.

Bourride: a Mediterranean fish soup that generally includes a mixture of small white fish, onions, tomatoes, garlic, herbs, and olive oil, thickened with egg yolks and *aïoli* (garlic mayonnaise); there are many variations.

Bourriole: rye flour pan-

cake, both sweet and savory; specialty of the Auvergne.

Boutargue, poutargue: salty paste prepared from dried mullet or tuna roe, mashed with oil; specialty of Provence.

Bouton de culotte: "trouser button"; tiny buttons of goat cheese from the Lyon area; traditionally made on farms, aged until rock hard and pungent; today found in many forms, from soft and young to hard and brittle.

Braiser: to braise; to cook meat by browning in fat, then simmering in covered dish with small amount of liquid.

Branche, en: refers to whole vegetables or herbs.

Brandade (de morue): a warm garlicky purée (of salt cod) with milk or cream or oil, and sometimes mashed potatoes; specialty of Provence; currently used to denote a variety of flavored mashed potato dishes.

Brassado: a doughnut that is boiled, then baked, much like a bagel; specialty of Provence.

Brayaude, gigot: leg of lamb studded with garlic, cooked in white wine, and served with red beans, braised cabbage, or chestnuts.

Brebis (fromage de): sheep (sheep's-milk cheese).

Brési: smoked, salted, and dried beef from the Jura.

Bretonne, à la: in the style of Brittany; a dish served with white beans; or may refer to a white wine sauce with carrots, leeks, and celery.

Bretzel: a pretzel; specialty of Alsace.

Brie de Meaux: "king of cheese," the flat wheel of cheese made only with raw cow's milk and aged at least four weeks; from Meaux, just east of Paris; brie made with pasteurized milk does not have the right to be called *brie de Meaux.*

Brie de Melun: smaller than *brie de Meaux,* another raw-cow's-milk cheese, aged at least one month, with a crackly, rust-colored rind.

Brillat-Savarin: (1755–1826) famed gastronome, coiner of food aphorisms, and author of *The Physiology of Taste;* the high-fat, supple cow's-milk cheese from Normandy is named for him.

Brioche: buttery, egg-enriched yeast bread.

Broche, à la: spit-roasted.

Brochet(on): freshwater pike (small pike).

Brochette: cubes of meat or fish and vegetables on a skewer.

Brocoli: broccoli.

Brouet: old term for soup.

Brouillade: a mixture of ingredients as in a stew or soup; also, scrambled eggs.

Brouillé(s): scrambled, usually eggs.

Brousse: a very fresh and unsalted (thus bland) sheep's- or goat's-milk cheese, not unlike Italian ricotta; specialty of Nice and Marseille.

Broutard: young goat.

Brugnon: nectarine.

Brûlé(e): "burned"; usually refers to caramelization.

Brunoise: tiny diced vegetables.

Brut: very dry or sugarless, particularly in reference to Champagne.

Buccin: large sea snail or whelk, also called *bulot.*

Bûche de Noël: Christmas cake shaped like a log (*bûche*), a sponge cake often flavored with chestnuts and chocolate.

Buffet froid: variety of dishes served cold, sometimes from a buffet.

Bugne: deep-fried yeast-dough fritter or doughnut dusted with confectioners' sugar, popular in and around Lyon at Easter.

Buisson: "bush"; generally a dish including vegetables arranged like a bush; classically a crayfish presentation.

Bulot: large sea snail or whelk, also called *buccin.*

Buron: traditional hut where cheese is made in the Auvergne mountains.

C

Cabécou(s): small, round goat's-milk cheese from the southwest, sometimes made with a mix of goat's and cow's milk.

Cabillaud: fresh codfish, also currently called *morue;* known as *doguette* in the North, *bakalua* in the Basque region, *eglefin* in Provence.

Cabri: young goat.

Cacahouète, cacahouette, cacachuète: prepared peanut—roasted, dry roasted, or salted. A raw peanut is *arachide.*

Cacao: cocoa; powdered cocoa.

Cachat: a very strong goat cheese; generally a blend of various ends of leftover cheese, mixed with seasonings that might include salt, pepper, brandy, and garlic, and aged in a crock; specialty of Provence.

Cachir: kosher.

Caen, à la mode de: in the style of Caen, a town in Normandy; a dish cooked in Calvados and white wine and/or cider.

Café: coffee, as well as a type of eating place where coffee is served.

allongé: weakened espresso, often served with a small pitcher of hot water so clients may thin the coffee themselves.

au lait or *crème:* espresso with warmed or steamed milk.

déca or *décaféiné:* decaffeinated coffee.

express: plain black espresso.

faux: decaffeinated coffee.

filtre: filtered American-style coffee (not available at all cafés).

glacé: iced coffee.

liègeois: iced coffee served with ice cream (optional) and whipped cream; also coffee ice cream with whipped cream.

noir: plain black espresso.

serré: extra-strong espresso, made with half the normal amount of water.

Caféine: caffeine.

Cagouille: on the Atlantic coast, name for small *petit gris* land snail, or *escargot.*

Caille: quail.

Caillé: clotted or curdled; curds of milk.

Caillette: round pork sausage including chopped spinach or Swiss chard, garlic, onions, parsley, bread, and egg and wrapped in *crépine* (caul fat); served hot or cold; specialty of northern Provence.

Caisse: cash register, or cash desk.

Caissette: literally, "small box"; bread, brioche, or chocolate shaped like a small box.

Cajasse: a sort of *clafoutis* from the Dordogne, made with black cherries.

Cajou: cashew nut.

Calmar: small squid, similar to *encornet,* with interior transparent cartilage instead of a bone. Also called *chipiron* in the southwest.

Calvados: a *département* in Normandy known for the famed apple brandy.

Camembert (de Normandie): village in Normandy that gives its name to a supple, fragrant cheese made of cow's milk.

Camomille: camomile, herb tea.

Campagnard(e) (assiette): country-style, rustic; (an informal buffet of cold meats, terrines, etc.).

Campagne, à la: country-style.

Canada: cooking apple.

Canapé: originally a slice of crustless bread; now also used to refer to a variety of *hors d'oeuvre* consisting of toasted or fried bread spread with forcemeat, cheese, and other flavorings.

Canard: duck.

Canard à la presse: roast duck served with a sauce of juices obtained from pressing the carcass, combined with red wine and Cognac.

Canard sauvage: wild duck, usually mallard.

Cancoillotte: spreadable cheese from the Jura; usually blended with milk, spices, or white wine when served.

Caneton: young male duck.

Canette: young female duck.

Cannelle: cinnamon.

Cannois, à la: in the style of Cannes.

Cantal: large cylindrical cheese made in the Auvergne from shredded and pressed curds of cow's milk.

Cantalon: smaller version of *Cantal.*

Cantaloup: cantaloupe melon.

Capre: caper.

Capucine: nasturtium; the leaves and flowers are used in salads.

Carafe (d'eau): pitcher (of tap water). House wine is often offered in a *carafe.* A full *carafe* contains one liter; a *demi-carafe* contains half a liter; a *quart* contains one-fourth of a liter.

Caramelisé: cooked with high heat to brown the sugar and heighten flavor.

Carbonnade: braised beef stew prepared with beer and onions; specialty of the North; also refers to a cut of beef.

Cardamome: cardamon.

Carde: white rib, or stalk, portion of Swiss chard.

Cardon: cardoon; large celery-like vegetable in the artichoke family, popular in Lyon, Provence, and the Mediterranean area.

Cargolade: a copious mixed grill of snails, lamb, pork sausage, and sometimes blood sausage, cooked

over vine clippings; specialty of Catalan, an area of southern Languedoc.

Carotte: carrot.

Carpe: carp.

Carpe à la juive: braised marinated carp in aspic.

Carré d'agneau: rack (ribs) or loin of lamb; also crown roast.

Carré de porc: rack (ribs) or loin of pork; also crown roast.

Carré de veau: rack (ribs) or loin of veal; also crown roast.

Carrelet: see *Plaice.*

Carte, à la: menu (dishes, which are charged for individually, selected from a restaurant's full list of offerings).

Carte promotionelle or *conseillée:* a simple and inexpensive fixed-price meal.

Carvi (grain de): caraway (seed).

Cary: curry.

Casse-croûte: "break bread"; slang for snack.

Casseron: cuttlefish.

Cassis (crème de): black currant (black currant liqueur).

Cassolette: usually a dish presented in a small casserole.

Cassonade: soft brown sugar; demerara sugar.

Cassoulet: popular southwestern casserole of white beans, including various combinations of sausages, duck, pork, lamb, mutton, and goose.

Cavaillon: a town in Provence, known for its small, flavorful orange-fleshed melons.

Caviar d'aubergine: cold seasoned eggplant purée.

Cébette: a mild, leek-like vegetable, sliced and eaten raw, in salads; native to Provence, but seen occasionally outside the region.

Cebiche: seviche; generally raw fish marinated in lime juice and other seasonings.

Cédrat: a variety of Mediterranean lemon.

Céleri (en branche): celery (stalk).

Céleri-rave: celeriac, celery root.

Céleri rémoulade: popular first-course bistro dish of shredded celery root with tangy mayonnaise.

Cendre (sous la): ash (cooked by being buried in embers); some cheeses made in wine-producing regions are aged in the ash of burned rootstocks.

Cèpe: large, meaty wild boletus mushroom.

Céréale: cereal.

Cerf: stag, or male deer.

Cerfeuil: chervil.

Cerise: cherry.

Cerise noire: black cherry.

Cerneau: walnut meat.

Cervelas: garlicky cured pork sausage; now also refers to fish and seafood sausage.

Cervelle(s): brain(s), of calf or lamb.

Cervelle de canut: a soft, fresh herbed cheese known as "silkworker's brains"; specialty of Lyon.

Céteau(x): small ocean fish, *solette* or baby sole, found in the gulf of Gascony and along the Atlantic coast.

Cévenole, à la: Cévennes style; garnished with chestnuts or mushrooms.

Chalutier: any flat fish caught with a trawl.

Champêtre: rustic; describes a simple presentation of a variety of ingredients.

Champignon: mushroom.

à la bague: parasol mushroom with a delicate flavor, also called *coulemelle, cocherelle,* and *grisotte.*

de bois: wild mushroom, from the woods.

de Paris: most common cultivated mushroom.

sauvage: wild mushroom.

Champvallon, côtelette d'agneau: traditional dish of lamb chops baked in alternating layers of potatoes and onions; named for a village in northern Burgundy.

Chanterelle: prized pale orange wild mushroom; also called *girolle.*

Chantilly: sweetened whipped cream.

Chaource: soft and fruity cylindrical cow's-milk cheese, with a 50 percent fat content; takes its name from a village in Champagne.

Chapeau: "hat"; small round loaf, topped with a little dough hat.

Chapelure: bread crumbs.

Chapon: capon, or castrated chicken.

Chapon de mer: Mediterranean fish, in the *rascasse* or scorpion-fish family.

Charbon de bois, au: charcoal-grilled.

Charentais: variety of sweet cantaloupe, or melon, originally from the Charentes, on the Atlantic coast.

Charlotte: classic dessert in which a dish is lined with ladyfingers, filled with custard or other filling, and served cold; in the hot version, the dish is lined with crustless white bread sautéed in butter, filled with fruit

compote, and baked.

Charolais: area of Burgundy; light-colored cattle producing high-quality beef; also, firm white cylinder of cheese made with goat's or cow's milk, or a mixture of the two.

Chartreuse: dish of braised partridge and cabbage; also herb and spiced-based liqueur made by the Chartreuse monks in the Savoie.

Chasseur: hunter; also, sauce with white wine, mushrooms, shallots, tomatoes, and herbs.

Châtaigne: chestnut, smaller than *marron,* with multiple nut meats.

Chateaubriand: thick filet steak, traditionally served with sautéed potatoes and a sauce of white wine, dark beef stock, butter, shallots, and herbs, or with a *béarnaise* sauce.

Châtelaine, à la: elaborate garnish of artichoke hearts and chestnut purée, braised lettuce, and sautéed potatoes.

Chaud(e): hot or warm.

Chaud-froid: "hot-cold"; cooked poultry dish served cold, usually covered with a cooked sauce, then with aspic.

Chaudrée: Atlantic fish stew, often including sole, skate, small eels, potatoes, butter, white wine, and seasoning.

Chausson: a filled pastry turnover, sweet or savory.

Chemise, en: wrapped with pastry.

Cheval: horse, horse meat.

Cheveux d'ange: "angel's hair"; thin vermicelli pasta.

Chèvre (fromage de): goat (goat's-milk cheese).

Chevreau: young goat.

Chevreuil: young roe buck or roe deer; venison.

Chevrier: small, pale green, dried kidney-shaped bean, a type of *flageolet.*

Chichi: doughnut-like, deep-fried bread spirals sprinkled with sugar, often sold from trucks at open-air markets; specialty of Provence and the Mediterranean.

Chicons du Nord: Belgian endive.

Chicorée (frisée): a bitter salad green (curly endive); also chicory, a coffee substitute.

Chicorée de Bruxelles: Belgian endive.

Chiffonnade: shredded herbs and vegetables, usually green.

Chinchard: also called *saurel,* scad or horse mackerel; Atlantic and Mediterranean fish similar to mackerel.

Chipiron (à l'encre): southwestern name for small squid, or *encornet* (in its own ink).

Chipolata: small sausage.

Chips, pommes: potato chips.

Chocolat: chocolate.
  amer: bittersweet chocolate, with very little sugar.
  au lait: milk chocolate.
  chaud: hot chocolate.
  mi-amer: bittersweet chocolate, with more sugar than *chocolat amer.*
  noir: used interchangeably with *chocolat amer.*

Choix, au: a choice; usually meaning one may choose from several offerings.

Chorizo: highly spiced Spanish sausage.

Choron, sauce: béarnaise sauce with tomatoes.

Chou: cabbage.

Chou de Bruxelles: brussels sprout.

Chou de mer: sea kale.

Chou de Milan: Savoy cabbage.

Chou-fleur: cauliflower.

Chou frisé: kale.

Chou-navet: rutabaga.

Chou-rave: kohlrabi.

Chou rouge: red cabbage.

Chou vert: curly green Savoy cabbage.

Choucas: jackdaw; European blackbird, like a crow, but smaller.

Choucroute (nouvelle): sauerkraut (the season's first batch of sauerkraut, still crunchy and slightly acidic); also main dish of sauerkraut, various sausages, bacon, and pork, served with potatoes; specialty of Alsace and brasseries all over France.

Choux, pâte à: cream pastry dough.

Ciboule: spring onion, or scallion.

Ciboulette: chives.

Cidre: bottled, mildly alcoholic cider, either apple or pear.

Cigale de mer: "sea cricket"; tender, crayfish-like, blunt-nosed rock lobster.

Cîteaux: creamy, ample disc of cow's-milk cheese with a rust-colored rind made by the Cistercian monks at the Abbaye de Cîteaux in Burgundy.

Citron: lemon.

Citron, orange, or *pamplemousse pressé(e):* lemon, orange, or grapefruit juice served with a carafe of tap water and sugar, for sweetening to taste.

Citron vert: lime.

Citronelle: lemon grass, an oriental herb.

Citrouille: pumpkin, gourd.

Also called *courge, potiron, potimarron.*

Cive: spring onion.

Civelle: spaghetti-like baby eel, also called *pibale.*

Civet: stew, usually of game, traditionally thickened with blood.

Civet de lièvre: jugged hare, or wild rabbit stew.

Civet de tripes d'oies: a stew of goose innards, sautéed in fat with onions, shallots, and garlic, then cooked in wine vinegar and diluted with water, and thickened with goose blood; from Gascony.

Clafoutis: traditional custard tart, usually made with black cherries; specialty of the southwest.

Claire: oyster; also a designation given to certain oysters to indicate they have been put in *claires,* or oyster beds in salt marshes, where they are fattened up for several months before going to market.

Clamart: Paris suburb once famous for its green peas; today a garnish of peas.

Clémentine: small tangerine, from Morocco or Spain.

Clouté: studded with.

Clovisse: variety of very tiny clam, generally from the Mediterranean.

Cocherelle: parasol mushroom with a delicate flavor; also called *champignon à la bague, coulemelle,* and *grisotte.*

Cochon (de lait): pig (suckling).

Cochonnaille(s): pork product(s); usually an assortment of sausages and/or pâtés served as a first course.

Coco: type of small white

bean, both fresh and dried, popular in Provence, where it is a traditional ingredient of the vegetable *soupe au pistou;* also, coconut.

Coeur: heart.

Coeur de filet: thickest (and best) part of beef filet, usually cut into chateaubriand steaks.

Coeur de palmier: delicate shoots of the palm tree, generally served with a vinaigrette as an hors d'oeuvre.

Coffre: "chest"; refers to the body of a lobster or other crustacean, or of a butchered animal.

Coiffe: traditional lacy hat; sausage patty wrapped in caul fat.

Coing: quince.

Col vert: wild ("green-collared") mallard duck.

Colbert: method of preparing fish, coating with egg and bread crumbs and then frying.

Colère, en: "anger"; method of presenting fish in which the tail is inserted in the mouth, so it appears agitated.

Colin: hake, ocean fish related to cod; known as *merluche* in the North, *merluchon* in Brittany, *bardot* or *merlan* along the Mediterranean.

Colombe: dove.

Colza: rape, a plant of the mustard family, colorful yellow field crop grown throughout France, usually pressed into vegetable (rapeseed) oil.

Commander avant le repas, à: a selection of desserts that should be ordered when selecting first and main courses, as they require longer cooking.

Complet: filled up, with no

more room for customers.

Compote: stewed fresh or dried fruit.

Compotier: fruit bowl; also stewed fruit.

Compris: see *Service (non) compris.*

Comté: large wheel of cheese of cooked and pressed cow's milk; the best is made of raw milk and aged for six months, still made by independent cheesemakers in the Jura mountains.

Concassé: coarsely chopped.

Concombre: cucumber.

Conférence: a variety of pear.

Confiserie: candy, sweet, or confection; a candy shop.

Confit: a preserve, generally peices of duck, goose, or pork cooked and preserved in their own fat; also fruit or vegetables preserved in sugar, alcohol, or vinegar.

Confiture: jam.

Confiture de vieux garçon: varied fresh fruits macerated in alcohol.

Congeler: to freeze.

Congre: conger eel; a large ocean fish resembling a freshwater eel *(anguille),* often used in fish stews.

Conseillée: advised, recommended.

Consommation(s): "consumption"; drinks, meals, and snacks available in a café or bar.

Consommé: clear soup.

Contre-filet: cut of sirloin taken above the loin on either side of the backbone, tied for roasting or braising (can also be cut for grilling).

Conversation: puff pastry tart with sugar glazing and an almond or cream filling.

Copeau(x): shaving(s), such as from chocolate or vegetables.

Coq (au vin): mature male chicken (stewed in wine sauce).

Coq au vin jaune: chicken cooked in the sherry-like *vin jaune* of the region, with cream, butter, and tarragon, often garnished with morels; specialty of the Jura.

Coq de bruyère: wood grouse.

Coque: cockle, a tiny, mild-flavored, clam-like shellfish.

Coque, à la: served in a shell. See *Oeuf à la coque.*

Coquelet: young male chicken.

Coquillage(s): shellfish.

Coquille: shell.

Coquille Saint-Jacques: sea scallop.

Corail: coral-colored egg sac, found in scallops, spiny lobster, and crayfish.

Corb: a Mediterranean bluefish.

Coriandre: coriander, either the fresh herb or dried seeds.

Corne d'abondance: "horn of plenty"; dark brown wild mushroom, also called *trompette de la mort.*

Cornet: cornet-shaped; usually refers to foods rolled conically; also an ice-cream cone, and a conical pastry filled with cream.

Cornichon: gherkin; tiny tart cucumber pickle.

Côte d'agneau: lamb chop.

Côte de boeuf: beef blade or rib steak.

Côte de veau: veal chop.

Côtelette: thin chop or cutlet.

Cotriade: a fish stew, usually including mackerel, whiting, conger eel, sorrel, butter, potatoes, and vinegar; specialty of Brittany.

Cou d'oie (de canard) farci: neck skin of goose (of duck), stuffed with meat and spices, much like sausage.

Coulant: refers to runny cheese.

Coulemelle: parasol mushroom with a delicate flavor; also called *champignon à la bague, cocherelle,* and *grisotte.*

Coulibiac: classic, elaborate, hot Russian pâté, usually layers of salmon, rice, hard-cooked eggs, mushrooms, and onions, wrapped in *brioche.*

Coulis: purée of raw or cooked vegetables or fruit.

Coulommiers: town in the Ile-de-France that gives its name to a supple, fragrant disc of cow's-milk cheese, slightly larger than *Camembert.*

Courge (muscade): generic term for squash or gourd (bright orange pumpkin).

Courgette: zucchini.

Couronne: "crown"; ring or circle, usually of bread.

Court-bouillon: broth, or aromatic poaching liquid.

Couscous: granules of semolina, or hard wheat flour; also refers to a hearty North African dish that includes the steamed grain, broth, vegetables, meats, hot sauce, and sometimes chickpeas and raisins.

Couvert: a place setting, including dishes, silver, glassware, and linen.

Couverture: bittersweet chocolate high in cocoa butter, used for making the shiniest chocolates.

Crabe: crab.

Crambe: sea kale, or *chou de mer.*

Cramique: brioche with raisins or currants; specialty of the North.

Crapaudine: preparation of grilled poultry or game bird with backbone removed.

Craquelot: smoked herring.

Crécy: a dish garnished with carrots.

Crémant: sparkling wine.

Crème: cream.

  aigre: sour cream.

  anglaise: light egg-custard cream.

  brûlée: rich custard dessert with a top of caramelized sugar.

  caramel: vanilla custard with caramel sauce.

  catalane: creamy, anise-flavored custard from the southern Languedoc.

  chantilly: sweetened whipped cream.

  épaisse: thick cream.

  fleurette: liquid heavy cream.

  fouettée: whipped cream.

  fraîche: thick, sour, heavy cream.

  pâtissière: custard filling for pastries and cakes.

  plombières: custard filled with fresh fruits and egg whites.

Crêpe: thin pancake.

Crêpes Suzette: hot crêpe dessert flamed with orange liqueur.

Crépine: caul fat.

Crépinette: traditionally, a small sausage patty wrapped in caul fat; today, boned poultry wrapped in caul fat.

Cresson(ade): watercress (watercress sauce).

Crête (de coq): (cock's) comb.

Creuse: elongated, crinkle-shelled oyster.

Crevette: shrimp.

Crevette grise: tiny soft-fleshed shrimp that turns gray when cooked.

Crevette rose: small firm-fleshed shrimp that turns red when cooked; when large, called *bouquet.*

Crique: potato pancake from the Auvergne.

Criste marine: edible algae.

Croque au sel, à la: served raw, with a small bowl of coarse salt for seasoning; tiny purple artichokes and cherry tomatoes are served this way.

Croque-madame: open-face sandwich of ham and cheese with an egg grilled on top.

Croque-monsieur: toasted ham and cheese sandwich.

Croquembouche: choux pastry rounds filled with cream and coated with a sugar glaxe, often served in a conical tower at special events.

Croquette: ground meat, fish, fowl, or vegetables bound with eggs or sauce, shaped into various forms, usually coated in bread crumbs, and deep fried.

Crosne: small, unusual tuber, with a subtle artichoke-like flavor, known as a Chinese or Japanese artichoke.

Crottin de Chavignol: small flattened ball of goat's-milk cheese from the Loire valley.

Croustade: usually small pastry-wrapped dish; also regional southwestern pastry filled with prunes and/or apples.

Croûe (en): crust; (in) pastry.

Croûte de sel (en): (in) a salt crust.

Croûtons: small cubes of

toasted or fried bread.

Cru: raw.

Crudité: raw vegetable.

Crustacé(s): crustacean(s).

Cuillière (à la): (to be eaten with a) spoon.

Cuisse (de poulet): leg or thigh (chicken drumstick).

Cuissot, cuisseau: haunch of veal, venison, or wild boar.

Cuit(e): cooked.

Cul: haunch or rear, usually of red meat.

Culotte: rump, usually of beef.

Cultivateur: "truck farmer"; fresh vegetable soup.

Curcuma: turmeric.

Cure-dent: toothpick.

D

Damier: "checkerboard"; arrangement of vegetables or other ingredients in alternating colors like a checkerboard; also, a cake with such a pattern of light and dark pieces.

Darne: a rectangular portion of fish filet; also a fish steak, usually of salmon.

Dartois: puff pastry rectangles layered with an almond cream filling as a dessert, or stuffed with meat or fish as an *hors-d'oeuvre.*

Datte (de mer): date shell (date-shaped prized wild Mediterranean mussel).

Daube: a stew, usually of beef, lamb, or mutton, with red wine, onions, and/or tomatoes; specialty of many regions, particularly Provence and the Atlantic coast.

Dauphin: cow's-milk cheese shaped like a *dauphin,* or

dolphin; from the North.

Daurade: sea bream, similar to porgy, the most prized of a group of ocean fish known as *dorade.*

Décaféiné or *déca:* decaffeinated coffee.

Décortiqué(e): shelled or peeled.

Dégustation: tasting or sampling.

Déjeuner: lunch.

Demi: half; also, an 8-ounce (250 ml) glass of beer; also, a half-bottle of wine.

Demi-deuil: "in half mourning"; poached (usually chicken) with sliced truffles inserted under the skin; also, sweetbreads with a truffled white sauce.

Demi-glace: concentrated beef-based sauce lightened with consommé, or a lighter brown sauce.

Demi-sec: usually refers to goat cheese that is in the intermediate aging stage between one extreme of soft and fresh and the other extreme of hard and aged.

Demi-sel (buerre): lightly salted (butter).

Demi-tasse: small cup; after-dinner coffee cup.

Demoiselle de canard: marinated raw duck tenderloin; also called *mignon de canard.*

Demoiselles de Cherbourg: small lobsters from the town of Cherbourg in Normandy, cooked in a court-bouillon and served in cooking juices. Also, restaurant name for Breton lobsters weighing 300 to 400 grams (10 to 13 ounces).

Dentelle: "lace"; a portion of meat or fish so thinly sliced as to suggest a re-

semblance. Also, large lace-thin sweet crêpe.

Dent, denté: one of a generic group of Mediterranean fish known as *dorade,* similar to porgy.

Dents-de-lion: dandelion salad green; also called *pissenlit.*

Dés: diced pieces.

Désossé: boned.

Diable: "devil"; method of preparing poultry with a peppery sauce, often mustard-based. Also, a round pottery casserole.

Dieppoise: Dieppe style; usually white wine, mussels, shrimp, mushrooms, and cream.

Digestif: general term for spirits served after dinner, such as *Armagnac, Cognac, marc, eau-de-vie.*

Dijonnaise: Dijon style; usually with mustard.

Dinde: turkey hen.

Dindon(neau): turkey (young turkey).

Dîner: dinner; to dine.

Diot: pork sausage cooked in wine, often served with a potato gratin; specialty of the Savoie.

Discrétion, à: on menus usually refers to wine, which may be consumed—without limit—at the customer's discretion.

Dodine: cold stuffed boned poultry.

Dorade: generic name for group of ocean fish, the most prized of which is *daurade,* similar to porgy.

Doré: browned until golden.

Dos: back; also the meatiest portion of fish.

Doucette: see *Mâche.*

Douceur: sweet or dessert.

Douillon, duillon: a whole pear wrapped and cooked in pastry; specialty of Normandy.

Doux, douce: sweet.

Doyenné de Comice: a variety of pear.

Dugléré: white flour-based sauce with shallots, white wine, tomatoes, and parsley.

Dur (oeuf): hard (hardcooked egg).

Duxelles: minced mushrooms and shallots sautéed in butter, then mixed with cream.

E

Eau du robinet: tap water.

Eau de source: spring water.

Eau-de-vie: literally, "water of life"; brandy, usually fruit-based.

Eau gazeuse: carbonated water.

Eau minérale: mineral water.

Echalote (gris): shallot (prized purplish shallot) elongated.

Echalote banane: banana-shaped onion.

Echine: sparerib.

Eclade de moules: mussels roasted beneath a fire of pine needles; specialty of the Atlantic coast.

Ecrasé: crushed; with fruit, pressed to release juice.

Ecrevisse: freshwater crayfish.

Effiloché: frayed, shredded.

Eglantine: wild rose jam; specialty of Alsace.

Eglefin, égrefin, aiglefin: small fresh haddock, a type of cod.

Elzekaria: soup made with green beans, cabbage, and garlic; specialty of the Basque region.

Embeurré de chou: buttery cooked cabbage.

Emincé: thin slice, usually of meat.

Emmental: large wheel of cooked and pressed cow's-milk cheese, very mild in flavor, with large interior holes; made in large commercial dairies in the Jura.

Emondé: skinned by blanching, such as almonds, tomatoes.

En sus: see *Service en sus.*

Enchaud: pork filet with garlic; specialty of Dordogne.

Encornet: small illex squid, also called *calmar;* in Basque region called *chipiron.*

Encre: squid ink.

Endive: Belgian endive; also chicory salad green.

Entier, entière: whole, entire.

Entrecôte: beef rib steak.

Entrecôte maître d'hôtel: beef rib steak with sauce of red wine and shallots.

Entrée: first course.

Entremet: sweet.

Epais(se): thick.

Epaule: shoulder (of veal, lamb, mutton, or pork).

Eperlan: smelt or whitebait, usually fried, often imported but still found in the estuaries of the Loire.

Epi de maïs: ear of sweet corn.

Epice: spice.

Epigramme: classic dish of grilled breaded lamb chop and a piece of braised lamb breast shaped like a chop, breaded, and grilled; crops up on modern menus as an elegant dish of breaded and fried baby lamb chops paired with lamb sweetbreads and tongue.

Epinard: spinach.

Epoisses: village in Burgundy that gives its name to a buttery disc of cow's-milk cheese with a strong, smooth taste and rust-colored rind.

Epoisses blanc: fresh white Epoisses cheese.

Equille: sand eel, a long silvery fish that buries itself in the sand; eaten fried on the Atlantic coast.

Escabèche: a Provençal and southwestern preparation of small fish, usually sardines or *rouget,* in which the fish are browned in oil, then marinated in vinegar and herbs and served very cold. Also, raw fish marinated in lemon or lime juice and herbs.

Escalope: thin slice of meat or fish.

Escargot: land snail.

Escargot de Bourgogne: land snail prepared with butter, garlic, and parsley.

Esargot petit-gris: small land snail.

Escarole: bitter salad green of the chicory family, with thick broad-lobed leaves, found in both flat and round heads.

Espadon: swordfish found in the gulf of Gascony, Atlantic, and Mediterranean.

Espagnole, à l': Spanish style; with tomatoes, peppers, onions, and garlic.

Estoficado: a purée-like blend of dried codfish, olive oil, tomatoes, sweet peppers, black olives, potatoes, garlic, onions, and herbs; also called *stockfish niçoise;* specialty of Nice.

Estofinado: a purée-like blend of dried codfish, potatoes, garlic, parsley, eggs, walnut oil, and milk, served with triangles of toast; specialty of the Auvergne.

BASIC SHORT-CRUST PASTRY

1½ cups (210 g)
  unbleached all-
  purpose flour
7 tablespoons (3½
  ounces; 105 g)
  unsalted butter,
  cubed, at room
  temperature
1 tablespoon sugar
1 large egg
Pinch of salt
1 tablespoon water,
  approximately

Place the flour in a large shallow bowl and make a well in the center. Add the butter, sugar, egg, and salt to the well and mix them together with your fingers. Very gradually work in the flour. Sprinkle the water as needed over the flour mixture and knead until well blended. Wrap the pastry in plastic wrap and refrigerate for about 30 minutes.

Yield: Pastry for one 10½-inch (27 cm) tart.

Estouffade à la provençale: beef stew with onions, garlic, carrots, and orange zest.

Estragon: tarragon.

Etoffé: stuffed.

Etoile: star, star-shaped.

Etouffé, étuvé: literally, "smothered"; method of cooking very slowly in a tightly covered pan with almost no liquid.

Etrille: small swimming crab.

Express: espresso coffee.

F

Façon (à ma): (my) way of preparing a dish.

Fagot: "bundle"; meat shaped into a small ball.

Faisan(e): pheasant.

Faisandé: game that has been hung to age.

Fait: usually refers to a cheese that has been well aged and has character —runny if it's a Camembert, hard and dry if it's a goat cheese; also means ready to eat.

Fait, pas trop: refers to a cheese that has been aged for a shorter time and is blander; also for a cheese that will ripen at home.

Falette: veal breast stuffed with bacon and vegetables, browned, and poached in broth; specialty of the Auvergne.

Fanes: green tops of root vegetables such as carrots, radishes, turnips.

Far: Breton sweet or savory pudding-cakes; the most common, similar to *clafoutis* from the Dordogne, is made with prunes.

Farci(e): stuffed.

Farigoule(tte): Provençal name for wild thyme.

Farine: flour.
  complète: whole wheat flour.
  d'avoine: oat flour.
  de blé: wheat flour, white flour.
  de maïs: corn flour.
  de sarrasin: buckwheat flour.
  de seigle: rye flour.
  de son: bran flour.

Faux-filet: sirloin steak.

Favorite d'artichaut: classic vegetable dish of artichoke stuffed with asparagus, covered with a cheese sauce, and browned.

Favou(ille): in Provence, tiny male (female) crab often used in soups.

Fenouil: fennel.

Fer à cheval: "horseshoe"; a

baguette that has that shape.

Féra, feret: salmon-like lake fish, found in Lac Léman, in the Morvan in Burgundy, and in the Auvergne.

Ferme (fermier, fermière): farm (farmer); in cheese, refers to farm-made cheese, often used to mean raw-milk cheese; in chickens, refers to free-range chickens.

Fermé: closed.

Fernkase: young cheese shaped like a flying saucer and sprinkled with coarsely ground pepper; specialty of Alsace.

Feu de bois, au: cooked over a wood fire.

Feuille de chêne: oak-leaf lettuce.

Feuille de vigne: vine leaf.

Feuilletage (en): (in) puff pastry.

Feuilletée: puff pastry.

Fève: broad, fava, coffee, or cocoa bean; also, the porcelain favor baked into the *galette des rois.*

Fiadone: Corsican flan made from cheese and oranges.

Ficelle (boeuf à la): "string"; (beef suspended on a string and poached in broth). Also, small thin *baguette.*

Ficelle picarde: thin crêpe wrapped around a slice of ham and topped with a cheesy cream sauce; specialty of Picardy, in the North.

Figue: fig.

Financier: small rectangular almond cake.

Financière: Madiera sauce with truffle juice.

Fine de claire: elongated crinkle-shelled oyster that stays in fattening beds *(claires)* up to two months.

Fines herbes: mixture of herbs, usually parsley, chives, tarragon.

Flageolet: small white or pale green kidney-shaped dried bean.

Flamande, à la: Flemish style; usually with stuffed cabbage leaves, carrots, turnips, potatoes, and bacon.

Flamber: to burn off the alcohol by igniting. Usually the brandies or other liqueurs to be flambéed are warmed first, then lit as they are poured into the dish.

Flamiche (au Maroilles): a vegetable tart with rich bread dough crust, commonly filled with leeks, cream, and cheese; specialty of Picardy, in the North; (filled with cream, egg, butter, and Maroilles cheese).

Flammekueche: thin-crusted savory tart, much like a rectangular pizza, covered with cream, onions, and bacon; also called *tarte flambée;* specialty of Alsace.

Flan: sweet or savory tart. Also, a crustless custard pie.

Flanchet: flank of beef or veal, used generally in stews.

Flagnarde, flaugnarde, flognarde: hot, fruit-filled batter cake made with eggs, flour, milk, and butter, and sprinkled with sugar before serving; specialty of the southwest.

flétan: halibut, found in the English Channel and North Sea.

Fleur (de sel): flower (fine sea salt).

Fleur de courgette: zucchini blossom.

Fleuron: puff pastry crescent.

Florentine: with spinach. Also, a cookie of nougatine and candied fruit brushed with a layer of chocolate.

Flûte: "flute"; usually a very thin *baguette.*

Foie: liver.

Foie blond de volaille: chicken liver; also sometimes a chicken-liver mousse.

Foie de veau: calf's liver.

Foie gras d'oie (de canard): liver of fattened goose (duck).

Foin (dan le): (cooked in) hay.

Fond: cooking juices from meat, used to make sauces. Also, bottom.

Fond d'artichaut: heart and base of an artichoke.

Fondant: "melting"; refers to cooked, worked sugar that is flavored, then used for icing cakes. Also, the bittersweet chocolate high in cocoa butter used for making the shiniest chocolates. Also, puréed meat, fish, or vegetables shaped in croquettes.

Fondu(e): melted.

Fontainebleau: creamy white fresh dessert cheese from the Ile-de-France.

Forestière: garnish of wild mushrooms, bacon, and potatoes.

Fouace: a kind of *brioche;* specialty of the Auvergne.

Foudjou: a pungent goat-cheese spread, a blend of fresh and aged grated cheese mixed with salt, pepper, brandy, and garlic and cured in a crock; specialty of northern Provence.

Fougasse: a crusty lattice-like bread made of *baguette* dough or puff pastry, often flavored with anchovies, black olives, herbs, spices, or onions; specialty of Provence and the Mediterranean. Also, a sweet bread of Provence flavored with orange-flower water, oil, and sometimes almonds.

Four (au): (baked in an) oven.

Fourme d'Ambert: cylindrical blue-veined cow's-milk cheese, made in dairies around the town of Ambert in the Auvergne.

Fourré: stuffed or filled.

Foyot: classic sauce made of *béarnaise* with meat glaze.

Frais, fraîche: fresh or chilled.

Fraise: strawberry.

Fraise des bois: wild strawberry.

Framboise: raspberry.

Française, à la: classic garnish of peas with lettuce, small white onions, and parsley.

Frangipane: almond custard filling.

Frappé: usually refers to a drink served very cold or with ice, often shaken.

Frémi: "quivering"; often refers to barely cooked oysters.

Friandise: sweetmeat, *petit four.*

Fricadelle: fried minced meat patty.

Fricandeau: thinly sliced veal or a rump roast, braised with vegetables and white wine.

Fricassée: classically, ingredients braised in wine sauce or butter with cream added; currently denotes any mixture of ingredients—fish or meat—stewed or sautéed.

Frisé(e): "curly"; usually curly endive, the bitter salad green of the chicory family, sold in enormous round heads.

Frit(e): fried.

Frite: French fry.

Fritons: coarse pork *rillettes* or a minced spread which includes organ meats.

Fritot: small organ meat fritter, where meat is partially cooked, then marinated in oil, lemon juice, and herbs, dipped in batter and fried just before serving; also can refer to any small fried piece of meat or fish.

Friture: fried food; also a preparation of small fried fish, usually whitebait or smelt.

Froid(e): cold.

Fromage: cheese.
  blanc: a smooth low-fat cheese similar to cottage cheese.
  d'alpage: cheese made in mountain pastures during the prime summer milking period.
  de tête: headcheese, usually pork.
  Echourgnac: delicately flavored, ochre-skinned cheese made of cow's milk by the monks at the Echourgnac monastery in the Dordogne.
  fort: pungent cheese.
  maigre: low-fat cheese.

Fruit confit: whole fruit preserved in sugar.

Fruits de mer: seafood.

Fumé: smoked.

Fumet: fish stock.

G

Galantine: classical preparation of boned meat or whole poultry that is stuffed or rolled, cooked, then glazed with gelatin and served cold.

Galette: round flat pastry, pancake, or cake; can also refer to pancake-like savory preparations; in Brittany, usually a savory buckwheat crêpe, known as *blé noir.*

Galette bressane, galette de Pérouges: cream and sugar tart from the Bresse area of the Rhône-Alpes.

Galette des rois: puff pastry filled with almond pastry cream, traditional Twelfth Night celebration cake.

Galinette: tub gurnard, Mediterranean fish of the mullet family.

Gamba: large prawn.

Ganache: classically, a rich mixture of chocolate and *crème fraîche* used as a filling for cakes and chocolate truffles; currently may also include such flavorings as wild strawberries and cinnamon.

Garbure: a hearty stew that includes cabbage, beans, and salted or preserved duck, goose, turkey, or pork; specialty of the southwest.

Gardiane: stew of beef or bull *(toro)* meat, with bacon, onions, garlic, and black olives; served with rice; specialty of the Camargue, in Provence.

Gargouillau: pear cake or tart; specialty of northern Auvergne.

Garni(e): garnished.

Garniture: garnish.

Gasconnade: roast leg of lamb with garlic and anchovies; specialty of the southwest.

Gâteau: cake.

  basque: a chewy sweet cake filled with pastry cream or, historically, with black cherry jam; also called *pastiza;* specialty of the Basque region.

  breton: a rich round pound cake; specialty of Brittany.

  opéra: classic almond sponge cake layered with coffee and chocolate butter cream and covered with a sheet of chocolate; seen in every pastry shop window.

  Saint-Honoré: classic cake of *choux* puffs dipped in caramel and set atop a cream-filled *choux* crown on a pastry base.

Gaude: thick corn-flour porridge served hot, or cold and sliced, with cream.

Gaufre: waffle.

Gave: southwestern term for mountain stream; indicates fish from the streams of the area.

Gayette: small sausage patty made with pork liver and bacon, wrapped in caul fat and bacon.

Gelée: aspic.

Gendarme: salted and smoked herring.

Genièvere: juniper berry.

Génoise: sponge cake.

Gentiane: gentian; a liqueur made from this mountain flower.

Germiny: garnish of sorrel. Also, sorrel and cream soup.

Germon: albacore or longfin tuna.

Gésier: gizzard.

Gibassier: round sweet bread from Provence, often flavored with lemon or orange zest, orangeflower water, and/or al-

monds. Also sometimes called *fougasse* or *pompe à l'huile.*

Gibelotte: fricassee of rabbit in red or white wine.

Gibier: game, sometimes designated as *gibier à plume* (feathered) or *gibier à poil* (furry).

Gigot (de pré salé): usually a leg of lamb (lamb grazed on the salt meadows along the Atlantic and Normandy coasts).

Gigot de mer: a preparation, usually of large pieces of monkfish *(lotte),* ovenroasted like a leg of lamb.

Gigue (de): haunch (of) certain game meats.

Gingembre: ginger.

Girofle: clove.

Girolle: prized pale orange wild mushroom; also called *chanterelle.*

Givré; orange givrée: frosted; orange sherbet served in its skin.

Glace: ice cream.

Glacé: iced, crystallized, or glazed.

Gnocchi: dumplings made of *choux* paste, potatoes, or semolina.

Goret: young pig.

Gougère: cheese-flavored *choux* pastry.

Goujon: small catfish; generic name for a number of small fish. Also, preparation in which the central part of a larger fish is coated with bread crumbs, then deep fried.

Goujonnette: generally used to describe a small piece of fish, such as sole, usually fried.

Gourmandise: sweetmeat.

Gousse d'ail: clove of garlic.

Gousse de vanille: vanilla bean.

Goût: taste.

Goûter (le): to taste, to try;

(children's afternoon snack).

Graine de moutarde: mustard seed.

Graisse: fat.

Graisserons: crisply fried pieces of duck or goose skin; cracklings.

Grand crème: large or double espresso with milk.

Grand cru: top-ranking wine.

Grand veneur: "chief huntsman"; usually a brown sauce for game, with red currant jelly.

Granité: a type of sherbet; a sweetened, flavored ice.

Grappe (de raisins): cluster, bunch (of grapes).

Gras (marché au): fatty; (market of fattened poultry and their livers).

Gras-double: tripe baked with onions and white wine.

Gratin: crust formed on top of a dish when browned in broiler or oven; also the dish in which such food is cooked.

Gratin dauphinoise: baked casserole of sliced potatoes, usually with cream, milk, and sometimes cheese and/or eggs.

Gratin savoyarde: baked casserole of sliced potatoes, usually with bouillon, cheese, and butter.

Gratiné(e): having a crusty, browned top.

Gratinée lyonnaise: bouillon flavored with port, garnished with beaten egg, topped with cheese, and browned under a broiler.

Grattons, grattelons: crisply fried pieces of pork, goose, or duck skin; cracklings.

Gratuit: free.

Grecque, à la: cooked in seasoned mixture of oil, lemon juice, and water;

refers to cold vegetables, usually mushrooms.

Grelette, sauce: cold sauce with a base of whipped cream.

Grelot: small white bulb onion.

Grenade: pomegranate.

Grenadin: small veal scallop.

Grenouille (cuisse de): frog (leg).

Gressini: breadsticks, seen along the Côte-d'Azur.

Gribiche, sauce: mayonnaise with capers, *cornichons,* hard-cooked eggs, and herbs.

Grillade: grilled meat.

Grillé(e): grilled.

Griotte: shiny, slightly acidic, reddish black cherry.

Grisotte: parasol mushroom with a delicate flavor; also called *champignon à la bague, cocherelle,* and *coulemelle.*

Grive: thrush.

Grondin: red gurnard, a bony ocean fish, a member of the mullet family, used in fish stews such as bouillabaisse.

Groin d'ane: "donkey's snout"; Lyonnais name for a bitter winter salad green similar to dandelion greens.

Gros sel: coarse salt.

Groseille: red currant.

Gruyère: strictly speaking, cheese from the Gruyère area of Switzerland; in France, generic name for a number of hard, mild, cooked cheeses from the Jura, including Comté, Beaufort, and Emmental.

Gyromite: group of wild mushrooms, or *gyromitra,* known as false morels.

H

Hachis: minced or chopped meat or fish preparation.

Haddock: small fresh cod that have been salted and smoked.

Hareng: herring, found in the Atlantic, the English Channel (the best between Dunkerque and Fécamp), and the mouth of the Gironde river.

Hareng à l'huile: herring cured in oil, usually served with a salad of warm sliced potatoes.

Hareng baltique, bismark: marinated herring.

Hareng bouffi: herring that is salted, then smoked.

Hareng pec: freshly salted young herring.

Hareng roll-mop: marinated herring rolled around a small pickle.

Hareng saur: smoked herring.

Haricot: bean.
  beurre: yellow bean.
  blancs (à la Bretonne): white beans, usually dried; (white beans in a sauce of onions, tomatoes, garlic, and herbs).
  de mouton: stew of mutton and white beans (also called *halicots*).
  gris: green string bean mottled with purplish black; also called *pélandron;* a specialty of the Côte-d'Azur.
  rouge: red kidney bean; also, preparation of red beans in red wine.
  sec: dried bean.
  vert: green bean, usually fresh.

Hâtelet, attelet: decorative skewer; currently used to mean meat or fish cooked on a skewer.

Herbes de Provence: mixture of thyme, rosemary, summer savory, and bay leaf, often dried and blended.

Hirondelle: swallow.

Hochepot: a thick stew, usually of oxtail; specialty of Flanders, in the north.

Hollandaise: sauce of butter, egg yolks, and lemon juice.

Homard (à l'Amoricaine, à l'Américaine): lobster; (a classic dish of many variations, in which lobster is cut into sections and browned, then simmered with shallots, minced onions, tomatoes, Cognac, and white wine; served with a sauce of the reduced cooking liquid, enriched with butter).

Hongroise, à la: Hungarian style; usually with paprika and cream.

Hors-d'oeuvre: appetizer; can also refer to a first course.

Hortillon: picturesque market garden plot built between crisscrossed canals on the outskirts of Amiens, a city in the north.

Huile: oil.
  d'arachide: peanut oil.
  de colza: rapeseed oil.
  de maïs: corn oil.
  de noisette: hazlenut oil.
  de noix: walnut oil.
  de pépins de raisins: grapeseed oil.
  de sésame: sesame oil.
  de tournesol: sunflower oil.
  d'olive (extra vierge): olive oil (extra virgin, or the first cold pressing).

Huître: oyster.

Hure de porc or *de marcassin:* head of pig or boar: usually refers to headcheese preparation.

Hure de saumon: a salmon "headcheese," or pâté,

prepared with salmon meat, not actually the head.

Hysope: hyssop; fragrant, mint-like thistle found in Provence, used in salads and in cooking.

I

Ile flottante: "floating island"; most commonly used interchangeably with *oeufs à la neige,* poached meringue floating in *crème anglaise;* classically, a layered cake covered with whipped cream and served with custard sauce.

Impératrice, à l': usually a rice pudding dessert with candied fruit.

Imperiale: variety of plum. Also, a large bottle for wine, holding about 4 quarts (4 liters).

Impériale, à l': classic *haute cuisine* garnish of mussels, cockscombs, crayfish, and other extravagant ingredients.

Indienne, à l': East Indian style, usually with curry powder.

Infusion: herb tea.

Isman bayaldi, imam bayaldi: "the priest fainted" in Turkish; a dish of eggplant stuffed with sautéed onions, tomatoes, and spices; served cold.

J

Jalousie: "venetian blind"; classic small, latticed, flaky pastry filled with almond paste and spread with jam.

Jambon: ham; also refers to the leg, usually of pork, but also of poultry.

à l'os: ham with the bone in.

blanc: lightly salted, unsmoked or very lightly smoked ham, served cooked; sold, cold, in *charcuteries* as *jambon de Paris, glacé,* or *demi-sel.*

cru: salted or smoked ham that has been cured but not cooked.

cuit: cooked ham.

d'Auvergne: raw, dry, salt-cured smoked ham.

de Bayonne: raw, dry, salt-cured ham, very pale in color.

de Bourgogne: See *Jambon persillé.*

de montagne: any mountain ham, cured according to local custom.

de Paris: pale, lightly salted, cooked ham.

de Parme: Italian prosciutto from Parma, air-dried and salt-cured ham, sliced thin and served raw.

de pays: any country ham, cured according to local custom.

de poulet: boned stuffed chicken leg.

de Westphalie: German Westphalian ham, raw, cured, and smoked.

de York: smoked English-style ham, usually poached.

*d'oie (*or *de canard):* breast of fattened goose (or duck), smoked, salted, or sugar cured, somewhat resembling ham in flavor.

fumé: smoked ham.

persillé: cold cooked ham, cubed and preserved in parsleyed gelatin, usually sliced from a terrine; a specialty of Burgundy.

salé: salt-cured ham.

sec: dried ham.

Jambonneau: cured ham shank or pork knuckle.

Jambonnette: boned and stuffed knuckle of ham or poultry.

Jardinière: refers to a garnish of fresh cooked vegetables.

Jarret (de veau, de porc, de boeuf): knuckle (of veal or pork), shin (of beef).

Jerez: refers to sherry.

Jésus de Morteau: plump smoked pork sausage that takes its name from the town of Morteau in the Jura; distinctive because a wooden peg is tied in the sausage casing on one end; traditionally, the sausage eaten at Christmas, hence its name; also called *saucisson de Morteau.*

Jeune: young.

Jonchée: rush basket in which certain fresh sheep's- or goat's-milk cheeses of Poitou (along the Atlantic coast) are contained; thus, by extension, the cheese itself.

Joue: cheek.

Julienne: cut into slivers, usually vegetables or meat.

Jurançon: district in the Béarn, the area around Pau in southwestern France, known for its sweet and spicy white wine.

Jus: juice.

K

Kaki: persimmon.

Kari: variant spelling of *cary.*

Kiev: deep-fried breast of chicken stuffed with herb and garlic butter.

Kir: an aperitif made with *crème de cassis* (black currant liqueur) and most commonly dry white wine, but sometimes red wine.

Kir royal: a *Kir* made with Champagne.

Kirsch: eau-de-vie of wild black cherries.

Knepfla: Alsatian dumpling, sometimes fried.

Kougelhoph, hougelhof, kouglof, kugelhoph: sweet crown-shaped yeast cake, with almonds and raisins; specialty of Alsace.

Kouigh-amann: sweet, buttery pastry from Brittany.

Kummel: caraway seed liqueur.

L

Laguiole: Cantal cheese from the area around the village of Laguiole, in southern Auvergne, still made in rustic huts.

Lait: milk.

demi-écremé: semi-skimmed milk.

écremé: skimmed milk.

entier: whole milk.

ribot: from Brittany, buttermilk, served with crêpes.

stérilizé: milk heated to a higher temperature than pasteurized milk, so that it stays fresh for several weeks.

Laitance: soft roe (often of herring), or eggs.

Laitier: made of or with milk; also denotes a commercially made product as opposed to *fermier,* meaning farm made.

Laitue: lettuce.

Lamelle: very thin strip.

Lamproie (à la bordelaise): lamprey eel, ocean fish that swim into rivers along the Atlantic in springtime (hearty stew of lamprey eel and leeks in red wine).

Lançon: tiny fish, served fried.

Landaise, à la: from the Landes in southwestern France; classically a garnish of garlic, pine nuts, and goose fat.

Langouste: clawless spiny lobster or rock lobster; sometimes called crawfish, and mistakenly, crayfish.

Langoustine: clawed crustacean, smaller than either *homard* or *langouste,* with very delicate meat. Known in British waters as Dublin Bay prawn.

Langres: supple, tangy cylindrical cow's-milk cheese with a rust-colored rind; named for village in Champagne.

Langue (de chat): tongue ("cat's tongue"; thin, narrow, delicate cookie often served with sherbet or ice).

Languedocienne: garnish, usually of tomatoes, eggplant, and wild *cèpe* mushrooms.

Lapereau: young rabbit.

Lapin: rabbit.

Lapin de garenne: wild rabbit.

Lard: bacon.

Larder: to thread meat, fish, or liver with strips of fat for added moisture.

Lardon: cube of bacon.

Larme: "teardrop"; a very small portion of liquid.

Laurier: bay laurel or bay leaf.

Lavaret: lake fish of the Savoie, similar to salmon.

Lèche: thin slice of bread or meat.

Léger (légère): light.

Légume: vegetable.

Lentilles (de Puy): lentils (prized green lentils from the village of Puy, in the Auvergne).

Lieu jaune: green pollack, in the cod family, a pleasant, inexpensive small yellow fish; often sold under name *colin;* found in the Atlantic.

Lieu noir: pollack, also called black cod; in the cod family, a pleasant, inexpensive fish found in the English Channel and the Atlantic.

Lièvre (à la royale): hare (cooked with red wine, shallots, onions, and cinnamon, then rolled and stuffed with *foie gras* and truffles).

Limaces à la suçarelle: snails cooked with onions, garlic, tomatoes, and sausage; specialty of Provence.

Limaçon: land snail.

Limande: lemon sole, also called dab or sand dab, not as firm or prized as sole, found in the English Channel, the Atlantic, and, rarely, in the Mediterranean.

Lingot: type of kidney-shaped dry white bean.

Lisette: small *maquereau,* or mackerel.

Livarot: village in Normandy that gives its name to an elastic and pungent thick disc of cow's-milk cheese with reddish golden stripes around the edge.

Lotte: monkfish or angler fish, a large firm-fleshed ocean fish.

Lotte de rivière (or de lac): fine-fleshed river (or lake) fish, prized for its large and flavorful liver. Not related to the ocean fish *lotte,* or monkfish.

Lou magret: breast of fattened duck.

Loup de mer: wolf fish or ocean catfish; name for sea bass in the Mediterranean.

Louvine: Basque name for striped bass, fished in the Bay of Gascony.

Lucullus: a classic, elaborate garnish of truffles cooked in Madeira and stuffed with chicken forcemeat.

Lumas: name for land snail in the Poitou-Charentes region along the Atlantic coast.

Luzienne, à la: prepared in the manner popular in Saint-Jean-de-Luz, a Basque fishing port.

Lyonnaise, à la: in the style of Lyon; often garnished with onions.

M

Macaron: macaroon, small cookie of almonds, egg whites, and sugar.

Macaronade: a rich blend of wild and domestic mushrooms and chunks of *foie gras,* smothered in fresh pasta; specialty of the southwest. Also, macaroni with mushrooms, bacon, white wine, and Parmesan cheese; an accompaniment to a beef stew, or *daube;* specialty of Provence.

Macédoine: diced mixed fruit or vegetables.

Mâche: Dark small-leafed salad green known as lamb's lettuce or corn salad. Also called *doucette.*

Mâchon: early morning snack of sausage, wine, cheese, and bread; also, the café that offers the snack; particular to Lyon.

Macis: mace, the spice.

Madeleine (de Commercy): small scalloped-shaped tea cake made famous by Marcel Proust; (the town in the Lorraine where the tea cakes are commercialized).

Madère: Madeira.

Madrilène, à la: in the style of Madrid; with tomatoes. Classically, a garnish of peeled chopped tomatoes for consommé.

Magret de canard (or *d'oie):* breast of fattened duck (or goose).

Maigre: thin, non-fatty.

Maïs: corn.

Maison, de la: of the house, or restaurant.

Maître d'hôtel: headwaiter. Also, sauce of butter, parsley, and lemon.

Maltaise: orange-flavored *hollandaise* sauce.

Malvoisie, vinaigre de: vinegar made from the malvasia grape, used for the sweet, heavy Malmsey wine.

Mandarine: tangerine.

Mange-tout: "eat it all"; a podless green runner bean; a sweet pea; a snow pea. Also, a variety of apple.

Mangue: mango.

Manière, de: in the style of.

Maquereau: mackerel; *lisette* is a small mackerel.

Maraîcher(e) (à la): market gardener or truck farmer (market-garden style; usually refers to a dish or salad that includes various greens).

Marbré: striped sea bream, Mediterranean fish that is excellent grilled.

Marc: eau-de-vie distilled from pressed grape skins and seeds or other fruits.

Marcassin: young wild boar.

Marchand de vin: wine merchant. Also, sauce made with red wine, meat stock, and chopped shallots.

Marée la: literally, "the tide"; usually used to indicate seafood that is fresh.

Marennes: flat-shelled green-tinged *plate* oyster. Also the French coastal village where flat-shelled oysters are raised.

Marinade: seasoned liquid in which food, usually meat, is soaked for several hours. The liquid seasons and tenderizes at the same time.

Mariné: marinated.

Marjolaine: marjoram. Also, multilayered chocolate and nut cake.

Marmelade: traditionally, a thick purée of fruit, or sweet stewed fruit; today, purée of vegetable, or stewed vegetables.

Marmite: small covered pot; also a dish cooked in a small casserole.

Maroilles: village in the north that gives its name to a strong-tasting, thick, square cow's-milk cheese with a pale brick-red rind.

Marquise (au chocolat): mousse-like (chocolate) cake.

Marron (glacé): large (candied) chestnut.

Matelote (d'anguilles): freshwater fish (or eel) stew.

Matignon: a garnish of mixed stewed vegetables.

Mauviette: wild meadow lark or skylark.

Médaillon: round piece or slice, usually of fish or meat.

Mélange: mixture or blend.

Méli-mélo: an assortment of fish and/or seafood.

Melon de Cavaillon: small canteloupe-like melon

BASIC TOMATO SAUCE

*I'm crazy about tomato sauce and feel particularly secure if I know that several jars of beauti-
ful red sauce are sitting in the cupboard, ready for pizza, pastas, whatever it is I'm in the
mood for that day. I like a well-seasoned sauce and sometimes even add a bit of grated orange
peel if the sauce needs perking up. This recipe offers proportions for about 1 quart (1 liter) of
sauce, and ingredients can, of course, be multiplied to make a larger batch.*

2 tablespoons virgin
   olive oil
4 medium onions,
   coarsely chopped
3 cloves garlic, coarsely
   chopped
4 pounds (2 kg) ripe
   tomatoes, quartered,
   or 3 large cans (each
   28 ounces; 794 g)
   Italian plum
   tomatoes
1 bay leaf
Handful of fresh herbs,
   preferably basil,
   chervil, thyme, and
   flat-leaf parsley,
   stemmed and
   minced
½ teaspoon dried red
   pepper flakes
   (optional)
Grated zest (peel) of 1
   orange (optional)
Salt and freshly ground
   black pepper to taste

1. Heat the oil in a large skillet over medium heat. Add
the onions and garlic and cook, stirring frequently,
until soft but not brown. Increase the heat to medium-
high and add the remaining ingredients, seasoning
lightly with salt and pepper. Cook uncovered, stirring
frequently, over medium heat until thick, 30 to 45
minutes. Check the seasoning.

2. Press the mixture through a fine-mesh sieve or food
mill.

3. The sauce will keep in the refrigerator for several
days or may be frozen for several months.

Yield: About 1 quart (1 liter).

from Cavaillon, a town
in Provence known for
its wholesale produce
market.
Ménagère, à la: "in the style
of the housewife"; usu-
ally a simple preparation
including onions, pota-
toes, and carrots.
Mendiant, fruits du: traditional mixture of figs, almonds, hazelnuts, and
raisins, whose colors suggest the robes of the
mendicant friars it is
named after.
Menthe: mint.
Merguez: small spicy sausage.
Merlan: whiting.
Merle: blackbird.
Merlu: hake, a member of
the codfish family, often
sold improperly in Paris
markets as *colin;* found in
the English Channel, At-
lantic, and Mediterra-
nean.
Mérou: a large grouper, an
excellent tropical or
near-tropical fish, generally imported from
North Africa but some-
times found in the Atlan-
tic and Mediterranean.
Merveille: hot sugared
doughnut.
Mesclum, mesclun: a mixture of at least seven

multi-shaded salad greens, from Provence.

Mets: dish or preparation.

Mets selon la saison: seasonal preparation; according to the season.

Méture: corn bread from the Basque region.

Meule: "millstone"; name for wheel of cheese in the Jura.

Meunière, à la: "in the style of the miller's wife"; refers to a fish that is seasoned, rolled in flour, fried in butter, and served with lemon, parsley, and hot melted butter.

Meurette: in, or with, a red wine sauce. Also, a Burgundian fish stew.

Mi-cru: half raw.

Mi-cuit: half cooked.

Miche: a large round country-style loaf of bread. Also, Basque name for aniseed cake-like bread.

Mie: interior or crumb of the bread (see *Pain de mie*).

Miel: honey.

Mignardise: see *Petit-four.*

Mignon de canard: see *Demoiselle de canard.*

Mignonette: small cubes, usually of beef. Also refers to coarsely ground black or white pepper.

Mijoté(e) (plat): simmered (dish or preparation).

Mille-feuille: refers to puff pastry with many thin layers; usually a cream-filled rectangle of puff pastry, or a Napoleon.

Mimosa: garnish of chopped hard-cooked egg yolks.

Minute (à la): "minute"; something quickly grilled or fried in butter with lemon juice and parsley (prepared at the last minute).

Mique: generally a large breaded dumpling, poached and served with stews and meats; specialty of the southwest.

Mirabeau: garnish of anchovies, pitted olives, tarragon, and anchovy butter.

Mirabelle: small sweet yellow plum. Also, colorless fruit brandy, or *eau-de-vie,* made from yellow plums.

Mirepoix: cubes of carrots and onions or mixed vegetables, usually used in braising to boost the flavor of a meat dish.

Miroir: "mirror"; a dish that has a smooth glaze; currently a fruit *mousse* cake with a layer of fruit glaze on top.

Miroton (de): slice (of). Also, stew of meats flavored with onions.

Mitonnée: a simmered, soup-like dish.

Mode de, à la: in the style of.

Moëlle: beef bone marrow.

Mogette, mojette, mougette: a kind of dried white bean from the Atlantic coast.

Moka: refers to coffee; coffee-flavored dish.

Mollusque: mollusc.

Mont blanc: rich classic pastry of baked meringue, chestnut purée, and whipped cream.

Montagne, de la: from the mountains.

Montmorency: garnished with cherries; historically, a village known for its cherries, now a suburb of Paris.

Morbier: supple cow's-milk cheese from the Jura; a thin sprinkling of ashes in the center gives it its distinctive black stripe and light smoky flavor.

Morceau: piece or small portion.

Morille: wild morel mushroom, dark brown and conical.

Mornay: classic cream sauce enriched with egg yolks and cheese.

Morue: salt cod; also currently used to mean fresh cod, which is *cabillaud.*

Morvandelle, jambon à la: in the style of the Morvan (ham in a piquant creamy sauce made with white wine, vinegar, juniper berries, shallots, and cream).

Morvandelle, râpée: grated potato mixed with eggs, cream, and cheese, baked until golden.

Mosaïque: "mosaic;" a presentation of mixed ingredients.

Mostèle: forkbeard mostelle; small Mediterranean fish of the cod family.

Mouclade: creamy mussel stew from the Poitou-Charentes on the Atlantic Coast, generally flavored with curry or saffron.

Moufflon: wild sheep.

Moule: mussel. Also a mold.

Moule de bouchot: small, highly prized cultivated mussel, raised on stakes driven into the sediment of shallow coastal beds.

Moule de Bouzigues: iodine-strong mussel from the village of Bouzigues, on the Mediterranean coast.

Moule d'Espagne: large, sharp-shelled mussel, often served raw as part of a seafood platter.

Moule de parques: Dutch cultivated mussel, usually raised in fattening beds or diverted ponds.

Moules marinière: mussels cooked in white wine with onions, shallots, butter, and herbs.

Moulin (à poivre): mill (peppermill); also used for oil and flour mills.

Mourone: Basque name for red bell pepper.

Mourtayrol, mourtaïrol: a *pot-au-feu* of boiled beef, chicken, ham, and vegetables, flavored with saffron and served over slices of bread; specialty of the Auvergne.

Mousse: light, airy mixture usually containing eggs and cream, either sweet or savory.

Mousseline: refers to ingredients that are usually lightened with whipped cream or egg whites, as in sauces, or with butter, as in *brioche mousseline.*

Mousseron: tiny, delicate, wild mushroom.

Moutarde (à l'ancienne, en graines): mustard (old-style, coarse-grained).

Mouton: mutton.

Muge: grey mullet.

Mulard: breed of duck common to the southwest, fattened for its delicate liver, for *foie gras.*

Mulet: the generic group of mullet, found in the English Channel, Atlantic, and Mediterranean.

Munster: village in Alsace that gives its name to a disc of soft, tangy cow's-milk cheese with a brick-red rind and a penetrating aroma; the cheese is also sometimes cured with cumin seeds.

Mûre (de ronces): blackberry (bush).

Muscade: nutmeg.

Muscat de Hambourg: variety of popular purple table grape, grown in Provence.

Museau de porc (or *de boeuf):* vinegared pork (or beef) muzzle.

Myrtille: bilberry (bluish black European blueberry).

Mystère: truncated cone–shaped ice cream dessert. Also, dessert of cooked meringue with ice cream and chocolate cake.

N

Nage (à la): "swimming"; aromatic poaching liquid (served in).

Nantua: sauce of crayfish, butter, cream, and, traditionally, truffles; also garnish of crayfish.

Nappé: covered, as with a sauce.

Natte: woven loaf of bread.

Nature: refers to simple, unadorned preparations.

Navarin: lamb or mutton stew.

Navarraise, à la: Navarre-style; with sweet peppers, onions, and garlic.

Navet: turnip.

Navette: "little boat"; small pastry boats.

Nèfle: medlar; tart fruit similar to a crab apple.

Neufchâtel: white, creamy, delicate (and often heart-shaped) cow's-milk cheese, named for village in Normandy where it is made.

Newburg: lobster preparation with Madeira, egg yolks, and cream.

Nivernaise, à la: in the style of Nevers; with carrots and onions.

Noilly: a vermouth-based sauce.

Noisette: hazelnut; also refers to small round piece (such as from a potato), generally the size of a hazelnut, lightly browned in butter. Also, center cut of lamb chop. Also, dessert flavored with hazelnuts.

Noix: general term for nut; also, walnut. Also, nut-size, typically *une noix de beurre,* or lump of butter.

Non compris: see *Service (non) compris.*

Nonat: small river fish in Provence, usually fried. Also known as *poutine.*

Normande: in the style of Normandy; sauce of seafood, cream, and mushrooms. Also refers to fish or meat cooked with apple cider or Calvados; or dessert with apples, usually served with cream.

Note: another word for *addition,* bill or tab.

Nougat: candy of roasted almonds, egg whites, and honey; specialty of Montélimar.

Nougat glacé: frozen dessert of whipped cream and candied fruit.

Nouilles: noodles.

Nouveau, nouvelle: new or young.

Nouveauté: a new offering.

O

Oeuf: egg.

　à la coque: soft-cooked egg.

　brouillé: scrambled egg.

　dur: hard-cooked egg.

　en meurette: poached egg in red wine sauce.

　mollet: egg simmered in water for 6 minutes.

　poché: poached egg.

　sauté à la poêle or *oeuf sur le plat:* fried egg.

Oeufs à la neige: "eggs in the snow"; sweetened whipped egg whites poached in milk and served with vanilla custard sauce.

Offert: offered; free or given.

Oie: goose.

Oignon: onion.

Oiselle: sorrel.

Olive noire (verte): black olive (green olive).

Olives cassées: fresh green olives cured in a rich fennel-infused brine; specialty of Provence.

Omble (ombre) chevalier: lake fish, similar to salmon trout, with firm, flaky flesh varying from white to deep red. Found in lakes in the Savoie.

Omelette norvégienne: French version of Baked Alaska; a concoction of sponge cake covered with ice cream and a layer of sweetened, stiffly beaten egg whites, then browned quickly in the oven.

Onglet: cut similar to beef flank steak; also cut of beef sold as *biftek* and *entrecôte;* usually a tough cut, but better than flank steak.

Oreille de porc: cooked pig's ear, served grilled, with a coating of egg and bread crumb.

Oreillette: thin, crisp rectangular dessert fritters, flavored with orange-flower water; specialty of Provence.

Orge (perlé): barley (pearl barley).

Orientale, à l': general name for vaguely Eastern dishes cooked with saffron, tomatoes, and sweet red peppers.

Origan: oregano.

Oseille: sorrel.

Osso bucco à la niçoise: sautéed veal braised with tomatoes, garlic, onions, and orange zest; specialty of the Mediterranean.

Oursin: sea urchin.

Oursinade: creamy sea urchin soup.

Ouvert: open.

P

Pageot: a type of sea bream or porgy. The finest is *pageot rouge,* wonderful grilled. *Pageot blanc* is drier and needs to be marinated in oil before cooking.

Paillarde (de veau): thick slice (of veal); also, piece of meat pounded flat and sautéed.

Pailles (pommes): fried potato sticks.

Paillette: cheese straw, usually made with puff pastry and Parmesan cheese.

Pain: bread. Also, loaf of any kind.

  aux cinq céréales: five-grain bread.

  aux noix (aux noisettes): bread, most often rye or wheat, filled with walnuts (hazelnuts).

  aux raisins: bread, most often rye or wheat, filled with raisins.

  azyme: unleavened bread, matzoh.

  bis: brown bread.

  brié: very dense, elongated loaf of unsalted white bread; specialty of Normandy.

  complet: bread made partially or entirely from whole-wheat flour, with bakers varying proportions according to their personal tastes.

  cordon: seldom-found regional country loaf decorated with a strip of dough.

  d'Aix: variously shaped sourdough loaves, sometimes like a sunflower, other times a chain-like loaf of four linked rounds.

  de campagne: country loaf; can vary from a white bread simply dusted with flour to give it a rustic look (and fetch a higher price) to a truly hearty loaf that may be a blend of white, whole wheat, and perhaps rye flour with bran added. Comes in every shape.

  de fantaisie: generally, any odd or imaginatively shaped bread. Even *baguette de campagne* falls into this category.

  de Gênes: classic almond sponge cake.

  de mie: rectangular white sandwich loaf that is nearly all *mie* (interior crumb) and very little crust. It is made for durability, its flavor and texture developed for use in sandwiches. Unlike most French breads, it contains milk, sugar, and butter, and may contain chemical preservatives.

  d'épices: spice bread, a specialty of Dijon.

  de seigle: bread made from 60 to 70 percent rye flour and 30 to 40 percent wheat flour.

  de son: legally, a dietetic bread that is quality controlled, containing 20 percent bran mixed with white flour.

  grillé: toast.

  paillé: country loaf from the Basque region.

  sans sel: salt-free bread.

  viennois: bread shaped like a *baguette,* with regular horizontal slashes, usually containing white flour, sugar, powdered milk, water, and yeast.

Paleron: shoulder of beef.

Palestine: classically, a garnish of Jerusalem artichokes.

Palmier: palm leaf–shaped cookie made of sugared puff pastry.

Palmier, coeur de: heart of palm.

Palombe: wood or wild pigeon, or dove.

Palourde: prized medium-size clam.

Pamplemousse: grapefruit.

Pan bagna: large round bread roll, split, brushed with olive oil, and filled with a variable mixture including anchovies, onions, black olives, green peppers, tomatoes, and celery; café specialty from Nice.

Panaché: mixed; now liberally used menu term to denote any mixture.

Panade: panada, a thick mixture used to bind forcemeats and *quenelles,* usually flour and butter based, but can also contain fresh or toasted bread crumbs, rice, or potatoes. Also refers to soup of bread, milk, and sometimes cheese.

Panais: parsnip.

Pané(e): breaded.

Panisse: a thick fried pancake of chickpea flour, served as accompaniment to meat; specialty of Provence.

Pannequet: rolled crêpe, filled and/or covered with sweet or savory mixture.

Pantin: small pork pastry.

Papeton: eggplant, fried, puréed, and cooked in a ring mold; specialty of Provence.

Papillon: "butterfly"; small crinkle-shelled *creuse* oyster from the Atlantic coast.

Papillote, en: cooked in parchment paper or foil wrapping.

Paquet (en): (in) a package or parcel.

Parfait: a dessert mouse; also, mousse-like mixture of chicken, duck, or goose liver.

Parfum: flavor.

Paris-Brest, gâteau: classic large, crown-shaped *choux* pastry filled with praline butter cream and topped with chopped almonds.

Parisienne, à la: varied vegetable garnish which generally includes potato balls that have been fried and tossed in a meat glaze.

Parmentier: dish with potatoes.

Passe Crassane: flavorful variety of winter pear.

Passe-Pierre: edible seaweed.

Pastèque: watermelon.

Pastis: anise-flavored alcohol that becomes cloudy when water is added (the most famous brands are Pernod and Ricard). Also, name for *tourtière,* the flaky prune pastry from the southwest.

Pastiza: see *gâteau basque.*

Pâte: pastry or dough.
  brisée: pie pastry.
  d'amande: almond paste.
  sablée: sweeter, richer, and more crumbly pie dough than *pâte sucrée,* sometimes leavened.
  sucrée: sweet pie pastry.

Pâté: minced meat that is molded, spiced, baked, and served hot or cold.

Pâtes (fraîches): pasta (fresh).

Patte blanche: small crayfish no larger than 2 ½ ounces (75 g).

Patte rouge: large crayfish.

Pauchouse, pochouse: stew of river fish that generally includes *tanche* (tench), *perche* (perch), *brochet* (pike), and *anguille* (eel); specialty of Burgundy.

Paupiette: slice of meat or fish, filled, rolled, then wrapped; served warm.

Pavé: "paving stone"; usually a thick slice of boned beef or calf's liver. Also, a kind of pastry.

Pavé d'Auge: thick, ochre-colored square of cow's-milk cheese that comes from the Auge area of Normandy.

Pavot (graine de): poppy (seed).

Paysan(ne) (à la): country style; (garnish of carrots, turnips, onions, celery, and bacon).

Peau: skin.

Pèbre d'ail: see *Poivre d'âne.*

Pêche: peach. Also, fishing.

Pêche Alexandra: cold dessert of poached peaches with ice cream and puréed strawberries.

Pêche Melba: poached peach with vanilla ice cream and raspberry sauce.

Pêcheur: "fisherman"; usually refers to fish preparations.

Pélandron: see *haricot gris.*

Pélardon: small flat, dried, pungent disc of goat's-milk cheese; specialty of the Languedoc.

Pèlerine: another name for scallop or *coquille Saint-Jacques.*

Perce-pierre: samphire, edible seaweed.

Perche: perch.

Perdreau: young partridge.

Perdrix: partridge.

Périgourdine, à la, or *Périgueux:* sauce, usually with truffles and *foie gras,* named for the Périgord in southwestern France.

Persil (simple): parsley (flat-leaf).

Persillade: blend of chopped parsley and garlic.

Persillé: "parsleyed"; describes certain blue-veined cheeses. See also *Jambon persillé*.

Pet de nonne: "nun's fart"; small, dainty *beignets*, or fried pastry.

Pétale: "petal"; very thin slice.

Petit-beurre: popular tea cookie made with butter.

Petit déjeuner: breakfast.

Petit-four (sucré or *salée):* tiny cake or pastry (sweet or savory); in elegant restaurants, served with cocktails before dinner or with coffee afterward; also called *mignardise*.

Petit-gris: small land snail.

Petit-pois: small green pea.

Petit salé: salt-cured portions of lean pork belly, often served with lentils.

Petite marmite (de langoustines): earthenware casserole; the meat and vegetable broth served from it.

Pétoncle: tiny scallop, similar to American bay scallop.

Pibale: tiny eel, also called *civelle*.

Picholine, pitchouline: a variety of green olives, generally used to prepare *olives cassées;* specialty of Provence.

Picodon (méthode Dieulefit): small disc of goat's-milk cheese, the best of which (qualified as *méthode Dieulefit*) is hard, piquant, and pungent from having soaked in brandy and aged a month in earthenware jars; specialty of northern Provence.

Pièce: portion, piece.

Piech: poached veal brisket stuffed with vegetables, herbs, and sometimes rice, ham, eggs, or cheese; specialty of the Mediterranean.

Pied de cheval: "horse's foot"; giant Atlantic coast oyster.

Pied de mouton: meaty cream-colored wild mushroom. Also, sheep's foot.

Pieds et paquets: "feet and packages"; mutton tripe rolled and cooked with sheep's feet, white wine, and tomatoes; specialty of Provence and the Mediterranean.

Pierre-Qui-Vire: "stone that moves"; a supple, tangy, flat disc of cow's-milk cheese with a reddish rind, made by the Benedictine monks at the Abbaye de la Pierre-Qui-Vire in Burgundy.

Pigeon(neau): pigeon or squab (young pigeon or squab).

Pignons: pine nuts, found in the cones of pine trees growing in Provence and along the southwestern Atlantic coast.

Pilau, pilaf: rice sautéed with onion and simmered in broth.

Pilchard: name for sardines on the Atlantic coast.

Piment: red pepper or pimento.

Piment (or poivre) de Jamaïque: allspice.

Piment d'Espelette: slender, mildly hot chile pepper from Espelette, a village in the Basque region.

Piment doux: sweet pepper.

Pimenté: hot, peppery, spicy.

Pimpernelle: salad burnet, a salad green with a somewhat bitter taste.

Pince: claw. Also, tongs used when eating snails or seafood.

Pineau des Charentes: sweet fortified wine from the Cognac region on the Atlantic coast, served as an aperitif.

Pintade(au): (young) guinea fowl.

Pipérade: a dish of pepper, onions, tomatoes, and often ham and scrambled eggs; specialty of the Basque region.

Piquant(e): sharp or spicy tasting.

Piqué: larded; studded.

Piquenchagne, picanchagne: a pear tart with walnut or brioche crust; specialty of the Bourbonnais, a province in Auvergne.

Pissaladière: a flat open-face tart like a pizza, garnished with onions, olives, and anchovies; specialty of Nice.

Pissenlit: dandelion green.

Pistache: pistachio nut.

Pistil de safran: thread of saffron.

Pistou: sauce of basil, garlic, and olive oil; specialty of Provence. Also a rich vegetable, bean, and pasta soup flavored with *pistou* sauce.

Pithiviers: a town in the Loire valley that gives its name to a classic large puff pastry found filled with almond cream. Also, lark pâté.

Plaice: a small, orange-spotted flounder or fluke, a flat ocean fish; also known as *plie franche* or *carrelet*. Found in the English Channel.

Plat cuisiné: dish containing ingredients that have cooked together, usually in a sauce.

Plat du jour: today's special.

Plat principal: main dish.

Plate: flat-shelled oyster.

Plateau: platter.

Plateau de fruits de mer: seafood platter combining raw and cooked shellfish; usually includes oysters, clams, mussels, langoustines, periwinkles, whelks, crabs, and tiny shrimp.

Plates côtes: part of beef ribs usually used in *pot-au-feu.*

Pleurote: very soft-fleshed, feather-edged wild mushrooms; also now being cultivated commercially in several regions of France.

Plie: see *Plaice.*

Plombière: classic dessert of vanilla ice cream, candied fruit, kirsch, and apricot jam.

Pluche: small sprig of herbs or plants, generally used for garnish.

Poché: poached.

Pochouse: see *Pauchouse.*

Poêlé: pan-fried.

Pogne: brioche flavored with orange-flower water and filled with fruits; specialty of Romans-sur-Isère, in the Rhône-Alpes.

Point(e) (d'asperge): tip (of asparagus).

Point (à): ripe or ready to eat, the perfect moment for eating a cheese or fruit. Also, cooked medium rare.

Poire: pear.

Poire William's: variety of pear; colorless fruit brandy, or *eau-de-vie,* often made from this variety of pear.

Poireau: leek.

Pois (chiche): pea (chickpea).

Poisson: fish.

  d'eau douce: freshwater fish.

  de lac: lake fish.

  de mer: ocean fish.

  de rivière: river fish.

  de roche: rock fish.

  fumé: smoked fish.

  noble: refers to prized, thus expensive, variety of fish.

Poitrine: breast (of meat or poultry).

Poitrine demi-sel: unsmoked slab bacon.

Poitrine d'oie fumée: smoked goose breast.

Poitrine fumée: smoked slab bacon.

Poivrade: a peppery brown sauce made with wine, vinegar, and cooked vegetables and strained before serving.

Poivre: pepper.

  d'ain: Provençal name for wild savory. Also, small goat cheese covered with sprigs of savory. Also known as *pèbre d'ail* and *pèbre d'ase.*

  en grain: peppercorn.

  frais de Madagascar: green peppercorn.

  gris: black peppercorn.

  moulu: grond pepper.

  noir: black peppercorn.

  rose: pink peppercorn.

  vert: green peppercorn.

Poivron (doux): (sweet bell) pepper.

Pojarski: finely chopped meat or fish shaped like a cutlet and fried.

Polenta: cooked dish of cornmeal and water, usually with added butter and cheese; also, cornmeal.

Pommade (beurre en): usually refers to a thick, smooth paste; (creamed butter).

Pomme: apple.

Pommes de terre: potatoes.

  à l'anglaise: boiled.

  allumettes: "matchsticks"; fries cut into very thin julienne.

  boulangère: potatoes cooked with the meat they accompany. Also, a gratin of sliced potatoes, baked with milk or stock and sometimes flavored with onions, bacon, and tomatoes.

  darphin: grated potatoes shaped into a cake.

  dauphine: mashed potatoes mixed with *choux* pastry, shaped into small balls and fried.

  dauphinoise: a gratin of sliced potatoes, baked with milk and/or cream, garlic, cheese, and eggs.

  duchesse: mashed potatoes with butter, egg yolks, and nutmeg, used for garnish.

  en robe des champs, en robe de chambre: potatoes boiled or baked in their skin; potatoes in their jackets.

  frites: French fries.

  gratinées: browned potatoes, often with cheese.

  lyonnaise: potatoes sautéed with onions.

  macaire: classic side dish of puréed potatoes shaped into small balls and fried or baked in a flat cake.

  mousseline: potato purée enriched with butter, egg yolks, and whipped cream.

  paillasson: fried pancake of grated potatoes.

  pailles: potatoes cut into julienne strips, then fried.

  Pont-Neuf: classic fries.

  sarladaise: sliced potatoes cooked with goose fat and (optionally) truffles.

  soufflées: small, thin slices of potatoes fried twice, causing them to inflate so they resemble little pillows.

sous la cèndre: baked under cinders in a fireplace.

vapeur: steamed or boiled potatoes.

Pommes en l'air: caramelized apple slices, usually served with *boudin noir* (blood sausage).

Pompe à l'huile, pompe de Noël: see *Gibassier.*

Pompe aux grattons: bread containing cracklings.

Pont l'Evêque: village in Normandy that gives its name to a very tender, fragrant square of cow's-milk cheese.

Porc (carré de): pork (loin).

Porc (côte de): pork (chop).

Porcelet: young suckling pig.

Porchetta: young pig stuffed with offal, herbs, and garlic, and roasted; seen in *charcuteries* in Nice.

Porto (au): (with) port.

Portugaise: elongated, crinkle-shell oyster.

Pot-au-feu: traditional dish of beef simmered with vegetables, often served in two or more courses; today chefs often use it to mean fish poached in fish stock with vegetables.

Pot bouilli: another name for *pot-au-feu.*

Pot-de-crème: individual classic custard dessert, often chocolate.

Potage: soup.

Potée: traditional hearty meat soup, usually containing pork, cabbage, and potatoes.

Potimarron: see *Citrouille.*

Potiron: see *Citrouille.*

Potjevleisch: a mixed meat terrine, usually of veal, pork, and rabbit; specialty of the North.

Poularde: fatted hen.

Poule au pot: boiled stuffed chicken with vegetables; specialty of the city of Béarn in the southwest.

Poule d'Inde: turkey hen.

Poule faisane: female pheasant.

Poulet (rôti): chicken (roast).

Poulet basquaise: Basque-style chicken, with tomatoes and sweet peppers.

Poulet de Bresse: high-quality chicken raised on farms to exacting specifications, from the Rhône-Alpes.

Poulet de grain: corn-fed chicken.

Poulet fermier: free-range chicken.

Pouligny-Saint-Pierre: village in the Loire valley that gives its name to a goat's-milk cheese shaped like a truncated pyramid with a mottled, grayish rind and a smooth-grained, ivory-white interior.

Poulpe: octopus.

Pounti: a pork meat loaf that generally includes Swiss chard or spinach, eggs, milk, herbs, onions, and prunes; specialty of the Auvergne.

Pousse-pierre: edible seaweed.

Poussin: baby chicken.

Poutargue, boutargue: salted, pressed, and flattened mullet roe, generally spread on toast as an appetizer; specialty of Provence and the Mediterranean.

Poutine: see *Nonat.*

Praire: small clam.

Pralin: ground caramelized almonds.

Praline: caramelized almonds.

Pré-salé (agneau de): delicately salted lamb raised on the salt marshes of Normandy and the Atlantic coast.

Presskoph: pork headcheese, often served with vinaigrette; specialty of Alsace.

Primeur(s): refers to early fresh fruits and vegetables, also to new wine.

Printanière: garnish of a variety of spring vegetables cut into dice or balls.

Prix fixe: fixed-price menu.

Prix net: service included.

Profiterole(s): classic *chou* pastry dessert, usually puffs of pastry filled with vanilla ice cream and topped with hot chocolate sauce.

Provençale: in the style of Provence; usually includes garlic, tomatoes, and/or olive oil.

Prune (d'ente): fresh plum; (variety of plum grown in the famed Agen region of the southwest).

Pruneau: prune.

Puits d'amour: "wells of love"; classic small pastry crowns filled with pastry cream.

Q

Quasi (de veau): standing rump (of veal).

Quatre-épices: spice blend of ground ginger, nutmeg, white pepper, and cloves.

Quatre-quarts: "four quarters"; pound cake made with equal weights of eggs, flour, butter, and sugar.

Quenelle: dumpling, usually of veal, fish, or poultry.

Quetsche: small purple Damson plum.

Queue (de boeuf): tail (of beef, oxtail).

Quiche lorraine: savory custard tart made with bacon, eggs, and cream.

R

Râble de lièvre (lapin): saddle of hare (rabbit).

Raclette: rustic dish, from Switzerland and the Savoie, of melted cheese served with boiled potatoes, tiny pickled cucumbers, and onions; also, the cheese used in the dish.

Radis: small red radish.

Radis noir: large black radish, often served with cream, as a salad.

Rafraîchi: cool, chilled, or fresh.

Ragoût: stew; usually of meat.

Raie (bouclée): skate or ray, found in the English Channel, Atlantic, and Mediterranean.

Raifort: horseradish.

Raisin: grape; raisin.
  de Corinthe: currant.
  de Smyrne: sultana.
  sec: raisin.

Raïto: red wine sauce that generally includes onions, tomatoes, garlic, herbs, olives, and capers, usually served warm over grilled fish; specialty of Provence.

Ramequin: small individual casserole. Also, a small tart. Also, a small goat's-milk cheese from the Bugey, an area in the northern Rhône valley.

Ramier: wood or wild pigeon.

Râpé: grated or shredded.

Rascasse: gurnard, or scorpion fish in the rockfish family; an essential ingredient of *bouillabaisse,* the fish stew of the Mediterranean.

Ratafia: liqueur made by infusing nut or fruit in brandy.

Ratatouille: a cooked dish of eggplant, zucchini, onions, tomatoes, peppers, garlic, and olive oil, served hot or cold; specialty of Provence.

Ratte de Grenoble: "Grenoble rat"; bite-size white potatoes.

Ravigote: classic thick vinaigrette sauce with vinegar, white wine, shallots, and herbs. Also, cold mayonnaise with capers, onions, and herbs.

Raviole de Royans: tiny ravioli pasta filled with goat cheese, from the Rhône-Alpes.

Ravioli à la niçoise: square or round pasta filled with meat and/or swiss chard and baked with grated cheese.

Reblochon: smooth, supple, creamy cow's-milk cheese from the Savoie in the Alps.

Réglisse: licorice.

Reine-Claude: greengage plum.

Reinette, reine de: fall and winter variety of apple, deep yellow with a red blush.

Religieuse, petite: "nun"; a small version of a classic pastry consisting of two *choux* puffs filled with chocolate, coffee, or vanilla pastry cream, placed one on top of another, and frosted with chocolate or coffee icing to resemble a nun in her habit.

Rémoulade (céleri): sauce of mayonnaise, capers, mustard, herbs, anchovies, and gherkins; (dish of shredded celery root with *rémoulade* sauce.

Repas: meal.

Rhubarbe: rhubarb.

Rhum: rum.

Rigotte: small cow's-milk cheese from the Lyon region.

Rillettes (d'oie): minced spread of pork (goose); can also be made with duck, fish, or rabbit.

Rillons: usually pork belly, cut up and cooked until crisp, then drained of fat; also made of duck, goose, or rabbit.

Ris d'agneau (de veau): lamb (veal) sweetbreads.

Rissolé: browned by frying, usually potatoes.

Riz: rice.
  à la impératrice: cold rice pudding with candied fruit.
  complet: brown rice.
  de Camargue: nutty, fragrant rice grown in the Camargue, the swampy area just south of Arles in Provence.
  sauvage: wild rice.

Rizotto, risotto: creamy rice made by stirring rice constantly in stock as it cooks, then mixing in other ingredients such as cheese or mushrooms.

Robe des champs, robe de chambre (pommes en): potatoes boiled or baked in their skin; potatoes in their jackets.

Rocamadour: village in southwestern France which gives its name to a tiny disc of cheese, once made of pure goat's or sheep's milk, now generally either goat's milk or a blend of goat's and cow's milk. Also called *cabécou.*

Rognonnade: veal loin with kidneys attached.

Rognons: kidneys.

Rollot: spicy cow's-milk

cheese with a washed ochre-colored rind, in small cylinder or heart shape; from the North.

Romanoff: fruit, often strawberries, macerated in liqueur and topped with whipped cream.

Romarin: rosemary.

Rondelle: round slice—of carrot, for example.

Roquefort: disc of blue-veined cheese of raw sheep's milk from southwestern France, aged in village of Roquefort-sur-Soulzon.

Roquette: rocket or arugula, a spicy salad green.

Rosé: rare; used for veal, duck, or liver. Also, rose-colored wine.

Rosette (de boeuf): large dried pork beef sausage, from area around Lyon.

Rôti: roast; meat roast.

Rouelle: slice of meat or vegetable cut at an angle.

Rouennaise (canard à la): in • the style of Rouen; (classic dish of duck stuffed with its liver in a blood-thickened sauce).

Rouget barbet, rouget de roche: red mullet, a prized, expensive rockfish, with sweet flesh and red skin; its flavorful liver is reserved for sauces.

Rouget grondin: red gurnard, a large, common rockfish, less prized than *rouget barbet.* A variety of *galinette.* An ingredient in *bouillabaisse.*

Rougette: a small red-leafed butterhead lettuce, specialty of Provence.

Rouille: mayonnaise of olive oil, garlic, chile peppers, bread, and fish broth; usually served with fish soups, such as *bouillabaisse.*

Roulade: meat or fish roll, or rolled-up vegetable soufflé; larger than a *paupiette,* and often stuffed.

Roulé(e): rolled.

Roussette: dogfish, also called *salmonette* because of its pinkish skin, found on the Atlantic coast. Good when very fresh.

Roux: sauce base or thickening of flour and butter.

Royale, à la: "royal-style": rich classic preparation, usually with truffles and a cream sauce.

Rumsteck: rump steak.

Russe, salada à la: cold mixed salad of peas and diced carrots and turnips in mayonnaise.

S

Sabayon, zabaglione: frothy sweet sauce of egg yolks, sugar, wine, and flavoring that is whipped while being cooked in a water bath.

Sabodet: strong, earthy sausage of pork, beef, pig's head and skin, served hot; specialty of Lyon.

Safran: saffron.

Saignant(e): cooked rare, for meat, usually beef.

Saindoux: lard or pork fat.

Saint-Germain: with peas.

Saint-Hubert: poivrade sauce with chestnuts and bacon added.

Saint-Jacques, coquille: see scallop.

Saint-Marcellin: small flat disc of cow's-milk cheese (once made of goat's milk) made in dairies in the Isère, outside Lyon. The best is well aged and runny, and seems to be found only in the Lyon area.

Saint-Nectaire: village in the Auvergne that gives its name to a supple, thick disc of cow's-milk cheese with a mottled gray rind.

Saint-Pierre: John Dory, a prized mild, flat, white ocean fish. Known as *soleil* and *Jean Doré* in the North, and *poule de mer* along the Atlantic coast.

Saint-Vincent: moist, buttery, thick cylinder of cow's-milk cheese from Burgundy with a rust-colored rind; similar to *Epoisses,* but aged a bit longer, therefore stronger.

Sainte-Maure: village in the Loire valley that gives its name to a soft, elongated cylinder of goat's-milk cheese with a distinctive straw in the middle and a mottled, natural blue rind.

Salade: salad; also, a head of lettuce.

Salade folle: mixed salad, usually including green beans and *foie gras.*

Salade lyonnaise: green salad with cubed bacon and soft-cooked eggs, often served with herring and anchovies, and/or sheep's feet and chicken livers; specialty of Lyon; also called *saladier lyonnais.*

Salade niçoise: salad with many variations, but usually with tomatoes, green beans, anchovies, tuna, potatoes, black olives, capers, and artichokes.

Salade panachée: mixed salad.

Salade russe: mixed diced vegetables in mayonnaise.

Salade verte: green salad.

Saladier (lyonnais): see *Salade lyonnaise.*

BASIC BREAD DOUGH

This yeast dough can be used for a variety of purposes—bread tarts, pizzas, fougasse, or a basic white loaf. I often keep a batch going in the refrigerator, for it will keep for several days in a sealed container. This recipe makes enough dough for two average-size tarts or pizzas or one loaf of bread.

1 cup (250 ml)
  lukewarm water
2½ teaspoons or 1
  package active dry
  yeast
2¼ to 2½ cups (315 to
  350 g) unbleached
  all-purpose flour
1 teaspoon salt

1. Place the water, yeast, and 1 cup of the flour in a large mixing bowl and stir until thoroughly blended. Let sit to proof the yeast, about 5 minutes.

2. Add the salt, then begin stirring in the remaining flour, little by little, until the dough is too stiff to stir. Place the dough on a lightly floured surface and knead, adding additional flour if the dough is too sticky, until the dough is smooth and satiny, about 10 minutes.

3. Place the dough in a bowl, cover, and let rise at room temperature until doubled in bulk, about 1 hour.

4. Punch the dough down, cover, and let rise again until doubled in bulk, about 1 hour.

5. After the second rise, the dough is ready to use. If it is to be stored, place it in a tightly sealed container and refrigerate.

Yield: About 1 pound (500 g) bread dough.

Salé: salted.
Salers: Cantal-type cheese, made in rustic cheese-making houses only when the cows are in the Auvergne's mountain pastures, from May to September.
Salicorne: edible seaweed, sea string bean; often pickled and served as a condiment.
Salmis: classic preparation of roasted game birds or poultry, with sauce made from the pressed carcass.
Salpicon: diced vegetables, meat, and/or fish in a sauce, used as a stuffing, garnish, or spread.
Salsifis: salsify, oyster plant.
Sandre: pickerel, perch-like river fish, found in the Saône and Rhine.
Sang: blood.

Sanglier: wild boar.
Sangue: Corsican black pudding, usually with grapes or herbs.
Sanguine: "blood" orange, so named for its red juice.
Sansonnet: Starling or thrush.
Sar, sargue: blacktail, a tiny flat fish of the sea bream family, best grilled or baked.
Sarcelle: teal, a species of wild duck.
Sardine: small sardine. Large sardines are called *pilchards.* Found year-round in the Mediterranean, from May to October in the Atlantic.
Sarladaise: as prepared in Sarlat in the Dordogne; with truffles.
Sarrasin: buckwheat.

Sarriette: summer savory. See *poivre d'ain.*
Saucisse: small fresh sausage.
Saucisse chaude: warm sausage.
Saucisse de Francfort: hot dog.
Saucisse de Strasbourg: red-skinned hot dog.
Saucisse de Toulouse: mild country-style pork sausage.
Saucisson: most often, a large air-dried sausage, such as salami, eaten sliced as a cold cut; when fresh, usually called *saucisson chaud,* or hot sausage.
Saucisson à l'ail: garlic sausage, usually to be cooked and served warm.
Saucisson d'Arles: dried salami-style sausage that

blends pork, beef, and gentle seasoning; a specialty of Arles, in Provence.

Saucisson de campagne: any country-style sausage.

Saucisson de Lyon: air-dried pork sausage, flavored with garlic and pepper and studied with chunks of pork fat.

Saucisson de Morteau: see *Jésus de Morteau.*

Saucisson en croûte: sausage cooked in a pastry crust.

Saucisson sec: any dried sausage, or salami.

Sauge: sage.

Saumon (sauvage): salmon ("wild," to differentiate from commercially raised salmon, half the price of wild).

Saumon d'Ecosse: Scottish salmon.

Saumon de fontaine: small, commercially raised salmon.

Saumon fumé: smoked salmon.

Saumon norvégien: Norwegian salmon.

Saumonette: see *Roussette.*

Saupiquet: classic aromatic wine sauce thickened with bread.

Sauté: browned in fat.

Sauvage: wild.

Savarin: yeast-leavened cake shaped like a ring, soaked in sweet syrup.

Savoie (biscuit de): sponge cake.

Savoyarde: in the style of Savoy, usually flavored with Gruyère cheese.

Scarole: escarole.

Schieffele, schieffala, schifela: smoked pork shoulder, served hot and garnished with pickled turnips or a potato and onion salad.

Sec (sèche): dry or dried.

Seiche: squid or cuttlefish.

Seigle (pain de): rye (bread).

Sel gris: salt, unbleached sea salt.

Sel marin: sea salt.

Sel (gros): coarse salt.

Selle: saddle (of meat).

Selles-sur-Cher: village in the Loire valley identified with a small, flat, truncated cylinder of goat's-milk cheese with a mottled blueish-gray rind (sometimes patted with powdered charcoal) and a pure-white interior.

Selon grosseur (S.G.): according to size, usually said of lobster or other seafood.

Selon le marché: according to what is in season or available.

Selon poid (S.P.): according to weight, usually said of seafood.

Serpolet: wild thyme.

Service: meal, mealtime, the serving of the meal. A restaurant has two *services* if it serves lunch and dinner; a dish *en deux services,* like *canard presse,* is served in two courses.

Service (non) compris: service charge (not) included in the listed menu prices (but invariably included on the bill).

Service en sus: service charge to be made in addition to menu prices. Same as *service non compris.*

Simple: simple, plain, unmixed. Also, a single scoop of ice cream.

Smitane: sauce of cream, onions, white wine, and lemon juice.

Socca: a very thin, round crêpe made with chickpea flour, sold on the streets of Nice and eaten as a snack.

Soissons: dried or fresh white beans, from the area around Soissons, northeast of Paris.

Soja (pousse de): soy bean (soy bean sprout).

Soja, sauce de: soy sauce.

Solette: small sole.

Sorbet: sherbet.

Soubise: onion sauce.

Soufflé: light, mixture of puréed ingredients, egg yolks, and whipped egg whites, which puffs up when baked; sweet or savory, hot or cold.

Soumaintrain: a spicy, supple flat disc of cow's-milk cheese with a red-brown rind; from Burgundy.

Soupir de nonne: "nun's sighs"; fried *choux* pastry dusted with confectioners' sugar. Created by a nun in an Alsatian abbey. Also called *pet de nonne.*

Souris: "mouse"; lamb shanks.

Spätzel. spaetzle, spetzli: noodle-like Alsatian egg and flour dumpling, served poached or fried.

Spoom: wine or fruit juice mixed with egg whites, whipped, and frozen to create a frothy iced dessert.

Stockfish, stocaficada, estoficada, estoficado, morue plate: flattened, dried cod found in southern France. Also, a purée-like blend of dried codfish, olive oil, tomatoes, sweet peppers, black olives, potatoes, garlic, onions, and herbs; specialty of Nice. Sometimes served with *pistou.*

Strasbourgeoise, à la: ingredients typical of Strasbourg including sauerkraut, *foie gras,* and salt pork.

Succès à la praline: cake

made with praline meringue layers, frosted with meringue and butter cream.

Sucre: sugar.

Supioun, suppion: cuttlefish, seen in the Languedoc.

Suprême: a veal- or chicken-based white sauce thickened with flour and cream. Also, a boneless breast of poultry or a filet of fish.

T

Table d'hôte: open table or board. Often found in the countryside, these are private homes that serve fixed meals and often have one or two guest rooms as well.

Tablier de sapeur: "fireman's apron"; tripe that is marinated, breaded, and grilled; specialty of Lyon.

Tacaud: pour or whiting-pour, a small, inexpensive fish found in the Atlantic and Mediterranean, usually fried.

Tagine: spicy North African stew of veal, lamb, chicken, or pigeon, and vegetables.

Talmouse: savory pastry triangle of cheese-flavored *choux* dough baked in puff pastry.

Tamié: Flat disc of cheese, made of cow's milk at the Trappist monastery in the Savoie village of Tamié. Similar to Reblochon.

Tanche: tench, a river fish with a mild, delicate flavor; often an ingredient in *matelote* and *pauchouse*, freshwater fish stews.

Tapenade: a blend of black olives, anchovies, capers, olive oil, and lemon

juice, sometimes with rum or canned tuna added; specialty of Provence.

Tarama: carp roe, often made into a spread of the same name.

Tartare (de poisson): traditionally chopped raw beef, seasoned and garnished with raw egg, capers, chopped onion, and parsley; (today, a popular highly seasoned raw fish dish).

Tarte: tart; open-face pie or *flan*, usually sweet.

Tarte encalat: name for cheesecake in the Auvergne.

Tarte flambée: thin-crusted savory tart, much like a rectangular pizza, covered with cream, onions, and bacon; specialty of Alsace; also called *Flammekueche*.

Tarte Tatin: caramelized upside-down apple pie, made famous by the Tatin sisters in their hotel in Lamotte-Beuvron, in the Sologne; a popular dessert, seen on menus all over France.

Tartine: open-face sandwich; buttered bread.

Tasse: cup; a coffee or tea cup.

Telline: a tiny violet-streaked clam, the size of a fingernail, seen in Provence and the Camargue; often served cooked in the shell with olive oil and garlic.

Tendre: tender.

Tendron: cartilaginous meat cut from beef or veal ribs.

Teurgoule: a sweet rice pudding with cinnamon; specialty of Normandy.

Terrine: earthenware container used for cooking

meat, game, fish, or vegetable mixtures; also the pâté cooked and served in such a container. It differs from a pâté proper in that the terrine is actually sliced out of the container, while a pâté has been removed from its mold.

Tête de veau (porc): head of veal (pork), usually used in headcheese.

Tétragone: spinach-like green, found in Provence.

Thé: tea.

Thermidor (homard): classic lobster dish; lobster split lengthwise, grilled, and served in the shell with a cream sauce.

Thon (blanc) (germon): tuna (white albacore).

Thon rouge: bluefin tuna.

Thym: thyme.

Tian: an earthenware gratin dish; also vegetable gratins baked in such a dish; from Provence.

Tiède: lukewarm.

Tilleul: linden tree; linden-blossom herb tea.

Timbale: small round mold with straight or sloping slides; also, a mixture prepared in such a mold.

Tomates à la provençale: baked tomato halves sprinkled with garlic, parsley, and bread crumbs.

Tomme: generic name for cheese, usually refers to a variety of cheeses in the Savoie; also, the fresh cheese used to make Cantal in the Auvergne.

Tomme arlésienne: rectangular cheese made with a blend of goat's and cow's milk and sprinkled with summer savory; also called *tomme de Camargue*; a specialty of the

Languedoc and Arles, in Provence.

Tomme fraîche: pressed cake of fresh milk curds, used in the regional dishes of the Auvergne.

Topinambour: Jerusalem artichoke.

Toro (taureau): bull; meat found in butcher shops in the Languedoc and Pay Basque, and sometimes on restaurant menus.

Torteau au fromage: goat cheese cheesecake from the Poitou-Charentes along the Atlantic coast; a blackened, spherical loaf found at cheese shops throughout France; once a homemade delicacy, today prepared industrially.

Tortue: turtle.

Toucy: village in Burgundy that gives its name to a local fresh goat cheese.

Tourain, tourin, tourrin: generally a peasant soup of garlic, onions (and sometimes tomatoes), and broth or water, thickened with egg yolks and seasoned with vinegar; specialty of the southwest.

Tournedos: center portion of beef filet, usually grilled or sautéed.

Tournedos Rossini: sautéed *tournedos* garnished with *foie gras* and truffles.

Touron: marzipan loaf, or a cake of almond paste, often layered and flavored with nuts or candied fruits and sold by the slice; specialty of the Basque region.

Tourte (aux blettes): pie (common Niçoise dessert pie filled with Swiss chard, eggs, cheese, raisins, and pine nuts).

Also, name for giant rounds of country bread found in the Auvergne and the southwest.

Tourteau: large crab.

Tourtière: shallow three-legged cooking vessel, set over hot coals for baking. Also, southwestern pastry dish filled with apples and/or prunes and sprinkled with Armagnac.

Train de côtes: rib of beef.

Traiteur: caterer, delicatessen.

Tranche: slice.

Trappiste: name given to the mild, lactic cow's-milk cheese made in a Trappist monastery in Echourgnac, in the southwest.

Travers de porc: spareribs.

Trévise: radicchio, a bitter red salad green of the chicory family.

Tripes à la mode de Caen: beef tripe, carrots, onions, leeks, and spices, cooked in water, cider, and Calvados (apple brandy); specialty of Normandy.

Triple crème: legal name for cheese containing more than 75 percent butterfat, such as Brillat-Savarin.

Tripoux: mutton tripe.

Tripoxa: Basque name for sheep's or calf's blood sausage served with spicy red Espelette peppers.

Trompettes de la mort: dark brown wild mushroom, also known as "horn of plenty."

Tronçon: cut of meat or fish resulting in a piece that is longer than it is wide; generally refers to slices from the largest part of a fish.

Trouchia: flat omelet filled

with spinach or Swiss chard; specialty of Provence.

Truffade: a large layered and fried potato pancake made with bacon and fresh Cantal cheese; specialty of the Auvergne.

Truffe (truffé): truffle (with truffles).

Truffes sous la cendre: truffles wrapped in paper or foil, baked buried in ashes.

Truite (au bleu): trout (a preferred method of cooking trout, not live, as often assumed, but rather in a "live condition." The trout is gutted just moments prior to cooking, but neither washed nor scaled. It is then plunged into a hot mixture of vinegar and water, and the slimy lubricant that protects the skin of the fish appears to turn the trout a bluish color. The fish is then removed to a broth to finish its cooking.)

de lac: lake trout.

de mer: sea trout or brown trout.

de rivière: river trout.

saumonée: salmon trout.

Ttoro: fish soup from the Basque region. Historically, the liquid that remained after poaching cod was seasoned with herbs and used to cook vegetables and potatoes. Today, a more elaborate version includes the addition of *lotte*, mullet, mussels, conger eel, langoustines, and wine.

Tuile: literally, "curved roofing tile"; delicate almond-flavored cookie.

Tulipe: tulip-shaped cookie for serving ice cream or sorbet.

Turban: usually a mixture or combination of ingredients cooked in a ring mold.

Turbot(in): turbot (small turbot). Prized flatfish found in the Atlantic and Mediterranean.

V

Vache: cow.

Vacherin: dessert of baked meringue, with ice cream and whipped cream. Also a strong, supple winter cheese encircled by a band of spruce, from the Jura.

Vallée d'Auge: area of Normandy. Also, garnish of cooked apples and cream or Calvados and cream.

Vanille: vanilla.

Vapeur, à la: steamed.

Varech: seaweed.

Veau: veal.

Velouté: classic sauce based on veal, chicken, or fish stock, thickened with a *roux* of butter and flour; also, variously seasoned classic soups thickened with cream and egg yolks.

Ventre: belly or stomach.

Vénus: American clam.

Verdure (en): garnish of green vegetables.

Verdurette: herb vinaigrette.

Vernis: large fleshy clam with small red tongue and shiny varnish-like shell.

Véronique, à la: garnish of peeled white grapes.

Vert-pré: a watercress gar-

nish, sometimes including potatoes.

Verveine: lemon verbena, herb tea.

Vessie, en: cooked in a pig's bladder (usually chicken).

Viande: meat.

Vichy: with glazed carrots. Also, a brand of mineral water.

Vichyssoise: cold, creamy leek and potato soup.

Viennoise: coated in egg, breaded, and fried.

Vierge: "virgin"; term for the best quality olive oil, from the first pressing of the olives.

Vieux (vielle): old.

Vieux Lille: thick, square cheese named for the old part of the north's largest city, made in the same way as *Maroilles,* with cow's milk, only salted more, then aged six months until stinking ripe. Also called *vieux puant,* or "old stinker."

Vinaigre (vieux): vinegar (aged).

Vinaigre de xérès: sherry vinegar.

Vinaigrette: oil and vinegar dressing.

Viognier (sorbet du): white grape of the Rhône (a sorbet made from this grape).

Violet or *figue de mer:* unusual iodine-strong, soft-shelled edible sea creature, with a yellowish interior. A delicacy along the Mediterranean, particularly in Marseille.

Violet de Provence: braid of

plump garlic, a specialty of Provence and the Côte-d'Azur.

Violette: violet; its crystallized petals are a specialty of Toulouse.

Viroflay: classic garnish of spinach for poached or soft-cooked eggs.

Vive or *vipère de mer:* weever, a small firm-fleshed ocean fish used in soups, such as *bouillabaisse,* or grilled. The venomous spine is removed before cooking.

Vol-au-vent: puff pastry shell.

Volonté (à): at the customer's discretion.

Vonnaissienne, à la: in the style of Vonnas, a village in the Rhône-Alpes. Also, crêpes made with potatoes.

X

Xérès (vinaigre de): sherry (vinegar).

Y

Yaourt: yogurt.

Z

Zeste: zest, or citrus peel with white pith removed.

Zewelmai, zewelwai: Alsatian onion tart.

Zingara, à la: gypsy style; with tomato sauce. Also classically, a garnish of ham, tongue, mushrooms, and truffles.

Recipe Index

Index

S